Shaman and Sage

Shaman and Sage

The Roots of "Spiritual but Not Religious"
in Antiquity

MICHAEL HORTON

WILLIAM B. EERDMANS PUBLISHING COMPANY
GRAND RAPIDS, MICHIGAN

Wm. B. Eerdmans Publishing Co.
4035 Park East Court SE, Grand Rapids, Michigan 49546
www.eerdmans.com

© 2024 Michael Horton
All rights reserved
Published 2024

Book design by Lydia Hall

Printed in the United States of America

30 29 28 27 26 25 24   2 3 4 5 6 7

ISBN 978-0-8028-7711-6

Library of Congress Cataloging-in-Publication Data

A catalog record for this book is available from the Library of Congress.

To Joshua Maloney

Contents

	Acknowledgments	ix
	List of Abbreviations	xi
	Introduction: Inventing the "Divine Self"	1
	Where We Are Headed	
1.	Survivor to Shaman	33
	Discovering the Divine Self	
2.	Dancing for Dionysus	71
	New Myths for the Utopian Stage	
3.	Shaman to Sage	121
	Religion of the One	
4.	"The True Mystics"	173
	Orpheus as Plato's Muse	
5.	"The Foes! The Foes!"	209
	Soul Saving in Alexandria	
6.	Hermes Trismegistus	252
	The Cult without Temples	
7.	Savior *of* or *from* the World?	285
	Christianity and Gnosis	

Contents

8. Orphic Exegesis — 312
   The Eternal Gospel

9. A Christian Reconstruction of Late Neoplatonism — 331
   St. Paul's Philosopher-Convert

10. Cosmotheism as Philosophical Religion — 373
    Eriugena's Dionysius

11. Prophetic Gnosis — 388
    Dreaming of Utopia

Works Cited — 427
Index of Authors — 479
Index of Subjects — 490

Acknowledgments

I cannot even remember when I began this project, but a significant episode was a series of lectures at Oxford by Keith Ward comparing mystical traditions in world religions. In any event, exploring this terrain has consumed four sabbaticals. Along the way I have accumulated many debts. They begin with the Center of Theological Inquiry for offering me a position as visiting scholar. In spite of gracious accommodations for our family, we could not make the move to Princeton for this period. However, the labor that went into the application and the feedback on the proposal from referees formed the nucleus of this project.

I dedicate this book to Joshua Maloney, who plied his training in literary arts, history, and theology to sharpening the focus and helping me to weed through labyrinthine chapters in search of a clear throughline. Whatever shortcomings remain are mine, but they would have been far greater without his skill, encouragement, critique, and hard work through many drafts.

Myriad conversations with colleagues at other institutions stimulated my interest and brought correction along the way. I am grateful especially to colleagues at Westminster Seminary California. Ryan Glomsrud, Julius Kim, and Steve Baugh have been particularly helpful, along with various students, especially Silverio Gonzalez, Tyler Moser, Caleb Wait, and Wes Viner.

I wish to express my thanks to Archbishop Samy Shehata and Mark Senada for hosting me in Cairo, and also to Sherif Fahim and his team in Alexandria for allowing me to share in their ministry and for giving me guided tours of ancient sites. Thanks also to Wageeh Mikhail and the monks at the monastery of St. Macarius the Great for introducing me to a living history.

I am grateful to Eerdmans for taking on this three-volume project. Michael Thomson captured my vision (more clearly perhaps than I), and when I thought I had to make the case for two volumes, he filled my sails with the reply, "No, I think that this requires three." James Ernest has encouraged me along the way and guided the project with his expert hand, bringing in two expert readers. I am

Acknowledgments

greatly indebted to copyeditor Blake Jurgens, whose expertise has gone far beyond copyediting, and to the project team, led by Jenny Hoffman. For all these editorial hands on deck, I am deeply appreciative and substantially less embarrassed than I would have been otherwise. Of course, all remaining errors are mine.

Finally, and foremost, my family deserves the deepest thanks for enduring my infatuation with the history of esoterism and showed hospitality toward arcane guests around the dinner table.

Abbreviations

Ancient and Late Antique Sources

1 Apoc. James	(First) Revelation of James

Aeschylus
Ag.	Agamemnon
Cho.	Choephori
Eum.	Eumenides
Prom.	Prometheus vinctus
Sept.	Septem contra Thebas
Suppl.	Supplices

Alcidamas
Od.	Odysseus

Alexander of Aphrodisias
Fat.	De fato
In Metaph.	Commentary on Aristotle's Metaphysica

Anth. gr.	Anthologie Graeca
Ap. John	Secret Book of John
Apoc. Paul	Revelation of Paul

Apollonius Rhodius
Argon.	Argonautica

Aristocritus
Theo.	Theosophia

Aristophanes
Av.	Aves
Ran.	Ranae

Aristotle
Cael.	De caelo
De an.	De anima
Hist. an.	Historia animalium
Metaph.	Metaphysica
Poet.	Poetica
Rhet.	Rhetorica

Augustine
Civ.	De civitate Dei
Conf.	Confessionum libri XIII
Ep.	Epistulae
Retract.	Retractationum libri II
Ver. rel.	De vera religione

BG	Bhagavadgita

Abbreviations

BP	Bhagavata Purana
BU	Brihadaranyaka Upanishad

CHALCIDIUS

In Plat. Tim.	Commentary on Plato's Timaeus

CICERO

Div.	De divinatione
Fin.	De finibus
Leg.	De legibus
Nat. d.	De natura deorum
Tusc.	Tusculanae disputationes

CLEMENT OF ALEXANDRA

Protr.	Protrepticus
Strom.	Stromateis
CO	Chaldean Oracles
Corp. herm.	Corpus Hermeticum

DAMASCIUS

De princ.	De principiis

DEMETRIUS

Eloc.	De elocutione

DIODORUS SICULUS

Bib. hist.	Bibliotheca historica

DIOGENES LAERTIUS

Vit. phil.	Vitae philosophorum

DIONYSIUS THE AREOPAGITE

CH	Celestial Hierarchy
DM	On the Mysteries
DN	Divine Names
EH	Ecclesiastical Hierarchy
Ep.	Epistles
MT	Mystical Theology
Disc. 8–9	Discourse on the Eighth and Ninth

EURIPIDES

Alc.	Alcestis
Bacch.	Bacchae
Heracl.	Heraclidae
Hipp.	Hippolytus

EUSEBIUS

Dem. ev.	Demonstratio evangelica
Hist. eccl.	Historia ecclesiastica
Orat.	Oratio de Laudibus Constantini
Praep. ev.	Praeparatio evangelica
Exeg. Soul	Exegesis of the Soul

GALEN

QAM	Quod animi mores

GELLIUS

Noct. att.	Noctes Atticae
Gos. Judas	Gospel of Judas
Gos. Mary	Gospel of Mary
Gos. Phil.	Gospel of Philip
Gos. Truth	Gospel of Truth

HERAKLEON

Comm. John	Commentary on the Gospel of John

Abbreviations

HERMIAS
In Plat. Phaedr. — Commentary on Plato's Phaedrus

HERODOTUS
Hist. — Historiae

HESIOD
Op. — Opera et dies
Theog. — Theogonia

HIPPOLYTUS
Haer. — Refutatio omnium haeresium

HOMER
Il. — Iliad
Od. — Odyssey
Hom. Hymn — Homeric Hymns

(PSEUDO-)HYGINUS
Astr. — Astronomica
Fab. — Fabulae

IAMBLICHUS
De myst. — De mysteriis
Theo. arith. — Theologumena arithmeticae
Vit. Pyth. — Vita Pythagorae

JOHN OF SCYTHOPOLIS
Prol. — Prologue
SchEH — Scholia: Ecclesiastical Hierarchy

JOHN SCOTTUS ERIUGENA
Div. praed. — De divina praedestinatione
Periph. — Periphyseon

JOSEPHUS
C. Ap. — Contra Apionem
J.W. — Jewish War

JULIAN
Ep. — Epistulae
Or. — Orationes

LACTANTIUS
Inst. — The Divine Institutes

LUCIAN
Musc. laud. — Muscae laudatio

LYDUS
De mens. — De mensibus

MACROBIUS
In somn. Scrip. — Commentary on the Dream of Scipio

MARINUS
Vit. Proc. — Vita Proclii

NONNUS
Dion. — Dionysiaca

OF — Orphic Fragments

OH — Orphic Hymns

OLYMPIODORUS
In Plat. Phaed. — Commentary on Plato's Phaedo

ORIGEN
Cels. — Contra Celsum
Comm. Jo. — Commentarii in evangelium Joannis
Comm. Matt. — Commentarium in evangelium Matthaei

Abbreviations

Or.	De oratione
Pasch.	De pascha
Princ.	De principiis

OVID
Metam.	Metamorphoses

PALAEPHATUS
Incr.	Incredibilia
Paraph. Shem	Paraphrase of Shem

PAUSANIAS
Descr.	Description of Greece

PHILO
Abr.	De Abrahamo
Contempl.	De vita contemplativa
Fug.	De fuga et inventione
Leg.	Legum allegoriae
Migr.	De migratione Abrahami
Opif.	De opificio mundi
Praem.	De praemiis et poenis
Somn.	De somniis

PHILOSTRATUS
Vit. Apoll.	Vita Apollonii

PHOTIUS
Bib.	Bibliotheca

PINDAR
Isthm.	Isthmionikai
Ol.	Olympionikai
Pyth.	Pythionikai

PLATO
Alc. maj.	Alcibiades major
Apol.	Apologia
Charm.	Charmides
Crat.	Cratylus
Ep.	Epistulae
Euthyd.	Euthydemus
Gorg.	Gorgias
Leg.	Leges
Phaed.	Phaedo
Phaedr.	Phaedrus
Phileb.	Philebus
Resp.	Respublica
Soph.	Sophista
Symp.	Symposium
Theaet.	Theaetetus
Tim.	Timaeus

PLETHON
Ad bess.	Ad bessarionem
De diff.	De differentiis

PLOTINUS
Enn.	Enneads

PLUTARCH
Adv. Colot.	Adversus Colotem
Alex.	Alexander
An. Procr.	De animae procreatione in Timaeo
Def. orac.	De defectu oraculorum
Is. Os.	De Iside et Osiride
Mor.	Moralia

(PSEUDO-)PLUTARCH
Strom.	Stromateis

PORPHYRY

Antr. nymph.	*De antro nympharum*
Christ.	*Contra Christianos*
Marc.	*Ad Marcellam*
Vit. Plot.	*Vita Plotini*
Vit. Pyth.	*Vita Pythagorae*

PROCLUS

De aeter. mundi	*De aeternitate mundi*
De mal.	*De malorum subsistentia*
Elem. theo.	*Elementatio theologica*
In Plat. Crat.	*Commentary on Plato's Cratylus*
In Plat. Parm.	*Commentary on Plato's Parmenides*
In Plat. Resp.	*Commentary on Plato's Respublica*
In Plat. Tim.	*Commentary on Plato's Timaeus*
Theo. Plat.	*Theology of Plato*
Pr. Paul	Prayer of the Apostle Paul

PSEUDO-APOLLODORUS

Bib.	*Bibliotheca*
RV	Rigveda

PSEUDO-DIONYSIUS

CD	Corpus Dionysiacum

SENECA

Ep.	*Epistulae morales*
Herc. fur.	*Hercules furens*
Oed.	*Oedipus*

SEXTUS EMPIRICUS

Math.	*Adversus mathematicos*
Pyrr.	*Pyrrhoniae hypotyposes*
SU	Shvetashvatara Upanishad

SIMPLICIUS

In Arist. Cael.	*Commentary on Aristotle's De Caelo*
In Arist. De An.	*Commentary on Aristotle's De Anima*
In Arist. Phys.	*Commentary on Aristotle's Physica*

SOCRATES SCHOLASTICUS

Hist. eccl.	*Historia ecclesiastica*

SOPHOCLES

Ant.	*Antigone*

STOBAEUS

Ecl.	*Ecloge*
Flor.	*Florilegium*

STRABO

Geogr.	*Geographica*
Teach. Silv.	Teaching of Silvanus

TERTULLIAN

Praescr.	*De praescriptione haereticorum*
Testim. Truth	Testimony of Truth
Treat. Res.	Treatise on the Resurrection
Tri. Trac.	Tripartate Tractate

Abbreviations

VERGIL
Georg. *Georgica*

XENOPHON
Mem. *Memorabilia*

Zost. Zostrianos

Secondary Sources and Other Abbreviations

AfO	*Archiv für Orientforschung*
AJP	*American Journal of Philology*
ANF	*The Ante-Nicene Fathers*. Edited by Alexander Roberts and James Donaldson. 1885–1887. 10 vols. Repr., Peabody, MA: Hendrickson, 1994
AR	*Archiv für Religionswissenschaft*
BG	Berlin Gnostic
CJ	*Classical Journal*
ClAnt	*Classical Antiquity*
ClQ	*Classical Quarterly*
CP	*Classical Philology*
DK	*Die Fragmente der Vorsokratiker*. Edited by H. Diels and W. Kranz. 1903. 3 vols. Repr., Berlin: Weidmann, 1974
fr(r).	fragment(s)
GOTR	*Greek Orthodox Theological Review*
GR	*Greece and Rome*
GRBS	*Greek, Roman, and Byzantine Studies*
HR	*History of Religions*
HSCP	*Harvard Studies in Classical Philology*
HTR	*Harvard Theological Review*
Int	*Interpretation*
JAAR	*Journal of the American Academy of Religion*
JAOS	*Journal of the American Oriental Society*
JECS	*Journal of Early Christian Studies*
JHS	*Journal of Hellenistic Studies*
JLARC	*Journal for Late Antique Religion and Culture*
JSSR	*Journal for the Scientific Study of Religion*
JTS	*Journal of Theological Studies*

KAR	*Keilschrifttexte aus Assur religiösen Inhalts*. Edited by Erich Ebeling. Leipzig: Hinrichs, 1919–1923
LCL	Loeb Classical Library
LM	*Early Greek Philosophy*. Edited by A. Laks and G. Most. 9 vols. Cambridge, MA: Harvard University Press, 2016.
LW	*Luther's Works*. Edited by Jaroslav Pelikan and Helmut T. Lehman. 55 vols. Philadelphia: Fortress; St. Louis: Concordia, 1955–1986
LXX	Septuagint
NAWG	*Nachrichten (von) der Akademie der Wissenschaften in Göttingen*
NHC	Nag Hammadi Corpus
NovT	*Novum Testamentum*
NPNF	*The Nicene and Post-Nicene Fathers*, Series 1. Edited by Philip Schaff. 1886–1889. 14 vols. Repr., Peabody, MA: Hendrickson, 1994
PG	Patrologia Graeca. Edited by J.-P. Migne. 162 vols. Paris, 1857–1886
PGM	*Papyri Graecae Magicae: Die griechischen Zauberpapyri*. Edited by Karl Preisendanz. 2nd ed. Stuttgart: Teubner, 1973–1974
Phil	*Philologus*
PL	Patrologia Latina. Edited by J.-P. Migne. 217 vols. Paris, 1844–1864
ProEccl	*Pro Ecclesia*
SJT	*Scottish Journal of Theology*
SPhilo	*Studia Philonica*
SPhiloA	Studia Philonica Annual
StPatr	Studia Patristica
SVTQ	*St. Vladimir's Theological Quarterly*
TAPA	*Transactions of the American Philological Association*
UF	*Ugarit-Forschungen*
VC	*Vigiliae Christianae*
ZNW	*Zeitschrift für die neutestamentliche Wissenschaft und die Kunde der älteren Kirche*
ZPE	*Zeitschrift für Papyrologie und Epigraphik*

INTRODUCTION

Inventing the "Divine Self"
Where We Are Headed

> Everything great in western civilization comes from a struggle against our origins.
>
> —Camille Paglia[1]

It is well known that many westerners today describe themselves as "spiritual but not religious."[2] Paul Heelas and Linda Woodhead define "spirituality" as a life based not on external authorities and expectations but "in deep connection with the unique experiences of my self-in-relation."[3] Religion represents a life of "subordinating subjective-life to the 'higher' authority of transcendent meaning, goodness and truth, whilst the latter (spirituality) invokes the sacred in the cultivation of unique subjective-life."[4] This is because subjective spirituality is individualistic. Though often practiced in community, it is not defined or disciplined by any community. The individual must be free "to relate in a pick-and-choose way to old and new religious narratives, constructing his or her own life-interpreting universe, loosely woven and therefore easy to change."[5]

Trend lines in the United States show that rising interest in "the sacred" is not a harbinger of religious revival among the 4 percent of the US population who identify as atheists.[6] Rather, it reflects a migration from organized religion,

---

1. Paglia, *Sexual Personae*, 40.
2. The category was coined in Erlandson, *Spiritual but Not Religious*.
3. Heelas and Woodhead, *Spiritual Revolution*, 3.
4. Heelas and Woodhead, *Spiritual Revolution*, 5.
5. Repstad, "Religious Individualism," 181.
6. This 2019 statistic was taken from the Pew Research Center, "Decline of Christianity."

1

Introduction

mainly Christianity, to a more self-defined spirituality.[7] Europe is further down the trail of secularization, and yet it has seen a similar spike in people identifying as "spiritual but not religious."[8] At the same time, 41 percent of Europeans consider astrology to be scientific (compared to 70 percent of Europeans considering astronomy scientific).[9] Overall, 58 percent of eighteen- to twenty-four-year-old Americans believe that astrology is scientific.[10] The number of US adults who believe in astrology is greater than the combined membership of all mainline Protestant denominations. Moreover, a 2018 Pew Research Center study found that 62 percent of US adults affirm at least one New Age tenet (e.g., spiritual energy in material objects, reincarnation, psychics, astrology), with the number rising to 77 percent among the "spiritual but not religious" category and 62 percent among self-designated atheists, agnostics, or "nothing in particular." Significantly, US Catholics (70 percent), mainline Protestants (67 percent), and nearly half of evangelicals (47 percent) affirm one New Age tenet as well.[11] In short, spirituality without religion is more open to views that both modern science and traditional religions (particularly Christianity) consider "superstitious."[12] Reincarnation is affirmed by 33 percent of US adults, and even more so by younger generations. Moreover, 29 percent of US adults say they have experienced a "direct revelation from God or other higher power."[13] Despite the claim that we live in a disenchanted age,

---

7. Burge, *Nones*, 2, 65. In 1996, 10 percent of US adults were self-identified "nones" (no religious affiliation). By 2018, this demographic reached the size of the two largest religious groups in the United States (Roman Catholic and Protestant), and by 2021 grew to 23 percent of the adult population. See Pew Research Center, "Religiously Unaffiliated."

8. Over a mere five years (2012–2017), the percentage of "spiritual but not religious" in Western Europe jumped from 19 to 27 percent. See Pew Research Center, "Being Christian in Western Europe," 119. Significantly, 53 percent claim to be "neither spiritual nor religious." However, I offer evidence below for the conclusion that even among these, spirituality (or at least interest in the "supernatural," particularly the occult) is quite high.

9. See https://ec.europa.eu/commfrontoffice/publicopinion/archives/ebs/ebs_224_report_en.pdf, accessed 6/20/2020.

10. National Science Foundation, "Science and Technology," 26.

11. Thirty-three percent of evangelicals believe in psychics, and 36 percent of Roman Catholics believe in reincarnation. See Pew Research Center, "'New Age' Beliefs."

12. See Pew Research Center, "'New Age' Beliefs." Although nearly half of evangelicals affirm at least one New Age tenet, it is noteworthy that the percentage rises significantly among more liberal Protestants and reaches 78 percent among the "nones." Statistically, the beneficiary of this decline in Christian participation (measured by behavior, belief, and belonging) is not atheism or scientific materialism but a pantheistic type of spirituality.

13. Belief that astrology is scientific is highest among eighteen- to twenty-nine-year-olds (40 percent) versus those sixty-five and older (23 percent). "Things happen that can't be explained by science or natural causes" was affirmed by 83 percent of respondents (atheists: 34 per-

only 4 percent of US adults say they are atheists, and, as noted above, most of them affirm supernatural forces. Reportedly, Wicca is "technically the fastest-growing religion" in America, and interest in witchcraft among the educated is rising.[14] Among political conservatives, the influence of mind-science theosophy is evident in the popularity of positive-thinking and prosperity-gospel movements.[15]

Spirituality without religion is not just a vapid way station to atheism, particularly when most atheists affirm some sort of spiritual reality.[16] Not even in post-Christian Europe is scientific naturalism the victor over religion. Instead, beliefs that would have been considered superstitious by Christians and scientists alike are considered scientific. Like American nonreligious spirituals or nones, Europeans—with a much longer history of secularization—are not less "superstitious" than they have been in the past but actually more so.[17]

---

cent; agnostics: 65 percent). Moreover, seven out of ten respondents agreed that the living can experience the presence of the dead, and half of respondents said they had been personally helped by them (even two-thirds of nones). Although Protestants traditionally deny the assistance of souls in heaven, 38 percent of evangelicals believe that one may receive help from the deceased, and 35 percent believe that one can communicate with them. See Pew Research Center, "Few Americans Blame God," 14.

14. Busker, "Witchcraft Is on the Rise"; Burton, "Rise of Progressive Occultism." See Burton's considerable documentation and explanation of the rise in *Strange Rites*.

15. On the evolution of the prosperity gospel (and much else in American religious culture) from New Thought, see the suberb study by Haller, *History of New Thought*. The prosperity gospel (also called "Word of Faith") has been enormously successful abroad, especially in Africa and South America. Though the object of a barrage of evangelical critiques in the past thirty years, many recent advocates (including close advisors of former president Trump) are now considered by the media—and political allies—as mainstream evangelicals. The list of evangelical critiques of the movement is too lengthy to include here. For one example, see McConnel, *Different Gospel*.

16. Steve Bruce offers compelling evidence that the interest in "alternative spiritualities," including the New Age movement, is simply part of the process leading from belief to unbelief. For example, those with "fuzzy" religious identities do not believe that there is only one way of salvation and so do not take "their" way with the same seriousness as traditional believers. Consequently, they neither proselytize outsiders nor catechize their young. The next generation joins the ranks of the "neither spiritual nor religious" (*Secularization*, 165–73). Even if Bruce is right, though, "spiritual but not religious" has persisted as a major tradition throughout our history to the present. If de-Christianization accounts for this phenomenon, then it has been happening for a long time and, in all likelihood, will continue. Without discounting Bruce's evidence, his conclusions seem a bit too dismissive of "spirituality" as nothing more than a way station to agnostic or atheistic positions.

17. "In Europe, there seems to be even more widespread belief [than in the United States] that astrology is scientific"—53 percent according to a European Commission study in 2001. See Allum and Stoneman, "Astrology in Europe," 302.

Consistently, sociologists of religion underscore the point that individual autonomy is the main driver of secularization. One may still be intensely engaged inwardly and privately while being disengaged from bodily and communal practices considered cages of the soul.[18] Even ideological secularism appears to be compatible with spirituality. As Charles Taylor points out, if one's measure is "the great historical faiths, or even with the explicit belief in supernatural beings, then it seems to have declined.... But if you include a wide range of spiritual and semi-spiritual beliefs, or if you cast your net even wider and think of someone's religion as the shape of their ultimate concern, then indeed, one can make a case that religion is as present as ever."[19] Like much of secularization itself, secularization theory arose within Christian societies and, for the most part, measures the waning influence of Christian beliefs and practices.

At least in Western modernity, spirituality without religion equates roughly to pantheism or panentheism without biblical monotheism, especially as interpreted in Christianity. And, as illustrated vividly in the cases of Socrates and Spinoza, polytheists and theists alike often find such spirituality indistinguishable from atheism. Emerging first as reinterpretations of and dissent from particular doctrines, antitheism has always been a secularizing phenomenon within monotheistic (especially Christian) religions, one led typically by mystics and critics who are ordained clergy. We should not forget that the Enlightenment itself was influenced significantly by "enthusiastic" alternatives to public religion. As Paul Tillich observed:

> It is entirely wrong to place the rationalism of the Enlightenment in contradiction to pietistic mysticism. It is popular nonsense that reason and mysticism are the two great opposites. Historically, Pietism and the Enlightenment both fought against Orthodoxy. The subjectivity of Pietism, or the doctrine of the "inner light" in Quakerism and other ecstatic movements, has the character of immediacy or autonomy against the authority of the church. To put it more sharply, modern rational autonomy is a child of the mystical autonomy of the doctrine of the inner light.[20]

Many figures of the Enlightenment were associated with mystical-pantheistic sects. Spinoza, whose work influenced them, belonged to a community of Anabaptists, Baptists, Quakers, and Remonstrants known as Collegiants after his ex-

---

18. Bruce, *Secularization*, 22, 103, 155.
19. Taylor, *Secular Age*, 427.
20. Tillich, *History of Christian Thought*, 286–87.

communication from the Amsterdam synagogue. Neither secular nor religious (in an orthodox sense), the Collegiants were nevertheless intensely spiritual—in the words of the Marxist historian Leszek Kołakowki, "Chrétiens sans Église."[21] This is not the whole story of secularization, much less of modernity, but it is a much larger part of the story than is usually told.

In fact, the phenomenon treated here so infuses our collective memory that we are often unaware of its influence. Rooted in the antipaganism of the Hebrew prophets, Christianity suppressed this aspect of the Western personality, and the Enlightenment folded Christianity itself into the immaturity of superstition. My goal is to conjure this repressed memory and to recognize it as a formative and enduring legacy in the narrative of modernity. In this volume I am interested especially in the emergence of the notion of the "divine self" that lies at the heart of a major transition from a locative to a utopian cosmos that I explain below.

Shaman and the Sage: Bronze Age Backdrop to the Axial Age

Arising in the fourth millennium BCE in the Fertile Crescent between the Tigris and the Euphrates, the Mesopotamian city of Sumer became one of the cradles of civilization where protowriting and technological advances flourished. Within a few centuries, Ur emerged as an even greater Sumerian city ruled by a king. Later the Akkadians, an East Semitic group, displaced the ruling class of Ur and established the first Mesopotamian empire there (2350–2150 BCE).

However, Indo-Iranian migrations from the steppes of Russia and central Asia in the next millennium would change history's course.[22] Sharing a common language, cult, and customs—including their invention of the war chariot—the Indo-Iranians branched into Iranian and Indo-Aryan peoples.

Launching the first wave, Indo-Aryans migrated to the Indus Valley civilization, which encompassed much of today's Pakistan, Afghanistan, and northwestern India.[23] From 1500 to 500 BCE, Indo-Aryans dominated all but southern India, with the Kuru Kingdom becoming the first organized state on the Indian subcontinent. The Indian branch also produced a number of significant migrations westward, including some to the Mediterranean where they became the ruling elite of the Hurrian-speaking Mitanni kingdom of the Levant and eastern Anatolia. In a sec-

---

21. Kołakowski, *Chrétiens sans Église*.
22. David W. Anthony provides an elegant and informed narrative in *Bronze Age Riders*; cf. Cavelli-Sforza, *History and Geography of Human Genes*.
23. Mallory, *Search of the Indo-Europeans*, 58–59.

Introduction

ond wave of migrations, Iranians settled in Mesopotamia, replacing the Akkadian Empire with the Old Babylonian Empire (1894–1598 BCE).

Across these Bronze Age societies, the following features are generally recognizable. Most of these Bronze Age societies possessed a cosmotheogonic myth of chaos-to-cosmos that justified the rites prescribed by the triumphant generation of deities ruling the holy city through a divine king. Signaling divine inspiration, these myths were written in epic poetry that had often been circulated orally in songs for centuries prior to being recorded. One of the earliest, written in Sumero-Akkadian cuneiform script, was the Mesopotamia Enuma Elish.[24] Several centuries later, Vedic Sanskrit emerged, forming the earliest layers of the Rigveda.[25] The Rigveda consists of 1,028 hymns whose earliest layers were transmitted orally from 1500 to 1200 BCE by Indo-Aryan tribes as they migrated from Afghanistan through Pakistan into northern India. The distinctively Iranian Avesta is a collection of texts written in Old Avestan. Like the early layers of the Rigveda, the oldest substrate of the Avesta consists of hymns and liturgical formulas, including hymns to individual divinities (*yazatas*). The common origin of Indic and Iranian peoples is evident in their shared use of cognate terms and especially the names of divinities.[26]

Significantly, these oldest forms of writing are religious epics—theogonic-cosmological myths relating the evolution of the visible world from the bodies of the gods. These epics are characterized by an emphasis on how the present generation of gods, after vanquishing their parents, came to rule the known world. Turning chaos into the beautifully ordered cosmos, the divine family in these myths establishes the social order along with the rituals that humans must perform in order to keep the polis from returning to confusion. These epic poems reflect the shift in Bronze Age civilizations from tribal warfare to settled life. Their chief concern is security within the walled city wherein culture flourishes from generation to generation. Like Russian dolls, the individual is embedded in the family, which is embedded in the polis of the divine warrior-king who guards the internal and external boundaries. The human king is the image of the king of the gods.

The supreme divinity of Indo-European mythologies is almost universally represented as the thunderbolt-hurling god of sky and storm.[27] However, not even

---

24. Mallory and Mair, *Tarin Mummies*, 257.

25. See Lowe, *Participles in Rigvedic Sanskrit*, 1–2.

26. These cognates include human (*manu*), spirits (*asura/ahura*), evil spirit (*druh/druj*), sun (*svar/hvar*), waters (*ap*), heaven (*ashman/asman*), prosperity (*usij*), priest (*bhaga/baga*), covenant (*mitra/mithra*), sacred spell (*mantra/manthra*). Many names of deities (*deva/daeva*) are shared: Supreme Lord of Wisdom (Asura Mahata/Ahura Mazda), Yama/Yima, Sarva (the Rigvedic attribute of Rudra that becomes hypostatized as Shiva), and others. See Griswold and De Witt, *Religion of the Rigveda*, 20–21.

27. Zeus fits the pattern we find with Set (Middle Egyptian), Indra (Indic), Ahura Mazda

this god is omnipotent. Due to a foolish mistake, Indra allows the evil spirits to enter the world, precipitating a career of perpetual war much like Ahura Mazda's battle against Ahriman and his demonic hosts. Moreover, the chief deity can behave in unpredictable ways as the cause of both prosperity and destruction. Set reflects this duality in Middle Egyptian myths. Although he can be destructive, Set also accompanies Ra in his solar barque, defeating the chaos serpent Apep. However, in the Osiris cycle of the Late Period, Set is unambiguously evil and the source of chaos.[28]

The founding myth also sanctions the cult. Only by performing perfectly the rites prescribed by the gods, including the annual renewal of the king's mandate by the chief deity ("Mandate from Heaven" in China), is prosperity assured. The gods do not exist outside the world, nor did they create it. Rather, they are the senior members of the community. Culture is cultic. The cult centers on rituals, and the rituals secure a long life of flourishing in the earthly city founded by the gods rather than in another world. If there is such an idea as immortality, it is achieved through offspring who contribute to the further good of the city.

Catastrophes of various sorts led to the Bronze Age Collapse (1200–1150 BCE), which occurred in northern India and throughout the Mediterranean.[29] The Hittite Empire was toppled and proud cities, after being plundered, were reduced to ruins.[30] Fleeing invaders from the sea, waves of refugees fled to other countries or to their own countryside to eke out a meager existence on small farms in villages.[31] The only semblance of civilization was the vast sea-bound "empire" of the Phoe-

---

(Iranian), Wotan (Germanic), Odin (Norse), Perun (Slavic), Ba'al (Canaanite/Phoenician), and Teshnub (Hurrian).

28. See Te Velde, "Seth," 3:269.

29. See Drews, *End of the Bronze Age*. The dates range more broadly depending on the civilization in question, but the most devastating impact generally occurs in this window.

30. Natural disasters such as volcanic eruptions and earthquakes have been suggested as causes for the Bronze Age Collapse, but the dominant theory for more than a century has been waves of invading "Sea Peoples." Some evidence suggests these Sea Peoples were Mycenaean Greeks, toppling the Hittite Empire and settling in Canaan as the biblical Philistines. Inscriptions in Egypt, Mari, and Syria mention "Caphtor," located in Crete, where the Minoans created the first European civilization. Moreover, Mycenaean pottery has been found all over southern Canaan (i.e., Philistia). In Amos 9:7, Yahweh declares, "Did I not bring up Israel from the land of Egypt, and the Philistines from Caphtor and the Syrians from Kir?" (cf. Gen 10:13–14; 1 Chr 1:11–12). See Redford, *Egypt, Canaan, and Israel*. A study found that the genetic makeup of Iron Age inhabitants of the region differs from that of the Bronze Age; see Feldman et al., "Iron Age Philistines." For a thorough review of the secondary literature see Woudhuisen, *Language of the Sea Peoples*.

31. At the same time, immigrants from the Balkans poured into teetering Mycenaean kingdoms. Many Mycenaean Greeks took refuge in recently founded colonies in Asia Minor and around the Black Sea, leaving the Aegean world a wasteland. See Meier, *Culture of Freedom*, 51.

nicians. Headquartered in modern Lebanon, it ringed the entire Mediterranean from Cyprus to Egypt and the Iberian Peninsula, but it was basically a company with commercial rather than political ambitions. The dissolution of the Kuru Kingdom in northern India around 900 BCE marked the collapse of the Rigvedic civilization. Egypt barely survived through these centuries, known as its Third Intermediate Period. Regardless of what may have caused this widespread collapse, Michael Grant represents the mainstream consensus when he says, "There was a gigantic series of migratory waves, extending all the way from the Danube valley to the plains of China."[32]

Throughout Asia and Egypt as well as Thrace and Greece a massive transformation occurred, which was marked by the ascent of the Assyrians. Growing steadily from a regional power, the Neo-Assyrian Empire lasted from the tenth to the seventh centuries. Like most of its successors, this empire was ruthless—for example, inculcating an imperial rather than local identity by deporting entire populations to other regions. Yet it was profuse in its advances, including a postal system and highways. In cultural life generally we discern a movement from chaos to order, from division to unity, from the many to the One.

A brief Neo-Babylonian Empire (612–539 BCE), marked by Judah's exile under Nebuchadnezzar II, was toppled by the Achaemenid Persian Empire led by Cyrus the Great. Johann P. Arnason observes, "Persian rule in the Near East was the culminating phase of a process that began when eighth-century Assyria embarked on an unprecedented project of world empire." Unprecedented exchange occurred within a realm that reached from the Danube to India and from the Black Sea to Egypt. Interactions between India and China during this period are hotly debated. While there are exaggerations on both sides, one conclusion seems obvious: "there was more interaction across the Eurasian microregion, before and during the Axial Age, than earlier historians tended to think."[33]

If civilization were to recover, it could never again depend on local kings invested with sacred authority but who were despotic and ineffective. India's new religions were born during its Second Urbanization period. Recovering from its "Dark Age" about a century later than these other civilizations, Greece began its migration from division toward unity. Among the chief signs of this movement are colonization, immigration of skilled workers, and urbanization. Coin currency rendered commerce more universal and mobile but also contributed to depersonalized social relations.[34] Security and prosperity required a new social order

---

32. Grant, *Ancient Mediterranean*, 79.
33. Arnason, "Rehistoricizing the Axial Age," 346–47.
34. See Seaford, *Money*. Surprisingly little work has appeared on the influence of factors

of laws and participation by free citizens (i.e., male landowners). Christian Meier calls it "the emergence of the political." Each group would choose a location for a settlement placed within a hilltop fort (*polis*) around which a new city grew.[35] While elsewhere power was still the dominant driver, Greeks were compromising and reasoning about the good city.

Phoenician immigrants brought alphabetic writing to the Greeks just in time for them to record the works of Homer, rendering obsolete the wide variations of these myths brought by traveling rhapsodes. Writing contributed to the shift from the local, concrete, diverse, and flexible communities based on oral communication to an emphasis on the universal, abstract, unified, and unvarying. The result was a massive disembedding and the rise of the autonomous individual. These trending shifts from the particular to the universal, the many to the One, the local to the global, the oral to the written, are bound up with the shift from locative to utopian. Uprooted from kith and kin, people belonged to an increasingly universal and abstract thing called society. No more than in an extensive canyon is the formation entirely homogeneous, yet distinct layers of sedimentation are recognizable and consistent along its length and breadth.

At the same time, across these diverse civilizations we see revolutions in religion. In its broadest horizon of meaning, this phenomenon represents a transition toward what Copleston described as the "Religion of the One."[36] During this period we witness a rather sharp and deliberate break with tradition, especially with its founding myths and ritualistic orientation focused on preserving the present order, in the direction of more abstract and philosophical doctrines. There are striking parallels even with respect to the new myths and concepts.

At the cosmic level, this is represented by the idea of the emanation of everything that is real from a single and absolute source, spreading like fireworks into a dazzling appearance of diversity and returning to its real being as a simple unity. At the microcosmic level, this idea is represented by the doctrine of transmigration (i.e., reincarnation). Emanating from the divine All, the Soul becomes divided into souls by falling into a body. Yearning for the All, souls hope to return to their proper unity after passing through many lives, meriting escape from the wheel of birth and rebirth. This doctrine of emanation-and-return ap-

---

in the Axial revolution other than ideas. Seaford overcorrects at points but draws insightful connections from detailed research.

35. Meier, *Culture of Freedom*, 52–53.

36. I take this from the title of Frederick Copleston's 1979 Gifford Lectures, *Religion and the One*. However, I argue that Zoroastrianism and the Hebrew prophets emphasize monotheism while the wider Axial trend is toward monism (i.e., pantheism or panentheism).

Introduction

peared in various civilizations at the same time without precedent in their earlier religious traditions.

That a major transition occurred around the sixth century BCE is difficult to deny. Under the astonishingly successful reigns of Cyrus the Great and Darius I, the Persian Empire became the most expansive power of its time, stretching from northern India to the Danube and from the Black Sea to Egypt. During this same century Confucius and Mencius, along with their mystical Taoist rivals Lao-Tse (Laozi) and Chuang Tzu (Zhuangzi); the Hinduism of the Upanishads; Jainism; Gautama Buddha; Zoroaster; the Hebrew prophets; and the Greek philosophers and tragedians all flourished. In short, the sixth century gave birth to universal religions that were more philosophical and oriented toward individual spirituality, transcendence, and unity with the divine All.[37] Across these diverse civilizations the so-called One and the Many Problem was a pressing issue on various levels: sociopolitical and economic no less than religious and philosophical.[38]

Axial Age

One prominent theory for this phenomenon was proposed in 1953 by the philosopher Karl Jaspers: "It would seem that the axis of history is to be found in the period around 500 B.C.," he says, "in the spiritual process that occurred between 800 and 200 B.C. . . . It is there that we meet with the most deepcut dividing line in history. Man, as we know him today, came into being. For short we may style this the 'Axial Period.'"[39]

Jaspers discerns clear features of such axiality. "What is new about this age, in all three areas of the world," says Jaspers, "is that man becomes conscious of Being as a whole, of himself and his limitations. He experiences the terror of the world and his own powerlessness. He asks radical questions. Face to face with the void he strives for liberation and redemption." Setting up for himself "the highest goals," this new self "experiences absoluteness in the depths of selfhood and in the lucidity of transcendence." This transcendence is twofold: the divine world above and beyond this one and the self's own ability to transcend the limits of the visible world. The highest point of transcendence is the deepest and truest self, expressed in the Upanishads' formula "Atman is Brahman" (4).

---

37. For reasons I explain later, the biblical prophets and Zoroastrianism are less susceptible to this generalization.

38. Turner, "Ontological Pluralism," 5–34.

39. Jaspers, *Origin and Goal of History*, 1. Subsequent references are given in the text.

No longer taking for granted one's boundedness, embeddedness, and embodiment in a concrete social, political, and historical context, this new self strives for universality. "As a result of this process, hitherto unconsciously accepted ideas, customs and conditions were subjected to examination, questioned and liquidated." From mythological thinking to a new stance of critical reasoning, religion became ethical and mythic, and rather than signifying particular events, "was turned into parable." In short, "This overall modification of humanity may be termed *spiritualization*.... In *speculative thought* he lifts himself up towards Being itself, which is apprehended without duality in the disappearance of subject and object, in the coincidence of opposites ... a coming-to-oneself within Being ... as becoming one with the Godhead" (1–3).

This transcendent orientation, Jaspers continues, led to a transition from mythological thinking to rationalization (*mythos* to *logos*). Rather than discovering an origin and a goal within history, the divine self finds this unity in an eternal cosmic process of emanation from the All into diversity and return to unity. "For the first time *philosophers* appeared.... Hermits and wandering thinkers in China, ascetics in India, philosophers in Greece and prophets in Israel all belong together, however much they may differ from each other in their beliefs, the contents of their thought and their inner dispositions.... He discovered within himself the origin from which to raise himself above his own self and the world" (3).

For Jaspers and many scholars who adopt his thesis today, "axiality" is like a Platonic form transcending actual historical particulars. Jaspers concentrates on "the common element." It is hardly a coincidence that Axial revolutions continue to be felt all around the world to the present, but they bear in themselves "this common element" that originated specifically in these civilizations simultaneously (9).

Jaspers is not ashamed to be an evangelist for the Axial Age. In fact, his zeal is evident in the epithets he attributes: "The whole of humanity took a forward leap.... Thus the higher we ourselves ascend, the more clearly do we see the Axial Period" (4). Though not subject to proof, "it can, however, be substantiated through a widening and deepening of the conception." As Jaspers writes, critics objected to Hegel's attempt to bring together "China, India and the West as stages in the dialectical sequence of the development of the spirit" on the basis that there is no historical evidence of such dependence. "Our thesis, however, involves something altogether different.... The true situation was rather one of contemporaneous, side by side existence without contact.... There are three independent roots of one history, which later—after isolated and interrupted contacts, finally only a few centuries ago and properly speaking not until our own day—become a single unity" (10–11). It is not a mere parallelism of certain features here and there, but a "total universal parallelism on the plane of world history" (12). Whenever and wherever such "breakthroughs to transcendence" appear, they are the effective history of the Axial Age.

It is clear that "breakthroughs" (or enlightenments) are measured by their correspondence to the development that has been most clearly achieved in Western mysticism. Writing in the aftermath of two world wars, Jaspers the existentialist philosopher is dedicated to a creed: "My outline is based on an article of faith: that mankind has one single origin and one goal," although (contra Hegel) these are completely unknowable and only discerned here and there in symbols (xv). It was "a deep breath bringing the most lucid consciousness" (2, 51).

Following Jaspers, many advocates of the Axial Age thesis are apologists for a nondogmatic, pantheistic/panentheistic, experientialist, and individualist spirituality. The Axial Age has also been called the "Great Leap of Being" and the "Great Transformation."[40] These epithets play up the generally sympathetic, sometimes even apologetic, character of the Axial Age thesis. Walter Burkert is certainly right in his observation that academic research has been a "battlefield between rationalists and mystics since the beginning of the nineteenth century."[41] Both assume a metanarrative of progress from immaturity to enlightenment. They agree that this path travels from dependence on authority to individual autonomy. Where they diverge is in the genealogy that led to modernity. In this sense, both are metanarratives as defined by Lyotard.[42]

Far from being a dispassionate historical account, the Axial Age thesis itself belongs to the reception history it seeks to explain. It emerges from a history of conservative Catholic interests to show that Christianity is the result of a fusion of Greek and biblical ideas.[43] Jan Assmann's criticism of the thesis is apt:

---

40. Voegelin, *In Search of Order*, esp. 37–47. As the latter two monikers imply, the thesis tends toward a metanarrative about where history *should* be going, which happens to coincide with a "new age" anticipated by Romanticism's antimodern trend. More recently, Karen Armstrong has called it "The Great Transformation," that is, when religious dogmatism was replaced by self-transformation and the idea that "All is One"; see Armstrong, *Great Transformation*. Given her expertise, this is a surprisingly shallow jeremiad, chockful of trite and vaguely New Age contrasts between dogmatists (i.e., theists) and "the great mystics, philosophers and poets" of the Axial Age. It is more about "our modern predicament" than a historical report. In a more nuanced version, Charles Taylor's *Secular Age* nevertheless perpetuates the disenchantment narrative of Max Weber and John Milbank with the Hebrew prophets (culminating in the Protestant Reformation) as the extinguishers of the sacred. Focused appropriation of the thesis is found throughout Taylor, *Secular Age*, 146–58, 308, 438–39, 578, 611–14, 685–89, 770–74. Critiques of the Axial Age thesis are plentiful. See for example Provan, *Conventional Myths*.

41. Burkert, *Babylon, Memphis, Persepolis*, 74. Defenders of the "Axial Age" thesis tend to be on the "mystical" side of Burkert's divide.

42. See the introduction to Lyotard, *Postmodern Condition*.

43. Joas, "Axial Age Debate," 10–24. In the aftermath of the Second World War, Jaspers, a

Inventing the "Divine Self": Where We Are Headed

Jaspers' theory of the Axial Age with its characteristic traits of "modernity" is not only a self-portrait or a cultural autobiography but also a normative mirror, confronting modern man with an image of how he should be. As far as the Western part of the Axial hemisphere is concerned, the concept of *Geist* [Spirit] ... plays in fact an enormous and ever-increasing role in the cultural texts of the ancient, especially (neo-)Platonic, Jewish, Christian, and, above all, Gnostic worlds.[44]

I share Assmann's suspicion that for Jaspers the Axial Age is equivalent to the way Christianity talks about the incarnation, even dividing history into before and after Christ.[45]

Jaspers's account also reads like a new myth of creation, fall, and redemption. Despite his repeated screeds against dogmatism, his thesis is quite dogmatic. Although he inveighs against the "exclusive truth" claimed by particular religions, he seems to endorse quite distinct dogmas.[46] As Assmann observes, Jaspers treats all of humanity as originating in the Axial Age, such that around 500 BCE "Man, as we know him today, came into being."[47] However, there was a fall: "When the age lost its creativeness, a process of dogmatic fixation and levelling-down took place in all three cultural realms." Obsession with rational organization and planning built universal empires, quenching much of the original spirit.[48] "The Axial Period too ended in failure. History went on." But that history "is determined, down to consequences I have only been able to hint at, by the conception of the Axial Period, irrespective of whether this thesis is accepted or rejected. It is a question of the manner in which the unity of mankind becomes a concrete reality for us."[49]

---

disaffected Protestant, contributed to a more cosmopolitan "enlightenment" than traditional descriptions of a "Greek Miracle." Nevertheless, he introduces a new division between "unawakened" and "awakened" cultures that, with his rigid definitions of the elements of the Axial Age, sounds a lot like "premodern" and "modern."

44. Assmann, "Cultural Memory," 373.

45. Assmann, "Cultural Memory," 375–76, referring to Voegelin, *Israel and Revelation*.

46. Jaspers, *Origin and Goal of History*, 20. An example of his "view from nowhere" is his judgment of Augustine. Reading Augustine brings the reader's conscience to the fore in a way unexamined by the Greeks. "Conversely, however, after spending some time on St. Augustine, he will experience an increasing desire to return to the Greeks and cleanse himself of the feeling of impurity that seems to grow with the pursuit of this type of thinking, to regain his health by immersion in the pellucid waters of Greek thought. *Nowhere on earth can we find final truth, authentic salvation*" (20, emphasis added). Combined with his metaphysics and eschatology, one might conclude with some justification that Jaspers accepts a gnostic verdict on history.

47. Jaspers, *Origin and Goal of History*, 1. Ironically, he says later that philosophy of history originated from a secularization of Christianity's notion of creation, fall, redemption, and consummation—particularly "St. Augustine's total conception" (186).

48. Jaspers, *Origin and Goal of History*, 5–6.

49. Jaspers, *Origin and Goal of History*, 20–21.

Introduction

Like the golden age of Hesiod and Vergil, the Axial Age is a myth by which history is measured. The eschaton is the unity of humanity, as Jaspers writes:

> Unity is not a fact, but a goal. The unity of history is perhaps produced by men's ability to understand each other in the idea of the One, in the one truth, in the world of the spirit, in which all things are meaningfully related to one another and belong together, however alien to each other they may be at the outset.... The goal is taken to be the manifestation of Being in man, the perception of being in its depths, that is, the manifestation of the Godhead.[50]

Indeed, as Jaspers declares later, "can I elude history, escape from it into the timeless?"[51] His concluding chapter, "Overcoming History," asserts that we move through history to the "supratemporal." "Here we overstep history to the everlasting present; as historical existence in history we are above and beyond history. We overcome history by entering into the unconscious.... What matters is the demand for presentness as eternity in time.... To the transcendent consciousness of existence, history vanishes in the everlasting present."[52]

In spite of the mythological character of Jaspers's thesis, it is difficult to resist the impression that he is generally correct about these features. He is wrong, as Assmann notes, in focusing on the *synchronicity* of the Axial revolution occurring all at once around the sixth century BCE. Hinduism, Buddhism, and Zoroastrianism did not exhibit all the features of "axiality" until they became part of a canon. "Decisive is the step to turn these visions into 'cultural texts,' to select these texts into a canon and to frame the transmission of this canon by institutions of exegesis ensuring its availability, readability, and authority over 3,000 years."[53] This process, which Assmann dates from 200 BCE to 200 CE, actually took much longer. Hindu and Buddhist "canons" were still being formed well into the twelfth century CE. Yet even critics generally concede the feature that Jaspers called "the common element" of the Axial Age. Most agree that it is the "Age of Transcendence."[54]

---

50. Jaspers, *Origin and Goal of History*, 257.
51. Jaspers, *Origin and Goal of History*, 271.
52. Jaspers, *Origin and Goal of History*, 273, 276.
53. Assmann, "Cultural Memory," 399. As Assmann notes, writing began long before the Axial Age as a sectoral (record-keeping) enterprise. However, the "primary canonization" of texts began as a process of oral transmission over many centuries. It is "secondary canonization"—the fixing of a particular set of texts as normative—that marks axiality. It generates "a culture of exegesis as its necessary complement" that makes it a living feature of the cultural memory.
54. Schwartz, "Age of Transcendence," 1–7.

Transcendence is a multivalent term.[55] In Jaspers's usage it has two connotations: the breaking out of the One from all limitations of the anthropomorphic gods, and the human self breaking through the limitations of time and space to unite with this One. Thus, Jaspers seems to imply that the theory of the emanation and return of all diverse things from the absolute simplicity of the One provides the metaphysical-mythical frame for other features of the Axial Age. Even critics like Assmann acknowledge, "The concept of the Axial Age refers to cultures and worldviews that distinguish between immanence (the this-worldly realm, home to the conditional and contingent) and transcendence (the other-worldly realm, home to the unconditional and absolute). On that basis, they tend to take a critical stance toward the world as it actually exists."[56] The invisible world is aloof to the boundaries and limitations of the visible world with its natural laws, but in its union with the body the soul forgets this. Analogously, the self takes for granted the limitations imposed by social and political embedding. The crowd will continue to mistake the shadows for the reality, but the philosopher, like the shaman, leads the few to escape these bonds.

What makes the Axial Age "axial," according to Bellah, is the "breakthrough" to a theoretical understanding or "reflexivity."[57] In other words, there is a discovery of the self, the world, and the beyond that encourages focused reflection on the meaning of existence.

> The first of these facts is the emergence in the first millennium B.C. all across the Old World, at least in the centers of high culture, of the phenomenon of the religious rejection of the world characterized by an extremely negative evaluation of man and society and the exaltation of another realm of reality as alone true and infinitely valuable. This theme emerges in Greece through a long development into Plato's classic formulation in the Phaedo that the body is the tomb or prison of the soul. In India we find perhaps the most radical of all versions of world rejection, culminating in the great image of the Buddha.[58]

"In China," Bellah adds, "Taoist ascetics urged the transvaluation of all the accepted values and withdrawal from human society," in contrast to "the virtual

---

55. Ingolf U. Dalferth offers an extensive and penetrating analysis of different connotations in his essay "Idea of Transcendence."
56. Assmann, *Invention of Religion*, 7.
57. Bellah, "Axial Age," 69.
58. Bellah, *Beyond Belief*, 22–23.

absence of world rejection in primitive religions."⁵⁹ "The Buddhist version of the Parable of the Cave is in an important sense the whole elaborate story of the Buddha's life as the tradition handed it down."⁶⁰ Bellah observes that "a very different formulation is found in Israel," though also with a greater stress on God's transcendence.⁶¹

Once it is accepted that there is another realm of absolute, unchanging, incorruptible, intelligible truth, goodness, and beauty, it follows naturally that people would begin to distance and disembed themselves from nature, history, society, and everything associated with bodily incarceration. The new myth is simultaneously a product of the new doctrines and a producer, since it provides the imagination with a new way of looking at things. And, as Socrates led Adeimantus to conclude, over a few generations these new myths might just take hold.

My purpose is not to engage Jaspers's thesis or its many subsequent articulations. Many of the features of the "Axial Age" I accept. However, it is definitely not a trend from polytheism toward *monotheism*, as frequently suggested, but rather toward *monism*, which I use in the modern philosophical sense.

There are several types of monism, but the most fundamental meaning is that reality is one, not many; diversity is apparent, not real.⁶² It is the "Religion of the One" that fosters (and is fostered by) this shift from a this-worldly frame to an otherworldly frame that encourages many of the other features that specialists associate with "axiality":

- **Cosmological Level:** The world emanates into diversity from the Absolute and returns to unity. Typically, this means that only incorporeal ideas are real and material things range from being mere appearances to shadows to deceptive

---

59. Bellah, *Beyond Belief*, 22–23. We see an example of this in Chuang Tzu, also known as Zhuangzi (310–230 BCE), who distinguishes the two realms sharply, referring to the "Genuine-Humans of old": "In their oneness, they were followers of the Heavenly. In their non-oneness, they were followers of the human." Chuang Tzu, "Great Source as Teacher," 55. The heavenly/human contrast appears throughout this chapter.

60. Bellah, "Heritage," 459.

61. Bellah, *Beyond Belief*, 22. Proponents of the axial thesis frequently overlook the extent to which Israel is an exception. There are parallels, which I indicate, but within a radically different outlook than is present in either primitive or "axial" periods. It would require more evidence to conclude with Bellah here that, despite the different formulation, "there too the world is profoundly devalued in the face of the transcendent God."

62. See for example Schaeffer, "Monism." I find often among Axial theorists the conflation of monism and monotheism, but pantheism/panentheism is of course radically different from theism. Sometimes monism is used to refer to the pre-Axial belief in one world with gods in it, but in this case monism is confused with polytheism.

illusions. "The great invention of the West," says Taylor, "was that of an immanent order in Nature, whose working could be systematically understood and explained on its own terms, leaving open the question whether this whole order had a deeper significance, and whether, if it did, we should infer a transcendent Creator beyond it."[63] The question would never have occurred to a pre-Axial person: "Is there something we're missing in our everyday lives because we focus so much on the here-and-now?" The question presupposes a "then-and-there."

- **Microcosmic (Psychological) Level:** The divine soul (the real part of us) falls into diversity through embodiment and returns to the Cosmic Soul through philosophical ascent. The doctrine of transmigration (reincarnation) was as new in India as it was in Greece. It is a unique contribution of the sixth century BCE with the Upanishads, Buddha's teaching (insofar as we know it), and Orphism in Greece.

- **Epistemology:** Experiential knowledge conveyed through the bodily senses never rises above opinion, while gnosis—an intuitive, unmediated, and mystical vision—yields the certainty of vision. In fact, in this act the subject becomes one with the object. Instead of assuming the traditional order, one begins to question it. Ironically, skepticism will lead to absolute certainty. The autonomous individual is one who knows directly without dependence on tradition and authority. The self takes a stance outside the embedded social order, leading to disembedding, distancing, and a critical attitude toward the status quo. As Taylor observes, most of the time human beings are "naïve" rather than "reflective" in their "background" assumptions.[64] However, a distinction between the visible and the invisible dimensions (i.e., being and becoming) provokes a host of other distinctions. This making of distinctions proliferates throughout the intellectual and social worlds, trying to create a cosmos out of a perceived chaos. The "Axial" revolution represents a massive shift resulting from making background presuppositions explicit and focal, examining them, and criticizing them in light of a new standard: reason (which is ultimately transrational gnosis).

- **Ethically:** The "Age of Transcendence" gives birth to a new tribe in every religion—the renunciate who rejects the body, the visible world, and society as a dangerous illusion. Ritual exactitude, which is concerned with the city's flourishing here and now, is eclipsed by ethics: universal rules for attaining individual life beyond. For the Buddhist, "The way to Nirvana involves renounc-

---

63. Taylor, *Secular Age*, 15.
64. Taylor, *Secular Age*, 13.

ing, or at least going beyond, all forms of recognizable human flourishing."[65] Pythagoras, Socrates, Plato, and the Stoics in Greece, Hindu *shramanas*, and Buddhist monks are preachers of salvation from everything associated with the body.[66]

- **Politically**: Rulers, especially "divine kings," lend authority to the status quo. When measured against universal truths that transcend this world, these traditions are revealed as oppressive illusions that oppose the individual soul's liberation from the shackles of the body and the social world. After beholding the eternal ideas of justice, goodness, love, truth, and beauty, the soul can never allow itself to be enslaved to earthly institutions. Utopian revolution takes two forms, usually in succession: trying to remake the social world according to its eternal archetype, or renouncing this world altogether. Having beheld these realities, the philosopher rather than the ruler is in a position to determine the proper blueprint for society.

More useful in my view than the Axial Age paradigm is the distinction drawn by J. Z. Smith between *locative* and *utopian* outlooks.

> The former is concerned primarily with the cosmic and social issues of keeping one's place and reinforcing boundaries. The vision is one of stability and confidence with respect to an essentially fragile cosmos, one that has been reorganized, with effort, out of previous modes of order and one whose "appropriate order" must be maintained through acts of conscious labour. We may term such locative traditions, religions of sanctification.[67]

In a locative outlook, the individual feels embedded in an ordered cosmos with boundaries that must not be crossed. One belongs to a family that belongs to a clan that belongs to a city, which is the earthly copy of the archetypal society of the gods above.

Rituals sanctify the order that unites heaven and earth. Smith explains that in this perspective, "Order is something won by the gods and it is this primordial act of salvation which is renewed and reexperienced in the cult."[68] This worldview is cyclical. In terms of place, the temple is the navel of the cosmos, where the ladder

---

65. Taylor, *Secular Age*, 17.

66. Differences are also apparent. For example, Orphic-Platonic asceticism is enflamed with desire for "flourishing" by achieving transcendence while Buddhist ascetics aim at the extinction of all desire as the root of suffering.

67. Smith, *Drudgery Divine*, 121.

68. Smith, *Map Is Not Territory*, 13.

Inventing the "Divine Self": Where We Are Headed

between gods and mortals is planted. Its time moves in the circle of annual festivals that mimetically preserve the participation of the lower world in the higher.[69]

In a utopian worldview, however, "the structures of order are perceived to have been reversed." Smith writes, "Man is no longer defined by the degree to which he harmonizes himself and his society to the cosmic patterns of order; but rather by the degree to which he can escape the patterns."[70] The star of the epic age Smith calls "Hero-That-Failed," but the star of the utopian world is the "Hero-That-Succeeded"—succeeded, that is, in breaking through the limits of a bounded cosmos.

It is the shaman who survived the Bronze Age and, across all these diverse civilizations, represents a new model for the type of individual that we recognize as the modern "self." Fascination with shamanism has returned with considerable force in Western culture, from academic studies to movies and video games. Even as I write, the current issue of the *Atlantic* includes the following insights from David Brooks on the success of U2's Bono:

> The band's other great strength is the pseudo-religious power of their concerts. Bono was influenced by an obscure book called *The Death and Resurrection Show: From Shaman to Superstar*, by Rogan P. Taylor, which argues that modern performance culture has its ancient roots in shamanism. When we go to a concert, we enter the presence of a mystic who interacts with the spirit world and brings spiritual energies into the physical one. "We're religious people even when we are not. We find ritual and ceremony powerful," Bono says. "We were always interested in the ecstatic. I think our music reflects that."[71]

In contrast with the picture of a cultural evolution toward an Axial "breakthrough," Smith's paradigm highlights that any society at any time can experience a revolution from a locative to a utopian stance or vice versa. Rather than a straight line, this narrative is filled with zigzags, reminding us that history is made by people, individually and socially, who often make deliberate decisions at key junctures about which parts of the cultural memory will be privileged or repressed.

I will be invoking key phrases in this project that I will define here briefly. They describe the same phenomenon, but from different vantage points.

---

69. The name of Mircea Eliade is associated with comparisons relating to sacred space and time. See especially Eliade, *Myth of Eternal Return*; Eliade, *Sacred and Profane*; Eliade, *Myth and Reality*.
70. Smith, *Map Is Not Territory*, 139.
71. Brooks, "Too-Muchness of Bono."

Introduction

Natural Supernaturalism

Natural supernaturalism refers to the pantheistic or panentheistic cosmotheology of this tradition.[72] Modern historians of philosophy recognize this Orphic cosmology by terms such as absolute idealism, pantheism, or panentheism. Coining the phrase, Thomas Carlyle described it as a gospel that proclaims "an altogether (totally) new (or hitherto unconceived) *species* of divineness, a divineness lying much nearer home than formerly. A divineness that does not come from Judea, from Olympus, Asgard, or Mt. Meru; but is in man himself, in the heart of every living man."[73] Theists believe that God created the world *ex nihilo* and therefore sometimes intervenes miraculously in nature; antisupernaturalists count nothing as a miracle. In contrast with both, this new mythology taught that nature itself is miraculous, loaded with inherent wonders of its own marvelous divinity that transcend materialistic explanations. Carlyle wrote:

> That the Supernatural differs from the Natural is a great Truth, which the last century (especially in France) has been engaged in demonstrating. The Philosophers went far wrong, however, in this, that, instead of raising the natural to the supernatural, they strove to sink the supernatural to the natural. The gist of my whole way of thought is to do not the latter, but the *former*.[74]

Although Carlyle assumed that this was a "new Mythus" constructed by anti-Enlightenment Romantic writers, the outlook he embraces is the Orphic myth that founded Western culture. As contemporary panentheist David Ray Griffin defines it:

> The word "panentheism," generally thought to have been coined by Carl Friedrich Christian Krause in the early nineteenth century, refers to the doctrine that our world exists within a divine being—a doctrine often expressed by speaking of God as the "soul of the world." This doctrine has, in the intervening period, become increasingly widespread.... This worldview is now widely called "scientific

---

72. Panentheism (all is in God) differs from pantheism (all is God) in conceiving the divine Absolute as transcending (i.e., "more than") the world that it includes in itself. See J. W. Cooper, *Panentheism*.

73. Quoted in Baumgarten, "Carlyle's 'Spiritual Optics,'" 514. I first discovered Carlyle's phrase (from his work *Sartor Resartus*, published in serial from 1833 to 1834) in Abrams, *Natural Supernaturalism*.

74. Carlyle, extracts from journal, in James Anthony Froude, *Thomas Carlyle: A History of the First Forty Years of His Life, 1795–1835* (New York: Harper and Brothers, 1882), 198.

naturalism," which in its most fundamental sense, is simply the doctrine that there are no supernatural irruptions of the world's normal causal processes.[75]

The deeper we descend into ourselves, the higher we ascend. Richard Kroner describes this well: "Man discovered that he was in the center of the world, and that he had to seek truth and guidance within himself. No outer authority can assume ultimate responsibility for the individual character of the person or for the faith that a man may accept as the ultimate source of all his decisions and norms of conduct."[76] Nature itself is divine at least in its incorporeal aspects, each organism and even plant or star animated by a soul. Where natural supernaturalism prevails, one views nature itself as possessing an inherently divine potency that awaits access and manipulation by human wisdom and magic.

> In this narrative, the official representatives of the mainstream (Christian theologians, rational philosophers, modern scientists) have always tried to suppress it, but never with any lasting success, because, like the unconscious, it is the hidden secret of their own existence, the vital source without which they could not exist. The positive religions, particularly the monotheistic ones, are "external" products of time and historical circumstance—they have had a beginning, and will have an end—but underneath them, there has always been this permanent and universal substratum: a kind of objective paganism expressing itself by symbols and myths, and grounded in the universal human search for self-knowledge, or gnosis.[77]

Natural supernaturalism does not deny that there are mysterious forces that transcend materialistic explanation. What it does reject is the idea of a personal deity who is independent of the world, created it out of nothing, and intervenes in nature and history. For most theorists of secularization, including Max Weber, "disenchantment" is measured by a distinctly biblical attack on images and superstition mediated to the modern world through the sixteenth-century Reformation. For the most part, Charles Taylor and many others assume this narrative.

Israel's monotheism is unique, Assmann notes, "For this monotheism did not evolve organically from polytheism, but broke with it by denouncing it as pagan."[78] Polytheism, or what Assmann calls "cosmotheism," was the "other," a gentile plague

---

75. Griffin, *Panentheism and Scientific Naturalism*, 1.
76. Kroner, *Speculation and Revelation*, 25.
77. Hanegraaff, *Esotericism and the Academy*, 295
78. Assmann, *Price of Monotheism*, 39.

Introduction

whose infectious spread in Israel the prophets condemned. By cosmotheism, he means something like what I am calling natural supernaturalism. The gods are cosmic and so easily translatable between cultures. Everyone has a sun god, sea god, and so forth; they're just called by different names and in the so-called Axial Age they become universal cosmic principles.

The first exception to this ecumenism is Israel, with what Assmann calls the "Mosaic distinction." Yahweh cannot be substituted for any foreign god; the prohibition of other gods or even images of Yahweh institutes a distinction between true and false, worship and idolatry, believers and unbelievers. Not in the myths of the nations but in the covenant history of Yahweh with his chosen people, revealed authoritatively in scripture, is the truth to be found.[79] The West opted for monotheism officially: "above all, however, we can see that the rejected alternative, the cosmotheism driven out by monotheism, has constantly shadowed the religious and intellectual history of the West, and in certain phases even struck at its heart."[80]

Throughout Western history, migrations from monotheism have almost always ended up in some version of Orphic cosmotheism. However, it has never been repressed entirely but "seems to be the common denominator of Egyptian religion, Alexandrinian (Neoplatonic, Stoic, Hermetic) philosophy, and Spinozism, including the medieval traditions such as alchemy and the cabala that might have served as intermediaries."[81] Thriving in esoteric circles, sometimes underground, it has been nevertheless the primary inspiration of philosophical religion in Jewish, Christian, and Muslim contexts. Instead of a steady cultural evolution, therefore, what we find is a cultural memory with a repressed other that haunts and sometimes revolts against the dominant consciousness.

Orphism

The survivor throughout the Bronze Age Collapse was the shaman, whose distinctive characteristics remain sufficiently consistent to allow some generalizations.

---

79. Assmann presented this thesis first with *Moses* and *Of God and Gods*. Conceding justifiable criticisms, he wrote a more nuanced version of his thesis in *Price of Monotheism* and a fuller treatment in *Invention of Religion*. I remain unpersuaded by several lines of his argument, especially his claim that the Bible's exclusive (or revolutionary) monotheism was the springboard for the Axial Age. Like many scholars, Assmann conflates monotheism with monism, and the trends identified with the Axial thesis are definitely pantheistic/panentheistic and not theistic. However, I find illuminating points along the way in his work.

80. Assmann, *Price of Monotheism*, 43.

81. Assmann, *Moses*, 141–42.

Originating in the Siberian steppes, the shaman, "one who knows," followed the Indo-Iranian migration as it separated into Iranian and Indian peoples.[82] More than a medicine man, he was the mediator between the underworld, this world, and the heavens. A seer of spirits, he could heal clients by controlling demons as well as bring back messages and even souls from the afterlife. He entered into trances, accompanied by dancing and drums, and conversed with animals. Often associated with shamanistic rituals were entheogens: drugs prepared for "generating the divine within."[83] One may even argue that the shaman's tribe increased under conditions of dislocation, disorganization, and decentering.[84]

The shaman is literally utopian, liberated to be anywhere at any time or even everywhere all at once: above, below, beneath. From ancient shamanic circles new myths emerged along with a new utopian outlook that transformed the ritualistic focus of their respective public religions into philosophical religions focused on the One. On the one hand, this utopian impulse sought to re-create the concrete social world according to its more abstract, transcendent, and divine model. On the other hand, especially after disillusionment with this ideal was realized, utopianism turned toward the need to escape the mundane realm altogether.

The survivor of epic poetry becomes the shaman, and the shaman becomes the sage. In the name of Orpheus new myths enciphered a radically novel cosmology in which all things emanated from a single principle and return. As the microcosm of this eternal process, the individual soul falls into various bodies and seeks eagerly to escape its bodily prison and recover its unity with the One. As M. L. West explains:

> [Orpheus] stands outside the Mycenaean world. . . . He was hauled inside the cultural horizons of classical Hellas by being made the son of Apollo and Muse, and the ancestor of Hesiod and Homer. Yet the stories portray him not as a distant forerunner of Homer, but as a singer of a different type: one who

---

82. Ronald Hutton adopts this derivation in *Shamans*; cf. Hoppál, *Sámánok Eurázsiában*, 15. However, the etymology is highly debated. Mircea Eliade argued that the word "shaman" originated in the Sanskrit *shramana*, which designated a mendicant visionary; see Eliade, *Shamanism*, 495. See also Eliade's summary of essential attributes of shamanistic practice on pages 3–7. Hutton relates that in 1692 Dutch scholar Nicholas Witsen in his work *Noord en Oost Tataryen* introduced the West to the term in his report of indigenous Siberian (Tungus-speaking) peoples. See Hutton, *Triumph of the Moon*, 32.

83. De Souza et al., "Jurema-Preta."

84. Davis-Kimball, Bashilov, and Yablonsky, *Nomads of the Eurasian Steppes*. Focusing on Britain, John Creighton demonstrates with considerable evidence (e.g., coins, rock art, round houses) wide familiarity with shamanic imagery. See Williams and Creighton, "Shamanic Practice"; Creighton, "Visions of Power"; Creighton, *Coins and Power*.

Introduction

can exercise power over the natural world and who can countermand death itself, a "shamanistic" figure. He entered Greek mythology, surely, not by way of Mycenaean saga but at a later period from Thrace, or through Thrace from further north, from regions where shamanistic practices actually existed or had existed.[85]

Hans-Georg Gadamer hints at the importance of this topic, referring to "the so-called Orphic, an idea which has influenced scholarship for a long time, and which still represents a completely open realm of problems for research."[86] Significant light has been shed in recent decades on this archaic mystery cult from Thrace that Pythagoras, Empedocles, and others mediated to Socrates and Plato. I summarize some of these findings in the second and third chapters of this volume.

Orphism is a catchall label for what ancients themselves understood as teachings concerning the soul's immortality, its fall into a bodily prison, and its reincarnation in various bodies "to pay the penalty" with the hope of escaping the wheel of rebirth to reunite with the One and All.[87]

In his *Symbolism of Evil*, Paul Ricoeur highlights four anthropological myths that vie for control of the Western imagination. The "Adamic Myth" distinguishes sharply between creation and fall. Given the term's ontological associations in other paradigms, "fall" is less apt than a "unique event" of human rebellion.[88] In sharp contrast, the "Orphic Myth," which he calls "The Myth of the Exiled Soul and Salvation through Knowledge," identifies the "fall" with embodiment.[89] According to the Orphic myth, the soul is divine, "not from here . . . from elsewhere," and its kinship with its origin can only be experienced through altered states of consciousness (e.g., ecstasy).[90] Much of what we would like to know about Orphism is lost to the hoary past, but Ricoeur's description is supported by the evidence I present in the early chapters of this volume. The doctrines of emanation and return, including the descent and return of the soul after various reincarnations, were essential to all the new universal religions associated with the Axial Age.

Contrary to the mainstream Axial thesis, however, I argue that this revolution is not the forerunner of modern disenchantment (a Romantic trope pressed by

---

85. West, *Orphic Poems*, 4.
86. Gadamer, *Beginning of Philosophy*, 38.
87. I will address historical debates over whether such a coherent phenomenon existed in the classical era. More important than this question, for my purposes, is the tradition that believed it did.
88. Ricoeur, *Symbolism of Evil*, 243.
89. Ricoeur, *Symbolism of Evil*, 279.
90. Ricoeur, *Symbolism of Evil*, 287–88.

Nietzsche in *The Birth of Tragedy* and followed by Max Weber). If anything, the turn to transcendence was more enchanted than ever. It was not a shift from *mythos* to *logos*, as Jaspers claims, but from traditional myths that founded rituals to new ones that inculcated natural supernature. To be sure, it fostered disembedding with an attitude of critically distancing of the individual from the material and social world but only toward a vision of divine spirit infusing the whole cosmos. Far from being vestiges of an archaic age, *mythos*, mystical enthusiasm, and magic were from the beginning integral to Western rationality, the repressed other of modernity.[91] Even within a broadly secular frame of pure immanence, as Casanova suggests, "the disenchantment of the world does not necessarily entail the disenchantment of consciousness, the decline of religion, or the end of magic. On the contrary, it is compatible with all forms of reenchantment."[92]

We will see strange shaman-like divinities—minor characters in Homer and Hesiod—take center stage, overwhelming initiates with divine madness. Not only in Greece but far away, as the dramatist Euripides said, "Barbarians everywhere now dance for Dionysus" (*Bacch.* 482).[93] Just as Dionysus conquered Attica with his mysteries, festivals, and plays, the legendary Orpheus sought to reconcile the god of ecstatic frenzy to his more reasonable half brother Apollo. Behind such myths are real-life transformations and negotiations among people who collectively shaped the direction of change.

As I shall show, this "Orphic" philosophy was part of a much broader transition under way in the sixth century BCE throughout Asia and Egypt. Even by the early fourth century BCE, Socrates routinely assumed his interlocutors would find Orphic tenets alien. Yet, not much later these doctrines were taken for granted and given varied combinations by creative bricoleurs.[94]

Orphism could never become a religion or a school precisely because of its own beliefs. As the soul is to the body, philosophy is to the public religion. Like the

---

91. The repression of these features actually begins with the antipathy of the Hebrew prophets toward idolatry, superstition, and magic, which was attenuated in the Middle Ages but revived in the Reformation. This point is underscored by Charles Taylor among many others, but their further argument that this led to secularization is persuasive only if enchantment (the opposite of secularization) is defined by a quasi-polytheistic and magical cosmos. At least for biblical traditions, defending monotheism can hardly be considered a secularizing move. On the contrary, "spirituality" would be a declension from orthodoxy.

92. Casanova, "Religion," 215.

93. All quotations of the *Bacchae* in this volume, unless otherwise noted, from Arrowsmith, *Euripides*.

94. In philosophy, Claude Lévi-Strauss used the term *bricolage* (making something from materials close to hand) to describe the way myths allow people to reconceive new ideas; see Lévi-Strauss, *Savage Mind*.

shaman, the sage must be free not only from the body but also from the limited, located, and bounded world of institutions. It is the individual's autonomous vision of the real that moistens the soul's wings, not the myths, opinions, and dogmas of "the many." Consequently, Orphism became a pervading influence precisely by not becoming a particular sect. It was a certain knowledge of who we are, where we came from, and where we are going. This knowledge was not based on historical events, particular things in this world judged by sense experience, or even reason, but rather upon direct intuition—gnosis.

Like the body, public religions are tombs or prisons of a soul that longs to return to the One: the flight of the alone to the Alone. The birthplace of such philosophical religion was the private mystery cult of the few over against the public religion of the many. As Harold Bloom notes, "Persistent to this day among Jews, Christians, Muslims, and even secularists, 'gnosis itself, in all its manifold forms and variants, also deserves to be called a *Weltreligion.*'"[95]

Moreover, far from abandoning the mythological outlook of the East, the new mythology borrowed heavily from oriental stories. We have only to listen to the sages themselves, for whom a journey to the East was *de rigueur*. Thales came to Egypt to learn its mysteries from its priests and convinced Pythagoras to do the same. Plato's tale of Atlantis in the preface to the *Timaeus* has the priest of Sais lecturing Solon on the ignorance of the Greeks regarding their own past. From Socrates onward, Greeks acknowledged that these ideas, though new to them, were gifts from more enlightened foreigners.

In the Greek enlightenment, we will see, the shaman became the sage. Several seventh-century shamanistic figures appeared on the Greek Ionian (i.e., Turkish) coast, where the first inklings of Presocratic philosophy emerged. Terpander, the founder of classical Greek music, was sent from Lesbos to Sparta on a purification mission.[96] Associated with Orpheus, he healed Sparta through "communal musical therapy."[97] Thaletas of Gortyn, a follower of Terpender and a pupil of Onomacritus (the editor of Orphic oracles), delivered Sparta from a plague around 670 BCE.[98] The soul of Hermotimus of Clazomenae went on nocturnal journeys while his body was in a trance.[99] According to Aristotle, Hermotimus formulated the dualistic theory of mind over matter before Anaxagoras and Parmenides.[100]

---

95. Harold Bloom, preface to Corbin, *Alone with the Alone*, xx, quoting Corbin, *Cyclical Time*, 193.
96. A helpful survey of Terpander's biography is found in Reese, *Music in the Middle Ages*, 11.
97. Power, *Culture of Kitharôidia*. Rich in information as well as analysis, this study is my principal resource for Terpander.
98. Burkert, *Orientalizing Revolution*, 42–43.
99. West, *Orphic Poems*, 149.
100. Preus, *Historical Dictionary of Greek Philosophy*, 190, citing Aristotle, *Metaph.* 984b20.

The seventh-century healer Aristeas from Proconnesus (a Greek colony in Asia Minor) converted himself into a raven at will to accompany Apollo and could die and reawaken at different times and places.¹⁰¹

Right at the dawn of the Greek enlightenment we find colorful shamanic figures like Pherecydes, Epimenides, Pythagoras, and Empedocles. All of them were involved in varying degrees with the rise of political democracy, natural philosophy, mathematics, and classical music. And they also projected the persona of the shaman, the "Divine Man" (*theios anēr*). Initiated in caves, they reappeared as gods.¹⁰²

Perennial Philosophy

Perennial philosophy refers to a genealogy of sages who taught the above doctrine. In short, the central doctrines identified as "Orphic" (macrocosmic cycle of emanation-reversion-unity; microcosmic incarnation-reincarnation-release) are part of an esoteric heritage that public religions disdain. Its most successful mediators have had to demonstrate that they remained in the bounds of established orthodoxy. Introducing the Renaissance version, Marsilio took Hermes Trismegistus as the fountainhead (along with Zoroaster in Persia), followed by Orpheus and Aglaophemus (who initiated the Orphic mysteries), Pythagoras and Philolaus, "teacher of our divine Plato." "In this way, from a wondrous line of six theologians emerged a single system of ancient theology, harmonious in every part."¹⁰³ By 1484, the date of his preface to the *Plotinus Commentary*, the perennial tradition led to Iamblichus and Proclus. For Jaspers, such a "single system of ancient theology, harmonious in every part" unified not only diverse sages but all the main disciplines that modernity divides sharply into the categories of secular and sacred.

In contrast with the modernist metanarrative of progress from the childhood of superstition to the adulthood of reason and science, the perennial-tradition metanarrative sees natural supernaturalism as the ideal toward which the most enlightened sages have oriented themselves. Instead of progress, modernity represents a decline. With roots in Romanticism, it is anti-Enlightenment and sees modernity

---

Supporting Aristotle's description is Sextus Empiricus, *Math.* 9.1.7. On the Pythagorean connection see Lucian, *Musc. laud.* 7 and book 8 of Diogenes Laertius, *Vit. phil.*

101. Herodotus, *Hist.* 4.13–16. See the excellent biography by Bolton, *Aristeas of Proconnesus*; cf. Phillips, "Legend of Aristeas."

102. Fascination with the shaman figure in scholarship over the last century is, in and of itself, fascinating. See Ginzburg, *Threads and Traces*, 83–95, 94.

103. Ficino, preface to *Corpus Hermeticum* (1462), translated in Copenhaver and Schmitt, *Renaissance Philosophy*, 147.

as a soulless materialism and calculative reason that has quenched the Western spirit, something Max Weber called "the disenchantment of the world."[104]

A good example of this theosophical account is Aldous Huxley's *Perennial Philosophy*. He defines perennial philosophy as "spiritual religion" exemplified in "the devout contemplatives of India, the Sufis of Islam, the Catholic mystics of the later Middle Ages," and, among Anabaptists, "[Hans] Denck, Sebastian Franck and Castellio, as Everard and John Smith and the first Quakers and William Law." In this best and highest religion, shorn of creeds and rituals, one finds the divine within. One finds the *ultimate* reality that his or her inner self is part of the divine All not in scriptures that relate mere historical events of the past but in the inner light that beholds eternal truths directly. As in the Orphic (Platonic) tradition, "spiritual religions" of all stripes regard the body as the individualizing and particularizing aspect that must be transcended in order to attain (or recognize) this unity.[105]

I am less interested in whether Neoplatonists, or for that matter Plato himself, represented an original Orphism correctly—or even whether there was such a phenomenon—than in the trail of sages who did. It is the effective history of the bricoleurs who claimed Orpheus's inspiration that blazed the trail of what has come to be called the perennial tradition. In fact, the first Greek references to Zoroastrianism are made by Plato and his circle.[106]

Philosophical Religion

Borrowing on Carlos Fraenkel's illuminating study, I mean by *philosophical religions* the idea that there is a universal and unchanging truth above all the opinions of diverse religions and schools. At their best, particular myths and cults point to reality, but philosophical contemplation rises above them. The goal of philosophical religion is to grow from the childhood of dependence on external authorities and the myths and rites associated with bodily life in the visible world to the autonomy of adulthood, which represents a direct and immediate vision of the truth itself with the inner eye. Since it first swept across Greece in the sixth century BCE as part of a much wider trend, it has become a default setting for what

---

104. For a survey of the secularization paradigm's development and consituent components, see Tschannen, "Secularization Paradigm."

105. Huxley, *Perennial Philosophy*, 1–34. Writing for a popular audience, Huxley highlights these characteristics of "spiritual religion" with a generous sprinkling of quotations from Eastern and Western mystics alike.

106. McEvilley, *Shape of Ancient Thought*, 171.

Inventing the "Divine Self": Where We Are Headed

is often signaled vaguely by the phrase "spiritual but not religious." It developed into what Fraenkel describes as "philosophical religion" that claims to transcend all particular religions.[107] Though nothing like an evolving institution, the Orphic tradition has been seen by proponents as a perennial wisdom accessed by the great sages across all religions.

Scouring miscellaneous wisdom from the archives of the Alexandrian library, Clement of Alexandria emphasizes that the greatest discoveries not only in philosophy but also in the arts, culture, and technology came to Athens from elsewhere.

> So philosophy reached a climax long ago among the non-Greeks as something precious, and shone brightly through the people and later reached the Greeks. Its main authorities were the prophets of the Egyptians, the Chaldaeans among the Assyrians, the Druids among the Gauls, the Samanaeans in Bactria [northern India], among the Celts their own philosophers, the Magi among the Persians (who by their magic powers actually foretold the Savior's birth, arriving in the land of Judaea led by a star), the Gymnosophists in India, and others called Sarmans [Hindu monks] and Brahmans [priests]. (*Strom.* 1.15.71[4–5])[108]

"I shall show a little later," he continues, "that the Greek sages were somewhat after the date of Moses" (*Strom.* 1.14.60[1]). This allowed Clement to display the borrowing of the Greeks not only from "barbarians" but from God's revelation to Israel.

Such genealogies synthesized what the Greeks had known all along; namely, that Athens had arrived rather late to the society of philosophers, receiving its wisdom and magic from the East. By the time of Hellenistic philosophers like Plutarch, it was generally known what Orphism was and that it represented the highest wisdom of all sages. Adding their own brushstrokes, Neoplatonists confirmed this portrait. According to Proclus, "All the theology of the Greeks comes from Orphic mystagogy."[109]

Unlike most religions, natural supernaturalism eschews the theistic package: a personal god wholly other than the self and the world with whom a relation is mediated by personal communication of truths and practices (i.e., revealed religion). The goal of life, then, is to enrich one's own inner experiences and interpretations—to *see* the realities rather than to be *told* about them. Descriptions

---

107. Fraenkel, *Philosophical Religions*.
108. Clement of Alexandria, *Stromateis: Books 1–3* (trans. Ferguson).
109. Proclus, *Theo. Plat.* 1.6. (= Testamenta 250 from Kern, *Orphicorum fragmenta*).

of contemporary spirituality versus religion suggest easy comparison: "The goal is not to defer to a higher authority, but to have the courage to become one's own authority."[110]

Autonomy is not only allowed by Orphic spirituality; it is the goal of philosophical religion. This is why it seems more plausible to believe, for example, in the soul's reincarnation than in bodily resurrection, in the mysterious forces of nature we experience directly than in the miraculous interventions of a creator mediated by external authority, in private spiritual beliefs and practices rather than in belonging to organized religion.

Philosophical religions invoke dogmas higher than anything in history. Jaspers himself employs this "god's-eye" view in his concluding chapter. The facts of the Axial Age are to be seen as "the basis of our universal conception of history . . . *common to all mankind*, beyond all differences of creed." How can Moses represent God as saying that he, Yahweh, alone is God? This requires everyone to embrace a local Jewish deity of whom they have never even heard. And how can Jesus say, "I am the the way, the truth, and the life; no one comes to the Father except through me" (John 14:6)? "The transcendental history of the revealed Christian faith is made up out of the creation, the fall, stages of revelation, prophecies, the appearance of the Son of God, redemption and the last judgement. . . . That which binds all men together, however, cannot be revelation but must be experience. Revelation is the form taken by particular historical creeds, experience is accessible to man as man." In contrast with "the erroneous claim to exclusive possession of truth by any one creed," Jaspers asserts, the Axial Age was a universal phenomenon. "The claim to exclusive possession of truth, that tool of fanaticism, of human arrogance and self-deception through the will to power, that disaster for the West—most intensely so in its secularised forms, such as the dogmatic philosophies and the so-called scientific ideologies—can be vanquished by the very fact that God has manifested himself historically in several fashions and has opened up many ways toward himself."[111]

In short, cosmotheism, pantheism/panentheism, natural supernaturalism, Orphism, perennial wisdom, and philosophical religions are synonyms for the phenomenon I am describing. "Orpheus brought the idea of Hen kai pan to Greece," says Assmann, "where it influenced the philosophies of Pythagoras, Herakleitus, Parmenides, the Stoics." "Hen kai pan—the conviction that one is all and all is one—was believed to be the nucleus of a great tradition that began in Egypt and

---

110. Heelas and Woodhead, *Spiritual Revolution*, 4.
111. Jaspers, *Origin and Goal of History*, 19–20.

was handed down to modernity."[112] Whatever the plight of traditional theistic religions in the world today, "spirituality" is flourishing, as it always has when monotheism loses its appeal. Orphic spirituality is far from the whole story, but it is a large part that is neglected except in specialized enclaves of esotericism scholarship. As contemporary polls and academic debates underscore, "secularization" is actually a spiritualizating distillation of existing religions considered too particular, this-worldly, and dogmatic. Yet such "philosophical religion" is an alternative religion with its own nonnegotiable dogmas and rituals.

The history of Western civilization cannot be reduced to Orphic philosophy and Hermetic magic. Yet it cannot be understood without it. The so-called Axial revolution was not something that happened once upon a time in the sixth century BCE. Rather, it has always been the native religion of Western culture. Challenges to the public religion of Athens and of Christendom have always asserted the "Religion of the One"—the perennial tradition of the One as everything and everything as the One.

---

112. Assmann, *Moses*, 141–42. Assmann notes that the term "cosmotheism" was coined by Lamoignon de Malesherbes, referring to the Stoic view held by Pliny as "non un Athée, mais un Cosmo-theiste," since Pliny believed the cosmos was god (142).

1

Survivor to Shaman
Discovering the Divine Self

> If you like, I will summarize another tale for you, well and skillfully—mind you take it in—telling how gods and mortal men have come from the same starting-point.
>
> —Hesiod, *Op.* 113–116[1]

> Prometheus: I caused mortals to cease foreseeing doom.
> Chorus: What cure did you provide them with against that sickness?
> Prometheus: I placed in them blind hopes.
>
> —Aeschylus, *Prom.* 250–253[2]

Regardless of what one makes of the Axial Age thesis, there is a significant turning point across many civilizations around the sixth century BCE. It is a shift from a locative to a utopian worldview. The hero of the earliest epics is the one who learned his or her limitations while the lead character in the age of tragedy is the boundary-breaker: the divine self.

---

1. Hesiod, *Theogony and Works and Days* (trans. West). Unless otherwise noted, I use this translation.
2. Translation of *Prometheus Bound* from volume 1 of Grene and Lattimore, *Complete Greek Tragedies*.

Chapter 1

SURVIVOR: THE LOCATIVE COSMOS OF THE EPIC AGE AND THE HERO-THAT-FAILED

Composed in cuneiform script on clay tablets before the second millennium BCE, the oldest recorded creation myth, Enuma Elish, begins with a primeval chaos or abyss from which heaven and earth (*an* and *ki*, or just *an-ki*) emerged.[3] The first parents are Apsu (freshwater) and Tiamat (saltwater ocean). From the "mingling of the waters" is born the generation that rules the present cosmos. According to Hesiod's *Theogony*, Gaia (earth) is the primordial mother who mates with her son Uranus (sky/heaven) to produce the second generation of gods: the Titans. Yet Homer reflects the influence of the Mesopotamian version, as Hera mentions Oceanus and Tethys—the two waters—as the parents of "all gods and men" (*Il.* 14.201, 302).[4] Tethys is a minor Titan in the standard Greek myth established by Hesiod, but here in Homer, as in the later version of Enuma Elish (still written over a millennium before Homer), the "mingling of the waters" generates the offspring of the primordial gods.[5]

In all these myths of the epic age, the human being is a survivor. One can imagine the cautious grin of the narrator concluding the Sumerian epic Atrahasis, "How we sent the Flood. But a man survived the catastrophe."[6] Survival is the most for which one can hope as a mortal, being part of a race that transgresses boundaries that the gods have set in place. Heroes strive for godlike immortality through reputation. Very rarely a mortal (almost always fathered by Zeus) is raised by Zeus

---

3. Covering much of modern Turkey, Iran, Syria, and Kuwait, the center of ancient Mesopotamia occupied the Fertile Crescent between the Euphrates and Tigris Rivers that emptied into the Persian Gulf. Recorded history begins with the city of Sumer where evidence of human settlements goes back to 10,000 BCE. A civilization of "firsts," Sumer is credited with inventing the wheel, the chariot, weapons of war, and the all-important sail as well as beer brewing, irrigation, writing, a legal code, and civil rights. However, recorded history—syllabic writing on clay (cuneiform) tablets—dates from the twenty-third century BCE; see Anthony, *Bronze-Age Riders*. Many inventions claimed by the West have turned out to have been achieved first in China and the Indus Valley. Since this is well beyond my competence, I will simply qualify the scope of the claim as excluding these civilizations.

4. See West, *East Face of Helicon*, 119–20; Gantz, *Early Greek Myth*, 1:11; Burkert, *Orientalizing Revolution*, 91–92. See also Hard, *Routledge Handbook of Greek Mythology*, 36–37.

5. Compare Homer, *Il.* 14.201, 302 with Hesiod, *Theog.* 126–128. Aristotle thought that this account probably informed Thales's cosmology (viz., all nature arising from water). See Aristotle, *Metaph.* 983b27; cf. Plato, *Crat.* 402b; *Theaet.* 152e.

6. Atrahasis 3.8. Translation from Dalley, *Myths from Mesopotamia*. In Atrahasis, the god Enlil is called Elill; to relieve confusion, I have changed the latter to the former.

to Olympian honors. For the most part, however, they fail. That is the point. It is good and proper for human beings to accept their fate.

In the Mesopotamian Epic of Gilgamesh, the eponymous legendary king of Uruk represents the epic hero who tests the boundaries yet by his failure teaches us to know our place and to keep it. We also learn how the Noah-figure Utnaphistim survived the flood, leaving the chief god Enlil so impressed by what Utnaphistim and his wife endured, following precisely Enki's instruction, that he agrees with Enki's desire to immortalize them both. From what we are told, Utnaphistim was an ordinary person who was granted the divinity he was not seeking. Gilgamesh stands in sharp contrast. A king in the long line of sacred representatives of the gods, he abuses his authority by sleeping with brides on their wedding night. The complaint of the grooms reaches the gods, who make a clay human as an opponent to curb Gilgamesh's vices. If he doesn't know his limits, the gods will help him to discover them.

Instead, Gilgamesh and the clay man Enkidu become like brothers, Enkidu tagging along in Gilgamesh's youthful projects of self-glorification. Together they slay the great monster guarding the forest. Protecting the walled city from foreign invaders and mythic intruders from the forest was the job of a king in a locative cosmos. But once again Gilgamesh steps outside of his domain to achieve a name for himself. One day, Ishtar herself—the queen of heaven—propositions the king, but he rejects her. More than that, he insults her dignity by listing her paramours. Even in relation to the gods, he does not know his place. In retaliation, Ishtar sends the Bull of Heaven to destroy the people of Uruk. Gilgamesh kills the divine bull, but Enkidu foolishly taunts the goddess by flinging its back parts at her. The gods agree that he must pay for this insolence with his life.

Heartbroken, Gilgamesh searches for Enkidu, hoping to reach him in the underworld.

> Enkidu my friend whom I love has turned to clay.
> Am I not like him? Must I lie down too,
> Never to rise, ever again? (Gilgamesh 10.3)[7]

Along the way, he hopes to discover not only Enkidu but the meaning of the afterlife and his own chances of becoming immortal. It is a turning point in his life. No longer seeking immortality through reputation—the hero who killed the forest monster and Ishtar's bull—which has led only to deep loss, Gilgamesh searches

---

7. Translation of the Epic of Gilgamesh, unless otherwise noted, from Dalley, *Myths from Mesopotamia*.

Chapter 1

frantically for Utnaphistim to guide him into wisdom, much as Odysseus takes pains to find the blind seer Teiresias in Hades.

> I am afraid of Death, and so I roam open country.
> I shall take the road and go quickly
> To see Utnapishtim. (Gilgamesh 9.1)

At last finding Utnaphistim, Gilgamesh relates all he has gone through in his search for Enkidu and his own immortality. In the deified survivor's speech we hear the central message of epic poetry:

> Why do you prolong your grief, Gilgamesh?
> Since the gods made you from the flesh of gods
> and mankind...
> Death is inevitable at some time, both
> for Gilgamesh and for a fool...
> Savage Death just cuts mankind down. (Gilgamesh 10.5–6)

A similar conclusion is drawn by a weary Odysseus—the survivor par excellence. During his stop on the island Phaiakia before returning home from the wars, Odysseus is entertained by the island's king, Alkinoös, at a sumptuous feast. Across books 6 through 13 of the *Odyssey* the hero recounts his many battles and trials to Alkinoös, who opines that his guests must be kin to the gods. Odysseus responds:

> Alkinoös, you may set your mind at rest.
> Body and birth, a most unlikely god
> am I, being all of earth and mortal nature.
> I should say, rather, I am like those men
> who suffer the worst trials that you know,
> and miseries greater yet, as I might tell you—
> hundreds; indeed the gods could send no more...
> Rough years I've had; now may I see once more
> my hall, my lands, my people before I die! (*Od.* 7.223–229, 240–241)[8]

Similarly, Achilles says in the *Iliad*:

---

8. Homer, *Odyssey* (trans. Fitzgerald). Unless otherwise noted, all translations of this text are from this edition.

> One and the same lot for the man who hangs back
> and the man who battles hard. The same honor waits
> for the coward and the brave.
> They both go down to Death,
> the fighter who shirks, the one who works to exhaustion.
> And what's laid up for me, what pittance? Nothing—
> And after suffering hardships, year in, year out,
> Staking my life on the mortal risks of war. (Homer, *Il.* 9.385–391)[9]

Another example from the Ramesside Period of Egypt, entitled the "Instruction of Any," instructs, "Say, 'Here comes one who has prepared himself for you,' and do not say, 'I am too young for you to take me.' Indeed, you do not know your death! Death comes, it steals the child from the arms of its mother, just like the one who has reached old age."[10]

We find similar poetry in the Bible, especially in the book of Ecclesiastes. After recounting his failure to find ultimate happiness in work, education and wisdom, wealth, and sex, Qohelet (the Preacher), identified as "the son of David, king in Jerusalem," comes to a similar realization as the king of Uruk and Odysseus:

> Vanity of vanities, says the Preacher,
> vanity of vanities! All is vanity.
> What does man gain by all the toil
> at which he toils under the sun?
> A generation goes, and a generation comes,
> but the earth remains forever.
> The sun rises, and the sun goes down,
> and hastens to the place where it rises ...
> All things are full of weariness;
> a man cannot utter it. (Eccl 1:2–5, 8–11)[11]

Wisdom, in a locative outlook, is accepting one's mortality. Death is an empirical fact, but it focuses our attention on what is truly important: "So teach us to number our days that we may get a heart of wisdom" (Ps 90:12).

---

9. Homer, *Iliad* (trans. Fagles). Unless otherwise noted, all translations of this text are from this edition.
10. Assmann, *Death and Salvation*, 13.
11. Unless otherwise noted, all biblical translations are from the English Standard Version (ESV).

Even when Utnaphistim tries to help Gilgamesh by giving him trials that the gods may regard as worthy of immortality, the king of Uruk fails. Finally, Utnaphistim tells him where he can dive into deep waters for a plant that at least returns one's youth. Setting off eagerly, Gilgamesh seizes the plant, but on his way home he discovers a fresh pool for a bath and leaves the plant on the shore. A snake steals his specimen and immediately sheds its skin, returning to its youth. In the words of Qohelet: "All is vanity."

Across the epic literature—Mesopotamian, Rigvedic, Greek, and Egyptian—the "Hero-That-Failed" and humans in general are almost passive instruments. This is apparent especially in the writings of Homer. The Trojan War was first sparked by petty jealousy among Aphrodite, Hera, and Athena about who is the most beautiful. As the vain dispute widens, the strife among the gods plays itself out on the ground through the bitter slaughter of human beings. Odysseus tells Teiresias, "my life runs on then as the gods have spun it" (*Od.* 11.158). It is the gods who closed his eyes "under slow drops of sleep" and "the mind of Zeus beyond the stormcloud stirred him" (*Od.* 12.434; 24.185). Not only Diomedes's courage and strength but Achilles's foolish fury is attributed to a god: "Hard, ruthless man," Ajax reproves, "the gods have planted a cruel, relentless fury in your chest!" Diomedes gives up on Achilles's reckless self-will, knowing that he will fight again "whenever a god fires his blood" (*Il.* 9.771, 778–779, 857–858). "Surely a goddess moved her to adultery," Penelope judges concerning Helen (*Od.* 23.250).[12] The heroes are spitting images of the god who controls their behavior at any given point, whether noble or vicious. Like the gods, they live by the code of warriors seeking honor and glory, yet they are mortals.

In short, the epic narrative is consistent with the view of human beings as pawns of the gods, formed to relieve their labors and provide their honors. Humans can only seek to placate and manipulate the gods by rituals, in contrast with the Genesis account of humans, male and female, as God's image and likeness, and endowed with royal authority. The gods of Mesopotamian and Greek epic seek to reduce the human population, while in Gen 1:28 we read, "And God blessed them. And God said to them, 'Be fruitful and multiply and fill the earth and subdue it, and have dominion over the fish of the sea and over the birds of the heavens and over every living thing that moves on the earth.'"

In the Epic of Gilgamesh, Siduri, "the divine barmaid," exhorts Gilgamesh "to enjoy the brief lifetime allotted to him as best he could" following the death of Enkidu, but instead he embarks on a headlong pursuit of immortality that leads to

---

12. In any event, Helen's abduction from Menelaus by Paris (based on the "reward" given to him by Aphrodite) is more accurately described as rape than adultery.

despair (10.1–8). "These ancient Near Eastern myths characterize the problem of human existence as a 'too much' rather than a 'too little,'" noted Nietzsche. "This 'too much,' this surplus causes man to fall outside the restrictions that characterize the animal world" and to "create an artificial world in which he can live—and that is culture."[13] The walled city, in contrast with the wilderness or desert, was the antidote to this feeling of anomie for the one who knew too much. It is this life that counts, so honor the gods and perform the rites that bring prosperity here and now. The secure fortress, separate from the mysterious forests and howling deserts, was where cult and culture could flourish. And it was in these activities that the locative community found its meaning and survival.

Those who mediated the epic order were likewise under the gods' control. Ancient poets, such as Homer or the author of Enuma Elish, were cult singers, whose inspired accounts became the basis for the public cult. Their shift into hexameter signaled that they were no longer in possession of themselves but had become a mere organ of the god's song. In this state, their own reasoning was thought to be suspended. The standard prophetic designations are derived from the Akkadian verb *maḫû*, "to become crazy, to go into a frenzy." As Martii Nissinen writes, "This verb is used for people who go out of their wits or, at least, behave in unexpected ways, and it is also used for a highly emotional performance."[14] In this vein, Enuma Elish says of Tiamat, "She became like a prophet, she changed her consciousness" (4.88).[15] We hear from another source, "I became affected [lit. struck, *lapâtu*] like a prophet, what I do not know I bring forth."[16] "Ecstatic priests and priestesses (*mahu, mahhutu*) were in fact common in Mesopotamia," notes Burkert.[17] Indeed, says Nissinen, along with the magician, they often were the same person described as a frenzied one, ecstatic, male-female, snake-charmer, chanter, or even, given associations with death and omens, a lamentation singer or wailer.[18] The same description appears across all Indo-Iranian languages.[19] The Greek word for "seer"

---

13. Nietzsche, *Birth of Tragedy*, 59–60.

14. Martii Nissinen relates that a high priest or exorcist is called *šangammāḫu, mašmaššu*, or *āšipu* whereas a prophet is called *maḫḫû*, seer (*ḫzh*), or magician (*naršindu, ēpiš ipši*). See *Ancient Prophecy*, 174. The Old Babylonian nouns are *muḫḫûm* (masc.) and *muḫḫûtum* (fem.); their Neo-Assyrian forms are *maḫḫû* (masc.) and *maḫḫûtu* (fem.).

15. Cited from Nissinen, *Ancient Prophecy*, 175.

16. Nissinen, *Ancient Prophecy*, 176. The mark of such prophecy, then, is that one is perceived as frenzied, not in possession of one's own faculties (i.e., *šēḫu* "possessed people").

17. Burkert, *Orientalizing Revolution*, 80.

18. Nissinen, *Ancient Prophecy*, 62.

19. West, *Indo-European Poetry and Myth*, 29. Inspired poetry bears the same meaning in the Old Avestan (Iranian) language of the Zoroastrian Gathas and in ancient Armenian, Lithuanian, and Germanic. "Poet" in Vedic Sanskrit means "inwardly stirred, inspired, wise" and the Rigveda

(*mantis*) is taken from the verb *mainesthai* "to be frenzied." The inspired poet in Greece was overcome with ecstasy (*ekstasis*) by divine possession (*enthysiasmos*). In the locative world of the epic, not only the mortal characters but the authors were passive instruments of divine agents.

While the poets told the epic tales, the priests and prophets administered the rituals based on these epics that kept society aligned with the cosmic order. Long before Dionysus became the founding patron of his mysteries and the Greek stage, religious rituals were the occasion for a public spectacle of raving. Wild chanting and music, especially drum beating, created a mood of enthusiasm signaling to the crowd that the gods were present. If the prophet did not lose his or her equilibrium, the musicians were dismissed.[20] Prophets also took part in mimetic rituals as actors on the stage, such as in the Marduk Ordeal where they would reenact Marduk's beating and imprisonment.

Prophet-seers were also expected to forecast horoscopes and, in the archaic age, says Burkert, "connections appear to run from Mesopotamia specifically to Delphi" in this practice.[21] Not only rituals and incantation texts but also amulets belong to the sphere of Mesopotamian magicians.[22] These amulets were meant to ward off evil spirits. The Sumerian and Mesopotamian *galla* (Akkadian *gallû*) are the *ghuls* of pre-Islamic Arabs and, much later, the ghouls of Western folklore.[23] A *gallû* was a female demon who, dying childless, was thought to assault pregnant women and to steal and eat children.[24] In Mesopotamian accounts, the dead are dragged to the underworld by the demonic *galla*, who are nonsexed but present themselves as female singers to Inana/Ishtar. Once in Kur, the dead are persecuted by demons, and this is the dwelling place of the child-devourer Lamashtu.[25] Babylonians would sacrifice a lamb to appease the *galla*, yet more was demanded. "It is evident that the Babylonian fire ceremony was observed in the spring season," says Donald A. Mackenzie, "and that human beings were sacrificed to the sun god."[26]

---

hymns were composed by priest-poets. The similarities of Indian and Iranian language and myth are well documented. Around 2000 BCE, Indo-Europeans migrated from northcentral Asia and separated into Iranian and Indo-Aryan peoples. The former displaced the native Semitic (Akkadian) rulers and language. Although Marduk dominated the new pantheon, the Mesopotamian myth remained largely intact.

20. Nissinen, *Ancient Prophecy*, 70.
21. Burkert, *Orientalizing Revolution*, 81.
22. Burkert, *Orientalizing Revolution*, 82.
23. Al-Rawi, "Arabic Ghoul."
24. D. R. West, "Gello and Lamia."
25. Black et al., "Inana's Descent to the Nether World." There was an order of official *galla* priests committed to lifelong lamentation.
26. Mackenzie, *Myths of Babylonia and Assyria*, 350, see also 248–51.

Indeed, child sacrifice was practiced among Ammonite and Canaanite worshipers of Molek.[27] By the seventh century, Burkert points out, this Babylonian-Akkadian demon appears in Greek lyric poetry. "The horrifying figure of Gello, an object of terror for children, is mentioned as early as the work of Sappho."[28]

A complex system of divination had been practiced in the Middle East going back at least to the second millennium, when we find a clay tablet used for hepatoscopy (mantic liver inspection).[29] There were other forms of divination such as haruspicy and extispicy (examining animal entrails), augury (inspection of birds in flight), and astrology, but the liver was seen as the source of microcosmic blood. Comparing the liver with the well-mapped clay model, a diviner might discover a "foot-mark" in the middle of the "finger" (caudate lobe) of the liver. On this basis, the diviner might prophesy invasion from an enemy nation.[30] In a locative cosmos, everything is connected—vertically and horizontally, inner and outer, self and other.

Not just anyone could perform such observations. It took considerable training to "read" these correspondences. Diviners were held in high esteem because of "their liminal position between the human and divine worlds."[31] Attached to the royal court and often belonging to an established family of prophets, diviners were state employees, very much a part of the elite.[32] The fame of Babylonians not only for astrology but also for hepatoscopy is attested in the

---

27. Biblical warnings against following the ways of their West Asian neighbors were enshrined in the law: "Say to the Israelites: 'Any Israelite or any foreigner residing in Israel who sacrifices any of his children to Molek is to be put to death'" (Lev 20:2–5). Ignoring this command (e.g., 2 Kgs 21:6; 2 Chr 28:1–4) is presented as primary evidence for the reason behind Judah's exile (Isa 30:33; Jer 19:12). The exact nature of this sacrificial ritual and its object are subjects of debate. See Heider, "Molech." Among others, John Day argues convincingly that Malik (Moloch) is an epithet for Nergal, the Mesopotamian ruler of the underworld; see *Gods and Goddesses of Canaan*, 213–15. On the basis of archaeological evidence and Greco-Roman testimonies, others argue that the Hinnom Valley (Gehenna) near Jerusalem was where these Canaanite sacrifices took place. See Stavrakopoulou, "Jerusalem Tophet Ideological Dispute"; Xella, "Tophet."

28. Burkert, *Orientalizing Revolution*, 82.

29. This liver tablet can be found in the British Museum (92668).

30. Nissinen, *Ancient Prophecy*, 62–63. The massive Mesopotamian compendium is the *Bārûtu* "Art of the Diviner," with eight thousand omens. See Robson, "Empirical Scholarship," 618–24.

31. Nissinen, *Ancient Prophecy*, 61–62. Many intriguing examples are collected in Koch-Westenholz, *Babylonian Liver Omens*. Some of the omens are quite specific: "a famous person will arrive riding on a donkey." Others are vague, not to mention gloomy: "long-term forecast: lament." Many are indecipherable apart from knowing the context: "If the pleasing word is split above and below: the man's teeth will come loose."

32. Nissinen, *Ancient Prophecy*, 68–69.

biblical book of Ezekiel: "For the king of Babylon stands at the parting of the way, at the head of the two ways, to use divination. He shakes the arrows; he consults the teraphim [cult objects]; he looks at the liver" (Ezek 21:21). Burkert judges, "The spread of hepatoscopy is one of the clearest examples of cultural contact in the orientalizing period," and thus assumes a "relatively high, technical level" of East-West exchange. "The mobility of migrant charismatics is the natural prerequisite for this diffusion, the international role of sought-after specialists, who were, as far as their art was concerned, nevertheless bound to their father-teachers."[33]

The Oracle of Delphi became the capital of Greek divination by the sixth century.[34] The Pythia, the priestess of Delphi, was merely a mouthpiece of Apollo as she sat upon her tripod in a trance (*enthysiasmos*, lit. possession by a god). People came with their questions and received enigmatic answers through oracles. Few reliable sources suggest that other forms of divination were practiced at Delphi. However, the important connection across these locative societies is the *mediation* of higher knowledge by authoritative experts. Meaning could not just be read off the surface of livers, bird flights, and oracles. It had to be interpreted according to strict formulas, and possession by a god was essential. Divination placed the official seer at the center of political life, determining the right time for a battle or royal succession, the reason for a public disaster, or the cause behind a disease. The Pythian priestess at Delphi was so embroiled in politics that she was sometimes accused of taking bribes from regimes favoring her cult.

Another important function of the seer-priest was purification. Not even disease was merely an individual affair. It threatened the whole community, not only as a physical contagion, but also because its spread indicated the gods' disfavor. If the operation failed, it was because it was not performed correctly and cult professionals paid for this with their lives, often including the execution of the priest's male offspring. Although obsession with ritual purification was characteristically Middle Eastern and Egyptian—it is also essential in India's early Rigveda—it came to Athens early in the sixth century. Across all these cultures, Bronze Age religion centered on outward rites publicly and perfectly performed. They represented the technology that preserved the alignment between the cosmic order above and its civic microcosm below. Religion was concerned primarily with the well-

---

33. Burkert, *Orientalizing Revolution*, 51.

34. For this dating I rely on Michael Scott, *Delphi*, 30. Herodotus reports that the Alcmaeonids, an important Athenian family from the late seventh to fifth centuries, "got a contract from the Amphictyons to build the temple which stands today at Delphi, but at that time did not exist" (*Hist.* 5.62–63).

being of the polis over the individual, ritual over doctrine and morality, and this life over the next.

As we see in Homer's epics, the gods are relatively uninterested in punishing moral failures unless they interrupt or corrupt their cult. The *Iliad* opens with Apollo sending "a fatal plague" throughout the army, "and all because Agamemnon spurned Apollo's priest." The victim is actually the priest's daughter, named merely "the girl," whom Agamemnon demanded as his war prize. Eventually, he is willing to give her back, proclaiming, "But fetch me another prize, and straight off too, else I alone of the Argives go without my honor. That would be a disgrace. You are all my witnesses, look—*my* prize is snatched away!" (*Il.* 1.39–41). Both Apollo and Agamemnon are jealous merely for their honor; the violence against the priest's daughter is beside the point. In fact, the gods themselves are far from being ethical models, as we will see in the abduction of Persephone by Hades, which is conducted with the approval of her own father, Zeus. Imitating the gods, heroes demand their "prize" and defend their honor and glory. But the gods are more powerful, of course, and slighting them may lead to the corruption of an entire family or city (*miasma*).[35] Ritual precision rather than moral or doctrinal exactness, or even sincerity, was demanded. Missteps in carrying out the rites could bring devastating reprisals. The public rites were overseen by the Areopagus, which functioned also as a supreme court for the city. Greek gods and heroes protected, defended, and blessed the city in every way in exchange for such ritual loyalty, delighting especially in the sacrifice of animals. The myths and rites of the public religion were not a self-chosen part of an individual's private life but the foundation of the city's whole existence.

However, in the sixth and fifth centuries, purification from bloodguilt (murder) also becomes an urgent matter. Diseases required ritual purification because they were bad omens or manifestations of curses that showed society had somehow become misaligned with the cosmic order. Such diseases could spread to the community or demonstrate visibly the displeasure of the gods toward the whole city. Therefore, ritual purifiers were held in high esteem; like expert craftsmen, they could be employed by foreign rulers to cleanse their city of *miasma*, the ritual impurity resulting from an unresolved sociopolitical crime.

In the ancient Orient, maladies were perceived to be caused by demons, particularly the souls of the dead who dared to cross their boundary into this world. These angry spirits were evil precisely because of this trespassing and had to be pushed into retreat by exorcists.[36] Violent threats and jeers directed at these spir-

---

35. Parker, *Miasma*, 118, 178.
36. Nissinen examines this phenomenon in relation to the ritual of Ishtar and Dumuzi in *Ancient Prophecy*, 71.

Chapter 1

its—and even to chthonic divinities—were a part of the Egyptian cult as well. Anyone successful in beating back menacing spirits from the underworld was a revered figure, a guardian of the boundary between life and death. In Uruk, the city of Gilgamesh, a four-day ritual included a prophetic trance with the furious beating of the kettledrum, cult singers, and dancers.[37] We read in a recently discovered fifth tablet of the Epic of Gilgamesh that Shamesh the sun-god has appeared to the king of Uruk in three dreams explaining how to defeat the forest monster Humbaba and Enkindu counsels,

> Be furious like a prophet (*āpilum*) go into frenzy!
> Let your shout boom like a kettledrum!
> Let stiffness leave your arm, let debility depart from your loins![38]

A purification ritual is an atonement that brings healing. These rituals address some committed offense that has disrupted the prosperity of the polis, one which usually involves a transgression of cultic rites or spaces.[39] Burkert observes that "social and physio-psychic ills were not clearly differentiated in archaic societies." Personal and civic illnesses were caused by some dishonor perpetrated against the gods.[40] A public illness calls for a public cleansing. There is an almost identical prescription in the Akkadian myth.[41]

Healing the body depended on expelling the demon and all other impurities of the soul, and healing the city required the expulsion of any person or family member suspected of bearing the curse. Burkert points out, "Among the practitioners of the rituals there are two main types: the seer (*bâru*), who was responsible for divination; and the actual magician-priest (*āšipu*).... The cathartic practice of the Greeks appears to concentrate on the purification of murderers from blood guilt: blood is purified through blood." As vase paintings exhibit, the reason for purification in the notable case of Proteus was not due to bloodguilt but to cure his daughters of their madness. In this case, it is not a good sort of madness that comes from the gods but a derangement brought on by evil spirits. "This madness had been caused by some

---

37. In Uruk, the first day of this ritual was led by the chanter and musicians. On the second day, a kettledrum was played for purifications. On the third and fourth days, there were mimetic rites with the "Lady of Uruk" taking her seat between the curtains and the prophet encircling it with a water basin three times with music, dancing, kettledrum, and a censer. See Nissinen, *Ancient Prophecy*, 71.

38. Quote from Nissinen, *Ancient Prophecy*, 175.

39. The *miasma* upon Athens, with a curse placed on the Alcmaeonids, was provoked by bloodguilt but, more importantly, by the violation of the temple of Athena as sanctuary.

40. Burkert, *Orientalizing Revolution*, 56–57.

41. Lambert, "Address of Marduk."

ritual transgression by the girls which varies in different versions of the myth; the cure is directed against the manifest sufferings which have resulted from it."[42]

A vivid example of such *miasma* and its cure is the story of Orestes introduced in a trilogy of plays known as the *Oresteia* by the founder of Greek tragedy, Aeschylus. Returning home from the Trojan War, Agamemnon finds his wife in the arms of a lover, who together kill the great warrior. Seven years later, Agamemnon's son Orestes returns from Athens and avenges his father's murder by killing his mother and her lover. Though Apollo himself commanded it, Orestes is targeted by the Erinyes (Furies), who brook no injustices and send madness upon him. During the birth of tragedy, occurring at the transition from archaic to classical Greece, purification was still socially conceived (Orestes is from the cursed house of Atreus). But here there is a greater sense of an individual as an active agent bearing his own consequences. This search for purification of Athens from a family curse returns below in our unfolding story.

Clear examples of this relationship between individual and social purification can be found in the instruction of Marduk and Aeschylus's *Oresteia*. Both involve ritual pollution that manifests itself in physical sickness. The former stipulates that the priest is to "take a suckling pig," remove the heart and "sprinkle its blood on sides of the bed," dividing the pig's limbs over the sick man, and "then cleanse that man with pure water from the Deep [*Apsu*]." The demons "shall take it. . . . May the evil spirit, the devil demon stand aside! May the kindly spirit, the kindly demon be present!'"[43] Similarly, in the case of Aeschylus's *Oresteia*, "in order to 'wash away the stain,' a piglet must be slaughtered in such a way that its blood pours over the polluted man; the blood is then washed off with running water; in this way the pollution 'has been driven out by piglet-killing purifications.'"[44] Burkert comments:

> The similarity is undeniable: the condition of sickness, the knowledgeable specialists, the sacrificial piglet, slaughter, contact with blood, and the subsequent cleansing with water. The torch and the incense bowl belong to the apparatus of Greek purification priests, too. . . . The Erinyes are imagined as beasts of prey, "dogs" who want to suck his blood, leech the life-force from him. Remarkably enough, already in Homer sickness is once described as an "attack by a hateful demon."[45]

---

42. Burkert, *Orientalizing Revolution*, 56–58.
43. Quoted in Burkert, *Orientalizing Revolution*, 58.
44. Burkert, *Orientalizing Revolution*, 56–57. The instruction adds, "Apollo himself is holding the piglet directly over the head of Orestes, who is seated; its blood will flow directly over his head. But then it can be made to disappear: Guilt 'can be washed away.'"
45. Burkert, *Orientalizing Revolution*, 59–60. See Homer, *Od.* 5.396. For the Erinyes, see Aeschylus, *Cho.* 1054; *Eum.* 264–267.

These Erinyes are the "Furies," born from the violent castration of Kronos, who execute wrath against all who break their oaths (Hesiod, *Theog.* 173–206). The Greek noun "Erinyes" is from the verb *orinein*, "to raise, stir, excite," and the noun *eris*, "strife," which underscores their similarity to the entourage of both Cybele and Dionysus. They are children of Night (Nyx) and Mother Earth and are associated with Dionysus in the Orphic Hymns: "Vociferous, Bacchanalian Furies!" (OH 68; cf. 66, 69). Sophocles's play *Oedipus at Colonus* has Oedipus and his associates pleading successfully with Apollo to offer a sacrifice to the Erinyes that will purify them of their bloodguilt.[46]

Even certain days were impure and required ceremonial cleansing. Presided over by Zeus Katharsios, lustrations involved a ritual sacrifice of birds, bulls, or sometimes a human scapegoat as "medicine" (*pharmakos*) on behalf of a whole town or city.[47] A sacrificed pig would be carried around the hall for ceremonial purification of an official meeting of Athenian assembly (*ekklēsia*). The growing obsession with hiring priestly purifiers to cleanse Athens or any other Greek city is of foreign—indeed, oriental—provenance.[48]

There is still no clear distinction between the religious purifier, diviner, or magician and the physician. The Hippocratic doctor assumes the role of the oracle or priest in "purifying" the *miasma* brought on by some sin. Mania and music were also intertwined at the Temple of Didyma, second to Delphi as the shrine of Apollo.[49] There a young shepherd, Branchos, was seduced by Apollo's kiss and became his loyal follower, "the prophet of Apollo."[50] Branchos is reputed to have delivered the Milesians of the plague: "he sprinkled the people with laurel branches . . . the people spoke the responses." The setting is clearly some sort of oath-making formula for mysterious rites, but there is more. "Callimachus has Branchos speak a formula two or three times which the people do not understand. Is there a foreign language involved here?" Burkert thinks perhaps it is related to a Mesopotamian cult of healing magic.[51]

The only place in the epic cosmos where individuals exist independently of the larger cosmic order is the underworld. There one discovers oneself alone, beyond the embeddedness of the bounded and locative world. Divorced from all

---

46. See Graves, *Greek Myths*, 33–34.
47. Bremmer, "Scapegoat Rituals." On the role of Zeus as Zeus Katharsios, see Parker, *Miasma*, 139. On the purification of a city, see 257–80.
48. Parker describes well the exile and purification of the killer as prominent in Greek mythology; see *Miasma*, 281–307, 393–94.
49. Nissinen, *Ancient Prophecy*, 199.
50. See Aeschylus, *Ag.* 1072–1340; cf. Fontenrose, *Didyma*.
51. Burkert, *Orientalizing Revolution*, 61.

social relations, and barely existing as a shadow of its former self, individualism is, literally, hell.[52]

Neither god nor mortal could break the moral law of nature but only break oneself against it. In the underworld the scalepans of justice were unerring, and mercy and forgiveness were absent because guilt was not a focal category but rather honoring the gods and their cult. The underworld acknowledged no heroes; the few mortals who had been blessed by the gods now dined al fresco on their patios in balmy Elysium. In Hades there were no great deeds accomplished, no victories achieved. For daring to cheat death, Sisyphus, the reputed founder of the Isthmian Games, became one of Hades's symbols of this vanity and absurdity of human existence. There were no possibilities, no measure of success or failure. All plans were in vain, all hopes frustrated, as Odysseus learns on his visit to Hades. Plato's Socrates describes Homer's underworld as "this dreary afterlife," and this is a good word for it. The underworld was simply where all but a few mortals went when they died.[53]

Long before Homer the great civilizations of the Orient took this view of the afterlife for granted. Mesopotamian pictures of the underworld are close to the descriptions given in book 11 of the *Odyssey*.[54] Odysseus makes the harrowing journey to the underworld to find the blind Theban seer Teiresias so he can find his way home to Ithaca. Upon coming ashore, Odysseus and his men sacrifice a black lamb and ewe, "letting their black blood stream into the wellpit" for the "breathless dead." Similar to Mesopotamian depictions, Homer narrates:

> Now the souls gathered, stirring out of Erebos,
> brides and young men, and men grown old in pain,
> and tender girls whose hearts were new to grief;
> many were there, too, torn by brazen lanceheads,
> battle-slain, bearing still their bloody gear.
> From every side they came and sought the pit with rustling cries; and
> I grew sick with fear. (*Od.* 11.40–46)

---

52. Condemned by the gods for his insolence toward Ishtar, Enkidu's spirit is nevertheless released and relates his experiences in the underworld. See Dalley, *Myths from Mesopotamia*, 47. Dalley offers here a number of intriguing comparisons.

53. Sourvinou-Inwood, *Reading Greek Death*, 198–200.

54. Burkert, *Orientalizing Revolution*, 65, acknowledges differences in the Greek development. "Nevertheless," as Burkert observes, "the extent to which the Homeric concept of Hades corresponds to the Mesopotamian is striking: a realm of mud and darkness that leaves no hope for mortals. . . . It is described in a famous scene in *Gilgamesh* when the ghost of Enkidu meets his friend, a scene which may have links with Homer even on a literary level."

Then Odysseus orders his men to make burnt sacrifice "to sovereign Death, to pale Persephone," preparing to search for Teiresias (11.49–53). Once he finds the blind prophet, he complains, "my life runs on then as the gods have spun it" (11.55).

"Then I saw Tantalos put to the torture," says Odysseus of Orestes's ancestor who elicited the family curse by chopping his brother's children up in a stew for their unwitting father. It is no wonder that Homer has him "tantalized" (the term originating from his name) in the underworld, stooping in vain to slake his parched throat with cool water from an illusionary pond. "For when the old man put his lips down to the sheet of water it vanished round his feet, gulped underground, and black mud baked there in a wind from hell." So too fruit-laden boughs drooped above his head, "but if he stretched his hand for one, the wind under the dark sky tossed the bough beyond him" (*Od.* 11.700–708).

The ruler (and namesake) of this dreary realm is Hades. His wife Persephone, the daughter of his siblings Zeus and Demeter, had been abducted and raped by Hades but grew accustomed to her new role as queen of the damned. Homer gives her such epithets as "dread Persephone." She granted to the blind seer Teiresias the gift of reason, "but the others flit about as shadows. . . . Never the flaming eye of Helios lights on those men." Hades's realm is filled with "unhappy spirits" and "shadowy halls," as Odysseus views "the cold dead and the joyless region." Odysseus learns the way home to Ithaca from Teiresias, who explains, "Any dead man whom you allow to enter where the blood is will speak to you, and speak the truth; but those deprived will grow remote again and fade." After a sip, Odysseus's mother stirs, looks up, and recognizes him. Three times he tries to embrace his mother, "but she went sifting through my hands, impalpable as shadows are, and wavering like a dream." He even wonders, "Or is this all hallucination, sent against me by the iron queen, Persephone, to make me groan again?" It is no illusion, his mother replies.[55]

Homer's eschatology is unsystematic and inconsistent, reflecting wide variations and influences. On the one hand, Odysseus's mother explains, "O my child—alas, most sorely tried of men—great Zeus's daughter, Persephone, knits no illusions for you" (*Od.* 11.245). "All mortals meet this judgment when they die. No flesh and bone are here, none bound by sinew, since the bright-hearted pyre consumed them down—the white bones long exanimate—to ash; dreamlike the soul flies, insubstantial" (*Od.* 11.245–252). On the other hand, the "soul" (*psychē*) here does not exclude the body. Rather, the whole self gradually vanishes. Hades is a real place to which Odysseus and his men can travel by ship, offering animal sacrifices that empty into a pool of "dark blood." Zombie-like inhabitants are

---

55. Homer, *Od.* 10.491–495; 11.15, 100, 160–245, respectively.

pathetic but recognizable, still bearing their fatal wounds and blood-spattered armor. Surprised to see the still-living hero in Hades, Teiresias's spirit asks, "Why leave the blazing sun, O man of woe, to see the cold dead and the joyless region?" (*Od.* 11.104–105). As in the Mesopotamian versions, darkness hangs in the air like a thick blanket. In fact, Helios threatens Zeus on one occasion to do his bidding: "Restitution or penalty they shall pay—and pay in full—or I go down forever to light the dead men in the underworld" (*Od.* 12.489–491). More than active suffering, the dominant images are of despair: existing too little to satisfy the meagerest want but existing too much to be relieved of desiring it.

This miserable afterlife, common to all, is also described in the recompense for the "suitors" of Penelope whom Zeus allowed Odysseus and his son to slaughter. Led by Hermes, "the newly dead drifted together, whispering . . . in black pain forever" (*Od.* 24.19–22). But did noble Teiresias, "prophet of Zeus," suffer anything less miserable? Was he not worthy of the Isles of the Blessed? He tells the fading Ajax, "dear son of of royal Telemon," that his death was due to Zeus's opposition: "and no one bears the blame but Zeus" (11.666). The great Herakles was supposed to be reclining with the gods. Yet in his sight of the underworld, "And Herakles, down the vistas of the dead, faded from sight" along with "other great souls who perished in times past" (*Od.* 11.717, 746–748). Who escapes from Homer's hell?

The Mesopotamian-Babylonian underworld entails the same kind existence for all people: "a shadowy version of life on earth."[56] Following his own visit to the underworld, Enkidu explains to Gilgamesh, whose semidivine lineage would seem to have assured him of better:

> Your wife, whom you touched, and
> your heart was glad,
> Vermin eat like an old garment.
> Your son whom you touched, and your heart was glad,
> Sits in a crevice full of dust. (Gilgamesh 12.4)[57]

Ancient Mesopotamians hoped that surviving family members would bring oblations of food and water to their grave. This was the principal cult in the Greek world also, long before the erection of temples to the gods. Yet Enkidu saw one

---

56. Black and Green, *Gods, Demons and Symbols*, 58, 180.
57. Burkert, *Orientalizing Revolution*, 65, acknowledges differences in the Greek development. "Nevertheless," as Burkert observes, "the extent to which the Homeric concept of Hades corresponds to the Mesopotamian is striking: a realm of mud and darkness that leaves no hope for mortals. . . . It is described in a famous scene in *Gilgamesh* when the ghost of Enkidu meets his friend, a scene which may have links with Homer even on a literary level."

"whose ghost has nobody to supply it: He feeds on dregs from dishes, and bits of bread that lie abandoned on the streets" (Gilgamesh 12.6).[58]

This twelfth and final tablet of the Epic of Gilgamesh depicts Gilgamesh returning to Uruk with secret instructions from the ferryman for bringing Enkidu back from the dead. True to character, Enkidu does not follow any of them and the earth seizes him. Enkidu pleads with Enlil to save him to no avail, and then entreats the deity Sin, who does not even answer him. Finally, it is kindly Enki— the creator and defender of humans—who once more obliges, commanding Ukur to open a hole in the earth. "And the spirit of Enkidu came out of the Earth like a gust of wind" to "return to his brother Gilgamesh. . . . They hugged and kissed, they discussed and agonized," as Enkidu explains the horrors of the underworld (Gilgamesh 12.6). If heroes with divine blood in their veins are rarely immortalized, what can the ordinary person expect?

The same dreary existence for all humans is another indication of a locative cosmos. The individual agency of mortals is submerged in the drama of the gods, who are themselves subject ultimately to Fate. As Bruno Snell observes, "In Homer every new turn of events is engineered by the gods. . . . In Homer the outstanding feats of man are said to spring, not from his individual character or from his special gifts, but from the divine force which flows through him. To formulate this more pointedly: There are personal fates, but no personal achievements."[59] What is clear implicitly is that the self is miserable and practically nonexistent when it leaves the locative, social, embedded world that, for all its woes and limits, is not without its joys whenever a god in a favorable mood puts wind in its sail. It is no wonder that the afterlife was virtually ignored in favor of whatever prosperity one could enjoy here and now. It was through the endurance of the family line and the city that one's existence continued.

In Homer's Greece, notes E. R. Dodds, there was "no unified concept of what we call 'soul' or 'personality.'" One may feel shame, which is mollified by a face-saving deed or propitiatory sacrifice, but it is strictly social and political, focused on how one is viewed publicly. Only in the transition to the classical era is the notion of guilt—a personal sense of moral failure and culpability—a feeling that one has deep within even if the sin is hidden to public view.[60] This inner pang had

---

58. Burkert, *Orientalizing Revolution*, 65, acknowledges differences in the Greek development. "Nevertheless," as Burkert observes, "the extent to which the Homeric concept of Hades corresponds to the Mesopotamian is striking: a realm of mud and darkness that leaves no hope for mortals. . . . It is described in a famous scene in *Gilgamesh* when the ghost of Enkidu meets his friend, a scene which may have links with Homer even on a literary level."

59. Snell, *Discovery of the Mind*, 29, 62.

60. Dodds, *Greeks and the Irrational*, 15–16.

to come from somewhere; it was a crucial part of the discovery of the self. If all of one's actions are actually those of the gods, then one can hardly be responsible for deeds, much less thoughts or desires. And if the only moral code, exemplified by the gods themselves, is shame or glory, the only course is to achieve immortality through fame because everyone faces the same fate after death. Like Gilgamesh, the hero has seen too much to settle for a dreary existence and has been driven to despair by that knowledge.

THE SHAMAN: UTOPIAN COSMOS AND THE HERO-THAT-SUCCEEDED

The diverse civilizations of the Bronze Age produced myths with some strikingly similar features. The earliest texts represent centuries of oral history written in poetic form. These epics celebrate the triumph of the gods turning a chaos into a cosmos, establishing boundaries above and below with laws to ensure stable, orderly rule and succession reflecting the current generation of reigning gods. Ancestors are honored and local heroes have their shrines. More than anything else, the purpose of epic myths was to provide a justification for the public rites that bound the earthly and celestial orders. The precise performance of these rites kept the cosmos from slipping back into chaotic darkness. It is the collective life in the city where the good life is to be found before one faces the inevitable end and passes into a dreary afterlife. One achieves security and prosperity—and, if possible, glory—here and now. The "Hero-That-Failed" reminds us of the futility experienced by precocious souls seeking to go beyond the limits.

Yet an episode lacking in Homer and Hesiod but found in Near Eastern and Egyptian myths from a millennium earlier is the sacrifice of a god in order to make humans intelligent.[61] Along with their body of clay, they have an *etemmu*, soul, spirit, *akh*, or mind that is divine. It is this idea that will enter the Greek world through Orphism with fanfare in the sixth century. In the *Iliad*, Athena breathes her "spirit" into Achilles. But this is not an anthropogony; it does not mean that Achilles now had *his own divine spirit* as a gift from Athena, but that Athena caused him to feel and act as she pleased, contrary to his own disposition and limitations. However, as these oriental breezes intensified, the Greeks would introduce their own versions of the Near Eastern anthropogonic myth, such as Athena blowing

---

61. The myth varies but with the same theme of a god being sacrificed to make humans divine as well as mortal. This unfortunate candidate is the vanquished Qingu in Enuma Elish, Ilawalla in Atrahasis, and, in the Sumerian-Akkadian "The Creation of Humankind" (*KAR* 4), the Alla-gods are sacrificed for the making of humans.

her spirit into Prometheus's clay models so that they have not only the best elements of animal souls but an immortal spirit or mind.[62] The myth of Dionysius would become the clearest analogue in the Greek world to the sacrifice of a god so that humanity might share in divine intellect.

Moreover, this is especially the case for those Bronze Age civilizations descended from the Iranian-Aryan peoples from the north who brought with them in their migration to Mesopotamia and India the figure of the shaman. In contrast with the "Hero-That-Failed," the shaman is the "Hero-That-Succeeded," breaking through the limits of the epic cosmos. Divine within, the shaman crosses frontiers between worlds, ignoring the confines of what was perceived as a natural order. He arrives in Athens suddenly and with spirited force. And, after giving birth to Greek mysteries, drama, and democracy, the Dionysian shaman—with the refinement of Orpheus—becomes known as the philosopher.

Profile of a Shaman

The shaman came from the Eurasian Steppe that stretches from Russian Siberia in the north to southeastern Europe, from the Danube to the Pacific Ocean, including Kazakhstan, Xinjan, Mongolia, and Manchuria.[63] Long before the rise of an official priestly class became tied to the ruler, the shaman was the original professional. In some modern cultures, the shaman remains the most respected figure of society.

In his magisterial study of the phenomenon from Asia to North America, Mircea Eliade identifies shamanism as "techniques of ecstasy."[64] Across the ethnographic data, he argues, the shaman (almost always male) recognizes three worlds: the underworld, this world, and the heavenly realms. And the shaman knows that there is a pole running through the middle of these worlds through which he ascends and descends at will. He is "regarded as having access to, and influence

---

62. Pseudo-Apollodorus, *Bib.* 1.7.1; Pseudo-Hyginus, *Fab.* 142; Ovid, *Metam.* 1.81.

63. Published originally in 1951, Mircea Eliade's *Shamanism: Archaic Techniques of Ecstasy* remains the starting point for such research. Covering two and a half millennia with mounds of ethnographic data, Eliade traces shamanism from Central Asia to its migration throughout the world.

64. Eliade, *Shamanism*, 4. Much has happened since Eliade first wrote this work in 1951, which has received a good deal of criticism for generalizing types lacking sufficient ethnographic specificity. See Hutton, *Shamans*. Throughout, Hutton provides a superb genealogy of research from the sixteenth century to the present as well as analysis of Eliade's descriptions. While Eliade's reductionism (e.g., three levels) is filled in by Hutton (e.g., more than three levels), it is not (to my mind) invalidated.

in, the world of good and evil spirits." According to Eliade, "Typically such people enter a trance state during a ritual, and practice divination and healing."[65] Hallucinogens sometimes facilitate the shaman's trance.[66] Although practices vary, many cultures know both benevolent (daytime) and malevolent (nighttime) shamans, not unlike the contrast between white and black magic in the Middle Ages.[67]

In his youth, the shaman is ostracized from other boys and given to bouts of depression, mania, and schizophrenia. Yet he learns gradually to master these afflictions and to see them as signs and tools of his divine powers. The next phases are incubation and initiation. This involves a period of seclusion in the wilderness and a "symbolic descent into the underworld; hypnotic sleep," including "drinks that make the candidate feel unconscious," and difficult ordeals: "beatings, feet held close to a fire, suspension in the air, amputations of fingers, and various other cruelties."[68] This initiatory experience is described in terms of one's dismemberment and cooking.[69] Not all magicians or ecstatics are shamans; "the shaman specializes in a trance during which his soul is believed to leave his body and ascend to the sky or descend to the underworld."[70]

Elaborate costumes as well as a large tambourine are the shaman's markers, though flutes have also been found to have played an important role.[71] Also essential is an association with animals.[72] He communicates with them, sometimes negotiating with their leaders on behalf of fishermen and hunters. He knows the animal that serves as his client's guardian spirit and channels their spirit, roaring like a bear or screeching like an eagle. Sometimes he takes the form of an animal, especially a bird, and he can locate human souls in animal bodies.[73]

---

65. See Eliade's entry "Shaman" in the *Oxford English Dictionary*. Mircea Eliade's *Shamanism* and its detailed ethnographic study has been the point of departure since it appeared. There Eliade reports, "Shamanism in the strict sense is pre-eminently a religious phenomenon of Siberia and Central Asia.... Throughout the immense area comprising Central and North Asia, the magico-religious life of society centers on the shaman ... the great master of ecstasy" (4).
66. Czigany, "Use of Hallucinogens"; Harner, *Hallucinogens and Shamanism*; Hurst, *Flesh of the Gods*.
67. Hoppál, "Eco-Animism of Siberian Shamanhood," 24–25.
68. Eliade, *Shamanism*, 64.
69. Eliade, *Shamanism*, 66.
70. Eliade, *Shamanism*, 5.
71. Fitch, "Biology and Evolution of Music," esp. 197.
72. This association emphasized by Eliade is explained well in Yakar, "Prehistorical Anatolian Religions," 297.
73. He assumes the role of the girl who leads souls in the Iranian version, Eliade says: "The girl goes down to the underworld to bring back her brother's head, that is, his 'soul,' just as the shaman brings the sick person's soul back from there; she sees infernal torments, which she

Recent ethnographic research, including genetic studies, has shown a consistent migration about 5,000 years ago from northern Asia through Siberia and across to Alaska with a remarkably uniform pattern of shamanistic technique.[74]

Detailed research demonstrates that the so-called dark tent ritual, unique to these northern regions, unifies these geographically disparate populations.[75] The common factor among these rituals is the shaman entering a tent without a fire and experiencing a dream-like state of perfect stillness in which he communicates with animal rulers. For example, he would be bound under a blanket and visit the fish ruler on behalf of fishermen. He would channel the growl of bears and other animals while the tent shook. Stépanoff argues that "this ritual played a crucial role in the intergenerational transmission, among people of the North, of a relationship to the world that could be described as *personal animism*." Without scriptures or institution, he adds, the "dark tent" was the product of "migration and borrowing."[76]

The shaman is therefore not a product of the locative world but rather preceded it.[77] As societies evolved from hunter-gatherer to agricultural and urban domesticity, the shaman was marginalized. However, he learned to flourish in that liminal space between worlds where he had always felt at home anyway. Not only his methods but his profession was considered illicit. Living on the periphery of traditional society, he became seen as a transgressive figure, the symbol of what might be called excommunicated spiritualities. The fact that the shaman could abandon his body as he searched for souls, flying on his magic arrow, contrasted sharply with the locative and bounded cosmos of his contemporaries. The shaman's worldview is utopian (i.e., placeless): not only disembedded but disembodied, his divine spirit glides freely across borders. "In other words, it would be more correct to class shamanism among the mysticisms than with what is commonly called a religion.... The shaman is the great specialist in the human soul; he alone 'sees' it, for he knows its 'form' and its destiny."[78] In other words, the shaman was spiritual, not religious.

On the surface, the ecstasy of traditional religious officials appears indistinguishable from that of the shaman. They even share the presupposition that the

---

describes and which, even though influenced by ideas from South Asia or the ancient Near East, contain certain descriptions of infernal topography which, all over the world, shamans were the first to communicate to the living." See *Shamanism*, 214.

74. Stépanoff, "Shamanistic Ritual," 242–43.
75. Stépanoff, "Shamanistic Ritual," 239–46.
76. Stépanoff, "Shamanistic Ritual," 241, 245.
77. Kolenkaya-Bostanci, "Evolution of Shamanism Rituals."
78. Eliade, *Shamanism*, 5, 8.

celestial realm of the gods, the earth, and the underworld are connected.[79] Thus, sacredness lies at the heart of all things, which is why every aspect of life is interpreted in a religious frame. But the differences are significant.

First, the shaman replaces the temple as the intersection of the three worlds. Navel of the universe, center, meeting place of heaven and earth, house of god, ladder to heaven: these were typical descriptions of the temple in the ancient Near East. In a locative environment, there is no divide between the individual, society, and public religion. The welfare of the society below depends on the satisfaction of the society above, and the ancient Near Eastern ruler was the mediator in whom both these societies met. His mandate from the chief of the gods was renewed at each New Year's celebration. Yet his mandate from the gods depended on a retinue of cult professionals to keep them aligned through precise performance of the stipulated rites. The gods were honored guests at these theatrical performances, expecting to see an annual imitation of their past victory over disorder. The relation between the divine and human realms was mediated and strictly controlled. The gods themselves existed within the bounded cosmos.

In contrast, the shaman is the temple, the intersection of the three worlds. He is utopian (placeless) because he is the place and his operations not only provide an imitative performance but gain access to the reality itself. The shaman is not only placeless but also timeless and unbound to a calendar of festivals. Ancestors were honored in archaic civilizations, but they had to be invited and their stay was limited and carefully monitored. "In Japan," we are told, "the souls of the dead are invited to return to this world for a day on August 15. Each family prepares itself to receive its dead and then accompanies them back to the cemetery."[80] At the festival of *frawasis*, Iranian magi allowed the return of spirits of the dead.[81] Yet these events were *exceptions*, underscoring the inflexible laws of nature.

For the ancient Near Eastern shaman, all of this merely bound the soul to the limitations of the present order. Public officials interpreted omens through physical media such as the flight of birds, entrails, and the stars or by reading a liver in comparison with a clay model. The credibility of the official rested on his or her ability to interpret the signs whereas the shaman just saw the reality directly and immediately. Religious officials in a locative environment are, for the most part,

---

79. Like Eliade, some specialists limit the designation "shamanism" to the distinctive characteristics summarized here. Others broaden the category, such as Peters and Price-Williams, "Experiential Analysis of Shamanism"; Samuel, *Mind, Body, Culture*; R. Wright, *Evolution of God*. Starting out with Eliade's restrictive definition, my account gradually broadens without losing the distinctions between prophets and priests in the public cult and the shaman.
80. Assmann, *Death and Salvation*, 15.
81. Malandra, "Zoroastrianism."

Chapter 1

ritual specialists. They are vessels of the gods. The shaman is not a priest of the gods but a divine spirit in his own right, a spiritual entrepreneur who devises his own magical rites. He does not need oracles from the gods to interpret the truth; he knows the truth already.

The religious officials in a locative situation are overwhelmed by the gods, their own faculties suspended, while the shaman is fully in charge. Here I find illuminating Gilbert Rouget's distinction between ecstasy and trance. The former is associated with immobility, silence, solitude, no sense of crisis, and sensory deprivation while the latter is announced by wild dancing, noise, witnesses, with a sense of crisis and sensory overstimulation. Ecstasy depends on recollection and hallucinations, while trance involves amnesia and no hallucinations. Instead of binary opposition, though, these should be seen as opposite poles of a continuum.[82] "Silence, solitude, immobility, three conditions that represent the exact opposite of those required by the shaman when he officiates or by the possessed person when he dances. . . . I could cite such other examples as Dionysiac dances in ancient Greece."[83] Trance begins with a convulsive stage of symbolic death, where the self passes away and is possessed.[84]

The poet-theologians of the epic age, like Homer, were possessed by a god. Indeed, the divine inspiration of their songs was measured by the suspension of their own faculties. However, the shaman was not the vessel of any god; he was not possessed but was in complete control of his mind as he employed his spiritual techniques. He made no inferences from the quasi-magical "science" of his day because he was a magician who simply knew what was wrong and had the spiritual technology to fix it.[85]

Second, the official priest is a border guard while the shaman is a border crosser. The royal prophets and priests of the ancient world were concerned with guaranteeing that the order below reflected the order above. The epic myths tell how the gods turned chaos into cosmos, and the corresponding rites explain how the terrestrial society remains in sync with this achievement. The most egregious trespasser was the soul of the dead. It was the vocation of religious officials to make sure that the dead remained dead, to police the boundaries so that spirits would not cross over to haunt the living. However, the shaman's ecstatic techniques transgressed these boundaries all the time. The reason people consulted

---

82. Rouget, *Music and Trance*, 3–62, here at 11.
83. Rouget, *Music and Trance*, 6.
84. Rouget, *Music and Trance*, 7.
85. Luck, *Arcana Mundi*, 499–510.

a shaman was precisely because he dealt with individual souls, communicating with them as a medium and sometimes bringing them back for a time.

Public religion was just that—public, corporate, concerned with keeping the earthly realm in harmony with the cosmic order established by the gods in the epic myth. State festivals guaranteed this harmony, but the shaman could not care less about the public order. If anything, the construction of society interfered with his divine calling in secret meetings. Oracles and divinations were concerned mostly with the security and prosperity of the city. The official priest served the public while the shaman had clients.

Lacking (in fact, eschewing) public authority for their work, ancient Near Eastern shamans depended on their own charisma and success. The trance was a prime advertisement of the shaman's spiritualist credentials. Typically, it involved "trembling, shuddering, horripilation, swooning, falling to the ground, yawning, lethargy, convulsions, foaming at the mouth, protruding eyes, large extrusions of the tongue, paralysis of a limb, etc."[86] Shamans attracted individuals whose main concern was not whether a neighboring people might attack the city, but whether their deceased son or daughter could be contacted and perhaps even retrieved. There is the "dramatic structure of the shamanic séance," including "the sometimes highly elaborate staging."

> But every genuinely shamanic séance ends as a *spectacle* unequaled in the world of daily experience. The fire tricks, the "miracles" of the rope-trick or mango-trick type, the exhibition of magical feats, reveal another world—the fabulous world of the gods and magicians, the world in which *everything seems possible*, where *the dead return to life* and the living die only to live again, where one can disappear and reappear instantaneously, where the *"laws of nature" are abolished*, and certain *superhuman "freedom"* is exemplified and made dazzlingly *present*.[87]

The shaman's entrepreneurial adventures contrast sharply with the epic myths and rituals that formed the locative horizon.

Third, traditional societies perceived shamans as outsiders to whom one turned in dire straits when the public cult seemed existentially inadequate. When the gods seemed aloof and heroes of the past could not help, one resorted to the shaman for results here and now. As official guardians of the boundaries, court

---

86. Rouget, *Music and Trance*, 13.
87. Eliade, *Shamanism*, 510–11. I have added italics to highlight the characteristics that mark the classical age.

prophets and priests entreated the gods. The shaman could only be perceived as threatening the order that had turned a chaos into a cosmos. This had political ramifications as well. The royal prophets and priests lived at the center of the city, usually in the king's palace, while shamans existed outside the city walls. The shaman circumvented the whole apparatus of public religion and royal protocol as well as traditional medicine. In short, shamans represented a potentially utopian and revolutionary rival.

Blazing the trail of the Silk Road, shamans were part of the Indo-Iranian people as they divided into Iranian and Indo-Aryan peoples around the second millennium BCE, the same time that the Enuma Elish was being etched into clay tablets by East Semitic Akkadians. While Sanskrit-speaking Indo-Aryans settled in northern India, the Iranian branch (Avestan) migrated to Mesopotamia, supplanting the Akkadian Empire in what became the Old Babylonian Empire. The earliest texts composed durng this period were religious, specifically epic myth and cultic rites. And in both language and religion, including names of deities, Avestan and Sanskrit texts from this period are remarkably similar.[88]

Yet even as the public religion swelled with a professional class of court priests, the medicine man continued to provide an esoteric alternative. Numerous healers, prophets, and seers followed well-worn trade routes as "craftsmen of the sacred."[89] Their product was not sanctification of the worldly order but salvation from it. They did not expel impurities from this world but escaped the bonds of mortality. They knew their true, inmost, and divine self transcended all limitations of the body, the public, and the external world. As we will see, this shamanic ideal comes rushing into Greece just after Homer and inspires a mysticism that stood increasingly in an awkward relationship to the public religion.

If Gilgamesh is in his proper place on a throne in Uruk, with an established priesthood and sacred rites, the early Bronze Age shaman belonged to an oral tradition of bricoleurs who depended on self-promotion and, above all, success. As McEvilley explains, "Both medical lore and religious lore were considered 'products' of this type." While the shaman-medicine man was not the sort of person to sell his wares in the public market, many shaman-like entrepreneurs traveled widely and were often sent by their rulers as "personal physicians" to friendly courts. "The specialized profession of 'physician' had not yet separated itself out from the larger profession of shaman or 'medicine man,' which included functions

---

88. Brereton and Jamison, *Rigveda*, 1:3–6; Samuel, *Origins of Yoga and Tantra*, 24–30; cf. Skjærvø, "Old-Avestan Scholarship."

89. This phrase was coined by Walter Burkert throughout *Orientalizing Revolution* and has become a standard way of classifying migrant healer-seers.

of magic, mythmaking, protophilosophy, and song or poetry, along with healing. Some of those whom we now regard as Greek philosophers would have appeared in the eyes of the Persian kings as 'physicians.'"[90] From such itinerant "craftsmen of the sacred," foreign ideas entered the Greek bloodstream.

Homer's blind seer, Teiresias, and the Pythian priestess of Delphi, not to mention Homer himself, were viewed as being under Apollo's inspiration or Hermes's magic.[91] "Divine madness" is not something that comes to a shaman, however, but it is inherent within him. Later, we will meet these two types of religious specialists that correspond to Socrates's distinction between "two kinds of madness, one produced by human illnesses, the other by a divinely inspired release from normally accepted behavior." And the prophetic madness of Apollo (Delphic) is further distinguished from the poetic madness of the Muses (Homeric) and the mystical madness of the shaman (Dionysian) (Plato, *Phaed.* 265a–b).[92]

---

90. McEvilley, *Shape of Ancient Thought*, 15; quoting Oppenheim, "Seafaring Merchants of Ur," 155. McEvilley cites an example from Herodotus, *Hist.* 3.1, who states when discussing how Amasis, the Egyptian pharaoh, sent an eye specialist to Cyrus that the Greeks were also beginning to win fame as physicians at this time. An unbroken line of Greeks was even "personal physicians" to the imperial Persian magi: Democedes to Darius I, Apollonides to Artaxerxes I, and Ctesias (and later, Polkritos) to Artaxerxes II.

91. M. L. West argues, "The Pythia resembles a shaman at least to the extent that she communicates with her god while in a state of trance, and conveys as much to those present by uttering unintelligible words. It is particularly striking that she sits on a cauldron supported by a tripod. This eccentric perch can hardly be explained except as a symbolic boiling, and, as such, it looks very much like a reminiscence of the initiatory boiling of the shaman translated from hallucinatory experience into concrete visual terms. It was in this same cauldron, probably, that the Titans boiled Dionysus in the version of the story known to Callimachus and Euphorion, and his remains were interred close by." See *Orphic Poems*, 147. This is one of a few places where I think West's analytical connections lack sufficient support. We know little about what the Pythia actually did, including whether she did it in a trance (any more than Homer or Hesiod), and people came all the way to Delphi for oracles (intelligible words). See Scott, *Delphi*, esp. 12–50. The explanation for the tripod is more strained, especially since boiling is a later story associated with Dionysus while the Pythia is the mouthpiece of Apollo who has no such associations.

92. Translation from Nehamas and Woodruff in Plato, *Complete Works* (ed. Cooper) (emphasis added). In this second category there are four types: "the inspiration of the prophet to Apollo, of the mystic to Dionysus, of the poet to the Muses, and the fourth part of madness to Aphrodite and to Love [Eros]." Plato also adds that people attribute to the Muses the divine madness of the poets (i.e., those who wrote the stories of the gods, mainly Homer and Hesiod) and the last (erotic desire) to Aphrodite and Eros. It is sometimes argued that the idea of a divine "madness" (*mania*) results from a mistranslation of Plato's *manikē*, which actually refers to divination, not madness. However, Socrates clearly distinguishes different types of "madness" and not only that of the poets. Socrates adds, "we said that the madness of love is the best," and then defines this as the love of dialectic.

Prophecy is external—an authoritative divine utterance mediated by a mortal representative. Mysticism is internal—an autonomous vision of the inmost self as one with divinity, requiring no mediation. People flocked to Apollo for a reliable word concerning their future but sought Dionysus for an experience with divinity in the present, in which their future destiny was suddenly known completely. The shaman not only was the survivor of the Bronze Age but entered a new age as both sage and savior.

A New Afterlife and the Utopian Turn

The discovery of the individual and, concomitantly, of the immortal soul aroused a sense of personal freedom. Only from a modern perspective can we assume that political and social changes were the drivers of this spiritual phenomenon. In reality, Athenian democracy was probably as much a product as a producer. We tend to assume that the notion of personal autonomy is a universal truth that rulers and their priests tried in vain to suppress. Often, the modern Enlightenment is seen as recovering this innate idea after centuries of Christian authoritarianism. However, the revolution that occurred in the sixth century BCE has remained a perennial tradition surging beneath the edifice of public religions. The utopian trend encouraged a shift in focus from keeping one's proper place in the polis here and now to a higher form of individual existence in the afterlife. Far from the dreary afterlife of the epic age, each soul could determine its own destiny.

Zoroastrianism emphasized the free will of individual souls to side with good or evil. Souls were presented with a choice of remaining in security with Ahura Mazda or descending into bodies to conquer the satanic Angra Mainyu. Deciding to join the battle, the souls descended. Upon death, the soul would appear on the Chinwad Bridge for judgment. The wicked would be dragged off by a demon while the righteous would be guided by their spiritual double to heaven.[93] Similarly, in Late Period Egypt (664–332 BCE) a radically new view of the afterlife developed that involved different judgments based on freely chosen lives.[94]

---

93. See hymn 30 in Agostini and Thrope, *Bundahišn*, 159–62.

94. Assmann, *Death and Salvation*, 12. Ancient Egyptian religion did not choose between the body and the soul or this life and the next. The body is distinguished from the *ba* and *ka* (i.e., the parts of the soul), but even the usual translations "soul" and "spirit" can be misleading, Assmann explains. The individual is always embedded in the network of society, even after death. The transfigured *ka* is one's ancestral spirit that remains part of the community. Death is a form of life and vice versa. The Egyptian body was not a "heap of dung" as in Greek thought but the mummified locus of individual and social bonds. "Even the tomb was a medium of such

A clear trend was emerging that pushed the individual agent to the center with personal choice determining one's postmortem future. And long before Socrates turned the attention of Athenian youths to ethical questions, Zoroastrianism had made the battle between good and evil the central task of humans. "In the beginning there were two Spirits, Twins spontaneously active. These were the Good and the Evil, in thought, and in word, and in deed. Between these two, let the wise choose aright; Be good, not base" (*Yasna* 30).[95] "With uplifted arms, O Mazda, I pray and humbly ask for happiness" through good thoughts, good words, and good deeds. "Thus, O Mazda Ahura, I come to You with Good Thought, so that I may learn through Righteousness the joy of both worlds, the physical and that of the mind."[96] The primacy of thoughts testifies to its vintage. Farhang Mehr explains, "The doctrine of moral dualism is at one end related to the principle of freedom of choice, and at the other end to the law of consequences. . . . In *The Younger Avesta* and Pahlavi books, the ethical dualism converts itself into cosmic dualism—a development contrary to the Gathic tradition, according to a Zoroastrian school of thought."[97] I return to Zoroastrian doctrines below, but Malanda's summary is worth bearing in mind:

> What emerged during the Achaemenid period was an eclectic Iranian religion, Zoroastrianism, which contained elements of Zarathustrianism, apocalyptic legends of the prophet, a full pantheon of deities that are almost entirely absent from the Gathas, an overriding concern over purity and pollution, the establishment of fire temples, a strong ethical code based on man's part in the cosmic struggle between the principles of Truth and the Lie, and an eschatology which saw history as an unfolding struggle between these principles, which would lead to the final Renovation of the Cosmos.[98]

In Egypt, too, the old gods had lost their magic (*heka*) and a new generation of central characters emerged in the Late Period. The shift from Re to Osiris and Isis was one of the most significant aspects of this phenomenon. The lament of "disenchantment" is always a prelude to the call for a new mythology. According to

---

'constellative embedding,' one intended to secure for the individual, for all time, a place in the social, geographical, and cultural space of the group."

95. Quoted in Mehr, *Zoroastrian Tradition*, 89.

96. *Gathas* (trans. Koupai), 20. The "soul of the just shall always be victorious and strong and the soul of the deceitful shall always live in pain. This is the doctrine that Mazda Ahura has established as the basis of creation" (10.7; cf. 16.1–17.7).

97. Mehr, *Zoroastrian Tradition*, 91.

98. Malandra, "Zoroastrianism."

one influential story, Re was becoming senile and agitated toward human beings. In this condition he sent his destroying Eye and then, shocked at the destruction, tricked the Eye into standing down. We have met versions of this irritated patriarchal deity repeatedly in the Bronze Age epics. Re is like Apsu, Enlil, and Kronos and his jealous son Zeus. After his Eye goes overboard in destroying humans, Re tricks the Eye into relenting and purposes simply to retire to heaven away from the noise of the unruly mortals. The other gods rule in his name and with his *heka*.

At this point, Isis determines to share the rule with the aged sun god. Capturing some of his drool, she kneads it into a clay snake that bites him. To save him, Isis asks Re to divulge his secret name, since this was the magic in the venom. "I am Khepera in the morning, Re at noon-day, and Temu in the evening," he says. But he resists revealing his secret name, explaining that his "begetter" planted it within him so that he would be immune to all magic. Isis will speak "efficacious words of power" if he yields, which finally he does in his agonizing pain. Possessing his name, Isis is now more powerful than Re himself.[99]

Isis is akin to Enki and Prometheus in her sneaky and even treasonous sympathy for mortals. But now she controls Re's magic. By that same magic (*heka*) she restores her husband Osiris. Set, the evil brother of Osiris and Isis who, like the Greek god Typhon, represents the forces of destruction, tears Osiris to pieces. Discovering his phallus, Isis reproduces Osiris from it. Osiris was thus worshiped as androgynous, providing fertility for men and women alike.[100] As Banebdjedet (the *ba* or soul of Osiris), he becomes "Lord of the Sky" and "Life of the Ra."[101] Simultaneously with Dionysus in Greece and Shiva in India, Osiris became more central even than Re in the Late Period. Once a chthonic and local deity of Busiris in Lower Egypt, Osiris became the resurrected king. Osiris and Isis with their son Horus (set in opposition to their villainous siblings Set and Nephthys), formed an all-powerful triad. As usual, behind the drama lies an actual political situation. It is the justification for Egypt's unification.[102] The turbulent road to this end is recounted mythologically in the Contendings of Horus and Set, which describes mutilations, a homosexual episode, and reunification with political

---

99. Budge, *Dwellers on the Nile*, 204–7.
100. Especially in Memphis, the cult centered on Osiris's soul (*ba*) was called Banebdjedet, which is grammatically feminine. See Smith, *Man and His Gods*, 45.
101. Roth, "Father Earth, Mother Sky." Even real-life political circumstances are reflected in the myth, as dismembered Egypt is united into one realm by Horus, Isis and Osiris produce Horus, the perfect king, and Ptah works through Horus to unite Upper and Lower Egypt, a political expression of the metaphysical scheme.
102. Griffiths, "Allegory in Greece and Egypt."

as well as metaphysical overtones.[103] Horus, the natural heir, prevails, assuming Osiris's throne.

The anxious could turn to the mother-savior Isis, who was not only compassionate and attentive but also all-powerful. During the Egyptian renaissance under Psametik, "It was not possible to resuscitate all the old gods, but Osiris and Isis became the favorites.... The influence of the Greeks upon Egypt was commercial and material; on the contrary, that of Egypt upon Greece was spiritual."[104]

In the Pyramid Texts of the Old Kingdom, the focus is on the celestial realm of Re (the equivalent of Zeus) and pharaohs becoming Re. The rest of humanity is resigned to a bare existence.[105] But in the later portions of the Book of the Dead the afterlife is opened to all, and it is no longer a celestial region but Duat—the underworld ruled by Osiris—a place of bliss for some and purgation for others.[106]

---

103. For a superb summary of the content within its setting see Griffiths, "Allegory in Greece and Egypt"; cf. Assmann, *Death and Salvation*, 367, where Set is linked to the perennial northern invader from Asia, especially Persians, Greeks, and Romans.

104. Sarton, *History of Science*, 1:181–82. After being a Neo-Assyrian vassal for a few months, Egypt was liberated by a native governor, Psametik, with the help of Greek and Carian mercenaries. It was a national unification campaign and, upon becoming king, Psametik established his capital at Sais and committed to an Egyptian renaissance. Part of the renaissance was the invention of Demotic script, a more popular form of writing. Like other civilizations, therefore, political reunification and writing were key factors. Taking advantage of Assyrian-Babylonian wars and the strength of Greek mercenaries, his son Necho invaded Judah in 609, defeating Josiah, but was defeated himself by Nebuchadnezzar four years later, losing all of his conquered territories in Asia. Solon admired Necho and made a special point to study his laws on a visit to Egypt, introducing some of them into the Athenian code. Cyrus invaded Egypt, which became part of the Achaemenid Empire in 525. See Sarton, *History of Science*, 1:183–84.

105. A fascinating Middle Egyptian text entitled "Debate between a Man and His Soul" exhibits beautifully the locative outlook of the epic age. The soul at first argues for a quick flight, similar to the advice of Plato's Socrates in the *Theaetetus*, and then the positions are reversed. The final speech is given to the soul, which suggests a compromise: endure hardship now and embrace death when it comes. "And you are dead, with your name alive. Yonder is a place of alighting, storage-chest of the mind. The West [netherworld] is a harbor to which the perceptive are rowed." The epic-age hero weeps not for "that one who was born" but for "her children.... Death is in my sight now, like a man longs to see home, when he has spent many years taken in captivity." The soul (*ba*), represented here as being caught in a bodily net, is not a savior but a survivor. See Allen, *Middle Egyptian Literature*, 334–55.

106. "Egyptian religion was developing into two main directions," says George Sarton, "leading respectively to Heaven and Hell—on one hand, a solar cult with the conception of an empyrean realm of the dead; on the other hand, the Osiridian cycle of myths suggested by the miraculous fertility of plants, animals, and men, together with the conception of underground mysteries." See *History of Science*, 1:221, 181–82. See also Breasted, *Dawn of Conscience*, 221. After being for a few months an Assyrian vassal, Egypt was liberated by a native governor, Psametik,

The soul's trial took place before Re in Old and Middle Egyptian texts. However, in the Book of the Dead, Osiris presides over this trial.[107]

The democratic afterlife is seen in the extensive spells and declarations of average people painted on simple wooden coffins from the Late Period.[108] In Osiris's courtroom, the inhabitant of the homeliest coffin can boast, as if he or she were Re, "I shall sail rightly in my bark, I am lord of eternity in the crossing of the sky." The goddess Heka will perform her magic for the pilot, and no one who knows the spell will ever be touched by the fire in the underworld.[109] Another announces, "I have made the four winds that every man might breathe thereof like his brother during his time." The same is said of the waters. "I have made every man like his brother."[110] What matters is not whether one is a prince or a parvenu but rather whether one is good or bad.[111] The justified—whatever their station—are beneficiaries of the liturgy reserved previously for pharaohs and few else. The deceased is addressed as "Osiris N," with "N" representing the name of the deceased. "This liturgy culminates in the solemn speech in which the newly arrived Osiris is presented to the gods of the netherworld as their new ruler: 'Rally round this N., do all he bids. Give praise to him, O gods. . . . Osiris N., come out, you being great and mighty, like the emergence of Re.'" As Osiris, the vindicated mortal is endowed with the authority to "threaten the gods with his *sekhem*-scepter."[112]

"Finally, the deceased is addressed as 'lord of *maat*.'"[113] This is the most audacious epithet so far. Ma'at is the law-and-order divinity, equivalent to the Greek Fate personified in the three sisters (Fates or Moirai) who determined the moments of birth, life, and death. Even Zeus is their subordinate, and they ensure that both gods and humans "pay the full penalty" for their misdeeds.[114] This view of

---

with the help of Greek and Carian (Semitic) mercenaries. It was a national unification campaign and on becoming king Psametik established his capital at Sais, committed to an Egyptian renaissance. Part of the renaissance was the invention of Demotic script, a more popular form of writing. Like other civilizations, therefore, political reunification and writing were key factors.

107. Allen, *Middle Egyptian Literature*, 334.

108. Assmann, *Death and Salvation*, 149. Assmann provides a number of supportive quotations from coffin texts on pages 170–77, 404–6.

109. Buck and Gardiner, *Egyptian Coffin Texts*, 7:262 (spell 1031).

110. Quoted in Breasted, *Dawn of Conscience*, 221.

111. From the time of Herodotus, it has been held that the Orphic and Pythagorean metempsychosis or reincarnation was derived from Egypt. However, while souls could definitely migrate from place to place in Egpyitan thought, sometimes even returning to their mummified body, reincarnation did not originate in Egypt.

112. Assmann, *Death and Salvation*, 289–91.

113. Assmann, *Death and Salvation*, 289–91.

114. See Hesiod, *Theog.* 221–225, where the Fates are daughters of Nyx (Night). In some later theogonies their mother is Themis, goddess of justice, and in Plato's *Republic* (617c) their mother

Fate as more ultimate than any gods is apparent in the Vedic Ṛta, the Avestan Asha (Arta) and the Egyptian Maat. However, since the Orphic soul is more ancient than all the gods, even this boundary no longer inhibits or rules her.

Neither Isis nor Osiris is a monarch like Re. It is not the action of the gods that is decisive in any case. The relevant gods in this episode are recorders of merits and weighers of hearts, the Egyptian Thoth being similar to the Indian Yama and the Greek Fates (or Themis holding out her scales). This was part of the depersonalization of the gods and the rationalization of theology. When it comes to gods, principles reign and not persons. When it comes to humans, it is the guilt of individual souls rather than the collective *miasma* of cities that requires purification. From this fountain sprang a new afterlife of different levels determined by one's own merits. The gods simply acknowledged what was essentially a natural law, karma, a divine decree. The human soul not only became identical with but actually replaced an external god and his judgment. As the afterlife became democratized and the soul rose to immortal and autonomous divinity, more freedom for personal agency was expected in this life as well.

Assmann explains that this changed already in the New Kingdom, so that instead of a hierarchy of divine royals and the merely human masses, "there was the distinction between good and evil, as well as that between knowing and the unknowing." We recall that the shaman's world is three-tiered with a pole running through the center. "The cosmos became three-tiered" in Egypt as well. The earth—this world—became contrasted with "the next world that included both sky and netherworld."

> As before, the deceased soared aloft to the sky, but now, the netherworld was equally important to him. Thus arose the concept of the next world as a place to which only the just and the knowing were admitted. This "moralizing" of the afterlife was a necessary consequence of the extension of the royal idea of the afterlife to lower social classes.[115]

The weighing of the heart in the scale, and the "Devouress" swallowing hearts heavy with guilt, became prominent. It was not who one was by physical birth but

---

is Ananke (Necessity). In fact, the sovereignty of Fate over gods and mortals alike characterizes Indo-European mythology. In *Il.* 16.705, Zeus's beloved son Sarpadon will be killed by Patroclus and there is nothing he can do about it because the Fates have willed it (16.433).

115. Assmann, *Death and Salvation*, 147–48. He says, "A formula that made its appearance in the Middle Kingdom and is attested to us hundreds of times, down to the end of the history of Egyptian religion, describes the status to which he aspired as
  Transfigured (*akh*) in the sky with Re,
  Powerful on earth with Geb,
  Vindicated in the realm of the dead with Osiris.

Chapter 1

how one conducted their life in spiritual and moral terms that came to determine their outcome. Mummification became essential in this period because the body had to be intact to live in the next life.[116] Osiris's Duat (underworld) was neither heaven nor hell but purgatory, where even the tardiest soul could catch up, but where even the most just could be overcome by evil forces. Here, both gods and human souls (*bas*) could regenerate, but they were still surrounded by dangers requiring spells and passwords. Magic had to be used sometimes even on gods who opposed the soul's transfiguration, just as Heka overcame Apep in the pitch-black underworld so Re-Osiris could rise again.[117] This was the rationale for the severe threats and spells that were directed at gods and daimons (demons) in Egyptian rituals, as we shall see in the Greek Magical Papyri.

To be reborn meant neither reincarnation nor resurrection; it meant becoming identical with Osiris.[118] The soul would progress to the two passes around the Island of Fire. Judgment would then be rendered according to Ma'at (the god of pure justice) with the possibility of a second death—being cast out of the ordered cosmos.[119] This was the final death, the annihilation of the soul. At the "End of Days," everything would return to primordial waters of chaos and there would

---

116. The arduous effort dedicated to mummification is sufficient to caution against generalizations. On the one hand, "gnostic" elements were always present in Egypt long before they appeared elsewhere. On the other hand, precisely because Egyptian religion developed more or less independently, these elements were always balanced with "antignostic" ones. Assmann writes, "The mummy was more than a corpse, it was an image of the god Osiris and a sort of hieroglyph of the entire person, on that, as the Egyptians put it, was 'filled with magic.'" See Assmann, *Death and Salvation*, 15. The whole process of mummification assumed that the body needed to be dismembered (its impurities removed) and knitted back together again. The transfiguration of the ancestral spirit was signified by the phrase "crossing the lake," which happened in the physical purificatory embalming process but also at the same time occurred in "its spiritual-magical aspect" (26–32). So, there was not a jarring shift from ritualistic, "this-worldly" formulas to metaphysical, "other-worldly" speculation. Nor was there anxiety about border crossing. The "ghost" (*akh* or transfigured spirit) of the departed was expected to come around for supper at the richly furnished table of the mummy. However, "In Egypt, the rule was the crossings between the realm of the living and the realm of the dead were subject to strict control" (33).

117. Teeter, *Religion and Ritual in Ancient Egypt*, 161–81.

118. The terms "reincarnation" and "resurrection" are often used in describing ancient Egyptian beliefs, but they are alien concepts. To be sure, the *ba* and *ka* fly freely to and fro, but there is no reincarnation of souls in other bodies, which would upset the entire cult of mummification. And a future resurrection of the body would void the main eschatological objective, which is that even at death (after judgment) the just are no longer distinct subjects but become identical with Osiris.

119. This is taught clearly in chapter 125 of the Book of the Dead.

Survivor to Shaman: Discovering the Divine Self

only be Atum (or Osiris, in some accounts). The end returns to the beginning, represented in the Ouroboros snake eating its tail.[120] Analogous to its counterparts, Late Period religion in Egypt was imbued with a cyclical consciousnesss, according to Assmann.[121] This is consistent with the cosmological myth emphasized by Orphic theogonies with emanation-return and reincarnation-escape as the correlates.[122]

The same type of succession myth spread across the Asian continent. The Upanishads (last parts or culmination of the Vedas) exhibit the same shift from concrete and bodily rituals to abstract philosophical doctrines focusing on cosmic emanation-and-return with its corollary, transmigration. Hinduism is a synthesis of many ideas, including Indo-Aryan rituals from the Rigveda and brahminic interpretation, but its doctrines appear to be mostly from a quite different origin. Among these new doctrines was the idea that upon separation from the body the soul ascends to Svargaloka (one of the seven highest heavens) from which it descends again into another body based on the cumulative karma of its previous lives. The goal ultimately is *moksha*, liberation from the cycle of rebirth. This is nirvana, the loss of self-identity in assimilation to *brahman* (the ultimate unchanging reality), analogous to the identification of the *ka* with Osiris and of the soul to the Cosmic Soul. Max Müller summarizes well the principal teaching of these texts: "know thy true self, that which underlines thine Ego, and find it and know it in the highest, the eternal Self, the One without a second, which underlies the whole world."[123] This is new with little connection to earlier Vedic traditions.

The *axis mundi*, ladder, world tree, or pole running through the middle of the three worlds belongs to the environment of the shaman, as we have seen. All these ideas intersect nicely in the Brihadaranyaka Upanishad, composed probably in the sixth century BCE. The true self (*atman*) is "the inner light within the heart," the vital essence or life force (*prana*). "He travels across both worlds, being common to both."

> Sometimes he reflects, somethings he flutters, for when he falls asleep he transcends this world, these visible forms of death. When at birth this person takes

---

120. Wilkinson, *Gods and Goddesses of Ancient Egypt*, 20–23.
121. Contrasting the Hebrew prophets with Egyptian religion, Assmann notes that ancient Egyptian religion is not gnostic—renouncing this world—but it is also not in step with Israel's horizontal vision of promise and fulfillment. "In this chain lay the historia sacra (sacred history) in whose horizon the drive for immortality satisfied its need for meaning—an idea that was entirely foreign to Egypt."
122. Assmann, *Death and Salvation*, 10–11.
123. Müller, *Upanishads*, lxxxvi n. 1.

on a body, he becomes united with bad things and when at death he leaves it behind, he gets rid of those bad things. Now, this person has just two places—this world and the other world. And there is a third, the place of dream where the two meet. Standing there in the place where the two meet, he sees both those places—this world and the other world. Now, that place serves as an entryway to the other world, and as he moves through that entryway he sees both the bad things and the joys. . . . In that place this person becomes his own light. . . . In that place there are no joys, pleasures, or delights; but he creates for himself joys, pleasures, and delights. In that place there are no pools, ponds, or rivers; but he creates for himself pools, ponds, and rivers—for he is a creator. (BU 4.3.6–10)[124]

Further, exactly as for the shaman, "Here, in dream, a man becomes his own light." In that realm "he has seen for himself the good and the bad" but has passed beyond good and evil. He does not perceive anything here by his senses because "there isn't a second reality here that he could see as something distinct and separate from himself. . . . He becomes the one ocean, he becomes the sole seer! This, Your Majesty, is the world of *brahman*. . . . This is the highest bliss!" (BU 4.3.14–32). Yajnavalkya, the sage attributed authorship of the Brihadaranyaka Upanishad, continues:

After this person has enjoyed himself and travelled around in that realm of dream and seen for himself the good and the bad, he rushes along the same path and through the same opening back again to the realm where one is awake. . . . As a heavily loaded cart goes along creaking, so this bodily self, saddled with the self of knowledge, goes along groaning as he is breathing his last. . . . As a mango or a fig or a berry detaches itself from its stem, so this person frees himself from these bodily parts and rushes along the same path and through the same opening back again to a new life (*prāṇa*). (BU 4.3.34–36)

Whenever one comes to know this, "all beings shout, '*brahman* has arrived!'" (BU 4.3.37). After this happens:

Then a mortal becomes immortal, and attains *brahman* in this world. . . . As a snake's slough, lifeless and discarded, lies on an anthill, so lies this corpse. But this non-corporeal and immortal lifebreath (*prāṇa*) is nothing but *brahman*,

---

124. All citations of the Brihadaranyaka Upanishad, unless otherwise noted, from Olivelle, *Upaniṣads*.

nothing but light. . . . If a person truly perceives the self, knowing "I am he"; what possibly could he want, whom possibly could he love, that he should worry about his body? . . . He's the maker of everything—the author of all! The world is his—he's the world itself! . . . Those who have known it—they become immortal. As for the rest—only suffering awaits them. When a man clearly sees the self as god, the lord of what was and of what will be, He will not seek to hide from him. (BU 4.4.7–15)

With the senses the self perceives only separate things, but this is illusion or magic (*maya*). "With the mind alone must one behold it—there is here nothing diverse at all! From death to death he goes, who sees here any kind of diversity. . . . The self is spotless and beyond space, unborn, immense, immovable. . . . There, in that space within the heart, he lies—the controller of all, the lord of all, the ruler of all!" (BU 4.4.19).

The new religions of Jainism and Buddhism arrived fully persuaded not only that the real self (*atman*) was identical with the All-Self (*brahman*) but that the former did not even exist. Paul Williams notes:

As far as we know, the Buddha himself dissolved away the unity we call the human being, or person, into an ever-changing series of physical matter, sensations, conceptions, further mental contents such as volitions and so on, and consciousness. Thus there is dissolved away any real Self, any unchanging referent for the name, the word "I." . . . Thus the forces which lead to continued rebirth [attachment and self-concern] come to an end and thence ends, to quote the scriptures, "this complete mass of frustration, suffering" (Pali: *dukkha*).[125]

The description of this life as "this complete mass of frustration, suffering" is still typical of the trend that longs for *moksha*, enlightenment, and release from rebirth. The Pali Canon of early Buddhism "still assumes the old binary model of 'this world and the next.'"[126] However, Gombrich argues, "It is only in Buddhism that the binary model of the sphere of action and the sphere of experiencing the results is superseded, and the whole universe is ethicized. In other words, according to the Buddha's teaching all sentient beings throughout the universe are morally responsible and can be reborn in a higher or lower station because of the good and evil they have done."[127]

---

125. Williams, *Mahâyâna Buddhism*, 2.
126. Gombrich, *What the Buddha Thought*, 35.
127. Gombrich, *What the Buddha Thought*, 35. Williams points out, "There is a Tibetan saying

Buddhism and Jainism sharply distinguished ritual and morality. "For them," says Richard Gombrich, "only what we call morality was relevant for soteriology, for determining one's destiny: ritual *per se* was utterly irrelevant." Hinduism never abandoned the ritualism of its Rigvedic heritage, he argues. Stuck, he says, in a heaven-or-hell eschatology, Hinduism cannot see reincarnation as opportunity but only as a threat.[128] In Jainism, "any rebirth is relatively undesirable."[129] At the same time that Greek Orphics were talking about the body as a prison of the soul, Taoism was teaching the goal of life was "release from the corpse" (*shijie*) so that that real self could ascend on wings.[130]

The three worlds of the shaman became the geographical horizon from the sixth century BCE to Dante and beyond. In these ancient societies, there was a striving for universality through these three worlds, from terrestrial division to eternal unity. By reconstructing, reducing, or replacing the stories and rites of local gods and the cult aimed at keeping their patronage of a particular city or kingdom, new scriptures expounded a philosophical religion that divulged eternal and universal ideas. Liberation from the alien world with its bodies and an earth-bound public religion in favor of assimilation to the One characterizes this utopian shift.[131]

---

that just as every valley has its own language so every teacher has his own doctrine.... This diversity prevents, or strongly hinders, generalization about Buddhism as a whole.... From earliest times in Buddhism there was a strong tendency to portray the Doctrine [Dharma] not as a series of tenets to be accepted or rejected, but rather as a medicine for curing quite specific spiritual ills." See *Mahâyâna Buddhism*, 2.

128. Gombrich, *What the Buddha Thought*, 34.
129. W. Johnson, *Harmless Souls*, 23–24, quoted in Gombrich, *What the Buddha Thought*, 34.
130. Kroll, *Dictionary of Classical and Medieval Chinese*, 509.
131. As noted above, the development in Egypt is more complex yet with definite transitions in the direction I have described.

2

Dancing for Dionysus
New Myths for the Utopian Stage

> Barbarians everywhere now dance for Dionysius.
>
> —Euripides, *Bacch.* 482

> [Orpheus] stands outside the Mycenaean world.... He was hauled inside the cultural horizons of classical Hellas by being made the son of Apollo and Muse, and the ancestor of Hesiod and Homer. Yet the stories portray him not as a distant forerunner of Homer, but as a singer of a different type: one who can exercise power over the natural world and who can countermand death itself, a "shamanistic" figure. He entered Greek mythology, surely, not by way of Mycenaean saga but at a later period from Thrace, or through Thrace from further north, from regions where shamanistic practices actually existed or had existed.
>
> —M. L. West[1]

In Greek tragedy, ritual becomes theater; the "flow" of the Eleusinian experience is continued on stage. In my view, locative contexts are characterized by what Victor Turner calls "flow." A chess player gives up her autonomy to participate in a rule-based game. The same is true of the actor, who surrenders his personal identity to the character and plot. In the transition from ritual to theater, "Flow reaches out to nature and to other men in... 'intuitions of unity, solidarity, repletion and acceptance'" and "we experience it as a unified flowing from one moment

---

1. West, *Orphic Poems*, 4.

Chapter 2

to the next, in which we feel in control of our actions, and in which there is little distinction between self and environment; between stimulus and response; or between past, present, and future."[2]

The myths that revise the horizon of classical Greece gravitated away from the bounded locative cosmos of the epic toward the utopian, boundary-breaking outsider: the shaman.[3] We do not meet a genuine shamanic figure in Homer. Sure, Odysseus tours the underworld, but only to confirm what everybody knows: the body is real; and gradually disintegrates. On the contrary, the Orphic/Vedic/Late Period Egyptian soul is *more real* than the body.[4]

Heracles may be a transitional figure. The son of Zeus's affair with mortal Alkmene enjoyed prestige quite early in the archaic period, appearing at many points throughout the *Iliad* and the *Odyssey*.[5]

New brushstrokes are added soon afterward that portray the hero in a more shamanistic light, beginning with Pherecydes, who is believed to have introduced Orphic doctrines and initiated Pythagoras in the Cave of Zeus. Gantz informs us, "Pherecydes is our first attested source for the idea that Zeus persuaded Helios not to rise for three days, so that his night with Alkmene would be three times the usual length."[6] The cave of nocturnal initiations is the "dark tent," the home of the shaman. There are similarities between Heracles and Dionysus.[7] As early as the eighth century BCE the story is told of Heracles and Apollo fighting over the golden

---

2. Turner, *From Ritual to Theatre*, 56–57, quoting from a 1972 unpublished manuscript by Mihaly Csikszentmihalyi, "Play and Intrinsic Rewards"; cf. Csikszentmihalyi, *Flow*.

3. Eliade, *Shamanism*, 510. Carolina López-Ruiz reveals the influence of West Asian (especially Semitic-Phoenician) myths in Greece during this period in *When the Gods Were Born*, esp. 5. Dwayne A. Meisner points out that West Asiatic groups (especially Phoenicians) brought with them to Greece "Semitic texts, such as the Ugaritic deity lists, the cycle of Ba'al myths, and the Hebrew Bible." Through intermarriage, Greek and foreign myths intermingled over generations. See *Orphic Tradition*, 19.

4. Fox, *Traveling Heroes*, 246–61. Teiresias the blind seer is able to prophesy future events but not on his own. Absent are the crucial incubation and initiation rites, intoxicants, tambourine, flutes (or pipes), and animal associates. He does not fly on an arrow or travel through the three worlds bringing back souls. He descends to Hades like all mortals but never returns. Teiresias still belongs to a locative cosmos: acted upon, not an actor.

5. Gantz, *Early Greek Myth*, 1:374.

6. Gantz, *Early Greek Myth*, 1:375.

7. Similar to Dionysus, Heracles is favored by Zeus over sons by Hera, who flies into jealous rage to foil Zeus's plan to place him on his throne. By the time of Pherecydes and especially the tragedians, Heracles strangled snakes sent by Hera into his crib and the blind magician-prophet Teiresias prophesies his heroic deeds and apotheosis. Gantz, *Early Greek Myth*, 1:377. He also wears the skin of a lion he had slain and his feats take him far north where shamanism still thrived; lying with a snake-woman, he sired Skythes, the founding king of Scythia (Herodotus 4.8–9).

tripod at Delphi.[8] This audacious act may suggest a polemic against the Delphic oracle and Apollo's cult more generally. A direct link with Dionysus is made when Heracles visits Pholos in his cave, refreshed by "a jar of wine sunk down in the earth which has been given to the Kentauroi by Dionysos, with orders to open it only when Herakles should come."[9] But the most evident links with shamanism (and Dionysus) are his death, descent to the underworld, and apotheosis.

While Homer and Hesiod include some Asiatic details, all of which support the locative cosmos portrayed in these texts, from the late seventh century BCE onward a significant tradition exists alongside the Homeric in which Middle Eastern and Egyptian elements "stand out undigested."[10] Explicitly, Anatolian (e.g., Phrygian) deities merged with Greek ones. Among the lost works of the Epic Cycle, *Alcmeonis* (late seventh or early sixth century) represents Dionysus alongside Gaia the earth goddess as "highest of all the gods."[11] In the so-called Homeric Hymns, the Hymn to Zeus is buried in the middle of the hymnal with a paltry four lines, while the hymnal begins with lengthy praises to Dionysus and Demeter.[12] An "orientalizing" of Homeric myths is evident across these songs.[13]

Uniting the new mythology is the theme of *separation, initiation,* and *return* that we have seen in the incubation and initiation experience of the shaman.[14]

---

8. Gantz, *Early Greek Myth*, 1:438.

9. Gantz, *Early Greek Myth*, 1:391.

10. Hesiod, *Theogony and Works and Days* (trans. West), 28–29. Observed in reference to Orphic literature, it nevertheless covers the broader trend of Dionysian/Eleusinian mysteries.

11. West, *Greek Epic Fragments*, 61; cf. 10–11, 58–63. See also Debiasi, "Alcmeonis." Drawing from several clues, Debiasi suggests that *Alcmeonis* was composed in "the second half of the seventh century, if not the beginning of the sixth century." It may have an Orphic provenance (270–76). The unfading fascination with Dionysus is evident in the growth of legends throughout the Hellenistic and Roman eras all the way to Nonnus in the fifth century CE, whose *Dionysiaca* fills forty-eight volumes.

12. The longer Homeric Hymns (including those related to Dionysus and Demeter) are from the late seventh or early sixth century. The ones to Delian Apollo and Aphrodite are perhaps datable to the eighth century. About 600 BCE the lyric poet Alcaeus alludes to lines from the Homeric Hymns to Hermes and to Dionysus. The first hymn, surviving only in fragments (representing 21 lines of text), may have originally had around 400 total lines. The god of frenzy returns for praise in two others hymns: Hymn 7 (59 lines) and Hymn 26 (13 lines), while another is dedicated to Demeter. See Richardson's notes in Cashford, *Homeric Hymns*, 149.

13. Prophet and healer are combined in the epithet "Iatromantic" often attached to Apollo's name, although he later gave to his son Asclepius oversight of healing. See Aeschylus, *Eum.* 62; *Suppl.* 263. Some Hellenistic Jews made Moses a *theios anēr* figure while endeavoring to stay within the bounds of monotheism; see Hamerton-Kelly, "Philo's Allegorical Commentary." Asclepius gains prominence as a shamanic figure in Pindar, *Pyth.* 3.55–58, as does Euripides, *Alc.* 3, and Plato, *Resp.* 408b.

14. *Separation, Initiation, Return* was the original title of Gennep, *Rites of Passage*. Jo-

These myths are all associated with the underworld and the nature of death and rebirth. They involve a story of dismemberment and return, transgression of boundaries (e.g., sex, gender, and social norms as well as underworld, earth, and heaven), and ecstatic raving (divine madness) with clamorous singing and dancing to loud drumbeats. Wherever there is a ritual of human dismemberment, these stories are nearby.[15] Naturally, given his "shamanic" profile, Dionysus moved from the wilderness to center stage.

The stories of Dionysus, Cybele, Demeter, and Persephone are, in fact, folded into one. They are about burial and resurrection, not in the Jewish or Christian sense but in terms of cutting up or burning of the mortal cocoon—"like a torch"—to release one's true self like sparks flying upward so that it can receive a new birth (Hom. Hymn Dem. 240).[16] In other words, they exhibit the features of the shaman's incubation. The last thing a shaman wants is to bind the soul to the same body forever.

Dionysus came from elsewhere in sudden and decisive conquest in the sixth century BCE.[17] Apollo, the god of prophetic oracles and inventor of the soothing lyre, turned a chaos ruled by Pytho into an ordered space for his cult (Strabo, *Geogr.* 9.3.12). His votaries came to him to hear calm and rational prophecies about what would happen and what had to be done to secure prosperity in this life. He was the inventor of music, but of the orderly and soothing kind. However, his half brother Dionysus was the god of wine, revelry, madness, and, eventually, theater. He was accompanied by uncouth, pipe-playing satyrs along with maenads, who were mostly female followers stung by madness from his thyrsus wand: Dionysus would have the Festival of Misrule year-round. Unwilling to remain in his tomb while Apollo prophesied for most of the year, the raucous god swept upon nation after nation in a frenzied trance, demanding allegiance to his universal religion. He would not be bound to the times and places of Eleusis or Athens. He did not care about the political, social, or religious polis he conquered but only the souls

---

seph Campbell adopts this typology in *Hero with a Thousand Faces*, 30, but with a more formulaic method.

15. As we see below, Demeter's interrupted rite of placing Demophon, the infant prince of Eleusis, in a fire to deify him, belongs in this category of immortalizing alchemy. See Burkert's summary of these episodes in *Homo Necans*, 98–119.

16. Unless otherwise noted, translations of the Homeric Hymns taken from Cashford, *Homeric Hymns*.

17. Dionysus was among the gods worshiped in the Mycenaean era; see Ventris and Chadwick, *Documents in Mycenaean Greek*, 463. However, as with other divinities, the characteristics and stories associated with him are quite different in the sixth century when he achieved prominence at Delphi. See Parke, *History of the Delphic Oracle*, 14 n. 2. According to Michael Scott, in fact, "there are more oracular responses recorded in the Delphic corpus relating to the worship of this god [Dionysus] than any other"; see *Delphi*, 86.

of their residents. His followers imitated his utopianism. Rather than being acted upon by a god, they embraced their inmost selves as divine and therefore *autonomous*, seeking gnosis rather than authoritative mediation.

Not one to be kept under a roof, Dionysus did not wait for followers to come to him but recruited his wild company in a vast network of caves. Dionysus happily surrendered to his brother the cultivated center; instead, he flourished on the boundaries, in the mountains around Delphi. However, he did have a place in Apollo's temple—a tomb—and an elaborate theatrical rite would reawaken him in order to occupy Delphi in the winter while Apollo vacationed northward in the legendary Hyperborea at the end of the world. "The dialectic between mountains and sanctuary is part of a broader set of polarities at the heart of the early *polis*," Jeremy McInerney observes. "The mountain was, as it were, brought into the sanctuary. The focal point for the movement between these difficult zones was the Corycian Cave, which marked the transition from the wilderness to culture."[18] While many came to Delphi for Apollo's prophecies concerning this life, Dionysus strode proudly across the stage in the sixth century as, in Carl Kerényi's words, "the archetypal image of indestructible life."[19]

Dionysus is also called Eleutherios (Liberator) and Mystes (Mystic) and Androgynous (like the Mesopotomian priests designated "male-female"). We recall the bisexuality of Egypt's new star, Osiris. This emerging "axial" theme underscores the comprehensive power of the burgeoning deity, both life-inseminating and life-bearing. Especially in Orphic circles Dionysus was called Zagreus, the first incarnation of Dionysus as the child who was torn apart by the Titans but returned a third time in another form thanks to Zeus's clever tactic of sewing him into his thigh as a womb.[20]

Here we have for the first time in Greece the equivalent of the episode in Enuma Elish of a god being sacrificed to provide a divine spirit to human beings. Iacchos (Iakchos), a minor deity, became assimilated to Dionysus in the Eleusinian mysteries.[21] Dionysus was also called Sabazios, clearly a foreign god.[22]

18. McInerney, "Parnassus," 263–64.

19. Kerényi, *Dionysos*, 205; cf. Bernabé et al., *Redefining Dionysos*.

20. The common noun *zagreus* denotes one who catches prey alive, as a *zagrē* was a pit for captive animals; see Kerényi, *Dionysos*, 82. I discuss the Titan myth in the following chapter.

21. We also hear it at the public Dionysus festival in September, at his Lenaia winter celebration, and in the theater at Great Dionysia in Aristophanes's *Frogs*, Euripides's *Bacchae*, and Sophocles's *Antigone* where Dionysus is invoked for the purification of Thebes from a plague with the choir hymning him as "god of many names . . . and son of deep-thundering [Zeus]" and as "*Iô*, leader of the dance of fire-breathing stars, lord of the night's voices, born of Zeus! Appear, master, with your Thyads [Maenads] crowding about you, frenzied, dancing all through the night Iacchus giver of blessings!" Sophocles, *Ant.* 1120–1150. Translation by Nisetich in Lefkowitz and Romm, *Greek Plays*.

22. Originally the sky-father god of Phrygia and Thrace, Sabazios was represented as a nomad

Bearing their thyrsus wand, Dionysus's initiates were called "wild ones" (*mainades*), women who imitated his hunting, tearing, and eating of raw animal flesh. Drinking wine from the krater of Dionysus, they would rush down a hill in pursuit of a wild animal, pricking each other with the Dionysian "madness" injected from the needle on the pinecone-topped thyrsus stick. Filled with his ecstasy, they became one with Dionysus. This myth was ritually enacted in "the frenzy of triennial feasts that bestow calm on us" (OH 52.6).[23] "'And they will set up many statues in the temples. As these things are three, so every three years forever shall mortals sacrifice to you perfect hecatombs at your festivals.' . . . Be gracious, you woman-maddening bull-god" (Hom. Hymn Dion. 1.14–18, 21–23).[24]

Cybele, the Phrygian mother goddess, was also assimilated into the Dionysian repertoire. Although forgotten along with the Titans in Homer and Hesiod, Gaia-Cybele is praised in Orphic hymns as "Mother of the Gods."[25] Depicted as a wild bushranger in a lion-drawn chariot attended by riotous drumbeating and wine-drinking dancers called the Korybantes, the hermaphrodite Cybele was castrated and expelled from the circle of the gods. She also fell in love with her son, Attis, and when he fell in love with a princess, she sent madness upon the marriage assembly and castrated him. Returning to his mother, he was rewarded with immortality as a pine tree, and by the late fourth century BCE Attis too had a place on the Athenian calendar.[26]

---

on horseback carrying a staff of power and was identified with both Dionysus and Zeus. The *Suda*, an important Byzantine encyclopedia, summarizes ancient testimonies to this connection under "Sabazios, Saboi." See Sider, "Two Epigrams of Philodemus."

23. Athanassakis and Wolkow, *Orphic Hymns*, 43.

24. See Macurdy, "Klodones, Mimallones and Dionysus Pseudanor," 191–92; Macurdy, *Troy and Paeonia*, 166. Every two years, Dionysian maenads (designated Thyades after the daughter of a Dionysian priest) from Athens would travel from Athens to join those of Delphi. The rituals took place not in Delphi but in the Parnassian Mountains. But there were other celebrations that were not part of the official calendar; see Scott, *Delphi*, 152, 220–21.

25. See Hom. Hymn 30. Discovered in central Turkey and dated from the sixth century BCE is the so-called Seated Woman of Çatalhöyük. The large-breasted woman appears, like Cybele, enthroned with her two lions at her side. David Leeming identifies this artifact with "Hittite-Hurrian mythology" and the forerunner of "the great Phrygian Goddess Cybele, the mother of the sacrificed Attis, and the many-breasted Artemis of Ephesus." See Leeming, *Oxford Companion to World Mythology*, 63–64, 155–56. A cache of Dionysus-related artefacts was discovered in Macedon. It includes volute kraters and the Maenad of Totovo (sixth century BCE). See Chulev, *Bronze Volute Wine Kraters*.

26. Lynn Emrich Roller explores the Cybele myth at length in *Cult of Anatolian Cybele*. A wide coverage of the Attis myth and cult is found in Lane, *Cybele, Attis, and Related Cults*. Cybele appears prominently in Euripides, *Bacch.* 21–22, 59, 73–88, 113–115, 125–150, 600. She was well known to Greeks probably from colonists in Phrygia; see Herodotus, *Hist.* 4.76; Pindar, *Pyth.* 3; Euripides, *Bacch.* 78–79.

The Cybele myth is a variation on the Dionysian theme, as a jealous Cybele visits her own violent misfortune upon others while her riotous Korybantes—castrated priests presenting as females—are identical to Dionysus's maenads with their whirling, frenzied dancing to loud drums.[27] Along with the Kouretes (their flute-playing companions), mountain Nymphs and Satyrs, the Korybantes attain prominence soon after Hesiod as Phrygian initiates to Dionysus and Cybele.[28] Epimenides was said to have composed five thousand lines dedicated to them, perhaps as a preface to his Orphic *Theogony*, and Pherecydes makes them offspring of Apollo and Rhetia.[29] Cybele is praised in many Orphic hymns, often folded into the personas of Demeter or Dionysus.[30] Homer would not have known what to make of this Orphic Rhea, daughter of the "firstborn" (*prōtogenos*): "you dance to the sound of drums and cymbals, O frenzy-loving maiden, O mother of Zeus . . . and do send death and the filth of pollution to the ends of the earth."[31] Through Cybele and Dionysius, the gods of order were either pushed to the background or put into the service of the Dionysian thrust. The shamanistic god par excellence was in charge. The "wilderness" of the other worlds was not a chaos to be contained but a vast territory to be explored.

These assimilations seemed natural to Greek colonists in Turkey, but Dionysus's conquest of Athens was prepared by Demeter. Worshiped as Sito, giver of

---

27. She especially prizes her Telchines or magicians; see Roller, "Phrygian Character of Kybele," 171–72. In imitation of her myth, the priests of Cybele were castrated and would present themselves as female; only initiates of the mysteries could be her followers, Korybantes, dancing to the beat of gongs and drums (225–32).

28. These playful dancers appear first in the Megalai Ehoiai (Hesiod, *Fragments of the Hesiodic Corpus* 10a.17–19, cited according to Merkelbach and West, *Fragmenta Hesiodea*; Gantz, *Early Greek Myth*, 1:147), which was regarded in antiquity as part of Hesiod's *Catalogue of Women*. See Hunter, *Hesiodic Catalogue of Women*; West, *Homeric Hymns*; West, *Greek Epic Fragments*; West, *Hesiodic Catalogue of Women*; Janko, *Homer, Hesiod and the Hymns*. Janko argues for Hesiodic dating (85–87, 198) while West dates the Ehoiai to 580–520 BCE (*Hesiodic Catalogue*, esp. 130–37). Strabo testifies to their Phrygian origin (*Geog.* 10.3.19; fr 3 cited according to Bernabé, *Poetae Epici Graeci*). Another group, the Idaian Daktyloi, discovered iron-working and were sorcerers (*goetēs*). "Pherecydes speaks of two groups, those of the 'left' (thirty-two in number, the sorcerers) and those of the 'right' (twenty in number, the dissolvers of spells)." See Gantz, *Early Greek Myth*, 1:148–49.

29. Gantz, *Early Greek Myth*, 1:147.

30. See OH 31 to the Kouretes. Unless otherwise noted, all translations of the Orphic Hymns taken from Athanassakis and Wolkow, *Orphic Hymns*. The Minoan civilization (2000–1450 BCE) in Crete was the only Greek culture that worshiped the mother goddess as supreme.

31. From OH 14 to Rhea. Pindar calls her "Cybele the Mother" (fr. 86). Euripides associates "Cybele the Mother" with Dionysus in *Bacch.* 64–186. Strabo, *Geogr.* 10.3.18, says that the rites merged in Athens at the Dionysus festival in March and January. See Roller, "Phrygian Character of Kybele," 125. See also OH 27.25 to the Mother of the Gods.

grain, Demeter's profile expands as it is caught up in the myth of Dionysus.[32] Demeter is the "Phrygian Mother of Gods," daughter of Kronos and Rhea—the same identity given to Cybele.[33] For Homer and Hesiod, Demeter's daughter Persephone is the dread queen of Hades.[34] But the Hymn to Demeter portrays her as a victim crying out for her mother (Hom. Hymn Dem. 6; cf. 8, 75). After Persephone's abduction by Hades, Demeter leaves her throne in grief and goes to Eleusis and, because of their hospitality, she creates her cult there (Hom. Hymn Dem. 205–270). With Demeter absent from her Olympian throne, grain is sown in vain, so Zeus sends Hermes on a diplomatic mission to Hades, who accedes on the condition that Persephone be returned to him for a third of every year (Hom. Hymn Dem. 350–355).[35] Racing with his immortal horses, Hermes delivers Persephone to her mother at her Eleusinian temple (Hom. Hymn Dem. 387). In Homer's perspective, there is good reason to avoid such contemplation and to focus instead on glorious achievements and domestic concerns here and now. Yet the Dionysian religion envisions a more cheerful afterlife, at least for his initiates, since the god of the underworld shows us how to be shamans, going back and forth as we choose.

Stories tied to agriculture—the cycle of seasons—are now associated with the cycle of dismemberment and union, alienation and reunion, which awakens initiates to their divine destiny.[36] This points to a marked shift from a locative interest (prosperity in this life) to the utopian search for a blessed afterlife previously reserved for the Olympian immortals. Persephone is found frequently on sarcophagi from the fifth century when Dionysiac mysteries were also focused

---

32. Fol and Marazov, *Thrace and the Thracians*, 26.

33. Philosophers from Pythagoras to Proclus will interpret both as examples of being deceived by visible appearances. Contemporary poet Louise Glück expresses this interpretation of Persephone in "A Myth of Devotion," 58–59; cf. her "Persephone the Wanderer," 16–19.

34. Arriving in Hades, Odysseus and his officers offer a burnt sacrifice "to sovereign Death, to pale Persephone" (*Od.* 11.50, 213). Hesiod's *Theogony* (around 600 BCE) relates that Demeter is the goddess of agriculture—in particular, corn, cereals, and grain born to Zeus and Rhea (453)—and gave birth to Pluton (god of fertile soil) by the hero Iasion (963). Demeter appears only twice in Homer, notes Gantz, with Zeus including her among those whom he has loved (*Il.* 14.326) but with no reference to offspring. In the *Odyssey* mention is made of her union with Iasion, which provokes Zeus to kill him with a thunderbolt (*Od.* 5.125–128). Hesiod does mention Persephone as a daughter (*Theog.* 912–914; 969–974). See Gantz, *Early Greek Myth*, 63–73. Hesiod also mentions her abduction by Hades but not her return (*Theog.* 913–914).

35. Taking any food in Hades required one to stay there permanently. When Hades slips a pomegranate seed into Persephone's mouth on her way home, he seals her fate of returning to the underworld every winter.

36. See Pindar, *Ol.* 2.60–88; *Isthm.* 1.55, 122; 7.1–4, 135.

on the afterlife.[37] "This much is clear," notes Burkert. "Dionysus and his followers have no terror of the underworld. He is good friends with Hades and Persephone, and even Cerberus [the guard-dog at its entrance] is no longer dreadful."[38]

The Mysteries: "Savage, Ineffable, Secretive"[39]

Athenian religion was nothing like a church with its own authoritative scriptures, creeds, clergy, and theological interpreters. Officiants were not spiritual guides. Belonging to priestly families, they performed rituals and returned to their mundane occupations.[40] Shrines were everywhere, including at home and in villages and cities. Temples housed gods, not worshipers. But all places were sacred. We read repeatedly, from the Presocratics to Damascius, that the world is full of gods. Rites were performed outside the temples in the open air, often in the marketplace where the gods were simply regarded as senior members of the community.[41] Homer's stories put the children to bed and taught them grammar. The metered myths were sung together by the fire and performed on stage. Each day of the week honored a god (e.g., Sun-Day, Moon-Day, etc.), and winter and spring were tied to Persephone's descent and return.[42] In the public religion based on the poets, a god was the director of a particular department of life (e.g., sky, earth, fertility, luck, etc.). The sociability of the worshipers, involving both comforts and threats, mirrored that of the gods.

The contrast of these traditional public religions with the mystery cults is considerable. The rites were not performed in public or in front of temples but in sacred groves or caves. These "temples" were not shrines of the gods but secret chambers of holy initiation apart from the madding crowd. Aristotle "said that those being initiated into the mysteries did not have to learn (*mathein*) but to

---

37. Burkert, *Ancient Mystery Cults*, 21, adding, "Scholars have been reluctant to acknowledge this dimension of Dionysiac worship, on the assumption that concern about the afterlife should be seen to have developed in later epochs; but the clearest evidence is concentrated right in the classical period."

38. Burkert, *Babylon, Memphis, Persepolis*, 84–85. Burkert supports this with a scene from a volute krater.

39. OH 27. Though the Orphic Hymns are from the opening centuries of our era, this characterization of Dionysus is consistent with descriptions from preclassical times.

40. Armstrong, "Pieties of the Greek World," 73.

41. Armstrong, "Pieties of the Greek World," 69–70.

42. Greeks and Romans observed in their week the Sun, Moon, Ares (Mars), Hermes (Mercury), Zeus (Jupiter), Aphrodite (Venus), and Kronos (Saturn). Germanic peoples substituted Ares, Hermes, and Aphrodite for Tiu (Tuesday), Woden (Wednesday), and Freya (Friday).

experience (*pathein*) and be changed by the experience."[43] As Dodds points out, "Religious experience of the shamanistic type is individual, not collective."[44]

Though secret, the mysteries were supported by the whole polis—but on a voluntary basis. The initiation into the god's mystery was a private choice—the only sphere in which this was conceivable for a Greek. Though testimonies relate a common experience of conversion and enlightenment, and crowd psychology contributed, the ecastasy was utterly individual. The traditional public religion was external, social, public, and focused on perfect performance of the ritual sacrifices that would secure the gods' protection of the city—the features of a locative worldview founded on the archaic epic. The mysteries offered a utopian alternative: an inward, individual, and private union with the god focused on the salvation of the soul. Such an experience could only be attained by a personal choice. "Mysticism" derives from these mysteries, meaning secrets, which assumes that they belonged to an inner circle.[45] Crucially, this inner circle consisted not of aristocrats but of individuals who chose to be initiated, whether male or female, rich or poor. When shoulder to shoulder at the mysteries, every person was equal. But those who did not choose initiation could expect nothing but "gloom and darkness below" in Homer's Hades (Hom. Hymn Dem. 475). The only divide that mattered was between the initiated and the noninitiated. Once savored at Eleusis, egalitarian liberty could not help but spread into the sphere of everyday life, law, and politics.

The Homeric Hymn to Demeter (ca. 650 BCE) relates the cycle of initiation with the three-stage ascent that would become nuclear to Orphic spirituality through all its permutations (Hom. Hymn Dem. 415–475).[46] For Eleusinian initiates, it was a ritual participation in Persephone's descent into bondage, Demeter's search, and Persephone's rebirth from her prison.[47] Singing the hymns and swinging branches on the sacred way, aspirants and *mystai* would stop at a certain point

---

43. Armstrong, "Pieties of the Greek World," 71.

44. Dodds, *Greeks and the Irrational*, 141–42.

45. Burkert, *Ancient Mystery Cults*, 13. See also Snell, *Discovery of the Mind*, 43–70; Berlin, "Birth of Greek Individualism." Berlin notes that individualism is typically thought to have begun with the Epicureans and Stoics. "Not public order, but personal salvation is all that matters" (302). However, he points out that individualism goes back further, to Antiphon (late fifth century BCE), Diogenes, Crates, and Aristippus. Antiphon sees the good life as "creeping into a corner of your own choosing and constructing a private life which alone can satisfy the deepest needs of men" (314). I am pushing the date back for individualism even further, with the origins of Orphic theology.

46. For helpful historical context, see Clay, *Politics of Olympus*.

47. Hearing conveys the presence of the other external to oneself and creates a social bond among hearers while the eye offers a direct, individual, and immediate union with what it sees.

to curse and tell bawdy jokes that, according to the story, "changed the mood of this sacred lady" (Hom. Hymn Dem. 203–204). Then they would ritually sprinkle themselves in the sea. Arriving at the sacred site, they would be overwhelmed by the complex of buildings and the main sanctuary, the telesterion, which seated thousands. Before entering, they would give the secret password: "I have fasted, I have drunk the *kykeon*, I have taken from the *kistē* (box) and after working it have put it back in the *calathus* (open basket)."[48]

It is worth noting parallels with the soma drink in Indian ritual: "We have drunk the soma; we have become immortal; we have gone to the light; we have found the gods. What can hostility do to us now, and what the malice of a mortal, O immortal one?" (RV 8.48.3).[49] The Bhagavadgita states, "Those who perform actions... [and] who drink from the juice of the pure Soma plant, are cleansed and purified of their past sins" (BG 9.20). Iranians called this drink haoma and identified it with a divinity designated by Ahura Mazda as the chief priest (Yasna 9.26).[50] Recent studies suggest that the recipe included ethnogenic mushrooms, similar to accounts of shamanic rituals.[51] Narcotics were used in the healing rites associated with Asclepius, poppy fields were abundant across Asia Minor and Greece, and the poppy was Demeter's favorite flower. Arguments for the *kykeon* drink including psychoactive ingredients seem largely conjectural at this stage.[52] The whole point of the rite was to recapitulate Demeter's refusal of wine or anything else but water with barley. Following Demeter's search for Persephone, this secret code represented the three stages initiates would go through for the next ten days of the Greater Mysteries: (1) Purification

---

The basic stock of Western philosophical terms for knowing is visual metaphors. A superb comparison of visual and oral cultures is found in Ong, *Presence of the Word*.

48. Clement of Alexandria, *Protr.* 2.18, which corresponds to lines 205–213 of the Homeric Hymn to Demeter. It has been suggested that besides water and barley something stronger was added to the drink; see Wasson, Hofmann, and Ruck, *Road to Eleusis*, 42. This argument is highly speculative. On this question see Burkert, *Ancient Mystery Cults*, 108–14. Without discounting the possibility of opium, Burkert points out that much of what reportedly happened at Eleusis was the opposite of what one might expect through hallucinogenic revelry. More importantly, the Homeric Hymn to Demeter specifically mentions that the goddess refused wine in such a state of sorrow, drinking only the barley-mint drink "for the sake of the rite," which had to be performed perfectly.

49. Jamison and Brereton, *Rigveda*, 1:129.

50. Toorn et al., *Dictionary of Deities and Demons*, 384.

51. Anthony, *Horse, the Wheel, and Language*, 454; Oldenberg, *Religion of the Veda*, 90–93; Wasson, *Mushroom of Immortality*.

52. See, e.g., Wasson, Hofmann, and Ruck, *Road to Eleusis*, 42. Burkert is more skeptical of this theory: see *Ancient Mystery Cults*, 108–14. Although the wine god Dionysus may have hosted wild parties in the public festival, Eleusis kept closer to the myth of Demeter.

(Demeter's anguish); (2) Illumination (discovering Persephone's captivity); and (3) Union (direct vision of Persephone herself).[53] It also followed the plot of Dionysus's dismemberment and reincarnation.[54] On the sixth night they sang and danced through the night in honor of Dionysus. Entering their incubation in the Adyton, healing temples of Asclepius, they had dreams, which they related to *Therapeutae* (therapists). Initiates entered the cave at Eleusis, journeyed through the underworld, and then returned to the staging, lighting, props, and actors in the telesterion reenacting the myth of Persophone's abduction and release.[55] The building bore a roof with a peak which could be opened to serve as a kind of chimney. The climax of the Greater Mysteries was the "sacred marriage" of the hierophant with a priestess (their union being consummated perhaps on the stage), followed by a flash of fire above the hierophant's throne and a gong with the announcement, "The Mistress [Demeter] has given birth to a Holy Boy! Brimo has given birth to Brimos! that is, the Strong One to the Strong One."[56] Brimos (from Thracian "terrifying/mighty") becomes one of the epithets of Dionysus. The Greater Mysteries lead from Demeter to Dionysus and Persephone, from harrowing descent and desparate searching to the release of postmortem existence. And "Iakchos," hailed in the torchlight procession, "was an alter ego of Dionysos, going to Eleusis as though in quest of his mother, Semele."[57] As expressed by the greatest lyric poet of the sixth century BCE, "Blessed is he who, having seen these rites, undertakes the way beneath the earth. He knows the end of life, as well as its divinely granted beginning."[58] In purification, eyes were closed; in the climactic union, opened to behold the truth. In Sophocles's version, Oedipus surrenders his physical vision in order to experience this genuine epiphany.[59] From a *mystēs* (one who closes his eyes), he became an *epoptēs* (one who saw), just as Heracles's mere vision of Persephone in the underworld enabled him to return with her to this world to conquer death (Euripides, *Heracl.* 613).[60] The whole process of silent stillness in a cave, dream-like searching for one's own lost soul along with Demeter's agonizing descent in search for Persephone in the depths of Hades, and the epiphany of life from death exhibit the vocation of a shaman.

53. Although little is known about the details, helpful background is provided in Bremmer, *Initiation in the Mysteries*, 48–55.
54. See Hom. Hymn Dem. 475; Clay, *Politics of Olympus*. See also Plato, *Euthyd.* 277d–e; *Ion* 533e; *Symp.* 215c–d. Cf. Bremmer, *Initiation in the Mysteries*, 51–52.
55. The mysteries and their commentators stress the visual aspect. See Petridou, "Ritual Framing in Eleusis."
56. See Kerényi, *Eleusis*, 92–95.
57. Kerényi, *Eleusis*, 64.
58. Pindar, fr. 121. See Nilsson, *Greek Popular Religion*, 42–64.
59. Kerényi, *Eleusis*, 83–85.
60. This distinction is described well by Foley, *Homeric Hymn to Demeter*, 66–71.

In her famous Hymn, Demeter *hears* her daughter's cries and Hekate, goddess of magic, relates what she too has heard about Persephone's abduction—in contrast with the male Helios who *sees*.[61] In the archaic age people believed what they heard: the stories of the poet-theologians, Homer and Hesiod. But now authority surrenders to autonomy of seeing for oneself what is true. "Blessed is the mortal on earth who has seen these rites," Demeter decrees in her famous Hymn, "but the uninitiate who has no share in them never has the same lot once dead in the dreary darkness" (Hom. Hymn Dem. 480–482).[62] "I came out of the mystical hall feeling like a stranger to myself," reported the rhetorician Sopatros (*Rhetores Graeci* 8.114–115).[63] These carefully veiled testimonies indicate a new experience of the self as something objective and worth knowing in its own right, an individual life that can be examined, alluding to Socrates's maxim taken from the Temple of Delphi: "Know Thyself."[64] Death is not loss, as in Homer's dreary afterlife, but is actually the gateway to rebirth. Separation is always the prelude to union. It is this life that is like a prison, wandering with Demeter in helpless sorrow. Withdrawing from society, one unites with her purgation and joyful reunion. At the end of the rites the illumined initiate was deemed a bacchant—someone who knew what happened when this life ended. Anyone could become a shaman.

"The Eleusinian mysteries—like other Greek mystery cults," says Foley, "inaugurated for humankind a different lot and experience of divinity than what we find in Homeric epic."[65] The domination by aristocratic families had no entrance to Eleuysis. Not only have the gods become kinder to humans, but Demeter has even attempted to transmute the infant prince of Eleusis, Demophoön, into a god. In what is in essence a labor strike against Zeus, she prefers her cult in Eleusis to the privileges of Olympus. She challenges the existing order.[66] In this she is on the side of Prometheus as well as Egypt's Isis. The old gods who have lost their magic (*heka*) are comparable to the tyrants of the various city-states.

Euripides, who had lost his faith in the gods of Olympus, became a devotee. The vision of Persephone, he said, allows one to return from the grave with her

---

61. Helene P. Foley points out that this is a theme running throughout the poem; see her *Homeric Hymn to Demeter*, 38.

62. Hom. Hymn Dem. 480–483. Cf. Pindar, fr. 121. The lodestar of the Mysteries' narrative, this hymn is dated between 650 and 550 BCE; see Foley, *Homeric Hymn to Demeter*, 28.

63. Quoted in Foley, *Homeric Hymn to Demeter*, 69.

64. The presence of these "toys" in the cult as well as the "egg" suggest that Orphic influences are present already at Peisistratus's establishment of the public cult in the sixth century BCE. Brought to Athens in this period, the Cybele cult merges with the Dionysian cult, the Greek mother of gods, Rhea, and Demeter. Athens also invoked her as the city's protector. See Parker, *Miasma*, 245–47.

65. Foley, *Homeric Hymn to Demeter*, 86.

66. Foley, *Homeric Hymn to Demeter*, 89.

(*Heracl.* 613). Sophocles says, "Thrice-blessed among the mortals are those who, having seen these sacred rites, enter Hades: for them alone there is life, but for the others all is evil."[67] Still, centuries later, Plutarch could divulge in his Neopythagorean idiom, the experience of an initiate:

> Wanderings astray in the beginning, tiresome walkings in circles, immediately before the end of all the terrible things, panic and shivering and sweat, and amazement. And then some wonderful light comes to meet you, pure regions and meadows are there to greet you, with sounds and dances and solemn, sacred words and holy views; and there the initiate, perfect by now, set free from all bondage, walks about crowned with a wreath, celebrating the festival with the other sacred and pure people, and he looks down on the uninitiated, unpurified crowd in this world in mud and fog beneath his feet. (Plutarch, fr. 168)[68]

Even for the more pragmatic Romans, Cicero could hail the Eleusinian mysteries as the means by which "we have been brought out of our barbarous and savage mode of life and educated and refined to a state of civilization." Moreover, Cicero adds, "we have learned from them the beginnings of life, and have gained the power not only to live happily, but also to die with a better hope" (*Leg.* 2.19.36).

It should not surprise us that such a dramatic spectacle gave rise to Greek theater, of which Dionysus—the wearer of many masks—was the designated founder. In fact, the theater picked up his story where the telesterion left off. As the connective tissue between cult and culture, the evolving Dionysus of the stage actually created most of the Dionysian myths.[69] The founders of the Greek stage attest to their own personal experience in the mysteries, often verging on divulging its secrets (punishable by death). Evoking their experience in the telesterion, the theater was its own cave of incubating initiates. Even in its architectural design, Sir Paul Harvey explains, "The Greek theatre appears to have been originally designed for the performance of dithryambic choruses in honour of Dionysus."[70]

---

67. Sophocles, fr. 837. Numeration of Sophocles fragments according to Pearson-Radt numeration; cf. Plato, *Leg.* 700b. Here Plato the "Athenian" contrasts these ordered distinctions with the confusion of music in his day, leading to "low standards" more generally.

68. Cited in Burkert, "Killing in Sacrifice," 77–79.

69. See Ober and Strauss, "Discourse of Athenian Democracy."

70. See the entry on "Theatre," in Harvey, *Oxford Companion to Classical Literature*, 422–23. Harvey notes, "The centre of it was the *orchēstrā* ('dancing-place'), a circular space, in the middle of which stood the *thumelē* or altar of the god. Round more than half of the *orchestra*, forming a kind of horse-shoe was the *theatron* ('seeing-place') proper, circular tiers of seats, generally cut out of the side of a hill. . . . Behind the orchestra and facing the audience was the *skēnē*, originally

Aristotle explains that the celebration of Dionysus, both in the mysteries and in the public festival, is the basis for both tragedy (based on the dithyramb, the wild dancing song) and comedy (based on the *kōmos* or phallus song), both unique to Dionysus (*Poet.* 1449a9–13). Long before Aristotle, Pindar stated that the dithyramb was invented for Dionysus (*Ol.* 13.18–19; cf. fr. 71, 115).[71]

Even the domain underscores the difference between Apollo and Dionysus: hearing the inspired stories versus beholding for oneself. Barely mentioned in Homer and Hesiod, Dionysus upstages even Demeter and Persephone (who becomes his wife). The propaganda for Dionysus's cult became aggressive in the hands of the tragedians, beginning with Aeschylus in the sixth century. He gave Dionysus a central place in his oeuvre, although these plays survive only in fragments.[72] Besides his *Bacchae*, Aeschylus wrote at least three trilogies (or tetralogies) related to Dionysus and Orpheus.[73]

A staple of tragic plays was the so-called *Lycurgeia*, a cycle based on the tale of Dionysus's claim over Lycurgus the king of Thrace.[74] It is an entire genre serving as a cautionary tale against rulers prohibiting the Dionysian cult.[75] The foolish Lycurgus mocks his cousin as effeminate.[76] Dionysus's followers were "practising

---

a wooden structure, a façade with three doors, through which, when the drama had developed from the dithyrambic chorus, the actors made their entrances." Cf. Aeschylus, *Panegyricus* 28.

71. See Pindar, *Complete Odes* (trans. Verity), 30, 153 n. 19. Cf. Plato, *Phaed.* 244a–245a.

72. The one surviving fragment (fr. 22) from his *Bacchae*, excerpted in Stobaeus, *Ecl.* 1.3.26–27, reads, "Evil, you see, comes swiftly upon mortals: the offence comes home to him who breaks the bounds of right." Unless noted, all translations of Aeschylus's fragments from *Attributed Fragments* (ed. and trans. Sommerstein), LCL. Fragments from Aeschylus's lost plays *Sisyphus the Runaway* (fr. 5 R) and *Egyptians* (fr. 228 R) identify him as Hades's son or Hades himself, respectively; see Sommerstein, LCL, 237. In *Sisyphus*, the escapee declares, "I now bid farewell to Zagreus [Dionysus] and his ever-hospitable father." Cf. Gantz, *Early Greek Myth*, 1:118.

73. According to Sommerstein, the trilogies were *Edonians, Lycurgus*, and *Bassarids* (LCL, 153); *Wool-Carders, Nurses of Dionysus*, and *Semele and Pentheus* (172); and *Ghost-Raisers, Penelope*, and *Bone-Gatherers* (193). The first may also have included *Youths* and the last may have ended with *Circe*. Both *Lycurgus* and *Circe* were satyr plays with both tragic and comic elements and the presence of satyrs with their large erection. These plays usually closed the Dionysus festival with a rather ribald finish. See Shaw, *Satyric Play*, esp. 2–4. An Attic cup by Exekias from 530 BCE portrays Dionysus turning the pirates into dolphins, as described in Hom. Hymn 7. See Richardson's Introduction to Cashford, *Homeric Hymns*, xxiii.

74. The first, according to Sommerstein, was Polyphrasmon, "son of his old rival Phrynichus, who produced a *Lycurgeia* in 467." See Sommerstein, LCL, 61.

75. Sommerstein, LCL, 60–65.

76. Aeschylus, frr. 59, 61: "What has a bass to say to a saffron gown, or a lyre to a hair-net? ... How incongruous! And what partnership can there be between a mirror and a sword? And as for yourself, boy, are you being brought up as a man? Then where's your prick? Where's your cloak? Where are your Laconian shoes? Or as a woman, then? Then where are your tits? What

the holy ecstatic rites of Cotyto," the Thracian goddess, says Aeschylus, as if her cult were already identified with Dionysus (Aeschylus, fr. 57). This thoroughly oriental, even shamanistic, form of worship shocks Lycurgus. The king of Thrace forbids the worship of Dionysus and locks up his votaries, then the god himself. Captive to no one, Dionysus takes command of the prison and causes the king to imagine that it is on fire. "Truly the house is possessed—the building is in bacchic frenzy!" (Aeschylus fr. 58).[77] So too in Thebes, Dionysus makes his universal cult supreme by severe measures, as Euripides celebrates:

> Here in Thebes I bound the fawnskin to the women's flesh and armed their hands with shafts of ivy. . . . I have stung them with frenzy, hounded them from home up to the mountains where they wander, crazed of mind, and compelled them to wear my ritual uniform. Like it or not, this city must learn its lesson: it lacks initiation in my mysteries, so I shall vindicate my mother Semele and stand revealed to mortal eyes as the god she bore to Zeus. (Euripides, *Bacch.* 23–25, 32–42)

Enveloped in new sights and sounds focused on separation, rebirth, and return, one's Eleusinian experience was triggered and reinforced. But it centered on stranger stories around the raw intensity of the impulsive bull-god and his mischievous supporting cast. Dionysus couldn't care less about bolstering Athenian patriotism. The world is his stage. Similar to the Eleusinian drama, one came to the theater a Greek but left as a liberated member of Dionysus's universal choir, reborn not by hearing (authority) but by seeing for oneself (autonomy).

The dramatists also create the narrative geography of Dionysus's trek to Athens. As Euripides narrates, the cult was founded in Lydia and Phrygia (Turkey) but touches down in Thrace, the gateway to Europe between the Black and Aegean Seas. The northern Thracian tribes of the Getae were known as "'the immortalizing ones' or 'those who make themselves immortal,'" and the Thracians were well known "for their ascetic practices and abstinence."[78] Some souls returned in

---

do you say? Why are you silent? Or shall I find you out by your song, seeing that you don't want to tell me yourself?"

77. The same episode, and even language, appears in Euripides, *Bacch.* 576–603, as noted by Sommerstein, LCL, 64. The quote is from Euripides, *Bacch.* 118–119. The same themes appear in fragments of Aeschylus's *Wool-Carriers* (frr. 169, 171), a satyr play that ordinarily concluded a series, so it may have been the last of a tetralogy, as proposed by Sommerstein, LCL, 249. See also Aristophanes's *Frogs*, as quoted in Bernabé, "Imago Inforum Orphica," 106. Painters also gave prominence to the Dionysian myth. A beautiful collection of frescoes from a secret gathering place of women devotees (maenads or bacchants) in Pompeii is reproduced in Adams, *Mystai*.

78. Stoyanov, *Other God*, 29, here citing Strabo, *Geogr.* 7.3.3–6, 11. Alexander Fol and Ivan

another body while others enjoyed a far greater existence apart from the body.[79] This outlook characterized Indo-European peoples who still had a strong shamanistic tradition.[80] Taking the myth literally, feral forms of Dionysian devotion involved wild orgies and pricking with thyrsus wands whose needle tips were laced with unknown substances.[81] Yet even on stage and in his public cult, the

---

Marazov add: "As early as the seventh century BC, the poet Archilochus called the Thracians (in his case the Abantes), the gods of battle, and was not ashamed to admit having once fled from the field, leaving his shield as booty to a Thracian warrior. The ancients were hard put to it to decide which of the many Thracian tribes was the most valiant: the Getae, Odomanti, Thyni, or Odrysae." See *Thrace and the Thracians*, 24. Similarly, of the Scythians and Thracians Herodotus, reports at length (*Hist.* 4.1–142). Interspersed throughout are connections with shamanism and Orphism: the story of Aristeas (4.13–15), Thracian belief in immortality (4.93–94) and the account of a freed slave of Pythagoras who disappeared in an underground chamber until returning three years later, persuading Thracians to adopt his Pythagorean doctrines (4.95–96). Scythians sacrifice without lighting any fires. "As soon as the animal is strangled, he is skinned, and then comes the boiling of the flesh." Next, they "strip the flesh from the bones and put it into a cauldron" (4.60–61).

79. Fol and Marazov, *Thrace and the Thracians*, 34–35.

80. Beginning with Eliade, ethnographic research has substantiated the remarkable commonalities of shamanism across all cultures, distinct from the various public religions. The shaman was common to Iranian and Indo-Aryan peoples, so it is not surprising that Iranians in their continuing migration throughout Central Asia and Eastern Europe carried many of the same traditions as their counterparts in East Asia. See Eliade, "Ideologies and Techniques among the Indo-Europeans," in *Shamanism*, 246, 387–427. Eliade focuses here on the Russian Yukagir people and adds, "To learn what ancestor had reincarnated himself, the Yukagir used to practice divination by the bones of shamans" (246 n. 86). Comparisons as well as contrasts with Egyptian religion are made by Assmann, *Death and Salvation*, 87–112. Notice the shamanic characteristics in the final play of Aeschylus's *Oresteia* trilogy, the *Eumenides*. See Lefkowitz and Romm, *Greek Plays*, 146.

81. McNicholl, "Reason, Religion and Plato," 75. Although drugs were not a part of the Eleusinian cult (in my view), they were involved in these illicit and very private cults. At Eleusis, the rites were tied perfectly to the myth, and Demeter did not even drink wine but a drink mixed with water and barley. Attempts to turn this into a hallucinogenic elixir (see, e.g., Ruck et al., "Ethnogens," 137–40) fail to appreciate the exactness of myth and rite. However, secret sects had their own rituals. Demeter was the "poppy goddess," and rituals at Greek temples of Asclepius (especially dream incubation) testify to the use of neopenthe (opium) and morphine (named after Morpheus, god of sleep) according to neurologist F. J. Carod-Artal. He observes that the oldest ritual use of opium is found in a Sumerian tablet in Mesopotamia—the "plant of happiness"—and ritual artifacts have been discovered in the remains of an Anatolian palace (nineteenth century BCE) and in Egyptian tombs. Note also the Ebers Papyrus (fifteenth century BCE), an ancient Egyptian medical text. Homer makes the first reference to the poppy in Greek literature (*Il.* 8.306), and it may have been the capsule that Helen added to the wine to make Menelaus's guests forget their anguish about Odysseus. On Crete, a Minoan shrine from 1300 BCE was dedicated to the "poppy goddess" of fertility. Thebes had poppy plantations as early as the fifteenth century BCE. See Carod-Artal, "Psychoactive Plants in Ancient Greece," 30–31.

Chapter 2

whole ambiance of Dionysus is shamanic. His realm is untamed nature, not the city. He descends to retrieve his mother in Hades and has her successfully immortalized. Pricking devotees with divine madness from cave to cave (similar to the shaman's tent), he rarely checks in with his father Zeus and siblings in the locative capitol atop Olympus. He is a utopian force of nature, dismembering his enemies and immortalizing his followers. "The sex drive is of course one such force," note Lefkowitz and Romm, "and goat-footed satyrs and Sileni, embodying the power of that drive with their erect phalluses, were depicted in Greek art as Dionysus' principal followers, along with the bacchae, women who have surrendered themselves, in nonsexual ways, to Dionysiac experience."[82]

Like the Eleusinian mysteries, the public festival, called City Dionysia or Great Dionysia, lasted seven days. It began with the *pompē*, a phallus procession based on the story of Dionysus sending a disease upon the genitalia of the Athenian men for initially rejecting his cult. After sacrificing a bull to purify the theater, five days of competition occurred, which were followed by the *kōmos* (comedy) that culminated in drunken citizens rushing madly through the streets.[83] It was a "feast of misrule" when ordinary norms were set aside or even reversed—a festival of chaos. In fact, women and children had leading roles in the cult. Afterward, probably contrary to Dionysius's wishes, everything returned to order. Precisely as exceptions, such festivals are reminders of the borders to be strictly maintained on other days.[84] Yet it is difficult to put the utopian genie back in the bottle. Additional "misrule" was associated with Dionysus, to the point that the Roman senate placed restrictions on the Bacchanalia.[85]

Hemp was especially popular in the shamanic ceremonies of Scythians and Thracians (Herodotus, *Hist.* 4.74, 164). Cf. Akeroyd, "Cannabis," 78.

82. Lefkowitz and Romm, *Greek Plays*, 738.

83. For a fuller itinerary of the Great Dionysia see Goldhill, "Great Dionysia and Civic Ideology"; Pickard-Cambridge, *Drama Festivals of Athens*.

84. Mikhail Bakhtin and others trace the "feast of misrule" to Rome, but the Dionysian festivals are no less a suspension of ordinary time. Still, Bakhtin's analysis is intriguing. See Bagshaw, *Mikhail Bakhtin*, 95. Important anthropological/ethnographic studies of this topic include Turner, *Ritual Process*, and Harris, *Sacred Folly*.

85. Kerényi, *Dionysos*, 239–40. Dionysus's first love was Aphrodite. Other lovers include Aura (Breeze or Wind), nymphs, mortals, the handsome satyr Ampelos, and the ferryman Prosymnus, who rowed Dionysus to the underworld through a cave in exchange for his promise that he would make love to him. By the time Dionysus returned, though, Prosymnus was dead. Carving a phallus from a tree branch, he fulfilled his vow and later writers reported an ongoing secret rite involving orgies at the prehistoric lake where the myth originated; see Ovid's *Fasti* 3.40; Pseudo-Hyginus, *Astr.* 2.5; Clement of Alexandria, *Protr.* 2.30. The first-century geographer Pausanias testifies that it was a very old rite involving orgies at the prehistoric lake where the myth originated. But he considered the rest of the story too indecent to comment on further (*Descr.* 2.37.6). Arriving in Rome around 200 BCE, Bacchanalia sects thrived especially in southern Italy

Ironically, the outsider became the insider, the private became public, and the forbidden became mainstream. Part of the shaman's mystique is a refusal to belong to the locative world, inhabiting instead the undomesticated wilds outside the city. Esoteric by design, mysteries were alternatives to the public religion. However, soon after Dionysus made his flamboyant appearance, the ruler Pisistratus (561–527 BCE) insisted on incorporating the cult into the national religion. Unifying Athens and Attica more generally, he envisioned a culture based on a cult that was in turn based on a new mythology. There was as usual a political aspect. The Alcmaeonids, led by Megacles, were the main opponents of Pisistratus, but they were under a curse (*miasma*) for their murder of Cylon's followers. This is why Solon recruited Epimenides to cleanse Athens. But the Alcmaeonids were the main architects and financiers of the Delphic cult. The son of the philosopher Hippocrates and related to Solon by his mother, Pisistratus took control of Athens from the factions that included Megacles. Suspecting with good evidence that the Pythian priestess was favoring her patron and his foe with bribes, Pisistratus snubbed the Oracle of Delphi and may have been behind the burning of the new temple complex.[86]

Instead, Pisistratus focused on establishing Athens as the center of all Attic cults. Not only did he invest in the erection of lavish temples that made Athens a recognizable capital, but he also set the mythologist Onomacritus over a commission to create an official edition of both Homer's epics and the Orphic poems.[87] This shows the esteem in which the latter were held at this point. Moreover, Pisistratus in effect created the public religion. Sparing no expense, he built the Temple of Artemis on the Acropolis and made Athena the patron of the city.

---

during the Roman era. See Ovid, *Metam.* 4.20; Seneca, *Oed.* 112–115; Pausanias, *Descr.* 10.29.4; Burkert, *Ancient Mystery Cults*, 5. The Roman Senate passed legislation against its excesses in 186 BCE and made it part of the Liber Pater (Free Father) cult of Rome. Given the dominance of women, the Senate determined that men would be excluded from the Bacchic priesthood, mingling of the sexes and its orgiastic rites were to be curtailed, and intoxicating substances limited. See Takács, "Bacchanalian Affair." Livy claims that the whole city was participating in the rites of Dionysus-Bacchus, engaging in heterosexual and homosexual orgies, and even murdering someone who refused to join, threatening the whole order of society. P. G. Walsh explains and evaluates Livy's charges in "Livy on the Bacchanalia."

86. The whole story is told by Herodotus, *Hist.* 1.59–64 and 5.62–66. On the burning of the temple see Scott, *Delphi*, 100.

87. See West, *Orphic Poems*, 248–50. Zopyrus of Heraclea, says West, "was the Pythagorean reputed to have written the *Krater* and perhaps the *Robe* and the *Net*" (250). Influential in Orphic and Pythagorean circles, these texts are discussed in the following chapter. On the whole Pisistratus-Onomacritus story, see Tsagalis, "Peisistratus," 193–95. This episode is related by Cicero and, subsequently, by many Roman writers. Consequently, some scholars consider it a legend since it "cannot be traced back beyond the first century B.C." See Pfeiffer, *History of Classical Scholarship*, 6. This is not true, strictly speaking, as the immediately following episode from Herodotus details.

He also established the calendar of annual festivals, with pride of place given to Dionysus, the newly arrived shaman-god. Pisistratus brought the Eleusinian mysteries under state patronage, erected its telesterion, and established the theater competitions and Panhellenic games, both of which inculcated and celebrated Dionysus-related figures and themes.[88]

A populist, Pisistratus was also a shrewd politician, and these were now the popular myths. He could not have made Eleusis an alternative to Delphi or favored Dionysus and Orphic theology by fiat. It had already happened. More mystical, individualistic, and focused on the soul and the afterlife, dismemberment, and rebirth, these myths were also more "oriental."[89] There is a greater emphasis on transcendence, but only to highlight the chasm that the shaman bridges.[90]

Even the public cult of Dionysus—celebrated in January and March—was based not on the stories of Homer and Hesiod but on those produced in mystery circles.[91] All of this was new. So was the Dionysian doctrine of reincarnation taught by the shamans, lawgivers, playwrights, painters, and philosophers of the golden age. If it surprises us that the Greek enlightenment rested on Dionysian-Orphic mysticism, it is even more astonishing that, contrary to its entire character, a utopian lion had been tamed into a locative lamb.

"Orpheus Famous by Name": Reconciling Apollo and Dionysus

Historically, the transitional figure between the shaman and the sage is the singer. The legendary Orpheus was the double heir of Apollo and Dionysus. From the former he acquired the temper of a prophet, possessed by the god of reason and foreknowledge. Yet he was theologically Dionysian, obsessed with stories of dismemberment and restoration as well as descent to and from the underworld, a

---

88. Besides the Olympic, Pythian, Nemean, and Isthmian Games. All these games were dedicated to the gods, with a hecatomb (sacrifice of a hundred bulls) and infused throughout with cultic rites. Pelops, mentioned above as a legendary victim of the Dionysian theme of dismemberment, boiling, and cannibalism, was the legendary founder of the Olympic Games. Hercules was viewed as the founder of the Isthmian Games, Zeus of the Nemean Games, and the Pythian Games were held at Delphi in honor of Apollo. The lyric poet Ibycus (sixth century BCE), who refers to "Orpheus, famous by name," invented the genre of the victory ode perfected by Pindar, who includes explicitly Orphic doctrines. "In his odes," says Anthony Verity, "Pindar stresses the inevitable gulf between men and gods, but also how the superhuman achievement of athletics in supreme competition can to some extent bridge the gulf." See Verity's introduction to Pindar, *Complete Odes*, x.

89. As observed in Burkert, *Orientalizing Revolution*, which I have cited frequently so far.

90. Nicholas Richardson makes this point well in his introduction to *Homeric Hymns*, xix.

91. Persephone's public cult was celebrated in the month of Anthesterion (midsummer). See Herodotus, *Hist.* 7.6.

denizen of the Eleusinian mysteries even more than the shrine at Delphi. The contrast between Apollo and Dionysus should not be overdrawn (as Nietzsche does in *The Death of Tragedy*), since both brothers were worshiped together in both places. Moreover, we shall see as the classical age unfolds that Apollo becomes something of a shaman himself.[92] Such a fusion of Apollo and Dionysus was precisely the intention of Orpheus—or, rather, the poet-theologians who, invoking his name, refashioned the horizon of ancient Greece.[93]

Orpheus appealed to intellectuals who transmuted ritualistic mysteries into the gold of philosophy and thereby gave Dionysius an enduring afterlife in the Western psyche.[94] At the birth of the classical age, the shamanistic *Meistersinger* became the bearer of the entire Greek tradition. Already in the sixth century BCE, Ibycus, the pioneer of victory poetry, mentions the prophet-singer as if he needed no introduction: "Orpheus famous by name."[95] In that same century, as noted above, Pisistratus commissioned Onomacritus to gather the Orphic poems into an official collection along with Homer and Pindar celebrated, "And sent by Apollo there came the lyre-player and father of song, greatly admired Orpheus" (Pindar, *Pyth.* 4.176).[96] Of course, "father of song" meant essentially that the legendary Thracian was the fountainhead of all inspired verse. It was taken for granted in ancient Greece that he preceded Homer and Hesiod and was the founder of all mysteries.[97] In the story of Jason and the Argonauts, set prior to the Trojan Wars, Orpheus even initiated the crew (including Heracles) in the mysteries.[98]

This antiquity lent prestige both to the mysteries even over the public religion and to Orpheus's priority over Homer. Like Dionysus (in fact, Homer as well),

---

92. In Homer, Paieon is the god of healing (*Il.* 5.401, 899; *Od.* 4.432). "But Sappo (44 LP) suggests and Sphokles (*OT* 145) confirms that the two figures have fused, and that Apollo is now the healer among the gods." He sends plagues and heals them. Gantz, *Early Greek Myth*, 96.

93. While rationalists and mystics of the nineteenth century conspire to drive them apart by anachronistic stereotypes of rational Apollo versus irrational Dionysus, it is important to see how Apollo's cult itself becomes more "mystical" in the hands of the Orphic-inclined tragedians and Presocratic philosphers.

94. See Guthrie, *Orpheus and Greek Religion*, and chapter 6 of Burkert, *Greek Religion*.

95. Reale, *History of Ancient Philosophy*, 1:294.

96. Pindar, *Pyth.* 4.176.

97. See for example Pausanias, *Descr.* 2.30.2. According to Bremmer: "The fifth-century mythographers Hellanicus, Pherecydes and Damastes all state that both Homer and Hesiod were descended from Orpheus," notes Bremmer, "and when the learned Sophist Hippias of Elis listed the most famous Greek poets he gave them in the order of Orpheus, Musaeus, Hesiod and Homer, as did Aristophanes, Plato and others after him." See *Initiation in the Mysteries*, 58. Contained in Pseudo-Apollodorus is the Orphic claim that he invented the mysteries (*Bib.* 1.3.2), which is also cited by Bremmer. See also Linforth, "Legend of Orpheus."

98. Apollonius Rhodius, *Argon.* 4.890–920; on the latter, see Simonides fr. 567 in Page, *Poetae Melici Graeci.*

Chapter 2

Orpheus is a pastiche of poets, playwrights, historians, philosophers, and geographers, and like Dionysius he reflects characteristics of the shaman.[99] The ancients saw him as the founder of the Greek renaissance.[100]

The Orpheus Myth

Around the end of the sixth century Pindar describes Orpheus as Apollo's son by the Muse Calliope and as known worldwide for the magical efficacy of his music, a story repeated by Euripides.[101] Apollo invented music, specializing in the distinctively Greek guitar (*kithara*), but under his instruction Orpheus perfected the instrument that accompanied his enchanting voice. Along with poetry and drama, music arose mainly in a religious context as a liturgical medium.

Like other shamans, including Dionysus, Orpheus descended to the netherworld, from which he brought back the soul of his wife, Eurydice. While he sang, his music made a heaven of even that dark place. Hades was so overwhelmed by its magic that he allowed Orpheus to bring back Eurydice on the condition that he would never look back on their return.[102]

Though a successful descent into Hades is characteristic of a shaman, Orpheus looked back, a fatal mistake that echoes Gilgamesh. It was a blemish that Plato would censure as a cautionary tale about looking back on earthly things even while breathing the empyrean air (*Symp.* 179d). Partisans of either Dionysus or Apollo wrote Orpheus's story in such a way that he could be either the Hero-That-Succeeded or the Hero-That-Failed. Nietzsche perceived that "the Dionysian and the Apollonian, in new births ever following and mutually augmenting one another, controlled the Hellenic genius."[103] However, his contrast is too stark.[104] Plato's "unmusical" interpretation of the failed rescue of Eurydice (in contrast with Ovid or Shakespeare's *Romeo and Juliet*) is surely more of an example of philosophical dogma ruining a good tragedy.[105] However, he arrives later. "Orpheus"

---

99. Though I remain a skeptic, Michael Schmidt improves considerably and winsomely on Thomas Taylor's defense of the historical existence of "Orpheus of Thrace" in *First Poets*, 3–20.

100. Burkert, *Babylon, Memphis, Persepolis*, 78.

101. Pindar, *Pyth.* 4.176–177; Euripides, *Alc.* 357–362.

102. Aeschylus in *Bassarids* knew the poem about Orpheus's descent into Hades; see West, *Orphic Hymns*, 12. Ovid's version in *Metam.* 10.8 is the most moving. In Plato, *Symp.* 179d–e Socrates reproves Orpheus for not being Orphic enough.

103. Nietzsche, *Birth of Tragedy*, 47.

104. A superb analysis of Nietzsche's immensely successful exaggerations is found in Detienne, "Forgetting Delphi."

105. Similarly, ever the Stoic, Seneca saw this as a warning against allowing one's emotions to cloud judgment (*Herc. fur.* 569).

represents a synthesis in which Dionysian madness is the highest form of knowledge, even for—indeed, especially for—Socrates. Beneath the cool abstractions lies the boiling blood of the tragic utopian.[106]

Orpheus's violent death was given several startling stories of dismemberment. According to the first, he was torn limb from limb by furious wives for introducing homosexuality to Thrace.[107] According to the second, the same fate befell him when Dionysus, infuriated that Orpheus ranked Apollo greatest of all gods, sent madness upon his maenads to carry out the deed.[108] A later account has Zeus executing Orpheus with a thunderbolt for upstaging his son.[109] With some contempt, Strabo said that leaders came to Lesbos to consult the "wizard's" oracle from as far away as Babylon.[110] Apollo's oracle at Delphi recedes, which may support this version. In a short space, Sommerstein concludes from Aeschylus fragments that Orpheus's fatal vision of the sunrise led him upon returning to turn his love toward Apollo rather than Dionysus. This is why the Thracian women (maenads) tore him to pieces and scattered his limbs, reprising Dionysus's own fate at the hands of Hera's Titans, but he too returns after the sweet burial by the Muses. "Aeschylus' story reflects a rivalry between the Pythagorean sect (whose most venerated deity was Apollo) and Dionysiac mystery-cults, which both claimed Orpheus as their prophet, and that the Dionysus-Apollo conflict provided the overarching theme of the whole trilogy, ending (in *Youths*) with the firm establishment in Thrace of cults of *both* gods. Like *Edonians*, this play clearly served in part as a model for Euripides' *Bacchae*."[111] In short, through Orpheus's ordeal Dionysus and Apollo are reconciled.[112]

There are also varied postmortem accounts. In one, his mother Calliope and her sister Muses bury the pieces of Orpheus in Thrace and place his lyre in the

---

106. Burkert, *Orientalizing Revolution*, 42–43.

107. Phanocles, *Florilegium* fr. 1, quoted in Aeschylus, *Bassarids* (fr. 23–24; see Aeschylus, *Attributed Fragments* [ed. and trans. Sommerstein], LCL, 18–19); Pseudo-Hyginus, *Astr.* 2.6.4; 2.7.1. Later authors include Pseudo-Apollodorus, *Bib.* 1.3.2; Ovid, *Metam.* 10.1–85; 11.1–84; Vergil, *Georg.* 4.453–527. Cf. Guthrie, *Orpheus and Greek Religion,* and chapter 6 of Burkert, *Greek Religion*.

108. This version appears in fragments of Aeschylus's *Bassarids* and also in Pseudo-Hyginus, *Astr.* 2.7.5; Ovid, *Metam.* 11.1–5; Pausanias, *Descr.* 9.30.5. Guthrie defends this account in *Orpheus and the Greek Religion*, 32.

109. Pausanias, *Descr.* 9.30.1–5. According to Alcidamas, Orpheus was slain by Zeus's thunderbolt, jealous that Orpheus was being preferred to his son Apollo. See Alcidamas, *Od.* 16; cf. 24. Apollo is the perpetrator according to Philostratus, *Vit. Apoll.* 2; see Godwin, *Lives of the Necromancers*, 46.

110. Strabo, *Geogr.* 7.7. Apollonius of Rhodes, Vergil, and Ovid, summarized in Reid, *Oxford Guide to Classical Mythology*, 797.

111. Aeschylus, *Attributed Fragments* (ed. and trans. Sommerstein), 18–19.

112. Along similar lines see West, *Studies in Aeschylus*, 26–50.

night sky as a constellation; in another, his head floats to Lesbos and Apollo buries it at Delphi.[113] This Apollo-Dionysus rivalry, settled finally by a fusion of sorts, seems to make the most sense of the reverence for both gods in Orphic lore. It is more conservative than the Dionysian cults, and yet the "bull-god" (a very Indo-European entity) remains central. In its philosophical tendency, Orphic theogonies are Dionysian, but Orpheus rationalizes the myths.

Behind these divergent myths are Orpheus propagandists as well as purists and partisans of either an Apollonian or Dionysian religion.[114] But a more reflective stage marks Orpheus's rise. His followers interpreted physical rites and myths in a mystical (i.e., allegorical) fashion. An obvious example is the transformation of the rending, boiling, and eating of animal flesh into cosmological and psychological theories (i.e., emanation and reincarnation).[115]

There was still the romantic Dionysus whose feral cult continued in secretive caves. However, as we shall see, this speculative Dionysian mysticism captured the imagination of Pythagoras, Parmenides, Anaxagoras, and other Presocratic philosophers. Even as early as Aeschylus, the "apostate" Orpheus is "more philosophical" and "reveres Apollo-Helios because of knowledge acquired in the underworld."[116] The rending-rebirth trope is given a philosophical interpretation with doctrines that were new in Greece, such as the immortality of the soul, the body as a prison, transmigration, and an emanationist cosmology. Drama becomes Gnosis.

Did Orphism Exist?

Of course, Orpheus is legendary, but does "Orphism" identify a genuine historical trend? Some scholars argue that Orphism is the reified construction of Neoplatonists. These minimalists have reacted against a generation that took a maximalist approach to the existence of "Orphic Religion."[117] To a large extent this scholarship reflected personal sympathies for a theosophical "perennial tradition."

---

113. Apollonius of Rhodes, Vergil, and Ovid in Reid, *Oxford Guide to Classical Mythology*, 797.
114. Kerényi, *Dionysos*, 205; cf. Bernabé et al., *Redefining Dionysos*.
115. Long ago the important specialist Michael Tierney argued that such animal rending and eating was merely minor in comparison with the Dionysian cult; see "Orphic Mysteries," 79–80. Yet we will see that Orphic practice was consistent with Pythagorean abstinence (e.g., Aristotle fr. 11 [Ross]). See for example OH 27 and 30. Though the Orphic Hymns are from the opening centuries of our era, this characterization of Dionysus is consistent with descriptions from preclassical times.
116. West, *Orphic Hymns*, 13.
117. To a large extent, these scholars are reacting against a maximalist approach that construed Orphism as an organized religion, often through the anachronistic lens of Christian (especially Protestant) categories. Respected specialist Jane Ellen Harrison could say in 1922

On its own terms, though, Orphism could never have been a religion or even a school; it was a spirit rather than a body, an idea rather than appearance. The minimalist Radcliffe Edmonds III argues that the only image that "Orphic" would have conjured in the mind of an ancient Greek is an excessive pretense to purity and "texts or rites that were exceptionally strange—alien rites or tales of perverse and horrifying deeds by the gods."[118] "There was no fixed set of Orphic myths or doctrines," Edmonds contends, "no Orphic mythology, just a bewildering array of rituals and myths to which different ancient authors and audiences, at different times and for different reasons, gave the magical name of Orpheus."[119] To whom, though, were such stories "perverse" and "strange"? By the sixth century, at least, Greek theatergoers were thoroughly catechized by these stories. Meanwhile Orphic thinkers criticized Homer and Hesiod precisely for the "perverse elements" of their stories. Rather than literally attribute to the gods all manner of vulgar practices (e.g., incest, child cannibalism, castration, deceit, and adultery), Orphic myths were riddles interpreted allegorically.

---

what no scholar today could say, viz., that Orpheus was the Martin Luther of his age, "a reformer, a Protestant." See *Prolegomena*, 461.

118. Over the last century, specialists have been divided over the extent to which Orphism even existed. At one end are the minimialists. In 1931 Ulrich von Wilamowitz-Moellendorff complained, "Moderns are obsessed with Orphism" (*Der Glaube der Hellenen*, 2:197). A decade later, I. M. Linforth extended Wilamowitz-Moellendorff's critique, convinced that "Orphism" had no identity other than texts that claimed connection to Orpheus in *Arts of Orpheus*. Recently, Radcliffe G. Edmonds III has presented a formidable case for the minimalist position in *Redefining Ancient Orphism*, 190–91. While eschewing such anachronisms, a number of prominent scholars today are convinced that there were actual Orphic communities based on distinct myths, doctrines, and rites. Recent discoveries (discussed below) have encouraged this position, represented especially by Alberto Bernabé. Equally eminent scholars may be found across this spectrum. My principal difference from Edmonds is less over what he affirms than what he rejects. For example, he contends, "The disjoined and fragmentary pieces of evidence we have are not the relics of secret canonical doctrines and scripture, but the productions of countless *bricoleurs* in competition with one another for religious authority" (9). This is a false choice, though. Every religious, philosophical, and political tradition could be described in such terms. Yet without some shared convictions, what could it mean to be "in competition with one another for religious authority"? A more nuanced account is offered in Meisner, *Orphic Tradition*.

119. Edmonds, *Redefining Ancient Orphism*, 190–91. Edmonds expands the general argument of Ulrich Wilamowitz and I. M. Linforth, who denied any coherent set of doctrines that define "Orphic" texts. See Linforth, *Arts of Orpheus*. In a more nuanced way, M. L. West cautions, "We must never say that 'the Orphics' believed this or that, and anyone who does say it must be asked sharply 'Which Orphics? . . . It is legitimate to talk about these Olbian or Tarentine Orphics, or any other specific group of Orphics that we can identify, but not talk about 'the Orphics' in general." See *Orphic Poems*, 3. Yet, throughout this learned volume West assumes and identifies typical features that distinguish Orphic literature generally in terms of myths, doctrines, and practices.

There is no evidence that ancients classified a text as Orphic simply because it seemed strange. Rather, they identified Orphism with distinct doctrines. Herodotus refers contemptuously to "rites known as Orphic and Bacchic (actually Egyptian and Pythagorean)" (*Hist.* 2.81).[120] Later he adds,

> The Egyptians say that Demeter and Dionysus are the chief powers in the underworld; and they were also the first people to put forward the doctrine of the immortality of the soul, and to maintain that after death it enters another creature at the moment of that creature's birth. It then makes the round of all living things—animals, birds, and fish—until it finally passes once again, at birth, into the body of a man. The whole period of transmigration occupies three thousand years. This theory has been adopted by certain Greek writers, some earlier, some later, who have put it forward as their own. Their names are known to me, but I refrain from mentioning them. (*Hist.* 2.123)

A century later, Aristotle includes the soul's transmigration as part of "the doctrine contained within the poems called 'Orphic'" (*De an.* 410b27–411a2).

A. H. Armstrong summarizes the core of the Orphic myth: "The divine in us is an actual being, a daimon or spirit, which has fallen as a result of some primeval sin and is entrapped in a series of earthly bodies, which may be animal and plant as well as human. It can escape from the 'sorrowful weary wheel,' the cycle of reincarnation, by following the Orphic way of life, which involved, besides rituals and incantations, an absolute prohibition of eating flesh."[121] Whatever anachronistic embellishments Neoplatonists may have added, this summary characterizes major philosophers from Pythagoras onward.

Based on this idea of the kinship of all living beings was the idea of a soul reincarnated from plants to animals to humans.[122] Even the minimalist E. R. Dodds was willing to acknowledge a sort of Orphic confluence around the ideas "that the body is the prisonhouse of the soul; that vegetarianism is an essential rule of life; and that the unpleasant consequence of sin, both in this world the next, can be washed away by ritual means," and even that "transmigration" is fairly well inferred.[123]

---

120. Translation of Herodotus, *The Histories*, unless otherwise noted, from de Sélincourt.
121. Armstrong, "Pieties of the Greek World," 99.
122. Burkert, *Babylon, Memphis, Persepolis*, 97; cf. Graf, *Magic in the Ancient World*, 170–74.
123. Dodds, *Greeks and the Irrational*, 149. The remarkable advance in discovery, translation, and interpretation is well represented by the labors of Alberto Bernabé. See his "La toile de Pénélope"; Bernabé and Jiménez San Cristóbal. *Instrucciones*. Cf. Graf, "Dionysian and Orphic Eschatology."

These doctrines were new in Greece, as they were in the East, but were part of a broader transition inspired by the utopian shaman over against the locative priest. As M. L. West says, "That Orpheus is to be seen in the context of northern shamanism is no new conclusion.... But from the late sixth century BC to the end of antiquity Orpheus' was the favourite name for pseudepigraphic poems of a religious, metaphysical, or esoteric nature." These writings focus on common themes, with titles such as "The Descent into Hades," recovering loved ones from the underworld, "the dismemberment and renovation of Dionysus," and the return of the soul into many different bodies (even of animals) until it is finally released from the wheel of rebirth.[124] Immortality, including reincarnation, which entailed the proscription against animal meat, was a foreign concept to the Greeks until it was advanced by Orphic philosophers such as Pythagoras.[125]

At this point, the Orphic transformation of Dionysus became widely adopted by philosophers as well as dramatists. Scenes on vase paintings tell the same story. One depicts Orpheus holding Cerberus the guard dog of Hades on a leash while he plays a lyre. "Thus at the borderline of life and death, marked by the herm, Orpheus controls the terror of the netherworld with his music."[126] Death and Hades are no longer to be feared but are the gateway to real life. Orpheus's lyre functions like the shaman's drum, attracting animals and even trees that uproot and descend the mountain to share the ecstasy.[127] Aeschylus (in *Bassarids*) knew the poem about Orpheus's descent into Hades.[128]

In Greek colonies from the Black Sea to southern Italy we find self-designated Orphic votaries buried with passports for the afterlife. These recent discoveries have caused considerable rethinking, suggesting strongly that there were actual communities that called themselves Orphic and attesting their distinctly Orphic doctrines.[129] The oldest of these thirty-five gold foils are from the fifth century BCE.[130] They speak of the body as a tomb, reincarnation, and the myth of Perse-

---

124. West, *Orphic Poems*, 5–6.

125. Although Zoroastrianism was the court religion under the Persian Empire, Bactria in northern India was a thriving center of interaction and synthesis with Hindu thought and ritual practice. In the Hellenistic period the region became an Indo-Greek kingdom, from which Alexander took a princess as his wife.

126. Burkert, *Babylon, Memphis, Persepolis*, 85.

127. Burkert, *Babylon, Memphis, Persepolis*, 85–86.

128. West, *Orphic Hymns*, 12.

129. West, *Orphic Poems*, 146.

130. The Greek is supplied by Philip Harland, "Orphic Bone Tablets." The first reads, "Life, Death, Life, Z | Truth | Za(greus) Z." The second: "Peace, War | Truth, Falsehood | Dio(nysios) | Dio(nysos) | Orphik-." The third: "Dionysos, Z. Truth | Body, Soul." I reversed "Peace, War | Truth, Falsehood" because it was correlated in Orphic circles with "Soul, Body." See Graf and Johnston,

Chapter 2

phone and Dionysus, designating initiates *bacchoi* with their thyrsus wand. They reveal an afterlife to which Plato's view of the body, the afterlife, and anamnesis (i.e., "all learning is remembering") bears striking resemblance.[131] These tablets, "instructions for the afterlife," were found in tombs on corpses and often in their mouths. These inscriptions allude to reincarnation and being deified, correlating the antithesis of death and life with that of embodiment and disembodiment.[132]

Three Olbian Bone Tablets (from the sixth or fifth century BCE) bear the names "Dionysus" and "Zagreus." The second of these tablets adds "Orphik-" and expresses the stark opposition of the "Soul, Body" correlated with "Peace, War" and "Truth, Falsehood."[133] These tablets were likely constructed in the same area and during the same time that, as Herodotus reports, Bacchic cults existed around the Black Sea.[134] Though distant geographically, these discoveries cluster mainly around circles within Greek colonies who called themselves *bacchoi* and *orphikoi* and praised Dionysos-Zagreus as their psychopomp.

Discovered in southern Italy in 1974, the Hipponion Tablet refers to *mystai* and *bacchoi* (the latter unmistakably linking it to Dionysus). In 1989 two tablets were published that include the line, "Say to Persephone that Bacchios himself freed you."[135] These ritual passwords not only laconically express Orphic mythology but also Orphic doctrines (body versus soul, death versus life) held by actual communities engaging in Orphic rituals. Voluntarily or not, Dionysus-Zagreus-Bacchios became the patron of a theosophical movement.

These painted vases and burial accessories recall the Orphic *hieros logos*, "sacred story." As philosophical alchemists, Orphic writers transmuted these myths into

---

Ritual Texts for the Afterlife, 4–41. Hipponion (400 BCE), Pelina, Petelia, Pharsalos, and Thessaly (fourth century); Entella (third century); five tablets from Eleutherna (Crete), Mylopotamos, Rethymnon (second to first centuries).

131. Palmer, *Plato's Reception of Parmenides*, 22–23.

132. Fritz Graf and Sarah Iles Johnston observe similarities to the Egyptian Book of the Dead in *Ritual Texts for the Afterlife*, 4–7, 16–17, 20–29, 34–35, 40–41. A clear sense of Dionysian-Orphic ritual is felt in the exhibit at the Getty Villa in Malibu, California, with one of these gold tablets surrounded by numerous vase paintings illustrating the rites.

133. West, "Orphics of Olbia." The first tablet suggests reincarnation: "Life, Death, Life, Z | Truth," and the third reads, "Dionysos, Z. Truth | Body, Soul."

134. Herodotus, *Hist.* 4.78.80; Burkert, *Babylon, Memphis, Persepolis*, 83–84. There are other artifacts that attest to an active Dionysian cult in Olbia, notes Chrysanthou, such as a mirror found in a grave inscribed with "euai!," which in the plays of Sophocles and Aristophanes is a cry of elation in Bacchic frenzy, and a fifth-century BCE vase stand with Dionysiac associations. "Also, Herodotus refers to the story of the Skythian king Skyles who around 460 B.C. wished to become initiated into the ecstatic cult of Dionysos Baccheios at Olbia." See Chrysanthou, *Defining Orphism*, 201–2.

135. Edmonds, *Redefining Ancient Orphism*, 60.

doctrines that became formative in the Greek enlightenment. Burkert points out the similarity of the Orphic password found on the gold Hipponian Tablet and a similar scene in the Egyptian Book of the Dead and the Phoenician silver plates. "They were deposited in tombs but also carried as amulets. In these Phoenician monuments it is not texts that recall Egypt but pictures of gods of the solar route, 'decans,' of unquestionable Egyptian character."[136] Not only did the Phoenicians bring alphabetic writing to Greece, but they also brought many of their West Asian (Semitic) myths along with those from Thrace and Egypt, who were included in the ring dominated by this seafaring people. "This strengthens the argument that Greek Dionysus, as he shows up in funerary contexts, has undergone the spell of Egypt," says Burkert, "and that Bacchic mysteries which claim to guarantee otherworldly bliss are influenced by the Osiris cult."[137] In addition, Phoenician and Hurrian-Hittite myths such as the Kumarbi myth seeped into Greek culture, especially in Orphic poetry.[138] Such a synthesis would make sense in Greek colonies of Anatolia.

Finally, we have Pisistratus in 540–530 BCE formally establishing the festivals and rites of Athens, with Dionysus nearly central there, and appointing Onamacri-

---

136. Burkert, *Babylon, Memphis, Persepolis*, 87. He adds, "Without documentation for the details of cultural contact, we can just postulate that this would have happened in the first half of the sixth century." See also Graf and Johnston, *Ritual Texts for the Afterlife*, and Bernabé and Jiménez San Cristóbal, *Instructions for the Netherworld*.

137. Burkert, *Babylon, Memphis, Persepolis*, 88, adding, "Even at Eleusis the mysteries proper, performed in a closed hall of initiations (*telesterion*), establish their presence by special architecture only in the sixth century. It is tempting to see the interrelation of personal mysteries with what has been called the discovery of the individual in the archaic epoch. The likelihood is strong that the old and traditional cult of Dionysus took a turn toward concern with afterlife through the Egyptian impulse. As Herodotus has it [2.49], after the original foundation of Dionysus worship some later 'sophists' imported Egyptian lore afresh. In our words, Orphic-Egyptian Dionysus came to overlay and to transform Mycenaean Dionysus—this seems a plausible thesis after all, even if it cannot be proved in detail to the skeptic."

In recent scholarship Algis Uždavinys has offered the most persuasive narrative and evidence for Egyptian influence, especially in *Orpheus and the Roots of Platonism*. However, Egypt was part of the Persian Empire during this period. The product of bricolage, Orphism was also the great bricoleur of Achaemenid gnosis. But Iranian and Hittite influences have been detected as well, which just points to the syncretism especially as Ionia fell to Cyrus of Persia in the second half of the sixth century. We are reminded also of Simon the *magos* much later in Acts 8:9–24, as Burkert himself observes in *Babylon, Memphis, Persepolis*, 88.

138. Chrysanthou, *Defining Orphism*, 205–56. The entire work builds methodically and carefully toward this conclusion. Consequently, instead of seeing the Eleusinian mysteries as a later development than the public cult, and Orphism as a still later offshoot of the mysteries, we should be open to the possibility that they flourished simultaneously, weaving in and out of each other as each writer, vase painter, or reader preferred. Even the cult of Apollo at Delphi appears in time alongside Dionysian and Orphic lore.

Chapter 2

tus to oversee the production of an authorized version of both Homer's epics and the Orphic poems, which demonstrates their equal authority as early as the sixth century BCE, when the "axial revolution" was simultaneous with the consolidation of the Persian (Achaemenid) empire.[139] Onamacritus's colleagues were among the inner circle of Pythagoras's immediate pupils, who were the likely authors of three important Orphic works entitled *Krater*, *Robe*, and *Net*.[140]

From the late seventh or early sixth century, the same artists who gave life to Dionysus were captivated by the Thracian singer. Calling Orpheus the "father of songs," the great lyric poet Pindar is taken with the doctrines of the body as a prison of the soul, reincarnation, and the hope for eventual disembodiment.[141] Aristophanes (*Ran.* 1032) and Euripides (*Hipp.* 952) also extol the Orphic myth.[142] Written just over a century or so after Homer, Heraclitus's statement that "the human Logos is sprung from the divine Logos" would have puzzled Greeks who had not been reading Orphic poems or philosophers influenced by them.[143]

Pindar seems to know Orphism as an insider (*Pyth.* 4.176–177). As early as Aeschylus, playwrights are aware of both the association of and difference between Dionysian and Orphic sects.[144] The Dionysian myth is woven throughout the Orphic Hymns in an unfolding narrative, praising each god as a character in the tragicomedy of Dionysius's life, including his violent dismemberment into multiplicity and his return to unity. Athanassakis and Wolkow observe, "Immortality is conferred by lofty song.... Immortality of the soul is the key Orphic belief in them. This central Orphic belief is the dominant theme of the Homeric *Hymn to Demeter*, composed sometime in the seventh century BC, whose origins specialists in Greek religion trace to an agricultural cult."[145] Column 22 of the Derveni Papyrus alludes to "Orphic Hymns" that must have existed in the sixth century.[146]

---

139. According to Diodorus Siculus, *Bib. hist.* 4.25.1–2, he was the son of Orpheus; cf. Herodotus, *Hist.* 7.6. Onamacritus's official edition of Orphic literature included the oracles and poems attributed to Orpheus as well as those attributed to Musaeus, considered variously as the son or disciple of Orpheus. His work was interrupted when it was discovered that he had forged an oracle.

140. West, *Orphic Poems*, 8–13.

141. Jaeger, *Early Greek Philosophers*, 86; Jaeger, "Greek Concept of Immortality"; Clarke, *Flesh and Spirit*, 294; Cornford, *Greek Religious Thought*, 62.

142. Hadot, "Spiritual Guide," 439.

143. Heraclitus as discussed in a fragment from Epicharmus (= DK 23B57), quoted in McNichoII, "Reason, Religion and Plato," 112.

144. West, *Orphic Poems*, 15, 16–17; cf. Herodotus, *Hist.* 2.81.

145. Athanassakis and Wolkow, introduction to *Orphic Hymns*, xv.

146. Bremmer, *Initiation in the Mysteries*, 65. Bremmer points out that there is an additional fifth-century Orphic hymn about Demeter's entrance in Eleusis, which may have been composed in Eleusis itself.

Any Orphic initiate was qualified to claim that he or she was of the "blessed race" of "immortal gods" and even "flew out of the circle of wearying heavy grief" of not only Zeus's sovereignty but of Fate as well, to which even Zeus is subjected. Persephone would then crown the initiate "a god ... instead of a mortal," which is the meaning of "A kid I fell into milk," an Orphic code for becoming immortal. The other two Thurii Gold Tablets add the following cryptic reference: "Recompense I have paid on account of deeds not just.... Now I come, a suppliant, to holy Phersephoneia [Persephone]." From the mysteries to the burial of actual initiates far from Eleusis, Persephone remains the gatekeeper. As we will see, the "deeds not just" are brought up again by the founders of Ionian science, particularly Anaximander, in a highly metaphysical explanation of emanation as a division from unity.

To be sure, maximalist scholarship usually takes its bearings from later Neoplatonists. Separated by many centuries from the original sources, Neoplatonists appropriated Orphism for their own philosophical religion. However, this is no different from what we call Aristotelianism, for example. Not a single complete book of Aristotle survives; all we have of Aristotle comes from fragments, student lecture notes, and testimonies. The Peripatetic scholiarch Andronicus of Rhodes collected what he had of Aristotle into a new edition in the first century BCE, which is the basis of today's surviving texts of the philosopher. Secondarily, the minimalist approach cannot account for the reception history of texts and fragments that testify to a very specific type of myths and dogmas that were widely regarded as "Orphic."

Yet even more importantly, our knowledge of Orphism no longer turns on whether we take our starting point from Damascius and other Neoplatonic sources. The publication of a new collection of Orphic fragments under the leadership of Alberto Bernabé, as well as his analysis of these materials, is an ongoing catalyst moving the trend away from a minimalist position.[147] It is precisely their doctrines that distinguish these Orphic texts from other writings.

Again, we cannot find an Orphic religion because the whole tenor of the shamanic enterprise is opposed to the official priesthood and poet-theologians. Private rather than public, its rituals were not external but internal: purification, contemplation, and mystical union. To advance from the Lesser to the Greater Mysteries, as it were, they sought out teachers and not temples. As Dodds points out, "Religious experience of the shamanistic type is individual, not collective."[148]

---

147. The bibliography of Bernabé's work is extensive. On the Gold Tablets, see Bernabé and Jiménez San Cristóbal, *Instructions for the Netherworld*. For the last century, Otto Kern's *Orphicorum fragmenta* has been the standard collection. Unless noted otherwise, all of my references to the fragments (hereafter OF) are from Bernabé Pajares and Romera, *Poetarum epicorum Graecorum*, 2.1:97–252 (fr. 90–359).

148. Dodds, *Greeks and the Irrational*, 141–42.

Chapter 2

Numenius and Plotinus described this mystical experience as "the flight of the alone to the Alone." To put it in Rouget's categories, the turn of Plato's Socrates from inspired poets (trance) to ecstatic philosophy (ecstasy) is not from revelation to reason, but from external authorities to inner intuition, from public religion to private spirituality—mystical, secret, and focusing not on the unity of the earthly polis but on the unity of the inmost self with the highest divinity.[149]

Orphic Myths: "Great Things in Riddles"

The opposite of modern connotations, in Hesiod's day the noun *logos* (from the verb *legein*) meant charming deceptive talk or idle chatter while the noun *mythos* (from the verb *mytheomai*) referred to truth conveyed through poets under divine inspiration.[150] By the sixth century, however, *mythos* came to mean false speech while *logos* came to mean true speech.[151] This false *mythos* was associated in particular with Homer and Hesiod. In reaction to such criticisms, Theagenes of Rhegium (late sixth century) explained away indecent passages by employing allegorical exegesis of Homer. He is generally considered to be the first to do so.

However, at the headwaters of Orphic writers, Pherecydes of Samos seems to have anticipated him by a generation.[152] In contrast with Theagenes, Pherecydes was not interested in the mere censorship of incest, murder, jealousy, and other

---

149. Rouget, *Music and Trance*, 5–12, especially the chart on page 11.

150. Lincoln, *Theorizing Myth*, 6–8. Lincoln points out that Hesiod typically uses the verb *legein* for deceptive talk and *mytheomai* for relating the truth, such as when he tells his brother Persus the truth: "I will tell [*mythēsaimēn*] real things." In Hesiod the myth is the truth, whereas words (*logoi*) are lies (4). Lincoln points out that Hesiod himself said that Hermes placed in Pandora's heart "falsehoods, seductive *logoi*, and a wily character" and even Zeus employed "plausible falsehoods" in his cunning triumph over Metis (10). He adds, "In Homer, *mythos* often denotes what it normally does in Hesiod: a blunt and aggressive act of candor, uttered by powerful males in the heat of battle or agonistic assembly" (17). In fact, this is true 93 percent of the time in the *Iliad* according to Martin, *Language of Heroes*, 22. Both Homer and Hesiod depict Hera deceiving Zeus quite frequently. Zeus notably deceives Agamemnon in a dream (*Il.* 2.1–40). And Hesiod himself says that the Muses only tell the truth when they choose (*Theog.* 27–28).

151. Heraclitus especially dismissed the Homeric myths and the popular religion associated with them, such as sacrificial rites and prayers to statues, as being "without any recognition of who gods and heroes really are." See Heraclitus, fr. 5; translation from Robinson, *Heraclitus*. Fragment from Aristocritus, *Theo.* 68 and Origen, *Cels.* 7.62. See also Lincoln, *Theorizing Myth*, 18. Clement says, "He complains that the procession in Dionysus' honor, where they even 'sing a hymn to the shameful parts,'" is a mere excuse for disorderly conduct, "But Hades and Dionysius, for whom they rave and celebrate the festival of the Lenaea, are one and the same!" See *Protr.* 22.2; 34.5, cited with Heraclitus, fr. 14 in Heralitus, *Fragments* (trans. Robinson).

152. Tate, "Beginnings of Greek Allegory," 214–15.

glaring problems. A completely new theological horizon, with new myths, was required, and this is echoed by a line of prominent writers with a clear Orphic affiliation. Like the soul, the real meaning must be released from the prison of the literal events in this world. The stories are *heard* but the truth is *seen*.

More than a century before Socrates, Xenophanes complained, "Homer and Hesiod attributed to the gods all the shameful things that are blameworthy among humans: stealing, committing adultery, and deceiving each other." He also said, "There is one god, . . . not at all like mortals in body, nor in mind," which could hardly accommodate a cast of divine characters who are exactly like mortals.[153] In the same period, Hecataeus says when opening his *Histories*, "For the stories of the Greeks, as they appear to me, are numerous and foolish," that is, nothing but human self-projections.[154] Pindar criticized these myths as well—again, out of respect for the gods.[155] It was not merely an episode here or there but myths in general had to be interpreted allegorically. The Orphic *hieros logos* (sacred story) reflects the growing criticism of traditional Homeric religion in its semantic reversal. After relating eccentric features of the Orphic-Pythagorean lifestyle, Herodotus adds, "They have a sacred story [*hieros logos*] which explains the reason for this."[156] For example, various reasons have been offered as to why Pythagoras forbade the eating of beans. But it was connected to Orphism, according to Pausanias. Demeter is the giver of grain, but he rebuffs those who attribute beans to the goddess. "Any one who has seen the mysteries at Eleusis, or has read what are called the works of Orpheus, knows what I mean."[157] "Seen" and "read" point up well the distinction between Eleusis and Orphism.

Despite learned efforts to reconstruct something like an original Ur-text, nearly all that we possess from classical Orphic literature is a patchwork quilt fashioned

---

153. Xenophanes, *Elegiacs* 1 (fr. B11–12 in Diels-Kranz ed.; cf. 13–24): "Not treating battles of the Titans or of the Giants, figments of predecessors [*plasmata tōn proterōn*], nor of violent civil war, in which tales there is nothing useful; but always to have respect for the gods, that is good." Translation of fragment from Freeman, *Pre-Socratic Philosophers*, 20. See also Lincoln, *Theorizing Myth*, 26–28.

154. Xenophanes, *Elegiacs* 15, in Freeman, *Pre-Socratic Philosophers*, 22. Thracians represent the gods with grey eyes and red hair, Ethiopians with black eyes and hair. The gods become a projection of ourselves. "But mortals believe the gods to be created by birth, and to have their own raiment, voice and body. But if oxen (and horses) and lions had hands or could draw with hands and create works of art like those made by men, horses would draw pictures of gods like horses, and oxen of gods like oxen, and they would make the bodies (of gods) in accordance with the form that each species possess." See also Snell, *Discovery of the Mind*, 143.

155. Lincoln, *Theorizing Myth*, 27.

156. Herodotus, *Hist.* 2.81. Translation by de Sélincourt, in Herodotus, *Histories*.

157. Pausanias, *Descr.* 1.37.3.

Chapter 2

by many hands over centuries. Scholars describe this as bricolage: using whatever is near at hand in a handyman sort of way.[158] Lacking an official canon, writers nevertheless recognized similar themes in other texts and freely molded them into their own version, which is also how the Epic Cycle that includes Homer's epics emerged.[159] Even when exploiting Hesiod's *Theogony*, Orphic myths engaged freely in reconstruction. For the most part, they are novel theogonies set in competition with Hesiod and with greater dependency on Middle Eastern and Egyptian inspiration.

Like the earlier epic form, Orphic myths represent a *hieros logos*, but instead of justifying certain rituals they lead beginners in a "riddling" way to metaphysical truth. At first one accepts the myths as they stand, merely on authority, until they discover how to behold the truth itself and for themselves. This spiritual pedagogy is what philosophy offers. The reflective, analytical, philosophical distillation of myths and rites is the hallmark of Orphism.

There were numerous theogonies associated by ancients with the Orphic ambiance. However, we have only fragments and testimonies from the fifth century BCE to the fifth century CE. Besides the Eudemian theogony (named after Aristotle's pupil who summarized it), the Hieronyman (or Hieronymus-Hellanicus) and Rhapsodic theogonies reflect distinctive accents. These latter two theogonies reflect the ongoing bricolage of Hellenistic Stoicism and Roman Neoplatonism, respectively, but the *hieros logos* of both theogonies has layers that go back probably to the fifth century BCE.[160]

However, in 1962 a carbonized roll was discovered on the funeral pyre of an Orphic initiate in modern Derveni, Thessaloniki. Only published as a whole in 2006, the Derveni Papyrus is Europe's oldest surviving text and perhaps the oldest Greek manuscript found anywhere.[161] It has aroused considerable discussion and debate since its discovery. UNESCO summarizes well its significance:

---

158. Based on Lévi-Strauss, *Savage Mind*, 16–36. The metaphor is used across the spectrum of specialists, from maximalists to minimalists, and is emphasized especially throughout Meisner's *Orphic Tradition*. While initially illuminating, its value fades to the extent that bricolage is seen as distinctive to Orphism. Virtually everything that has come to us from the ancient world may be described in similar terms.

159. We have hints of the same phenomenon of bricolage in the Epic Cycle with the same stories as Homer's being given rather different renditions. Not even the *Iliad* and *Odyssey* as we have them are purely the product of the blind poet called Homer but have passed through many editorial hands. Raising again the question of a real-life "Homer," Barbara Graziosi's *Inventing Homer* is meticulous if controversial at points.

160. I discuss this further in the following chapter.

161. Gábor Betegh describes the challenging process from discovery to publication in *Derveni Papyrus*, 56–73.

The Derveni Papyrus is of immense importance not only for the study of Greek religion and philosophy, which is the basis for the western philosophical thought, but also because it serves as a proof of the early dating of the Orphic poems offering a distinctive version of Presocratic philosophers. The text of the Papyrus, which is the first book of western tradition, has a global significance, since it reflects universal human values: the need to explain the world, the desire to belong to a human society with known rules and the agony to confront the end of life.[162]

The work is a commentary on an early fifth century BCE or older theogony, dubbed the Protogonos theogony because its central character is the firstborn (*prōtogonos*) god, Phanes.[163] Its twenty-two reconstructed columns preserve much of this fourth-century commentary on a fifth-century poem.[164] The first surviving columns pertain to ritual practices, sacrifices to the Erinyes, removing daimons, and beliefs of Persian magi with quotations of Heraclitus and Parmenides.[165] The Derveni commentary is eclectic, reflecting Anaxagoras's theory of Mind as the efficient cause of all but also quoting Heraclitus, Parmenides, and Diogenes of Apollonia.[166]

Analogous to the graduation from the Lesser to the Higher Mysteries of Eleusis, instruction in theology was essential as a propaedeutic to the experience of mystical union.[167] The *hieros logos* of the Orphic Rhapsodies, for example, relates what Orpheus saw when he was searching for his wife/mother in Hades, offering a guide for the initiate's successful passage that includes passwords for Persephone.

---

162. UNESCO, "Derveni Papyrus."

163. Kirk, Raven, and Schofield argue it may be earlier than the fifth century in *Presocratic Philosophers*, 30–31.

164. Richard Janko produced an interim text in 2002; see "Derveni Papyrus: An Interim Text"; Betegh, *Derveni Papyrus*. With the assistance of infrared photographs by Makis Skiadaressis, an improved copy appeared in 2006 in Tsantsanoglou, Parássoglou, and Kouremenos, *Derveni Papyrus*. See also Kotwick, *Der Papyrus von Derveni*, based on Janko's improved text.

165. See P. Derveni 7 in Betegh, *Derveni Papyrus*, 17.

166. Although this is easily conformed to Orphic beliefs (and likely shaped by them), it is Epimenides who adds the characteristically Orphic eschatological orientation. Bremmer thinks the *Theogony* on which the Derveni commentary is based was produced in southern Italy under the influence of Parmenides. Bremmer, *Initiation in the Mysteries*, 62. Bernabé, "Derveni Theogony." Cf. Laks and Most, *Studies on the Derveni Papyrus*. Janko, "Derveni Papyrus: An Interim Text," 1–62, points up the reference to Parmenides, which is not apparent in Betegh's version. See also Bernabé Pajares and Romera, *Poetarum epicorum Graecorum*, 2.1:97–252 (fr. 90–359).

167. *Heiros logos*, "sacred discourse," identifies inspired speech particularly in Orphism; it is a figure of speech that Plato uses several times, as we will see in context.

Chapter 2

THE SHAMAN BECOMES A SAGE

Bronze Age myths differed significantly from Indo-European myths, yet this shift too happened across many civilizations. For example, the cosmogonic analogies of fire overcoming the storm-god, chariots versus footmen and horses, bronze versus stone, indicate important changes.[168] The shift from the Bronze Age warrior-king to "the divine self" as utopian hero had an even greater long-term impact. Indra becomes Shiva; through Dionysus, Zeus assumes a demiurgic role absent from Homer and Hesiod. Allegorical interpretation is the hermeneutical corollary of Orphic anthropology. Like the body and everything else known by physical senses, the outer meaning of a myth must be cast away as the soul ascends to its inner truth. Remaining prisoners of the body, the uninitiated "many" are unqualified for the ascent of the initiated "few." The hierophant began the Greater Mysteries by commanding the doors to be shut; Orphic writers use this to instruct the uninitiated to close their ears. The author of the Derveni Papyrus explains:

> [Orpheus's] poetry is something strange and riddling for people. But Orpheus did not intend to tell them capatious riddles, but momentous things in riddles. Indeed, he is telling a holy discourse [*hieros logos*] from the first and up to his last word. As he also makes clear in the well-chosen verse, for having ordered them to put doors to their ears he says that he is [not legislating] for the many [?] . . . [?] [But only for] those pure in hearing. (P. Derveni 7)[169]

There is a public meaning of Homer's myths, but a private one for "the true mystics," says Plato, "by which I mean—the philosophers" (*Phaed.* 69c).[170] Not only did

---

168. It is helpful to read West's *Indo-European Poetry and Myth* alongside Anthony's *Horse, the Wheel, and Language.*

169. Translation by Betegh, *Derveni Papyrus,* 17.

170. Plato refers to the "Hymns of Orpheus" (*Leg.* 829d–e). This could not have been the Orphic Hymns known to us since this was a Hellenistic composition. In any case, *all* theological (which included philosophical) writing was composed in hexameter verse, as poetry was the mark of divine inspiration. Some hymns (or at least earlier layers) may have been from the classical era. For excellent summaries of the dating and context see Athanassakis and Wolkow, *Orphic Hymns,* x–xxi; West, *Orphic Poems,* 1–38. Some scholars include among Orphic theogonies the mid-third century BCE Gurôb Papyrus; see Bernabé and Jiménez San Cristóbal, "Orphic Papyrological Tradition." However, this text seems to belong to the Dionysian cult or perhaps the Eleusinian mysteries. Besides the invocation of Dionysus by his distinctive epithets, the most conspicuous mark of this provenance is the mention of sacrificing raw flesh for "ancient crimes." It is also closer to the Greek Magical Papyri than to the usual Orphic themes. Bernabé

ancient Greeks equate philosophy and mysticism; they were quite certain that the former was the offspring of the latter. Indeed, before Plato the distinction would not have made much sense. After all, the highest vocations—those of hierophant, poet-theologian, and lawgiver—were guided by divine inspiration. It was the aim of Socrates and especially of Plato to claim all three for true philosophers.

The partisans of allegorizing latched onto Orpheus, distilling doctrines from myths and physical rituals. Philosophers considered the Bacchic-Orphic cults to be mired still in the ritualistic world of the archaic age, a childhood of authority. They needed to follow Orpheus in translating Dionysian sensuality into Apollonian reason. Yet such reason was imbued with mythology and mysticism. Gold plates and bone tablets are still being discovered along the path from the Black Sea near ancient Thrace southward through Macedonia all the way to Greek colonies of southern Italy where Pythagoras and Parmenides were active.[171] This geographical trail, I believe, aligns with the historical development of a mystery cult into philosophy. That many of these gold tablets were discovered in the area of Pythagoras's activity is evidence of the school's Orphic affinities. Yet it was in Orphism's genes to gradually transcend cultic ritualism as it was tied to the body, the visible world, and the external meaning of nature and texts. Pythagoras may be as close as we come to the real-life Orpheus.

It is a false dilemma therefore to classify these texts as either Pythagorean or Orphic; they are integrally related. Pythagoras was not the originator, his teacher Pherecydes of Syros having introduced these doctrines for the first time in written form, but he is the most identifiable figure who transformed the shaman into a sage. If we had more of his work, I am confident we would be talking more about Pherecydes than Pythagoras as a father of Western thought. His constant presence in the drafting of minor Homeric divinities into the Orphic ambit is noted frequently throughout Gantz's *Early Greek Myth*. The Orphic poems, Physika and Hieros Logos, also reflect Pythagorean thought and are often attributed to Pythagoras.[172] Meisner observes that Orphic theogonies "were a means by which Orphic poets asked questions about their universe, often addressing the same concerns

---

tends to assimilate the Dionysian cult to Orphism, but the two developed independently; the prohibition of animal sacrifice (or consumption) is a *sine qua non* of the latter. Parts of the Rhapsodic theogony appear to be much earlier than the version summarized by Damascius. On this widely disputed question, see West, *Orphic Poems*, 250–511; Edmonds, *Redefining Ancient Orphism*, 45; Jones, "Orphic Cosmo-Theogony"; Jourdan, *Orphée et les chrétiens*, 2:101, 291–94, 318; Bernabé, "La teogonía órfica citada."

    171. Shellie A. Smith summarizes many of these finds very well in "Identifying an Archetype."
    172. West, *Orphic Hymns*, 13.

as contemporary philosophers."[173] These first works of Greek science and metaphysics were embedded in hymns.[174]

As we discussed in the introduction, through the seventh century shaman-like figures appear on the Greek Ionian (i.e., Turkish) coast, where the first inklings of Presocratic philosophy emerged. We meet Terpander, associated with Orpheus, who is the founder of classical Greek music, sent from Lesbos to Sparta on a purification mission through musical therapy.[175] One of his followers, Thaletas of Gortyn, was a pupil of Onomacritus the editor of Orphic oracles, and he delivered Sparta from a plague around 670 BCE.[176] The soul of Hermotimus of Clazomenae went on nocturnal journeys while his body was in a trance.[177] According to Aristotle, he formulated the dualistic theory of mind over matter before Anaxagoras and Parmenides.[178] The seventh-century healer Aristeas from Procennesus (a Greek colony in Asia Minor) converted himself into a raven at will to accompany Apollo and could die and reawaken at different times and places.[179]

It is significant that all of these figures come from the north, Scythia and Thrace, where shamanism was still a living tradition. As Herodotus describes, it was a region distinguished by belief in the immortality of the soul and transmigration (*Hist.* 4.93–94). They observe "a triennial festival, with the appropriate revelry, . . . held in honour of Dionysus" (4.108). There are sacred tents thick with hemp-smoke (4.74–75) and cauldrons ready to receive meat dismembered, boiled, and eaten (4.59–61). It was here where Heracles was seduced by the snake-woman to bear the founder of Scythia, where Dionysus destroyed his cousin to establish his cult, and where the royal heir Scylas was executed by his kinsmen for being "initiated into the mysteries of Dionysus," since "no Scythian can see sense in imagining a god who drives people out of their wits" (4.79). It is here the land where the popular disappearing-reappearing shaman Aristeas achieved fame in Greece (4.13–15). It is also where Orpheus of Thrace launched his career, perhaps through Pythagoras's former slave (4.95–96).

---

173. Meisner, *Orphic Tradition*, 43.
174. Meisner, *Orphic Tradition*, 39–43.
175. A helpful survey of Terpander's biography is found in Reese, *Music in the Middle Ages*, 11. On his musical therapy see Power, *Culture of Kitharôidia*.
176. Burkert, *Orientalizing Revolution*, 42–43.
177. West, *Orphic Poems*, 149.
178. Preus, *Historical Dictionary of Greek Philosophy*, 190, citing Aristotle, *Metaph.* 984b20. Supporting Aristotle's description is Sextus Empiricus, *Math.* 9.1.7. On the Pythagorean connection see Lucian, *Musc. laud.* 7 and Diogenes Laertius, *Vit. phil.* 8.
179. Herodotus, *Hist.* 4.13–15.

Beginning with Pherecydes of Samos in the early sixth century, we discern a misty trail of shaman-sages. Ancients considered him a wonderworking, cave-dwelling healer, and also the first to introduce Orphic theogonies and doctrines, especially the soul's immortality and transmigration. Aristotle praised him as the first Greek thinker to produce a systematic examination of the world.[180]

Epimenides, around the same time, is another figure clearly at the center of Athenian shamanism, philosophy, and democracy. As the story goes, he wandered into a cave where he slept for fifty-seven years and returned many decades later, aware now of his status as a "divine man" (*theios anēr*). "So he became famous throughout Greece, and was believed to be a special favourite of heaven.... Some writers say that the Cretans sacrifice to him as a god; for they say that he had superhuman foresight," warning Athenians of future dangers, "and that he claimed that his soul had passed through many incarnations" (Diogenes Laertius, *Vit. phil.* 1.109, 114). Though mostly lost to us, ancients possessed his *On the Birth of the Kouretes and Korybantes* and a *Theogony*. "He is stated to have been the first who purified houses and fields, and the first who founded temples. Some are found to maintain that he did not go to sleep but withdrew himself for a while, engaged in gathering simples" (1.112). Solon sent a ship to bring him to Athens to purify the city, and the plague was lifted (1.109).[181] It was simultaneously a political moment for Epimenides's defense of liberty.[182]

Poets, theologians, philosophers, lawgivers: shamanic sages were establishing monastic-like communities beyond the reach of tyranny and violence. Diogenes Laertius adduced a letter from Epimenides to Solon that decries "the enslavement of citizens" and the plague of tyrants. "For it is hard to contrive that men brought up as free men under the best laws should be slaved. But instead of going on your travels, come quietly to Crete to me; for here you will have no monarchy to fear" (*Vit. phil.* 1.113). More than just a representative of the early Greek shaman, Epimenides was a Pythagorean and Orphic actor at the intersection of mysteries,

---

180. Aristotle, *Metaph.* 1091a29–b12. More generally, see Schibli, *Pherecydes of Syros*, and Granger, "Theologian *Pherekydes of Syros*."

181. Arriving in Athens in the forty-sixth Olympiad (595–592 BCE), "He stopped the pestilence in the following way. He took sheep, some black and others white, and brought them to the Areopagus; and there he let them go whither they pleased, instructing those who followed them to mark the spot where each sheep lay down and offer a sacrifice to the local divinity. And thus, it is said, the plague was stayed." See Diogenes Laertius, *Vit. phil.* 1.110. Translation unless otherwise noted is from *Lives of Eminent Philosophers* (trans. Hicks). St. Paul alludes to Epimenides in Titus 1:12 when he states, "all Cretans are liars," but quotes him directly in Acts 17:28: "for 'In him we live and move and have our being'; as even some of your own poets have said, 'For we are indeed his offspring.'"

182. On the historical context of Epimenides's arrival and claims, see especially Duplouy, *Construire la Cité*. See also Kingsley and Parry, "Empedocles."

dramatic theater, and politics.[183] As difficult as it may be for modern westerners to swallow, Epimenides the Orphic cult-leader was a major catalyst of the Greek enlightenment.

Admittedly, the historical Pythagoras is only a little less encrusted with legends, but fact and fiction converge in the image of a shamanic sage. After his Egyptian experience and being initiated into the mysteries by Epimenides in the Cave of Zeus, Pythagoras came to believe that he was Hermes's son and his father told him he could have any wish but immortality. To remember his past lives was Pythagoras's request (*Vit. phil.* 8.3–4). He recalled his transmigrations through human heroes, animals and even plants (8.5). We have no extant record of any writings from Pythagoras, but Diogenes Laertius claims *On the Mysteries* and, "According to Ion of Chios in his *Triagmi* he ascribed some poems to his own making to Orpheus" (8.8).

The legends that grew up around Pythagoras involve distinctively shamanic features. Pythagoras was confronted by Abaris the Hyperborean, a Scythian or Mongolian shaman mentioned above, and "identified him as the god [Apollo] of whom he [Abaris] was the priest." According to Iamblichus, he even gave Pythagoras the magic arrow on which he traveled great distances, and in response Pythagoras certified the truth of Abaris's recognition of his divine identity (*Vit. Pyth.* 19).[184] Pythagoras communicated with animals (*Vit. Pyth.* 13).[185] He traveled great distances and spoke in different cities at the same time (28). He healed by his music and lived many interesting lives (14–15).[186] West observes, "Pythagoras too, perhaps from an early date, was said to have descended to Hades and returned."[187] As for shamanic credentials, there is hardly a box he does not tick. Herodotus identified him as "Orphic and Bacchic."[188] Pythagoras favored political democ-

---

183. Duplouy, "Epimenides the Cretan." See also Burkert, *Orientalizing Revolution*, 63. Aeschylus, *Sept.* 800; Herodotus, *Hist.* 6.57.2.

184. Unless otherwise noted, translation of Iamblichus's *Life of Pythagoras* from Guthrie, *Pythagorean Sourcebook and Library*, 80. This legend probably goes back to Aristotle according to Burkert, *Lore and Science*, 143. Cf. Griffiths, "Abaris," 1. See Herodotus, *Hist.* 4.36.1–2; Pausanias, *Descr.* 9.10; Strabo, *Geogr.* 7.3.8; Nonnus, *Dion.* 11.132.

185. A bear that injured inhabitants was so soothed by the philosopher's teaching, we are told, that it swore an oath not to disturb the city. Similar stories are told of conversations with an ox and birds, including an eagle he drew down for company; see Guthrie, *Pythagorean Sourcebook and Library*, 71.

186. He had once been Euphorbus, a Trojan War hero in Homer, *Il.* 17.81, as well as Hemotimus of Clazomenae!

187. West, *Orphic Poems*, 12; Burkert, *Lore and Science*, 155–61.

188. Herodotus, *Hist.* 2.81.1–2. See also Meisner, *Orphic Tradition*, 115, citing Plato, *Leg.* 782c–d; cf. Aristotle, fr. 195 and 191, and Diodorus Siculus, *Bib. hist.* 1.92.2; 1.96.3–5.

racy, but like Dionysus refused to allow his thriving community (indeed, cult) of Kronos to be absorbed into any polis. At some point, following Thales's advice and example, Pythagoras spent time in Egypt with the priests, who gave him access to the temples and their libraries, a rare privilege for foreigners. Drawing on earlier sources, Porphyry says that he became a priest of the Temple of Diospolis in Egypt (Porphyry, *Vit. Pyth.* 18–19). Instructed by Pherecydes, Thales, and Anaximander, Pythagoras formed the first actual school of Greek philosophy in the sixth and early fifth centuries.[189]

About a half-century older than Pythagoras, Parmenides formed a school in a nearby Greek colony of Elea. We will have an occasion to investigate his controversial poem.[190] For now, though, it is sufficient to observe that he too was in the line of shaman-sages and was at least initially a Pythagorean. We now know that he was associated with "a cult of priest-healers (iatromantis) of Apollo who practiced incubation, usually in caves, in order to receive wisdom and truth." Reason by itself is insufficient but must be "accompanied by divine inspiration and metis (cunning wisdom)."[191] In Homer, the god of healing is Paieon, but by the time of the tragedians "the two figures have fused" and Apollo is "one who sends plagues [and] he is also the one who can halt them."[192] In Orphic hands, the god of prophecy is given a shamanic character. Yulia Ustinova has discovered over forty caves associated with the cult of Apollo Oulios—Apollo the Healer—into which priests descended to receive oracles.[193] This was clearly an alternative to the oracle of Delphi. Strabo refers to shrines in Anatolia near Dionysus's childhood Nysa with a charonium, a cave, "above the sacred precinct" of the Plutonium with its shrine of Hades and Persephone,

> by nature wonderful; for they say that those who are diseased and give heed to the cures prescribed by these gods [Hades and Persephone] resort thither and live in the village near the cave among experienced priests, who on their

---

189. This according to Plato, *Soph.* 242c–d, and Aristotle, *Metaph.* 986b18–27. I return to Pherecydes in another chapter. Dubbed by ancients "the first theologian," he was the first Greek to teach reincarnation.

190. The only thing we have from him is the superb and nearly complete transcription by Simplicius of the poem's first half on the way of truth versus falsehood. Of the second half (on cosmology) we have fifty-four fragments and a number of testimonies. See "A-Fragments" under the Parmenides section of Diels and Kranz, *Die Fragmente der Vorsokratiker*. A more comprehensive collection is found in Coxon, *Fragments of Parmenides*, 99–267, and the "D" section of Laks and Most, *Western Greek Thinkers*, part 2, ch. 19 (Parmenides).

191. Rickert, "Parmenidean Ontological Enaction," 472.

192. Gantz, *Early Greek Myth*, 1:95–96.

193. Ustinova, *Caves*, noting that several are dedicated to Apollo (53–54).

behalf sleep in the cave and through dreams prescribe the cures. These are also the men who invoke the healing power of the gods [*theôn iatreian*]. And they often bring the sick into the cave and leave them there, to remain in stillness [*hêsychia*], like animals in their lair [*phôleos*], without food for many days. And sometimes the sick give heed to dreams of their own, but still they use those other men, as priests, to initiate them into the mysteries and counsel them. To all others the place is forbidden and deadly.[194]

In 1958, while excavating an ancient medical compound in Velia (Roman Elea), archeologists discovered a first-century CE sculpture of a man with the inscription "Oulis son of Euxinus of Hyele [Elea] *iatros pholarchos* in the 379th year."[195] Two others with the same inscription were discovered: one for the year 280 and another for 446. In his description above, Strabo calls an incubating priest "*pholarchos*," meaning those who lie down in a cave like an animal in its lair. Thus, Ustinova concludes, there was a flourishing tradition of "incubating priests" in Elea since at least the fifth century BCE.[196] Moreover, Parmenides is one such priest, as a bust was discovered above an incubation chamber (cryptoporticus) with the inscription "Parmenides son of Pyres *Ouliadēs physikos*," physician or physicist.[197] "He would lie down in a cave, like Epimenides and Orpheus before him, and incubate," says Rickert, "and with his visions came wisdom."[198]

In this light, his poem may be seen as a "performative text," argues Rickert. Speaking in the dactylic hexameter of inspired verse, he relates a vision he received in the Cave of Night. Rickert says, "Aspects of Parmenides' poem directly invoke shamanistic practices," such as the feeling of "rush," "yawning abyss," "sounds of piping [*syrinx*] from the spinning of the chariot's axles ... and the grand doors opening. ... Taken together, these images and sensations evoke the embodied sensation of incubation." During the absolute stillness of incubation, cave-dwelling priests of Apollo became "'sky-walkers' [*aithrobates*] like Abaris Skywalker who delivered an arrow to Pythagoras." Parmenides's immensely formative poem therefore was not chiefly a reflection on but an enactment of the meaning of reality: the healing of the soul.[199] As Eliade reminds us, "The principal function of the shaman in Central and North Asia is magical healing."[200] However one interprets

---

194. Strabo, *Geogr.* 14.1.44; see Rickert, "Parmenidean Ontological Enaction," 482–84.
195. Ustinova, *Caves*, 192.
196. Ustinova, *Caves*, 197.
197. Ustinova, *Caves*, 192.
198. Rickert, "Parmenidean Ontological Enaction," 483.
199. Rickert, "Parmenidean Ontological Enaction," 485–86.
200. Eliade, *Shamanism*, 215.

his revelation from Night, Parmenides can hardly be considered the turning point from mythology and religion to metaphysics and reason. A final comparison with the trail of Orphic shaman-sages is that Parmenides is the lawgiver of Elea, just as Epimenides and Pythagoras had been of their communes.[201]

A similar pose is struck by Empedocles from Greek Sicily, active in the middle of the fifth century, and the last philosopher to write in verse. Diogenes Laertius tells us that he was a pupil, along with Zeno, of Parmenides, but then became a student of Anaxagoras and the Pythagorean school, revering Pythagoras as "a man of superhuman knowledge" (*Vit. phil.* 8.54–56). Empedocles's identification of the four elements (earth, air, water, and fire) and evolution through the interaction of Strife (separation) and Love (recombination) provoked enduring debates (Aristotle mentioning him more often than anyone else except for Plato). Yet he was chiefly "a preacher of the new religion which sought to secure release from the 'wheel of birth' by purity and abstinence. Orphism seems to have been strong at Akragas in the days of Theron, and there are even some verbal coincidences between the poems of Empedokles and the Orphicising Odes which Pindar addressed to that prince."[202] Discoursing at length on reincarnation, he professes, "For by now I have been born as boy, girl, plant, bird, and dumb sea-fish."[203] A political reformer, "he declined the kingship when it was offered to him" because "Empedocles favoured democracy" (*Vit. phil.* 8.64). Yet he appeared in city after city as a rock-star deity akin to Dionysus's profile, wearing gold robes with purple ribbons, bronze shoes, and a laurel wreath for a crown (8.70).[204] Addressing his poems to his fellow citizens of Acragas, he declared:

> I go about you as an immortal god, no longer mortal, held in honour by all, as I seem, crowned with fillets and flowing garlands. When I come to them in their flourishing towns, to men and women, I am honoured; and they follow me in thousands, to inquire where is the path of advantage, some desiring oracles,

---

201. Speusippus appears to be the first testimony to Parmenides as lawgiver (fr. 1, in Diogenes Laertius, *Vit. phil.* 9.23; cf. Strabo, *Geogr.* 6.1.1; and Plutarch, *Adv. Colot.* 1126a.
202. Burnet, *Early Greek Philosophy*, 199.
203. Empedocles fr. 117.
204. Diogenes Laertius says at this place, "Diodorus of Ephesus, when writing of Anaximander, declares that Empedocles emulated him, displaying theatrical arrogance and wearing stately robes." See also McEvilley, *Shape of Ancient Thought*, 67: "He is credited in late sources with accomplishments such as controlling the wind (D. L. VIII.60), raising the dead and, like Orpheus, soothing violent passions by playing the lyre (Iambl. *Vit. Pyth.* 113). Heraclides Ponticus relates that Empedocles revived a woman who had been in a trance without pulse or respiration for thirty days (D. L. VIII.60–61, 67)."

while others ask to hear a word of healing for their manifold diseases, since they have long been pierced with cruel pains.[205]

In one account, after Empedocles purified them from a plague, the crowd "rose up and worshipped and prayed to him as to a god" (Diogenes Laertius, *Vit. phil.* 8.71). In another episode, after offering a sacrifice and enjoying the feast, Empedocles remained alone at the table as if in a trance, but in the morning his friends could not find him. After a vision of light, his friend and physician Pausanias "bade them to take no further trouble, for things beyond expectation had happened to him, and it was their duty to sacrifice to him since he was now a god" (8.68). Aristotle acclaimed him the inventor of rhetoric and a pioneer of physical science, while crediting reports of his miracles (8.57).[206] He was a physician and philosopher, yet he also had a good deal of "the medicine man" about him.[207] Gorgias, the Sophist after whom a Platonic dialogue is named, claimed that "he himself was present when Empedocles performed magical feats," and Heraclides called him not merely a physician but "a diviner [*iētron kai mantin*] as well" (2.375). To see these as contradictions is to project our own modern dichotomies. No more than his Orphic predecessors is Empedocles a paradox in his historical context.

The close connection between philosophy and medicine is evident in Empedocles's claim that from his philosophy "you shall learn all the drugs [*pharmaka*] that exist as a defence against illness and old age; for you alone will I accomplish all this." His votaries will control wind and rain. "And you shall bring out of Hades a dead man restored to strength."[208] Anyone can be a shaman by learning the techniques of ecstasy, especially secrecy and silence. And this belief is evident in the paradoxical view of an immortal soul as the mediator between the divine One and the human Many. McEvilley summarizes it well: "The soul, insofar as it is One with Mind is god; insofar as it is lower embodied Soul it is a daimon—Empedocles' term for the fallen Orphic god. Plotinus preserves not only the Empedoclean-Orphic tone but, at times, the tone of the Egyptian *Book of the Dead* which lay behind it: 'Becoming man, he has ceased to be the All; ceasing to be man ... he soars aloft and administers the Cosmos entire; restored to the All, he is the maker of the All' (*Enn.* V.8.7)."[209]

Behind this conception that will come to dominate Western consciousness is the Orphic myth enshrined laconically on the gold foils and bone tablets described above. "Clearly the myth in which Empedocles presents himself is the

---

205. Empedocles, fr. 112. Translaton in Freeman, *Ancilla to the Pre-Socratic Philosophers*, 64.
206. See also Kingsley and Parry, "Empedocles."
207. Burnet, *Early Greek Philosophy*, 199.
208. Empedocles fr. 111.
209. McEvilley, *Ancient Thought*, 563.

same in outline as that intimated by the gold plates."[210] Even after describing classical Athens emerging from superstition to become the enlightened "city of reason," Vernant acknowledges Epimenides as the "very model of the inspired shaman."[211] However, McEvilley is closer when he concludes that "of all the pre-Socratics he has been reported as the most perfect example of the cultural transition from shamanic to philosophical activities."[212]

Conclusion

Reflecting the utopian revolution, this phenomenon we're calling Orphic is more mystical, philosophical, and spiritual than the public religion of the locative environment. On its own terms more of an essence than an institution, it could not be contained in any single sect or school. Edmonds is correct to point out that Orphic literature is bricolage, with each writer reaching for whatever materials were near at hand that jibed with their own speculations.[213] Each contributed to an evolving tradition that nevertheless appealed not to tradition but to the immediate authority of private revelation.[214] As Edmonds suggests, "the ancient label Orphic was more like the contemporary term 'new age,' which is associated, not specifically with particular religious ideas or organizations, but more vaguely with a set of ideas loosely defined by their distance from mainstream religious activity, especially by claims to extra-ordinary purity, sanctity, or divine authority."[215] Yet Orphism names a phenomenon that is both more coherent in doctrinal commitments and more mainstream than minimalists contend. The question is not whether there are much later embellishments but whether there is a living tradition to which they could recognizably belong. From the sixth century BCE onward, Greeks knew what "Orphic" connoted. It is *only* the doctrines that distinguish Orphic writings.

Where does "Orphism" come from? Herodotus was sure it came from Egypt, as he thought regarding all Greek mythology. Different gods were worshiped in differ-

---

210. McEvilley, *Ancient Thought*, 107, adding, "Empedocles' association with Orphism became so strong that at some time his second poem, which Aristotle knows by another title (*Rhet.* 1373b14), was renamed *Katharmoi* ('Purifications'), a title that Plato used for Orphic rites and books (*Rep.* 364e)."
211. Vernant, *Origins of Greek Thought*, 70.
212. McEvilley, *Ancient Thought*, 67.
213. Edmonds, *Redefining Ancient Orphism*, 6.
214. Edmonds, *Redefining Ancient Orphism*, 4: "As Redfield has pointed out, to connect the name of Orpheus to a story or ritual is 'to bypass tradition and claim (as it were) a fresh revelation,' the claim to the authority ... of a specially privileged individual."
215. Edmonds, *Redefining Ancient Orphism*, 4, quoting Redfield, "Politics of Immortality," 106.

Chapter 2

ent centers—"the only two to be universally worshipped are Isis and Osiris, who, they say, is Dionysus" (*Hist.* 2.42). Indeed, Dionysus was given his own festival in Egypt.[216] Herodotus speculates that Melampus, mentioned by Homer as the progenitor of a great lineage of magician-seers (*Od.* 15.223–242), learned his art from Egyptian priests just as had Pythagoras a few centuries later.[217] However, scholars continue to debate over whether Pythagoras first brought Orphic doctrines like transmigration to the Greeks, as Herodotus maintains.[218]

On the other hand, Herodotus himself offers conflicting evidence. On the one hand, as already observed, he discerns clear connections between Pythagoras and the Thracian Orpheus. He connects Dionysus with Thracian and Scythian tribes in the north, bordering Apollo's legendary winter home of Hyperborea. It is the land of magic, the land of shamans like Aristeas, who accompanied Apollo in the form of a raven and would die and later appear somewhere else (*Hist.* 4.13–15). It is the land of the Neuri who "practice magic," and "once a year every Neurian turns into a wolf for a few days, and then turns back into a man again." Even more savage are the Androphagi, "Man-eaters," who have "no notion of either law or justice" (4.105–106). The Scythians offer a sacrifice without any fire. "As soon as the animal is strangled, he is skinned, and then comes the boiling of the flesh" (4.60). And in the ceremonies of Scythians and Thracians hemp smoke fills the tent (4.75). The

---

216. Herodotus, *Hist.* 2.42, 145–146, 156. There is no choral dance. "Instead of the phallus they have puppets, about eighteen inches high; the genitals of these figures are made almost as big as the rest of their bodies, and they are pulled up and down by strings as the women carry them round the villages. . . . Flutes lead the procession, and the women as they follow sing a hymn to Dionysus" (2.48–50).

217. Herodotus, *Hist.* 2.48–50. He adds, "I will never admit that the similar ceremonies performed in Greece and Egypt are the result of mere coincidence—had that been so, Greek rites would have been more Greek in character and less recent in origin. Nor will I allow that the Egyptians ever took over from Greece either this custom or any other." See also Kampakoglou, "Melampus in Callimachus and Hesiod."

218. In the notes of Herodotus, *Histories* (trans. de Sélincourt), John Marincola comments on this passage: "The unnamed writers are the Pythagoreans and the Orphics, who probably did not owe their doctrine of transmigration of souls to the Egyptians" (641 n. 67). In Egyptian eschatology there is one final judgment by Osiris and his assayers, weighing one's works, and this determines one's fate. Rebirth is not being born in another earthly body but the complete liberation of the *ahk* (glorified spirit) in bliss or annihilation. See Assmann, *Death and Salvation*, 173, 404–5. Another birthplace, suggested by Carl Kerényi, is the Minoan civilization on the island of Crete; see Kerényi, *Dionysos*, 4–50. However, this culture disappeared during the Greek Dark Age around 1100 BCE and the parallels seem unconvincing. However, Crete was situated between the Anatolian coast, Egypt and Attica. Flourishing in the sixth century BCE as a major trading center, it could well have facilitated the path of Dionysus (along with Cybele and Demeter) into Athens.

familiar episode of the tragedians, of Dionysus being at first rejected along his path, is related by Herodotus in the story told by Greek colonists.[219]

Thrace is especially central in the legends of Dionysus and Orpheus. Thrace is located midway on the trade route of Phoenicians from Asia to Greece, and Demeter and Dionysus followed the same track. Like the founder of the Eleusinian mysteries, Orpheus was Thracian.[220] In fact, "After Orpheus succeeded in making peace between Apollo and Dionysus, they became one and the same god in the Thracian mind."[221] Dionysus can be connected to Egypt and Phrygia as well as Greece. However, as West notes, Thrace, "Orpheus' country," has no place in Hesiod's genealogy of the gods. "He stands outside the Mycenaean world ... who can exercise power over the natural world and who can countermand death itself, a 'shamanistic' figure. He entered Greek mythology, surely, not by way of Mycenaean saga but at a later period from Thrace, or through Thrace from further north, from regions where shamanistic practices actually existed or had existed."[222]

Amid layers of legend there are actual disciples who are creating sacred stories to justify their circle of shaman-sages. "To the Thracians," relate Fol and Marazov, "the souls of the dead were not pale shadows in Hades." Death was welcomed and suicide was even respected.[223] The Thracians, Herodotus relates, were the last people Darius subdued before he reached the Danube. The Getae tribe in particular "believe that they never die. . . . The belief of these people in their immortality takes the following form: they never really die, but every man, when he takes leave of this present life, goes to join Zalmoxis, a divine being who also called by some of them Gebeleizis" (*Hist.* 4.93–94).[224]

Just at this point Herodotus adds a very important twist. According to the report of "the Greeks who live on the Hellespont and the Black Sea," this Zalmoxis was actually a Thracian who had been a slave in Pythagoras's household.

---

219. Scylas the Scythian king happened upon a Greek colony and decided to be "initiated into the mysteries of Dionysus." Such rites appalled the Scythians: "when the Schythians saw their king in the grip of the Bacchic frenzy," they reported it back home. When he heard a rebellion was afoot, Scylas "fled the country and took refuge in Thrace" but was eventually beheaded (4.78–80).
220. Fol and Marazov, *Thrace and the Thracians*, 27.
221. Fol and Marazov, *Thrace and the Thracians*, 32.
222. West, *Orphic Poems*, 4.
223. Fol and Marazov, *Thrace and the Thracians*, 34–35.
224. Considering him a model shaman from his own Romanian heritage, Mircea Eliade offered the fullest treatment of Zalmoxis/Gebeleizis. See Eliade, *Zalmoxis*. He also founded a journal called *Zalmoxis*. Eliade and Trask, "Zalmoxis." Cf. Drugaş, "Name of Zalmoxis." However, as is usually the case, etymological theories result in more questions than answers.

Amassing a fortune after his release, Zalmoxis returned to teach immortality and reincarnation to his people.

> All the time that he was trying to promulgate this new doctrine, he was occupied in the construction of an underground chamber, and when it was ready he entered it and disappeared from sight. For three years he lived in this room underground, and his fellow countrymen missed him sadly, and mourned for him as if he were dead; then in the fourth year, he reappeared, and in this way persuaded the Thracians that the doctrine he had taught was true. (*Hist.* 4.95–96)[225]

If Hermippus is to be relied on, Pythagoras built exactly the same underground chamber upon his arrival in Italy and declared to the assembly that "he had been down to Hades, and even read out his experiences to them.... They were so affected that they wept and wailed and looked upon him as divine, going so far as to send their wives to him in hopes that they would learn some of his doctrines; and so they were called Pythagorean women" (Diogenes Laertius, *Vit. phil.* 8.41).[226] We have encountered nearly the same account concerning Empedocles. Explaining the usefulness of charms to heal the soul as well as the body, Socrates says, "I learned it while I was with the army, from one of the Thracian doctors of Zalmoxis, who are also said to make men immortal [*apathanitizein*]."[227]

Around the time Herodotus was relating this story, various Orphic sects in Greek colonies from the Black Sea to southern Italy were inscribing cultic messages on bone tablets and gold leaves. The clustering of "passwords for the afterlife" in the area of Pythagoras and Parmenides shows that there was an actual cult.[228] Pythagoreans and Orphics follow similar customs.[229] Ion of Chios ascribed Orphic poems to Pythagoras, and others appear to have been written by his immediate students (who were also engaged for Onomacritus's edition).[230] Apollo,

---

225. "For my part," he concludes, "I neither put entire faith in this story of Zalmoxis and his underground chamber, nor wholly disbelieve it."

226. Josephus relates in *C. Ap.* 1.162–165 that, according to Hermippus (DK I 111.36), Pythagoras incorporated Mosaic laws into his system. On this claim and Hermippus's background, see Bar-Kochva, *Image of Jews in Greek Literature*, 164–205.

227. Plato, *Charm.* 156d–157c. Translation from Sprague in Plato, *Complete Works* (ed. Cooper).

228. Zhmud, "Pythagorean Communities."

229. Bremmer, *Initiation in the Mysteries*, 67. Bremmer adds, "We know that the Pythagoreans also wore white clothes and Pythagoras himself, according to Aelian (*VH* 12.32), dressed in white clothes, trousers and a golden wreath. It seems likely that the Orphics followed the Pythagoreans in this respect, as in several others."

230. "According to Ion of Chios in his *Triagmi* he ascribed some poems of his own making to Orpheus" (Diogenes Laertius, *Vit. phil.* 8.8). West points out that Epigenes "is recorded as

music, animal communication, and of course cave incubation also connect Pythagoras to Orpheus.[231] Instead of Delphi, many flocked to Kroton to hear the oracles of the one who was believed to be the actual incarnation of Apollo. Among Aristotle's descriptions is mention of Empedocles's wide travels, which included Thurii where the gold leaves mentioned above were discovered.[232]

Along with Egypt and Thrace, Persia has been conjectured since antiquity as the incubator of Orphic ideas. West argues that the monistic metaphysics, a real world beyond the one we perceive, reincarnation, and ten-thousand-year cycles—all of this was "the gift of the Magi."[233] Regardless, we see remarkably similar doctrines ascending simultaneously in India.

In short, all roads lead finally not to a single place but to a person: Pythagoras, who spread the new theology-cum-philosophy across Greece. From the Eleusinian mysteries to the effusion of new mythology around Dionysus and Orpheus, the "divine self" emerged, fueling the rise of democracy and classical culture. Kings and tyrants are toppled, and even those among the latter rule by the common consent of citizens. "Accordingly," Duplouy writes, "one can also consider how excessive is the alleged shift from myth to reason, when considering that Cleisthenes, the so-called 'Grand architect' of the new democratic Athens, and Pericles, the promoter of the city as the 'School of Hellas', actually referred to the mediation of a Cretan 'inspired shaman' in order to absolve their family from a hereditary sin."[234]

Of course, Pythagoras himself is preceded by shamanic figures like Hermotimus of Clazomenae, Pherecydes of Syros, and Epimenides, and he was not their

---

having stated, in a discussion of Orphic poetry, that the *Descent to Hades* and the *Hieros Logos* were really by Cercops the Pythagorean, and the *Robe* and *Physika* by Brontinus." See West, *Orphic Poems*, 9 n. 15; Clement of Alexandria, *Strom.* 1.131. For more on these figures, see West, *Orphic Poems*, 9–10. Given my point above, and Ion of Chios's mention of hymns by Pythagoras attributed to Orpheus, it seems plausible that Pythagoros is the author of *Krater*.

231. For example, Pythagoras invented the numerical relations of tones to divisions on a stretched string. See also Müller, *Literature of Ancient Greece*, 1:149. Alcidamas says, "Orpheus was the first to introduce writing, having learnt it from the Muses, as the inscription on his tomb shows: 'The Thracians buried Orpheus here, the ministers of the Muses / Whom lofty-ruling Zeus slew with the smoking thunderbolt / The dear son of Oiagros, who taught Herakles / Having discovered writing and wisdom for mankind.'" Through his brother Linus and son Musaeus, Orpheus's influence spread, he adds. "Linos discovered music and furthermore Mousaios . . . discovered numbers as his poems too show: a straight hexameter of four and twenty measures / So that a hundred men live as a tenth generation." See Alcidamas, *Od.* 16.

232. See Kingsley and Parry, "Empedocles."

233. West, *Early Greek Philosophy*, 67. However, he maintains that it was the outlook of pre-Zoroastrian Persia. Richard Reitzenstein pioneered the Iranian-source theory in *Das iranische Erlösungsmysterium: Religionsgeschichtliche Untersuchungen* (1921).

234. Duplouy, "Epimenides the Cretan."

sole heir. Nevertheless, he became the first semi-historical figure in the gradual transition from shaman to sage. As such, he himself becomes bricolage symbolizing what was recognized increasingly as a new horizon spreading across the great expanse of the Persian Empire. Besides enlightenment in Egypt, he is said by the third century BCE to have studied at the feet of Jewish teachers in Palestine; by the third century CE, Philostratus has him in India among the gymnosophists, and Iamblichus adds Celtic Druids and Iberian sages to his curriculum vitae.[235] Not unlike Orpheus, Pythagoras emerges from the cave as the "divine man" (*theios anēr*) of a local cult to become a psychopomp for a universal faith in the "divine self" in everyone.

To be sure, "Orphism" is the product of the imagination, a canvas on which countless mythographers, playwrights, painters and sculptors, musicians, natural philosophers, physicians and metaphysicians, even politicians, have plied their own brushstrokes. Yet the landscape is familiar to us—or should be, anyway. In it we recognize the divine madness in Western reason, the mysticism at the heart of modernity, and the magic that bears seeds of cures as well as curses. Shamanism is not the graveclothes of Attica's gradual emergence from enthusiasm to reason but a conspicuous midwife of classical Greek music, politics, theater, science, and philosophers, and the divine self that would haunt Western culture long after the glory of Greece had faded.

---

235. Riedweg, *Pythagoras*, 8.

3

Shaman to Sage
Religion of the One

> Zeus is all things,
> he who makes appear all things in a cycle, Zeus, beginning, middle, and accomplishment,
> and Zeus is all almighty, Zeus has everything within himself.
>
> —Anonymous Hymn to Zeus (OF 243)[1]

> The self has entered this body, this dense jumble.
> If a man finds him,
> Recognizes him,
> He's the maker of everything—the author of all!
> The world is his—he's the world itself!
>
> —Brihadaranyaka Upanishad 4.4.13[2]

> First [Pythagoras] declares that the soul is immortal; then that it changes into other kinds of animals, . . . that nothing is absolutely new, and that all things that come to be alive must be thought akin. Pythagoras seems to have been the first to introduce these opinions into Greece.
>
> —Porphyry, *Vit. Pyth.* 19[3]

---

1. Quoted in Bernabé, "Gods in Ancient Orphism," 430. Aeschylus's fragment, "Zeus is all things . . . ," is too close to this Orphic hymn to be random. Therefore, Nietzsche's opposition between Aeschylus (who introduced this phrase) and Socrates's ostensibly "Apollonian" command over Euripides is inaccurate. See Nietzsche, *Birth of Tragedy*, 47–93.

2. Translation from Olivelle, *Upaniṣads*.

3. *Vit. Pyth.* 19 (= DK 14, 8a). Quoted in McKirahan, *Philosophy before Socrates*, 84.

Chapter 3

More than four millennia ago, the Indo-Iranians separated into Indo-Aryan and Iranian peoples, speaking Sanskrit and Avestan, respectively. Centuries later, a native speaker of one language could still understand with some challenges the other language. These languages even shared some names of divinities.[4] Both civilizations spread out in waves westward and eastward, creating remarkable hybrids as they mixed with local cults. But the Bronze Age Collapse brought widespread devastation to once-flourishing cities. Recovering about a century before Greece, Asia saw scattered populations migrating to new cities, cities forming alliances and kingdoms. In India the axial shift coincided with its Second Urbanization, filling the Ganges plain with large population centers that enjoyed flourishing agriculture, technology, and ironworking.

On the foundations of the Assyrian Empire, the Achaemenid Persians erected the most expansive empire yet, from northern India to the Danube and from the Black Sea to Egypt. Monetary currency, writing and literacy, and a bustling network of trade routes contributed to the migration from locative communities based on oral traditions and kinship ties to more universal and utopian societies.[5] In the sixth century BCE we see also the rise of universal religions: what we know today as Hinduism, the founding of Jainism and Buddhism in India, the founding of Taoism and Confucianism in China, the rise of Zoroastrianism in the Persian capital, and the return of Judean exiles to Jerusalem with the prophets bearing a message of a messiah as judge and savior not only of Israel but of the world.[6]

---

4. For example, a god is a *daeva* in Avestan and a *deva* in Sanskrit. They overlap even in some of the names of their gods: Mithra/Mitra; Vayu/Vayu; Thworestar/Tvastar. Both religions were sacrificial cults that had a special affinity for fire (Atar/Agni). See Malandra, "Zoroastrianism." C. Watkins explores some of the common myths in *How to Kill a Dragon*.

5. On the influence of monetization see Seaford, *Money and the Early Greek Mind*. Although he overstates the case for coinage as the main driver of rationalization, his research and arguments are enlightening.

6. As I elaborate below, Hinduism evolves out of Vedic ritualism into the more philosophical current of the sixth century, while Buddhism goes further in abandoning earlier Indic religion in favor of monism. Zoroastrianism is a more complicated phenomenon, as it seems to have arisen as a prophetic monotheism with a sharp ethical dualism rather than as monistic system. In this regard, it is comparable more to the Hebrew prophets. I am not persuaded by comparisons of Zoroaster (Zarathustra) to a shaman (e.g., Widengren, *Die Religionen Irans*). However, as the century unfolds, the broader trend of philosophical gnosis (and magic) draws the ethical battle between Light and Darkness into a metaphysical conflict that paves the way for Zurvainism and Manichaeism. Dating ranges for the life of Zoroaster vary widely among specialists (1200–500 BCE), with some doubting whether he lived at all (see Kellens and Pirart, *Les textes vieil-avestiques*). Shaul Shaked observes that the written form of the Bundahishn is the ninth century CE, but argues that the earliest material goes back to oral tradition around 1000 BCE. See his foreword to *Bundahišn*, xi. For all these new religious philosophies, the length of

THE RISE OF THE ONE: PANTHEON TO PANENTHEISM

For many other reasons also, religions became more philosophical in the sixth century BCE, and that philosophy reflected the shift from a locative cosmos with its emphasis on that which is concrete, particular, and varied to a utopian cosmos focusing on that which is more abstract, universal, and a complete unity. We may call it the religion of the One.[7] This universal principle, the One, was known by various names: Zeus-Dionysus, the infinite Apeiron, Cosmic Soul, Logos, Mind, Monad, and Harmony. It is utterly transcendent, beyond knowing, and yet the source of all. *Brahman* was its name in India.[8] Long before Parmenides, the Upanishads emphasized this notion of the real behind the veil of appearance and the concept of macrocosm and microcosm. In China, it is the *tai chi*, the Great Ultimate, or *tao*, "Way"; Persians knew an Infinite Time (Zurvan) above the duality of his twins good (Ahura Mazda) and evil (Ahriman). In Egypt, Ma'at was the personification of a transcendent and universal law.

In this chapter I use the term "monism" broadly to include priority monism (all things come from and return to the One) and substance monism (there is only one substance). And, for the most part, it is idealist monism (only spirit or mind is real).[9] This is true, I argue, even for the Miletian (Ionian) thinkers. In theology, it is a passage from polytheism to pantheism/panentheism.[10] In anthropology, it is a shift from many bodies to the unified Soul Itself; in cosmology, from many sources to a single, divine, unchanging, and incorporeal one. Ficino expresses it well: "The ancients considered things divine as the only realities, and that all others were only the images and shadows of things."[11] Among these "axial" thinkers there are exceptions to this broad trend, but, as I argue below, fewer than is often thought.

What is not part of this trajectory is monotheism, contrary to the tendency of Axial Age scholars to conflate monotheism with monism.[12] Except for the short-

---

time between hypothesized layers of oral transmission and written texts renders any definitive dating illusive.

7. I adapt this phrase from Frederick C. Copleston's 1979–1981 Gifford Lectures, published as *Religion and the One*.

8. See Brereton and Jamison, *Rigveda*, 1:349–55.

9. As I point out in this chapter, this broad tendency accommodates a variety of metaphysical positions identified by contemporary philosophers. In addition to different formulations of monism itself, there are idealist and material (physicalist) versions. See Jason Turner's taxonomy in "Logic and Ontological Pluralism."

10. The best survey of panentheism I have found is Cooper, *Panentheism*.

11. Ficino, as quoted in Taylor, *Eleusinian and Bacchic Mysteries*, 47–48.

12. Generally, when the Axial Age paradigm is deployed, it charts a trek from polytheism to

lived reign of Egypt's pharaoh Akhenaten (r. 1353–1336 BCE), Israel was an island of monotheism surrounded by a sea of polytheism that became increasingly monistic in the so-called Axial Age.[13] Attributes accorded by monists to the cosmos are considered by monotheists to be unique to the creator who made all things by his own loving choice and creativitiy. The qualitative distinction between God and creatures entails that the latter are also real but in a creaturely (and therefore analogical) way. Thus, difference is just as real as unity.[14]

Souls falling from unity (World Soul) into divided bodies, returning, and then being reborn in different bodies, is a microcosm of the cosmic cycle. Which came first—the psychology or cosmology—remains a mystery. Regardless, the great achievement of the Greeks according to Diogenes Laertius (discounting the "barbarians"), from Orpheus to Musaeus and Linus and Eumolpus and on to the Presocratic philosophers, is the doctrine that "all things proceed from unity and are resolved again into unity" (*Vita phil.* 1.3).[15] Like a fountain, the nozzle jettisons a single flow that separates into many sprays with myriad droplets, cascading into broadening tiers of basins before returning to its source. The source is not itself a part of the flow; it must transcend the variety in order to produce it. The flow is a decline from its pristine source, but this is necessary for the filling of the whole cosmos with divine being and goodness. Assmann calls this view "Cosmotheology."[16]

---

monotheism, typically considered from better to worse. In addition to the examples cited above, see Sanderson, *Religious Evolution*, 37–38, 48–49, 51–178. Of these "religions of salvation," the Hebrew prophets represent the only unequivocally monotheistic tradition. Such conflation is rooted in Friedrich Delitzsch's frankly anti-Jewish disdain for the Old Testament. He sought to show especially the dependence of Genesis 1 on (rather than being a parody of) Enuma Elish. The best refutation remains that of noted Assyriologist Alexander Heidel, *Gilgamesh Epic*.

13. It is debated whether Akhenaten was a henotheist or monotheist. See for example Ridley, *Akhenaten*, 13–15, and Hart, *Egyptian Gods and Goddesses*, 44. (Regardless, he was declared a heretic after his death.) The same question (henotheism versus monotheism) is raised in connection with Zoroastrianism. The nucleus of the Zoroastrian scriptures, called the Avesta, is the five Gathas (meaning "songs" in both Avestan and Sanskrit) containing seventeen hymns addressing various divinities. See Irani and Tagore, *Divine Songs of Zarathushtra*. Similar to the Rigveda, the Gathas are hymns (*gāthā* meaning "song" in both languages), and they form the core of the Zoroastrian liturgy (*Yasna*). The oldest Avestan manuscript is from 1323 CE, and most of the original material has been lost. This left a lot of room for invention, just at the time when metaphysical questions of the one and the many and the source of good and evil were converging.

14. "Humanity" (unity) is "male and female" (plurality). In Christianity, in fact, the three persons (*hypostaseis*) are as real as their consubstantial unity.

15. This is as good a statement of this chapter's thesis as possible. See also Cornford, "Pattern of Ionian Cosmology," 23.

16. See Assmann, *Price of Monotheism*, who praises "Cosmotheism" for its "rapt assent" and veneration of nature especially in contrast with the dull, mundane, and "secular" wisdom of

Attributed to Linus of Thrace, Orpheus's legendary brother, are the following lines from *On the Nature of the World*:

> So through discord all things are steered through all.
> From the whole are all things, all things form a whole,
> all things are one, each part of all, all in one;
> for from a single whole all these things came,
> and from them in due time will one return,
> that's ever one and many.[17]

This process is one of universalizing, rationalizing, and assimilating from the concrete to the abstract, from the oral and local to the written and universal, from locative embeddedness to utopian liberation—above all, from the many to the One.

This universalizing process happened simultaneously across cultures that, in the sixth century, became absorbed into a single empire. While this took five to seven centuries in India, McEvilley explains, "The process from polytheism through Orphic pantheism to philosophical monism seems to have taken a century or so.... In Greece, where the transition is more abrupt and discontinuous than in India, even more attention should be paid to external forces that may have upset the internal balance of Greek mythology and tumbled it into a new form overnight."[18] This transition appears in the following stages.

Assimilating Gods to Natural Elements

In a locative cosmos, the gods retain their individual personalities. They are above us, but they are like us. Though they never die, they are born. They ride on horses

---

Israel (9, 69). However, he acknowledges that this divinization of nature has a dark side as well. Not distinguishing God from the world, it fuses religion and the state with a tendency toward mastery (57). According to Assmann, Hermeticism, Gnosticism, Spinozisim, Freemasonry, Rosicrucianism, Naziism, and the New Age movement are offspring of "Cosmotheism" (75).

17. Quoted in West, *Orphic Poems*, 57, from Stobaeus, *Ecl.* 1.10.5 with emendations from West, "Conjectures on 46 Greek Poets," 155–56. West notes in 57 n. 73, "The doctrine in line 3 is mentioned as that of Linus and Pythagoras by Damascius, *De principiis* 25 bis, 27 (i. 45.12, 48.13 Ruelle)." Linus may be a personification of the *linos*, a song of lament. In antiquity he was considered the founder of melody, the teacher of Hercules and Orpheus, and, according to some accounts, Orpheus's elder brother, who was exposed by his mother at birth and torn by dogs but returned (Nonnus, *Dion.* 41.376; Homer, *Il.* 18.541; Pausanias, *Descr.* 9.29.6). He is said also to have introduced writing (i.e., the Phoenician alphabet) to Greece (*Suda*, s.v., Λίνος). See also Diogenes Laertius, *Vit. phil.* 1.4.

18. McEvilley, *Shape of Ancient Thought*, 60–61.

and chariots, eat, and drink. Lightning is literally a thunderbolt from Marduk or Zeus. The gripping drama of gods fighting on opposite sides of the Trojan War really happened as told, more or less. One feels embedded in this cosmos, surrounded by the gods at every turn.

In a utopian cosmos, however, the gods are everywhere but nowhere. "Zeus's thunderbolt" refers to a meteorological phenomenon, just as rain is called "Tears of Zeus." "Fates Clothed in White" refers to phases of the moon, "Workless" to nighttime, and "Aphrodite" to the time for sowing seed, and so on.[19] The war of the gods in the Trojan War refers allegorically to the opposition of elements: Fire (Apollo, Helios, and Hephaestus) versus Water (Poseidon and Scamander).[20] In Egypt the primordial gods are abstract and unknowable principles.[21]

In Greece, this abstracting and universalizing tendency was the work of Orphic poets, not atheists. In formulating the theory of the four elements—fire, air, water, earth—the Orphic-Pythagorean shaman Empedocles correlated each respectively with Zeus, Hera, Nestis (or Persephone), and Aidoneus. The older biomorphic mythology was absorbed into the emanative process. Everything that exists became a combination of opposites governed by Love (Eros/Aphrodite) and Strife (Eris/Dionysus).[22] In Orphic lore, Persephone was now all-pervading nature.[23] Thus, her profile expanded considerably but she lost her distinct place within the cosmos and her distinct character in mythology.

Gods no longer *entered* our social world, bestowing courage or malice upon mortals; instead, they *became* our natural world, sacred souls that animate the celestial gods, that is, the planets and stars. Orphic metaphysics elides the distinction between ruler and realm, theology and cosmology. Poseidon is not the god of the sea but is the sea (OF 413). The world is divine from top to bottom

---

19. From Epigenes's *On Orpheus* via the testimony by Clement of Alexandria; see Freeman, *Pre-Socratic Philosophers*, 6.

20. Xenophanes, *Elegiacs* 32; Freeman, *Pre-Socratic Philosophers*, 23.

21. The Ogdoad of Hermopolis consists of four paired (male-female) abstractions: Darkness (Kek-Kauket), Endlessness (He-Hauket), Hiddenness (Amon-Amaunet), and Watery Abyss (Nun-Naunet). As for Heliopolis's Ennead, Shu and Tefnut are not only creators or rulers of Air and Moisture but are also fundamental elements. Geb and Nut are Earth and Water, from which Osiris, Isis, Set, and Nephthys are born. And it is not that the gods act upon us; the newly discovered divine soul is itself each person's inner animator. Yet it is less the case that the supernatural is naturalized than that nature is supernaturalized. The gods are not remote, as in modern deism, much less denied; on the contrary, they are so immanent that divinity permeates the cosmos in declining degrees from top to bottom.

22. Empedocles, fr. B6 (= D 57). Translation by Freeman, *Pre-Socratic Philosophers*, 52.

23. *See* OH 29.16 and Julian's "Hymn to the Mother of Gods" (*Or.* 5.162a) in *Works of the Emperor Julian* (ed. Wright).

but in descending grades. Orpheus teaches "in riddling form" that Night is called the "nurse" of becoming since the sun heats and dissolves and the night cools and unites (P. Derveni 10.23). In contrast with action adventures about a mythical past, these stories are allegories of what happens always and everywhere, eternally: namely, cosmological emanation and return.

Assimilation to an Erstwhile Minor Shamanic Deity

Across ancient myths, we find the grouchy divine patriarchs who created humans as slaves grow senile and become done in by the younger generation of deities. Enki/Marduk intervenes on behalf of humans repeatedly, as does Prometheus, who despite being damned by Hesiod still attains the status of benefactor of humankind on the Athenian stage. (Humans attain a status disallowed by the archaic emphasis on their being mere drones of ritual honors for the gods.) Homer's "dread Persephone" becomes "Great Goddess" and "Savior," equivalent to Isis. Hekate likely derived from Egyptian Heka. In fact, this mere chthonic goddess of magic and crossroads absorbs many of the functions of Hermes until she becomes the World Soul by the Hellenistic era. Even Zeus takes on a Dionysian character. Indeed, Dionysus's first birth by Persephone (as Zagreas in Orphic versions) and next, by Semele, is consummated in his third incarnation as the offspring of Zeus both by insemination and birth. The old gods of the locative and bounded cosmos are rendered moribund except as precursors to the utopian and universal deity. In India, too, minor gods ascend while the major gods of the early Rigveda are marginalized or absorbed. These deities strive not only for local or even national recognition but for universal fame as virile benefactors rather than senile tyrants of humanity.

By the time of Herodotus in the fifth century, the gods of Greece were viewed as universal and simply called by other names elsewhere. This ambition for a universal religion that transcended any national cult was precisely what Dionysus's profile highlights. Out of nowhere, Dionysus quite literally steals the stage and, as we have seen, he brings his own cast.

Indians called Dionysus "Nysian," considering him the founder of Nysa in India. Significantly, in the Rigveda, the oldest Sanskrit writing, Shiva is a minor epithet for a minor god (Rudra). This contrasts sharply with Shiva's prominence in classical Hinduism (200 BCE–500 CE). Brereton and Jamison observe that "on the one hand, he is fierce and malevolent, with an often inexplicable anger that needs to be appeased; on the other, he is a healer, who controls remedies for disease . . . young and ferocious: the flame-red 'boar of heaven' (I.114.5), or the one 'pouncing like a terrifying wild beast' (II.33.11), or the red-brown bull (II.33.5, 8, 15)." His storm deities known as *maruts* (or *rudras*) imitate his characteristics as they follow him from place to place. He is "an 'outsider' divinity."[24] As with the Egyptian Osiris, comparisons of Dionysus with Shiva were recognized from the beginning. Cosmic dancer, naked ascetic ("Gymnosophist," as coined by the Greeks), androgynous lord of fertility and snakes who kills with poison and heals with medicine, Rudra-Shiva is a kindly herdsman yet slaughterer of "beasts" (i.e., souls).[25]

Shaivists formed "groups outside the normal social orders of clan and settlement." The earliest devotion to Rudra-Shiva emerged among the extreme mystical-ascetic *shramanas* whose behavior and customs reflect shamanistic techniques.[26] According to Geoffrey Samuel, *shramana* originally refered to ascetic devotees of Shiva, who "has always retained a more transgressive side to his image," and he argues convincingly that the word "shaman" derives from *shramana*. The earliest of the ascetic groups, the Pashupatas, "were practitioners of a style of spirituality that involves deliberately shocking behaviour and the conscious courting of disrepute," similar to Greek Cynics, whose habits were "intended to attract rejection and dishonour and lead them to be regarded as crazy.... These involved wandering from place to place and indulging in deliberately shocking and improper acts."[27]

These Indian renunciates were "committed to withdrawal from not only everyday society but the entire cycle of rebirth (*saṃsāra*)," but this was "a new development" arising around 400 BCE.[28] The "seeking of dishonor" was a characteristic of Pashupata Shaivism, McEvilley explains. Its *brahmins* imitated Shiva as recounted in texts such as the Bhagavata Purana:

> Like a madman he haunts horrid cemeteries, surrounded with ghosts and evil spirits. He is naked, his hair in disorder. He laughs, he weeps, he smears himself with ashes and wears as his only garment a necklace of skulls and human bones.... He is mad, adored by madmen, and reigns over the spirits of darkness. (BP 4.207)[29]

---

24. Brereton and Jamison, *Rigveda*, 1:66–67, 102–3. On comparisons see Daniélou, *Gods of Love and Ecstasy*.
25. Vanamali, *Shiva*.
26. Brereton and Jamison, *Rigveda*, 1:102–3.
27. Samuel, *Origins of Yoga and Tantra*, 239–41. Eliade also argued that Western ethnographers coined shaman from *shramana*; see *Shamanism*, 495. The etymology remains a debated point. For instance, Christopher Beckwith argues that ancient Greeks identified *shramanas* with Buddhists in his *Greek Buddha*, esp. 129–30. However, Olivelle identifies its presence in the Upanishads and the Bhagavadgita; see *Asraman System*, esp. 9–14. The Sanan (perhaps the root of *shaman*) is related to the Soma sacrifice (CU 8.1.1–8; see Olivelle, *Upaniṣads*).
28. Samuel, *Origins of Yoga and Tantra*, 120–23.
29. Quoted from McEvilley, *Shape of Ancient Thought*, 220–33.

We are reminded of the association of the Erinyes (Furies) with Dionysus in the Orphic Hymns: "Vociferous, Bacchanalian Furies!"[30] "The poet of the Hesiodic *Catalogue*," notes West, "associated the mountain Nymphs and Satyrs with 'the divine Kouretes, dancers who love to sport.' ... Their name means simply 'young men,' and corresponds to Koruai 'Maids,' a name sometimes used of the Nymphs." They are "mischief-makers," *kobalos*, meaning "an impudent rogue or trickster." Though they faded from archaic Greece generally, they were revered in Crete, related to Zeus's birth. Returning to the stage, they become "*daimones* in the entourage of Dionysus, which suggests something like the Satyrs or Sileni."[31] And, as we will see, Parmenides is greeted by the goddess as "kouretes" and "initiate."

The renunciate tradition of Brahmanism employed "the vocabulary of 'magical power,'" and the outsider group took them seriously "because they have acquired the genuine skills needed to carry it off." Moreover, "the renunciates have placed themselves outside society," assuming early on "the cult of dead spirits in marginal places outside the city."[32] The act of prayer presupposes that "the outcome depends on the deity's will." However, "The incantation or ritual, if correctly uttered or performed, automatically produces the desired result. If supernatural powers are involved in bringing it about, they are not persuaded but compelled. If the magic is unsuccessful, some mistake must have been made in the words used or the actions executed." Prayers are about content, whatever the wording or ritual practice. New prayers could be added easily. "Spells and incantations, on the other hand, were esoteric knowledge supposed to be fixed and unchanging."[33] To cite a Vedic example, a woman asks the gods to inflame her object of desire with a burning for her. "Send him wild Maruts" (Atharvaveda 6.130.2–4).[34] Herbs were also used with incantations and spells.[35] Maledictions (in the form of "I bind so-and-so") are well attested in Greek as well as Indian and Egyptian magic, often by naming each part of the person to be cut up, just as in healings.[36]

Shiva mendicants also imitated animals and could transport themselves magically, going through mountains easily.[37] "In some cases the shamanic current

---

30. OH 68; cf. 66 and 69.
31. West, *Indo-European Poetry and Myth*, 294–95.
32. Samuel, *Origins of Yoga and Tantra*, 239–41 and 239 n. 15. On comparisons with the Greek Cynics see McEvilley, *Shape of Ancient Thought*, 231.
33. West, *Indo-European Poetry and Myth*, 326.
34. West, *Indo-European Poetry and Myth*, 327.
35. West, *Indo-European Poetry and Myth*, 331–32.
36. West, *Indo-European Poetry and Myth*, 332–33.
37. For magi, see RV 6.49.11. For tongues and eyes see RV 1.174. For travelers see RV 5.54.9; 5.55.9.

Chapter 3

may have been segregated in certain secret or sheltered priesthoods" known for their "mastery over fire" as well as "sorcery and goblinism." Interestingly, the Upanishads themselves instruct that the most esoteric philosophy must be recited in the wilderness.[38]

As the esoteric community became more prominent, so did its divine patron. Osiris became indistinguishable from Dionysus in Egypt. Osiris, god of the underworld, was dismembered by his evil brother Set, god of violent chaos. Osiris's wife, Isis the savior, recovered and revived all but his lost phallus and so commanded priests to set up an image of an erect phallus in all her temples (Diodorus Siculus, *Bib. hist.* 1.21.1–3).[39] Egyptians insisted that their Dionysus came first (*Bib. hist.* 3.74.1).[40]

There is little point in identifying Orphic literature with "whatever is strange." Hesiod's *Theogony* strikes us as unusual, sometimes bizarre and even offensive. Moreover, "what is strange" is happening across Asia, Egypt, and Greece at the same time. In Greece, it is under Orpheus's inspiration that various shaman-like writers plot their own versions of a new mythology aimed at the same doctrinal point: that all things come from a transcendent One and return to it. In some Orphic poems, this absolute principle is Infinite Time (e.g., Pherecydes, Epimenides, the Rhapsodic theogony); in others, Night (e.g., the Protogonos theogony found in hymns, *testimonia*, and the Derveni papyrus). Even in the latter's succession myth, there may have been an Infinite Kronos above and before the Kronos we know, but this is lost to us. Regardless, there is a primordial divine principle beyond light and darkness, being and becoming, good and evil, male and female: the absolutely simple One from which the stream of unity-and-difference flows.

Like the Many-and-One, the relation of Being to Becoming does not cross one's mind in a locative cosmos: The actual world is as it has always been; the gods just move into their respective domains. But since theogony has merged with cosmogony in Orphic hands, the Being-Becoming question is acute. Though still eternal,

---

38. Olivelle, introduction to *Upaniṣads*, xxxii. Fire rites were nuclear to Vedic and Iranian religions. Demeter's attempted initiation-deification of the royal toddler Demophoön by placing him in the fire suggests possible influences from Indo-Iranian quarters.

39. See also *Bib. hist.* 4.6.3 on the centrality of the Osiris myth and his phallus cult in Egypt. Edmonds points out striking parallels drawn by ancient Egyptians between Epaphos and Dionysus. Epaphos is also a son of Zeus and his mother Io, and with his wife Memphis was the founder of Egypt and sired Lybia and Ethiopia. Diodorus lists Io as one of many Dionysian incarnations and as "a ruler in Egypt who established the Dionysiac rituals there." See Edmonds, "Dionysos in Egypt?," 415–16. He refers here to Diodorus Siculus, *Bib. hist.* 3.74.1.

40. Quoted in Edmonds, "Dionysos in Egypt?," 416. The "first Dionysos" is the "son of Ammon and Antheia" whereas "the second Dionysos, men say, who was born to Zeus by Io, the daughter of Inachus, became king of Egypt and appointed the initiatory rites of that land; and the third and last, sprung from Zeus and Semele, became among the Greeks, the emulator of the first two."

the cosmos is an emanative procession from the One. But if the One is beyond the process it causes, how do many things come into being? What remains constant, unscathed by the strife of opposites in the realm of becoming? Are these changes an illusion derived from sense experience or are they constantly blending in new combinations? As we will see, Orphic bricoleurs have not nailed all of this down. While a major trend is toward mixing metaphor, strict (numerical) monism is not ruled out. In either case, though, everything comes from the One and returns to it.

Following ancient Near Eastern precedents, Orphic theogonies offered a royal succession of six rulers.[41] "First came the Chasm," says Hesiod (*Theog.* 116). Originally, chasm is the literal meaning of the word "chaos" and it bears no connotation of disorder; it is simply a void, as in Genesis 1:2. Out of the Chasm came Earth, Eros, Underworld (Erebos), and "dark Night." With Night (Nyx) begins succession through sacred marriage (*hieros gamos*): In "shared intimacy" with Erebos, Night gives birth to Air and Day. Earth gave birth to her husband Heaven, and from their union came Eros, Oceanus and others, the last of whom was "crooked-schemer Kronos, most fearsome of children, who loathed his lusty father" (*Theog.* 116–138).

Instead, most Orphic theogonies begin with either Night or Time (Kronos). Either way, it is a primordial and transcendent absolute above the gods we know. In Homer, even Zeus is afraid of the primordial Nyx, and Hesiod refers to "the horrible dwelling of dark Night" (*Theog.* 744). However, in Orphic lore she is the origin and goal of all things. The *Eumolphia* ascribed to Orpheus's associate Musaeus has all things descending from a union of Tartarus and Nyx (2B14), and Epimenides has "Aer and Nyx as the two first principles."[42] Whether by herself or in union with a non-Homeric natural principle, the cave of Night is the womb of gods and mortals.[43] Night also leads the Eudamian Theogony. Since Eudamus, who preserved it, was a pupil of Aristotle, it is not suprising that Aristotle refers to "the theologians who generate everything from Night" (*Metaph.* 1071b26).[44] Instead

---

41. West argues that the Derveni Papyrus is an abridgement of the Protogonos theogony because of its central character. Based on the Rhapsodic theogony, West argues that there are six generations characterizing the Orphic succession myth; see *Orphic Poems*, 68–69. Much of Meisner's argument in *Orphic Tradition* militates against reconstructing a common theogony in favor of recognizing the diverse perspectives of bricoleurs. Although sympathetic on most of his points, I agree with West on these two points: there was obviously an earlier text on which the Derveni author comments, and its agreement with the Rhapsodic theogony on the six generations is probably essential to the Orphic scheme.

42. Gantz, *Early Greek Myth*, 1:2–3.

43. This includes the Protogonos theogony known to the Derveni commentator and the Eudemian theogony known to Aristotle and his pupil Eudemus. Epimenides and Parmenides also took this view.

44. Quoted in Meisner, *Orphic Tradition*, 94.

of being terrified by Night, the Orphic Zeus enters her cave often to receive his powers and prophecies, just as Parmenides does to receive his inspired poem. John Palmer observes, "The goddess Night serves as counselor to Zeus in some of the major Orphic cosmologies, including the Derveni cosmology (P. Derveni 11.10). In the closely related Orphic *Rhapsodies*, Night instructs Zeus on how to preserve the unity produced by his absorption of all things into himself as he sets about initiating a new cosmogonic phase."[45] Specifically, Zeus asks her, "How may I have all things one and each one separate?" (OF 164 and 165).[46] This is the One-and-Many question in a nutshell, and it never would have occurred to Homer or Hersiod.

It is not surprising that Greek shamans would find the origin of all things in a cave. At the beginning of the sixth century BCE, Pherecydes "the theologian"—credited by ancients with shamanic powers—seems to have been the first to introduce the new Orphic myths and doctrines that Presocratics, beginning with Epimenides and Pythagoras, would absorb into their pores.[47] Herbert Granger says, "He is more relevant than scholars generally think to the project of patching together a good idea of the intellectual milieu that fostered cosmology and ultimately led to philosophy as we have come to appreciate it, in the arguments of Parmenides's unnamed goddess. That milieu is primarily theological," but this means primordially philosophical. Examining "Pherecydes the Theologian" leads us to conclude that the speculative tradition that came to be identified as Orphic and Pythagorean is "a more unified group than is usually acknowledged."[48] What emerges initially is not a paper trail between India and Greece but a pattern of ideas. Yet as the sixth century unfolded, considerable interaction occurred in the imperial court. "It is certain," says McEvilley, "that Pherecydes imported Oriental ideas into the Greek tradition, including some from India. The Indian doctrines he brought entered Greece enmeshed in a net of Persian ideas. It is a plausible hypothesis that Pherecydes called them the teachings of Orpheus in order to naturalize them."[49]

---

45. Palmer, "Parmenides." Yet, as Meisner argues convincingly, the Derveni commentator, like the author of the original text, is most likely writing a hymn used in actual rituals, not a systematic theology (*Orphic Tradition*, 53–85).

46. See Betegh, *Derveni Papyrus*, 175 n. 173.

47. Although nothing has survived of his writing, much of it did endure to the Hellenistic era and received wide attention in commentaries. From these testimonies we may discern strong similarities with the cosmotheology of Orphic texts. See Cicero, *Tusc.* 1.16. Hermann Schibli provides a useful summary drawn from various ancient sources in *Pherecydes of Syros*, 128–29. See also Kirk, Raven, and Schofield, *Presocratic Philosophers*, 59. According to Laertius, he was one of the Seven Sages of Greece (*Vit. phil.* 1.119, 122).

48. Granger, "Theologian Pherekydes of Syros," 135. See Kirk, Raven, and Schofield, *Presocratic Philosophers*, 59.

49. McEvilley, *Shape of Ancient Thought*, 171.

Beginning with Pherecydes, other Orphic writers have Infinite Time (Kronos) as the origin and absolute principle above all division.[50] Kronos, Zas (Zeus) and Chthonie "always existed," he says, "but Chthoniê acquired the name of Gê, since Zas gives earth to her as a gift of honour."[51] Kronos ejaculates the seeds of gods and mortals in various caves—signaling where the realm of becoming and difference begins. After defeating Ophion, Zas assumes the throne and Kronos happily retires from the emanative process. Zas marries Chthonie. On the third day of the wedding he presents her with a robe embroidered with the whole topography of the earth. Thereupon he pronounces her Ge, the terrestrial earth. In other words, Kronos and Zas never turned into someone or something else, while Chthonie became Nature. Above earthly time of becoming, there remains infinite time of being (Kronos), and above the Zeus we know, the archetypal Zas. Water, air, fire, and earth represent more than natural elements. For him, they are the primal forces of mythology, though of his own creation. The chaos became a cosmos when the elements collided and produced a new mixture. But the ultimate father of all remains transcendent.[52]

There is a similar idea in Persia with Zurvan (Infinite Time) producing the twins of Ahura Mazda and Ahriman along with the Pythagorean notion of a transcendent Monad above the division of one and many. Similarly, Indian thought places *brahman* above all duality. Taoisim's *tai chi* above the *yin* and *yang* all point in the same direction. In Late Period Egypt also, the first god we know—the cosmos-forming demiurge—is generated by primeval forces in the hidden darkness of divine chaos waters.[53]

---

50. On Time (Kronos) as preeminent in Orphic cosmogonies see Kirk, Raven, and Schofield, *Presocratic Philosophers*, 24. By my calculation, this includes Pherecydes and the Rhapsodic Theogony, but we do not have complete copies of any Presocratic theogony. It is possible, in my view likely, that our fragments and testimonies pick up at the first *participation* in the emanation process, where unity is divided into the plurality of the cosmos.

51. Freeman, *Pre-Socratic Philosophers*, 14. West notes, "'Zas' seems to be a conflation of Zeus and the Anatolian weather-god Santa or Sandon. Pherecydes had a father with the Anatolian name of Babys, and he may perhaps have drawn on Anatolian as well as Greek myth for his inspiration" (*Indo-European Poetry and Myth*, 182).

52. For summaries of his two theogonies with helpful commentary, see West, *Indo-European Poetry and Myth*, 347–48, 355, 373; Kirk, Raven, and Schofield, *Presocratic Philosophers*, 66–68; Schibli, *Pherecydes of Syros*, 89–90. Meisner summarizes well: "In Pherecydes' cosmogony, Chronos is the first principle who creates the elements of fire, air, and water 'from his own seeds' and from the mingling of these elements the gods are created" (*Orphic Tradition*, 145).

53. Paired in male-female couples, they are He and Hauket (formlessness), Kek and Kauket (darkness/night), Amun and Amaunet (hiddenness). Then, from Nun and Naunet (the chaos waters) emerged the mound from which Re was born and began forming the world, beginning

Whatever its identity, there is a hidden abyss—Night's cave within space or Infinite Time—from which everything emanates. The seventh-century choral lyricist Alcman makes the female nymph Thetis goddess of water and the first deity-demiurge. She produces Poros (the *archē*) and Tekinos (*telos* or boundary). Poros produces Eros, the principle of differentiation.[54] Also striking is the trend toward female divinities as the primordial principle. The upshot is that there is a completely undifferentiated, unchanging, unbegotten One on whom all difference and oppositions depend. In the Rhapsodies, Kronos mates with Ananke (Necessity) to produce Aither and Chaos (sameness and difference), which produces the cosmic egg from which Phanes emerges, mating with Night, to generate Ouranos. When he was born, the aither split in halves: sky and earth (OF 109–119 B).[55]

Meisner concludes that in the earliest Orphic poems Night was the source of all, while later theogonies made Kronos the unbegotten progenitor, followed by Phanes, who produced the cosmic egg. In any event, he adds, it is Dionysus—in his third incarnation as the offspring of Zeus functioning as father and mother (sewing him in his thigh)—who is the ruling demiurge. In the Hieronyman Theogony, "Zeus takes on the form of a snake to have sex with Rhea/Demeter, who gives birth to Persephone and in turn, Zeus has sex with Persephone who gives birth to Dionysus."[56]

In short, whatever the gaps and divergences, the main point is that there is a primordial principle of divinity transcending the process that it generates *and* a demiurgic figure responsible for ensuring the participation of the many in the One.

The Orphic demiurge Phanes is where participation in the One begins.[57] Like his successor Dionysus, he is "two natured," signaling the bisexuality that allows him to inseminate and give birth. Phanes is "the begetter of blessed gods and mortal men; ineffable, hidden, brilliant scion, forever in whirring motion . . . yes, I call you Lord Priapos . . . of the many seeds." Borrowing from Near Eastern iconography, Phanes is represented here with bright and golden flapping wings,

---

with the creation of the new gods. On the emergence of these new cosmotheologies see Hornung, *Conceptions of God in Ancient Egypt*.

54. The choral lyricist Alcman in the seventh century already breaks from Homer and Hesiod in an "Orphic" direction. See West, "Three Presocratic Cosmologies." West compares the papyrus to RV 10.129.2–3.

55. West, *Orphic Poems*, 86–87. However, I am not persuaded by his argument that it was Protogonos "the firstborn" who sprang from the egg; rather, this was Phanes.

56. Meisner, *Orphic Tradition*, 121.

57. The Derveni commentator at least seems convinced that it is teaching the doctrine of Parmenides as well as Heraclitus. The Protogonos theogony is not only the earliest to which we have some access through the Derveni commentary, but the most intriguing and consistent. Plato does not refer to this name, but his intellectual demiurge is consistent with Phanes.

whirls like the wind, and has several heads of different animals.⁵⁸ From Phanes the scepter passes to his much older wife Nyx (Night), succeeded by Ouranos, Kronos, and, finally, Zeus.⁵⁹ For all her male successors, Night remains sovereign. Night is responsible for Zeus's power, which grows as he listens to her oracles.⁶⁰ She instructs Zeus to castrate Kronos and to swallow Phanes.⁶¹ By swallowing Kronos, Zeus contains "in his belly" all of his predecessors—except of course for the female Night on whom they all depend for their power.

Preparing for the next succession, Zeus sews Dionysus's fetus into his thigh, which makes him both the father and mother and leads to Dionysus being the sixth and final ruler of the cosmos. It was important for Mesopotamian myths like the Enuma Elish to get right the "six generations." Egyptians had also been struggling long before the Greeks to relate the One and the many.⁶² In this telling, from Phanes to Dionysus, all of the rulers are shamanic figures. They must be, since each one is the culmination of his predecessors: Phanes's epithets include Protogonos (Firsborn), Zeus, and Bromios/Dionysus.⁶³

Not only does this shamanic deity become preeminent among the heavenly rulers, but he also becomes fashioner of the cosmos. While Genesis 1 is the most uncompromising example of a *technomorphic* (creation) cosmology, Bronze Age myths typically are *biomorphic* (pairs of gods generating other gods).⁶⁴ However, as Meisner points out, "Phanes is born biomorphically but functions as a demiurge in the Hieronyman theogony and the Rhapsodies." ⁶⁵ Demiurgic fashioning intro-

---

58. "Hymn 6 to Protogonos" in Athanassakis and Wolkow, *Orphic Hymns*, 8–9. See also West, *Orphic Poems*, 205.

59. Regardless of whether Night was the primordial goddess, she only becomes the first ruler when Phanes passes her the scepter.

60. Translation from Betegh, *Derveni Papyrus*, 19. The upshot is that Zeus's father Kronos is his strength but Nyx is his enlightenment.

61. P. Derveni 13.4 and 16.3: αἰδοῖογ κα[τ]έπινεν, ὃς αἰθέρα ἔχθορε πρῶτος . . . πρωτογόνου βασιλέως αἰδοίου. I am not persuaded by Brisson's alternative reading: "He (= Zeus) swallowed down the reverend one (Phanes), who was the first to leap forth into ether [and not: "which ejaculated in the ether"] . . . of the first-born king (Phanes), the reverend one" See Brisson, review of Meisner, *Orphic Tradition*.

62. See Hornung, *Conceptions of God in Ancient Egypt*.

63. OF 70 (= Damascius, *De princ.* 1111.17). For Protogonos, see OF 86 (= Hermias, *In Plat. Phaedr.* 247c) and "Hymn to Protogonos" (OF 87). For Eros, see OF 74 (= Proclus, *In Plat. Tim.* 31a). For Zeus and Bromios, see OF 170 (= Proclus, *In Plat. Tim.* 29a). See Betegh's summary in *Derveni Papyrus*, 141, including notes 32–35. Formerly just another epithet for Dionysus, Phanes became the first god absorbed by the sixth and final ruler, Dionysus. See OF 60; 492.3, cited in Bernabé, "Gods in Ancient Orphism," 434.

64. Burkert, *Babylon, Memphis, Persopolis*, 63.

65. Meisner, *Orphic Tradition*, 24.

duces an intelligent craftsman who borrows what is near at hand to compose the visible world as close as possible to its ideal paradigm. For Orphic poets, this too is a myth, but it gestures toward the truth and provides a link between the birth of the gods and the formation of the cosmos. Homer and Hesiod knew nothing of this sort of demiurgic figure: gods, like mortals, were inhabitants of the cosmos—rulers of existing realms, not their artisans.

Taking on this demiurgic role, Dionysius became mainstream, much like Osiris in Egypt and Shiva in India at about the same time. Indeed, they seem like one and the same character. They are all outsiders who became insiders, oddballs who demanded respect, icons of an alternative spirituality that became mainstream. Finally, the gods collapse into a unity. The Derveni poem talks about the birth of the gods and their relations with each other. "All this must disappear," however, "as the personal identity of the individual gods is absorbed into the monumental figure of the one cosmic Mind."[66]

This Shamanic Deity Becomes the Divine One-and-All

Besides the Derveni Papyrus, Empedocles and Pindar cite the Protogonos theogony. Dionysus, the present ruler, has all gods—even Zeus—in his belly, signifying his consummate power. More gruesome than Hesiod's castration of Kronos by Zeus, the episode is taken directly from the Kumarbi myth of the Hittites.[67] He inherits the cumulative powers of them all as the ruler of the sixth generation. This transformation of myth reflects pantheism or panentheism, not atheism. Earth (Ge), Mother (Meter), Rhea, and Hera are all the same god (P. Derveni 22). Parker argues that "the Orphic myth of succession in heaven takes on a new colour if Protogonos and Zeus and Dionysus are in some sense the same god, if Zeus was implied in Protogonos and Protogonos reincarnated in Dionysus."[68] We encounter "different names of a single Nature" because "all that is one."[69]

---

66. Betegh, *Derveni Papyrus*, 219.

67. Burkert, *Orientalizing Revolution*, 217 n. 21; cf. 5, 94. Much else is drawn from this Hittite text, Burkert notes in *Babylon, Memphis, Persepolis*, 92: "This famous Hittite text has Kumarbi doing just the same to Anu, 'Heaven.' In consequence Kumarbi becomes pregnant with the Weather god, another god, and with the river Euphrates. And we find that Orpheus is following the Hurrian-Hittite model even here: in consequence of his dealings with the *aidoion* [phallus], Zeus now is carrying springs and rivers, together with all the other gods, in himself (col. 16 [12])." See also Meisner, *Orphic Tradition*; West, *Theogony*, 18–31; Kirk, *Myth*, 214–20. See also P. Derveni 13. Cf. Beckman, "Primordial Obstetrics."

68. Parker, "Early Orphism," 493–94. This was Proclus's interpretation. See Brisson, "Proclus et l'orphisme," 57.

69. OF 413, quoted in Bernabé, "Gods in Ancient Orphism," 431.

> Zeus is all things,
> he who makes appear all things in a cycle, Zeus, beginning,
> middle, and accomplishment,
> and Zeus is all almighty, Zeus has everything within himself.
>
> (OF 243)[70]

We catch the transition in mid-flight, as it were, in the *Mikroteros Krater* poem (OF 413–416). After a litany of identifications of gods with natural principles, the poem concludes, "all that is one."[71] The Rhapsodic theogony displays the same inconsistency: on the one hand, the world is the body of Zeus, while, on the other, Zeus is the demiurge.[72] However, this paradox is resolved by recourse to the emanation-return scheme: the many are really in the One. Zeus fashions the cosmos as demiurge precisely *as* his own body, as appearances or images of his absolute idea. There is a primeval One above all division, so that it can be the All in its incorporeal, intellectual, and immutable simplicity. Zeus is "Pan" (All), in both the Hieronyman and the Rhapsodic theogonies.[73]

But then how do the many participate in the One? In answer to this question Phanes-Zeus-Dionysus is represented as androgynous or bisexual, as both the male inseminator of ideas and the womb that brings forth individuals that bear them. The verb used here to describe conception (*mēsato*) is two-toned, signifying both a physical and an intellectual gestation, that is, the birth of a thought.[74] Biomorphic theogony has been absorbed into emanationism. Like produces like, as in the birth of a child to parents. Zeus—Universal Mind—becomes also his ancestor and son, spanning three generations of deities and both sexes.[75] It is worth remembering that "Male-female" was an epithet of Mesopotamian priests just as it was for Dionysus, Cybele, and their votaries: the raving maenads and Korybantes.[76] The old gods must reproduce offspring with their mate, but this one produces all things out of himself and by himself. Performed at the City Dionysia

---

70. Translation from Bernabé, "Gods in Ancient Orphism," 430.
71. Quoted in Bernabé, "Gods in Ancient Orphism," 431.
72. Bernabé, "Gods in Ancient Orphism," 428. M. L. West believes that the Rhapsodic theogony "was a composite work, created in the late Hellenistic period by conflating earlier Orphic poems, in particular the Hieronyman (a descendant of the Protogonos), Eudamian, and Cyclic Theogonies." See *Orphic Poems*, 69. On this basis, he believes, the basic outline of a founding Orphic theogony is possible and that it is substantiated by the Protogonos theogony known to the Derveni commentator. For his argument, see especially *Orphic Poems*, 68–139.
73. Bernabé, "Gods in Ancient Orphism," 428; cf. the Stoic-infused "Hymn to Zeus" (OF 243).
74. Bernabé, "Gods in Ancient Orphism," 428.
75. For Rhapsodies (OF 240–241) and Hieronyman theogony (OF 85), see Bernabé, "Gods in Ancient Orphism," 437.
76. See Aristophanes, *Av.* 690–702, and "To Dionysos" (OH 30).

in 414 BCE, Aristophanes's *Birds* uses the same bisexual language (*Av.* 690–702) as Orphic Hymn 30: "I call upon loud-roaring, reveling Dionysos, primeval, two-natured, thrice-born Bacchic lord, savage, ineffable, secretive, two-horned and two-shaped."[77] Just as the previous rulers are collapsed into an abstract Unity, androgyny represents this principle as transcending all dualities: one/many, male/female, light/darkness, good/evil, mind/matter. So "he became solitary," "Mind itself, being alone" (P. Derveni 13). In short, everything ultimately is a spark of divinity inasmuch as it is mind, soul, logos, air, etc.

Various types of monism can be accommodated in such a tale, but existence monism (pantheism) or priority monism (panentheism) fit most comfortably. Everything is Mind, whose single thought unfolds into a multiplicity of appearances, as witnessed in the poem attributed to Linus above: "all dies that's mortal, but the substrate was and is immortal forever, fashioned thus, yet with strange images and varied form will change and vanish from the sight of all."[78] What is *real* is one, indivisible, immutable being; the changing images visible to the physical eye are *appearances* that vanish.[79] In this way, generation and passing away are seen merely as illusions. The real always remains, despite appearances. Mind is all.

A similar assimilation of minor shamanic deities to a utopian "All" occurred in Hinduism. As in other traditions, the shaman becomes the sage; the erstwhile heretic becomes the pioneer of a new orthodoxy.[80] In Vedic religion, still focused on rituals, *brahman* was the sacred power that made effectual the sacred formulas spoken in the liturgy. But in the Upanishads *brahman* is Absolute Reality.[81] Depending on the school, Shiva or Vishnu assumed "a universal or cosmic role" that he never enjoyed through the Vedic age.[82] Samuel adds, "One can certainly see signs of a movement in this direction in some of the later Brahmana specu-

---

77. See also Locke, "Orpheus and Orphism," 11. The Orphic Hymn is a late testimony but is probably more consistent with the warp and woof of the early theogonies than many of the modern alternatives. Colored as it may be by Neoplatonism, it is nevertheless more in touch than modern scholarship with classical ways of thinking.

78. Quoted in West, *Orphic Poems*, 57.

79. Athanassakis and Wolkow, *Orphic Hymns*, xvi.

80. As Patrick Olivelle observes, "Some of the fundamental values and beliefs that we generally associate with Indian religions in general and Hinduism in particular were in part the creation of the renouncer tradition. These include the two pillars of Indian theologies: samsara—the belief that life in this world is one of suffering and subject to repeated deaths and births (rebirth); moksa/nirvana—the goal of human existence." See Olivelle, "Renouncer Tradition," 273–74.

81. See RV 10.90 in Brereton and Jamison, *Rigveda*, 243–44. See also 32–37 for a helpful discussion of later appropriation for the *varna* system of social and political organization.

82. Samuel, *Origins of Yoga and Tantra*, 201.

lations and the earlier *Upaniṣads*. These texts suggest a coming together of the philosophical and metaphysical tendencies of the *Upaniṣads with a commitment to a specific universal deity that derives from other sources.*"[83] Various deities came to be "treated as emanations (*vyûha*) of Nārāyaṇa/Viṣṇu as supreme godhead."

> This is the basis of the later [third century BC] Pāñcarātra ritual tradition, as well as a precursor to the eventual concept of the multiple avatars or divine manifestations of Viṣṇu in the *Bhagavadgîtâ*.... Another fairly early Vedic text, the *Śatarudrīya*, is a litany accompanying offerings to Rudra: Gonda describes it as representing Rudra-Śiva "in his ambivalent character, both as a malevolent and as a benevolent deity" and notes that *Rudra-Śiva in this text is "unmistakably on the way to become an All-God."*[84]

Moreover, there is a new figure, Prajapati, who is a demiurge. The "Lord of creatures," Prajapati becomes identified with the creator Brahma (distinct from *brahman*) in this period. Like the Orphic Protogonos-Phanes, Prajapati is bisexual, which means that he both generates and gives birth to himself and to all gods and nature. And also like Dionysus and Osiris, he is associated with sacrifice through ritual dismemberment.[85] In Zoroastrianism as well, the many gods of Iranian polytheism become assimilated to emanations of Ahura Mazda.[86] Some descendants of the Jewish exiles who remained in Persia developed this concept more fully, planting the seeds of kabbalah that would be harvested centuries later. Behind Ahura Mazda himself is "Infinite Time." Yet Ahura Mazda is "the Being par-excellence."[87] One could say that Ahura Mazda now has "all gods in his belly."

Similarly, in the Egyptian Book of the Dead, the deities become attributes, emanations, or aspects of Re.[88] Amun (Hidden One) is Re's ineffability, for example,

---

83. Samuel, *Origins of Yoga and Tantra*, 201, emphasis added.

84. Samuel, *Origins of Yoga and Tantra*, 203–4, emphasis added. Samuel quotes Gonda, "Śatarudriya," 82.

85. See especially the Hiranyagarbha Sukta, where the father/mother of all is identified with the sun and Prajapati. M. L. West discusses other parallels with the Rigveda in West, *Early Greek Philosophy*, 28–34; West, *Orphic Poems*, 104. The parallels are described well in Gier, *Spiritual Titanism*, 59–76. This is true also in Jain and Buddhist religions; see Gombrich, *What the Buddha Thought*, 34.

86. Peter Clark considers "pre-Zoroastrian" sources in *Zoroastrianism*, 56; cf. Dhalla, *Zoroastrian Theology*, 96–142, see also 19–25; McEvilley, *Shape of Ancient Thought*, 60–61.

87. Dhalla, *Zoroastrian Theology*, 19–25.

88. The world's earliest recorded writings are the Pyramid Texts of the Old Kingdom, reaching back to the twenty-sixth century BCE. Moreover, there were four major centers of Egyptian religion—Heliopolis, Hermopolis, Memphis, and Thebes—that generated distinct theologies.

and in his flights Horus is Re-Horakhty, and so forth. A similar trail emerges in the Memphite theology.[89] Osiris replaces Re in the same way that Dionysus subsumes Zeus, and Shiva eclipses not only his epic-era Rudra but, for Shaivists at least, the entire pantheon. The old gods of the epics are dying.[90]

"He swallowed the phallus of [Phanes/Protogonos] which ejaculates the ether first . . . the phallus of the first born," the Protogonos theogony relates, "and he himself became solitary." "By this," says the Derveni commentator, "he makes clear that the Mind itself, being alone, is worth everything, as if the others were nothing. For it would not be possible for the subsisting things to be such without the Mind. And in the following verse after this he said that the Mind is worth everything: 'Now he is king of all and will always be . . . Mind'" (P. Derveni 13 and 16).[91]

MIND EMANATES WORLD: COSMIC EGG AND COSMIC HUMAN

The emanation of our unborn and undying soul is prior logically to that of the born but undying gods. "In this way," according to Aristophanes's *Birds*, "we are by far the oldest of all the blessed ones" (*Av.* 702–703). This message, repeated on the Athenian stage, is found in the passwords for the afterlife discovered in tombs of Orphic initiates.[92] The shaman traversed the three worlds, but now the

---

In all of them, Ra the sun god represented the chief deity, sailing on his golden barge from sunrise to sunset and repeating the cycle the next day. The cult of Ra the sun god became the state religion in the twenty-sixth century as well.

89. In Memphite theology, "Ptah is the fountain of life for the gods and all material realities," according to the Shabaka Stone (early seventh century BCE). "The gods who came into being as Ptah: Ptah upon the Great Throne." Ptah is "the heart and tongue of the Ennead" (the nine gods as Ptah's manifestation). Ptah is therefore in all gods and all gods are in Ptah: they are interchangeable: "[T]he Great, that is the mighty Great One is Ptah, who caused all the gods [to live], as well as their kas [spirits], through his heart, by which Horus became Ptah, and through this tongue by which Thoth became Ptah." The single thought and speech of Ptah makes these other gods identical with Ptah himself. Atum emerges next from the waters as the demiurge, identified with the sun and fire. See line 64 of the Shabaka Stone in Bodine, "Shabaka Stone," 17–19. See also Wilkinson, *Gods and Goddesses of Ancient Egypt*, 77–78; Redford, "Ptah"; H. Smith, *Man and His Gods*, 45; Lesko, "Ancient Egyptian Cosmogonies," 95–96. Henri Frankfort's *Ancient Egyptian Religion*, 53–55, is very insightful.

90. Vos, "Atum," 121.

91. See also Vyas, "Concept of Prajapati in Vedic Literature." Wendy Doniger makes frequent comparisons throughout her provocative study, *Splitting the Difference*.

92. Aristophanes, *Av.* 702–703 (= OF 1), quoted in Betegh, *Derveni Papyrus*, 148. Luc Brisson thinks that *Birds* was a major source of Orphic theogonies; see "La figure de Chronos," 38.

human being is the three worlds in microcosm. This microcosm/macrocosm was as novel in the Vedic world as it was in Greece.⁹³ For the Derveni commentator all the gods, even Zeus, were just different names for the activities and powers of the "monumental figure of the one cosmic Mind," which alone is unborn. Yet in spite of this "pantheistic and monistic moment," the Derveni commentator finally separates Mind from the "other beings."⁹⁴ This is panentheism in a nutshell: the world is Mind but Mind transcends the world.⁹⁵

Natural supernaturalism is an apt epithet for this new utopian outlook.⁹⁶ Cosmic Mind pervades all things—in fact, it is all things—and yet in truth transcends things. This doctrine of emanation lies at the heart of the Western tradition of metaphysics from Pythagoras to Proclus.

The only question is whether the many changing things are nonentities—merely appearances (absolute idealism)—or are opposites that an intelligent mixer blends into a harmony (dualism merging into monism). In Diogenes Laertius's succinct formulation once again, "all things proceed from unity and are resolved again into unity" (*Vit. phil.* 1.3).

There are two themes that help us to gain a clearer picture of this emergent worldview. The first is the golden egg from which the demiurge is hatched, using the materials of the shell's upper half to form the world above and the lower half to shape the sensible world. The second is the image of a cosmic human whose higher and lower halves make much the same point. It is this latter myth that brings into sharp focus the highly influential notion of a correspondence between microcosm and macrocosm.

McEvilley suggests that in the Middle Vedic period "when the monistic impulse takes ascendancy," there was an "importation of late Akkadian texts involving the concept of a Cosmic Person."⁹⁷ In Rigveda 10.90, the "Hymn of the Cosmic Man"

However, Betegh thinks the egg motif appears later and was perhaps even influenced by Aristophanes's *Birds*, but that Aristophanes "created a comic pastiche of different theogonies" and should not be used as a source for Orphism; see *Derveni Papyrus*, 148–49. The debate reminds us of the dangers of looking for a single source of anything in this period.

93. Gombrich elaborates the Buddhist use of this correlation in *What the Buddha Thought*, 38–44.

94. Betegh, *Derveni Papyrus*, 221, 223.

95. But we can see how pantheistic Stoics thought that they had every right to the Orphic-Pythagorean and even Platonic tradition, like the Platonists. See Copleston, *History of Philosophy*, 47–53; cf. Rubarth, "Stoic Mind."

96. Thomas Carlyle coined the term and M. H. Abrams used it in the title of his enormously helpful book, *Natural Supernaturalism*.

97. McEvilley, *Shape of Ancient Thought*, 60–61.

represents a human (ideal, incorporeal, and divine) as the divine All from whom all things emanate. "The Man alone in this whole world: what has come into being and what is to be . . . a quarter of him is all living beings; three quarters are the immortal in heaven. With his three quarters the Man went upwards, but a quarter of him came to be here again" (10.90.2–4). The cosmos is not something created all at once but is generated again and again in the sacrifices and rituals. From it horses, cows, goats, and sheep appeared.

> The brahmin was his mouth. The ruler was made his two arms. As to his thighs—that is what a freeman was. From his two feet the servant was born. . . . From his head heaven developed. . . . From his two feet the earth . . . when the gods, extending the sacrifice, bound the Man as the sacrificial animal. With the sacrifice the gods performed the sacrifice for themselves: these were the first foundations. (RV 10.90.9–16)[98]

This formative myth quite clearly identifies the upper part with divinity (three-quarters remaining in the upper world) and the lower part with the physical world. The hierarchical ontology is supported by the strict ranking of social and political life, a point that was emphasized in the evolution of the *varna* (caste) system.[99] There is considerable similarity between Ilawela, sacrificed by the gods to provide intelligence for clay creatures, and stories like the one above from the Rigveda as well as Dionysus and Orpheus myths.[100] As we will see, Plato offers a calculus quite similar to the *varna* scheme.

Even before Pherecydes was Hermotimus of Clazomenae (late seventh or early sixth century).[101] Aristotle said Hermotimus taught the view of Mind over matter long before Anaxagoras, and he is classed with Parmenides and Empedocles by Sextus Empiricus.[102] Like the demiurgic intellect of other philosophical religions at the time, Zoroastrianism's Gayomart is the cosmic body. Everything is one of his limbs, in a finite way.

---

98. Brereton and Jamison, *Rigveda*, 243–44.
99. See Brereton and Jamison, *Rigveda*, 32–37, for a helpful discussion of later appropriation for the *varna* system of social and political organization.
100. See tablet 1 of the Atrahasis in Dalley, *Myths from Mesopotamia*, 15–16.
101. Though he was identified as a Pythagorean by Lucian, a number of Hellenistic sources refer to traditions in which Pythagoras mentions him as one of his previous incarnations. Nineteenth- and early twentieth-century specialists (including Diels) dismissed him as a mystic and magician (such strictures would exclude many of our pioneering figures). His profile has risen considerably in recent decades to match the esteem in which he was held by ancients.
102. Aristotle, *Metaph.* 984b20; Sextus Empiricus, *Math.* 9.1.7.

Only in the sixth century BCE does the cosmic egg become a trope for an emanationist cosmology. There is no cosmic egg lying around anywhere in Homer, Hesiod, or early Vedic and Egyptian lore.[103] However, all at once across Asia and the Mediteranean, the egg becomes central to cosmologies.[104] In all these myths, it shows how the absolute One is the source of duality. Returning to Aristophanes's play, *Birds*, we read:

> First there was Chaos and Night, black Erebus and wide Tartarus, but neither earth nor air nor sky existed. In Erebus' boundless bosom first of all black-winged Night produced an egg, a wind-egg, from which, as the seasons came around, there grew the lovely Eros, whose back gleams bright with golden wings, whose flight is swift as winds. This [Eros], mingling by night with winged Chaos throughout wide Tartarus, hatched our race, and first brought us into the light. At first there was no race of immortals, until Eros mixed up everything, but once each one was intermixed with the other, then sky and ocean formed and earth, and the immortal race of all the blessed gods. (Aristophanes, *Av.* 693–703 [= OF 64 B = 1K])

Night's curious "wind-egg" (*hypenēmion ōon*) reflects a Semitic influence.[105] Aristophanes must have assumed that his audience was familiar enough with these strange West Asian myths to understand the point.[106]

In Greece, Pherecydes initiates speculation on everything emerging from the golden egg.[107] As noted above, Kronos (Time) places his seeds in caves from which

---

103. It is interesting that in rejecting separate forms, Aristotle seems to parody this view, referring to the "vacuous egg" (*Hist. an.* 559b24).

104. For example, see the myths surrounding Babylonian Belos (Marduk), Egyptian Ptah, Hurrian-Hittite Kumarbi, Syrian Dagan, Indic Prajapati, and Chinese Pangu. On the contrast with Homer and Hesiod, see Betegh, *Derveni Papyrus*, 180–81.

105. West, *Orphic Poems*, 201–2; cf. Meisner, *Orphic Tradition*, 89–91.

106. On the Indian side, see RV 10.129 in Brereton and Jamison, *Rigveda*, 246–47. On the Iranian side see Kreyenbroek, "Cosmogony and Cosmology," 303–7; cf. Bundahishn Ibd., providing both milk (43.15) and semen (94.4). *Yasna* 13.85 refers obliquely to the episode and there are prayers on behalf of the great white bull (13.13, 35, 39). The Cow's Lament (*Yasna* 29b) is an allegory supporting Zoroaster's mission against the lies of Ahriman. Meisner writes, "Around the second century BC in Persia, Zoroastrian cosmologies also seem to have involved a time-god and a cosmic egg. Zurvan Akarana ('Infinite Time') has sex with himself and produces two sons, Ohrmazd and Ahriman. Each is responsible, respectively, for good and bad things. However, closer in time and space were 'three Phoenician cosmogonies that involve the motif of the egg.'" Meisner, *Orphic Tradition*, 90–91. Cf. West, *Orphic Poems*, 103–4. Significantly, in this picture there is a transcendent God above the principles of one and many, similar to Pythagoreanism.

107. The first philosopher-theologian to write in prose, Pherecydes created a myth in which Kronos ejaculated fire, air, and moisture, depositing the seeds in five caves. From the mixture

the first gods we know appear, the first and supreme of them being Eurynome, a nymph-goddess of water. Impregnated by the serpentine Ophion, she lays an egg around which Ophion entwined to fertilize it and from this egg the world was hatched. But Ophion boasted he had accomplished this by himself. Ophios the god of chaos reminds us of Typhon, known in Egypt as Set. Similar to Horus, Zeus defeats Ophios.[108] West notes that the cosmic pole and the cosmic tree on which Zas hung his embroidered robe for Chthonie are common shamanic tropes, "but wherever Pherecydes got this idea from, it can hardly have been from any ancestral Greek tradition."[109] So far as we can tell, this myth of Ophion is the "eccentric cosmology of Pherecydes."[110]

"Closer in time and space to the Greeks, there are three Phoenician cosmogonies that involve the motif of the egg," notes Meisner. Aither and Aer produce Oulomos (Semitic for time). "Oulomos has sex with himself and produces 'Chousoros the opener' and an egg, and 'when [the egg] broke in two, heaven and earth appeared from the halves.'"[111] Epimenides has Aer and Night generating Oceanus and Tethys, who produced the egg from which the first gods emerged and thence all life.[112]

> In each of these cosmogonies, the primordial deity is a personification of Time, like Chronos in the Hieronyman and Rhapsodic theogonies. This Time deity does not create the world, but produces the deity who will create the world: in Phoenician cosmology, Oulomos produces both the egg and the creator god

---

of these seeds he made another generation of gods: the fiery gods of Ouranos and shining Ether, gods of wind in gusty Tartarus, watery gods in Chaos, and gods of darkness in the cave of Night. Zeus became Eros and married Chthonie (Earth). On the third day of the wedding, Zeus presented her with a robe embroidered with Earth and Ogenos and its mansions, causing Chthonie to rejoice, "Henceforth, I will be called Gē!" See Schibli, *Pherecydes of Syros*, 128–29. In other words, she is no longer merely terrestrial but heavenly.

108. Apollonius summarizes this myth, identifying it as Orphic in *Argonautica* 1.49. Schibli summarizes the fragments and *testimonia* in *Pherecydes of Syros*, 128–29; cf. 89–90. Pherecydes is the first Greek to include Ophios in a myth. See West, "Three Presocratic Cosmologies," 161–63; cf. West, *Indo-European Poetry and Myth*, 347–48.

109. West, *Indo-European Poetry and Myth*, 346–47.

110. West, *Indo-European Poetry and Myth*, 348. West adds, "The Greek myth might be derived from the Near East and the Indic and Germanic ideas of a pillar from the shamanistic cosmologies of the Finno-Ugric and other peoples of central and northern Asia. . . . It is a form of the *axis mundi* associated with the shaman's passage between higher and lower worlds" (346).

111. Meisner, *Orphic Tradition*, 90–91.

112. See Fowler, *Early Greek Mythography*, 2:7–8. See similarly Rhapsodic theogony (OF 109–119B); Meisner, *Orphic Tradition*, 36, 95.

Chousoros, who opens the egg; in Persian cosmology, Zurvan produces Ohrmazd, who creates the sky in the form of an egg with the earth inside; and in Vedic cosmogony, Kala produces Prajapati, who in earlier accounts is equated with an embryo and in later accounts is born from an egg. The similarities between these narratives and the later Orphic theogonies are striking, since they also being with Time (Chronos), who produces the cosmic egg out of which the creator deity Phanes is born.[113]

However, the Orphic myth is closest to the Vedic in which "the time-god Kala produces the creator god Prajapati by means of a cosmic egg."[114]

In India, Prajapati not only emerges from the cosmic egg but actually is the cosmic egg celebrated in the Hiranyagarbha: "He is the God of gods, and none beside him."[115] He is Brahma the creator also called the Manifest in the Mahabhar (Manu Smrti 1.1.9). Floating in the emptiness and darkness of nonexistence for a year, the cosmic egg broke into halves, forming the heavens (*svarga*) and the earth (*prithvi mata*). In the Upanishads he becomes the World Soul or *brahman* itself.[116] The new religion of Taoism represents the primordial chaos mythically

---

113. Meisner, *Orphic Tradition*, 90–91.
114. Meisner, *Orphic Tradition*, 90–91.
115. RV 10.121. Translation by Griffith in Brereton and Jamison, *Rigveda*, 121–22. As we have seen, one obvious point of contrast between locative and utopian epochs is the shifting focus in sacred texts from rituals to philosophical religion. Like the early Gathas in comparison with Zoroastrianism and Orphic myths in relation to Homer, the Upanishads mark the beginning of a transformation from Vedic ritualism to Hinduism. They are called *vedanta*, "last parts of the Vedas," because they are seen as their culmination. The actual school of Advaita Vedanta arrives centuries later but is arguably the most natural reading of the Upanishads, along with the Bhagavadgita and Brahmasutra. The oldest parts of the Mahabharata (including the Bhagavadgita), like the oldest layers of Upanishads, originate around the beginning of the fifth or fourth century BCE.
116. Deusson and Geden, *Philosophy of the Upanishads*, 198. On the Pelasgian myth of Eurynome (proto-Gaia) laying an egg, see Graves, *Greek Myths*, 27–30. Parallel to Mesopotamian and Greek developments, the older layers of Vedic materials are epics with hymns and spells while the classical texts (fourth century BCE to fifth century CE) are more philosophical (a good example being the Chandogya Upanishad). See Flood, *Introduction to Hinduism*, 40. As we have seen, one obvious point of contrast between locative and utopian epochs is the shifting focus in sacred texts from rituals to philosophical religion. Like the early Gathas in comparison with Zoroastrianism and Orphic myths in relation to Homer, the Upanishads mark the beginning of a transformation from Vedic ritualism to Hinduism. and it is also one of the most important sources of Advaita monism (or nondualism). The oldest parts of the Mahabharata (which includes the Bhagavadgita) originate around the beginning of the fifth or fourth century BC. Three main subschools include Nondualism (Advaita), Qualified Nondualism (Vishishtadvaita), and Dualism (Dvaita). Yet all Vedanta schools agree that Brahman is the material as well as

as Hundun, an innocently reckless, confused, unintelligible, and messy child also identified with the cosmic egg.[117]

According to what can be pieced together from earlier and later Gathas, a similar pattern was emerging in Persian religion.[118] Infinite Time (Zurvan), in a moment of forgetfulness, produced the opposing twins: Ahura Mazda, the supreme deity of goodness and truth, and Ahriman the principle of evil and falsehood. The former shaped his creations in the form of "bright, white fire" (Bd 1.44) while Ahriman made his creation from darkness. "Time" (Zurvan) is the transcendent absolute from which good and evil emanate. Even in "orthodox" Zoroastrianism, "the original, motionless state was described as ideal and motion, procreation, and diversity were indirectly attributed to the incursion of Ahriman."[119] The upper eggshell of the first creation is sky while water filled the egg's lower half. Fire is the principle of life while water is Ahriman's evil chaos.[120]

In Egypt's version, the boiling waters produced the cosmic egg from which emerged Atum, ejaculating Shu (dry air, preservation) and Tefnut (moist air, change and time).[121] So in this case there is a primordial divinity transcending opposite male and female principles and hence, in a riddling way, is androgynous and generates the first pair of gods by himself. The demiurge produced by this transcendent One ejaculates the seeds of diversity. Thought and word are Atum's means of creation, and all gods and living creatures have his spirit or *ka*.[122] In an-

---

instrumental cause of the world, the self is the agent of his or her actions for which he or she is responsible (*karma*), and transmigration (*samsara*) with the goal of final release (*moksha*) from the wheel of rebirth.

117. Girardot, *Myth and Meaning in Early Taoism*, 134.

118. The main text for Iranian cosmology during this time is the Bundahishn, which exists in a shorter Indian recension (IBd) and a longer Iranian recension (Gbd or simply Bd). My references are to the latter (Bd). See Agostini and Thrope, *Bundahišn*.

119. Kreyenbroek, "Cosmogony and Cosmology," 303–7.

120. Kreyenborek, "Cosmogony and Cosmology," 303–4.

121. A good English translation of the Shabaka Stone is found in Pritchard, *Ancient Near Eastern Texts*, 4–5. The following story is central to Memphite theology. The first emanation is the Ogdoad (eight gods in four pairs): Amun/Amaunat (Hiddenness), Huhe/Hauket (Formlessness), Kuk/Kauket (Darkness) and Nun/Naunet (Watery Abyss). Ptah communicates to Atum all his attributes—thought and speech—in order to create the world. From Atum-Ptah proceed Shu (Air), Tefnut (Moisture), Geb (Earth), and Nut (Sky). They give birth to Osiris, Isis, Set, and Nephthys (the purely intellegible form of female). A similar triad to Osiris, Isis, and Horus in the Late Period is more cosmological than eschatological: Nefertem, son of Ptah, and Sekhnet. A youthful Nefertem emerges from the primal waters on the egg-like mount sitting in a lotus flower. He is represented as a warlike lion, bearing a scimitar and a falcon's head with a lotus headdress. See Hart, *Egyptian Gods and Goddesses*, 99.

122. Wilkinson, *Gods and Goddesses of Ancient Egypt*, 18, 99–101.

Shaman to Sage: Religion of the One

other account, the cosmic egg was laid by Thoth, the god of writing and recorded judgments. The sun king Re hatched first, creating the world.[123] In spite of different theogonies, the origin of the world from a cosmic egg is consistent. The divine elements (Ogdoad or Ennead) emanate through a combination of opposites.[124]

In all its forms, the cosmic egg presents dualism as a form of monism and a monism that presupposes dualism. The upshot of the division of the egg is that the demiurge formed the cosmos from ideas (the upper shell) and lower matter. Much like his teacher Pherecydes, Pythagoras believed that opposites formed a unity. The universe is a constant mixing of this strife and love, but in its essence are the same elements in ever-diluted mixtures.

Thus, even dualism is ultimately monistic, since the opposites are mixed into a single substance. Pythagoras's Monad is like the male principle of *purusha* (symbolized as Vishnu): ultimate reality identical with *brahman*. Yet beneath the Monad is the Dyad, which (like Plato's World Soul) is the source of multiplicity.[125] From this opposition all others unfold. As Aristotle records it, Pythagoras listed ten opposites that are essential to the overall good of the cosmos.[126] This list of opposites is virtually identical to that of Taoism's *yin* and *yang* and the Dvaita Vedanta school: male/female, rational/irrational, spiritual/material, and so forth, but their mixture fills out the cosmos into a unity with descending grades of being. Yet just as all things multiply from the simple unity of the Absolute (Zeus/*brahman*/*tai chi*), so they return. The opposites, like male and female producing a child, resolve in a united substance.[127] In contrast, Parmenides and the Advaita Vedanta school

---

123. Dunand and Zivie-Coche, *Gods and Men in Egypt*, 42–57. On the egg specifically, see 9–10, 50–51, 293. Ra is also depicted as a child (or scarab) emerging from a lotus.

124. Wilkinson, *Gods and Goddesses of Ancient Egypt*, 78, 206–7. See Leeming, *Creation Myths of the World*, 104. In Heliopolis, Nun (primeval waters) engendered the primal mound and the self-begotten Amun (who is also Re). Amun then spat or masturbated air (Shu) and moisture (Tefnut). They begat Geb (Earth) and Nut (Sky), the parents of Osiris, Isis, Set, and Nephthys. See Dunand and Zivie-Coche, *Gods and Men in Egypt*, 42–57.

125. To offer just a few insightful examples, see Astore, "Unveiling Ultimate Reality."

126. They are good/evil; one/many; infinite/finite; male/female; light/darkness; right/left; even/odd; rest/motion; straight/crooked; square/oblong. See Aristotle, *Metaph.* 988a7–15; cf. *Cael.* 279b17–280a10, 27–32.

127. The Taoist opposites are: female/masculine; black/white; dark/light; north/south; fire (i.e., creativity)/water (i.e., transformation); passive/active; moon/sun; cold/hot; old/young; even numbers/odd numbers; valleys/mountains; poor/rich; soft/hard; gives spirit to all things/gives form to all things.The I Ching Hexagram is explained in Wilhelm, *Book of Changes*, esp. 209–324. The dualism-in-monism (along with the emergence of a demiurgic figure from a cosmic egg) is found also in chapter 11 of Chuang Tzu (Zhuangzi) in Watson, *Complete Works of Chuang Tzu*, 122. See also Mair, *Tao Te Ching*, 90. Mair compares Chuang Tzu to Zeno of Elea and Socrates

Chapter 3

simply denied that there are opposites. There is only Being, which is simple and unchanging thought.[128]

For dualists and nondualists alike, the highest enlightenment leads one ultimately to the realization that there is nothing and no one except the One. Max Müller writes, "Thus the pupil is led on step by step to what is the highest object of the Upanishads, viz. the recognition of the self in man as identical with the Highest Self or Brahman."[129]

---

in Mair, "Chuang Tzu," 2:24; Mair, *Wandering on the Way*. See also Girardot, *Myth and Meaning in Early Taoism*, 134.

128. Katz, *One*, 1–2. Cf. Michaels, *Hinduism*, 264; Larson and Bhattacharya, *Sāmkhya*; Ruzsa, "Sankhya"; Bhattacharji, *Indian Theogony*, 35–37. Just as in the Orphic-Platonic tradition, the One is the realm of reality: one ideal, unchanging, unmoving thought contrasted with the realm of appearance. In Hindu thought (especially the school of Advaita Vendanta), this contrast between reality and appearance is represented by *brahman* and *maya*, respectively. *Brahman*—Ultimate Reality—is the single cause (*upadina*) of all emanation. Gough, *Philosophy of the Upanishads*, 47–48. Though often translated illusion, *maya* is used typically to denote appearance. See Vroom, *No Other Gods*, 57.

Hinduism is notoriously resistant to tidy Western categories, but there are six "orthodox" schools, two of which are the Samkhya (dualist) and Advaita Vedanta (monist) schools. Nondualist Upanishads include the Brihadaranyaka (4.3.32) and Chandogya (6.2). See also Timalsina, "Purusavāda." For the identification of the "Universal Being" as "supraessential," see the Purusha Sukta of the Rigveda. See for example Krisnananda, *Daily Invocations*, esp. 6 and 13–16. On p. 13 the "Universal Being" is described as "indivisible supraessential." Cf. Paramananda, *Plato and Vedic Idealism*; Ram, "Plato and Vedanta"; Staal, *Advaita and Neoplatonism*. McEvilley emphasizes the influence of Indian philosophy on Greek thought in *Shape of Ancient Thought*. While the Samkhya school holds that *brahman* is personal and *purusha* is manifold (e.g., individual spirits or souls), Vedanta denies the former and teaches that there is one all-pervasive spirit or soul (*purusha*). Moreover, over against the nontheistic Samkhya tradition, the Advaita school teaches that only an intelligent *brahman*, not an unintelligent *prakriti*, can be the cause of the world; see Sharma, *Critical Survey of Indian Philosophy*, 242–44. Consequently, unlike the Samkhya school, Advaita Vedanta does not require a liberation of *purusha* from *prakriti*, since the latter is but the former's illusory appearance in the realm of phenomena. This is the basic difference between the two types of monism emerging *across* these civilizations: opposites mixed versus opposites denied.

The Dvaita Vedanta school, formulated by Ramanuja (1017–1137 CE), is one of the three major schools of Hindu philosophy, *dvaita* meaning "two." According to Dvaita Vedanta, the world is real, created, and exists externally to the self. Although souls are similar to the divine essence, there is no merging of identities. Each soul exists independently from others and has its own qualities and destinies. See Sharma, *Dvaita School of Vedanta*. See also Stafford, "Dvaita, Advaita, and Viśiṣṭādvaita." Changing things are not as good as unchanging things but they really exist distinctly. However, even Ramanuja's dualist philosophy is considered a form of qualified monism (Vishishtadvaita). See also Stoker, "Madhva."

129. Müller, *Upanishads*, 15.

The individual âtman or self, however, was with the Brahmans a phase or phenomenal modification only of the Higher Self, and that Highest Self was to them the last point which could be reached by philosophical speculation. It was to them what in other systems of philosophy has been called by various names, the One, the Divine, the Absolute. The highest aim of all thought and study with the Brahman of the Upanishads was to recognise his own self in the Highest Self, and through that knowledge to return to it, and regain his identity with it. Here to know was to be, to know the Âtman was to be the Âtman, and the reward of that highest knowledge after death was freedom from new births, or immortality.[130]

The so-called "lower" (*para*) *brahman* is known by identifiable attributes while the "higher" (*apara*) *brahman* remains utterly transcendent. Similar to Parmenides, the Prameya Ratnavali teaches that the latter is the real unity. "Viṣnu who is the Self of all embodied being . . . called figuratively the Lord of Paramâ. . . . There is one ruler, all-pervading, the Lord Kriṣna, the adored of all and *though one, shines forth as many.*"[131]

Everything other than the One (*apara brahman*) is an appearance or illusion (*maya*).[132] Only to the extent that we are attached to the body do we imagine a distinction between subject and object, self and other, whether other beings or divinity. We find it in many places, such as the "That art Thou" (*tat tuam asi*) dictum of the Chandogya Upanishad.[133] Consequently, the world of multiplicity, subject to the bonds of finitude—time, change, body, etc.—must either denied, overcome, or escaped.[134] *Moksha* is the supreme good (freedom from the possibility of suffering) "in the realization of the Self as Self pure and simple."[135]

---

130. Müller, *Upanishads*, 17.

131. For the *Prameya Ratnavali*, see Basu, *Sacred Books of the Hindus*, 15–16, emphasis added. It should be noted that Jainism and Buddhism, both founded in the sixth century, do not see any need to affirm the existence of any personal god. Some Buddhists worship Gautama, and Mahayana Buddhism considers other buddhas to be divine beings. See Williams, *Mahâyâna Buddhism*, 21.

132. Indich, *Consciousness in Advaita Vedanta*, 50.

133. Chandogya Upanishad 6.8.7: "The finest essence here—that constitutes the self of this whole world; that is the truth; that is the self (*atman*). And that's how you are, Śvetāketu." Translation from Olivelle, *Upaniṣads*, 152.

134. See Samkhyakarika 57. Quoted in Larson, *Classical Sāṁkhya*, 273.

135. Samkhyakarika 1.3. Similarities between Shiva and Dionysus also are not difficult to draw, as I have pointed out. See also Sinha, *Samkhya Philosophy*, 1; Larson, *Classical Sāṁkhya*, 36–47. Essential also are the SU 3.11.15, 20; 4.1–4, 10; 51; 258–261, and BU 5.4.3–4 in Olivelle, *Upaniṣads*, 73–74. Larson, *Classical Sāṁkhya*, 75, identifies four main stages of development: the oldest Upanishads and Vedic hymns (900 to 600 BCE), early metaphysical speculations (fourth

The emanation-return scheme unites all metaphysics emerging in this period. The effects are in the cause (*satkaryavada*). All that exists emanates dependently from something else above it (*pratityasamutpada*).[136] The pure spring from which Being surges is not affected by the mixing with muddy sediment downstream. Like the visible sun it shines regardless of the darkness of matter. On the one hand, Parmenides and Indic Advaita insist that the One/*brahman* must appear just as the individual soul appears in a body, yet this is a "show" (*maya*), a magical illusion. Cornfield observes that Parmenides makes humans—their senses in particular—responsible for the illusions but never provides an account for why this is so.[137]

This ontological antithesis of body and soul is the microcosm projected onto the cosmos itself. Even in its monism there remains a conflict-dualism, as suggested by the male-female opposites of Egypt's Ogdoad, Brahma the creator and Vishnu the preserver on the one side and Shiva the destroyer on the other, or Ahura Mazda and Ahriman. Yet, as in Orphic theogonies, there is a further trend to absorb them into either Vishnu or Shiva.[138] Even when biomorphic genealogies appear, there remains a simple Absolute transcending all multiplicity. From this One all things emanate and return.

At the level of the macrocosm, this means that we should treat all the variety of sense as a shadow or illusion. At the microcosmic level, the goal is return from the diversity of bodies to the unity of spirit. In Hundun perhaps we find our shamanic deity of Chinese philosophy.[139] Chuang Tzu has Hundun exhort:

> Smash your form and body, spit out hearing and eyesight, forget you are a thing among other things, and you may join in great unity with the deep and

---

to first century BCE, including the Bhagavadgita), classical Samkhya (first to tenth centuries CE), and a Samkhya renaissance (fifteenth to seventeenth centuries).

136. McFarlane, "Process and Emptiness."

137. See Cornford, *Plato and Parmenides*.

138. Not to be confused with *brahman*, Brahma was cursed by Shiva for being bound to human sexual passions. Consequently, his cult is insignificant, but there is a general trend toward identifying a supreme god among various Hindu schools, including Vaishnavism, Shaivism, and the Bhakti movement and especially Krishnaism, both of which consider Krishna, the eighth avatar of Vishnu, the supreme deity. However, we see especially in Vedantic Hinduism the same trend toward metaphysical abstraction.

139. Victor H. Mair compares Chuang Tzu to Zeno of Elea and Socrates in "Chuang Tzu," 2:24. Cf. Mair, *Wandering on the Way*.

boundless. Undo the mind, slough off spirit, be blank and soulless, and the ten thousand things one by one will return to the root—return to the root and not know why. Dark and undifferentiated chaos—to the end of life none will depart from it. But if you try to know it, you have already departed from it. Do not ask what its name is, do not try to observe its form. Things will live naturally and of themselves.[140]

The idea of the body as an illusory prison is as evident in the Upanishads as in Orphic lore.[141] The body is nonexistent, and as soon as the soul (*atman*) releases itself from this illusion, it merges with the Universal Consciousness (*brahman*).[142] "Salvation" is therefore an immediate gnosis, a realization of what is already the case. One is no longer limited by the body and its emotions but cosmic. In the categories I am using, one no longer experiences a locative outlook but a utopian one. After death there is no awareness of self and other, since "the Whole has become one's very self (*atman*).... It is the immortal; it is *brahman*; it is the Whole" (BU 2.5.2).

In terms of metaphysical doctrines, this cosmology is indistinguishable from that of Parmenides (OF 488.3).[143] Aristophanes could take for granted his audience's familiarity with the idea that while gods were born souls are without beginning or end.[144] Rohde observed that in Pindar the soul survives the body's death "'since this alone is derived from the gods' (fr. 131), which, of course, is not Homeric belief."[145] There are many distinctive themes and emphases, observes Bernabé. "Yet the most un-Olympic of the features of Orphic gods is the idea that human beings are of divine origin and can be reintegrated into their primitive condition."[146] More than two millennia later, Goethe could summarize eloquently the basic substance of the Orphic myth:

---

140. Chapter 11 of Chuang Tzu in Watson, *Complete Works of Chuang Tzu*, 122.

141. After he tells his pupil that everyone venerates *brahman* in all things, the pupil says, "'It is the person here in the body (atman) that I venerate as brahman.' Ajâtasatru replied: 'Don't start a conversation with me about him! I venerate him only as the one possessing a body. Anyone who venerates him this way will come to possess a body, and so will his children'" (BU 2.1.9).

142. The synthesizer of Advaita is Adi Shankara (eighth century CE), whose central thesis is "*atman* is *brahman*." The longest chapter of his main text is a meditation on *tat tvam asi* "That thou art." See Nakamura, *Indian Buddhism*, 176–77.

143. Quoted in Bernabé, "Gods of Later Orphism," 432.

144. As quoted above: "In this way, we are by far the oldest of all the blessed ones" (*Av.* 702–703).

145. Rohde, *Psyche*, 7.

146. Bernabé, "Gods in Ancient Orphism," 440–41.

Chapter 3

> The spirit of Man
> Resembles water.
> Coming from heaven,
> Rising to heaven,
> And hither and thither,
> To Earth must then
> Ever descend.[147]

But why must the soul "ever descend"? Orphic theology had a ready answer: to "pay the penalty for ancient crimes."[148] Here there is considerable controversy over whether this "ancient crime" refers to the Titans tearing Dionysius apart and Zeus making humans from their divine soul and smoldering flesh. Already in the classical age Pindar implies it.[149] And Pindar winks at his Pythagorean patron as if he knows the truth in what he is saying.[150]

Regardless, descent into a body itself is the mechanism for penalty-paying. We do not need the so-called Titan anthropogony to establish the Orphic dualism of body and soul. Athanassakis and Wolkow summarize this well:

> Central to Orphism is the idea that the body is evil and the soul is divine. In fact, the body is a tomb which serves as a prison for the spiritual entity we call the soul. The material part of man, the body, is the evil inheritance of the Titans. The spiritual part, the soul, comes from Dionysos, an immortal god and the son of Zeus. It is obvious that the Homeric concept of the living body as the man himself and of the soul as a pale lifeless shadow of him is completely inverted in Orphism.[151]

---

147. Goethe, "Song of the Spirits over the Water."
148. The story is summarized and explained in Bernabé and Jiménez San Cristóbal, *Instructions for the Netherworld*, 115–88. See also Plato, *Leg.* 701b–c, where he refers to "the titanic nature" in humans. Edmonds argues at length that the Titan anthropogony is a late Neoplatonist invention. See Edmonds, "Tearing Apart the Zagreus Myth" and *Redefining Ancient Orphism*, 269–391. For the opposing view see Bernabé, "La toile de Pénélope"; Bernabé, "Autour du mythe orphique," 76–77; Bernabé, "Gods in Ancient Orphism," 436–37.
149. Pindar, *Ol.* 2.17–33, 67–68.
150. Pindar, *Complete Odes* (trans. Verity), 142 n. 1. Pindar also says in *Ol.* 2.85–88, "I have many swift arrows in the quiver under my arm. They speak to those who understand, but for the most part they require interpreters. Wise is the man who knows much by nature, while those who have acquired their knowledge chatter in pointless confusion, just like a pair of crows against the divine bird of Zeus." Translation from Verity. Cf. Bremmer, *Initiation in the Mysteries*, 61; Burkert, *Babylon, Memphis, Persepolis*, 95–96.
151. Athanassakis and Wolkow, *Orphic Hymns*, xiv. Cf. West, "Orphics of Olbia."

Whatever additional penalties need to be paid during one's life, incarnation itself is a sentence. The sharp antithesis (soul | body [=] life | death) in the Orphic bone tablets of Olbia expresses this point laconically. The gold leaves also promised release from guilt through initiation in the mysteries. The passwords that came with such initiation guaranteed atonement and safe passage.[152] It is not because of an ethical transgression by Titan ancestors that humans are sinful but because they are embodied. They have done something in their past life to merit their current incarnation. Yet the soul remains the indestructible, immortal, and divine.

It is not the Titan myth, therefore, that is "the cardinal point of the Orphic doctrine," as Martin P. Nilsson suggested.[153] Rather, it is the *sōma-sēma* (body-prison) doctrine that is central. A common trope for this idea that emerges in Egypt, India, and Greece is "lying in the mud." Werner Foerster even suggests that "the totality of Gnosis can be comprehended in just this image."[154] Lying in bodily mud, the soul becomes forgetful of its divine identity.[155] We are in judgment now, by embodiment; the future represents perfect freedom and purity that we can begin in this life. For Egyptians, the "mire" of mud represented death, but for Orphics it symbolized the present existence in the body. Adapting an Egyptian ritual, Orphics lay in the mud to endure their ritual death, surrendering their Titanic nature.[156] It is after relating this Titan anthropogony that the initiate declared joyfully to the gods, "I, too, boast that I belong to your blessed race" (OF 488.3). The throng above looks down on "the uninitiated, unpurified mob here on earth" that is "murky and deep mire," says Aristophanes (*Av.* 703).[157] Like other playwrights, Aristophanes may have come dangerously close to the capital crime of divulging an actual part of the Eleusinian mysteries.

Orphism is a philosophy, but it is also a way of salvation—from the wheel of rebirth Dionysus's tomb in the Parnassus shows him mortal and then after the

---

152. Bremmer, *Initiation in the Mysteries*, 76.

153. Nilsson, "Early Orphism," 221. See also his 1935 monograph by the same title.

154. Foerster, *Gnosis*, 1:2–3, quoted by Kalligas, *Enneads of Plotinus*, 1:205. Kalligas observes, "The 'alchemical' figuration of the soul's relation to bodily desires as gold steeped in mud has a markedly dualistic character that made it especially attractive to the Valentinian Gnostics. See Iren. *Adu. Haer.* I 6.2, 623–29." He also points out that the metaphor is used twice in Plotinus (*Enn.* 1.5.51–58 and 4.7 [2].10.47–50), both prior to his confrontation with the gnostics.

155. Graves, *Greek Gods and Heroes*, 16. In Chinese mythology, the goddess Ming Po serves a soup of forgetfulness. See Murdock, "Lethe and the Twin Bodhisattvas."

156. Parker, *Miasma*, 286. Other Orphic rituals are described at 302–7.

157. Aristophanes, *Frogs*, quoted above from Bernabé, "Imago Inforum Orphica," 106. Cf. Graf and Johnston, *Ritual Texts for the Afterlife*, 4–7, 16–17, 20–29, 34–35, 40–41. Cf. Bremmer, *Initiation in the Mysteries*, 59–60, quoting Burkert, *Ancient Mystery Cults*, 87, emphasis added.

ritual is performed, "returned to his divine condition."[158] Reborn from Zeus's thigh, the soul—one's real self—remains constant in every incarnation.[159]

PRESOCRATICS AND ORPHISM

It is usually said that the Milesian natural philosophers broke through religion and mythology to embrace critical thinking. However, the main critics of traditional religion and mythology were associated with Orphism. Moreover, their new myths were intended at the outset to be riddles for a philosophical doctrine rather than to be taken seriously as literal truth. Myths in general facilitate critical thinking as the first stage of imagining a radically different way of conceiving the world. Advancing beyond the authority of inspired verse, the Milesian thinkers developed critical investigation into nature itself and Eleatic philosophers introduced deductive logic. Nevertheless, we have seen that Orphic myths encoded an infinite and immutable One above the apparent world of becoming. When we are told that the demiurge "ejaculated first" a particular element—be it aether/aer, water and chaos, aer and night, moving time, mud and water (earth), etc.—we are in the atmosphere of what we know of Presocratic natural philosophy. More than this, we are at the origins.

A common assumption in modern surveys is that even if Orphic influences may be detected in the more metaphysical Eleatic school of southern Italy, Milesians pioneered Western science by seeking purely naturalistic explanations. However, no actual schools existed until Pythagoras established his in Croton. Thales did not give formal lectures, and Anaximander (610–545 BCE) was not his successor but his "compatriot and companion" (*politēs kai hetairos*).[160] Moreover, as we will see, Presocratics do not fit neatly into these camps. Pythagoras was a

---

158. See OF 323–326.

159. Moreover, if we go all the way back to the Canaanite myth, the Marduk-Zeus figure Ba'al is dragged down to the underworld by Death, "El's darling." Death boasts, "I put him in my mouth like a lamb; he was crushed like a kid in my jaws" (6.2.5–24). Translation from Coogan and Smith, *Stories from Ancient Canaan*, 110–53. However, Ba'al turns this misfortune into redemption. Death threatens, "If you do not give up one of your brothers . . . then I will consume humans, I will consume the multitudes of the earth" (6.5.1–25). Ba'al complies. "See now," exults Death, "Baal gave my brothers for me to eat, my mother's sons for me to consume" (6.6.10).

160. Sarton, *History of Science*, 1:173. Aristotle called for special mention for those thinkers he believed anticipated his own views, and his student Theophrastus was the first to suggest different schools. Expanding on Theophrastus, Sotion's *Successions* created the Ionian and Italian schools as we know them today, mainly through Diogenes Laertius, who quotes this work often. See Kirk, Raven, and Schofield, *Presocratic Philosophers*, 135 n. 2.

pupil of Thales and Anaximander, the pioneers of the so-called Milesian (Ionian) school, and Anaximander's postulation of an Infinite (Apeiron) is no less metaphysical than the Monad of Pythagoras or the One of Parmenides.[161] Xenophanes is supposed to have founded the Eleatic school, yet his natural investigations were crucial in the development of Ionian philosophy.[162] Though a pioneer of metaphysics, Parmenides made important scientific discoveries as well. Daniel Graham goes so far as to call the Eleatic "the premier figure in Early Greek astronomy."[163] By the time we reach Anaxagoras and Empedocles, any definitive contrast between these schools is untenable.[164] Orphic ideas do not account for the whole development of early Greek thought, but all of the Presocratic philosophers were connected to it in some way.

The Seven Sages

The ancient list of the "Seven Sages" varies, but Thales leads them all, joined (according to most lists) by Solon, Epimenides, Anaxagoras, Anacharsis, and Orpheus.[165] All of these names figure prominently in the Orphic lineage, while others (notably Homer and Hesiod) are absent (Diogenes Laertius, *Vit. phil.* 1.42–45). According to Diogenes Laertius, "philosophy, the pursuit of wisdom, has had a twofold origin; it started with Anaximander on the one hand, with Pythagoras on the other. The former was a pupil of Thales, Pythagoras was taught by Pherecydes" (*Vit. phil.* 1.13). For this reason, the one is called Ionian and the other Italian.[166]

---

161. Also anachronistic is the portrait of the Greeks emerging from the childhood of mythology and religion into the maturity of reason and natural investigation. The gods are alive and well in Presocratic cosmotheologies, and reality is not reduced to a material substrate. Aristotle called them *physiologoi*, which does not mean physicalists (i.e., material monists) but simply "those interested in nature" (*Metaph.* 986b).

162. See Copleston, *History of Philosophy*, 47–53.

163. Graham, *Explaining the Cosmos*, 182.

164. McKirahan concludes that while there was definitely a Pythagorean "school," "The Milesian 'school' therefore seems to be an invention of the doxographers who wrote at a time when philosophy was largely associated with 'schools' and who assumed that the association which evidently took place between Thales and Anaximander and between Anaximander and Anaximenes must have take place in a school" (*Philosophy before Socrates*, 77–78).

165. Sarton, *History of Science*, 1:169.

166. The principal Ionian (or Milesian) philosophers—Thales, Anaximander, and Anaximenes—flourished in the sixth century, but it is uncertain whether they wrote any books, and even if they did none of them have survived. Anaximenes wrote one, but only one sentence survives. Freeman, *Pre-Socratic Philosophers*, 18–19. In contrast, a fair number of fragments from the philosophical poetry of the Eleatics has come down to us—just enough to generate vigorous debates among modern interpreters. See Curd, *Legacy of Parmenides*, 15–18.

However, as even Laertius points out in a letter we will encounter below, Pherecydes and Thales were friends and Anaximander and Pythagoras were taught by both of them. A closer look at these figures draws back the curtain to peek at the birth of natural philosophy.

We have seen that for Pherecydes the great battle was not between the Titans above and the Greeks and Trojans below but between the triumph of "Zeus" over the chaos-serpent Ophion. From this strife between opposites the cosmos is formed by the first demiurgic figure in Greece. Above these Zeus and Ophion Infinite Time (Kronos) is the single source. This model would become popular among philosophers of an Orphic-Pythagorean persuasion (seen especially in Empedocles's conception of Love and Strife). For Hesiod's epic-age Zeus, bringing order out of chaos was a political-military affair limited to the cosmos the gods shared with mortals. From Pherecydes on, however, theogonies blend into cosmogonies without acknowledging any distinction. This is consistent with what already happened in Late Period Egypt and spread across India westward.

Even before Thales, Alcmon and Pherecydes supposed water to be the first cause, identifying it with chaos. Yet whereas Hesiod understood chaos according to its normal Greek usage to mean merely an empty abyss (i.e., space), Pherecydes saw it as a primeval threat associated with matter.[167]

Diogenes Laertius claims to have access to a letter from Thales to Pherecydes occasioning when Solon was dispatched to Crete to fetch Epimenides for Athens's cleansing. "I hear that you intend to be the first Ionian to expound theology to the Greeks," says Thales in the letter, apparently without first having it reviewed by others but offering to come to Syros for that purpose. "For surely, Solon of Athens and I would scarcely be sane if, after having sailed to Crete to pursue inquiries there, and to Egypt to confer with the priests and astronomers, we hesitated to come to you." In a customary way of deference, Thales implies that he is a well-informed ear for Pherycides's speculations, especially for one who stays at home applying himself "to one thing, namely writing, while we, who never write any-

---

167. See Freeman, *Pre-Socratic Philosophers*, 14. See also West, *Orphic Hymns*, 9. This close circle of students was recruited by Onamacritus to assist him in compiling the standard edition of Orphic poems. Confusing it with the later Rhapsodic theogony, according to West, Epigenes attributed the *hieros logos* to either Cerops the Pythagorean or to Theognetus the Thessalian. "The *Descent* is given to Herodicus of Perinthus, while the *Robe*, together with a *Net*, is given either to Brontinus or to Zopyrus of Heraclea.... The *Net* was in all probability the Orphic poem known to Aristotle in which the formation of a living creature was likened to the knitting of a net (fr. 26; Kern, *Orphicorum fragmenta*). The image, already alluded to in the *Timaeus*, suggests that the soul is air occupying the interstices of a material body. It savours of Pythagoreanism.... Related ideas may have inspired the *Robe*."

thing, travel all over Hellas and Asia." He adds, "For Solon too will come, with your permission" (*Vit. phil.* 1.43–44).

If it is genuine, this letter places Thales in the middle of the Orphic shamanism of his day. The shaman-sage, democrat, and self-proclaimed reincarnated deity Epimenides of Crete was considered by some to be the founder of the Eleusinian mysteries.[168] Sarton comments, "Those complicated mysteries relative to Demeter, Persephone, and Triptolemos are really nature myths concerned with fertility and immortality; they had been introduced from Crete by the 'wise man' Epimenides in 596.... It is as if all the beliefs and religions that had grown up in the countries surrounding the Eastern Mediterranean had been put in a crucible for centuries and millennia; the most sacred rites of Hellas were like the residue and the quintessence of that alchemy."[169]

Epimenides was believed to have descended into the underworld as a shamanic god (as Pythagoras is said to have done). Damascius says, "Epimenides gave the first elements as Air and Night, from which were created Tartarus, from which sprang two Titans; these having united produced the Egg, from which again another generation sprang."[170]

Pythagoras, we have seen, is the clearest link between Orphic and Presocratic thought, who posits a transcendent Monad above the Dyad (principle of plurality). The cosmos expands into diversity by a constant mixing of opposites. This cosmology is consistent with Milesian natural philosophy. The Pythagorean Empedocles fits the shamanic profile and advances the doctrine of reincarnation: "I have already been a bush and a bird, a boy and a girl, a mute fish in the sea," he said, implying that his soul now incorporates consciousness of these past lives.[171] Yet he formulated the basic elements (earth, wind, fire, water), whose interaction through a process of Strife (separation) and Love (union) was the élan of emanation. His influence on Presocractic natural philosophy and metaphysics, not to mention rising democracy, is considerable.

---

168. Diodorus Siculus attributes the Eleusinian mysteries (and others) to Epimenides. See Sarton, *History of Science*, 1:169. Again, my interest is not in evaluating these claims but in tracing the effective history.

169. Sarton, *History of Science*, 1:197. Cf. West, *Orphic Poems*, 6–7.

170. See Freeman, *Pre-Socratic Philosophers*, 10. A fragment from his epic poems reads, "I too am of the race of the fair-tressed moon, who with a dread shudder shook off the wild lion; and strangling him in Numea because of revered Hera, the divine strength overcame him" (3.2). According to Aristotle, "Epimenides gave his oracles not about the future, but on things in the past which were obscure" (*Rhet.* 1418a).

171. Quotations of the fragments of Empedocles's poem *On Purifications* from Lombardo, *Parmenides and Empedocles*, here 58.

Chapter 3

Presocratic philosophers, in different ways, assumed the Orphic divide between the immortal and therefore divine element in the human being (soul) and the human body (outer shell). Even for Hesiod, humans were somehow distant relatives of the gods, but unlike Hesiod the Orphics envisioned humans as immortals, which for the Greeks meant divine. Indeed, as we have seen, Orphic theology taught that, unlike the gods, souls were unborn and eternal. With this immortality and transmigration of the soul (microcosm), they were able to link the many to the One (macrocosm). The process of the soul's descent into a body and its return in another body, with the hope eventually of breaking free of the cycle to realize their identity with the One, became the broader cosmological horizon of emanation and return.[172] The process no doubt moved in both directions—from microcosm to macrocosm and vice versa—but they were integrally related.

Some Presocratics seem to lean toward what we would call pantheism while others are more inclined toward panentheism. Again, this is a modern distinction as these thinkers moved freely across these boundaries. As we have seen in other civilizations at this time, there were monists and dualists, but even dualism could finally resolve into a single mixture. Emanation and return governed the horizon, whether it was conceived as mere appearance of the real (i.e., unchanging unity) or as a combination of opposites into a harmony. Paths diverged mainly over whether there was change (e.g., coming into being and passing away) or genuine plurality.

Thales and the Ionians

Living between the mid-seventh and mid-sixth centuries, Thales was designated "the first philosopher" by Aristotle (*Metaph*. 983b27–33). He advanced his own version of natural supernaturalism with a concern nonetheless to test hypotheses by studying nature.[173] Regardless of what he meant by "water," Thales was not a materialistic monist except with regard to the physical-visible world. "Of all things that are, the most ancient is God, for he is *uncreated*," testimonies relate. "The most beautiful is the universe, for it is *God's workmanship*. . . . What is the

---

172. I am not committing myself to a historical generation of cosmology from psychology but only to a logical interdependence and coherence. Nevertheless, I suspect tentatively that reflection on the soul expanded in widening circles to encompass a pattern of cosmic unity-emanation-return.

173. He rose to fame, according to testimonies, by predicting a solar eclipse, even though the event could not have had any meaning given his view of earth as a disk floating on the ocean. See Sarton, *History of Science*, 1:170–71. Regardless of whether such stories are later fabrications, the study of nature itself was a distinctive of Ionian/Milesian philosophy.

divine? That which has neither beginning nor end" (Diogenes Laertius, *Vit. phil.* 1.35). This distinction does not necessarily entail creation ex nihilo, but it excludes reductive physicalism. Thales, Anaximander, and Anaximenes thought that the earth was a flat disk floating in water, in infinite space, or on air.[174] Thus, they were not looking for a god but for a natural element as a created "one." Thales held according to Cicero that matter was not all there is: "God is that Mind which shaped and created all things from water" (*Nat. d.* 1.10).[175] If Cicero is accurate, this would place Thales in the Orphic camp with Hermotimus of Clazomenae and Pherecydes, anticipating Anaxagoras. Diogenes Laertius even tells us that Thales "was the first to maintain the immortality of the soul. . . . His doctrine was that water is the universal primary substance, *and* that the world is animate and full of divinities" (*Vit. phil.* 1.24, 27, emphasis added). Since Thales did not write anything, we do not know how closely this resembles his teaching. Nevertheless, Cicero and Diogenes Laertius were drawing on testimonies unavailable to us today.

This notion of a supreme god creating a limited and finite world is not monotheistic (and neither was it the position of Cicero or Diogenes). Aristotle's testimony is centuries earlier than most: "Some say that [soul] is mixed in the whole universe. Perhaps that is why Thales thought that everything was full of gods" (Aristotle, *De an.* 411a7).[176] Of course, this is Aristotle's own view: the divine form is in the matter, and this is what makes all material things alive, as the soul animates the body. If Aristotle is accurate in his conjecture, though, this would mean that Thales proffered nothing different from Hermotimus, Pherecydes, or Orphics generally: Everything in nature is animated (hence, deified) by a single Mind or Soul. "The world is full of gods" *means* that "soul is mixed in the whole universe." If Thales did not intend this, his disciples did.[177]

We can be fairly sure from ancient testimonies that Thales was, in our terms, a philosopher—even a theologian—and not simply a scientist. Diogenes Laertius summarizes a familiar tradition: "Thales had no instructor, except that he went to Egypt and spent some time with the priests there" (*Vit. phil.* 1.27). Simplicius says Aristotle disagreed with Thales's view that earth rests on water, "which was

---

174. Sarton, *History of Science*, 1:169. In terms of natural cosmology (including astronomy, geometry, and mathematics), the Egyptians and Babylonians were way out ahead of the Greeks. Ionian philosophers did not have to travel to learn about astronomy (along with astrology and magic), since those with the best practical knowledge were sailors and merchants from Iran and Egypt. Babylonians had long charted the zodiac, but Cleostratos formulated the "twelve 'signs' of the zodiac" in his lost *Astrologia*, See *History of Science*, 1:179.
175. Note also Aristotle, *Metaph.* 983b6, 8–11, which is our main early witness to Thales's view.
176. Aristotle, *On the Soul* 411a7. Quoted in McKirahan, *Philosophy before Socrates* (4.11), 30.
177. Aristotle, *De an.* 405a19. Cf. Sarton, *History of Science*, 1:171–72.

prevalent perhaps because the Egyptians recounted it in mythological form and Thales may have imported the doctrine from there."[178] He would have encountered the idea of a golden egg or mound emerging from primordial chaos waters to set about forming a cosmos. Thales would have known that this was also part of the Orphic cosmogony. Indeed, William Smith argues that Thales derived the idea of water as the primary cause from Orphism but tested it by natural methods.[179] The upshot is unity in difference, different "things" being simply varying forms of one primary and ultimate element.

What did "water" mean for Thales's contemporaries? For Orphics and Egyptians with whom he studied as well as Indian and Chinese philosophers, it was the chaos waters from which the cosmic egg emerged that produced the demiurgic Re/Phanes/Prajapati/Pingu. Plato appeals to an Orphic theogony to explain Homer's odd and very Mesopotamian claim that the two waters—Oceanus and Tethys (i.e., Apsu and Tiamat)—were the originating pair for all gods and mortals.[180] Everything comes from water: the chaos waters or the mixing of the waters (fresh and salt). According to the second-century CE church father Athenagoras, "Orpheus was the first theologian. He gave Water as the beginning of the Whole." Is this not Thales's view? And "from Water came Mud, and from both came a serpent, Heracles or Time. . . . This Heracles produces a huge Egg, which split into two, forming Ge (Earth) and Ouranos (Heaven)" (*Leg.* 18).[181] Nietzsche concluded, "In his dogma that water is the origin of things, that is, that it is that out of which every thing arises, and into which every thing resolves itself, Thales may have followed Orphic cosmogonies, while, unlike them, he sought to establish the truth of the assertion."[182]

Hovering between pantheism and panentheism, emerging Hinduism and the new religions of Jainism and Buddhism similarly embraced hylozoism. In the West, this was Aristotle's position that everything is alive. Even panpsychism—that everything including animals, plants, and rocks had a soul (*jiva*)—was ad-

---

178. *In Arist. Cael.* 522.16–18 (= DK 11A14). Quoted in McKirahan, *Philosophy before Socrates*, 28. Aristotle says, "Some believe that the people of remote antiquity, long before the present generation, who were the first to speculate about the gods, had this idea about nature too. For they made Ocean and Tethys parents of coming to be and made water, which the poets called Styx, the oath by which the gods swore. For the most ancient is the most honored, and the most honored thing is what is used to swear by" (*Metaph.* 1.3 983b27–33 = DK 11A12; McKirahan, 28).

179. Smith, "Thales," 1016.

180. Plato, *Crat.* 402b and *Tim.* 40d–e, interpreting Homer, *Il.* 14.193–210, 245. See Burkert, *Orientalizing Revolution*, 92–95.

181. As quoted in Freeman, *Pre-Socratic Philosophers*, 3.

182. Nietzsche, *Tragic Age of the Greeks*, §3.

opted in Indian philosophy. The *jiva* represents the spiritual substance that emanates from *brahman* as part of itself. In early Jainism, panpsychism was inclusive of plants and even stones.[183] Far from atheistic, this outlook is pantheistic or at least panentheistic. Nature is a self-organizing system not because the divine is excluded but because divinity animates everything. In contrast with the perpetual intervention of the Olympian gods, the divine substrate of nature is sufficient to account for the existence of things. Divine Soul permeates nature.

Regardless of whether Thales was following Orphic cosmogonies, his disciples certainly were. Order is immanent to nature, not imposed from outside. This would follow the growing criticism of arbitrary kingship and tyranny in favor of universal and unchanging ethics that the soul recognizes. As André Laks puts it, the Milesian cosmologies "in which most scholars generally recognize the first manifestations of the birth of 'philosophy'" actually return to theogonies.[184]

> Pherecydes of Syros, who composed, probably a little earlier than Anaximander, a theogony in prose that Aristotle located halfway between mythology and natural philosophy, stated at the beginning of his treatise that Zeus (named Zas) had *always* been; just like Kronos (time) and Chthoniê (the earth). The same configuration is found at a higher level of abstraction in Anaximander, who, according to a possible interpretation of an indication that goes back to Theophrastus, was the first to use the term *archê* ("beginning") in the sense of "principle"; for this principle (in the present case, the "unlimited") also turns out to be "at the beginning."[185]

However, it becomes evident in the thought of Thales's younger colleague Anaximander (610–546 BCE) that water—even primeval chaos waters—could not account for the diversity of the cosmos. His work *On Nature* (*peri physeōs*) is considered the "first treatise on natural philosophy in the history of mankind."[186] Like Thales, Anaximander drew upon the pioneering work of Egyptians and Babylonians.[187] If Thales believed that "the whole universe is full of gods" because divine "soul" pervades it, Anaximander does not diverge as much as we thought

---

183. BG 2.20; cf. SU 3.21 in Olivelle, *Upaniṣads*, 259; Schmithausen, *Sentience of Plants in Early Buddhism*, 3. Later Buddhism excluded plants and stones. See Gombrich, *What the Buddha Thought*, 48; cf. ch. 1 in W. Johnson, *Harmless Souls*.
184. Laks, *Concept of Presocratic Philosophy*, 70.
185. Laks, *Concept of Presocratic Philosophy*, 71, 74.
186. Sarton, *History of Science*, 1:173.
187. Sarton, *History of Science*, 1:174, 176.

when he posits the Apeiron (Indefinite/Infinite) as the source.[188] Pherecydes had taught that there must be something beyond all opposites, not itself any element at all, that accounts for the elements, something unchanging that is the basis for all changing things. In other words, there must be a transcendent One above even the opposition of the One and the many in order to keep the system from collapsing into dualism. Similarly, Anaximander's Apeiron is something divine behind, above, and beyond that generates all things and does not decay.[189] We may compare it to the Chinese *tao*, the Vedic *brahman*, or the Pythagorean Monad above the difference between one and many.[190] Anaximander's Unlimited is clearly not merely the source of nature (as water seemed to be for Thales) but an all-encompassing divinity—above the gods—since it is not only immortal but unbegotten, and separate from all plurality and change. The Apeiron cannot be any element of which it is the cause but remains eternally unchanged and above all opposites of fire and water, dry and moist, hot and cold, etc.

Simplicius says that according to Anaximander this *apeiron* is "both principle [*archē*] and element [*stoicheion*] of the things that are.... He says that it is neither water nor any other of the so-called elements, but some other indefinite [*apeiron*] nature, from which come to be all the heavens and the worlds in them; and those things, from which there is coming-to-be for the things that are, are also those into which is their passing-away, in accordance with what must be." This intimation of an Orphic provenance—"in accordance with what must be"—is confirmed by the following sentence: "For they *pay the penalty* and recompense to one another for their injustice in accordance with the ordering of time—*speaking of them in poetical terms*." The four elements change into each other, so none is a candidate for being the simple and immutable cause of all complexity and change. Everything comes from the *apeiron*, returning to be destroyed and reborn not as new elements (which are immutable) but as a new combination.[191] Emanation is not merely the overflow of the Good but a fault or crisis, an ontological estrangement. It is a fall from unity to division. However, echoing the demiurgic figures we have encountered (and anticipating Plato's *Timaeus*), Anaximander's One at least behaves like an agent intellect at work in separating and uniting. It actively com-

---

188. Herbert Granger points out this dependence of Anaximander on Pherecydes in "Theologian Pherekydes of Syros," 135.

189. Quotation of Anaximander from Aristotle, *Phys.* 204b (= DK 12A15).

190. Vernant, *Pensée grecque*, 128; English translation in *Origins of Greek Thought*, 112–15; cf. 119–27.

191. Quotation of Anaximander from Simplicius, *In Arist. Phys.* 24.13 (= DK 12A9, 12B1; LM 6P5, 6D6, 6D12), emphasis added.

bines and separates opposites (hot-cold, wet-dry, etc.).[192] But if it is a purposeful intellect, and coming-to-be and passing-away represent some sort of fault, is not the Apeiron itself to blame?[193]

From Anaximander on, the assumption is that everything flows from the One and returns to it. The scheme once again is not atheistic materialism but natural supernaturalism. A god cannot intervene in the world because the world *is* god (i.e., immortal), at least in its real substratum: incorporeal mind or soul. This is a higher level of abstraction attended by measurements and empirical arguments, but it is no less mythological than prior accounts. In other words, it is no more "scientific" to endow nature with a universal divine spirit than it is to speak about a cosmic egg or creation from nothing. Indeed, everything arises from and returns to the Apeiron, but it has no characteristics and there is no way of observing it; it can only be deduced as a necessary postulate.[194] Yet this is the approach of Parmenides's Eleatic school as well.

Anaximander's student Anaximenes believed that the rationalizing process had gone too far, so he "tried to reintroduce a physical principle. . . . Water would not do because it was too tangible, too determinate. But what of wind or air, permeating everything?"[195] Anaximenes noticed how actual things were distinguished qualitatively by differences in temperature.[196] Air is the one element that changes into many things through condensation (thickening; *pyknōsis*) and rarefaction (thinning; *manōsis*). When rarefied, *aēr* becomes less dense, thinner, and ultimately transforms into fire. In condensation, it becomes concentrated, taking the form of water and eventually stone. All things come into existence by this harmonization of opposites. In positing fire as the unifying force, Heraclitus may have had this most rarefied state of *aēr* in mind.

Just as humans breathe in air (emanation) and exhale it (return), the cosmos breathes an "air" (*aēr*) that is far more celestial than we know.[197] It is clear that Anaximenes's *aēr* is more than the air we breathe. He even calls this source of all

---

192. See Lloyd, "Hot and Cold."
193. Heraclitus, fr. B25 in Heraclitus, *Fragments* (trans. Robinson).
194. Anaximander quoted in Simplicius, *In Arist. Phys.* 24.13 (= DK 12A9, 12B1); cf. Aristotle, *Phys.* 204b22.
195. Sarton, *History of Science*, 1:177. Only three short fragments have come down to us, but testimonies (including Aristotle) give us some idea of his thought.
196. Sarton, *History of Science*, 1:177.
197. From a monotheistic perspective, this is unfortunate for theology, eliding the creator-creature distinction, but it also contributes significantly to the abortion of science in the classical era. The world cannot be explained *on its own terms purely as nature*, distinct from divinity. The macrocosm/microcosm paradigm forces nature to fit into a preformed metaphysical system.

existence *aithēr* or *pneuma* (soul). While the Septuagint, the Greek translation of the Old Testament, would later use the word *pneuma* to translate the Hebrew *ruaḥ* ("the breath of life"), Anaximines was the first to employ *pneuma* in philosophy.[198] "Just as our soul ... being air holds us together," he said, "so *pneuma* and air encompass and guard the whole world."[199] The microcosm is like the macrocosm. According to Hippolytus, "From *aēr*, he said, the things that are, and have been, and shall be, the gods and things divine, took their rise, while other things come from its offspring" (*Haer.* 1.7). Cicero comments, "Anaximenes held that air is god, and that it has a beginning in time, and is immeasurable and infinite in extent, and is always in motion; *just as if formless air could be god*" (*Nat. d.* 1.26).[200] We also cannot forget the Orphic account of how Zeus became the All by swallowing the phallus of "the first born" Phanes, "which ejaculates the aether first" (P. Derveni 13 and 16). And, closer to Anaximander's Apeiron than Thales's water, *aēr*/breath is imperceptible. In the only surviving fragment of Anaximenes's works we read, "Just as our soul, being air, holds us together and controls us, so do breath and air surround the whole kosmos."[201] The *archē* of life is the spiritual *aēr* breathed by the gods, comparable to soul. By the time we reach the end of the pioneering trail of Milesians, Anaxagoras posits Mind as the One. Everything is composite, just as the human body is made up of many parts. Yet although Mind pervades all things, it remains simple.[202]

As Max Müller observes, "Anaximenes' Air will inspire Plato's notion of the World Soul just as Anaxagoras' Mind will become the demiurgic Intellect."[203] The natural processes of rarefaction and condensation are modifications (accidents in Aristotle's terminology) of this single underlying substance. In condensation, air becomes water, and in rarefaction it becomes fire, which was Heraclitus's prime element. This would certainly become a suggestive thought for the Stoics: "The great rhythm of the cosmos was somewhat like the respiratory rhythm of our own life."[204] It is another picture of emanation-return, another myth that is quasi-scientific in its naturalism. Heraclitus's fire is not a terrestrial substance but the

---

198. Benso, "Breathing of the Air," 13.
199. Aetius 1.3.4, quoted in Vamvacas, *Presocratics*, 45–51, here at 47.
200. Quotations of Hippolytus and Cicero from Burnet, *Early Greek Philosophy*, 73 and 78, emphasis added.
201. Anaximenes, DK 13B2; quoted in McKirahan, *Philosophy before Socrates*, (6.6), 53.
202. See DK 59B11. This and many of the other fragments included in McKirahan, *Philosophy before Socrates*, 193–95, "are all quoted by Simplicius—ample evidence that he had the text (or at least some of the text) of Anaxagoras before him" (193n1).
203. Max Müller, preface to *Upanishads*, 15.
204. Sarton, *History of Science*, 1:169.

divine Logos that informs the perpetual dialectic of separation (Strife) and union (Love).[205] Fire indicates what it is like, but Logos is its first principle.[206] Mary Boyce demonstrates the significant influence of Iranian theology on Ionian philosophers, including the Ephesian Heraclitus who considered fire the divine Logos animating all things.[207] It is not surprising that the most Stoic of the Orphic theogonies, the Heironyman theogony, is similar.[208] A universal Absolute—whether called the *apeiron, aēr/aithēr, nous*, or fiery Logos—reduces to different names a single, unchanging, ultimately real substance that lies at the heart of the cosmos. Indeed, according to the fragments and *testimonia*, these thinkers regarded their fundamental principle as similar to if not synonymous with intellectual soul.

Bartender versus Thinker

For Milesians and Eleatics alike, science and metaphysics were integrally related. Both studied nature and sought a supernatural explanation for why there is something rather than nothing. Both relied ultimately on deduction rather than empirical observation for their imperceptible One. And they agreed that the many emanate from unity to division and return to simple unity. The real difference is not between Ionian scientists and Italian theologians but between religious philosophers who believed either that this process involved a blending of opposites

---

205. Heraclitus as quoted in Sextus Empiricus, *Math.* 7.126–127 (= DK 22A16). See Kirk, Raven, and Schofield, *Presocratic Philosophers*, 206–7. Megino explores this more fully in "Presence in Stoicism," 139–47.

206. Clymer, *Philosophy of Fire*, 18. This work is an example of the theosophical imagination of the early twentieth century. Nevertheless, this terse summary underscores the important point that the *name* of the god was less important than its symbolic function in relation to the natural world.

207. On divine fire in Zoroastrianism see Boyce, "Zoroastrian Temple Cult of Fire." On influences among Ionian thinkers, see her *History of Zoroastrianism*, 150–63. See also Sharples, "Fire in Heraclitus," 231–35.

208. Like the "Unknown Darkness" (Kek/Kauket) of Egyptian religion, the transcendent source of being cannot be within being itself and so is not included in the genealogy that begins therefore with Water and Sand (Earth). See Wilkinson, *Gods and Goddesses of Ancient Egypt*, 77–78. Similarly, the Heironyman (Heironymus-Hellanicus) theogony begins with Water (stable) and Matter (susceptible to producing change). By the commingling of Water and Matter, Earth emerges. Earth gives birth to a serpentine Kronos (distinct from Kronos, Zeus's father), representing the eternal cycle of Time winding its way back to the beginning. This Kronos is "double-bodied," that is, male and female. His consort is Ananke (Necessity/Nature) and "Andrastea, having her arms stretched out in the whole cosmos, and touching its limits." See Betegh, *Derveni Papyrus*, 143–44. Although most scholars give it a later date, Edmonds makes a good argument for a fifth-century BCE composition. Edmonds, *Redefining Ancient Orphism*, 18–20.

Chapter 3

by a demiurgic intellect or that there is *only* unity and the many things are merely appearances or illusions that we mistake for being the reality.

The similarity of these "schools" is evident as early as Xenophanes, who was born near Miletus around 570 BCE and yet is considered the founder of the Eleatic school. Xenophanes reflects the usual distinctives attributed to this school, particularly natural investigation. For example, the twins Castor and Pollus, called the Dioskouroi, won immortality from their father Zeus by forming the Gemini constellation, known to sailors as St. Elmo's Fire. "Those star-like apparitions mariners call the Dioskouroi," Xenophanes counters, "they are in reality clouds: small ones that glow because of some agitation."[209]

Yet he was not reducing reality to matter. A traveling rhapsode meant an inspired poet-theologian, which indeed he was. Xenophanes was a fierce critic of the myths of Homer and Hesiod for theological reasons: they misrepresented the gods as if they were like us. "God is one," he said, "greatest among gods and men, not at all like mortals in bodily form or thought." He denied any hierarchy among gods, along with the belief that they were born or that they are anthropomorphic meddlers in earthly affairs.[210] God is "eternal, self-sufficient, independent, master of everything, unmoving." As McKirahan describes, "The world for all its diversity and change possesses an underlying unity. All its movements are controlled by the unitary divinity that pervades it. Moreover, god controls things through thought. . . . [I]ntelligence, not the whims of the Olympians, governs the world."[211]

From these fragments McKirahan concludes, "Most important, and contrary to earlier Greek views, Xenophanes is a monotheist" and in natural philosophy was "the first dualist, positing earth and water as the basic substances from which all things are made."[212] I disagree on both counts. As I've noted, frequently the movement from the many to the One is described as a shift from polytheism to monotheism, but this erroneously conflates monotheism and monism. Along with many contemporary scholars, McKirahan thinks Plato misidentified Xenophanes as "the founder of monism" (*Soph.* 242d4–5); similarly, Aristotle: "Xenophanes who was the first of these to preach monism (Parmenides is said to have been his student) made nothing clear . . . but looking off to the whole heaven he declares that the one is god" (*Metaph.* 986b10–25).[213] If Aristotle is correct, this view is

---

209. Aetius 2.18.1 (= DK 21A39). Quoted in McKirahan, *Philosophy before Socrates*, 67.
210. McKirahan, *Philosophy before Socrates*, 61, quoting Xenophanes, fr. 7.11.
211. McKirahan, *Philosophy before Socrates*, 63.
212. McKirahan, *Philosophy before Socrates*, 62–63.
213. McKirahan, *Philosophy before Socrates*, 58, 64.

monistic rather than monotheistic: "the one is god," not "there is one god." Plato's Parmenides in the so-named dialogue is pure fiction, but in the *Sophist* Plato represents the Eleatic position as stating "that only one thing is" (244b). Although this interpretation has been challenged vigorously in recent years, I remain convinced that Parmenides was a strict (or existence) monist: difference, plurality, change, and corporeality are apparent (due to sense perception) instead of real.[214] Like Pythagoras (and later, Plato), Xenophanes is more of a substance monist with the procession from unity to division occurring through mixing of opposites. The analogous development in classical Hinduism is represented, respectively, by Advaita and Dvaita schools. The picture is similar to the Infinite (*apeiron*) of Anaximander (under whom Xenophanes is said to have studied along with Pythagoras) as well as Anaxagoras's *nous*.

It seems counterintuitive that one whom moderns regard as the father of rationalism identified the way of truth not with a rational ascent from darkness to daylight but with a revelation he received in the cave of Night. Rickert reminds us, "Parmenides is led by mares, daughters of Helios, the goddess Dikē, and finally an underworld goddess (again, probably Persephone) to a revelation of 'well-persuasive truth.'" Persephone addresses Parmenides as a *kouros* (initiate).[215] We have seen that his actual cave of incubation and healing was considered the gateway to Hades. Regardless of how one interprets the ontology in his poem, it is clear that he is enacting in it precisely the sort of soul-healing that he practiced in the cult of Apollo Oulios. Shifting into dactylic hexameter, he is "sky-walking" like Abaris, Empedocles, Pythagoras, and, later, Empedocles.[216]

Night does not give Parmenides an erudite lecture explaining nature but speaks words meant to "enchain and paralyze the thought of the *kouros* and guide him to the experience of eternity, immobility, and completeness."[217] The doctor becomes the patient. It is not surprising that his successor Zeno is famous for his *Paradoxes*. Night is the cave or womb that conceives both day and night in our perceptual world. It becomes typical of all later mysticism that reality is hidden behind a veil of images that mortals mistake for truth and, however one ends up defining his ontology, the introductory proem indicates that this is his starting point.[218] Par-

---

214. Key critics of the strict monist interpretation of Parmenides include Mourelatos, *Route of Parmenides*; Barnes, *Presocratic Philosophers*; Kirk, Raven, and Schofield, *Presocratic Philosophers*; Curd, *Legacy of Parmenides*.

215. Rickert, "Parmenidean Ontological Enaction," 480–81.

216. Rickert, "Parmenidean Ontological Enaction," 486.

217. Marciano, "Images and Experience," 44.

218. While I find myself tossed on the waves of the current debate over the poem's meaning (e.g., strict, aspectual, predicational monism among other interpretations), I am inclined toward

menides may not embrace strict monism but he may as well, since everything that is perceived by the physical senses is an illusion. The way of truth (*alētheia*) is a revelation beyond reason that leads to an intellectual vision of reality as it is in itself. The way of opinion (*doxa*) is deceived by perceptible appearances. The primordial goddess tells Parmenides that they are wrong who speak of "male [embryos] on the right, female on the left . . . [m]an and woman mixing the seeds of love, mingling of bloods" (Parmenides fr. 6–8).[219] This Pythagorean harmony of opposites is what the foolish acknowledge. In short, "This is the world in common Opinion, things coming to be and passing away in their season, and to everything men have given a distinctive name" (fr. 17 and 18). There is no coming-into-being and passing-away or mixing of opposites. The Real—what is (*to eon*)—is "ungenerated and deathless, whole and uniform, and still and perfect" (fr. 8.1–4).[220] In short, where Pythagoreans would agree that unity mixed with plurality, maleness with femaleness, infinity with finitude, is *less* real, Parmenideans deny that it is real in any sense. We cannot even think what is not, "for to think and to be are one and the same."

Being is one—*What Is*. (Parmenides fr. 2–3)

The Pythagorean "divine man" Empedocles has four elements—fire, earth, water, and *aithēr* (the rarefied atmosphere of the gods)—constantly mixing and separating. The elements never change, but the constant union by Love and separation brought about by Strife accounts for why things seem to come into being and pass away. Empedocles tried to solve the One-many problem by combining Ionian and Eleatic ideas. Between the One and the many he posited the Few, which were the four elements. However, he introduced the provocative notion that the One and the many do not exist simultaneously but at different moments in a cyclical process. McEvilley explains:

The cosmos is said to evolve through four stages which are repeated infinitely, as the hand of a clock circles continually through the four compass points.

Aristotle's view that Parmenides is engaged in metaphysics, not physics. What-is-one (*hen to on*) cannot be subject to plurality or change. Being (what-is) is one in essence, plural in perception. See Aristotle, *Metaph.* 986b14–18; *Phys.* 184a25b–12. The way of truth (*alētheia*) is a revelation beyond reason that leads to an intellectual vision of reality as it is in itself. The way of opinion (*doxa*) is deceived by perceptible appearances. As we will see, this is the upshot of Plato's myth of the cave, and he too depends on Orphic sources as divine revelation.

219. Translation of Parmenides fragments, unless otherwise noted, from Lombardo, *Parmenides and Empedocles*.

220. Translation here from Coxon, *Fragments of Parmenides*.

In the Age of Love, or of the One, Love melts all things together into an undifferentiated unity which, not unlike the Being of Parmenides, is called the Sphere. In mythological terms, this is a Golden Age, an age before strife and separate identities. In the following age, the counterforce—Hate, or Strife, or Separation—gradually disrupts this unity, separating things out into different forms. The next or third age is the Age of Hate proper, the opposite of the Age of Love; the unifying force of Love has been driven altogether from sight and the universe is a hell of Hate and Strife. In the fourth age, the force of Love reappears and gradually expands again as Strife gradually recedes, restoring unity for a new Age of Love.[221]

One is reminded of the cycle of peace and strife represented in Egypt by the myth of Horus versus Set. The cyclical process of cosmology assimilates the temporal register. In Empedocles's view nothing really changes since the elements are immutable (like Plato's Forms). Nothing new comes into being or passes away. Yet in this cosmic alchemy everything is changing, as new separations and unions, rarefactions and condensations, give rise to novel combinations. The concept of reincarnation is the logical provocation of this new outlook. Something has to transcend the whole process of change. This was the dominant position among Presocratic philosophers.[222] Whereas Pythagoreans taught that unity mixed with plurality, maleness with femaleness, mind with matter, and infinity with finitude are all *less* real than unity itself (viz., the Monad), Parmenides denies that it is real in any sense (Parmenides fr. 2–3).

All Presocratics agreed that reality emanated from one source. The principal sticking point between Parmenides and his erstwhile Pythagorean comrades is stated well by Plato's Eleatic visitor:

> They each appear to me to tell us a myth, as if we were children. One tells us that there are three beings, and that sometimes they're somehow at war with each other, while at other times they become friendly, marry, give birth, and bring up their offspring. Another one says that there are two beings, wet and dry or hot and cold. And our Eleatic tribe, starting from Xenophanes and even people before him, tells us that what they call "all things" are just one. Later on, some Ionian and Sicilian muses both had the idea that it was safer to weave the two views together. They say *that which is* is both many and one, and is bound

---

221. McEvilley, *Shape of Ancient Thought*, 68.
222. Empedocles, frr. B6 and B10, quoted in Curd and Graham, *Oxford Handbook of Presocratic Philosophy*, 419.

Chapter 3

by both hatred and friendship. According to the terser of these muses, in being taken apart they're brought together. (*Soph.* 242c–e)

CONCLUSION

In all of these schemes, dualism resolves into monism just as monism presupposes dualism. Both schools agree that ultimately the various gods are merely "different names of a single Nature ... all that is one."[223] The cosmos is seen increasingly as the unfolding and enfolding of a divine source transcending it. The world in its many parts is seen either as identical with Zeus (pantheism) or as merely apparent reflections of a nonpersonal "Zeus" that transcends these images (panentheism). Either way, it is emanation *ex deo* rather than a creation *ex nihilo*.[224]

Although the Derveni Papyrus is later (mid-fourth century BCE), it includes a good deal of a mid-fifth century commentary on the Protogonos theogony. The commentator begins with an allusion to Parmenides. Active in the early fifth century, Parmenides also calls Zeus "only one" (*monogenēs*).[225] All the other gods "grew onto him." That is, all the other gods are aspects of the one god, as in the theogonies above.[226] Burkert observes:

> The god, who has become the only one, creates the world through thinking: "He thought out" (*mesato*). The parallel to Parmenides, who has his *daimon* "thinking out" Eros (B 13), is immediately apparent. But once more, so are parallels to Egypt ... [which] celebrates Ptah as the one who produces the gods "by heart and lips," that is, by thinking and speaking.[227]

Creating by means of thought, Zeus "becoming the only one," and everything coming from Night are all from Orphism, which means the Orphic theogony "is firmly dated to the sixth century."[228] At the same moment in history, *brahman* is the great "illusionist" according to the Shvetashvatara Upanishad: "the illusionist creates this whole world, and in it the other [soul] remains confined by the illusory power. One should recognize the illusory power as primal matter, and the

---

223. OF 413 in Bernabé, "Gods in Ancient Orphism," 431.
224. Ficino as quoted in Taylor, *Eleusinian and Bacchic Mysteries*, 47–48.
225. Parmenides, fr. 8.4.
226. OF 21a; cf. OF 167.
227. Burkert, *Babylon, Memphis, Persepolis*, 95.
228. Burkert, *Babylon, Memphis, Persepolis*, 95.

illusionist, as the great Lord. This whole living world is thus pervaded by things that are parts of him."[229]

Focusing on Indian developments, Samuel draws an observation that is just as true in Egypt and Greece: "What is notable though is the similarity between these schools, all of which tend in one way or another to collapse phenomenal reality into a single substrate or underlying principle."[230] Instead of collapsing divinity into nature, they assimilated nature to a simple divine force. What little we possess from the Presocratics is tempting to read as if it represents a transition from religious mythology and belief to reason, science, and atheism. On the contrary, it is difficult to find personal divine agents in their cosmos because *everything* belongs to a single divine process of emanation and return. If they strike us sometimes as emptying the universe of the gods, it is only to discover a single divinity as the unifying reality that animates all things from a blade of grass to celestial bodies.

Presocratic thought may seem like a forerunner of modern naturalism and it is often treated as such. Like Spinoza's critics, the opponents of Orphic cosmotheology from Anaxagoras to Diogenes of Melos to Socrates could not conclude otherwise than that Orphic sages were atheists.[231] Yet how so? From Thales on, "the world is full of gods," and even Democritus—the father of atomism—is no exception.[232] His cosmos may consist of swerving atoms, but each atom contains the whole sacred universe, a microcosm of the macrocosm. It is not until the fifth century with Protagoras that we meet an openly agnostic philosopher, claiming that "man is the measure of all things."[233]

But the problem from a theistic (even polytheistic) perspective is that if everything is divine, do gods actually exist? If God is everything, does he have independent existence? Despite their polytheism and anthropomorphism, the

---

229. SU 4.9–10 and 5.1 in Olivelle, *Upaniṣads*, 260–61.

230. Samuel, *Origins of Yoga and Tantra*, 218. Without reducing this trend to politics—viz., a single empire claiming universal rule—this may have played a role, Samuel observes.

231. While atheism denies the existence of God, acosmism denies the existence of the world. See Kuehn, "Acosmism," 6. Janko argues that the author of the Derveni Papyrus was an atheist along with a trail of sympathizers from Anaxagoras through Diogoras to Socrates; see Janko, "Diagoras of Melos"; Janko, "Derveni Papyrus"; Janko, "Physicist as Hierophant." However, Betegh argues just as persuasively that the commentator was not an atheist in Betegh, *Derveni Papyrus*, 350. Janko replies to Betegh in Janko, review of *Derveni Papysus* (by Betegh). I am suggesting that the whole debate is moot, since pantheism/panentheism rather than atheism can look to theists (even polytheists) a lot like atheism.

232. Wright, "Presocratic Cosmologies," 419.

233. "Concerning the gods," Protagoras said, "I have no means of knowing whether they exist or not, nor of what sort they may be, because of the obscurity of the subject, and the brevity of human life." See DK 80B4 from a lost work entitled *On the Gods*.

stories of Homer and Hesiod had the gods entering the world as distinct beings. Of course, they did not create anything but were superior beings within a shared cosmos. Nevertheless, if Zeus himself has now become a cipher for an abstract One, Zeus himself does not actually exist. From one perspective they are driving out the gods, but from another they are conceiving the whole cosmos as divine. Gods do not intervene in the world because the divine is the animating Mind, the World Soul.

Though attended by greater natural investigation, Milesian no less than Italian philosophers were deducing their rationalizations from Orphic myths in search of this universal principle. Things in nature were supernatural because they represented one immortal and therefore divine substratum separated (i.e., "paying the penalty") into myriad bodies.[234] What distinguishes these early thinkers is not a rejection of mythology but a *new* mythology that is "prophetic and riddling" for the uninitiated; to repeat the Derveni commentator. "But Orpheus himself did not wish to utter disputable riddles, but important things in riddles. In fact he is speaking allegorically from his very first word right through to his last."[235]

---

234. See Aristotle, *De an.* 410b 27–411a 2. An especially clear example of an Orphic intersection of Stoic and Aristotelian thought is explained in Megino, "Presence in Stoicism," 139–41. See also Sarton, *History of Science*, 1:178.

235. I follow here the translation of Janko, "Reconstructing (Again) the Opening of the Derveni Papyrus."

4

"The True Mystics"
Orpheus as Plato's Muse

> But we ought always truly to believe the ancient and holy doctrines which declare to us that the soul is immortal and that it has judges and pays the greatest penalties, whensoever a man is released from his body.... And I fancy that those men who established the mysteries were not unenlightened, but in reality had a hidden meaning when they said long ago that whoever goes uninitiated and unsanctified to the other world will lie in the mire, but he who arrives there initiated and purified will dwell with the gods. For as they say in the mysteries, "the thyrsus-bearers are many, but the mystics few"; and these mystics are, I believe, those who have been true philosophers.[1]
>
> —Plato, *Ep.* 335a; *Phaed.* 69d[2]

> Plato paraphrases Orpheus everywhere.
>
> —Olympiodorus, *In Plat. Phaed.* 10.3.13[3]

---

1. The first part of the quote from the *Letters* is from *Plato IX* (trans. Bury). The second part from *Phaedo* is from *Plato I* (trans. Fowler). The authenticity of the *Letters* is disputed, but the seventh letter is judged the most likely to have come from Plato's pen. See Bury, "Pref. Note to "Epistle VII"; Kenny, *Ancient Philosophy*, 49; Ledger, *Re-Counting Plato*, 148–50. Against authenticity, see Schofield, "Plato and Practical Politics."

2. Quoted in Guthrie, *Orpheus and Greek Religion*, 15.

3. As quoted in Uždavinys, *Orpheus and the Roots of Platonism*, 42. Uždavinys explains, "Like Orpheus, Plato's Socrates is a servant of Apollo, maintaining that the best music is philosophy. Hence, philosophical talk is analogous to the prophetic song of Orpheus or the theological hymn of 'Apollo's philosophical swan who sings that this life is a prelude to a discarnate afterlife.'" Yet I argue that for Socrates/Plato (as well as Orphism generally), Dionysus remains the central character.

Chapter 4

There is no question that Socrates's reindoctrination program was more austere than the Orphic writers had recommended to this point. However, Nietzsche's argument in the first part of *The Birth of Tragedy* is one-sided. Despite his Apollonian reputation, Plato's Socrates is smitten by Dionysus's ecstasy. Indeed, he exults, "Our greatest blessings come to us by way of madness, if perchance the gods will grant it" (*Phaedr.* 244a–b).[4] Like Orpheus himself, Socrates seeks to domesticate Dionysian enthusiasm without losing the central upshot of the myth. A key figure in the transition from shaman to sage, he completes Orpheus's mission of domesticating the Dionysian cult. Turning its outward fanaticism inward, he transforms cultic mysteries into philosophy.

By the time of Socrates this trend has been well under way, substituting Homeric for Orphic myths.[5] Indebted above all to Pythagoras, Plato borrowed also from Anaxagoras, Parmenides, and Heraclitus as another bricoleur in an evolving and diverse tradition. By Socrates's time, says Dodds, "the idea was there; it looks as if all the new mythology did was to generalise it."[6] The trail that leads to Socrates and Plato can only be explained by "the so-called Orphic influence," as Gadamer observes:

> What the figure of Pythagoras has to do with all of this seems obvious to me. If one reads the biographies of the Presocratics, the same thing shows up again and again: every one of them, from Anaximander to Parmenides and so on, is portrayed as a follower of Pythagoras. . . . In my estimation, it means that Pythagoras brings together fundamental motifs, like the riddle of numbers and the riddles of the soul, the transmigration of the soul, and the purification of the soul.[7]

It makes little difference whether we call these doctrines Orphic or Pythagorean, since Pythagoras became the standard-bearer for the tradition leading to Socrates.

Much of the origins of Orphism as well as Pythagoras's original teaching will remain buried in the distant past, but it is this reception history that shaped the

---

4. See esp. ch. 3 of the seminal work of Dodds, *Greeks and the Irrational.*
5. Sarton, *History of Science*, 1:401.
6. Dodds, *Greeks and the Irrational*, 142, 137. According to Dodds, there are significant parallels with Norse and Irish myths and he traces the "irrational" from the tattooed shamans of the Asiatic Steppes (Russia) to Scythian tribes and thence to Greece and Italy (143). Thrace would certainly have been a clearinghouse for these heterogeneous religious beliefs, as I have narrated with dependence on specialists.
7. Gadamer, *Beginning of Philosophy*, 38.

horizon of the Western imagination. Encrusted with discrepancies, pseudepigrapha, and legends, it is the effective history of the Orphic myth that still fascinates. Percy Shelley expresses well in his elegy of Keats what is so familiar that we do not even recognize it as a myth at all:

> Thou canst not soar where he is sitting now.
> Dust to the dust! but the pure spirit shall flow
> Back to the burning fountain whence it came,
> A portion of the Eternal, which must glow
> Through time and change, unquenchably the same.[8]

But such assumptions must have seemed alien when they first arrived in Athens. As Dodds says, "It was here that the new religious pattern made its fateful contribution: by crediting man with an occult self of divine origin, and thus setting soul and body at odds, it introduced into European culture a new interpretation of human existence."[9]

Like the legendary Orpheus, Plato's Socrates preserved the Dionysian cult and Eleusinian mysteries precisely by domesticating them to philosophical reason. Given its own central axioms, Orphism could never remain in its native shell of external mystery cults. As the body is the prison-house of the soul, not only material rites but all public, visible, corporate, and institutional religion had to give way to individual ascent. External authority must yield to the autonomy of the inner self: the flight of the alone to the Alone, as Socrates's later heirs would put it. The result was philosophy. This also helps to explain Socrates's turn to ethics. The same trend was happening in Egypt and across Asia. "To turn away from the world, to turn inward into the self, and finally to return (*fu li*) to society or break with it forever—this is the pattern of response of Chinese thinkers to the crisis of the ethical life."[10] The key dogmas of the Orphic tradition Socrates defended as central to his reeducation program in Athens. Echoing the shaman, the philosopher adopts the "Divine Man" mystique, exhibiting and teaching the "techniques of ecstasy" that release the soul from its prison.[11] Plato affirms this program explicitly as "the Orphic way of life."[12] And, as we see below, Orphic myths and doctrines are alluded to explicitly and implicitly across the dialogues. Yet, as Kenneth Seeskin

---

8. Shelley, "Adonais," stanza 38, lines 337–42, in Reiman and Powers, *Shelley's Poetry and Prose*.
9. Dodds, *Greeks and the Irrational*, 139. Cf. Turchi, *Le religion dei misteri*, 52; Albert, *Grieschische Religion*, 22.
10. Roetz, *Confucian Ethics*, 267.
11. As we have seen in Eliade, shamanism offers "techniques for ecstasy."
12. Plato, *Leg.* 782c.

observes, "only a small fraction of Plato's commentators have deemed this aspect of his thought worthy of discussion, let alone critical evaluation."[13]

Philosophy as Mystical Theater

It is a modern anachronism, therefore, to picture the Greek enlightenment as a retreat from religion; rather, it was a flight from what we might call organized religion. The goal remained nothing less than salvation of the soul and assimilation to God (*Theat.* 176a–b).[14] As I demonstrate in this chapter, we do not have to speculate about Orphic influence because Plato refers us repeatedly to this source to ground his main philosophical arguments.

Instead of seeking immortal fame on the battlefield of Troy, the hero of the new stories is the immortal soul. Remembering her preincarnate bliss, the soul fastens her gaze to the unchanging forms in a direct, unmediated, and autonomous vision. Especially in the *Symposium,* Plato skates perilously close to betraying details of the Eleusinian rites, which he seems to have known as an initiate or at least through Socrates. The mysteries of Eleusis form the semantic ambiance of Platonic philosophy while Orphic myths—along with their doctrinal upshot—become authoritative references. The philosopher-shaman just sees the reality, the way advanced initiates in the Greater Mysteries become *epoptēs*: beholders. These stages of initiation—*teletē* (purifying preparation), *muesis* (closing one's eyes), and *epopteia* (beholding the vision)—became the familiar pedagogy of ascent in all subsequent mysticism (purification, illumination, union). The beatific vision prior to incarnation is free of all earthly distraction. "That was the ultimate vision, and we saw it in pure light because we were pure ourselves, not buried in this thing we are carrying around now, which we call a body, locked in it like an oyster in its shell" (*Phaedr.* 250c).[15] This highest attainment is the "divine madness" in which the soul's highest intellect becomes identical with its formal object.[16]

---

13. Seeskin, "Platonism, Mysticism and Madness," 574.

14. Amazingly, modern scholarship had been mostly embarrassed by this major thesis until Julia Annas and David Sedley. See ch. 3 in Annas, *Platonic Ethics*, and Sedley, "Becoming like God."

15. Unless otherwise noted, all translations of the *Phaedrus* from Nehamas and Woodruff in Plato, *Complete Works* (ed. Cooper), 524, emphasis added.

16. See Plato, *Phaedr.* 244a–b as well as ch. 3 of Dodds, *Greeks and the Irrational.* One may take exception to a rather modern aversion to this element of Dodds's views on Platonism (especially his treatment of later Neoplatonist theurgy) while absorbing his insights and thorough documentation.

"The True Mystics": Orpheus as Plato's Muse

As Aristotle divulged concerning the mysteries, "It is not necessary for those being initiated to learn something but to experience and to be put into a certain state."[17] Similarly, Socrates explains that one can only prove Orphic truths from other Orphic doctrines. Rationalism is born in an *a priori* mystical leap. One must first surrender to the Orphic doctrine of the soul; from this presupposition, the experience of recollection proves itself.[18] This is the upshot of Plato's new myths, anticipated at the beginning and introduced throughout his *Republic*. After descending into the cave, the initiate enters the intelligible telesterion to behold the truth. In book 7 the soul of the prisoner in the cave is set free by turning herself away from the shadows and stepping into the light of being.[19] The most shamanic experience occurs at the end, in which the deceased soldier Er is sent back from the underworld to explain the Orphic afterlife. The whole Eleusinian experience has been intellectualized into a philosophical allegory, as previous Orphic bricoleurs had done with less imagination.

Just as each person had to choose whether to be initiated into the Eleusinian mysteries, one had to choose his or her own destiny based on a specific and unvarying law of merits. Dodds observes that the archaic age closed with a shift from shame to guilt, an "internalizing of conscience." Ritual purification could deal with external and collective pollution, but with this new emphasis on the autonomy of the divine self came a deeper sense of personal guilt. Not sacrifices but inner justice of the soul was required.[20] "The transference of the notion of purity from the magical to the moral sphere was similarly a late development: not until the closing years of the fifth century do we encounter explicit statements that clean hands are not enough—the heart must be clean also."[21] This is when Plato's Socrates enters the picture, pioneering the field of natural ethics. The soul, contaminated by the body and its senses and rendered sluggish, requires *katharsis*—purification from guilt or defilement. The lead must be distilled out of the gold through spiritual exercises.[22]

---

17. Aristotle fr. 15, quoted in Foley, *Homeric Hymn to Demeter*, 69.

18. In his own words, "I assume the existence of a Beautiful, itself by itself, of a Good and a Great and all the rest. If you grant me these and agree that they exist, I hope to show you the cause as a result, and to find the soul to be immortal" (*Phaed.* 100b). Translation from Grube in Plato, *Complete Works* (ed. Cooper). Unless otherwise noted, all Plato citations of the *Phaedo* are from this edition.

19. Cf. the allegory of the sun in book 6.

20. Anna Lännström explains this very well in "Religious Revolution."

21. Dodds, *Greeks and the Irrational*, 36–37. Dodds comments further that this coincided with a greater emphasis in secular law on motive, underscoring once again a new sense of individual responsibility.

22. For example, *Phaed.* 66b–69d; *Resp.* 363c–366b; *Leg.* 909a–910d.

Chapter 4

This purification, for Socrates, required Orphic *doctrines* but not the ritualism of the itinerant Dionysian and Orphic cults. Philosophy—the path of virtue and wisdom—is enough to guide the soul to Persephone (*Ep.* 333e).[23] Indeed, no one disdained *orpheotelestai* (traveling ritual specialists) more than Orphic philosophers. The Derveni commentator says that "all those who hope to acquire knowledge from someone who *makes craft* of the holy rites deserve to be wondered at and pitied" (P. Derveni 20, emphasis added).[24] Socrates and Plato stand with "Orpheus" in transmuting the lead of earth-bound myth and ritual into metaphysical doctrines. "Wisdom itself is a kind of cleansing or purification. It is likely that those who established mystic rites for us were not inferior persons but were speaking in riddles long ago when they said that whoever arrives in the underworld uninitiated and unsanctified will wallow in the mire, whereas he who arrives there purified and initiated will dwell with the gods. There are indeed, as those concerned with the mysteries say, many who carry the thyrsus but the Bacchants are few. These latter are, in my opinion, no other than those who have practiced philosophy in the right way" (*Phaed.* 69c–d).[25] Such sentiments reveal Socrates and Plato as legatees in a long line of Orphic bricoleurs, turning the outward spectacle into an inner one. The emotional intensity that in the Bacchic experience happened outside and with others is channeled inside for what Plotinus called "the flight of the alone to the Alone" (*Enn.* 6.9.11).[26]

Rather than abandoning mysticism for rationalism, Plato teaches "the best things we have come from madness, when it is given as a gift of the god." The first is the prophetic gift sent by Apollo and the Muses, associated with the priestesses of Delphi and Dodona. "We will not mention the Sybil or the others who foretell many things by means of god-inspired prophetic trances and give sound guidance to many people—that would take too much time for a point that's obvious to everyone." Plato describes the "weeping, and violent beating of the heart," manic dances that leave initiates "out of their minds," yielding finally to a trance

---

23. Translation from Morrow in Plato, *Complete Works* (ed. Cooper).
24. Like serious Christian teachers versus television evangelists today, religious salesmen go through the motions "without even asking further questions"; they imagine they will attain knowledge of mysteries just by performing some external (magical) ritual. Translation from Betegh, *Derveni Papyrus*.
25. Translation from Grube in Plato, *Complete Works* (ed. Cooper).
26. These famous words, *phygē monou pros ponon*, conclude the *Enneads* according to Porphyry's ordering.

in which they are possessed by a god (*enthysiasmos*; lit. divine possession).[27] "The people who designed our language in the old days never thought of madness as something to be ashamed of or worthy of blame; otherwise they would not have used the word 'manic' for the finest experts of all—the ones who tell the future—thereby weaving insanity into prophecy" (*Phaedr.* 244b–c).

"Next," he says, "madness can provide relief from the greatest plagues of trouble that beset certain families because of their guilt for ancient crimes . . . it gives prophecies and takes refuge in prayers to the gods and in worship, discovering mystic rites and purifications that bring the man it touches through to safety for this and all time to come. . . . Third comes the kind of madness that is possession by the Muses, which takes a tender virgin soul and awakens it to a Bacchic frenzy of songs and poetry" (*Phaedr.* 244d–245a). It is interesting that Plato refers this inspiration of poet-theologians to Dionysus rather than to the Apollonian Muses who gave Homer and Hesiod their songs. "If anyone comes to the gates of poetry and expects to become an adequate poet by acquiring expert knowledge of the subject without the Muses' madness, he will fail, and his self-controlled verses will be eclipsed by the poetry of men who have been driven out of their minds" (245a).[28] For Plato, inspired verse was a necessary stage for beginners. Children needed the sorts of training, authority, stories, and rituals that prepared them to outgrow them. The problem was that the stories of Homer and Hesiod were misleading, and the masses preferred to live as children and not continue their pedagogical ascent. Even Plato's own myths were meant to begin the ascent and were not to be taken literally. The goal of philosophy for Plato was to mature beyond authority toward autonomy, beyond the body and the visible world to the pure ideas.

Thus, the last stage of divine madness is philosophy: the love of wisdom, an intellectual eroticism, that comes as a gift of Aphrodite. "Now we must first understand the truth about the nature of the soul. . . . Every soul is immortal. . . . And since it cannot have a beginning, then necessarily it cannot be destroyed . . . and if this is so—that whatever moves itself is essentially a soul—then it follows necessarily that soul should have neither birth nor death" (245c–e). Thus, it is not philosophy in general as an academic discipline but a particular spirituality, of

---

27. Dodds, *Greeks and the Irrational*, 78–79. See also Rouget, *Music and Trance*, esp. 11. Affirming the value of such "madness," Plato here goes out of his way to offer a dubious philological explanation that "nowadays people don't know the fine points, so they stick in a 't' and call it '*mantic*'" (244c).

28. The dialogue *Charmides* reinforces this perspective of the suspension of the poet's faculties.

Orphic provenance, that yields safe passage from life in the body (which is death) to the celestial vision (which is life).

Initiates in the Dionysian-Orphic cult are related to true philosophers as appearance is related to reality. Yet appearances are only deceiving if one takes them for the truth itself. At least in the *Phaedrus* passage above (and in the *Symposium*), one must use appearances as signs directing the soul higher. Analogous to the Lesser Mysteries, these lower rungs of madness are youthful stages toward adulthood initiation in the Greater Mysteries of philosophy.

In all the types of divine mania Plato uncovers, the truth revealed (or attained) "is not knowledge," Hackforth notes, "but *excludes knowledge*."[29] So we might expect at this highest stage that knowledge would be attained. But one never graduates from mysticism to reason; on the contrary, in this highest stage of divine madness not only corporeal vision but rational contemplation is left behind. That this ultimate state is *ignorance* may strike us as odd for the founder of Western rationalism, but this is just what Plato's Socrates says. The wise are those who "recognise an immaterial reality, in other words Platonists and some fellow-Socratics and Pythagoreans."[30] Socrates's model is Empedocles, whom he calls a "divine man" (*theios anēr*; *Leg.* 642d–e). Diotima, the hierophant who taught Socrates the theory of love, even bears a striking resemblance to Empedocles. In his recollection of her speech, Socrates invokes sacrifice, prophecy, purification, and the language of mystery cults (e.g., initiation and initiates, *teletai*), reaching its climax in a revelatory vision (*Symp.* 210d–e). "Even you, Socrates, could probably come to be initiated into these rites of love," she tells him. "But as for the purpose of these rites when they are done correctly—that is the final and highest mystery, and I don't know if you are capable of it" (210a). From there Diotima explains the ladder of love, moving from beautiful bodies upward to Beauty, along the lines of the Lesser and Greater Mysteries (210a–211e).

"Shamanistic themes begin to be repeatedly associated with all these themes," Todd M. Compton observes.[31] Like Orpheus, the shaman is situated between the poet and the sage on this ladder of ecstasy. Like Dionysus as well as the Eleusinian mysteries, the shaman's tent is recognized by external sights and sounds. "Then many strange people will be philosophers." It would include "lovers of sights" as well as "lovers of sounds," those who "run around to all the Dionysiac festivals, omitting none, whether in cities or villages, as if their ears were under contract

---

29. Plato, *Phaedrus* (trans. Hackforth), 60, emphasis added.
30. Plato, *Phaedrus* (trans. Hackforth), 62.
31. See ch. 16 of Compton, *Victim of the Muses*.

to listen to every chorus." Are we to call *these* individuals "philosophers"? "No," Socrates replies, "but they are *like* philosophers." The Lesser Mysteries lead to the Greater. "And who are the true philosophers? Those who love the sight of truth" (Plato, *Resp.* 475d–e).[32]

The philosopher is one who has acquired the expertise and the virtue to reflect critically on myths, decipher their meaning, and discern which myths are closer to conveying the truth. Plato's contrast of the poet's divine possession and the philosopher's contemplative recollection is similar not to the usual modern antithesis of religion and reason but to Rouget's distinction between trance and ecstasy.[33] Prophets and poets *hear* a divine word and relate it to other hearers, but the shaman *sees* the other world with his own eyes directly and immediately apart from any external authority. That is what initiates in the Greater Mysteries experienced.

> But beauty was radiant to see at that time when the souls, along with the glorious chorus (we [philosophers] were with Zeus, while others followed other gods), saw that blessed and spectacular vision and were ushered into the mystery that we may rightly call the most blessed of all. And we who celebrated it were perfect, and simple, and unshakeable and blissful. That was the ultimate vision, and we saw it in pure light because we were pure ourselves, not buried in this thing we are carrying around now, which we call a body, locked in it like an oyster in its shell. (Plato, *Phaedr.* 250b–c)

It cannot be stressed too highly that the Western lexicon for knowing is bound up with seeing. Derrida put it crisply: according to this instinct, "c'est-à-dire-à la forme visible pour l'oeil metaphysique."[34] The entire history of Western philosophy is a discourse on light and vision.[35]

The shaman's soul is never locked in his body. He beholds what is real while the public religion perpetuates illusions based on what the people hear from authori-

---

32. All translations of the *Republic,* unless otherwise noted, from Grube in Plato, *Complete Works* (ed. Cooper).

33. Rouget, *Music and Trance,* 11.

34. Derrida, *L'écriture et la Différence,* 45. In translation, "the form that is visible for the metaphysical eye"; see *Writing and Difference,* 27. Metaphors of vision dominate the Western lexicon: "I see," "clear and distinct ideas," "worldview," "contemplation" (to behold: *theoria* in Greek, *contemplatio* in Latin); from *specere,* "inspection," "perspective," "speculate," etc.

35. Derrida, *L'écriture et la Différence,* 45–47. Cf. Levin, *Modernity and the Hegemony of Vision,* especially the essays by Hans Blumenberg (30–62) and Andrea Nye (361–78).

ties (viz., the poet-theologians) and see with their physical eyes. Plato's mysticism cannot be dismissed as a stubborn habit from a superstitious age or as merely rhetorical ornamentation. On the contrary, it is intrinsic to his metaphysics. Empirical investigation, because of its object (sensible appearances), yields only opinion; discursive reasoning can jog the soul's memory of a preincarnate vision of the Beautiful, but the highest union and therefore knowledge is ineffable, nonrational, unmediated, and purely intuitive gnosis reserved in past ages for the shaman. For Plato, reason soars but loses oxygen, surrendering to mystical ecstasy in the final stage of union. Echoing the passports for the afterlife in the Orphic gold plates, Socrates relates the journey of the departing soul to the underworld, aided by a spirit-guide, and returning to this world. In fact, he says, "As it is, it is likely to have many forks and crossroads, and I base this judgment on the sacred rites and customs here" (*Phaed.* 108a). Proclus seems justified in concluding, "every part of which is fully of a symbolical representation, as in a dream, and of a description which treated of the ascending and descending ways, of the tragedies of Dionysus, the crimes of the Titans, the three ways in Hades, and the wandering of everything of a similar kind."[36] Just as the shaman differs from the typical prophet-priest by circumventing natural signs, the philosopher knows without mediation, *which includes discursive reasoning*.

Prior to the sixth century BCE, *mythos* meant true while *logos* was unreliable or even deceitful speech.[37] Gradually, a stream of Presocratic writers—all with Orphic associations—turned sharp criticism toward the stories of Homer and Hesiod as misrepresentations of the gods. Socrates's litany in the *Republic* of offensive examples is virtually identical to that of Xenophanes decades earlier.[38] The meaning of *mythos* and *logos* has been reversed now, so that the former connotes falsehood and the latter truth. Yet Plato does not dispense with myth, as Aristotle will recommend.[39] On the contrary, good myths conceal truth just as the body hides the soul. Every such story is a "lie" (*pseudos*) simply because it draws on the

---

36. Taylor, quoting Proclus, in *Eleusinian and Bacchic Mysteries*, 33–34.

37. Lincoln, "Competing Discourses." As Lincoln points out, this construct contains some truth but the reality is more complicated.

38. Xenophanes fr. 1–6 in *Fragments and Commentary* (ed. and trans. Fairburns), 66–67. All quotes from Xenophanes are from Fairburns. I am following his order of the fragments 1–30, which correlate with DK 21B23–26.

39. Aristotle, *Rhet.* 1407a35 (= DK 31A25). According to Aristotle, Empedocles, for example, is full of "stammering" because of his reliance on myth (*Metaph.* 985a4). Alasdair MacIntyre repeats Aristotle's evaluation in "Myth," 5:435. A similar argument is made in Brisson, *Plato the Myth Maker*.

realm of appearances. Yet it is with such shadows that embodied souls begin their upward journey. "Then we must first of all, it seems, supervise the storytellers," Socrates instructs in his manifesto for cultural revolution. The worst stories will have to go. "Which ones do you mean?" asks Adeimantus. "Those that Homer, Hesiod, and other poets tell us, for surely the composed false stories, told them to people, and are still telling them." They represent the gods as jealous, cruel, afraid, fickle, and deceitful. They tell *misleading* myths about the gods punishing and sending evil as well as good. The gloomy stories of Hades inculcate dread instead of courage and pleasure in the face of death (Plato, *Resp.* 377b–392d).

SOCRATES'S VOCATION AS ORPHIC PROPHET

From his earliest period, Plato's Socrates exhibits a deep sense of having been entrusted by Apollo with a prophetic mission (*Apol.* 30a–b). Orpheus himself had been Apollo's prophet—some said even son. The *Apology* reports Socrates as saying in his trial that the earthly judges are doing him a favor. "At all previous times," he says, "my familiar prophetic power, my spiritual manifestation, frequently opposed me, even in small matters." It would appear that not merely the Muses but Apollo himself is his alter ego, perhaps even his soul. In facing "what is generally thought to be the worst of all evils, my divine sign has not opposed me" in concluding that "those of us who believe death to be an evil are certainly mistaken.... If, on the other hand, death is a change from here to another place, and *what we are told* is true and all who have died are there, what greater blessing could there be, gentlemen of the jury?" There in heaven he has true judges—among whom he names Triptolemus, cofounding priest of the Eleusinian mysteries. "Again, what would one of you give to keep company with Orpheus and Musaeus, Hesiod and Homer?" (*Apol.* 40c–41b).[40] The order of names reflects the common belief that Orpheus was the founder of all poetry (i.e., theology and mysteries). Assuring his despondent friends that his impending death is a blessing, Socrates compares himself to Apollo's swans that are silent until they sing in prophecy at their death. Afraid of their own death, people think they "sing in sorrow." "I believe that as they belong to Apollo, they are prophetic, have knowledge of the future and sing of the blessings of the underworld, sing and rejoice on that day beyond what they did before. As I believe myself to be a fellow servant of the swans and dedicated to the

---

40. Translated by Grube in Plato, *Complete Works* (ed. Cooper), emphasis added.

same god, and to have received from my master a gift of prophecy not inferior to theirs, I am no more despondent than they on leaving life" (*Phaed.* 85a–b).[41]

Also, though without the bombast, this vocation is reminiscent in form and content of the philosopher, shaman, and early Orphic priest Empedocles. Addressing the citizens of Akragas, he announces himself in *On Purifications* "as an undying god, mortal no longer, honored by all and fittingly crowned with sacral ribbons and flowering wreaths" (Empedocles, fr. 112).[42] He continues:

> There is an old condition, *a decree of Gods eternal* and sealed with extensive oaths, that if a spirit blessed with long-lasting life should by sin or error defile itself with slaughter, or forswear on oath in the spirit of Strife, he shall wander *thirty thousand years* apart from the blest, *born through time in various mortal forms*, switching through the painful tracks of life.... *I have already been a bush and a bird, a boy and a girl, a mute fish in the sea.* (fr. 115)

A little later he adds, "*From the living he made the dead*, changing their forms, and *from the dead the living*, clothing them in *the unfamiliar tunic of flesh*," from plants to animals to humans (fr. 124, emphasis added). All of these italicized ideas are integral to Plato's outlook. Typically, when Plato's Socrates introduces his distinctive doctrines he grounds it in an Orphic *hieros logos* (sacred story) with which he assumes his auditors are familiar.

Metempsychosis, as expressed in exactly these same terms, is a hallmark of the Orphic theology that Plato weaves throughout even his earliest dialogues. Some recent commentators have attempted to demythologize the beliefs associated with the Orphic mysteries.[43] This strategy, in my view, misses Plato's distinctions between the myths and the doctrines (*logoi*). The former must be interpreted allegorically, to be sure, for because they are drawn from the realm of becoming, they always fall short of being itself. But they contain the truth in a riddling fashion. Of course, Plato didn't believe a soldier named Er actually existed. However, as Hackforth concludes, "I do not believe that Plato could have written thus at

---

41. Aeschylus referred to a "seer of the signs" who now lies dead, "like a swan, whose song and dance were rites of death" (Aeschylus, *Ag.* 1440–1445) in Lefkowitz and Romm, *Greek Plays*, 93.

42. "To whatever flourishing cities I come with my followers here, men and women both," he adds, "I am revered, sought by thousands, some inquiring of the road to wealth, some in need of prophecy, others trying to hear a healing word for the long afflictions that pierce their bodies through with pain." Translation of Empedocles from Lombardo, *Parmenides and Empedocles*.

43. As two of many examples, see, for example, Annas, *Introduction to Plato's Republic*, 348–53; Bloom, *Republic of Plato*, 409–36.

the end of a myth which involves reincarnation and transmigration if he had not believed in them both."⁴⁴

In the *Gorgias* Plato says, "*Give ear* then—*as they put it*—to a very *fine account*" of "the prison of payment and retribution" (523a–b).⁴⁵ "Give ear" is code for the Orphic interpretation of the mysteries, which begin with the hierophant's command to shut the doors and allow only the initiated to hear. Typically in Plato's dialogues a meditation on death is a device for repeating a formula that includes three elements: an appeal to *hieroi logoi* (i.e., stories we've been told, ancient theory, the sacred and ancient words) followed by the distinctively Orphic doctrine of the soul (preexistence and immortality, paying the penalty, reincarnation). Often this formula is concluded by an acknowledgment (either by Socrates or an interlocutor) that this doctrine is difficult for most people to understand much less to believe. Once aware of this formula, one is struck by how often it appears.

The beginning of the *Republic* has Socrates and Glaucon returning from Piraeus, Athens's harbor town, which had just added the Thracian goddess Bendis to the cultic calendar. "I wanted to say a prayer to the goddess," Socrates explains, "and I was also curious to see how they would manage the festival, since they were holding it for the first time" (*Resp.* 327a). Opening this important dialogue with the arrival in Athens of the dazzling Bendideia (celebrated May-June) may have been more than a *mise-en-scène*. Bindis was the Thracian "Great Mother Goddess" who was often shown not only as Artemis but as Hekate and Persephone alongside Dionysus.⁴⁶ As the spot where Homer has Dionysus touch down from Asia Minor, Thrace was also where Orpheus was thought to have united the cults of Apollo and Dionysus. On the way back, Socrates and the others stop off at the home of Polemarchus and his nobly aged father Cephalus where the dialogue is set. Always in pursuit of wisdom, Socrates asks Cephalus, "What's the greatest good you've received from being very wealthy?" "What I have to say probably wouldn't persuade most people," the old man replies. "But you know, Socrates, that when someone thinks his end is near, he becomes frightened and concerned about things he didn't fear before. It's then that *the stories we're told about Hades*, about how people who've been unjust here must *pay the penalty* there—stories he used to make fun of—twist his soul this way and that for fear they're true" (*Resp.* 330d).⁴⁷

As the opening scene of this crucial dialogue, the salute to the new cult from Thrace can hardly be casual. What is especially worth recognizing is that these "sa-

---

44. Hackforth's comment in Plato, *Phaedrus* (trans. Hackforth), 89.
45. Translation by Zeyl in Plato, *Complete Works* (ed. Cooper).
46. Fol and Marazov, *Thrace and the Thracians*, 22–24.
47. Translation from Grube in Plato, *Complete Works* (ed. Cooper), emphasis added.

cred stories" or accounts function in these instances as authorities even prior to and apart from reasoning. But these authorities are not Homer and Hesiod. In the voice of the Athenian, Plato expresses in the *Laws* his belief that "the Orphic life" (*bios*) is the natural condition of humanity before bloody sacrifices polluted the gods' altars and this statement is supported by Clinias: "So it's *commonly said*, and it's *easy enough to believe*" (*Leg.* 782c–d).[48] Another *hieros logos* reference appears later:

> In addition, we must tell *the story* which is so strongly believed by so many people when they hear it *from those who have made a serious study of such matters in their mystic ceremonies*. It is this: *Vengeance is exacted* for these crimes in the after-life, and when a man *returns* to this world again he is ineluctably obliged to *pay the penalty* prescribed by the law of nature—to undergo the same treatment as he himself meted out to his victim, and to conclude his earthly existence by encountering a similar fate at the hands of someone else. (*Leg.* 870d–e, emphasis added)

Socrates relates in his dialogue with Meno, "I have heard wise men and women talk about divine matters."

> The speakers were among the *priests and priestesses* whose care it is to be able to give an account [*hieros logos*] of their practices. *Pindar too* says it, and many others of the divine among our poets. What they say is this; see whether you think they speak the truth: *They say that the human soul is immortal*; at times it comes to an end, which they call dying, at times it is *reborn*, but it is *never destroyed*, and *one must therefore live one's life as piously as possible*. (*Meno* 81a–b, emphasis added)[49]

---

48. Unless otherwise noted, translation of the *Laws* from Saunders in Plato, *Complete Works* (ed. Cooper). The full section of *Leg.* 782b–e reads: The Athenian: "Well, we believe, don't we, that at a certain point virtues made their appearance, not having existed before, and olives likewise, and the gifts of Demeter and Kore [Persephone], which Triptolemus, or whoever it was, handed on to us? . . . We observe, of course, the survival of human sacrifice among many people today. Elsewhere, we gather, the opposite practice prevailed, and there was a time when we didn't even dare to eat beef, and the sacrifices offered to the gods were not animals, but cakes and meal soaked in honey and other 'pure' offerings like that. People kept off meat on the grounds that it was an act of impiety to eat it, or to pollute the altars of the gods with blood. So at that time men lived a sort of 'Orphic' life, keeping exclusively to inanimate food and entirely abstaining from eating the flesh of animals."

49. Unless otherwise noted, translation of the *Meno* from Grube in Plato, *Complete Works* (ed. Cooper).

Then he quotes a fragment of Pindar to that effect: "Persephone will return to the sun above in the ninth year the souls of those from whom she will exact punishment for old miseries, and from these come noble kings, mighty in strength and greatest in wisdom, and for the rest of time men will call them sacred heroes" (*Meno* 81b–c).[50] He adds:

> As the *soul is immortal*, has been *born often* and has *seen all things* here and in the underworld, there is nothing which it has not learned; so it is in no way surprising that it can recollect the things it knew before, both about virtue and other things. As *the whole of nature is akin*, and the soul has learned everything, nothing prevents a man, after recalling one thing only—a process men call learning—discovering everything else for himself, if he is brave and does not tire of the search, for searching and learning are, as a whole, *recollection*. (*Meno* 81c–e)

More examples of this formula are found in the *Cratylus*: "Don't you agree with Anaxagoras that [everything] is ordered and sustained by mind or soul? Thus *some people say* that the body is the tomb of the soul, on the grounds that it is entombed in its present life, while others say that it is correctly called 'a sign' because the soul signifies whatever it wants to signify by means of the body." Whether or not these "others" are also Orphic, Plato adopts the equation of the body (*sōma*) with a prison (*sēma*), adding: "I think it is most likely *the followers of Orpheus* who gave the body its name, with the idea that the soul is being *punished for something*, and that the body is an enclosure or *prison* in which the soul is securely kept [*sōzetai*]—as the name '*sōma*' itself suggests—*until the penalty is paid*; for, on this view, *not even a single letter of the word needs to be changed*" (*Crat.* 400c).[51]

Not surprisingly, the formula is found frequently in the *Phaedo*, as in these examples:

> We recall *an ancient theory* that souls arriving there [in the underworld] come from here, and then again that they arrive here and are *born here from the dead*. If that is true, that the living could not come back if they did not exist, and this is a sufficient proof that these things are so if it truly appears that *the living never come from any other source than from the dead*. (70c–d)

---

50. Socrates's words here parallel fr. 15 (Kern, *Orphicorum fragmenta*).
51. Translation from Reeve in Plato, *Complete Works* (ed. Cooper), emphasis added.

Chapter 4

> It is likely that *those who established the mystic rites for us* were not inferior persons but were speaking in riddles long ago when they said that whoever arrives in the underworld *uninitiated and unsanctified* will *wallow in the mire*, whereas he who arrives there *purified and initiated* will *dwell with the gods*. (69c–d)

> There is the explanation that is put *in the language of the mysteries*, that we men are in a kind of *prison*. (62b)

> *We are told* that when each person dies, the guardian spirit who was alotted to him in life proceeds to lead him to a certain place, whence those who have been gathered together there must, after being judged, proceed to the underworld with the guide who has been appointed to lead them thither from here. Having there undergone what they must and stayed there the appointed time, they are led back here by another guide after long periods of time. *The journey is not as Aeschylus' Telephus describes it.* He says that only one single path leads to Hades, but I think it is neither one nor simple, for then there would be no need of guides; one could not make any mistake if there were but one path. As it is, it is likely to have *many forks and crossroads*, and *I base this judgment on the sacred rites and customs here*. (107d–108a)[52]

It suffices to offer a final example of the *hieros logos* formula followed by Orphic teaching, this one from *Letter 7*:

> And we must always firmly believe *the sacred and ancient words* declaring to us that *the soul is immortal*, and when it has *separated from the body* will go before its judges and *pay the utmost penalties*. (*Ep.* 335a, emphasis added)[53]

The sixth-century father of tragedy Aeschylus was clearly taken with Dionysus but still under the thrall of Homer's view of the afterlife—one dreary existence for all. The Orphic doctrine of different destinies based on personal judgments of the soul was just then appearing. Plato in *Phaed.* 62b does not base this on reason but on a "secret doctrine" (*ho en aporrē tois legomenos logos*).

Continuing, he explains that Oceanus is the great river (or sea) that encompasses the earth, while the Acheron flows through deserted places into Tartarus, the underworld. It is to "the Acherusian lake to which the souls of the majority

---

52. All translations of the *Phaedo* in this collection of block quotes from Grube in Plato, *Complete Works* (ed. Cooper), emphasis added.
53. Translation from Morrow in Plato, *Complete Works* (ed. Cooper), 1654.

come after death and, after remaining there for a certain appointed time, longer for some, shorter for others, they are sent back to birth as living creatures" (*Phaed.* 113a). Upon arriving, the souls are judged.

> Those who have lived an *average life* make their way to the Acheron and embark upon such vessels as there are for them and proceed to the lake. There they dwell and are *purified by penalties for any wrongdoing* they may have committed; they are also suitably rewarded for their good deeds as each deserves. Those who are deemed *incurable* because of the enormity of their crimes ... [are] *hurled into Tartarus never to emerge from it.* ... Those who are deemed to have lived an *extremely pious* life are freed and *released from the regions of the earth as from a prison.* ... Those who have purified themselves sufficiently by philosophy live in the future altogether *without a body*; they make their way to even more beautiful dwelling places. (113d–114c)[54]

Significantly, Socrates adds, "No sensible man would insist that these things are as I have described them, but I think it is fitting for a man to risk the belief—for the risk is a noble one—that *this or something like this*, is true about our souls, and their dwelling places, since the soul is evidently immortal, and a man should repeat this to himself *as if it were an incantation*, which is why I have been prolonging my tale" (114d, emphasis added). With Orphic bricoleurs generally, he considers mythological details about oceans and rivers flowing in and out of Tartarus of little consequence, but the doctrine contained in these riddles should be repeated "as if it were an incantation." He equates "practicing philosophy in the right way" with despising everything associated with the body and its deceptions. "A soul in this state makes its way to the invisible, which is like itself, the divine and immortal and wise ... [and], as is said of the initiates, truly spend the rest of time with the gods" (81a). Socrates, therefore, distinguishes "a mere tale" from "an account" that contains the truth in a riddling way (*Gorg.* 523a). He is unequivocal that Orphic myths—over against Homer and Hesiod—communicate "an account" rather than "a mere tale."

Everything comes from opposites, he argues in defense of the soul's immortality (*Phaed.* 70c–71b). Exactly as Empedocles has it in *On Purifications*, Socrates says that life comes from death, death from life; passing from this life initiated in the mysteries versus wallowing in the mire. The cycle of reincarnations is the prison from which the soul longs to be freed, making this world Hades.[55] In fact, he

---

54. Translation from Grube in Plato, *Complete Works* (ed. Cooper), emphasis added.
55. Jáuregui, "Construction of Inner Religious Space," 685; cf. Stoyanov, *Other God*, 32.

sides explicitly with "the followers of Orpheus" who render *sēma* "prison" instead of "sign" and who believe the soul is kept in this prison "until the penalty is paid" (*Crat.* 400c). This distinctively Orphic notion of reincarnation as paying a debt for "ancient crimes" appears frequently across the dialogues.[56] Guthrie summarizes this well, "Plato makes frequent use of the term [*hieros logos*] and expresses great reverence for that which it describes. Moreover, the teachings which he takes from this storehouse correspond with what we know from other sources to be Orphic and are certainly nothing to do with, say, Homer or Hesiod."[57]

Socrates's view has become so deeply ingrained in the West that it is hard for us to imagine how jarring it must have been even for his closest friends, as related in the *Apology* and *Phaedo*. They will bury a corpse, not Socrates. "Catch me if you can," he jokes (*Phaed.* 115d–116a). In the meantime, a soul is always led astray by the body it temporarily animates (65a–67a).

> The lovers of learning know that when philosophy gets hold of their soul, it is imprisoned in and clinging to the body, and that it is forced to examine other things through it as through a cage and not by itself, and that it wallows in every kind of ignorance. Philosophy sees that the worst feature of this imprisonment is that it is due to desires, so that the prisoner himself is contributing to his own incarceration most of all. (*Phaed.* 81a)

Every pleasure or visible observation is but "another nail to rivet the soul to the body" and it even "makes the soul corporeal" so that "it soon falls back into another body and grows with it as if it had been sewn into it. . . . Because of this, it can have no part in the company of the divine, the pure and uniform" (83d–e).

Plato's Socrates even adopts the same words from Empedocles's reference to "a decree of gods eternal" stipulating the calculus for the wheel of rebirth, all the way down to being reincarnated as "a mute fish in the sea" (Empedocles, fr. 117). The *Timaeus* relates a solemn divine decree that the soul is first implanted as a human being: a man, if it is a good soul, but if not, then as a woman or worse, down to a "dumb fish" until it finally allows the Same (unity, intellect) to rule over the Different (irrational diversity associated with the body). Only "with reason

---

56. This explicit connection is made throughout the dialogues, e.g., *Crat.* 400b–c; *Gorg.* 492a–493a; *Phaed.* 61e–62e; 107d; *Resp.* 586a; 614b–621d.

57. Guthrie, *Orpheus and Greek Religion*, 15: "As an example out of many the 7th Letter will serve (335a = O.F.10): 'We must ever maintain a belief in the ancient and sacred stories which reveal that our soul is immortal, and has judges, and pays the utmost penalties whenever a man is rid of the body.'"

thus in control," the soul may return "once more to [their] first and best form" (*Tim.* 41e–42d).⁵⁸

A corollary trend was occurring in India. As in archaic Greece, metempsychosis or reincarnation was unknown in Vedic India.⁵⁹ Yet rather quickly it attained an important position around the same time that Pherecydes taught it to Pythagoras, causing it to become a central doctrine of classical Hinduism. It would become the basis for the *varna* (caste) system.⁶⁰ The elaborate calculus in the *Phaedrus* has a similar sociopolitical application for the lives that a soul will take up depending on their actions in a previous life. Like *karma*, reincarnation is based on what Plato refers to as "the law of Destiny." Explaining the beatific vision and how the soul lost her wings, Plato continues,

> If any soul becomes a companion to a god and catches sight of any true thing [i.e., a Form], it will be unharmed until the next circuit. . . . If, on the other hand, it does not see anything true because it could not keep up, and by some accident takes on a burden of forgetfulness and wrongdoing, then it is weighed down, sheds its wings and falls to earth. At that point, according to the law, the soul is not born into a wild animal in its first incarnation. (*Phaedr.* 248c–d)

According to Plato, the "soul that has seen the most" will become a philosopher. The "second sort" will be a "lawful king or warlike commander." The third will become "a statesman, a manager of a household, or a financier; fourth will be

---

58. Unless otherwise noted, translation of the *Timaeus* from Plato, *Timaeus and Critias* (trans. Lee).

59. As Axel Michaels explains in *Hinduism*, 38: "all the key terms of Hinduism either do not exist in Vedic or have a completely different meaning." He adds, "The religion of the Veda does not know the ethicised migration of the soul with retribution for acts (*karma*), the cyclical destruction of the world, or the idea of salvation during one's lifetime (*jivanmukti; moksa; nirvana*); the idea of the world as illusion (*maya*) must have gone against the grain of ancient India, and an omnipotent creator god emerges only in the late hymns of the rigveda. Nor did the Vedic religion know a caste system, the burning of widows, the ban on remarriage, images of gods and temples, Puja worship, Yoga, pilgrimages, vegetarianism, the holiness of cows, the doctrine of stages of life (*asrama*), or knew them only at their inception. Thus, it is justified to see a turning point between the Vedic religion and Hindu religions."

60. A key text is the Purusha Sukta (RV 10.90.11–12), where, in his immanence, the universal mind is the Cosmic Human sacrificed for the emanation of his intellect to creation. The *brahmins* are his mouth, his arms are the rulers and warriors (*kshatriyas*), while his thighs are the farmers and merchants (*vaishyas*) and his feet are the common laborers and servants (*shudras*). See Olivelle, "Caste and Purity." 199–203.

a trainer who loves exercise or a doctor who cures the body." The fifth will become "a prophet or priest of the mysteries," and the sixth, "a poet or some other representational artist." The seventh will become "a manual laborer or farmer; to the eighth the career of a sophist or demagogue, and to the ninth a tyrant" (*Phaedr.* 248d–e).

However, no soul is released from this cycle of embodiment "for ten thousand years, since its wings will not grow before then." The exception is a true philosopher. Upon choosing a philosophical life three lifetimes in a row, such souls return to their original bliss "in the three-thousandth year."

> As for the rest, once their life is over, they come to judgment; and, once judged, condemned to go to places of punishment beneath the earth and pay the full penalty for their injustice, while the others are lifted up by justice to a place in heaven where they live in the manner the life they led in human form has earned them. In the *thousandth year* both groups arrive at a choice and allotment of second lives, and *each soul chooses the life it wants. From there, a human soul can enter a wild animal, and a soul that was once human can move from an animal to a human being again.* But a soul that never saw the truth cannot take a human shape, since a human being must understand speech in terms of general forms, proceeding to bring many perceptions together into a reasoned unity. That process is the recollection of the things our soul saw when it was traveling with god, when it disregarded the things we now call real and lifted up its head to what is truly real instead. . . . [O]rdinary people think he is disturbed and rebuke him for this, unaware that he is possessed by god. (*Phaedr.* 248e–249d)

With reincarnation according to an impersonal law of Destiny, the dogma of the divine self reaches its apogee. Instead of being acted upon by the gods, individuals possess their own inner divinity: a self-moving soul. One's destiny lies in one's own hands, not in the wrath or mercy of a personal deity. This karmic scheme is also quite an incentive to become a philosopher, especially an "Orphic" one. Indeed, it appears that the philosophers have replaced Homer's heroes living in the Isles of the Blessed.

The sort of Orphism that Plato (or at least his brother Adeimantus) criticizes is the "begging priests and prophets" who imagine they can change the law of Destiny by gimmicks. "If the rich person or any of his ancestors has commited an injustice, they can fix it with pleasant rituals" or persuade the gods to harm an enemy by "spells and enchantments." It is beneath the dignity of the gods to picture them as angry, much less as being pacified by "sacrifices and incantations." And it is beneath the dignity of the human soul to assume that its fate lies in anyone or anything other than its own justice and merits (*Resp.* 363c–366b).[61] In short, Orphic *ritualism* is opposed to Orphic *doctrines* and the itinerant Dionysian and Orphic cults—mere thyrsus-bearers are a parody of the true mystics, meaning philosophers (*Phaed.* 69d).

Cosmic Alchemy from *Republic* to *Laws*

As the microcosm of the universe, the individual human being is body, soul, and mind, with its lower nature bound to the body and the higher part of the soul reaching toward divine mind.[62] This Eastern doctrine, going all the way back to Enuma Elish and the Rigveda myth of the "Cosmic Human," tells of Phanes emerging from a cosmic egg and fashioning the cosmos from the upper (intelligible) and lower (sensible) parts of the shell. This dualistic psychology becomes the basis for metaphysics. In Orphic lore the *psychē* takes the place of the anthroporphic gods.

Even Hackforth, who is generally reticent to draw such connections, says:

> In his description of the fall of the soul Plato is of course drawing on Orphic doctrine and imagery. That the human soul is a fallen daimon is one of the main tenets of Orphism, most familiar to us through the fragments of Empedocles's religious poem Purifications. . . . With the mention of the "ordinance of Necessity" the myth passes fully into an Orphic milieu. . . . [T]he period of revolution has in fact become the Orphic period of 1000 years (the actual figure

---

61. This passage is often quoted as evidence of Plato's rejection of Orphism in general. Two things should be noted. First, we have seen the same criticism by Orphics themselves. "But all those (who hope to acquire knowledge) from someone who makes a *craft* of holy rites deserve to be wondered at and pitied," according to the Derveni commentator. Going through the motions, "without even asking further questions," they imagine somehow they will attain knowledge of mysteries just by performing a ritual. They are to be pitied "because it is not enough for them to have spent their money in advance, but they also go off deprived of understanding as well" (P. Derveni col. 20, trans. Betegh). Second, the speaker in *Resp.* 363c–366b is not Socrates but Plato's brother, Adeimantus, who is arguing that since people find ways to get themselves off the hook, true justice is a chimera. This is certainly not Socrates's view. Nonetheless, given what we know of Plato's criticisms of Homer for representing the gods as angry or jealous and of the strict calculus of birth and rebirth, we may assume some sympathy for Adeimantus's characterization.

62. See Heraclitus as quoted in Stobaeus, *Ecl.* 1.180.1 (= DK 22B115), as quoted in McNicholl, "Reason, Religion and Plato," 111. Sometimes it seems that Plato regards the intellect as separate from the soul, at other times the highest part of the soul.

is given in the next section [Tim. 249A]), which elapsed between one incarnation and the next. Finally we come to the "order of merit" of lives, the highest of which falls to the lot of those who have had the fullest vision of the Forms, the lowest to those who have seen least.[63]

Indeed, Socrates says, "you are accustomed to mention frequently that for us learning is no other than recollection.... So according to this theory too, the soul is likely to be something immortal." Simmias has no doubts about recollection either, even stating, "I want to *experience* the very thing we are discussing, recollection" (*Phaed.* 72e–73a).[64]

Dodds describes this new sense of the "divine man" transferred from the realm of shamans to anyone who chooses the philosophical life: "the daemon becomes a sort of lofty spirit-guide, or Freudian Super-Ego, who in the *Timaeus* is identified with reason in man. In that glorified dress, made morally and philosophically respectable, he enjoyed a renewed lease of life in the pages of Stoic, Neoplatonic, and even medieval Christian writers."[65]

The soul's flight from the body and the visible world is sometimes expressed as a calm process: upon death "the soul departs gladly" (*Tim.* 81d). Yet elsewhere the danger of embodiment is hightened: Plato says that because of "the evils that haunt this region of our mortal nature, we should make all speed to take flight from this world to the other" (*Theaet.* 176a).[66] One of Plato's most sustained and unequivocal passages of Orphic dualism comes in the *Phaedo* 64a–68d: "For whenever [the soul] attempts to examine anything with the body, it is clearly deceived by it.... And indeed the soul reasons best when none of these senses troubles it, neither hearing nor sight, nor pain nor pleasure, but when it is most by itself, taking leave of the body and as far as possible having no contact or association with it in the search for reality.... Then he will do this most perfectly who approaches the object with thought alone, without associating any sight with his thought, or dragging in any sense perception, ... freeing himself as far as possible from eyes and ears, and in a word, from the whole body, because the body confuses the soul and does not allow it to acquire truth and wisdom whenever it is associated with it." In this life the soul is receiving its just recompense for deeds committed in a previous life. Hence, the purification that is synonymous with philosophy is "to separate the soul as far as possible from the body ... and to dwell by itself as

63. Plato, *Phaedrus* (trans. Hackforth), 82–83.
64. Translation from Grube in Plato, *Complete Works* (ed. Cooper), emphasis added.
65. Dodds, *Greeks and the Irrational*, 42–43.
66. Quoted from Cornford, *Plato's Theory of Knowledge*, 87.

far as it can both now and in the future, freed, as it were, from the bonds of the body." The philosophical life, then, is an embrace of death, "and this release and separation of the soul from the body is the preoccupation of the philosophers." The goal is not merely "not to get swept off one's feet by one's passions, but to treat them with disdain" and "is this not suited only to those who most of all despise the body and live the life of philosophy?"

The journey is therefore cyclical, with the end being like the beginning before our first incarnation. Falling from unity into a body, the soul aims in ever ascending circles to return finally to its original and eternal state. But if particular things, especially bodies, fall far down the ladder of being, what accounts for this apparent ontological separation? If the universe is one *and* many, how are the two related? Prior to Plato, the religion of the One had spread across a vast region, including Greece. Building on his Presocratic predecessors, Plato attempted across several works to give a more complete philosophical account, a new and better story of the One and the many.

Theory of Forms: Linking Being to Becoming, One to Many

For Plato, things in the realm of becoming can be more or less like being by virtue of something intelligible in them. Even a particular tree subject to perpetual change remains constant because of the idea or form of "tree" that transcends the participant. The more divided, corporeal, sensible, and mutable something is, the less real it is. Yet even the lowest appearances receive some existence from the things above them. The whole idea of *degrees* of being was what Parmenides's goddess condemned as introducing composition into the utterly simple One. Plato looks for a way of affirming the simplicity of the One while accounting for the quasiexistence of the many. So, without flinching, he makes the cosmic Mind (*Nous*) a demiurge containing a complex unity of multiple forms.[67]

While the *Republic*'s allegory of the cave underscores the near oblivion of the realm of becoming, the *Timaeus* emphasizes the gradual extension of cosmic goodness from the forms to nature. Souls are made from the leftover mixture from which the Cosmic Soul itself was made (*Tim.* 41d). The Pythagorean Monad is the intellectual demiurge who inseminates the indefinite Dyad with his rational ideas so that she will give birth to good souls in bodies. Parmenides strictly rejects the existence of any principle of plurality (viz., the Dyad). Early on (in the *Parmenides*), Plato was already searching for a *via media*. The *Republic* offers a

---

67. All of this comes from *Resp.* 392a–399e, translation from Grube, in Plato, *Complete Works* (ed. Cooper).

more developed theory, with the realm of diverse and ever-changing appearances possessing at least some degree of existence.

It is key for Plato that in this mixing there is no change in the ingredients themselves—that is, the forms, which are the real existence of many participants. Socrates may have been shorter and became taller—that itself is relative to other individuals. But Large and Small never commingle with or convert into each other. One may be added to one, but one never becomes two or vice versa (*Phaed.* 96e–97b). "And," he adds later, "it is through Bigness that big things are big" and through Small that smaller things are small. There is not "any other cause of becoming two except sharing in Twoness" (100e–c). "But Tallness, being tall, cannot venture to be small" or vice versa, "nor does any other of the opposites become or be its opposite while still being what it was," which would otherwise destroy its being (103a). These immutable forms replace the mutable gods and even the elements of Empedocles. For Empedocles, these unchanging underlying elements were empirical: fire, water, air, earth. But for Plato they are forms—many of them, one for every type of thing. The rest of the argument is important (to 104c), but the upshot is that the soul can never be mindled with death: it is immortal (105d–e).

By the time we reach the *Timaeus*, the Pythagorean picture of mixing opposites has the edge. In fact, the cosmic Intellect or demiurge is now the One and the Good in its activity of world formation.[68] It is not that everything *is* a simple unity and nothing diverse exists, but the demiurge facilitates the emanation from the One through the World Soul and back, through the Soul, to the One. Significantly, with the exception of Plato's nephew and immediate successor Speussipus, all Platonists until the first century BCE interpreted the One "beyond being" (*Resp.* 509b) hyperbolically instead of literally.[69] Thus they followed Plato's own Pythagorean trend.

The *Timaeus* envisions the demiurge mixing the cosmic cocktail with each mixture being less pure than the previous, but there is always some good even in

---

68. His influences are many, but Parmenides (via Zeno), Heraclitus (via Cratylus), and the Pythagoreans with whom he sojourned in southern Italy stand out especially. At least as Plato mediates him, Socrates's "Unlimited" (distinguished from "Limit") comes from Anaximander (610–546 BCE) via the Pythagoreans, while his unifying concept of mind (*nous*) opposed to matter (*hylē*) was taught by Anaxagoras (500–428) and his contemporary, Parmenides. See Diogenes Laertius, *Vit. phil.* See also Lindberg, *Beginnings of Western Science*, 29. Overall, however, the materialistic monism of Anaximenes's system had its most lasting effect on the Stoics.

69. Only with Eudorus of Alexandria do we find a "One" above the Monad and Dyad in the realm of being. For this development see Dillon, *Heirs of Plato*, 40–63, 98–111. Cf. Burkert, *Lore and Science*, 88–89.

"The True Mystics": Orpheus as Plato's Muse

the more diluted stages. Following the moves we have seen before: (1) gods are identified with natural principles; (2) a minor shamanic deity rises to prominence; (3) this god becomes a universal principle from which (4) all things emanate and return. Consequently, (5) the end is like the beginning.

But there is no cocktail without a bartender. It is Philolaus who mediated most of what we know as the teachings of Pythagoras. The fragments we have from Philolaus's *Nature* suggest something like Plato's later moves. The demiurge does not create anything, since matter is as eternal as ideas, but plies his intellect to mix being and becoming. While there is no demiurgic figure in traditional Greek religion, many examples exist in the ancient Near East. Using modern categories, we may say that in a pantheistic view, the One is simply all there is. In a panentheistic perspective, all there is emanates from the One into apparent diversity and returns to the simple Unity it has always been in its real essence. Both are opposed to the biblical concept of creation *ex nihilo* (out of nothing). Marduk, Brahma, and Phanes all make the cosmos from preexisting materials. The Pythagorean metaphor of weaving opposite threads echoes the Orphic cosmologies (Krater, Net, and Robe) written by Pythagoreans recruited to assist Onomacritus in compiling an official Orphic collection.[70] The cosmology of the *Timaeus* is the product of this weaving, like a hanging mobile or macrame plant holder with each rung suspended from the One. This opens up possibilities Plato could not have envisioned in his Parmenidean stage while avoiding the Pythagorean tendency toward absolute dualism.

Plato posits in *Republic* 509b that the Good is "beyond being." If we take this literally, there is a Monad *above* the duality of the Monad and Dyad (i.e., the One and the many) of Pythagorean dualism. This secures a monism in which everything emanates from the One, which transcends the one-many opposition. Plato's doctrine of participation (*methexis*) in separate forms is an answer to this question. Things at the bottom share at least minimally in the goodness of things near the top because there is no missing link in the chain. There can be many forms—one for every type of thing in the universe—as long as each is absolutely

---

70. West, *Orphic Hymns*, 9. Confusing the Krater with the later Rhapsodic theogony, according to West, Epigenes attributed the *hieros logos* to either Cerops the Pythagorean or Theognetus the Thessalian. "The *Descent* is given to Herodicus of Perinthus, while the *Robe*, together with a *Net*, is given either to Brontinus or to Zopyrus of Heraclea. . . . The *Net* was in all probability the Orphic poem known to Aristotle in which the formation of a living creature was likened to the knitting of a net (fr. 26; Kern, *Orphicorum fragmenta*). The image, already alluded to in the *Timaeus*, suggests that the soul is air occupying the interstices of a material body. It savours of Pythagoreanism. . . . Related ideas may have inspired the *Robe*."

simple.[71] The theory of forms, therefore, is Plato's resolution to the problem of the One and the many.

But then how do the many particulars participate in universal being? A particular bee shares in the form of bee (*Meno* 72b–c). All of these forms are contained in—or even constitute—the demiurgic Intellect, which is itself a one-many and thus the beginning of participation in the One. There is no other cause of things coming to be than their participation in reality (i.e., form) (*Phaed.* 101c). Tallness can never become small (or vice versa). Opposites never come from each other; nor do they coalesce. Instead, they separate and even "flee" from each other (102a–103a). Tallness remains even in the presence of many short things (103a–e). A person may participate in tallness and shortness and thus possess a medium height, but the forms themselves are unchanging. Since forms are inconvertible and immutable for Plato, the invisible never becomes visible or vice versa, and the soul never becomes body or vice versa. It is the soul that makes the body living. But the World Soul herself is living by her very nature. The opposite of being alive is being dead, but the soul will never admit the opposite, so the soul is "deathless" (105a–e). In the macrouniverse, the question is how many things can come from a single substance; in the microcosm the question is how the individual soul is divine.[72] Neither Socrates nor Plato invented the idea of the soul as divine in its highest aspect and as mortal in its lowest aspect, or that this was a microcosm of the Whole. But Plato drew together these doctrines in a recognizable and powerful synthesis.

Within such a scheme, mediation becomes a focal concern. In this period Plato's interest in finding "something in the middle" is displayed across his thought: "something intermediate between being and non-being," something "between pure imitation and pure narration," "something between Dionysian frenzy and philosophical eros . . . between knowledge and ignorance," and so forth. Parmenides said the real is one and unchanging, while Heraclitus (like Empedocles) held that reality is an ever-changing process of violent opposition of Love and Strife. These middle things mean, for Plato, that instead of a binary choice—an "off-on" switch—reality has a dimmer that ranges from "beyond being" to "being," "becoming," and "nonbeing," lower and higher.

---

71. Patricia Curd argues throughout *The Legacy of Parmenides* that this is precisely what Parmenides also believed: a predicative rather than numerical monism. It is Melissus (after Zeno) who adopts the latter position, she argues. Yet Plato's descriptions of "our father Parmenides" favor numerical monism. Curd acknowledges this but believes Plato conflated the positions of Parmenides and Melissus (240 n. 49). She may be right (the arguments are strong), but I am more interested here in what Plato did with Parmenides.

72. Guthrie, *History of Greek Philosophy*, 1:132.

Making the World Go Around: Souls and World Soul

There is a danger of dipping into Plato's dialogues at any one point. He is like a bird in flight, wrestling not only with his inheritance but with his own synthetic imagination. The most significant mediating spirit emerging in Plato's middle period is the World Soul. The trilevel human soul (rising from animal to sensual to intellectual) is the microcosm of the World Soul. From her uppermost level, she receives the ideas that inform particular souls and then, as the "womb of becoming," incarnates them in diverse bodies. The Intellect (demiurge) is already less unified than the One, since it is a unity consisting of many forms (contra Parmenides). The World Soul beneath it is more diversified still, since its single substance of unified Soul becomes many souls by virtue of being placed in physical bodies. At a macrocosmic scale, the World Soul herself is the lowest of the intelligibles after the One and the Intellect. Parmenides did not require any mediation because there was no higher and lower, one and many; all was one with the illusion of plurality and change arising due to our senses (*Resp.* 479b–c).

The World Soul herself was created from a mixture of Indivisible (unchanging intellect) and Divisible, and thus the ideal Soul was born. In Pythagorean terms, it is the Dyad through which the "many" appear. From what was left over from this mixture, the craftsman made human souls and the younger gods fashioned bodies from fire and earth combined with air and water as well as the mortal part of the soul.[73] After receiving the indivisible essences (forms implanted in her womb by the demiurgic Intellect), the World Soul generates the many souls of particular things in nature (*Tim.* 34b–35b). Poised on the threshold between the two worlds, the World Soul is "the womb of becoming," who gives birth to Nature, "the nurse of all becoming and change" (49a–50a). From 41a to 42d, Plato reintroduces the Orphic myth of reincarnation and the demand of the soul to emancipate itself

---

73. See Lee, introduction to Plato, *Timaeus and Critias*, 15. As Desmond Lee observes, "This analysis of a single *observed* movement into a combination of two or more actual movements had been one of the triumphs of the Pythagoreans. It was taken up by Plato and carried still further by Eudoxus, who as a member of the Academy took up Plato's challenge to produce an analysis which would 'save the phenomena,' that is, account in terms of a combination of movements for the observed facts. This he did with his system of concentric spheres, which was adopted by Aristotle and dominated astronomy until the time of Copernicus." In fact, "it was at this time in the Academy that European mathematical astronomy was born; for the line of descent leads directly from Eudoxus (390–37 BCE) to the great Hellenistic astronomers and so to Ptolemy." There is nothing new in talking about atoms (Leucippus and Democritus being major precursors), but Eudoxus "limited the number of forms which the basic particles could take to four of the five regular solids. . . . The association was not made until Dalton, and then it formed the basic of modern chemistry."

from the body. Souls are shards of the World Soul and can only return to unity by anticorporeal philosophy. By virtue of the Soul, everything is soaked with divinity in various degrees. Even plants have souls, but they are fixed and rooted, lacking the power of self-motion (77a–c). Soul is "the best of the generated beings by the best of the intelligible and eternal beings" (37a). Moving away from the idea of the soul as simple, Plato's tripartite psychology not only distinguishes aspects or levels in the soul but finally, in the *Timaeus* and the *Laws*, places them in their own "local habitats" with immortality held out only for the rational part (69c–d).

Next, in the same bowl the demiurge forms a less pure mixture that he divides into "as many souls as there are stars, and allotted each soul to a star . . . and humankind being of two sexes, the better of the two was that which in future would be called man" (*Tim.* 41d–42a). The cosmos has now become a changing and imperfect copy of the realm of being, "a visible god, supreme in greatness and excellence, beauty and perfection, a single, uniquely created heaven" (92d). Even the "later" mixtures such as human beings have a noble trace of the original ingredient. The existence of the *celestial* gods Plato thinks is self-evident even in the visible heavens at night with the "X" (i.e., the Milky Way).[74] Thus even "the fixed stars," the *Timaeus* relates, "are living beings divine and eternal" while "the earth [is] our foster-mother, winding as she does about the axis of the universe he [the Demiurge] devised to be the guardian of night and day and first and oldest of the gods born within the heavens" (40b). Whatever shares in the World Soul also participates in the demiurge and therefore in the Good. Although bodies themselves are not good, they benefit from the goodness of their soul, if they yield to it.[75]

Aporias and contradictions remain in the *Timaeus*. As Hackforth observes, Plato wavers between insisting that soul is the power of all motion (including emotion) and a "religious, Orphic-Pythagorean" picture of "a divine soul essentially (in its 'true nature') divorced from all physical functions, all lower activities."[76] There are "tensions concerning the number of world souls and the nature of their respective relationships to the body of the universe, both within the *Timaeus* and between the *Timaeus* and other dialogues." The cosmos is already in motion even in its precosmic chaotic condition, so (based on his own theory) some soul must have moved it (*Tim.* 30a; 52d–53b). Implied is "a second, irrational

---

74. See Latura, "Plato's Visible God," 880–86.
75. Wilberding, "World Soul," 17, as derived from *Leg.* 894e–896b.
76. Plato, *Phaedrus* (trans. Hackforth), 76: "It is significant that the two dialogues in which the moving function of soul is prominent—*Phaedrus* and *Laws*—are the only two in which passions (emotions) and desires are clearly attributed to discarnate soul. The *Laws* in effect, though not explicitly, regards discarnate soul as tripartite, and, if for that reason alone, we ought to take the explicit statement of the *Phaedrus* to that effect as seriously meant."

world soul."⁷⁷ This becomes more prominent in Plato's late period. To put it more positively, it seems that Plato's choice of the mixing metaphor already reflects his attempt to break out of a strictly binary opposition between soul and body. It remains unclear that he has found a way to do this.

When the Craftsman Lets Go

In the *Statesman*, the immanent World Soul is an inherently unstable mediator. Its "backward movement" is the slightest change possible, but it is a departure from the best nonetheless. Only "the most divine things of all" can remain perfectly calm, constant, and unchanging, "and by its nature body is not of this order." (It is analogous to the dialectical monism of Taoism, with the active, stable, and rational [male] principle operating upon the receptive and unstable [female] principle.) Body is the source of change for both the comos and the individual participants of the Soul. Whenever the "craftsman" leaves it to itself, it changes; when he restores it to immortality, it acquires life again (*Pol.* 269c–270).⁷⁸ Body allows soul to become a visible, radiant, appearance of the good, but it also corrupts and confuses soul to whatever degree the soul allows it to do so. All the craftsman has to do for things to go wrong is take his hand off the tiller at any point, which apparently he does (271a–c).

The Eleatic visitor says "the steersman of the universe let go—as it were—of the bar of the steering oars and retired to his observation post." This eventually "produced a great tremor in itself, which in its turn brought about another destruction of all sorts of living things" (*Pol.* 272e–273d). Things started developing forward again: smaller to larger, younger to older, "fire from Prometheus, crafts from Hephaestus and his fellow craftworker, seeds and plants from others" (274d). After finishing eight periods of uniform motion around the circle of the same, the *Timaeus* (39d) teaches that there was a "great year" when the stars and planets returned to their original configuration (about 36,000 years). In the *Timaeus* the Egyptian priest suggests something similar in the Greek's own (but forgotten) myth of Phaëthon.⁷⁹

---

77. Wilberding, "World Soul," 24.

78. Unless otherwise noted, translations of the *Statesman* from Rowe in Plato, *Complete Works* (ed. Cooper).

79. See *Tim.* 22c–d: "Your own story of how Phaëthon, child of the sun, harnessed his father's chariot, but was unable to guide it along his father's course and so burnt up things on the earth and was himself destroyed by a thunderbolt, is a mythical version of the truth that there is at long intervals a variation in the course of the heavenly bodies and a consequent widespread destruction by fire of things on the earth."

Chapter 4

The World Soul (Dyad) is at the center of this drama. Able to look up to the demiurgic Intellect who inseminates her with his forms, she can also look down to nature to which she gives birth and become confused. But in the *Statesman*, the Soul's lure toward her wilder side becomes a more ominous possibility. Though not evil in herself, the Soul tends to evil by herself. "So while it reared living things in itself in company with the steersman, it created only slight evils, and great goods." In separation from the steersman, she starts out well "but as time moves on and forgetfulness increases in it, the condition of its original disharmony also takes greater control of it, and, as this time ends, comes to full flower. Then the goods it mixes in are slight, but the admixture it causes of the opposite is great, and it reaches the point where it is in danger of destroying both itself and the things in it." Just then the steersman takes the helm again, concerned that the Soul "should not, storm-tossed as it is, be broken apart in confusion and sink into the boundless sea of unlikeness" (*Pol.* 273c–e).

Then why cannot evil be attributed to the demiurge himself for taking his hands off the rudder? And if the demiurge is none other than the Good/Monad, there is a possibility that this source of all could be implicated. After all, the Dyad/World Soul receives her definition from this superior principle. No worries, Plato insists, because the demiurge possesses the forms, impregnating the World Soul—the womb and nurse of becoming—with his ideas. He brings her back to stability. The Pythagorean picture of the Monad imposing its reason as best as possible on the indefinite Dyad is the *Timaeus*'s view of the demiurge limiting the World Soul. The further from the sun, the less light, but it is light nonetheless. The key to understanding how Plato's cosmos works is found in *Timaeus* 48a: "Reason overruled Necessity by persuading her to guide the greatest part of the things that become towards what is best."[80] Like matter, necessity is identified with evil, but it is not an active agent; it is just the muddy riverbed that the stream needs in order to flow, however murky it becomes downstream. This is the source of the privative doctrine of evil simply as nonbeing, a lack of goodness.

However, privation is not Plato's last word on the subject. From the middle to the late period Plato attributes evil to no fewer than the following: (1) Necessity (*Tim.* 48a) or the World Soul (*Tim.* 72d; *Pol.* 286e; *Leg.* 897b–898c; 897d); (2) a providential good that we do not recognize as such (*Leg.* 903b–c); (3) punishment for sins in a previous life (*Tim.* 41e–42d; 48a–b; 91d; *Resp.* 613a), and, of course, (4) Matter (*Tim.* 35a, 48a–b; *Resp.* 613a).

Matter is a weak spot in the lower world, a problem that "is compounded," as Johnson cautions, "when Matter is not seen as the creation of the Monad, but of

---

80. Cornford, *Plato's Cosmology*, 35.

the level directly above itself, sometimes referred to as the Soul and sometimes as the Demiurge, depending on the school concerned." By Plato's division of the *one world* mixed together (Pythagoras) into *two worlds*, one higher and one lower, "the way is open then for the error of certain Gnostic schools and others in regarding Matter as an evil creation in opposition to the spiritual creation of the Monad, and thus to the devaluing of physical existence."[81] As Armstrong points out, unlike Pythagoras, Plato can affirm cosmic goodness only in a "very qualified" sense, leading to "darker and more passionate dualisms . . . with varying feeling-tones and shades of emphasis, throughout the later Platonic-Pythagorean tradition."[82] Evil cannot exist in the higher realm of reality, so it must be a quality of the lower world of appearances due to an ontological distance from the Good *or* two opposing sources of good (incorporeal) and evil (corporeal). He sometimes verges on placing these worlds in antithesis. The divided line in the *Republic* (509d–511e) is susceptible to such interpretations.

Gradually, to preserve the integrity of the Monad "One," the Dyad becomes more independent, a source of her own products alongside those of the Monad. She becomes closer to matter, which increasingly becomes a principle alongside and set over against the intelligible realm. The forms that mediated goodness to their many participants disappear from the late dialogues. Aporias and contradictions ensue by the time we reach the *Laws*.

In Plato's *Laws*, reflecting the latest phase of his thinking, he is more Pythagorean, which means more dualistic, yet more worried that the helmsman may not be able to contain his recalcitrant spouse. There may even be more than one World Soul. For Pythagoreans, the indefinite Dyad was the wild card, and this is Plato's World Soul. Despite her origin from the paternal Monad, the World Soul is our mother and, as in Pythagoras's table of opposites, she must be less rational but is also the necessary link to nature.[83] Speaking for Plato, the Athenian says, "Soul is the master, and matter its natural subject. . . . And the next unavoidable admission, seeing that we are going to posit soul as the cause of *all* things, will be that it is the cause of good and evil, beauty and ugliness, justice and injustice and all the opposites" (*Leg.* 896c–d).

This is a contradiction of Socrates's judgment against Homer's stories in the *Republic*: "It is "the foolish mistake Homer makes about the gods. . . . And, as for saying that a god, who is himself good, is the cause of bad things, we'll fight that in every way, and we won't allow anyone to say it in his own city" (*Resp.* 370b–381b).

---

81. P. Johnson, "Neoplatonists and the Mystery Schools," 145.
82. Armstrong, "Dualism," 35.
83. Plato, *Phaedrus* (trans. Hackforth), 71.

Yet even in this work the World Soul requires the Intellect to keep her rationally stable. But in the *Laws* (896c–d) there is a Soul that is called "evil" (*kakē*). This raises the question, "One soul, or more than one? I'll answer for you both: more than one. At any rate, we must not assume fewer than two: that which does good, and that which has the opposite capacity." The latter's motions cause false opinion, "grief," "fear," and "hate" (*Leg.* 896e–897a; 898c–e).

The general consensus in recent studies is that in his late period Plato moves in a more dualistic direction, which is also substantiated in his seventh *Letter* and in the so-called unwritten doctrines. These latter teachings, reserved for select students in oral seminars, were preserved by his pupils Aristotle and Xenocrates and have received renewed interest in recent decades.[84] Consistent with the unwritten doctrines is the seventh *Letter*. The Monad (or the One/Good) does not transcend being (contra *Resp.* 508e–509b). Instead, there are *two* supreme principles.[85] "There are *two primary ontological principles* that are the causes of all things," according to these fragments and testimonies.[86] Alexander of Aphrodisias, head of the Peripatetic school in the early third century CE, said that for Plato these two divine principles become even "more important than the Ideas" he had earlier made the touchstone of his cosmology (*In Metaph.* 88.1).[87] In short, the single emanation from the Good to the Intellect with its perfect forms from the Intellect to the Soul and individual souls is replaced with a dualistic map. The source of evil is not a privation of being but a divine cause of movement. This is a concept full of portent for Hellenistic philosophy.

---

84. See especially Hans Joachim Krämer (founder of the Tübingen-based working group) in "Plato's Unwritten Doctrine"; cf. Krämer, *Plato and the Foundations of Metaphysics*; cf. Nikulin, *Other Plato*. Only with the later Platonists did "esoteric" obtain the meaning that it has today. In its original context, secret simply meant closed to the public, like an advanced seminar. Dmitri Nikulin observes that in his *Life of Pythagoras*, "Iamblichus distinguishes between exoteric and esoteric Pythagoreans." The esoteric type left behind enigmatic statements "that had to be interpreted as pointing to hidden allegorical meanings," said the later Neoplatonist. See Nikulin, "Plato," 10.

85. See Aristotle, *Metaph.* 1086a11–12, quoted in Nikulin, "Plato," 16. Nikulin adds, "From the ideal numbers come dimensional (geometrical) entities. . . . After the intermediates come physical appearances, or sensual material bodies."

86. Nikulin, "Plato," 15, emphasis added. Accepting the existence of the unwritten doctrines and the possibility of identifying its distinctive teachings, Dillon is reticent to go as far as the Tübingen scholars. See Dillon, *Heirs of Plato*, 16–29.

87. Translation from *Complete Works of Aristotle* (ed. Barnes), 2:2440. Cf. Nikulin, "Plato," 17.

Conclusion

Instead of limiting the *mythos* to the intrigues of the all-too-human residents of Olympus, Plato opened the Western consciousness to a wholly new horizon: a cosmic spirituality with a noetic sun shedding its intellectual rays down even to the lowest worm. Not atheism but panentheism is the theological horizon. The Orphic self that Plato both inherited and bequeathed to future generations came from this sun and could return to it through the mystical philosophical ascent. Whatever truth may have been revealed in the Eleusinian rites, Plato's Socrates keeps returning to "what we are told" by sages who teach Orphic doctrines. Not the "thyrsus bearers" of the cult but the mystics are "the true philosophers" (*Phaed.* 69d).[88]

In Plato's synthetic imagination, Parmenides's absolute One could be affirmed as the *most* real while acknowledging some existence for the Heraclitean realm of flux. More like a dimmer than a binary switch, Plato's cosmos is divine in descending degrees. His triadic metaphysics (terrestrial, celestial, ideal) is carried forward into anthropology (humans as body, soul, and spirit or mind—the highest part of the soul), and his epistemology follows this scale: initiate (*teletē*), illumined (*muesis*), and *epopteia* (beholder of the vision), correlative to prophecy/poetry (from Apollo), divine madness (from Dionysus), and erotic passion for the One (from Aphrodite). In the details much can be criticized but the comprehensiveness of his Orphic vision justifies his central place in the "perennial tradition."

As with the shaman, there is a process of bringing divinity indoors, into more intense rings of privacy: from the public space (the *polis* and *agora*) to the mysteries, the philosophical community sharing "the Orphic life," as Plato calls it, and finally the inner chamber of the individual soul. The inwardness and individualism, over against the external ritualism of the public religion, helped to form the concept of the autonomous individual and remains a core conviction of Western culture. The true mystic is the philosopher, Plato insisted. Socrates did not disagree with Alcibiades's conclusion, "I need not mention Socrates himself—and all the rest, have all shared in the madness, the Bacchic frenzy of philosophy" (*Symp.* 218b).

From Zoroaster and Indian gymnosophists (naked philosophers) the thyrsus wand passed to Hermes Trismegistus and thence to Orpheus, Pythagoras, Philolaus, and Plato. Such genealogies are replete in later Neoplatonism to bolster the authority of the so-called Orphic theogonies. Testimonies from the fifth century

---

88. Translation from Plato, *Euthryphro, Apology, Crito, Phaedo* (trans. Jowett). It will be this positive equation of "speculative" and "mystical" that Hegel also adopts for his system.

Chapter 4

BCE to the imperial era relate Pythagoras's expeditions to the Middle East, Egypt, and India in search of higher wisdom. More importantly, he was taught by Orpheus himself, wrote works in the name of Orpheus, and became a priest in the Orphic mysteries. Iamblichus adds the Celts and Iberians to his travelogue of spiritual tourism.[89] Whether Plato actually went to Egypt, as his epigones claimed, Cicero put it well: "They say Plato learned all things Pythagorean" (*Tusc.* 1.17.39).

Another example of the transition from shaman to sage is Diogenes of Sinope. Born at the end of the fifth century BCE, he inhabited the streets and marketplace of Athens and Corinth. Practically naked, he hurled profanities at, gave the middle finger to, and even urinated on unfortunate interlocutors. Otherwise, he was sleeping in a wine jar or teaching his new philosophy, Cynicism, which he learned from Socrates's pupil Antisthenes.[90] Patching together earlier reports, Diogenes Laertius includes the story of Alexander the Great, who, being eager to meet the philosopher, asked Diogenes if he could do any favor for him. Relaxing under the morning sun, Diogenes replied, "Yes, stand out of my sunlight." Unfazed, Alexander responded, "If I were not Alexander, then I should wish to be Diogenes," to which the philosopher replied, "If I were not Diogenes, I would still wish to be Diogenes" (*Vit. phil.* 6.6.18, 21, 38).[91]

Cynic means "dog-like" (*kunikos*) and Diogenes accepted the epithet warmly. Flouting conventional morality, he literally hounded passersby, even masturbating after delivering a moving speech. Reportedly, he said that "other dogs bite their enemies, I bite my friends to save them."[92] Believing that *eudaimonia* (healthy-mindedness) was achieved by casting off tradition and the vanity of riches, power, and honor, Cynics found salvation in *autarkeia*: independence from anyone or anything other than themselves. This was achieved through shamelessness (*anaideia*) and a hard life (*ponos*) of asceticism (*askēsis*). Cynic philosophy fiercely defended freedom of speech (*parrhēsia*). According to ancient testimonies, Cynics taught two rules: "Know yourself" and "deface the currency" (i.e., deconstruct conventional society).[93] Emotions confuse the mind while reason calms it; philosophy persuades while laws merely command.[94]

89. Riedweg, *Pythagoras*, 7–9.
90. John M. Dillon summarizes these accounts from Plutarch, Diogenes Laertius, and others in *Morality and Culture in Ancient Greece*, 187–88.
91. Translation by Hicks, in Diogenes Laertius, *Lives of Eminent Philosophers*. Cf. Plutarch, *Alex.* 14. See Desmond, *Cynics*.
92. Quoted in Stobaeus, *Flor.* 3.13.44.
93. See Dobbin, *Cynic Philosophers*, 29, 195.
94. Dobbin, *Cynic Philosophers*, 45, 68.

Diogenes also coined the term "cosmopolitan" (*kosmopolitēs*) when questioned about his identity, declaring himself to belong to no nation but to the whole world (Diogenes Laertius, *Vit. phil.* 6.2.63). As developed by Stoics, it meant that all people belong to the human race, not to any one nation, race, or socioeconomic class. Nature, expressed in universal laws and rights, take precedence over local laws and customs.[95] In Corinth, Diogenes passed his philosophy on to Crates, who taught it to Zeno of Citium, the founder of Stoicism. It was mainly in Stoic thought that the Cynic ideal was most fully realized. Cynicism nearly died out, however, until it was revived in the Roman era. Critics complained of mischievous ascetics claiming Diogenes's mantle, but even the emperor Julian commended the Cynic philosophy.[96]

Diogenes himself seems like an unlikely formulator of this radically novel concept—cosmopolitanism—that has shaped the modern imagination. Nevertheless, he presents us with another vista in the transition from shaman to sage. A devotee of Cybele and Dionysus, he uses deliberately offensive tactics to experience and to help others experience the folly of depending on worldly things for happiness. We are reminded of Shiva's ribald ascetics from whose number the shamanic monks of Hinduism and Buddhism arose. It is with Shiva's followers, the first Indian ascetics, to whom Thomas McEvilley compares the Cynics.[97]

Strongly anti-Vedic, Pashupata devotional practices (*bhakti*) included muttering unintelligibly, smearing ashes on the face and body to release the devotee from bodily bonds, and a practice called "the seeking of dishonor." Only by performing "despicable" acts could the devotee "efface his ego by courting contempt": "Ill-treated, he should wander," according to the sect's texts.[98] The shaman's smearing of ashes on their face (which I have personally witnessed in Varanasi) reflects the ascetic's close connection with the dead and the afterlife. Reportedly, Alexander came upon Diogenes staring at a pile of bones. "I am searching for the bones of your father but cannot distinguish them from those of a slave," he explained to an astonished but admiring emperor (Diogenes Laertius, *Vit. phil.* 6.6.18, 21, 38).[99] Accompanying Alexander in his conquest of India, the Cynic Onesicritus brought his delegation to the gymnosophists where he is said to have witnessed a suicide by self-immolation.[100] In fact, Pashupatas believed not only in reincarnation but

---

95. G. W. Brown, "Cosmopolitanism."
96. See Julian's sixth oration in Dobbin, *Cynic Philosophers*, 187.
97. McEvilly, *Shape of Ancient Thought*, 225–36.
98. McEvilly, *Shape of Ancient Thought*, 226.
99. Cf. Plutarch, *Alex.* 14; Desmond, *Cynics*.
100. Dobbin, *Cynic Philosophers*, 83.

in reanimation, which "holds that a sorcerer can inhabit a corpse and act through it."[101] Similarly, Shaivist Pashupatas sought a state of consciousness free of dependence on anyone or anything. Over against Vaishnavist theology, Pashupatas rejected dependence even on divinity, with which the highest part of the soul in any case is identical.[102] There is even a parallel to the Stoic *apokatastasis*, the cycle of emanation and destruction in the Mahabharata, where the day of Brahama is used to refer to the cycle of creation and destruction.[103] It is not surprising that Diogenes's teaching inspired Stoic thought and practice, including the doctrine of *apokotastasis*.[104]

With Diogenes of Sinope and Indian followers of Shiva the presence of the shaman in the Axial revolution is further evident, reflecting the utopian and universalizing tendency. Nowhere and everywhere, the wandering cosmopolitan is free of earthly bonds, including the geopolitical boundaries to which the masses are attached. The locative world of his contemporaries is an iron cage they don't even recognize as such. Autonomy, freedom, distancing, dislocation and disembedding, universalism, and reflexivity all provoke sharp criticism of tradition. Once more, these features of the Axial Age find their patron in the shamanic sage.

---

101. McEvilley, *Shape of Ancient Thought*, 226.
102. Conwell and Gough, *Sarva-Darsana-Samgraha*, 103.
103. González-Reimann, "Cosmic Cycles, Cosmology, and Cosmography," 1:415.
104. Carlos Megino explores the Orphic-Stoic link in "Presence in Stoicism," 139–46.

5

"The Foes! The Foes!"
Soul Saving in Alexandria

> The foes, the foes, seven are they, seven are they; evil are they, evil are they; seven are they, seven are they. Seven gods, seven evil gods. . . . Seven demons of oppression. . . . Roaring above, gibbering below, they—the seven—they are the voices which cry and pursue mankind.
>
> —Babylonian Spell[1]

> Do not hasten to the light-hating world, boisterous of matter, where there is murder, discord, foul odors, squalid illnesses, corruptions, and fluctuating works. He who intends to love the Intellect of the Father must flee these things. . . . [For] from the hollows of the earth leap chthonian dogs, who never show a true sign to a mortal.
>
> —Chaldean Oracles, fr. 134 and 90[2]

> To ascend to another world of freedom and openness becomes the aim of Hellenistic man and the chief concern of his religion.
>
> —Jonathan Z. Smith[3]

---

1. Quoted in Thompson, *Semitic Magic*, 47–50. See Wiggermann, *Mesopotamian Protective Spirits*, esp. 1–40, 117–95; Dalley, *Myths from Mesopotamia*, 282–316, with "Sebetti" in glossary.

2. Unless noted otherwise, all translations of the Chaldean Oracles (CO) are from Majercik, *Chaldaean Oracles*.

3. Smith, *Map Is Not Territory*, 140.

Chapter 5

Whether considering justice, goodness, beauty, love, or truth, Plato's Socrates came to the same conclusion: These virtues only truly exist in another world. Athenian democracy was a parody of the good city. Imagining they were free, the people were easy prisoners of experts in flattery, marketing, and instant gratification. Their souls were enslaved to their passions. Education was entertainment, stoking private ambition without forming virtuous citizens. Precisely because they did not believe the archetypes of these virtues existed above, they could not even imitate them below. Simulacra and simulation kept the many amused in the cave and dull to reality.

A real revolution would require the virtual destruction of the existing order, separating children from their families and starting fresh with new myths. The utopian cannot accept the present order, so there are two options: revolution or retreat. If this world cannot be made into an image of the other world, then one must escape alone or with a dedicated band of those willing to mend their wings and take flight. Disillusioned after his mentor's death, Plato searched for wisdom abroad in just such a community in Tarentum in southern Italy. This Greek colony was led by the Pythagorean Archytas. A pupil of Philolaus, Archytas was the leading Pythagorean of the time. Founder of mathematical mechanics, he was also elected general of the colony seven times in a row, achieving the fame that Pericles enjoyed in Athens.[4] It was through his friendship with Archylas and experience in his community that Plato became involved in the politics of Syracuse and came to realize once again the futility of earthly regimes.

Both types of utopianism, revolution and retreat, are illustrated by different readings of the *Republic* and have exercised an enormous influence on Western culture. Eliade documents "countless examples of shamanic ascent to the sky by means of a ladder," just as Egyptian funerary texts emphasize. "'I set up a ladder to heaven among the gods,' says the Book of the Dead.... An ascent to heaven by ceremonially climbing a ladder probably formed part of the Orphic initiation."[5]

I have suggested this second interpretation of the *Republic*. Evil belongs intrinsically and eternally to this visible world. It cannot be eradicated, Socrates tells Theodorus, "nor is it possible that [evil] should have its seat in heaven.... But it must inevitably haunt human life, and prowl about this earth.... That is why a man should make all haste to escape from earth to heaven; and escape means becoming as like God as possible; and a man becomes like God when he becomes just and pure, with understanding" (Plato, *Theaet*. 176a–b).[6]

---

4. Lang, *Science*, 154.
5. Eliade, *Shamanism*, 487–88.
6. Translation from Levett in Plato, *Complete Works* (ed. Cooper).

This "haste to escape from earth to heaven" was a call to calm ascent through the pedagogy of Platonic philosophy: from beautiful things to Beauty itself. There is always something in the middle, better though not quite perfect, to let us catch our breath before continuing the ascent. Yet the lower rungs are seen as more unstable and surrounded by evil spirits set on thwarting the soul's escape. To keep the highest intelligibles from being implicated, the One and the Intellect are pushed upward and made increasingly transcendent, and this world grows darker, colder, and more menacing.

Platonic wing-mending therapy was utopian, but there was still a sense of a faint image of the Good even in the visible world. In the Hellenistic era, a more anxious exit strategy emerged—a "cosmic paranoia," where "man sees danger and threat everywhere." "Looking up at the heavens," says J. Z. Smith, one "no longer sees the signs and guarantors of order, the guardians of a good cosmic and human destiny, the positive limits placed on the chaotic powers above and below and on the span of human existence; but rather a grim system of aggressors."[7] Thanks to Persia, astrology plays a larger role and in Greece and Egypt as well as Asia there is a fear of celestial gods—planets and stars—impeding the soul's ascent. The "Hero-That Failed," which taught us to accept our place, such as Gilgamesh, is exchanged for the "Hero-That-Succeeded" in "escaping the tyrannical order."[8] Drawing anxiously on religious texts and rites, mystical schools and sects advertised their exit strategies. Platonism itself, along with Stoicism and Neopythagoreanism, drew upon darker cosmological strands of the Orphic tradition.[9] Indeed, it is an era in which the explicit label "Orphism" was invoked for oracles laden with panic and directions for escape.

We must exercise historical sympathy to imagine a world in which a distinction between sacred and secular or cult and culture was unknown. A more accurate dichotomy is between exoteric and esoteric: the public cult(ure) sanctioned by the gods and the charismatic "divine human" who transgressed the boundaries. This latter utopian figure is the shaman, but a much broader retinue of "craftsmen of the sacred" travelled widely throughout the Persian Empire and Greece.[10] "'High' literature and practical incantations come together on the same level, at any rate in the East.... Turning from this to the Greek civilization, we find the double aspect of cathartic practice and speculative mythology combined in Orphism in particular."[11]

---

7. Smith, *Map Is Not Territory*, 138. See Sargent, "Thinking Utopia," 11.
8. Smith, *Map Is Not Territory*, 139.
9. Smith, *Map Is Not Territory*, 140.
10. Burkert surveys "craftsmen of the sacred" at length in *Orientalizing Revolution*, 41–127.
11. Burkert, *Orientalizing Revolution*, 125.

Chapter 5

In the ancient world, the classic shaman-sage is laureled with epithets of expansive authority. Orpheus, Zoroaster, Manu, Moses, and Hermes Trismegistus are not only the original singer-songwriters, theologians, and framers of the cult but are also founders of all arts and sciences and the ancestors who gave the people their laws. As the search for wisdom, philosophy covered the same expanse. It is not surprising in such a culture that changes in the field of spirituality could have wide effects not only across all disciplines but across all classes. The enormous spiritual energy spent in turning the wheel from a locative to a utopian direction came with costs though. As in our own age, gaining a greater sense of freedom and individual autonomy and a spirit of exploration has resulted in the corresponding loss of a sense of security and community as well as the ability to accept this life with all its limitations.

With this chapter we move toward Alexandria, where the most conspicuous and influential Orphic movements emerged in a kaleidoscope of patterns. Nietzsche is exactly right: "Our whole modern world is entangled in the net of Alexandrian culture."[12] This is essential to the rest of my narrative in this volume. Hermeticism, Gnosticism, and Neoplatonism—along with a distinctive Alexandrian Christianity—both competed and combined with each other in response to similar questions provoked at least in part by philosophy. The main Orphic doctrines could be adapted to any religion, as evident in the Greco-Egyptian cult of Serapis as well as Greco-Buddhism and similar hybridizations.[13]

Alexandria became the laboratory for an all-encompassing vision of integrating philosophy and religion with technology, medicine, and the arts. Even its coins display the fusing of Greek, Persian, and Egyptian religion.[14] MacLeod explains that Alexandria "was a religious site, and a site of religions, a place where all the gods were worshipped, where Jews, pagans and Christians debated theologies influenced by the Zoroastrianism of Persia, and the Buddhism and Hinduism of India."[15] Early in the second century CE the emperor Hadrian grumbled to his consul, "Here, the servants of Serapis are Christians, and those who call themselves Christian presbyters serve Serapis. Here there is no synagogue leader, no Samaritan, no Christian presbyter who is not also an astrologer; a soothsayer, and a quack."[16]

12. Nietzsche, *Birth of Tragedy*, 110.
13. The Greco-Indian kingdom of Bactria was an especially fertile laboratory of hybridization. See Tarn, *Greeks in Bactria and India*. Many studies have shown this crossfertilization, including Thomas McEvilley's *The Shape of Ancient Thought*, from which I have drawn several times. Cf. Beckwith, *Greek Buddha*.
14. Ferguson, introduction to Clement of Alexandria, *Stromateis, Books 1–3*, 6.
15. MacLeod, introduction to *Library of Alexandria*, 9.
16. Quoted in Haage, *Alchemie in Mittelalter*, 63.

"Leaving It in Twilight": Tying Up Plato's Loose Ends and Fissures in the Academy

Numenius judged, "Plato taught neither in the usual manner, nor did he make his teachings very clear; but he treated each point just as he thought wise, leaving it in twilight, half way between clearness and unclearness [and thus] became the cause of the subsequent discord and difference of opinions about his teaching."[17] An indefatigable promotor of the Pythagorean tradition in the second century CE, Numenius nevertheless is hard to refute on this point.

At least in the *Timaeus*, the cosmos itself is identified as a visible god, studded with beautiful stars and planets that are themselves mortal bodies with immortal souls. There is a marvelous synchronicity of macrocosm and microcosm: the highest part of the soul, moving in a circular fashion, repairs the circuits of the mind just like celestial bodies. The naked eye could behold at night the "X" (i.e., the Milky Way) that formed the visible body of the World Soul. Pythagoras even assimilated it to his number mysticism for a cosmic theory of music: the "harmony of the spheres" with each planet and star possessing its own number-note. The beautiful things in this world are appearances of reality but as such they are symbols leading to Beauty itself.

However, Plato's later thinking moves in a Pythagorean direction. The *Timaeus* bears this out obviously, especially in its mathematical-geometrical cosmology.[18] But there is more to it than this. If Plato the monist wants still to see all of reality emanating from the One, he is faced with the problem of how evil creeps up the ladder of being. In book 10 of the *Laws*, Plato endorses the Athenian stranger's idea of an evil World Soul (*Leg.* 286e); there is a Soul that is bad (*kakē*, 897d and 986e), with neither understanding nor excellence (897b; 898c). Is this the one and only World Soul or its evil twin? The soul controls the body (892a; 896c), but even the Soul is not unequivocally good; there are benevolent and malicious Souls (896e). The World Soul is inherently unstable (*Pol.* 273c–d; *Phileb.* 43a; 59a–b; *Crat.* 439d; *Phaedr.* 245e). Even a little later in the *Timaeus*, after teaching that all is good that proceeds from "the god," we find that evil is attributed to the Soul (43a–b). Although the demiurge inseminates her with his pure ideas, she can be unstable in her lower extremities nearest the body (*ousia peri tōn sōmatōn*; *Tim.* 28a). In all these later teachings it is emphasized that the demiurge intervenes periodi-

---

17. Translation from Guthrie, *Numenius*, 66.

18. The influence of Pythagoras is in full color in the *Timaeus*, with its mystical-mathematical model of the cosmos, including the Tetrad (or *Tetraktys*), which forms the Decad. For Aristotle's definition and critique see book 3 of his *Cael.*; *Metaph.* 987b; *De an.* 404b24.

Chapter 5

cally to keep the Soul from irrational behavior. But *if* she finally came completely unhinged, wouldn't the demiurge be responsible?[19] According to Alexander of Aphrodisias, even Plato said that "when *limited by the One* the Indefinite Dyad becomes the Numerical Dyad."[20] Surely this pushes any blame up the ladder to the One itself. Realizing this, he seems to veer in an increasingly dualistic (Pythagorean) direction. But instead of there being harmony there is conflict and even total opposition between two World Souls.

As I have emphasized, the monists are dualists deep down, and the dualists are monists at the end of the day. Monists deny the reality of evil while dualists harmonize it with the good in an ultimate unity. Either way, the more the World Soul is identified with the visible world, the more ambivalent the latter becomes.[21]

The same internal debates appear in the "Axial" religions. We find the Dvaita (twoness) and Advaita (not-twoness) Vendata schools of Hinduism, analogous to Parmenidean and Pythagorean traditions.[22] Upon the death of Gautama in 483 BCE, Buddhism splintered into "Eighteen Schools," but more than two centuries passed before Buddhist scriptures appeared in textual form.[23] During the final period of Iranian rule (the Sasanian Empire: 224 BCE to 651 CE), a fierce debate

---

19. Dillon, *Middle Platonists*, 45.

20. Alexander, *In Metaph.* 88.1, translated in *Complete Works of Aristotle* (ed. Barnes), 2:2398, emphasis added. Alexander (late second to the early third century CE) was an Aristotelian, so it is especially interesting that he (like Aristotle) interprets Plato in this Pythagorean manner.

21. Dillon, *Middle Platonists*, 7: "There is not really room in a coherent metaphysics for an Active Intellect *and* a Rational World Soul, so the World Soul of later Platonism tends to be seen as irrational, or at least sub-rational, merely receptive of reason-principles and requiring 'awakening' by God. . . . As for the Young Gods, they could either be taken as the sub-rational World Soul, or as the class of Daemons, subservient to the World Soul. One can discern vacillation on this point in such men as Albinus and Apuleius."

22. The earliest Upanishads appeared between 600 and 300 BCE, receiving numerous interpolations along the winding path toward what we know as Hinduism a millennium later during its Classical Age (200 BCE to 500 CE). See Basham, *Classical Hinduism*; Flood, *Introduction to Hinduism*, 40. Patrick Olivelle says that "in spite of claims made by some, in reality, any dating of these documents [early Upanishads] that attempts a precision closer than a few centuries is as stable as a house of cards." See *Early Upanishads*, 12–14. The Muktika canon was formed from the beginning of the Common Era to the fifteenth century, and new Upanishads have been added as recently as the modern era; see Olivelle, *Upaniṣads*, 5–9. Dividing further into subschools, these divisions continued to be formalized well into the Middle Ages. See Michaels, *Hinduism*, 38; Sullivan, *A to Z of Hinduism*, 9. Evidence appears throughout Geoffrey Samuel's *Origins of Yoga and Tantra*.

23. Yet the oldest Buddhist scriptures (Pali Canon) were said to have been written on palm leaves during the Fourth Buddhist Council in 29 BCE, but most specialists date the text to the fifth century CE. See Schopen, *Bones, Stones, and Buddhist Monks*, 24, 27; Sujato and Brahmali, *Authenticity of the Early Buddhist Texts*.

arose over just this point. To ensure a dualism that resolved into an ultimate monism, Zurvanists contended that a Monad called Time exists above the principles of the One and the Dyad. Favored at court, Zurvanism was nevertheless declared heretical by the priestly magi, as was the radical dualism of Mani and his followers (Manichaeans). This focus was motivated not by ivory tower speculation but by the acute sense of the evil in this world. How far up the ladder does it go? Or are there two ladders? Either way, people needed to know. This became a vexing issue for all philosophy in the Hellenistic period.

With a heavy infusion of Stoic and Neopythagorean thought, Hermeticists, gnostics, and Neoplatonists were all wrestling with internal debates over this issue. Many philosophers of the Roman era were committed to a harmonization of the philosophers but often with a broad tendency toward a darker cosmos, a more transcendent light, and more unstable World Soul. When one does catch a glimpse of utopia, elation could turn quickly to terrifying dread and disappointment.

Plato's nephew Speussipus took the helm that some thought would pass to Aristotle. But Aristotle had become critical of some of his teacher's main ideas. First, Aristotle's supreme divine principle, the "Unmoved Mover," was, if anything, even more transcendent than Plato's "Good." His supreme God is a thinker, contemplating himself, and, in doing so, drawing reality toward its fulfillment in him. Theology is therefore the beginning of all philosophy for Aristotle because the supreme God—the Prime Mover—is the ultimate (final) cause of all that exists.[24] Deleting God as the *efficient* as well as final cause voided the procession from the One through the rational agency of the demiurge—in other words, providence. This became the dividing point between Platonists and Aristotelians. Yet the primacy of *nous* even over *pneuma* that emerges in Middle Platonism and later in Neoplatonism (as well as in Origen) is due to Aristotle's influence. Moreover, we will see that his supreme self-thinking Thinker is Plotinus's *nous* or Intellect.

Second, Aristotle found several problems with Plato's theory of forms.[25] He thought that the concept of separate forms existing somewhere in an ideal world as the model for the demiurge's work was as mythological as the stories of the

---

24. Aristotle, *Metaph.* 1026a16; cf. 984a1–b30. Cf. Gilson, *God and Philosophy*, 32.

25. The vexing problems set out in the *Parmenides* are premised on the idea that the forms existed in a transcendent realm. Using the example of "greatness," Parmenides raises serious difficulties (at 132a–b) for this view that Plato (through the young Socrates and other speakers in other dialogues) recognizes and seeks to resolve. Aristotle offered his own version of the argument in the *Metaphysics* (990b17–1079a13; 1039a2; 1059b8). In both versions, the argument is multipronged and potentially lethal. Stated briefly, Aristotle's "Third Man Argument" judges that every particular existent would have to have its own form and then there would have to be another form to unite them into one essence *ad infinitum*.

poets (*Metaph.* 997b10). For Aristotle, the forms inhere in the material things themselves. So the only real world is *becoming*, except for the fully actualized Mind. Being *is* becoming, a dynamic movement toward the divine *telos*.

Third, Aristotle diverged from Plato's dualistic trajectory.[26] Having dispensed with separate forms, he argues that everything is on its way to becoming what it is. Instead of drawing a line between an unchanging realm of *being* and an apparent world of *becoming*; like Speusippus, he distinguishes between *potency* and *act*. An acorn contains everything that the oak tree is potentially and realizes this telos in actuality. The Prime Mover itself is not developing because it is perfect thought—Pure Act—and rather than *causing* all things (efficiently) it lures them (teleologically) to their final end. Consequently, evil is just a lack of actuality: a failure to fulfill something's inherent form or nature. The goal of a watch is to tell time, so it is not matter that keeps a timepiece from realizing its telos but a lack of perfection. A bad human being is one who has a good nature that he or she has failed to bring to realization.

The third pupil of Plato's inner circle, Xenocrates, succeeded Speusippus as the head of the Academy and incorporated many of Aristotle's insights into his interpretations. In fact, Aristotle's position on the problem of evil and other points dominated the Academy for centuries until the Middle Platonists reverted to Speusippus's interpretation.[27] Yet for Xenocrates himself, Plato's later and darker thoughts pressed him to conclude that the World Soul was the "evil and disorderly principle."[28] Yet, Xenocrates also held that the demiurgic Intellect infuses all.[29] The traditional gods—perhaps Plato's younger gods of the *Timaeus*—return but in a conflict-dualist framework.[30]

Polemon (350–267 BCE) was the third successor of Plato's Academy and, along with Xenocrates, was a teacher of Zeno of Citium.[31] Polemon could not have anticipated, much less inspired, Stoic materialism or its *logos* doctrine. Nevertheless, as Dillon says, "it is he above all who gives Antiochus, two hundred years after him, the stimulus for his synthesis of Platonism, Aristotelianism and Stoicism

---

26. See Aristotle, *Metaph.* 1091b32–35 in Nikulin, "Plato," 22. Jens Halfwassen defends the reading of Speusippus and Plotinus in "Monism and Dualism"; cf. Halfwassen, "Speusipp und die metaphysische Deutung."

27. Dillon, *Middle Platonists*, 13.

28. Dillon, *Middle Platonists*, 26.

29. See Stobaeus, *Ecl.* 1.62. One can understand how this thought would be developed by Zeno and the Stoics.

30. Rulers during the Golden Age, the Titans (viz., the first twelve offspring of Mother Earth, Gaia, and Father Sky, Uranos), were offspring of the primordial deities but parents of the Olympian gods. Making war on their children, the Titans were overthrown (Zeus taking the lead over Kronos) and cast into the underworld (except for Kronos, who must dream eternally).

31. Dillon, *Middle Platonists*, 39–40.

which was to prove so fruitful in the succeeding centuries."[32] Stoics embraced a full-fledged pantheism in which Heraclitus's fiery *logos* was the active principle of all things. Everything in the cosmos represented a modification of a single divine being.[33] Thus, the various gods of popular myth became *attributes* of the divine Whole.[34] Diogenes Laertius explains, "Zeno says that the whole world and heaven are the substance of god" (*Vit. phil.* 7.147–149; cf. 7.132–160). It is a variety of natural supernaturalism. Though significant, the only difference between idealism and materialism was that the former construed the "All" as strictly immaterial. Even the Stoics taught that there were declining grades of matter, from gross to ethereal, but it was a single material divinity from the fiery Logos to the heavy bodies that fall to the center, which is why the earth lies at the center of the universe.

In the late sixth and early fifth centuries, Xenophanes inherited the Orphic trend of viewing the Mind as the all-pervading and active principle, a movement away from anthropomorphic deities to *a* god to the idea of *divinity* as pervading the Whole. "He is mind alone, holy and beyond description," says Empedocles, "darting through the whole cosmos with swift thoughts."[35] And Aeschylus, the father of Greek tragedy, said long before Zeno, "Zeus is *aithêr*, Zeus is earth, Zeus is heaven, Zeus, surely, is all things, and whatever is higher than these."[36] As West points out,

---

32. Cicero tells us (*Fin.* 4.6) that the Stoics adopted Polemon's theory of self-consciousness (*oikeiōsis*). Wayne M. Martin provides an excellent exploration of this idea in his essay "Stoic Self-Consciousness."

33. Long and Sedley, *Hellenistic Philosophers*, 1:163–64. For example, Seneca (*Ep.* 113.2) says, "Virtue is nothing other than the mind disposed in a certain way" (quoted on 1:176). Nevertheless, "The Stoic world is occupied exclusively by particulars." There is, for example, no universal "humanity" in actual existence (contra Plato's and Aristotle's forms) (1:164). Stobaeus relates that Stoics deny the existence of ideas; "what we 'participate in' is the concepts" in our own mind (*Ecl.* 1.136.21–137.6; quoted on 1:179). Laertius quotes are from Inwood and Gerson, *The Stoics Reader*, Sel 51–55, 52.

34. As Cicero describes the view of Chrysippus: "god is the world itself, and the universal pervasiveness of its mind" (*Nat. d.* 2.12–15), quoted from Long and Sedley, *Hellenistic Philosophers*, 1:323. Seneca praises the divine element suffused throughout the whole and particularly in human reason: "Why shouldn't you think that there is something divine in him who is a part of god? All of that which contains us is one and is god. And we are his allies and parts" (*Ep.* 92.30), quoted from Inwood and Gerson, *The Stoics Reader*, 72, 97. Even Boethius argued much later, "And since the heavenly bodies are born in the aither, it is reasonable that they should possess the powers of sense-perception and intelligence; from which it follows that the heavenly bodies should be counted among the gods" (Diogenes Laertius, *Lives of the Philosophers*, 60, referring to Boetheius, *On Nature* 30.42).

35. Empedocles fr. 397, as quoted in Raven, Kirk, and Schofield, *Presocratic Philosophers*, 376–77.

36. Aeschylus fr. 34, quoted from Smyth, *Aeschylus*, 2:403. See also Kenney, "Monotheistic and Polytheistic Elements," 276–78.

the formative Stoics Cleanthes and Chrysippus "clearly did know the story of Zeus swallowing the gods." Only the Whole (Zeus) was a deathless god, "periodically consuming the rest and regenerating them out of himself."[37] The whole conception is a logical extension of natural supernaturalism. Every physical process is nothing other than god's activity.[38] Since everything was a part of a single divine whole, identified with Fate, the Stoics saw evil as necessary. Evil was intrinsic to nature itself and a necessary opposite to good—just as sweet needs sour, moistness needs dryness, and so forth.[39] Since all is God and God is all, nothing occured contingently; events large and small fall like dominos in a logical order that cannot be altered.[40]

Instead of Mind (*nous*) shedding its rays downward, the Stoics conceived of it as radiating its animating reason outward to every part of its cosmic body. The "fire" of the Logos at the heart of the cosmos was the Orphic soul. But it did not transcend embodiment; rather, the Whole simply was the body of god. If Plato could call the cosmos a god, then it is not surprising that some might, literally, flesh out that idea. There was certainly room for Stoics to suggest that "soul" (*psychē*) animates the whole cosmos as "breath" (*pneuma*). This is the basis for their theory of "cosmic sympathy" (*sympatheia*).[41] This idea was implied throughout the whole tradition of Presocratic Orphism: Pythagoras's harmony of opposites, Empedocles's combination of Love and Strife, and so forth. Yet in Stoic materialistic monism it was possible that one part of the god's physical body could affect other parts. The divine soul animated stars and planets, animals and plants, and even metals possessed not just an animal soul but a *rational* soul. This makes it possible to imagine that various plants and metals correspond to celestial forces

---

37. West, *Orphic Poems*, 113.

38. "The Stoics found much to criticise in what popular belief contained over and above this," Eduard Zeller observes. "The real content of mythology . . . was to be determined by philosophical theology; the one God of the Stoics was to be worshipped partly directly and partly indirectly in the form of the gods of mythology." See Zeller, *History of Greek Philosophy*, 225–26.

39. Gellius (*Noct. att.* 7.1.1–13) says that, according to Chrysippus, evil must exist necessarily as the antipode to good. "And there is no such opposite without its matching opposite. For how could there be perception of justice if there were no injustices? . . . For goods and evils, fortune and misfortune, pain and pleasure, exist in just the same way: they are joined to each other head to head, as Plato said [*Phaedo* 60b]. Remove one, and you remove both." Chrysippus calls this "relationship of oppositeness" (*kata parakolouthēsin*). Quoted in Long and Sedley, *Hellenistic Philosophers*, 1:329.

40. Calcidius 144; Aetius 1.28.4; Gellius, *Noct. att.* 7.2.3; Cicero, *Div.* 1.125–26; Stobaeus, *Ecl.* 1.79.1–12; Alexander, *Fat.* 191, 30–192, 28; all quoted in Long and Sedley, *Hellenistic Philosophers*, 1:331, 336–37. But it would be ridiculous to conclude that you shouldn't call a doctor because you will recover regardless, Cicero replies to critics, as the doctor's intervention is also predetermined. Chrysippus's "term for these cases is, as I said, 'co-fated'" (*On Fate* 28–30); see Long and Sedley, *Hellenistic Philosophers*, 1:340.

41. Salles, "Stoic World Soul," 45–46.

that could be used in alchemical medicine, amulets containing the energy of a sympathetic star or planet, and other activities that we see exploding in the Hellenistic era. The reason within a plant, animal, or amulet could be used to heal the reason in humans. As in a human body, everything in the universe is related.[42]

The cosmos generates rational seeds that determine the nature each entity has as a part of its single body. Zeno says that when a man "shoots forth" his seed, "a portion of his soul" is implanted in the womb; "it is seized by another breath and becomes part of the soul of the female and something that coalesces with it."[43] Being also corporeal, the soul upon death is reabsorbed into the *logos spermatikos* like a spark into its flame.

In the meantime, Polemon's successor Arcesilaus (315–240 BCE) initiated the New Academy, taking Plato's school in the direction of epistemological skepticism, though not quite as far as that of Pyrrho of Ellis (360–270 BCE).[44] About three centuries later, in 90 BCE, Antiochus of Ascalon restored the Academy to the search for certainty, embracing a Stoicized Platonism that becomes the basic future direction of what is called Middle Platonism.

Cosmic Paranoia in the City of Alexander

Much like Florence for Edwardian aristocrats, a trip to Egypt for higher wisdom was *de rigueur* for Greek philosophers since at least the sixth century BCE.[45]

---

42. Galen, *QAM* 4, translation provided in Inwood and Gerson, *The Stoics Reader*, 99. According to this theory, blood is correlated with spring, infancy, air, the liver, warm and moist, and a sanguine personality; yellow bile with summer, youth, fire, the gallbladder, warm and dry, and a choleric temperament; black bile with autumn, adulthood, earth, the spleen, cold and dry, and melancholy (in fact, the Greek word comes from "black bile"); phlegm with winter, old age, water, the brain and lungs, cold and moist, with a phlegmatic personality. Like the *logos* itself, the physician must regulate these humors through *eukrasia* (good mixing). This idea of balancing humors was part of ordinary medicine until the middle of the nineteenth century. Given the sympathy and kinship of all things, maintaining a balanced harmony at the microcosmic and macrocosmic levels was considered essential.

43. Zeno, fr. 128 (from Eusebius, *Praep. ev.* 15.20.1) in von Arnim, *Stoicorum Veterum Fragmenta*, 1.36. Quoted in Salles, "Stoic World Soul," 51.

44. Any argument can be used to prove the opposite, so nothing can be known according to Pyrrhonic skepticism. Rather than certain knowledge, the goal is *epochē*, the suspension of certainty in order to arrive at tranquility (*ataraxia*). Academic skepticism was a softer position, allowing that one could discern more probable views even if certainty is unattainable.

45. Searching for a pedagogue for his son, Phillip of Macedon skipped over Speusippus (who was willing to leave his helm at the Academy) and picked Aristotle. Aristotle was joined by his childhood friend Ptolemy, who became the first Greek king of Egypt and fused the Greek and Egyptian religions in the cult of Serapis. See Fox, *Alexander the Great*, 48.

Chapter 5

"Herodotus and other Greeks of the fifth century BC recognized that Egypt was different from other 'barbarian' countries.... Like India, it was full of old and venerable wisdom."[46] Plato himself played up the superiority of Egyptians to Greeks in the opening story of the *Timaeus*.

Conquering Egypt in the name of his schoolboy friend, Ptolemy I built Alexandria from scratch with a sophisticated grid that included wide boulevards with the world's first streetlighting. The Library of Alexandria along with its Museon and expansive research center was a wonder of the world and attracted the best and the brightest in various fields.[47] Alexandria became a rival cultural center to Athens even in Aristotle's final years. After his death, many students of his Lyceum took up residency in Alexandria, and other wisdom-seekers from all over the empire joined the city's swelling ranks. Schools mixed freely, creating eclectic philosophies, although by the first-century CE followers of Plato seemed to have the clear edge.

Approaching the Common Era, the vast reaches of Alexander's conquests had been Hellenized, even as the conquered peoples transformed what it meant to be Hellenic. Upon the death of Cleopatra in 30 BCE, Egypt became a Roman vassal. Expanding far beyond the reaches of the Greek conquests, the Roman Empire incorporated still more indigenous gods and rites. Still, Alexandria, the nexus of several trade routes including India, would remain the second most important city in the empire, and Egypt remained a land of mystery and magic. Besides, the Isis cult offered something beyond civil religion. People were "craving for a more personal relation to the deity and for a redemptive religion," as H. Isris Bell puts it.[48] By the second century CE, Isis temples were as prominent in Rome as they were in Alexandria. As Griffiths says, "Salvation was one of the key concepts of the age for all who were seeking hope and assurance from religion."[49] She notes further, "In Hellenistic and Roman phases it is Isis who is mostly honored as the savior. Yet the pattern of belief throws the limelight unmistakably on Osiris. He is the prototype both of victory in the tribunal that awaits the souls after death and of triumph over death itself."[50] As the scribe and recorder, the canine-headed Thoth, identified with Hermes, gained greater prominence as well.[51] And by the beginning of the imperial era, this amalgamated figure became Hermes Trismegistus.

Then, around the beginning of the Common Era, alarm spread across the empire, and nowhere was this angst felt more than in Alexandria. Cries of panic

---

46. Matthews and Roemer, introduction to *Ancient Perspectives on Egypt*, 43.
47. MacLeod, introduction to *Library of Alexandria*, 8.
48. Bell, *Cults and Creeds*, 2.
49. Griffiths, "Great Egyptian Cults," 49.
50. Griffiths, "Great Egyptian Cults," 50.
51. Griffiths, "Great Egyptian Cults," 44.

were heard across all classes, including—even especially—the privileged. Rather than a unified world bathed in the rays of the noetic sun, the cosmos was now a battlefield. How widespread this cosmic paranoia was we cannot be sure, but it was pervasive enough to engender a cluster of Orphic movements, centered in Alexandria, that spread their message of salvation far and wide. These are the movements we will be exploring for the next few chapters: Hermeticism, Gnosticism, and Neoplatonism.

The Orphic Soul in the Ptolemaic Cosmos

As we reach the Alexandrian port during the Roman period, Plato's well-ordered cosmos is more like a battlefield. The darker thoughts have come to the fore. The world is foreboding, compromised by evil powers, as shown in this spell from the Mesopotamian tablet in the epigraph above. These "seven foes" are no less than the Pleides. They are divine but not wholly beneficent. Combining this Babylonian influence with a similar Egyptian cosmology, the planets and stars become threatening divine beings. Astrological signs are seen no longer as unequivocally auspicious. Each contributed a distinct temperament to the human soul on its descent that was returned on its purgative reascent. In the Greek Magical Papyri, Egyptian religion, and Hermetic theurgy, sinister daimons formed a harrowing army demanding a password at each station. Higher-ranking daimons would send down despicable spirits, evil daimons that could slither under doors to keep ardent souls from regrowing their wings. The earth was a nasty and dangerous place, the center of the cosmos, but the heavens held threats as well.

This anxiety was encouraged by the rise of a new cosmology that conceived of the cosmos in terms of various spheres nested in each other from the earth outward to the crystalline sphere, beyond which stood heavenly salvation. Ptolemy (100–168/170 CE), a Roman Alexandrian, formulated this cosmology in his foundational text in astronomy and mathematics, the *Almagest*, as well as in its companion, the *Tetrabiblios*, both of which were equally important for astrology. Ptolemy was a distinguished yet typical specimen of his Alexandrian context, shaped by Babylonian and Hellenized Egyptian influences and especially by the Stoic philosopher Posidonius.[52]

In *On Heroes and Demons*, Posidonius teaches that humans originated from the sun and descended to the moon and then to the earth. Humans were thereby a bridge between the two spheres; some souls became humans, others heroes,

---

52. Boll, *Studien über Claudius Ptolemaus*, 131–40.

and still others daimons. Fate and astrology played a major role in his thinking.[53] Plutarch thought that souls returned to the moon, while spirits (possessed by the few) returned to the sun. For Ptolemy as well, each planet "was the Lord of a sphere," notes F. C. Burkitt. "If then the planets (or their spheres) had an influence on men, that influence came inevitably and inexorably. Astrology as a doctrine of Fate, of inevitable and inexorable Fate."[54] The more bounded—even imprisoned—one felt, the greater the sense of urgency in controlling fate or perhaps escaping its bonds altogether.

The development of this Ptolemaic cosmology was not responsible for wild speculations, strategies, and ritual operations for the soul's return to its spiritual Ithaca past the hazardous Sirens and Cyclopes of the celestial realm, but it did provide a scientific map that confirmed widespread spiritual beliefs. Ptolemy's speculations included an atlas of the various signs of the zodiac and the point at which the soul descended, entered the earth, and then returned. The soul incarnated through Cancer and returned through Capricorn. Drawing on Ptolemy's conclusions, Numenius delineated the soul's descent downward from heaven through the Milky Way and the intersection of Capricorn and Cancer to the "gates of the sun."[55]

For Numenius, the descent of the soul in the first place was not a cheerful experience. He writes, "These theologians and Plato teach that before the souls descend into material bodies, they must go through a struggle with the physical demons who are *of western nature*, inasmuch as, *according to the belief of the Egyptians, the West is the abode of harmful demons.*"[56] In Egyptian religion, the West is the place of the underworld over which Osiris presides. Egyptian funerary rites include magical declamations of the dark gods Apep and Set (both symbolized as a crocodile) along with their "demons of the West" who threaten the solar barque on its way to the afterlife.[57] Valentinian gnostics also refer to "demons of the West" (e.g., in the *Pistis Sophia*).[58] Not unlike the American Wild West, these ominous rogues lie in wait for traveling souls.[59] However, a further sign of grow-

---

53. See Posidonius fr. 111 and 112 in Edelstein and Kidd, *Posidonius*.
54. Burkitt, *Church and Gnosis*, 32–35.
55. Numenius fr. 34 (Test 47 L; 105.19–106.18), quoted in Macrobius, *In somn. Scrip.* 1.121–4. Published in Petty, *Fragments of Numenius of Apamea*, 73.
56. Numenius, fr. 62a, quoted in Guthrie, *Numenius*, 50.
57. Fontenrose, *Python*, 221.
58. Guthrie, *Numenius*, 136.
59. It is worth noting for Homer as well that Elysium (Isles of the Blessed) is situated in the West (*Od.* 4.561), and Hesiod places it in the western ocean at the end of the earth. See Westmoreland, *Ancient Greek Beliefs*, 70.

ing pessimism is that "the West"—associated with the afterlife—becomes darker and more sinister in connotation. Gnostic, Hermetic, and Neoplatonic schools offered different strategies of escape, but they all felt in varying degrees the same existential plight.

The Wild Card: Evil and the World Soul

A modern category, the label Middle Platonism roughly refers to the period between the rejection of skepticism by Antiochus of Ascalon in 90 BCE to Plotinus in the third century CE. In an atmosphere of growing cosmological pessimism, the primary concern of skepticism was to seal off the Good from the ladder of being. In Greco-Roman theology, there are good and evil daimons (similar to angels and demons); however, they are divine beings (albeit lower in rank). As the distance expanded between the supreme principle and its lowest products, good daimons became much more important as intermediaries and as allies against evil daimons.[60] Average people in the imperial period made friends with good daimons as allies in their defense against palpably real villains. By the dawn of the Common Era we find evil daimons, bad souls, and an anxious dread that this terrestrial world was teeming with foes bleeding upward, implicating the World Soul especially in association with matter at her lower extremities.

A strict monism allowed for a merely privative view of evil, as we have seen. Brushing the dust off of Speusippus, as it were, strict Platonists emphasized the transcendence of the One beyond being. Yet this had the effect of making people feel that the Good was more remote, unknowable, and aloof to their anxieties. A host of intermediaries was required, but the lowest ones were precisely where one may expect bad operators.

Dualism was simpler, and this is why it became attractive not only to Pythagoreans but to some Platonists. Not merely distanced from evil, the Good represented the principle of an entirely separate genealogy. However, this came at the expense of promoting what Armstrong calls "conflict-dualism."[61] The usual proponents are the Neopythagoreans, with the Good identified as the Monad and matter as the Dyad—a score that gnostics would play *fortissimo*. Agreeing that the One (the Good or Monad) was beyond being (based on Plato, *Resp.* 509b),

---

60. Reale, *History of Ancient Philosophy*, 227.
61. Armstrong, "Dualism," 34. In this insightful essay, Armstrong distinguishes conflict-dualism from the more benign form, "Two Worlds dualism," that he associates with Plato. While I find this distinction helpful heuristically, I am arguing here that the line between them can be blurry.

monists and dualists acknowledged that such infinite transcendence needed to be balanced with the immanence of divinity near us. Instead of overcoming the ontological distance by addition of intermediaries, though, dualism prefered division: Soul and even the Intellect were divided into higher and lower, good and bad, entities, which spread to lower gods and daimons. The rococo theogonies among Valentinian gnostics is a logical, if absurd, extension of this outlook.

A strict Platonist (and monist) like Albinus in the mid-second century CE identified evil with matter.[62] However, most of the notable Neopythagorean Platonists (e.g., Plutarch, Numenius, Albinus) were dualists who identified evil not with matter but with the indefinite Dyad (World Soul).[63] But this meant that there was no mixture of good and evil; some things (especially sensible ones) were just bad—pure and absolute evil. Despite this tendency, there is no necessary correlation between dualism and pessimism or between monism and an optimistic cosmology. However, even a Pythagorean like Eudorus of Alexandria, who emphasizes the Good's transcendence, attributes matter to no less than the Monad (equivalent to the Platonic Intellect or demiurge), a view developed by the later theurgic Neoplatonists. There are two Pythagoreans who contributed significantly to the growing dualism of this period: Plutarch and Numenius.

Absolute Dualism: Plutarch

Plato's speculation about an evil soul in the *Laws* became for Plutarch a cosmological dogma, Reale observes, one used "to achieve a vision of reality in which the two opposed principles of good and evil eternally face each other." This is how Plutarch interprets Egyptian mythology in *On Isis and Osiris*.[64] In careful detail and with the primary sources available to him, Plutarch not only helps us understand the conflict-dualism that fed these Alexandrian movements, but his *Isis and Osiris* is also a lodestar for discerning the particular Greco-Egyptian context in which Hermetic, gnostic, and Neoplatonic schools emerged.

---

62. Dillon, *Middle Platonists*, 45.

63. Since the time of Plotinus we have tended to interpret Plato as a monist—the pure Good/One emanating its rays downward in ever diminishing grades. However, no major Platonist after Speusippus read Plato as teaching that the Good was beyond being until Numenius and Plotinus five centuries later; see Dillon, *Middle Platonists*, 18. Speusippus also interprets Plato, oddly, as teaching that the One is potential (not actual) and is not the cause of all things. Dillon mentions Plotinus as the one who revived this view, but as I argue below, Numenius pioneered its recovery. Given Plato's gravitation toward Pythagoras in his later years, the more dualistic Neopythagoreans may well have been closer than Plotinus to Plato's mature view.

64. Reale, *History of Ancient Philosophy*, 225–26.

"The Foes! The Foes!": Soul Saving in Alexandria

The Isis-Osiris myth is remarkably similar to the myths of Dionysius and Orpheus, as Plutarch underscores with the former interpreted in an Orphic way. It reaches back more than two millennia before Christ and is told in the Pyramid Texts and the Book of the Dead. Egyptian religion did not spiritualize the myth and its corresponding rituals but saw them as essential to the magic that made Egypt the destination for practical wisdom-seekers throughout the empire.

There had been a number of variations of the Isis-Osiris myth by Plutarch's time, but the main outline is clear enough. Osiris, primeval king of Egypt, is murdered by his brother Set, who then takes Isis for his own wife. Summarizing the myth, Plutarch explains that Set, representing chaotic evil, set his dogs upon Osiris, cutting up his body and strewing the pieces across Egypt. Finding his phallus, Isis reconstructs the body and restores Osiris to life; hence the elaborate phallus-processions that incorporate Dionysius. Eventually, the gods proclaim Horus legitimate and although he triumphs over Set/Typhon, Isis feels sorry for him and frees him. When Horus gains ground, *ma'at*—cosmic harmony—is restored, but Set's triumphs lead to misery. From Osiris's recovered phallus, Horus becomes the "Osiris" who wrestles with the evil Set for control of history (*Is. Os.* 17.1–5).[65]

Plutarch exhorts, "Now, we should make use of the myths [*mythoi*] not as though they were altogether sacred sermons [*hieroi logoi*], but taking the serviceable [element] of each according to its similitude [to reason]" (*Is. Os.* 58.1). The "under-meaning," Plutarch says, is "a reflexion of a certain reason" that he sets out to decode. For example, since the gods are impassible, it is better to believe "that the things related about Typhon and Osiris are passions neither of gods nor of men, but of mighty *daimones*." Like the myths, the rituals of Greeks and Egyptians alike are silly if taken literally and lead some by reaction to atheism (69.2).

Plutarch explains detailed priestly regulations as significant only as allegories of a higher truth. Even the fact that the priests wear simple linen and are clean-shaven symbolizes them cutting themselves off from matter as far as possible. "The many" do not understand even this simplest "secret," Plutarch says (*Is. Os.* 4.1–2).[66] In searching for mythological fodder for philosophical doctrines, Egypt can compete with Athens, Plutarch claims.[67] The dismemberment of Dionysus by the Titans corresponds remarkably to that of Osiris at the hands of his brother Typhon-Set, the serpentine god of destruction (also a Greco-Roman fusion).[68] "Greeks consider Dionysius to be lord and prince not only of wine, but

---

65. Mead, *Thrice-Greatest Hermes*, 200–245. All translations of *On Isis and Osiris* from Mead.
66. Quoting Plato, *Phaedr.* 67b.
67. Mead, *Thrice-Greatest Hermes*, 191.
68. Yuri Stoyanov observes, "In Orphism the body and the soul were brought together as a

of every moist nature," Plutarch notes, just as Egyptians consider Osiris (35.2, 5, 7). It is no wonder that Greeks translated the name Osiris as Dionysus.[69]

Interpreted allegorically, Plutarch exhorts, it all makes sense: Typhon (Set) is the principle of multiplicity and therefore disorder, tearing reason to pieces. But his dogs are thwarted when Isis regathers his body "and transmits [his reason] to those perfected in the art of divinizing." In Pythagorean fashion, he says that this occurs through abstinence from "many foods and sexual indulgences" and "service in the sacred [rites], the end of which is gnosis of the First and Lordly One, the One whom mind alone can know, for whom the Goddess calls on [them] to seek, though He is by her side and one with her" (2.2). His reference to "those perfected in the art of divinizing" suggests a Hermetic or at least theurgic context, as the *Asclepius*, attributed to Hermes Trismegistus, describes "the art of making gods" (Corp. herm. Ascl. 37).[70]

Plutarch no doubt performed such rituals with devotion, but did so as noetic-symbolic exercises. Dillon surmises, "This position can, I think, be characterized as 'gnostic.'"[71] In his opening address to Klea, Plutarch exhorts, "For the Divine is neither blest through silver and through gold, nor strong through thunderings and lightnings, but [blest and strong] by gnosis and by wisdom" (*Is. Os.* 1.1–4). Here Plutarch is trying to persuade readers to embrace a more gnostic (Hellenistic) practice over against the literalism and physicality of Egyptian religion. The truth about the gods is "more holy than is all and every purging rite and temple-service ... gnosis is more suitable to [the Goddess] than any other title" (2.1). Deification was accomplished through gnosis. The antithesis between ritual and reason would

---

result of the primordial crime of the Titans—the dismembering and the devouring of Dionysus. The revived Dionysus appears to have been perceived as a savior-god, releasing entrapped souls from a 'Titanic' prison, and Orphism is credited with introducing into European religiosity the pattern of soul-body dualism, whether in terms of distinct antithesis or mere separation." See Stoyanov, *Other God*, 32.

69. Stoyanov relates, "The Orphic myth of the dismemberment of Dionysus, which was represented in the rites initiated by Orpheus (Diodorus 5:75,4), recalls the myth of Osiris' dismemberment in Egypt and, indeed, Diodorus refers to the Greek translation of Osiris as Dionysus (1:11.3). Zeus avenged the horrible death of Dionysus by destroying the Titans with lightning and, while Dionysus was later revived, it was out of the ashes of the Titans that man was created." Stoyanov, *Other God*, 31.

70. Copenhaver, *Corpus Hermeticum*, 67–92.

71. Indeed, as Dillon remarks, "Plutarch plainly holds that knowledge of God is not simply a matter of philosophizing in the modern sense, but rather of training and disciplining the mind through ascetic practices and the observance of ritual." See "Plutarch and Second Century Platonism," 216.

have been as strange to devotees of the Egyptian religion as that between body and soul.

All of the groups we will consider—not only gnostics but also Neoplatonists and Hermeticists as well as Clement and Origen—were "gnostic" in Plutarch's sense. The idea is that particular religions clothe universal truths (i.e., Orphic philosophy) in their own myths and rituals that are in themselves dispensable. To quote Plato again, "There are indeed, as those concerned with the mysteries say, many who carry the thyrsus but the Bacchants are few. These latter are, in my opinion, no other than those who have practiced philosophy in the right way" (*Phaed.* 69c–d). Thus began a long line of demythologizing, one characteristic of the critique of religion and religious texts found even in the present day.

Plutarch finally interprets the whole myth of Isis and Osiris by first presenting the options (clearly limited to a Greek horizon). Pythagoreans interpret the riddles of religious mythology as signifying Orphic doctrines, especially the dualism of spirit and matter.[72] The same is true of "Dualists" (i.e., Platonists) especially over against atomistic (Democritan-Epicurean) and monistic (Stoic) ontologies. If "God is the cause of all," then the cosmos must consist of "'harmony, as that of lyre or bow,' according to Heraclitus, and according to Euripides: 'There could not be apart good things and bad, But there's a blend of both so as to make things fair.'" According to so many ancient and worthy poets and philosophers, "both non-Greek and Greek," the cosmos "is many things and these a blend of evil things and good" (*Is. Os.* 1.9, 224–225).

The metaphor of blending opposites into a single mixture, as in the *Timaeus*, yields itself to a monistic interpretation. The alternative would be two bowls, good and bad, each one generating its own products. However, as if he had caught himself, Plutarch offers a key qualification implicitly criticizing the *Timaeus*: "It is *not* that from two jars a single mixer, like a tavern-keeper, pouring things out like drinks, mixes them up for us, but that from *two opposite principles* and *two antagonistic powers*" that all things, good and bad, derive. "For if nothing has been naturally brought into existence without a cause, and Good cannot furnish cause of Bad, *the nature of Bad as well as Good must have a genesis and principle peculiar to itself*" (*Is. Os.* 45.6–8, emphasis added).

Having moved gradually toward his own view, Plutarch casts his lot with the Zoroastrian magi, "the most wise" who teach that "there are two craft-rival Gods,"

---

72. As Plutarch writes: "Moreover, what is said by the Pythagorians, namely, that the sea is the tears of Kronos, would seem to riddle the fact of its not being pure and cognate within itself" (*Is. Os.* 32.10).

sources of good and evil Egyptian rites also engage in fiery denunciations of evil daimons without blasphemy to the higher gods (as Iamblichus tries to explain to Porphyry). Like Horus and Set, Zeus and Typhon, or Apollo and Dioynsius, the two gods are "at war with one another," Plutarch continues (*Is. Os.* 1.9).

However, there is an eschatological triumph of the Good in the Zoroastrian myth, which Plutarch even acknowledges. The Egyptian myth also promised that Horus would eventually win. Yet for Plutarch, there can be no *denouement* to history because the world is eternal and cyclical. With Plato, he agrees that evil cannot be eliminated from this lower world. The myths tell us not what happened or will happen, but what is happening everywhere and always.

For Plutarch the World Soul is not inherently evil, but her indefiniteness and difference from the One renders her susceptible to "movement" (code for "mistake"). His fellow Neopythagorean Numenius completes this dualistic tendency, and Plotinus assumes much of it even as he criticizes it at significant points, especially after his confrontation with gnostics.[73] However, Numenius rejects any identification of the Dyad (World Soul) with evil in no uncertain terms: "these conceptions are unacceptable to people of even middling education."[74] Rather, the evil World Soul is matter. It is not surprising that such acute legatees of Orphism and Pythagoras would identify evil with matter; what *is* surprising is that some of them would identify evil with the World Soul. Against this move, Numenius draws the no less shocking conclusion that there are *two* World Souls, one good and the other evil.[75] Maybe this was actually the mature position of Plato (see book 10 of *Laws*). Even Philo of Alexandria identifies the World Soul with the Dyad. Philo calls her Sophia (as the gnostics did in their more extreme theogony) while Plutarch refers to her as Isis.[76]

From a Neopythagorean perspective, the indefinite Dyad is the first offshoot from the definite One, and therefore the most susceptible to blame for evil. What

---

73. Dillon, *Middle Platonists*, 45. As we will see, the confrontation with the gnostics pushed Plotinus away from the more "Numenian" tendencies of earlier formulations.

74. This testimony concerning Numenius comes from Chalcidius, *In Plat. Tim.* 295–96. Quoted in Reale, *History of Ancient Philosophy*, 268. If this is accurate, then the indefinite Dyad is not actually indefinite at all, but *is* multiplicity (twoness). This is how Numenius himself understood the position, rejecting it on the grounds that if the Dyad (which Numenius considered to be matter itself) were generated by the Monad not only would evil be attributed to the Monad, but the Monad would be transformed into the Dyad.

75. Chalcidius's description of Numenius's view can be found in frr. 44–47, 52, and 55–56 in Petty, *Numenius of Apamea*. See also Baltes, "Numenios von Apamea," 247–48.

76. Dillon, *Middle Platonists*, 45–46. "And for Philo, this Dyad is also identified with the figure of Sophia, while Plutarch identifies it with Isis in the preface of *On Isis and Osiris*, though toward the end he makes Isis rejoice at 'impregnation' by the Logos of God."

comes after the One and the Intellect but the World Soul—the womb of nature? Could she be the source of evil here below? To put the matter frankly, the stable father—not just the transcendent One, but the demiurgic Intellect—has become remote from the life of the family. It is the mother, who is often irrational and unstable, who garbles the information put into her by the paternal demiurge. "Especially with Neopythagorean influences," says Dillon, "Middle Platonism tends to give a larger role to the World Soul than it has in the *Timaeus*."[77] But the more she is identified with the visible world, the more ambivalent her nature becomes.[78] That makes her susceptible to being identified as the weak spot in the triad. Plutarch does not think that matter is evil intrinsically, but it is animated by the restless, irrational Dyad (*An. procr.* 1014d). Yet if the One sets the Dyad (World Soul) on her course by his limiting and defining action, how is evil not to be attributed to this first principle?

The Middle Platonists wrestled with the loose ends present in Plato not only to harmonize Aristotle with Plato but also to harmonize Plato with himself. If one chooses a monistic scheme, the worry remains concerning how high evil bleeds upward, while the alternative provokes the danger of "conflict-dualism."[79] One thing is clear. There is a growing obsession with the problem of evil, and Orphism remains a powerful resource in answering that existential as well as philosophical question. At the dawn of the Common Era, Plutarch, Atticus, and Numenius would take this dualism as far as it could go within a Pythagorean-Platonist system, while gnostics would press it even further. Yet, as Dmitri Nikulin judges, it is Plato's esoteric teachings themselves that pushed against "a strict monism."[80] In so doing, Plato followed through with greater consistency the ontological dualism at the heart of Orphism.

From all of this it would seem that the real progenitor of "underground Platonism" is Plato. Plutarch comes nearer than Plotinus to Plato's late positions. Jerry S. Clegg puts it well, "It is hard to escape the thought that Plato's creation myth is incompatible with his doctrine."[81] In fact, there are contradictions in the myth itself at this point (*Tim.* 30a–b versus 43a–b). But the *Laws* leaves little doubt of Plato's direction toward a view ready to be exploited centuries later by Plutarch, Numenius, Atticus, and, more radically, by gnostics.[82] Indeed, the Christian theo-

---

77. Dillon, *Middle Platonists*, 45.
78. Dillon, *Middle Platonists*, 7.
79. Armstrong, "Dualism," 34.
80. Nikulin, "Plato," 15.
81. Clegg, "Plato's Vision of Chaos," 52.
82. Yet, most gnostics (like Platonists generally) affirmed a dualism subordinated to an ultimately monistic scheme. Sophia, analogous to the World Soul, is the "wild card" whose foolish

logian Hippolytus (170–235 CE) argued that Pythagoreanism, which Pythagoras himself derived from Egypt, was the source of gnostic teaching (*Haer.* 6.23–25).[83] This indicates at least that similar views were being debated outside of gnostic, Platonic-Neopythagorean circles.

Given the ineffable transcendence of the Monad and the Dynad's being pregnant with evil products, where does that put us? What about all of the bad souls, daimons, and gods generated by the Dyad–World Soul herself? While disagreeing about how high the blame could go, Roman-era philosophers in general agreed that the terrestrial world was the haunt of evil daimons. Such imprecations are frequent in the magical papyri and were a large part of Egyptian ritual. However pristine the highest principles of the cosmos may be, the gods we know are often terrifying according to this outlook. The Good is not jealous and does not begrudge all things a share in its goodness, but it was also a common rule among Middle Platonists that "gods do not have dealings with humans."[84] "Whatever the differences in detail, however, it is common ground for all Platonists that between God and Man there must be a host of intermediaries, that God may not be contaminated or disturbed by a too close involvement with Matter."[85]

Persian magic and astrology, but especially Egyptian ritual, gave vexed souls a sense that they could do something about their situation. In this environment Neoplatonism, Hermeticism, and the various gnostic communities emerged, offering different schemes of escape. Calmer Platonists like Plotinus exhorted a steady course of contemplation that would eventually yield ascent and reunion with the One. The Hermetic strategy was for the individual to become the magus uniting heaven and earth, Mind and mind, by discovering the sympathetic attractions that could prolong life and deify the soul. Gnostics wanted to burn any bridges between the two worlds and take flight with all speed from the physical realm.

---

mistake sets in motion the fall of souls into matter. However, she is an emanation (albeit the last one) of the divine beings, and even the evil creator is her divine offspring. Thus, while gnostic dualism was darker, the dualism of the Neopythagoreans was more complete.

83. On Hippolytus's interpretation of this connection generally, see Mansfield, *Heresiography in Context*. Actually, however, gnostics were more monistic and followed Middle Platonists in affirming a transcendent Good beyond being and sequestering it from the poles of good and evil. Their Sophia may have made a foolish mistake of enormous consequence, but they never said (as Plutarch and Atticus did) that the "father of all" set the wheels in motion by his limiting action upon the maternal Dyad.

84. Reale, *History of Ancient Philosophy*, 227.

85. Dillon, *Middle Platonists*, 47.

Offshoots proliferated, especially in the fertile delta of Alexandria, that would spread quickly throughout the empire and into succeeding epochs. However, the Orphic myth was common to them all: the fall and rise of the divine self trapped in a world of bodies, fate and laws, astral and planetary powers, gods and daimons both good and bad.

Numenius of Apamea

Numenius's influence looms large in the Alexandrian milieu. True to his ancient master, Numenius saw philosophy as oriented more toward transformative experience than to abstract theories.[86] Plato in the *Theaetetus* defined the goal of philosophy and life itself as being conformed to God as much as possible. To this end, Numenius, like Plutarch, scoured the half-forgotten Eleusinian mysteries.[87] The Orphic mysteries had cast their spell, and, notes Shaw, he was so well acquainted with the Greco-Egyptian mysteries of Serapis that he must have been initiated into it.[88]

The world, which Numenius also considered "a beautiful god," was in its corporeal aspect actually frightening; matter threatens, like an angry sea, to take the captain down. Plato said the same about the World Soul (especially in *Pol.* 273b), but definitely not about the demiurge. Here as well, anxiety over the problem of evil keeps moving up the ladder. While the World Soul–Dyad was held increasingly responsible for irrational urges by Middle Platonists, Numenius implicated the demiurge, locating the cosmic tragedy in the "forgetful" passion of the creator-legislator. But this means that this world is intrinsically evil, although the second god sows the seeds of the first god within creatures.

Numenius believed he was simply clarifying Plato's doctrine, but in doing so he describes a darker conception of emanation. Taking the table of opposites to its logical extreme, he split the demiurge through the entire hierarchy. There are Two

---

86. Shaw, foreword to Numenius, *Fragments* (trans. Petty), iii.

87. Guthrie, *Numenius*, 42: "Among the philosophers Numenius was one of the most eager for Mysteries. A dream announced to him that the Divinities were offended, because he had published the Eleusynian mysteries by interpretation. He dreamed, namely, that the Eleusynian divinities, garbed like prostitutes, stood before a public house of ill fame; and as he was wondering how the Goddesses came to such an ignominious attire, they had angrily answered that by himself they had been violently torn out of the sanctuary of their modesty, and had been exposed for hire to every passer-by."

88. Shaw, foreword to *Fragments*, iv. However, although this idea is certainly Hermetic, it is Stoic first, as were many of Numenius's other ideas encountered below.

World Souls, good and evil.[89] The same is true for the microcosm: each person has a rational soul, which is divine, and an irrational soul that is from matter.[90] Like Plato, he affirms that the cosmos is a mixture: "the goodness of the Idea," ruled by Providence, and "the badness of Matter," ruled by Necessity. However, it is a long way from the *Timaeus* in which pure goodness emanates from a single source in descending grades. While Plato himself wavered between this two-worlds dualism and conflict-dualism, Plutarch, Atticus, and especially Numenius pressed into the latter territory.[91]

Numenius's conflict-dualism regards descent as punishment. This is *one* of Plato's accounts, but Numenius takes the darker path of his later teaching influenced by Empedocles's Orphic doctrine: "The reason for the descent of the souls is that they are guilty."[92] Thus, all incarnations are evil.[93] Suffering is an "inevitable evil" for beings associated with matter.[94] The harmony of opposites does not encompass soul and body.[95] Generation, including biological reproduction, is a mark of such depravity, over against the contemplative life of immobile attachment to the immobile. Indeed, Numenius interpreted the war between the Athenians and Atlantians in the *Timaeus* as "the conflict between men of philosophic interests, and those who carry on generation [begetting children]," notes Guthrie.[96]

Numenius's allegorical interpretation of the Homeric cave (fr. 30) is characteristically Orphic. Incorporating much of it into his own Cave of Nymphs (esp. at 10 and 34), Porphyry explains, "Here Numenius is important, as are the interpreters of Pythagoras' hidden meanings who understand the river Ameles in Plato, the Styx in Hesiod and the Orphics, and the outflow in Pherecydes as semen" (*Ad Gaurum* 34.26–35.1).[97] This cave is the material cosmos, in contrast with the intelligible one. Numenius associates water with matter and moistness with em-

---

89. Reale, *History of Ancient Philosophy*, 269. As Reale interprets Numenius, the Monad is the Second God in its activity of contemplating the higher realm, while the Third God is actually the Second God "in its specifically demiurgic function, that is, in its function ordered to informing matter (Dyad)"—what Numenius also calls not just the Soul of the World but "the 'good soul' of the world. For him the Dyad is the sensible principle opposed to the intelligible world, a principle evil in itself and the source of every evil."

90. Porphyry as quoted in Stobaeus, *Ecl.* 1.49.25.

91. Armstrong, "Dualism," 38–39.

92. Guthrie, *Numenius*, 138–39.

93. See Domaradzki, "Of Nymphs and Sea," 146–47; cf. Guthrie, *Numenius*, 52, 131.

94. Guthrie, *Numenius*, 130.

95. Guthrie, *Numenius*, 138–39.

96. Guthrie, *Numenius*, 132–33.

97. Translation, unless otherwise noted, from Wilberding, *Porphyry to Gaurus*. Numenius refers explicity to Pherecydes's "efflux" (DK 7B7 = Schibli F 87).

bodiment. The rational soul floats like a nymph on or above the river/semen while the irrational soul enters the embryo with it.[98] Thus the river or semen represents "the fluid border between the sensible and intelligible world."[99]

Indeed, continues Numenius, the soul faces a perilous journey to its fatherland. Following his own allegorical-Orphic reading of the *Odyssey*, Numenius develops a travelogue for the soul's reascent through the Zodiac. After delineating Numenius's astrological views, Porphyry endorses his interpretation of Plato:

> For I do not think it irrelevant that for Numenius and his school Odysseus in the Odyssey also seemed to serve Homer as the symbol of the one passing through successive generation, and thus being restored to those apart from every wave and without experience of the sea: "Until you reach those who know not the sea, 'Men eating food not mixed with salt.'" And the material world is an ocean and sea and wave for Plato also.[100]

Porphyry explains that those who know not the sea and who eat food not mixed with salt are disembodied souls. The rest wander, tossed about by the waves like Odysseus and his crew.[101]

Numenius takes to the sea again, as he did with the image of the ship's pilot, for this Homeric flight home. If the soul should reach the pure light of being, it must exist like a "solitary fishing boat, sailing along between the waves.... Thus, far from the visible world, must he commune with the Good, being alone with the alone (solitude), far from man, or living being, or any body, small or great, in an inexpressible, indefinable, immediately divine solitude."[102]

The phrase "flight of the alone to the alone" associated with Plotinus was actually coined by Empedocles and is repeated often by Numenius.[103] From its descent to its return, the life of the soul in this world must be a constant struggle; evils cannot be eliminated. For this flight the soul must put aside the visible world and draw energies from the third god, the "intellectual food" from the second,

---

98. Fraenkel points out in *Philosophical Religions*, "The same doctrine he finds in the Pythagoreans, who claim that 'the souls settled upon the waters which was god-inspired [thepnoon],' and in Genesis 1:2, according to which the 'Spirit of God moved over the waters'" (101; Numenius fr. 30).

99. Domaradzki, "Of Nymphs and Sea," 139–50.

100. Numenius, fr. 33 (Test. 45 L) from Porphyry, *Antr. nymph.* 34.11–13. Published in Petty, *Fragments of Numenius of Apamea*, 73.

101. Domaradzki, "Of Nymphs and Sea," 49.

102. Numenius quoted in Guthrie, *Numenius*, 4.

103. Guthrie, *Numenius*, 107.

and the "sciences" from the first. "These are the three successive elements of the ecstasy."[104] It is the usual Orphic ascent: purgation (turning away from everything visible), illumination (gnosis), and, finally, union (ecstasy).

Numenius also follows the Orphic-Pythagorean abstension from meat and sex, which stir passion and exercise a "charm enough to entrap souls into the imprisonment of incarnation." And yet, "love is divine; and, after all, this attraction, in a lower sphere, is no more than the same desire which drew the First Divinity on to create the second, and the second to create the world." Salvation comes when the lower part yields to the good soul, he says. "The reward of good choice is a fresh happy incarnation; but in this world we may hope to achieve the bliss of ecstasy, and the knowledge of Good."[105] Yet if all incarnations are inherently evil and punishment for guilt, one wonders how "a fresh happy" one is possible.

Numenius's dualism deepens the well-trodden path of escape from the world. It is not quite right to call this pessimism, since he believes all truly spiritual substances are reunited. Usual modern dichotomies do not quite work to describe his thought. As I have shown thus far, monistic systems harbor an underlying dualism. This dichotomy breaks down especially when correlated with pessimism/optimism. Perhaps the most appropriate term for this growing conflict-dualism is "anticorporeal": a negative view of the physical world and embodiment that would characterize Orphic philosophy generally but is taken to an extreme by Numenius and still further by the gnostics. With Plato conflict-dualism was a possibility, but with Plutarch, Numenius, and Atticus in the first two centuries of the Common Era it became a reality. As Armstrong says, "There is the principle of light, form and order, the dark, disorderly evil soul, and between them matter, which is sharply distinguished from the evil soul."[106] Either way, monistic or dualistic, the visible world—that is, corporeality—is either merely apparent or, if it really exists, is evil.

Yet even the highest principles below the One have evil doppelgängers. Dillon is surely right when he says, "Numenius's view of the world is more starkly dualist than that of Plutarch," adding:

> Not only does he believe in an evil principle at work in the world, which he identifies with the Indefinite Dyad of Pythagoreanism (fr. 52), but he feels a dualism within the individual soul, to the extent of postulating two souls within each

---

104. Guthrie, *Numenius*, 134.
105. Guthrie, *Numenius*, 133, emphasis added.
106. Armstrong, "Dualism," 38.

individual (fr. 43), a rational and an irrational. The descent of the rational soul into body he sees as an unqualified misfortune (fr. 48), and no reconciliation, only constant struggle, can come about between these two souls. This "gnostic" view he shares with the Chaldaean Oracles (fr. 102–4, 107, 112), and it adds up to a distinctly world-negating attitude, in distinction to that of Plutarch.[107]

Monism here has been replaced by a conflict-dualism with two sources of existence: good and evil. Numenius has pushed to their extreme edges both the inherent tendency within Platonism toward acosmism and the conflict-dualism of his Neopythagorean sources.

For Numenius it was Pythagoras the Orphic priest, and not Plato, who was the original genius. He holds, as Fraenkel points out, that "Plato provides the best access to the philosophy of Pythagoras which, in turn, has its source in the ancient wisdom traditions of the Greeks—from Homer and Hesiod to the Eleusinian mysteries (Fragments 31, 33, 34, 36, 55, 58)" and encompasses the best philosophical religion of "'the Brahmans, the Jews, the Persians, and the Egyptians,' as well as the Romans and Christians (Fragments 1a, 10a, 31)."[108] Colonizing the barbarians, Orphism had not replaced these public religions. On the contrary, Greek philosophers could respect foreign religions as concealing in their own way the universal truth in a diversity of myths, rites, and laws. Through this consistent allegorizing, Orphic teaching became synonymous with what Westerners called reason.

To be sure, Numenius is a radical and innovative figure in the tradition. Yet he was read so eagerly in Plotinus's circle that Plotinus was accused of plagiarizing him. Clement, Origen, and Eusebius held Numenius in such high esteem that they preserved most of the fragments that we possess of him, and the later Neoplatonists absorbed many of his ideas. The ideas of a precosmic fall of souls that determines their level of incarnation and a final restoration of all souls will be adopted by some gnostics but especially by Origen.

Not surprisingly, Numenius was especially intriguing to Marcilio Ficino in the Renaissance when he sought to charm the spirit of Hermes Trismegistus into taking up residence in a much later and much different age. All of this presses us to ask: Has what is often identified as esoteric, underworld, irrational, and conflict-dualist Platonism actually become the main current of the tradition in the imperial age? And is it simply one plausible outcome of Orphic philosophy?

107. Dillon, "Plutarch and Second-Century Platonism," 228.
108. Fraenkel, *Philosophical Religions*, 101.

Chapter 5

Philo of Alexandria: Orphic Moses

Hellenistic Judaism is a significant phenomenon especially since the fall of the Jerusalem Temple in 70 CE.[109] Philo of Alexandria (20 BCE–50 CE) is more representative than formative of this trend. Numenius encouraged philosophers to "invoke the nations of renown, citing the initiations, dogmas, and fundamental rituals which they celebrated in agreement with Plato—all those which the Brahmans, Jews, Magi, and Egyptians have established."[110] Plato, he said, is simply a "Greek-speaking Moses."[111]

Generally, a "harmony of the philosophers" was the goal of all schools during this period, but with a preferred fountainhead as the unifying factor. Only in a few cases, notably Albinus (*fl.* 150 CE), do we meet a strict Platonist who polices the borders.[112] The "harmony of philosophers" even became the epithet of Middle Platonism all the way to Ammonius, the founder of Neoplatonism, who wrote a work entitled *Harmony of Moses and Christ*. Of course, while this preferred fountainhead may have been the unifying factor, the Orphic myth remained the main ingredient of each school's eclectic mixtures. For Philo, the arbiter was a quite Platonic Moses.[113] Plato had said that the arduous and hazardous search for truth is like sailing on a raft, "unless he can sail upon some stronger vessel, some divine revelation, and make his voyage more safely and more securely" (*Phaed.* 85c–d). Philo finds this "stronger vessel" in the Hebrew scriptures, which he identifies repeatedly as "the Mosaic philosophy."[114] Numenius called Moses "the prophet" the same way Homer is simply "the poet."[115] Perhaps with Philo in mind, he added, "Among the nations that believed God was incorporeal" were "the

---

109. Neusner and Green, *Dictionary of Judaism*.

110. Numenius, fr. 1a (9a L). Fragment from Numenius's first book of *Concerning the Good*, as quoted in Eusebius, *Praep. ev.* 9.7.1. See Petty, *Fragments of Numenius of Apamea*, 3.

111. Numenius, fr. 8 (Des Places). From Edwards, *Neoplatonic Saints*, 15. It is worth noting that according to Josephus (*J.W.* 2.477–480), Apameans would not allow the Jews to be killed or taken into captivity during the Jewish Wars.

112. For Albinus the first god was utterly transcendent and unknowable (anticipating Pseudo-Dionysius in some of his arguments). He also believed that each soul had its own star and returned ultimately to that star after a cycle of various reincarnations.

113. Giovanni Reale does not exaggerate when he says, "With Philo . . . the history of 'Christian' philosophy (i.e., religious philosophy) and hence 'European' philosophy begins"; see *History of Ancient Philosophy*, 170.

114. Reale, *History of Ancient Philosophy*, 178–79.

115. Guthrie, *Numenius*, 101.

Hebrews, not scrupling to quote the expressions of the prophets, and expounding them allegorically."[116]

According to David Runia, Philo was "an exegete of scripture who drew on the Greek philosophical tradition to unfold and expound the hidden wisdom of Mosaic philosophy."[117] While Runia is correct, "the hidden wisdom of Mosaic philosophy" turned out in many instances to be identical with "the Greek philosophical tradition." If Numenius could remark not long afterward, "What else is Plato than Moses speaking Greek?" it is probably because he had been reading Philo. At the same time, Philo's commitment to monotheism—indeed, to a transcendent, omnipotent, and personal God—introduces considerable tensions with Platonism.

Not surprising for an Alexandrian of any stripe, and especially for a Middle Platonist, Philo was eclectic in both his influences and contributions. For his Logos doctrine (along with *sophia*, "wisdom") he was indebted to the Stoics. There is evidence of the influence of the Neopythagorean Eudorus on his thinking as well, and Clement of Alexandria even calls him "the Pythagorean Philo" (*Strom.* 1.72.4). However, Philo was also a devout adherent of a religion whose cornerstone was the Shema: "Hear, O Israel: The LORD our God, the LORD is one" (Deut 6:4). Moreover, the God of Israel is personal. The name revealed to Moses, translated from the Greek Septuigint, "I am" (*ego eimi*, Exod 3:14) is not a principle but "the God of Abraham, Isaac and Jacob" (Exod 3:6).

Lacking any definite article to distinguish it from other gods (polytheism) and eschewing the term "divinity" (pantheism), the word "God" (*theos*) with Philo acquires a density that it lacked in Hellenic wisdom. As Andrew Louth points out, Philo exhibits "a much clearer conception of a transcendent God."[118] God is even above the One and the Monad—indeed, beyond even the Good itself.[119] Moreover, the main attributes of "He Who Is" are sovereignty and goodness.[120]

Matching his stress on divine transcendence is Philo's interest in God's nearness. Contrary to the logic required of an emanationist scheme or Aristotle's absolute denial of any relation, Philo holds that God is not related to the world

---

116. Guthrie, *Numenius*, 2.

117. Runia, *Philo and the Church Fathers*, 189.

118. Louth, *Origins of the Christian Mystical Tradition*, 17.

119. *Praem.* 40; *Fug.* 198; *Contempl.* 2. See also Reale, *History of Ancient Philosophy*, 186.

120. Louth, *Origins of the Christian Mystical Tradition*, 20. Giovanni Reale observes that, based on the Septuagint rendering, "*Elohim* [= *theos*] expresses the power and the force of good and hence of the act of creation, *Yahweh* [= *kurios*] the legislative and punishing force." See Reale, *History of Ancient Philosophy*, 194.

Chapter 5

yet freely chooses to relate the world to himself. Moreover, Philo speaks of the emanation of divine powers from the Torah, a doctrine that will become fertile soil for later Jewish-gnostic kabbalah.[121] The first to invoke this important distinction between divine essence and energies, Philo was able to conceptually protect monotheism by positing emanations only with respect to God's energies (i.e., actions), not his essence.[122] The rays of God's energies shine through even to the lowest worm, but his essence does not.

Whatever divergences Philo makes from heathen philosophy, he nevertheless presupposes the Orphic doctrines. This may be seen, for example, in his *Migration of Abraham*, which interprets the patriarch's journey from his moon-worshiping family in Haran to the land of promise as an allegory of the stages in mystical ascent.

In traditional Jewish and Christian interpretations, Abraham's historical and physical migration from Haran was essential to the fulfillment of God's promise. Abraham never returns, but goes to a place that he has never known based solely on this pledge. The narrative distance of Athens and Alexandria from Jerusalem is measured well by Emmanuel Levinas's poignant contrast: "To the myth of Ulysses returning from Ithaca, we wish to oppose the story of Abraham who leaves his fatherland forever for a yet unknown land and forbids his servant to even bring back his son to the point of departure."[123] The end is definitely not like the beginning.

In Philo's version, however, Abraham's migration is a cycle of descent and return, an eternal journey between two worlds. Thus, his interpretation of scripture was much like Plato's Orphic interpretation of Odysseus's departure and return to Ithaca and Plutarch's exposition of the myth of Isis and Osiris. The end is always like the beginning. As Reale explains,

> Beginning with the Orphic mysteries, there was a considerable effort in the first two centuries to penetrate the myth's "inner hidden meaning." Towards the end of the second century CE the grammarian Dionysius Thrax significantly placed in opposition to the Delphic Oracle, which communicated in clear language

---

121. Johnson, "Neoplatonists and the Mystery Schools," 149.
122. On this distinction and Philo's role in formulating it, see Bradshaw, *Aristotle East and West*, 59–67. Cf. Louth, *Origins of the Christian Mystical Tradition*, 18.
123. Levinas, "Trace of the Other," 348.

and literal expressions, Orpheus who used symbols and thus Dionysius emphasized the superiority of "speaking by means of symbols."[124]

Philo claims Jewish counterparts of this procedure in the Therapeutae who settled in Egypt, Reale notes. "Philo says that they systematically practiced allegorical interpretation and they likened the literal sense to the body of a living thing, the allegorical method to its soul."[125] Just as Abraham made many "steps" (Philo strains to suggest that Abraham's journey was intellectual, not physical), so too must all humans in the ascent of mind.

First, the soul must be purified. "Its first step is to relinquish astrology, which betrayed it [the mind] into the belief that the universe is the primal God instead of being the handiwork of the primal God, and that the causes and movements of the constellations are the causes of bad and good fortune to mankind" (Philo, *Migr.* 194–195).[126] Dillon notes that this first step entails a stronger sense of both God's sovereignty and human responsibility than heretofore seen in Platonism, which typically allowed astral fatalism in the bodily world.[127] Turning away from "adoration of the cosmos (the Chaldaic mentality, as Philo called it)," notes Reale, the soul can begin to fulfill the Delphic maxim "Know thyself."[128] However, the goal is to discover one's dependence on God alone.

Just as Plato taught that the soul cannot take flight until it has turned itself wholly away from sensible things, God's summoning of Abraham from his land, people, and father's house is understood by Philo as a call to leave the visible world. "Land" symbolizes "body," "kindred" equals "sense-perception," and "father's house" is the speech revealing the "Mind's living-place" (*Migr.* 2–3). "Depart, therefore, out of the earthly matter that encompasses thee: escape, man, from the foul prison-house, with all thy might and main, and from the pleasures and lusts that act as its jailors" (9). The pure mind "will stay no longer in Haran, the organs of sense, but withdraw into itself. For it is impossible that the mind whose course

---

124. Reale, *History of Ancient Philosophy*, 174.
125. Reale, *History of Ancient Philosophy*, 175, referencing Philo, *Contempl.*
126. Translation of *On the Migration of Abraham*, unless otherwise noted, from *Philo's Works* (ed. Colson and Whitaker).
127. Dillon, *Middle Platonists*, 45. "All in all," Dillon remarks, "the Middle Platonists, though producing many scholastic formulae on the subject, failed to solve the problem, and bequeathed it in all its complexity to Plotinus, who writes a magnificent, if inconclusive, treatise on the topic in *Enneads* III 2–3." However, Philo introduced to Platonists a new and more consistent defense of human freedom and responsibility.
128. Reale, *History of Ancient Philosophy*, 202.

still lies in the sensible rather than the mental should arrive at the contemplation of Him that is" (*Migr.* 195).

Second, Philo introduces despair of oneself as a counterweight to the intellectual pride of philosophers. "Faith in God, then, is the one sure and infallible good," he says in another work on the Jewish patriarch (*Abr.* 268). He says elsewhere, "The man who has despaired of himself is beginning to know Him that is" (*Somn.* 1.60).[129] To suggest that the wise person has "despaired of himself" is alien to any confidence in the soul's ability to penetrate the heavens or to find God within oneself.

Third, Philo's transcendent God is not only personal but establishes a covenantal relationship with creation based on speech (*logos*) when he calls Abram out of Haran. *Logos* here means word or speech, more so than reason, and is based on the idea of God "as one who speaks—*ho legon*—an idea of God without parallel in Greek thought."[130] Throughout the Hebrew scriptures, God acts by speaking and not just by thinking or emanating. The soul cannot steal into God's chamber, but God reveals himself as he pleases and on his terms, so that, as Reale interprets, "it is not so much the man who sees God, but it is 'God who let himself be seen by man.' ... We are, then, in the presence of an idea completely unknown to Greek philosophical thought, that of a gratuitous gift which God makes to men for love of them."[131] Truth is not something that the people of Yahweh arrive at, but is Yahweh's gift of law and promise.

Nevertheless, the journey from Haran, the realm of the senses, is a flight from the visible world to this God. This too mixes biblical and Platonist elements. For Platonists, salvation is the flight of the true self—that is, the soul—from this world to the One. Philo, however, says that this flight is not the *self's leaving* but a "leaving *from* self," which Reale says "is identical with a mystical and ecstatic union with God."[132] Yet such self-abandonment represents a different type of mysticism than the traditional Platonist self-preoccupation. The soul is immortal, even God's image and likeness, but not divine.

While Jewish monotheism plays an important role in Philo's cosmology, the Orphic doctrine of the body as prison (*sōma-sēma*) structures his anthropology and, consequently, his soteriology. "This is the most admirable definition of immortal life," he stipulates, "to be occupied by a love and affection for God unem-

---

129. Translation of *On Dreams*, unless otherwise noted, from *Works of Philo* (trans. Yonge).
130. Louth, *Origins of the Christian Mystical Tradition*, 27.
131. Reale, *History of Ancient Philosophy*, 186.
132. Reale, *History of Ancient Philosophy*, 204, emphasis added.

barrassed by any connection with the flesh or with the body." He paraphrases Plato's remark in the *Theaetetus* that "we ought to endeavor to flee from this place as speedily as possible" (*Fug.* 63).[133] To know oneself is to realize that the body is a prison.[134] Echoing the *Phaedrus*, Philo expresses beautifully the Orphic vision in *On the Creation*:

> And again, being raised up on wings, and so surveying and contemplating the air, and all the commotions to which it is subject, it is borne upward to the higher firmament, and to the revolutions of the heavenly bodies. And also being itself involved in the revolutions of the planets and fixed stars according to the perfect laws of music, and being led on by love, which is the guide of wisdom, it proceeds onwards till, having surmounted all essence intelligible by the external senses, it comes to aspire to such as is perceptible only by the intellect: and perceiving in that, the original models and ideas of those things intelligible by the external senses which it saw here full of surpassing beauty, it becomes seized with a sort of sober intoxication like the zealots engaged in the Corybantian festivals, and yields to enthusiasm ... till it appears to be reaching the great King himself. (Philo, *Opif.* 70–71)[135]

In sum, from Philo's Judaism comes something completely foreign to Hellenists: descending into ourselves in order to *despair* of finding God there, so that we will cast ourselves upon the God who is outside of our soul. For the rest of the journey to God, Philo interprets biblical narratives as quarries for what is in the main the Orphic-Plato cosmogenic myth.

Philo had prepared the soil for a type of Judaism that could survive the destruction of Jerusalem in 70 CE two decades after his death. Without land, temple, or sacrifice, Philo's spiritualization of the Hebrew Bible was expanded vigorously by Rabbi Akiva (50–135 CE), whose focus on the soul's ascent past harrowing obstacles reflected a cosmology quite foreign to rabbis of the previous generation.[136]

---

133. Translation from *Works of Philo* (trans. Yonge).
134. Quoted in Reale, *History of Ancient Philosophy*, 203.
135. Translation from *Works of Philo* (trans. Yonge).
136. See the fascinating essay by Nathaniel Deutsch, "Dangerous Ascents." Cf. Sholem, *Major Trends in Jewish Mysticism*, 53. After Philo's death there was a profusion of mystical texts emerging out of Hellenistic Judaism (e.g., 4 Ezra, 2 Baruch, Apocalypse of Abraham). Though excluded from the canon, ascent literature (*hekhalot* and *merkabah*) began to flourish near Philo's time and especially among the Alexandrian diaspora. *Hekhalot* (palaces) and *merkabah* (chariot) mysticism flourished around the time of Philo, and especially in Alexandria, sowing the seeds

Chapter 5

Alexandrian Middle Platonism was the milieu in which Neoplatonism, both Hellenistic and Christian, was born. It was also the birthplace of what Dillon has designated famously as "the Platonic underworld," that esoteric elixer represented by the Corpus Hermeticum, the Chaldean Oracles, and gnosticism, all of which in varying degrees became mainstream Platonism and part of the continuing story of the Orphic myth.[137]

THE GODDESS OF MAGIC BECOMES THE WORLD SOUL

Plato did not reject wholesale what we would call magic; it just did not interest him much, because it bound the soul to physical nature. He thought that most of these spirits were benevolent: guardian angels aiding and directing us in our ascent. Indeed, Kronos delegated not humans but daimons to rule as a superior race (*Leg.* 713c–d).[138] In any case, a philosopher rises above the fray in union with supreme Intellect. For him, philosophers were the "true mystics," but magic and mysticism are rather different enterprises. Plato simply was not bothered by the ominous "foes" that original Orphics seemed to worry about.

But for Plato's heirs in the Hellenistic era the ascent is fraught with peril and one must fight magic with magic. It is not surprising that the goddess of magic became the World Soul. "It cannot be considered an accident," says Hans Lewy, "that the origination of the Chaldaean system should be temporally coincident with the most flourishing period of the Oriental mystery-religions, of the Hermetic theosophy and of western Gnosticism, as well as with the revival of the metaphysical tendencies of Platonism."[139]

Popularity of Mystery Religions

One sign of the restless soul was the popularity and proliferation of mystery cults throughout the Roman Empire in the first two centuries of the Common Era. Suddenly, Romans were flocking to Isis shrines and participating in the festivals and flamboyant processions of Artemis, the many-breasted Ephesian

---

of later kabbalism. Accompanying the ascents is familiar shamanistic imagery. See Graf, "Bridge and the Ladder." See also Reed, "Heavenly Ascent, Angelic Descent." For a broader survey of this literature see Collins, *Apocalyptic Imagination*.

137. Dillon, *Middle Platonists*, 384–96.
138. Shaw, *Theurgy and the Soul*, 9.
139. Lewy, *Chaldaean Oracles and Theurgy*, 312.

goddess identified with Diana. Yet, above all, the mystery cults attracted tremendous interest, and Orphic mysteries continued in Alexandria into the fifth century. Patrick Atherton observes that "a not uncommon sight was the religious devotee moving from city to city on a sort of pilgrimage, offering himself as a candidate for initiation."[140] "It was mostly in Egypt, however, which was always a sort of mirage for the ancients, that a real religious tourism occurred," says Saffrey. "The great period for pilgrimages was the second and third centuries of our era, and the most famous pilgrim was the emperor Hadrian, who endorsed a fashion that would continue long after him." Isis and Osiris were easily blended with Orphic-Dionysian myths, as we saw with Plutarch. The pilgrimage to Egyptian shrines "was international, and all regions of the ancient world were represented: Greece, Asia Minor, Syria, Spain, the Gauls, and of course many local areas."[141] The mysteries of the lion-headed Mithras, identified originally with Ahriman in Zoroastrian lore, was a seven-level cult popular among the imperial army, and its underground temples have been found from Africa to Britain. The cult of Sol, the sun, spread rapidly under the emperor Elagabalus early in the third century.

The Eleusinian mysteries continued until Theodosius closed pagan temples in the fourth century. The Dionysian cult, fused with the mysteries of Osiris, flourished (Diodorus Siculus, *Bib. hist.* 1.13–15, 23). In 215 BCE Ptolemy IV Philopater received the *teletai* of Dionysus at court and decreed that "those initiating to Dionysus" in the countryside must register themselves, along with their books, in Alexandria. This seems less a suppression of the cult than an attempt to include and perhaps supervise it.[142] The registering of books suggests a concern to weed out texts considered spurious. In any case, it is significant that the cult was worthy of royal notice. It fared better than the Bacchanalia celebrations that the Roman Senate reined in by official legislation in 186 BCE. When the Sarmatians (a Scythian tribe) destroyed the telesterion in 170 CE, Marcus Aurelius rebuilt it.

Philosophy grew, at least in part, out of mystery religions. Yet it went beyond them, transposing myths and rites into doctrines. As we have seen, Pythagoras, Socrates, and Plato saw philosophy as a purified mystery religion. As such, it was the antipode of the public religion even when the rites of Demeter and Dionysus were celebrated. The mystery cults drew initiates away from the common life of

---

140. Atherton, "City in Ancient Religious Experience," 332.
141. Saffrey, "Piety and Prayers," 206.
142. Seaford, *Dionysos*, 58.

Chapter 5

the nation, city, and family to participate in spiritual rather than physical sacrifices and more ascetic and otherworldy forms of religious life.[143]

Johnson observes, "the Mystery religions . . . converged on Alexandria to become an essential ingredient of public life: the lesser rites colourful and histrionic, but the higher levels of initiation more akin to the metaphysics of transcendence, and thus to the Platonic theory of Ideas."[144] And the so-called return to "religion" among Middle Platonists and Neoplatonists from Porphyry onward was explicitly Orphic. This is the moniker they chose to describe their theology, including the Platonic dialogues and the Chaldean Oracles. It has been seen by many, both then and now, as the perennial wisdom, the *prisca theologia*, of all the best religious oracles of the world.

We are landing at the port of Alexandria and what John Dillon famously calls the "Platonic underworld."[145] Such sobriquets strike us intuitively as apt, but they may obscure more than illuminate the context. We are not surprised that in his landmark work *The Greeks and the Irrational*, E. R. Dodds places Hermetic, gnostic, and theurgic Neoplatonism on the "irrational" side.[146] "At Alexandria," as Giovanni Reale expresses it, "the most important attempts at a synthesis occurred—between the typically Hellenic rationalistic spirit and the Eastern which was, on the contrary, religious and radical in nature."[147] It was "a rococo religiosity of Eastern inspiration."[148] In the late nineteenth century Eduard Zeller offered the same perspective, noting that the "religious influence" in Greek thought was of Eastern origin.

> This was Orphism, which with its separation of body and soul, matter and mind, god and the world grafted dualism upon Greek thought and relied on divine revelations instead of rational proof. The Greek mind in men like Pythagoras and his pupils, Empedocles and Plato endeavored to comprehend

---

143. This distinction was not airtight; some philosophers were priests of mystery cults while participating also in the public religion (though none was a priest). However, the tension remains between poet-theologians serving the state religion and philosophers seeking a deeper magic.
144. Johnson, "Neoplatonists and the Mystery Schools," 143–44.
145. Dillon, *Middle Platonists*, 384, 394.
146. Dodds, *Greeks and the Irrational*.
147. Reale, *History of Ancient Philosophy*, 169–70.
148. Reale, *History of Ancient Philosophy*, 285.

this doctrine and elaborate it on rational grounds. But it remained something foreign in Greek intellectual life.[149]

Yet I find this modern construct of rational Greeks being infected by alien Eastern influences quite dubious. As novel as Orphic myths and doctrines were in the beginning, by the Hellenistic era they were as Greek as the Isis cult whose imposing temples were found in Rome, Alexandria, and other important cities. To whatever extent Pythagoras, Socrates, and Plato tamed the cult of Dionysus, its orgiastic enthusiasm merely turned inward. The doctrines of the immortality and divinity of the soul, reincarnation, and the struggle of the soul to ascend from its bodily prison by being overcome by a suspension of reasoning in favor of mystical ecstasy, along with the ideal of a small circle of pupils initiated into the school of a sage and the individual's assimilation to god (*homoiōsis theō*): these were indeed new developments in Greece. But similar departures from the locative myths and rituals were occurring elsewhere during the same period. Regardless, by the time of Alexander's conquests "Orphism" was mainstream Hellenistic thought and Greeks recognized a kinship with Egyptian, Hindu, Zoroastrian, and Buddhist religions. This made Platonism a philosophy of salvation in the ultimate sense.[150] Porphyry is the one who endorsed the Chaldean Oracles as inspired scripture and accepted theurgy until he thought his student Iamblichus had taken it too far. As embarrassing as it may be for many moderns, Western philosophy is the offspring of an ancient mystery religion.

Yet Plato's Socrates bequeathed an Orphism without its physical cult, and this became more problematic in a place like Roman Alexandria, where one felt the need to see and hear the gods and to know that he or she had friends in high places to assist against the foes. Bertrand Russell says of Plato, "He is not an orthodox Orphic; it is only the fundamental doctrines that he accepts, not the superstitions and ceremonies of purification."[151] Although Socrates left behind the external rites of the mystery, he did not dispense with the formalities but instead put them to use as noetic stages in ascent.[152] In the main, magic was distilled in allegory until it became philosophy.

149. Zeller, *History of Greek Philosophy*, 313.
150. Far from being marginal (e.g., *Theaet.* 176b), this goal is identified (explicitly and implicitly) in the *Resp.* 352a; 383c; 501b; 613a; 621b; *Phaed.* 78c; 79d; *Phaedr.* 248a; 249c; *Tim.* 90a; *Leg.* 715c–716d.
151. B. Russell, *History of Western Philosophy*, 111.
152. Plato's direct correlation of philosophical ascent with the mysteries is made in *Phaed.* 81a–e; *Resp.* 378a; 560e. Note also the association of ascent with allusions to Dionysian (*Symp.*

Chapter 5

But the line between mystical prophet and magical priest was permeable.[153] And it became even more so in Middle Platonism and the theurgic Neoplatonism after Plotinus. Mysticism and magic are both a species of secret gnosis, the former being theoretical and contemplative and the latter practical and technological. Those who were more prone to the latter did not want merely to understand the world but to change it. These more esoteric—to us, magical and superstitious—souls would have said that such spiritual technology was required by the ominous circumstances on the ground.

Neither Socrates nor the Chaldean Oracles reject outright what we would call magic, but both excoriate "vulgar mechanics" who make "images without intellect." For both, the ultimate goal is ascent and assimilation to God, and mystical contemplation remains an essential part of their method. What is new is "theurgy," which was added as a necessary part of that process. Physical, outward rites and not only inner ascetic practices became essential. Theurgists arose because some Platonists came to believe that the ascent was more difficult than Plato imagined, given the obstacles, threats, and inherent weakness of the incarnate soul. All of the other eccentricities of theurgy can be put down to influences that had long been incorporated into Egyptian religion: Greco-Egyptian ritual, Persian (i.e., Chaldean) and Ptolemaic astrology, and, above all, the Greek Magical Papyri, albeit interpreted in a more philosophical (Orphic) frame.

Hearing from the Gods: The Chaldean Oracles

When one feels anxious, it is not enough to behold the gods in steady contemplation; the gods must speak to us. Philosophy became more enveloped in religious ritual, magic, astrology, and alchemy. "Barbarian" sages held particular fascination among Greek intellectuals.

Oracles were always a part of Greek and Roman life not only at Delphi but elsewhere, especially in Egypt, including Thebes, Karnak, and the Siwa Oasis where Alexander the Great traveled to hear that he had been given the empire. Yet these oracles concerned mostly insider information on the seeker's life in this world. Belonging more to the locative environment, these oracles focused mainly on this-worldly politics. The Eleusinian mysteries and Orphic theologies had already reoriented the search for salvation to the afterlife. Plato acknowledged that in

---

218b; *Leg.* 672b; *Phaedr.* 250b–c; 265b) and Orphic mysteries (*Phaed.* 62a–b; 69b–d; 79d; 82d; *Resp.* 533c; *Phil.* 400b–c).

153. See Shaw, "Living Light," 59–87.

escaping this world one may hope for "some stronger vessel" than reason and investigation, "some divine revelation [*logou theiou tinos*; lit. 'some word of god'], and make his voyage more safely and more securely" (*Phaed.* 85c–d).[154] Philo was convinced he had this in the Hebrew scriptures, and Numenius recommended appropriating the oracles of Hindus, Egyptians, Zoroastrians, and Jews (albeit by allegorizing it all into Orphic interpretations). Christians had now entered the lists with the New Testament, to which gnostic Alexandrians soon would apply their own allegorizations. In fact, the interest of Neoplatonists in forming a canon of Orphic-Chaldean literature was motivated in part as a response to Christianity.[155]

But by the second century CE many of Plato's heirs grew impatient waiting for "some stronger vessel." A new oracular genre of Orphic literature emerges during this time, which included rhapsodies, hymns, and theogonies. Hermeticists and gnostics used the oracular form to cut to the chase with Hermes or Jesus giving encyclopedic knowledge on a variety of topics. One senses across the diverse examples of this genre impatience with reasoned arguments and seemingly insignificant historical details and narratives. We need the gods to *tell us* the truth and, more importantly, what to do in this mess. The Chaldean Oracles became just as important as Plato's dialogues, exerting profound influence not only on school Neoplatonism but on Hermeticists and gnostics as well.[156] For philosophers like the Stoic Chaeremon (also an Egyptian priest), the Thoth literature was incorporated into the writings attributed to Hermes Trismegistus.

While Plotinus's calm speculations reflect the philosophical tradition of rational ascent, his successor, Porphyry, expresses the anxiety of the age in his *Philosophy from Oracles*. He speaks of the weariness of the human heart in longing for some revelation from the gods to give security and certainty after the "birth-throes of truth," that is, metaphysical speculation.[157] Philosophers begin appealing to oracles, at least in part because of the sense of remoteness from the Absolute Good in a demon-haunted world. People wanted to know the Good, and they wanted a certainty that transcended the bickering and seemingly arbitrary formulas of competing philosophical and religious sects.

154. Grube renders this "some divine doctrine," but the Greek is better rendered in Fowler: "some divine revelation."
155. Merlan, "Religion and Philosophy."
156. We will explore their influence on all these groups later. For an especially good treatment of the relation to gnostics, see Turner, *Sethian Gnosticism*, esp. 40.
157. Lewy, *Chaldaean Oracles and Theurgy*, 8.

The spiritual environment seemed to call for a Neoplatonist canon that included the Chaldean Oracles and various "Orphic" hymns and theogonies along with their vast array of deities.[158] Composed by Julian the Theurgist in the second century, perhaps with the aid of Numenius, the Chaldean Oracles introduce the term "theurgy" for the first time. By the time of Porphyry the Chaldean Oracles had become as important as Plato's dialogues.

Hekate—the goddess of magic—figures prominently in the Chaldean Oracles as the oracle-giver.[159] From Porphyry on, the Platonic dialogues, the Chaldean Oracles, and various pieces designated "Orphic" (e.g., the Orphic Hymns and Rhapsodies) were considered inspired and infallible scripture: the canon of Neoplatonists.[160] Orpheus himself at this time even came to occupy a more prominent and explicit place in the genealogy of philosophical religion. Johnston notes, "The century preceding the Oracles' composition gave birth to Apollonius of Tyana, who followed a Pythagorean/Platonic creed, but who also performed traditional magical or shamanistic feats. Such was the general atmosphere."[161]

Hekate Becomes the World Soul

Said to have been composed in a trance by Julian the Theurgist in the second century CE, the Chaldean Oracles reflect a more original Orphic doctrine that characterizes Zoroastrian and Egyptian religions even as they reflect the mood (viz., pessimistic dualism) of their own day:

> Do not hasten to the light-hating world, boisterous of matter, where there is murder, discord, foul odors, squalid illnesses, corruptions, and fluctuating works. He who intends to love the Intellect of the Father must flee these things.... [F]or from the hollows of the earth leap chthonian dogs, who never show a true sign to a mortal. (CO fr. 134, 90)

The Oracles teach that daimons "enchant souls, forever turning them away from the [holy] rites" (CO fr. 135). However, in Zoroastrianism there is a near parity between the good and bad gods, with 3,300 evil spirits under the leadership of

---

158. Lewy, *Chaldaean Oracles and Theurgy*, 5.
159. Lewy, *Chaldaean Oracles and Theurgy*, 6–7.
160. Lewy, *Chaldaean Oracles and Theurgy*, 5. Lewy explains that the original title was "Oracles in Verses" (*logia di' epôn*)—interestingly, logia—sayings or teachings.
161. Johnston, *Hekate Soteira*, 72.

Angra Mainyu (Ahriman). Demons play an important role in Buddhist thought as well.[162] That is an astounding council of oppressors! As we will see, these barking dogs of Hekate—the goddess of magic raised in the Oracles to the World Soul— are souls of the dead, avenging ghosts.

Hekate represents yet another Greco-Egyptian fusion that intensified in the Roman period as people were looking frantically for the exit.[163] As we have seen, Hesiod gave her much wider attention than Homer. Yet it was only under Orphic influence that she gained prominence. Pausanias relates: "Of the gods, the Aeginetans worship most Hecate, in whose honor every year they celebrate mystic rites which, they say, Orpheus the Thracian established among them" (*Descr.* 2.30.2).[164]

The ineffable and supreme Good was utterly remote, so a bevy of mediators was required. Liminal earthly spaces at roads and the thresholds of homes and other buildings were considered sacred intersections where ghosts loitered. These souls of the dead, often referred to as Hekate's barking dogs, could help or haunt depending on whether specific rites were performed. It is not surprising, then, that Hekate was the goddess of crossroads and magicians. Magicians would manipulate souls at crossroads, and even rocks, sticks, or other substances taken from these spaces were thought to hold daimonic energy. Despite his sharp criticism of superstition, "Pliny advocates that women in labor wear an amulet filled with plants that have grown up inside a sieve thrown onto the crossroads," and when he "advises burying frogs at crossroads as a precaution against fever (H. N. XXXII 113), perhaps this acted as an amulet to keep pinned to the crossroads the troublesome spirits imagined to bring disease."[165] As usual, Hellenists sought to allegorize such stories, with Platonists mapping them onto their existing theogony and cosmology.

The Chaldean Oracles, which became the charter of Neoplatonism, raised Hekate's profile considerably. Following the Middle Platonist trend, as emphasized especially by Philo, the Chaldean Oracles regards the ultimate God (First Father) as utterly transcendent and unknowable.[166] The father we know is the Intellect or Mind (*nous*) and, below it, the World Soul, which Philo called Sophia and Plutarch

---

162. Associated with birth, rebirth, and desire, Mara and his beautiful daughters seek to thwart the Buddha's enlightenment. See Boyd, "Symbols of Evil in Buddhism."

163. Johnston, "Crossroads," 217–19.

164. Translation of Pausanias provided by W. H. S. Jones, LCL.

165. Johnston, "Crossroads," 224.

166. Majercik, introduction to *Chaldean Oracles*, 5. As we will see, even the gnostics agreed that the supreme principle is the "Father" or "Abyss," removed from any association with the

identified with Isis. And, as we have seen, the World Soul was the weak spot in the intelligible triad. In her proximity to nature as the womb of becoming, the World Soul could become unstable and require the demiurge to save her from irrational movement. At the same time, she was the medium through which the seminal ideas of the demiurgic Intellect came to birth in the natural world.

Hekate, the humbler chthonic guardian of liminal spaces and patron of witches and magicians, emerges as the World Soul in the Oracles, the cosmic boundary protecting the intelligible world from matter.[167] This meant that magic was now essential to protection against the menacing influences of stars and planets, daimons above and below, seeking our ruination. And yet, Hekate never loses her wilder side. Repeatedly in the Oracles we discover that even if the rites are perfectly performed and Hekate deigns to descend to her statue and give an oracle, she still must be entreated not to harm her devotees as she departs. Moreover, she never loses her barking dogs—the ghoulish souls that she can set upon anyone at her whim. Indeed, as Plutarch argues, if we got rid of this vast chain of daimons merely because they represent the evil side of the family line, it would be as if one removed the air between the Earth and the Moon. To eliminate the daimons would disconnect the chain of being and "make the relations of the gods and men remote and alien" (*Def. orac.* 415e–f).[168] We cannot help but go through Hekate-Soul. Shifty moon-and-magic goddess that she is, especially in her proximity to nature, she could be unpredictable, but she was also at her highest and most rational "flower of intellect" our only connection to divine Mind. There were close affinities with gnostic sects, even in terms of the names given to these entities and the attribution of bisexuality to the female power.[169]

We may sum up this chapter with one of Porphyry's favorite hymns from the Chaldean Oracles. The "supreme Father," he says, is "exalted above the 'Eternal

---

material world (6). Porphyry identified this figure with the Plotinian One, while Proclus placed him beneath the One in the first rank of the realm of Intellect.

167. Johnston offers a persuasive and succinct argument from the sources for this equation in her Appendix to *Hekate Soteira*, 153–63.

168. Plutarch, *Moralia* (trans. Babbitt)..

169. Majercik, introduction to *Chaldean Oracles*, 7. Majercik says, "Indeed, the linking of 'Power' with the Chaldean 'Father' (or 'Abyss') suggests a primordial bisexual deity akin to the Gnostic Abyss-Ennoia or Abyss-Sigê (see fr. 4 and notes). . . . A 'triple-powered' Monad is also a familiar figure in various Gnostic systems, sometimes understood as the Supreme God (e.g., Allogenes, NHC XI, 49, 36–38), other times as a lesser being (e.g., Steles Seth, NHC VII, 121, 32–34)." In the Oracles, her bisexuality means that she is impregnated by the demiurge and, in turn, inseminates nature.

Strength'" (maternal principle) and the demiurgic Intellect, who are likened to mother and son. Apparently combining the Neopythagorean Dyad and the World Soul, as in Plutarch, the oracle switches the roles of demiurge and the Soul as attested in the *Timaeus* and in Plotinus's system, and Porphyry follows Hekate willingly.[170] Now the Intellect nurses at the breast of the World Soul–Hekate, imbibing her "eternally flowing rays" (i.e., the forms) not only as his nourishment but as his very being.[171] Hence, the power of "oracles" to justify even serious departures from revered authorities.[172] Without a doubt, we have arrived in Alexandria.

---

170. Hekate is prominent in Porphyry's *On Statues* (fr. 351–360 in Smith, *Porphyrii philosophi fragmenta*, 407–35). Augustine's *City of God* preserves Porphyry's appeal to an oracle from Hekate against Christians (NPNF² 6:416–17). From his examination of *De abstinentia* Guiseppe Muscolino concludes that Porphyry not only drew upon Persian (Zoroastrian) science but was "also a practicing sorcerer" (based especially on 11.41.5). See Muscolino, "Porphyry and Black Magic," 146. See also Smith, "Religion, Magic, and Theurgy in Porphyry," 1–10.

171. Lewy, *Chaldaean Oracles and Theurgy*, 12–13.

172. Traditionally, the Intellect is either the "Father" (in the *Timaeus* line of thinking) or the "Son" (in the view of Speusippus, Philo, and Plotinus). But never is the Intellect (i.e., demiurge) considered the child of the World Soul. Rather, the Intellect inputs the data from the forms into the World Soul, who then gives birth to individual souls.

6

Hermes Trismegistus
The Cult without Temples

> In things pertaining to theology there were in former times six great teachers expounding similar doctrines. The first was Zoroaster, the chief of the Magi; the second Hermes Trismegistus, the head of the Egyptian priesthood; Orpheus succeeded Hermes; Aglaophamus was initiated into the sacred mysteries of Orpheus; Pythagoras was initiated into theology by Aglaophamus; and Plato by Pythagoras. Plato summed up the whole of their wisdom in his letters.
>
> —Marsilio Ficino[1]

> Thus that religion of the world which runs as an undercurrent in much of Greek thought, particularly in Platonism and Stoicism, becomes in Hermeticism actually a religion, a cult without temples or liturgy, followed in the mind alone, a religious philosophy or philosophical religion containing a gnosis.
>
> —Frances Yates[2]

After decades of academic research, Gilles Quispel concluded that "modernity originated in Egyptian magic."[3] More nuanced is Jan Assmann's assessment:

---

1. Ficino, *Philebus Commentary*, 181, 247. A similar genealogy appears in various places throughout Ficino's works. See Hankins, *Plato in the Italian Renaissance*, 2:460–64. It is interesting that Ficino singles out Plato's *Letters*, since (as we will see) these letters (especially the second and the seventh), regardless of their authenticity, belong to the so-called esoteric teachings rather than the published dialogues and contain more controversial doctrines.

2. Yates, *Giordano Bruno*, 4–5.

3. Quispel, "Reincarnation and Magic," 231.

"Hermeticism is one of the undercurrents of Western cultural memory; it has never been a main current, but neither has it been entirely marginal or entirely forgotten."[4] A revival of Hermeticism lay at the heart of the Renaissance and the rise of modern science all the way to Isaac Newton, and it has reemerged clearly in Romanticism and contemporary theosophy including New Age circles. However, its significance is wider and deeper than explicit retrievals. To some extent, modern scientific rationality is the offspring of a long, romantic, and quarrelsome relationship between Christianity and Hermeticism.

While traveling magician-priests abused the name of Orpheus by their quackery, more importantly for Plato salvation could not be sold; one could only "pay the penalty," just as Orphic texts stipulated. The solemn decree of necessity could not be suspended by the gods, much less by the material rites, sacrifices, incantations, and passwords of mortals. Philosophy guided the soul upward while magic—like religious rituals—kept the soul bound to bodily things.[5]

However, one person's superstition was another's science. Plato's Socrates did not discount charms, for example, while Aristotle was convinced of telepathy. The latter's student, Theophrastus, represented superstition with initiates going constantly to the sea to sprinkle themselves, as in the Eleusinian rites.[6] In Roman Alexandria advances in engineering and other mechanical arts as well as astronomy and mathematics rose together with the magical arts. Some of the real engineering advances were even gimmicks for the Serapis temple, such as a hydraulic pump that opened the massive doors and set a fire upon the altar. It is difficult in our modern context to appreciate a culture in which science, religion, and magic were not distinctly marked and fiercely defended territories. This is the problem with the narrative of Western progress from magic to religion to science.[7]

In the third century, however, as cosmic paranoia intensified, this Roman disposition toward mechanics found its religious embodiment in Hermes Trismegistus, the fountainhead of all wisdom and teacher of theurgy, that is, the techniques that brought the gods to the aid of desperate souls. Dodds calls it an "age of anxiety."[8] And in all such eras, the locative cosmos frays. In panic, souls turn to the shaman. In Hermes, philosophy and magic merged, forging new itineraries of

---

4. Assmann, foreword to *Secret History of Hermes Trismegistus*, vii.
5. See Plato, *Alc. maj.* 122a; *Meno* 81a; *Resp.* 364b–365a; *Leg.* 871d–e.
6. Versnel, "Deisidaimonia."
7. Ludwig Wittgenstein makes this point effectively. Reminding us that ritual actions often involve eating and drinking, he says, "But then it is nonsense if we go on to say that the characteristic feature of *these* actions is that they spring from wrong ideas about the physics of things. (This is what Frazer does when he says magic is really false physics, or as the case may be, false medicine, technology, etc.)." See Wittgenstein, "Remarks on *The Golden Bough*," 33.
8. See Dodds, *Age of Anxiety*.

Chapter 6

Orphic ascent and a new branch of the Western philosophical tradition that culminated in Proclus, whose elegant cosmic hierarchy was perhaps the final pagan theological vision, although its influence on Western philosophy and mysticism would long outlive its creator.[9]

Hermes Trismegistus: "The Egyptian"

On an unknown day near the turn of the third century, Alexandrians were drawn to the main thoroughfare for a parade of books. In most cities a book parade would not attract an audience. But this was no ordinary city, and the prized volumes were not just ordinary books. It was a solemn procession for the cult devoted to Hermes Trismegistus. Among the enthralled spectators of such events was the Christian teacher Clement of Alexandria, who reported:

> At the start of the procession were the Hermetic divine hymns and royal biography. Astrological books dealing with the fixed stars and the planets and their movements were followed by hieroglyphic inscriptions on geographical themes; following these were books dealing with education and cult practices. There were also hieratic books about the laws, the gods, and the training of priests. There were, altogether, thirty-six books of Hermes containing the entire philosophy of the Egyptians, and these were complemented by six books on medical questions. (*Strom.* 6.4)

From Clement's report of the Hermetic parade we enter further into the colorful origins of how we became "spiritual, not religious," that is, ostensibly modern but in reality part of a long conversation between Plato, Hermes, and Christ.

As Clement's description attests, there was virtually no sphere of life and learning that fell outside the purview of Hermes Trismegistus's inspiration. Hermes became the legendary founder of a tradition—Hermeticism—with a wide array of metaphysical, astrological, magical, medical, alchemical, legal, and religious texts attributed to his name.[10] For many, however, it was not just a tradition; Hermes Trismegistus was simply "the Egyptian."

---

9. Among others attesting to the popularity of this worldview expressing affinities for pantheism or panentheism are Einstein, Spinoza, Nobel Prize–winning physicists, the Eranos group, and a number of prominent scientists working today. The literature is vast, but see for example Clayton and Peacocke, *In Whom We Live*; Buckareff and Nagasawa, *Alternative Concepts of God*.

10. See Ebeling, *Secret History*, 9. Ebeling writes, "These numbers are modest compared to the 36,525 books noted by Manetho or the 20,000 mentioned by Seleucus. . . . Both the

254

Besides Clement we may also imagine among the crowd Ammonius Sakkas, an Indian immigrant from a Christian family who turned to philosophy (Hindu, Persian, and Platonic) and was the teacher of both Origen and Plotinus.[11] It is not far-fetched to imagine among the spectators some students of Basilides and Valentinus, founders of the two largest known gnostic sects who had taught at their own schools in Alexandria just a half-century earlier. By the time of this Hermetic procession, gnostic teachings, although challenged fiercely by Irenaeus and other church leaders, were still spreading.

We have in this snapshot of a day in third-century Alexandria a gathering of the main schools of thought that would shape the Western mind even to the present day. Weaving in and out of each of these tributaries, this stream has made its way to us even today in ways that we hardly realize.

Like the state cult to Serapis more generally, Hermes Trismegistus represented a fusion of gods: the Egyptian Thoth and the Greek Hermes. Egypt, we recall, had already fused Dionysus with Osiris, which is why Herodotus attributed Orphic and Pythagorean doctrines to Egypt.[12] Diodorus Siculus ascribes to Hermes the invention of language, the rites of the public religion, astronomy and music, wrestling, and the lyre (its strings representing the seasons). He writes, "And he taught the Greeks eloquence [hermeneutics], which is why he is called Hermes" (*Bib. hist.* 1.16).[13] Hermes also carried the *kerykeion* (Latin, *caduceus*), a winged staff that still today is the symbol of medicine. Thoth, the scribe of Osiris, was the Egyptian counterpart of Hermes, so the two were easily fused.[14] The grandson of the messenger god Hermes who conducted souls to the afterlife, Hermes Trismegistus possessed the accumulated powers of his progenitors, hence his moniker "Thrice-Great" (*trismegistus* in Latin).

---

figure and the writings of Hermes Trismegistus were the product of the syncretic, Hellenistic philosophy of nature, which itself was a conglomeration of Aristotelian, Platonic, Stoic, and Pythagorean doctrines, interspersed with motifs from Egyptian mythology and themes from Jewish and Iranian origin."

11. On the identity of Ammonius as the founder of the Neoplatonic school, see Porphyry, *Vit. Plot.* 3.

12. According to Diodorus Siculus, there were three incarnations of Dionysus in Egypt. The "first Dionysos" was the "son of Ammon and Antheia"; "the second Dionysos, men say, who was born to Zeus by Io, the daughter of Inachus, became king of Egypt and appointed the initiatory rites of that land; and the third and last, sprung from Zeus and Semele, became among the Greeks, the emulator of the first two." See *Bib. hist.* 3.74.1, as quoted in Edmonds, "Dionysos in Egypt?," 416 n. 2.

13. Translation of *On Egypt*, book 1 of the *Historical Library* of Diodorus Siculus, unless otherwise noted, from Murphy.

14. Copenhaver, *Hermetica*, xiv.

Chapter 6

Hermes Trismegistus was an ecumenical symbol. Stoics associated him with the demiurgic *logos*, Garth Fowden notes, and in the so-called Greek Magical Papyri (which are actually more Egyptian than Greek), he became "a cosmic power, creator of heaven and earth and almighty world-ruler (*pantokratōr, kosmokratōr*)."[15] According to both sources, Ebeling observes, Hermes was an omniscient deity who taught Isis and Osiris. "Yet he was mortal: it is stressed that when he died, he ascended to the heavens and became the like-named planet Mercury."[16] Throughout the Roman Empire he was simply "the Egyptian," although the particular texts attributed to Hermes, such as the philosophical Hermetica known as the Corpus Hermeticum, were unknown outside of Egypt until the third century.[17] Beginning with Tertullian and Clement, our earliest references to these texts come from African Christians.[18] Hermetic literature was preserved (and interpolated) mostly in Arabic translation.

Specialists have described Hermeticism as "a thing without corners and edges," its teachings "characterized by resistance to the dominance of either pure rationality or doctrinal faith."[19] This eclecticism made Hermetism attractive to many who refused to belong to any school or church—those who we might today call "spiritual, not religious." Its influence was enormous and enduring, but inner debates kept Hermeticism from forming a sufficient center around which a coherent school could survive in any organized form. Just as migrant Orphic priests were identified by "their great smoke of books," Hermeticism was more like an early republic of letters than a religion or philosophical school.

Modern scholars distinguish between the philosophical and technical Hermetica. The former type is represented by the Corpus Hermeticum, with the Chaldean

---

15. Fowden, *Egyptian Hermes*, 24–25.
16. Ebeling, *Secret History*, 27.
17. Fowden, *Egyptian Hermes*, 196.
18. Fowden, *Egyptian Hermes*, 198: "Tertullian of Carthage is the first writer who indisputably quotes from the philosophical books of Hermes, in the *Adversus Valentinianos* and the *De anima*, both written in 206/207." By the way, we should note, this is true of most groups that we have mentioned. Despite Numenius's obvious importance, Clement of Alexandria is the first to mention him, and much of what we have of Numenius is from Clement and Eusebius. The enduring legacy of Philo (including many of his writings) is due to Christian preservation, and the same is true of the gnostic writings preserved by Irenaeus and his heirs. In spite of their hostility to those teachings, the Nag Hammadi discovery has shown their accounts have been remarkably accurate. This says something, I think, about the openness of Christians in this milieu to engaging real disagreements rather than to build straw opponents. This quite broad procedure stands in contrast with Celsus, Porphyry, and others who recklessly misrepresent Christians.
19. The first quote is from Dörrie, *Platonica Minora*, 104, as quoted in Ebeling, *Secret History*, 11. Ebeling miscites Dörrie's volume here as *Opera Minora*. The second quotation is from van den Broek and Hanegraaff, introduction to *Gnosis and Hermeticism*, vii.

Oracles as a constant companion.[20] The latter type includes the Greek Magical Papyri (second to fourth centuries; one suriving text dates from the era of Augustus) and medical, astrological, alchemical, and ritual texts.[21] In short, Thoth-Hermes was a household name throughout the empire.[22]

Hermetic Theology: "All Names and No Name"

The term "perennial philosophy" was coined in the Renaissance by Vatican librarian Agostino Steuco (1497–1548). However, the idea that there is a core of true religion—a *prisca theologia*—underlying all religions was also assumed by ancient Roman philosophers. This core was basically Orphic, which Roman writers made clear in their genealogy of key figures: Orpheus, Zoroaster, Pythagoras, Hermes Trismegistus, and Plato. It was a philosophical religion that could be held by anyone; allegorical transmutation of their scriptures and rites yielded the same golden truth. In Alexandria, Jews and Christians placed Moses at the head of this stream but incorporated as much as they could of the remaining genealogy.[23] In doing so, they claimed that Orpheus was taught by Musaeus (Moses).[24] The late Neoplatonist Proclus put it baldly: "All the Greeks' theology is the offspring of the Orphic mystical doctrine."[25] And in the first few centuries of our era, Hermes Trismegistus became the psychopomp behind it all.

The substance of this perennial tradition is that God is everything but nothing. This paradox derived from the Orphic metaphysics that controled both later and original Neoplatonism. On the one hand, the "first Lord and Maker" transcends

---

20. Majercik, *Chaldaean Oracles*.

21. As with the Oracles, it is important to bear in mind that Hermeticists did not know of any division between philosophical and technical (or practical) wisdom: these are our modern divisions. We will see that Platonism dominates the philosophical Hermetica, but the authors allude to rituals and would have been engaged in the sort of activities described in the Magical Papyri.

22. Lucillius in the time of Nero refers to Petosiris, the ancient Egyptian high priest of Thoth at Hermapolis and guardian of the books of Thoth-Hermes, "as if he were a household name" (Lucillius in *Anth. gr.* 11.164). See Fowden, *Egyptian Hermes*, 3. Fowden adds that some astrological and iatromathematical (medical-mathematical) Hermetica "were already in circulation in the first century B.C., and perhaps earlier." Byzantine censorship of magical texts accounts for the loss of much of this material (8–9).

23. Assmann, foreword to *Secret History*, ix. "Josephus Flavius recounted that the grandchildren of Adam, the sons of Seth, had inscribed this primeval knowledge on two columns, one of them made of bricks in the case of an outbreak of fire, the other of stone in case of a catastrophic flood. The column of stone survived the Flood and supposedly could still be seen in Syria."

24. Copenhaver, *Hermetica*, xxviii.

25. Proclus, *Theo. Plat.* 1.6 (Testamenta 250 in Kern, *Orphicorum fragmenta*).

the realm of being, yet, on the other hand, this Maker *is* all things because they exist in the One in an undifferentiated unity. Thus God and the cosmos must be thought together in terms of reality and appearance, cause and effect, fountain and flow. This relation is unidirectional; the rays do not make up the sun but the sun makes the rays. It is the familiar cosmology of Parmenides.[26]

Plato taught both that the One is beyond being (*Resp.* 509b), yet the *Timaeus* myth at least implies that the One is the Intellect (demiurge) in its world-forming activity. Plato does not seem to resolve this tension, leaving a contradiction that could be appropriated equally by monists and dualists. We find just this inner debate throughout the philosophical Hermetica (and in contemporary Hindu, Buddhist, Zoroastrian, and Chinese schools). What is new in Hermeticism (and in the theurgic Neoplatonism that continued its basic outlook) is that human beings now have a role to play in "marrying" opposites not just within themselves but in the whole cosmos as co-demiurges.[27]

In general, the Hermetic texts fully absorb both the Orphic *sōma-sēma* dualism, including the superiority of the invisible-intellectual world, and the Stoic emphasis on universal sympathy of above and below. Precisely because the lower world (including humans) is a microcosm of the Ideal World, theurgical practices may assist the soul in its ascent from the material world. But like their Orphic

---

26. Aristotle was the first to identify Parmenides as the founder of a univocity of being (*Phys.* 986b27–34), but I have shown that this was part of a wider trend. In Chinese thought, the duality of *yin* and *yang* (symbolized in the Taijitu diagram) is merely conceptual, while the reality is the *tao* or Taiji (Supreme Ultimate) before, above, and beyond all dichotomies. See Feuchtwang, "Chinese Religions." Foundational for Taoism as well as Confucianism, the Book of I-Ching divides the world into good (*yang*) and evil (*yin*), which are correlated with higher and lower, spiritual and bodily. In fact, the body is an illusion. This idea runs throughout the Taoist text, the Secret of the Golden Flower: "People create the body by attention." The lower soul can rise into higher soul by transformation through various lives. "If you are dull and depressed on awakening, that is a sign of clinging to the body, which means clinging to the lower soul" Translation from Cleary, *Secret of the Golden Flower*, 14–15. The Book of I-Ching also posits a limitless god (*wu-ji*) who produces a limited god (*tai-chi*), who produces *yin* and *yang* (*Tao Te Ching*, ch. 28). I am grateful to my student Michael Xu for pointing out this connection in his paper "A Separated God" (Fall 2021). For a similar doctrine in Jewish kabbalah see Cordovero, *Introduction to Kabbalah*. Moreover, according to the Islamic Sufis, God is the Unity of Being (*Wakhdat al-wujud*). On the other hand, *wakhdat ash-shuhud* means "apparentism" and refers to the distinction of creator and creation. See Nasr, *Islamic Philosophy*, 154–48.

27. As we will see much later, Hegel's doctrine of sublation (*Aufhebung*) carries forward the useful contradiction of male and female, spirit and matter, infinite and finite, preserving and abolishing the latter in the process of producing a "child of the Work." This is not Hegel's invention but was suggested to him by the history of Orphic mysticism that I am recounting, and he recognized fully the parallels with Indian and Chinese thought.

predecessors, Hermetic writers are bricoleurs. Not only do they disagree with each other, but they also disagree with themselves, often times within the same text.[28] The inner debates alternate between Stoic and Platonic tendencies but remain within the broader ambit of Orphic metaphysics.[29]

The overall trend of Hermetic ontology is pantheistic. Zielinski calls it "pantheistic realism" and offers a suggestive argument that when Poimandres (Sovereign Mind) corrects Hermes's assumption that "god is unseen," the author is trying to persuade the Poimandres community to adopt "the newest, Gnostic-pantheist revision of Hermeticism."[30] "It hardly needs spelling out," says Fowden, "that anyone who accepted the basic Hermetic teachings about the three spheres of being, God, the World and Man, and their unity through sympathetic interlinking, was committed to a more or less immanentist or monist position." And yet, ironically, there is still an emphasis on the transcendence of the supreme god. Indeed, ascending "from *epistêmê* to *gnôsis*," the Hermetist increasingly came to devalue the cosmos and humanity "and to undermine their integral relationship with God—in other words to cultivate a philosophy of dualist tendency and to emphasize the transcendent nature of the Divinity."[31] The absolute idealism of Parmenides is not the only trajectory of the Hermetica, but it is a major one. The upshot is this: even if Platonists cannot go so far as to embrace the Stoic's materialistic monism, all of *spiritual* reality (i.e., Mind) is one. Copenhaver notes, "For 'all are one' as a Hermetic theme with roots in Greek thought reaching as far back as the Pre-Socratics."[32]

We also find antithetical propositions in the Corpus Hermeticum with respect to the distinction drawn by Festugière between pessimistic and optimistic gnosis.[33] Adopting Festugière's distinction, Frances Yates writes:

---

28. Corp. herm. 9.9, entitled "On Understanding and Sensation." Unless otherwise noted, all translations of the Hermetica from Copenhaver, *Hermetica*. In fact, Walter Scott argues that this text represents a "Stoicized Platonism" and it was "probably written between 280 and 300 A.D." He further suggests, interestingly, that it was a reaction to Christian disdain for Egyptian (Alexandrian) Hermetists. See W. Scott, *Hermetica*, 2:204–5.

29. This "pantheistic moment" that finally yields to the view that supreme Mind transcends everything else is even visible in the classical Orphic poem and its commentary in the Derveni Papyrus (around 400 BCE). In fact, there are close affinities between many Hermetic treatises and the Derveni Papyrus.

30. Zielinski, referring to in Corp. herm. 11, in his "Hermes und die Hermetik I," 336–38, 350–55.

31. Fowden, *Egyptian Hermes*, 102.

32. Copenhaver, *Hermetica*, 216 n. 2, citing Nock and Festugière, *Corpus Hermeticum*, 2:358 n. 15; W. Scott, *Hermetica*, 3:9–11; Moreschini, *Studi*, 94–95.

33. Yates, *Giordano Bruno*, 22, discussing Nock and Festugière, *Corpus Hermeticum*, 1:84; 2:x–xi.

Chapter 6

> For the pessimist (or dualist) gnostic, the material world heavily impregnated with the fatal influence of the stars is in itself evil; it must be escaped from by an ascetic way of life which avoids as much as possible all contact with matter, until the lightened soul rises up through the spheres of the planets, casting off their evil influence, as it ascends to its true home in the immaterial divine world. For the optimist gnostic, matter is impregnated with the divine, the earth lives, moves, with a divine life, the stars are living divine animals, the sun burns with a divine power, there is no part of Nature which is not good for all are parts of God.[34]

It is hard to imagine more antithetical worldviews, and yet we find both in the Corpus Hermeticum. This underscores the preferability of "procorporeal" and "anticorporeal" to "optimistic" and "pessimistic." Some texts of a more Platonic bent are procorporeal, but, for the most part, this way of thinking is more Stoic. As a rule, the more Stoic writers incline toward a practical theurgy, while the more Platonic stress that being "born again" is a matter of gnosis: mind plugging in to the Mind with a more explicitly Orphic emphasis on the soul's release from matter.

One important indicator of the anticorporeal outlook is the trope of the body as a "tunic (*chitōn*) of skins." Genesis 3:21 says, "And the Lord God made for Adam and for his wife garments of skins and clothed them." The phrase appears in many places in Philo, where he gives it a Platonic meaning.[35] Philo thought that the tunics here and in Lev 10:5 were "irrational coverings for the soul's rational part."[36] Similarly, Corp. herm. 7 includes a colorful litany of Orphic tropes: "But first you must *rip off the tunic* that you wear, the garment of ignorance, the foundation of vice, the bonds of corruption, the *dark cage*, the *living death*, the *sentient corpse*, the *portable tomb*, the *resident thief*, the one who hates through what he loves and envies through what he hates. Such is the odious tunic you have put on . . . *blocked up with a great load of matter*" (Corp. herm. 7.2–3).[37] In the background here is the concept of the soul's *okhēma* ("subtle body" or "astral vehicle"). On its descent the soul would add layers of clothing until it acquired finally a gross body; on its return, the soul would gradually return heavier tunics (*chitōnōn*) to the star or planet from which they had been loaned.[38] However, this became an important notion when the fragile soul required more armor for its embattled ascent.[39]

---

34. Yates, *Giordano Bruno*, 22.
35. J. Z. Smith, *Map Is Not Territory*, 17 n. 52.
36. Copenhaver, *Hermetica*, 147 n. 72. C. H. Dodd traces this trope (i.e., "tunics of skin") from Philo to Valentinus in *Bible and the Greeks*, 191–94. Cf. Philo, *Leg.* 2.15.55–59.
37. Translation from Copenhaver, *Hermetica*, emphasis added.
38. See Bos, "Vehicle of Soul."
39. Copenhaver, *Hermetica*, 162: "Festugiere (NF I, 131, nn. 57–58; cf. Layton, *GS*, p. 295) refers

Moreover, Hermetic writers alternate between identifying evil with the terrestrial body and identifying it with celestial bodies. Apparently targeting gnostics (and the authors of Corp. herm. 6 and 10), Corp. herm. 9 underscores Plato's point that evil exists only in this lower world (9.4). But the text goes on to say that surrounding the sun are "many troops of demons," each arrayed "under the regiments of stars," sent by the gods to oversee humankind, repaying irreverence "through torrents, hurricanes, thunderstorms, fiery alterations and earthquakes; with famine and wars" (9.10–13).[40] This is the work that Socrates expressly forbids being attributed to the gods in the *Republic* but that we have seen Plato ascribe to an evil Soul in the *Laws*. Yet whether it is identified with celestial or terrestrial forces, evil is attributed to bodies.

Composed before and during Plotinus's lifetime, the philosophical Hermetica reflect Plotinus's specific way of formulating theophany—"no name yet all names."[41] In the first treatise, Hermes Trismegistus is preoccupied with the question about "What Is?" He relates, "once my bodily senses were restrained, an enormous being completely unbounded in size seemed to appear to me and call my name and say to me: 'What do you want to hear and see; what do you want to learn and know from your understanding?'" (1.1). Poimandres explains, "This is what you must know: that in you which sees and hears is the word of the lord, but your mind is god the father; they are not divided from one another for their union is life. . . . In your mind you have seen the archetypal form, the preprinciple that exists before a beginning without end" (1.6, 8). Once more, the shamanic vision of reality—without mediation—is the highest gnosis. From there we have a tale of cosmotheology—theophany—similar to that of Plotinus. The archetypal human looking at his reflection (Narcissus) united with nature, so that now the human is "twofold—in the body mortal but immortal in the essential man. . . . This is the

---

to similar Gnostic ideas about removing the garments and cites texts from Porphyry, Proclus, Iamblichus and others to show that this fiery body is demonic." We encounter this soul-vehicle in Origen as well. Gregory Shaw suggests that it originated with Plutarch or Numenius in his foreword to *Fragments of Numenius of Apamea*, iv. However, although this idea is certainly Hermetic, it was Stoic first. Proclus attributed it to Atticus and Albinus (*In Plat. Tim.* 4.234.9). Plotinus conceives a descent in which the soul adds increasingly heavy layers of bodiliness and lays aside each garment on the return (*Enn.* 1.6 [1].7.10; 4.3 [27].15.1–8). E. R. Dodds attributes it to Posidonius in *Proclus*, 366; cf. Proclus, *Elem. theo.* 209. John Dillon offers a survey of testimonies in *Iamblichi Chalcidensis*, 371–72.

40. I highlight "good and evil according to their natures" because according to the gnostic "doctrine of natures," it was the eternal substance of a soul that determined whether it was elect or reprobate. A similar view seems to be advanced here but in relation to daimons rather than humans.

41. See Plotinus, *Enn.* 5.1.6.45; 5.1.7.1; 5.3.11.1–4. Unless otherwise noted, quotations of the *Enneads* in this chapter are from Armstrong, LCL.

final good for those who have received knowledge [*gnōsis*]: to be made god" (1.15, 26, emphasis added). The "Cosmic Human" we have met in Indian and Chinese philosophy as well as in Orphic myths is alive and well in Hermetic cosmology.

The Divine Self: Microcosm, Prisoner, and Magus

From Democritus ("Man, a little world") to Leonardo da Vinci, the idea of humans as a microcosm—body, soul, and mind—of the cosmic hierarchy has been a powerful idea.[42] The additional concept especially from Stoics of a universal sympathy of things above and below contributed to the idea of humans as the link. Even in the most "optimistic" Hermetic texts, the Self as a divine cocreator is identified solely with the highest part of the soul, not with the body. Yet it is precisely through embodiment that the soul achieves its great work: deification. Mind and soul need the body in order to carry out the work of uniting correspondences.

Humans are not only prisoners of their body but, precisely in and through their bodies, mediators between heaven and earth. What we have here, then, is a positive—even exalted—view of the human being as microcosm and one with the supreme Mind, but only when it is abstracted from all bodily association. "For when soul has looked on the beauty of the good, my child, it cannot be deified while in a human body" (Corp. herm. 10.6). Repeating Plato, the author says that the cosmos is both good and evil. "But the human, because he moves and is mortal, is evil" (10.12). Those who use their temporary incarceration to help inferiors will win back their wings first as a daimon and then as an astral god. "For the unfaithful it goes differently: return to heaven is denied them, and a vile migration unworthy of a holy soul puts them in other bodies" (Corp herm. Ascl. 12).[43] In other words, embodiment affords an opportunity to improve one's next life by serving the souls of lower life-forms.

Despite the more positive justifications for embodiment, the baseline anthropology of the Hermetica remains in the thrall of conflict-dualism. The first treatise, *Poimandres*, exhibits the familiar Orphic division between material and spiritual reality with the body as a prison, just as we found in Plato.[44] The human being experiences tension between communion with the gods according to the divine part and the material and sensual nature that is shared with animals over which the human is placed. Ranged in the middle, the divine self experiences embodiment as a prison that is to be despised.[45]

---

42. On Democritus, see Schmidt-Biggemann, *Philosophia Perennis*, 132. On da Vinci, see Wallace, *World of Leonardo*, 103.

43. Cf. W. Scott, *Hermetica*, 2:226.

44. Plato, *Crat.* 400c; *Phaed.* 61e–62c; *Gorg.* 493a, *Resp.* 586a and elsewhere.

45. Yet I disagree with Shaw's conclusion that Plotinus's position was therefore closer to the gnostics. On the contrary, in opposition to the gnostics (and Numenius), Plotinus was drawing

Whereas Plotinus regards matter as evil and embodiment as something merely to be escaped (though calmly, not like gnostic hysteria), Iamblichus's view is more complex. Plotinus thinks that true philosophers such as himself keep their head above the water of becoming, but Iamblichus dives into the deep end, embracing matter as the way to escape it. To be sure, the soul undergoes shock as it awakens to its fleshly embodiment. It is exiled completely from its divine company, wholly changed from immortal to mortal. The soul becomes alienated (*allotriōthen*)—in the words of Ralph Waldo Emerson, "Man is a god in ruins."[46] Yet this painful event is necessary for the soul to become a cocreator with the demiurge and attain deification.

> The soul sews itself into the fabric of the material world, yet its collaboration with the Demiurge comes at a cost. Although immortal, the soul becomes mortal and is exiled from the circle of the gods. Iamblichus presents this in stark terms: The soul is a mean not only between the undivided and the divided, the remaining and the proceeding, the noetic and the irrational, but also between the uncreated and the created. . . . "Thus, that which is immortal in the soul is filled completely with mortality and no longer remains only immortal."[47]

Although the daimons have been involved in the dispersal or exile of the soul and transporting it into its earthly prison, they also play an important role in revealing the divine signatures in this world to lead them back home. Ranged midway between the two worlds, the shaman-magus was able to bring them together, just as Isis reunited the scattered parts of Osiris's body. In short, human beings have work to do, not just to contemplate what is always and everywhere, but to play our part in the demiurgic art.[48]

While gnostics took Orphic theology as far as it could go, van den Broek is correct when he says that "a Gnostic could never have said of man that he is

---

a sharper line between the two worlds to preserve the intelligible realm from any taint of evil. Where the gnostic felt trapped in her body, Plotinus is convinced that the truest and inmost self was even now present to the Mind of which it was a part.

46. Quoted in Shaw, "Demon est Deus Inversus," 179.

47. Shaw, "Demon est Deus Inversus," 180, quoting Simplicius, *In Arist. De An.* 89.33–37; 90.21–23.

48. Fowden, *Egyptian Hermes*, 88, from *Cyr.* 18. Similar to Plotinus, it is said that this is possible at any moment, even in the body, but only if mind transcends it. See Corp. herm. 12.9; cf. Corp. herm. 11.19. Again, comparisons with gnostic texts suggest themselves. See van den Broek, "Gnosticism and Hermeticism in Antiquity," 5–6. Significantly, van den Broek adds, "However, these similarities cannot conceal the great differences that separate Gnostics and Hermetists with respect to the three fundamental issues—namely, the doctrine of God (theology), of the visible world (cosmology), and of man (anthropology)."

a *magnum miraculum*, a most astonishing being, as he is called in the Asclepius."[49] Indeed, one fragment from the Chaldean Oracles expresses a more positive view of the body: "through the holy rites not only the soul, but even the body is thought worthy of much help and salvation: 'Save also the mortal covering of bitter matter,' the gods announce to the most holy of the theurgists when they are encouraging them."[50]

The heavenly gods remain above, as does the uppermost part of the soul, while the true human (the inmost mind) "rises up to heaven" and understands all "and—greater than all of this—he comes *to be on high without leaving earth behind*, so enormous is his range.... *Therefore, we must dare to say that the human on earth is a mortal god but that god in heaven is an immortal human*. Through these two, then, cosmos and human, all things exist, but they all exist by action of the One" (Corp. herm. 10.25, emphasis added).

Daring indeed is this thought that the human—at least one's spirit or mind—is a mortal god and that God is an immortal human. One side of Hermetic thinking is typically Platonic (bodily imprisonment), but the other side is practically Promethean in its spiritual optimism. It is not adding anything new to the Orphic and Titan myths, or the *Timaeus*, for Asclepius to say, "God, the father and master, made gods first and then humans, taking equal portions from the more corrupt part of matter and from the divine" (Corp. herm. Ascl. 22a).[51] But there is no precedent in Platonism for the belief that humans are mortal gods. Though the soul is divine, it is precisely such corporeality and mortality that disqualifies the composite human as such from being called divine. It is one thing to assert that a human soul may become *like* god, as Plato taught (*Theaet.* 176b), and quite another to suggest that "mankind was ordained to be *better* than the gods." Given this kinship, Asclepius is exhorted to "recognize mankind's power and strength. Just as the master and father—or god, to use his most august name—is maker of the heavenly gods, so it is mankind *who fashions the temple gods* who are content to be near to humans.... He *not only advances toward god; he also makes the gods strong*.... Mankind certain deserves admiration, as *the greatest of all beings*" (Corp. herm. Ascl. 22b–23).[52] Theurgists are cocreators, fellow demiurges of the demiurge. After enduring not only the trials but the rituals of embodiment, they can become more than they ever imagined in their preexistence.

---

49. Van den Broek, "Gnosticism and Hermeticism in Antiquity," 12.
50. CO fr. 129 (= Julian, *Or.* 5.178d).
51. In Copenhaver, *Hermetica*, 79.
52. In Copenhaver, *Hermetica*, 80, emphasis added.

"Unspeakable Acts Perfectly Performed": The Art of Making Gods

There is a lot of theology in the Corpus Hermeticum and theurgic Neoplatonism, but the main interest is in doing and not dogma. Magicians were utopians, wanting to bend the rules of fate. They were the vanguard of natural scientists because they wanted to change nature, not just to understand it. They did not imagine that they could transform a substance by mere whimsy, but that by combining different substances they could produce a new one. Nature herself is the divine offspring of the Soul, and sooner or later she divulges her secrets. To invoke Hadot's categories, they combined the Orphic respect for nature's secrets with the Promethean impulse to decode and exploit them.

We see this already in the Greek Magical Papyri (much of which is Egyptian), a loose collection of spells that were prior to and contemporary with the production of the Chaldean Oracles. Without any weakening of the emphasis on the transcendence of the supreme and unknowable Father, the Oracles launched a new phase of accounting for divine immanence. There the visible world is connected to the primordial Triad by a chain of lesser divinities, and they are not unambiguously benevolent.[53] To promote an optimistic interpretation, there is a strong emphasis on good daimons in their ranks from the archangels downward.[54] Priests in particular are identified as connectors (*telestai*), like the shamans of old. The priest has the map and knows how to distinguish the angels from the demons. He knows the right rituals for uniting heaven and earth, that is, the practice known as theurgy.[55] Ironically, Hellenistic Orphism is more congenial to the public religion of Egypt than to that of Athens.

More easily felt than articulated, late Roman Orphism was a catchall for Hermetic, gnostic, and Platonic forms of gnosis. But by the end of the fourth century it included rituals such as those described in the Greek Magical Papyri, the Chaldean Oracles, and Iamblichus's *On the Mysteries*. These rituals were revived with vigor for three years under the emperor Julian.

Not only Greek contemplation but also the religious intensity of rituals drawn from the Orient, especially Egypt, constituted a perennial tradition from Zoroaster and Indian gymnosophists to Orpheus and thence to Pythagoras and Plato. Underscoring the superiority of Persian education, Socrates explains that "the boy is entrusted to 'royal tutors.' . . . The first of them instructs him in the worship of their

---

53. Majercik, introduction to *Chaldean Oracles*, 8.
54. Majercik, introduction to *Chaldean Oracles*, 13–14.
55. CO fr. 177 (= Damascius, *De princ.* 1.290.15–17).

gods, the Magian lore of Zoroaster" (*Alc. maj.* 122a). In the usual genealogy related by Platonists of the age, Zoroaster lived six millennia before Plato and injected astrology and alchemy into the Hellenic bloodstream via Orpheus, Indian sages, Pythagoras, and Philolaus all the way to Plato. The impact of the Zoroastrian magi had already been felt in Egypt under two centuries of Persian rule (527–332 BCE) when Darius I, himself a magus, rebuilt temples and encouraged Egyptian religion. Although the Persians invented the terms *magus* (the ritual practitioner) and *magu* (the practice of the *magus*), for the Greeks they functioned much the same as did their notion of "philosophy," covering wisdom generally from metaphysics and mathematics to music and medicine as well as astrology and alchemy. "One can connect this with the notion of Pythagoras as a 'wise man,' a kind of shaman," says Celenza.[56]

Hermeticism was infused also with Egyptian religion. One treatise charges the Greeks with corrupting Egyptian rites, as if the potent magic of Egyptian words could be translated. "The very quality of the speech and sound of Egyptian words have in themselves the energy of the objects they speak of. . . . For the Greeks have empty speeches . . . and this is the philosophy of the Greeks, an insane foolosophy of speeches. We, by contrast, use not speeches but sounds that are full of action" (Corp. herm. 16.1–2). In Greco-Roman Egypt, Hermes Trismegistus reigned over this whole field. Theurgic Neoplatonists were not radicals belonging to an "underground Platonism"; if any modern categories apply, they were reactionary conservatives clinging fervently to the vision of Iamblichus and Julian of a rejuvenated pagan empire.

Theurgy: "The Art of Making Gods"

Theurgy is the place where magic and philosophy meet. Pierre A. Riffard observes, "Theurgy is a type of magic. It consists of a set of magical practices performed to evoke beneficent spirits in order to see them or know them in order to influence them, for instance by forcing them to animate statues, to inhabit a human being (such as a medium), or to disclose mysteries."[57] Plotinus argues that a select few—sages like Socrates and Plato—enjoy this distinction. For them, "the god"—no less than the One or *nous*—was the guiding spirit (*Enn.* 3.4.6).[58]

Just as the Egyptian priest informed Plotinus that his guiding daimon was actually a god, the Chaldean Oracles announce, "For the theurgists do not fall

---

56. Celenza, "Pythagoras in the Renaissance," 670.

57. Riffard, *Dictionnaire de l'ésoterisme*, 340.

58. John M. Rist offers an intriguing comparison of Porphyry's account and Plotinus's treatment of the subject in "Plotinus and the 'Daimonion' of Socrates."

into the herd which is subject to Destiny."⁵⁹ This is at once gnostic, Hermetic, and Plotinian. Gnostics agreed with Plotinus that they are divine in their uppermost part of the soul and could therefore transcend all material associations. In contrast with Plotinus, however, Hermetic theurgy assumes that the soul is wholly enmeshed in matter and requires material substances and operations to ascend to its homeland. Combining divine spirit with terrestrial nature, the human being is the mediator of the two worlds.

The Chaldean Oracles introduce the term "theurgy" for the first time. Supposedly delivered by the gods to Julian the Chaldean and his son Julian the Theurgist (late second century CE), "Chaldean" advertises the oracles' connection with Eastern magic.⁶⁰ They reflect "that type of Middle Platonism which had affinities with both Gnosticism and Hermeticism as well as links with Numenius." Majercik's summary of this milieu ticks the Orphic boxes:

> a) their elaborate and often exasperating metaphysical constructions; b) an extreme derogation of material existence; c) a dualistic understanding of human nature that envisions the soul or mind as a "spark" of the Divine trapped in matter; d) a method of salvation or enlightenment that generally involves a spiritual and/or ritual ascent of the soul; e) a mythologizing tendency that hypostasizes various abstractions into quasi-mythical beings.

They typically involve a highest deity "described in Pythagorean terms as a 'Monad' who either exists alongside of or extends into a 'Dyad'" with "a complex proliferation of cosmic entities" and a "dominant female principle . . . directly responsible for material creation as we know it."

> In certain Gnostic systems, for example, she is Ennoia or Sophia; in the Chaldean system, Dynamis or Hecate; in the Hermetica (esp. *C.H.* I), Life or Nature. Despite the abstract qualities of most of these names, a definite personal function is assigned to each: the Gnostic Sophia experiences feelings of grief and fear, she gives birth to the Demiurge, Ialdabaoth; the Chaldean Hecate generates life from her right hip; the Hermetic Nature entices and unites with the primal Anthropos. This female principle ultimately reflects the World Soul of Plato's *Timaeus*, refracted in varying degrees through the prism of Middle Platonism; along the way, Plutarch will have assimilated this figure to the Egyp-

---

59. CO fr. 153 (= Lydus, *De mens.* 2.10; 31.16–19). Porphyry refers to this episode in *Vit. Plot.* 10.
60. Majercik, introduction to *Chaldean Oracles*, 1–2.

tian Isis; Philo, to the Jewish figure of Wisdom; and Numenius will have split it into opposed good and evil entities.[61]

Since Gregory Shaw's study of Iamblichus in 2003, it has become customary to distinguish theurgy (*theourgia*) from magic (*goēteia*).[62] Key in that agreement is the definition of *theourgia* as "the work of the gods" (a subjective genitive) rather than "the making of gods" (an objective genitive). Magic sought to place the initiative in human hands, manipulating and commanding chthonic daimons and disembodied souls, Johnston observes. "Theurgy, however, placed the power the magician sought in the celestial realm." "In theurgy and philosophy," she adds, "as celestial mediators and mediation became ever more important to man's spiritual self-improvement and salvation, Hekate [goddess of magic] became increasingly beneficent, ever more the savior."[63]

However, the relationship of theurgy and magic is more complicated. The connection with Hekate of course associates theurgy with magic, but she had now been elevated to the position of the World Soul. In short, magic looks down to nature to conjure salvation, while theurgy looks up to Hekate to send it down. While magicians imagine that they conjure marvels, Iamblichus argued, theurgy depends on the cooperation of the gods.[64] Magic is trapped in this world, the prisoner of Physis, concerned only with terrestrial transformations, coercing the gods to act against their will; theurgy is pious and reverent dependence on the gods for spiritual grace.[65] As Shaw argues, focusing on Iamblichus, the differences in theurgic actions is based on different cultic needs: beginners need physical rites before they can advance to higher gnosis.[66]

It is true that in the Oracles and the philosophical Hermetica the goal is not common magic, the mere transformation of nature into nature, but using natural

---

61. Majercik, introduction to *Chaldean Oracles*, 3–4.
62. G. Shaw, *Theurgy and the Soul*. For his definition see especially 11. Generally, mainstream twentieth-century scholarship dismissed theurgic Neoplatonism as an aberration, an oriental contagion that caused pupils of Plotinus's school to wander dizzily into the weeds of irrationalism. Especially since Shaw and the Radical Orthodoxy circle with which he is associated, there has been an overcorrection with a decidedly apologetic intent.
63. Johnston, *Hekate Soteira*, 147.
64. Iamblichus, *De myst.* 1.12, 14; 2.6, 11; 3.1, 10, 18; 4.2. Unless otherwise noted, the translation is from Iamblichus, *On the Mysteries* (trans. Clarke, Dillon, and Hershbell).
65. Majercik, introduction to *Chaldean Oracles*, 23.
66. Beginners require more familiar "earthly" steps, while intermediates advance to prayer and hymns, but the highest level is silent contemplation, as noted by G. Shaw, *Theurgy and the Soul*, 25–26. Johnston offers a concise summary of debates in recent scholarship over this question in *Hekate Soteira*, 77.

elements sympathetic to their divine archetype in order to release the divine from the bonds of nature altogether. It is religious, oriented to the gods descending and speaking through statues composed of sympathetic elements. This is the metaphysics I am describing as "natural supernaturalism." In one sense, the magician shares this horizon, imagining that there are natural substances that, when combined, have supernatural qualities. However, the theurgist's aim is not merely this-worldly; it is nothing less than salvation, understood by Middle Platonists generally as Plato's notion of assimilation to god as far as possible (*Theaet.* 176b).

However, the line between theurgy and magic is blurrier than Shaw suggests even in the case of Iamblichus.[67] Many of the formulas in the Oracles are taken directly from the Magical Papyri. More importantly, it is anachronistic to assume that Iamblichus was the singular source for understanding the Chaldean Oracles, which appeared a century before his birth. And yet there is plenty in the Oracles to suggest that daimons and even gods were bound and loosed by the hierarch through rituals perfectly performed.[68] "And, again, another (god), being compelled, said: 'Listen to me, although I do not wish it, since you have bound me by Necessity.' And still, more clearly, (Hecate says): 'Why from the eternally coursing ether, do you need to invoke me, the goddess Hecate, by constraints which bind the gods'" (CO fr. 220–221). Similarly, Asclepius in the Corpus Hermeticum explains "the art of making gods" (i.e., fabricating and enlivening statues). The purported author of the Oracles, Julian the Theurgist, even exhibited this by making a clay head with which he claimed to have produced rain. These oracles were thought to have been transmitted directly from Plato's soul.[69] Nevertheless,

---

67. Even Iamblichus engaged in practices that we would call magic, including levitating and, in two local springs, summoning gods who greeted him as their father. The report is found in the fourth-century *Lives of the Philosophers and Sophists* by Eunapius, discussed helpfully in Fowden, "Pagan Holy Man." Majercik says, "it is clear that the Chaldean system included a complex ascent ritual involving purifications, trance, phantasmagoria, sacred objects, magical instruments and formulas, prayer, hymns, and even a contemplative element, all of which was practiced (most likely) in the context of a 'mystery community.'" See his introduction to *Chaldean Oracles*, 5. Regardless of their distinct metaphysics, in terms of practices theurgy incorporates magic and, far from being an avocation, was an integral part of the instruction and experience of Athenian and Alexandrian schools. Moreover, ancient writers did not distinguish philosopher-magicians like Apollonius of Tyana from theurgists.

68. Contra Shaw, *Theurgy and the Soul*, the reference range of *theourgia* in the ancient sources cannot be reduced to the objective genitive "work of the gods." This is apparent not only in Iamblichus's *De mysteriis* but in the Asclepius (with instructions on "the art of *making* gods") and the Chaldean Oracles.

69. Saffrey, "Les Néoplatoniciens," 218–19. On the appropriation of this idea by Julian the Theurgist, see Lewy, *Chaldaean Oracles and Theurgy*, 461.

Hermeticism and its vigorous afterlife in theurgic Neoplatonism was a return to a more original, magical, and ritualistic type of Orphism that Plato had censured.

Especially by introducing the shift from theology to theurgy, the Oracles represent a liminal crossing from a locative to a utopian outlook that characterizes in different ways and degrees all of the movements designated by Dodds as the Platonic underworld. For the various groups that read the Oracles eagerly, the higher soul shares in the Intellect and can escape while the lower soul (and world) is ruled by Fate or Destiny (*heimarmenē*), threatened by evil daimons of the material world, and, of course, trapped in bodies.[70]

The tragicomedy of the divine self promised the same starring role to every patron. Whatever the differences over the analysis of the plight, solutions, and methods, philosophy was about soul-saving. But magic is one thing and mysticism is another, with plenty of the latter in the Corpus Hermeticum. Human reasoning can examine the ideas (i.e., the forms), but not the Mind itself. For the latter only the "flower of intellect," akin to Plato's "divine madness," would suffice.[71]

But the Chaldean Oracles represent a more practical side of Hermetic theurgy influenced by magical texts. After suitable preparation, we learn in the "Hymn to Apollo" in the Greek Magical Papyri that the magician chants his invocation to various deities and angels, including not only Apollo and Zeus but also "Michael, who rule[s] heaven's realm," and "archangel Gabriel" (*PGM* 1.301).[72] The theurgist is a demiurge; he is, in effect, the creator.[73] According to the liturgy, the priest declares to the god, "I have been attached to your holy form. I have been given power by your holy name. I have acquired your emanation of the goods, Lord, god of gods, master, daimon." The priest is further instructed, "Having done this, return as lord of a godlike nature ... which is accomplished through this divine encounter" (4.220–222). Hebrew names are especially sacred in the Greek Magical Papyri, and these texts have been compared with Jewish ascent apocalypses.[74]

The theurgist at this point is no longer merely a human being. Theurgists are not even conscious of themselves, or even human, which is why they can endure

---

70. This is not to overlook radical differences between the Oracles and gnostic writings that entail a more optimistic versus pessimistic outlook, respectively. In this respect, Hermeticism is closer to the spirit of the Oracles.

71. Jaruszynski, *Science in Culture*, 72.

72. See the translation of the "Hymn to Apollo" from the Greek Magical Papyri in Bradshaw, *Aristotle East and West*, 130. Hereafter all quotations are from Betz, *Greek Magical Papyri*.

73. Bradshaw, *Aristotle East and West*, 130.

74. Himmelfarb, "Revelation and Rapture," 79–90, esp. 86. See also Sholem, *Major Trends in Jewish Mysticism*, 43.

walking on glowing coals without being burned (Iamblichus, *De myst.* 3.4). The sacred sounds and rites become the transmitter of the divine voice. Iamblichus explains, "The theurgist, through the power of arcane signatures, commands mundane natures, no longer as man, nor as employing a human soul; but as existing superior to them in the order of the Gods, he makes use of greater mandates than pertain to himself, so far as he is human." He even uses threats against the gods because these beings are actually lower while he is in this state of divine possession. It is only "through a union with the Gods, which he obtains from the knowledge of arcane symbols," that he has this quality or power (*De myst.* 6.5–6).[75]

As Augustine recognized, Porphyry opened the door to Hermes Trismegistus and theurgy. When his student Iamblichus went headlong into Egyptian religion, Porphyry drew back, slamming the door that he had opened. It was too late, however. It was theurgy, not theory, that mattered most now to Plato's distant heirs.[76] With Iamblichus the Neoplatonic tradition becomes theurgic all the way to the closing of the pagan schools.

Magus *at Work*

In theurgy, perfect performance of rituals, not perfect conceptions, ideas, or even virtue, was the key. Theurgists often borrowed what was at hand, including divination, astrology, and alchemy, but in a way that was different from what they called "vulgar magicians." Like Julian the Theurgist, Hermeticists insisted that authentic theurgy depended on the natural sympathy of everything in the cosmos: natural supernaturalism.

Chants and Invocations: "Sounds Full of Power"

Demetrius in the first century reports, "In Egypt, the priests, when singing hymns in praise of the gods, employ the seven vowels (*phōnēis*), which they utter in due succession" (*Eloc.* 71).[77] The seven vowels correlated with the seven planets. As the body-soul fulcrum between the two worlds, the magus imitated the work of God in the beginning, "'Let there be light!' And there was light" (Gen 1:3–4). The Hebdomad was central in Zoroastrian astrology as well, consisting of seven star-

---

75. Cf. Copenhaver, *Hermetica*, 72–73.
76. Anton, "Theourgia-Demiourgia," 18: In Plato's day, poetry was seen as a threat to philosophy, but as Anton observes this "hardly compares to the magnitude of the challenge the art of theurgy presented to the theoretical man of wisdom seven centuries later."
77. Demetrius, *On Style* (trans. Roberts).

Chapter 6

daimons (represented as archangels) ruling over each sphere.[78] The same mystical utterance of the seven vowels of the heavenly spheres is found in gnostic writings along with references to the Ogdoad (the eightfold primordial deities of ancient Egypt).[79] We might recall from earlier the terror expressed at the "seven foes" that stalked and impeded the soul's progress to the heavens, but theurgists promised to bind them and harness their powers for the ascent.

Besides the hierophant, "ecstatics" assist in the ascent. Iamblichus explains that "the Bacchic frenzy is aroused" by loud and sensuous music and by other tunes calmed (*De myst.* 3.9). Orpheus, we recall, plied his Apollonian reason to the Dionysian cult. Iamblichus acknowledges the supervisory power of the Korybantes (Cybele's attendants) but distinguishes theurgy's ultimate aim from those of "Bacchic frenzies." Further, Porphyry is misinformed in thinking that it is men who are possessed by the "Mother of the gods." Rather, "very few are males, and those who are tend to be rather effeminate. And this form of possession has a life-engendering and fulfilling power, in which respect it differs completely from every form of frenzy" (*De myst.* 3.10).[80]

Astrology and Horoscopes

A star-ruled cosmos was hardly novel in the ancient world. Far from being the effluence of an irrational underground, such astrological ideas were simply the astronomy of the day encouraged by the Ptolemaic cosmology. However, Hermeticism is distinguished by an ingredient that charges it with an especially "modern" impulse to not merely understand and predict one's fate but also change it—in effect, to master the stars and thereby the universe through spiritual technology. Can this be done? At least some Hermetic writers believed so, through manifold

---

78. Shaw, *Theurgy and the Soul*, 185. He notes that in his *Theologumena arithmeticae* Iamblichus says, "Hence, in a similar way, they [Babylonian priests] call the stars and *Daimones* that rule over each of these herds 'Angels' and 'Archangels,' and these are seven in number. So, according to the truest etymology the Hebdomad is called *angelia*'" (*Theo. arith.* 57.6–9).

79. Shaw, *Theurgy and the Soul*, 208. Shaw explains, "Iamblichus believed that the seven vowels were connatural (*sungenia*) with the seven planetary gods, and certain Gnostic writings suggest that one-to-one correlations were ritually developed. For example, Valentinus's disciple Marcus associated the vowels with heavenly spheres," from the first heaven to seventh respectively (i.e., $a, e, ē, i, o, y, ō$). See also Pearson, "Gnosticism as Platonism"; Pearson, "Theurgic Tendencies."

80. Clarke, Dillon, and Hersbell note, "The priests of Cybele used to castrate themselves in imitation of Attis, and wandered about as begging prophets, wonder-workers, and quacks. They did not have a good reputation; see [Lucian], *Asin.* 35ff. and Apuleius, *Metam.* 7.24" (Iamblichus, *On the Mysteries*, 139 n. 185).

Hermes Trismegistus: The Cult without Temples

practices such as the use of horoscopes, talismans, stones, and plants as well as the veneration of images.[81] With the aid of Stoic ideas, Hermeticists believed in a correspondence between all things. Yet they grafted this onto their eclectic Platonic stalk, with celestial gods (viz., souls of planets and stars) having a certain sympathy for particular objects, smells, colors, and sounds. This affinity could be exploited through theurgic wooing of the god to his or her natural symbols.

Statues Enlivened

First, a statue would be made from materials that were sympathetic signatures of the god to be invoked. Apparently, Hekate had her own color palette and specific leaves and scents she liked. These would be mixed with lizard guts and smeared onto the statue. Second, the worshipers are called in their ascent to "sing a hymn to Paean" followed by the command, "keep silent, initiate" (CO fr. 131–132). This difference is probably explained by the two groups addressed: intermediates and advanced adherents respectively.[82]

Then initiates were sprinkled with salt water, perhaps in imitation of bathing in the sea prior to participation in the Eleusinian mysteries. Although the various rites for propitiating or repelling the avenging souls differ considerably (offering cakes versus swearing at them), the goal is similar to the old Orphic rituals. Next, as Majercik explains, the adept would call upon a supreme god or various other gods "by uttering his divine names, which amounted to a lengthy recitation of unintelligible vowel and consonant sounds," such as we find in gnostic and Hermetic sources but also in usual magical incantations in the antique Roman period.[83] Also, there was the animating of statues, which was Egyptian.[84] Being given the ontological character of a god, the theurgist "enlivened" the statue—that is, made the bodily symbol the receptacle of the World Soul, identified with Hekate. The statues did not just represent the gods; they were the material vehicles through

---

81. Lactantius, Irenaeus, Epiphanius, Hippolytus, Augustine, and other ancient Christian writers criticized the gnostics for introducing images of God (including Jesus) into their practices. However, for theurgic Neoplatonism such images were seen as essential in the practical work of liberation from the world. Once again, I differ slightly with Gregory Shaw's interpretation of theurgy in general through the lens of Iamblichus. I am not disputing the importance of the complete descent of the soul in Iamblichus, which Shaw marvelously explains, but I doubt that this is the view of our Hermetists. Rather, they agree with Plotinus and Porphyry that fate affects only the lower soul while the higher remains above.

82. Once more, to Gregory Shaw's helpful insight in *Theurgy and the Soul*, 25–26.

83. Majercik, introduction to *Chaldean Oracles*, 25–26.

84. Majercik, introduction to *Chaldean Oracles*, 26.

which the gods revealed themselves and spoke to the initiates. There was also binding and loosing gods in the statues.[85]

Despite the obvious Greco-Egyptian ritualism, Platonic contemplation remains essential to such theurgy. One of the Chaldean Oracles instructs something similar to Buddhist meditation: "You must not perceive it intently, but keeping the pure eye of your soul turned away, you should extend an empty mind toward the Intelligible in order to comprehend it, since it exists outside of (your) mind."[86] According to Proclus and Damascius, the Oracles invoke "You (gods) who know the supermundane, Paternal Abyss by perceiving it."[87] Such ideas, even the title "Paternal Abyss," suggest the possibility of gnostic influence.

These exhortations remind us that in spite of the obvious methodological overlaps, we are dealing with a different outlook from common magic. In fact, these fragments are likely targeting magicians as their closest competition. They never marry the visible with the invisible but are deceived into thinking that irrational material substances can be transformed into other ones. "Many are swept away by the crooked streams of matter" (CO fr. 172).[88] Johnston notes, "Astrology, bird auspices and haruspicy are called 'toys, the supports of a deceptive trade.'"[89] Like Plato, such theurgists identified magic with the rites of the public religion, keeping the soul bound to the body and the material world. The statue was not naturally divine but became inhabited by a god when the sympathies were present. This is what the "enlivening of statues" means. The statues they passed along the street were mere matter, "images without intellect."

Next we enter one of the most fascinating scenes in the theurgy of the Oracles: "Operate with the magic wheel of Hectate."[90] Spun by the theurgist, these golden balls held by a leather thong whirled and made animal or laughing sounds as they whipped the air.[91] The hierophant, himself a human "connector," used these magic wheels as "transmitters."[92] When "whirled inwardly," says Damascius, the iynx "calls forth the gods; outwardly, it sends them away."[93] "And Proclus says

---

85. Majercik, introduction to *Chaldean Oracles*, 27. See CO frr. 112 and 163 (= Damascius, *De princ.* 2.317.3–7), as quoted in Johnston, *Hekate Soteira*, 82–83.
86. CO fr. 1 (= Damascius, *De princ.* 1.154.14–26).
87. CO fr. 18 (= Proclus, *In Plat. Crat.* 57.25–26; Damascius, *De princ.* 2.16.6; 2.65.16).
88. Johnston, *Hekate Soteira*, 82–83.
89. CO fr. 107 (= Psellus in PG 122:1128b8–c7), cited in Johnston, *Hekate Soteira*, 86.
90. CO fr. 206 (= Psellus in PG 122:1133a4, 12–14).
91. Psellus (PG 122:1133a), as quoted in Johnston, *Hekate Soteira*, 90. Johnston also notes here that this magic wheel is mentioned all the way back to Pindar.
92. Johnston, *Hekate Soteira*, 93.
93. Damascius, *De princ.* 2.95.15, quoted in Johnston, *Hekate Soteira*, 90.

that they transmit all things from the noetic sphere to the material sphere and back again" (*In Plat. Parm.* 1199.36–38).[94] As the World Soul, mediating intellectual and sensible realms, Hekate sends forth her iynx-daimons and they return to her through this operation of the magic wheel. "Theurgically," Johnston explains, "the iynx-wheel, whose whirling and sounds both symbolize and strengthen cosmic sympathy upon which the theurgist relies, depends on Hekate; it works by her grace."[95]

"Magical materialism," a concept employed by Lewy, is not the best description of this outlook. Rather, it is a version of "natural supernaturalism." There are many points of difference with Plato, but the Chaldean system is not Stoic. The two worlds, soul and body, are forever distinguished as much in the Oracles as in they are in the *Republic*. Technological images are striking. The priests are connectors, and the telestic statues that they make are transmitters, which still assumes a divided line with Hekate as the border. Theurgy lives in the liminal space of mysticism and magic, fed by Chaldean (Persian) and Greco-Egyptian rituals and the Magical Papyri. However, this spiritual technology is above all a magical Platonism. Johnston summarizes this well: "The Cosmic Soul of the *Timaeus* became identified with Hekate, patroness of ritual magic. The Platonic daemon, as described in the Symposium, became identified with the iynx-wheel, a witch's and magician's tool.... The Oracles made philosophical and spiritual concepts more immediately practical by allying them with the tenets of popular religion and magic."[96]

All these rituals are preparatory to the theurgist sending his soul upward.[97] The soul can only prepare itself for the work of the gods. And yet, even if she sends down the recipe, words, and rites to use, the god must appear and deliver her oracle if the performance is correct.[98] In ordinary divination, the priest would try to discern the future through the body of the animal itself, but "all these are playthings, the props of commercial fraud." In theurgy the god spoke directly to the

---

94. Johnston notes in *Hekate Soteira*, 91 that according to CO fr. 78 (= Damascius, *De princ.* 2.201.3–4) "they are established as 'ferrymen' (diaporthmioi)."

95. Johnston, *Hekate Soteira*, 110. Marinus refers to the iynx wheel used by Proclus in *Vit. Proc.* 28, quoted in Johnston, *Hekate Soteira*, 90 n. 2; cf. also Josephus, *J.W.* 2.154: "who describing the descent of the soul into the body, says that it enters into the body just as if it were 'pulled down into the prison of the body by some iynx from nature.'" See Johnston further in *Hekate Soteira*, 96–98.

96. Johnston, *Hekate Soteira*, 84.

97. Johnston, *Hekate Soteira*, 83.

98. CO fr. 147 (= Psellus in PG 122:1133b5–8) and CO fr. 148 (= Psellus in PG 122:1136b11–c1), respectively quoted in Johnston, *Hekate Soteira*, 118–19. See also Lewy, *Chaldaean Oracles and Theurgy*, 247–48.

theurgist (CO fr. 107).[99] Having prepared oneself by the previous rituals, Hekate appears and addresses the theurgist:

> Having spoken these things, you will behold a fire leaping skittishly/ like a child over the aery waves; or a fire without form, from which a voice emerges; or a rich light, whirring around the field in a spiral. But [it is also possible] that you will see a horse flashing more brightly than light, or a child mounted on the swift back of a horse, a fiery child or a child covered with gold, or yet again a naked child; or even a child shooting arrows, standing upon a horse's back.[100]

Upon the marvelous epiphany, Hekate delivers her oracle and the theurgist becomes a god.

So far, the theurgic drama has followed the Chaldean Oracles closely, and this is true in the final stage of enlivening the statue as well. According the Hermetic Asclepius, statues—like human beings—are composed of two natures: one "which is purer and more divine by far" and a base materialilty (Corp. herm. Ascl. 23). Central to theurgic art was the "enlivening" of statues. By themselves these statues were just a mixture of lizard guts, plants, and stones. But the desired god had an affinity for each of these signs. The "telestic art" of enlivening statues was, as Lewy says, "accomplished by special magical actions." The "vivification" of Hekate's statue in the Chaldean Oracles along with her magical wheel that "provided another means of compelling the presence of gods or demons," was nuclear to the practice of Maximus, to whom the emperor Julian entrusted himself.[101]

Statues were media through which the gods would appear, rolling up their sleeves to get something done. Like the theurgist himself, correct words and correctly crafted statues were a combination of earthly material and divine substance. The Roman state priests looked down, expecting matter itself to reveal secrets, but the theurgists looked up, calling down the gods to their statues that consisted of perfectly applied sympathetic materials and through perfectly performed rites. This operation occurred simultaneously on the plane of nature, the heavens, and within the operator's soul.[102]

---

99. Majercik, *Chaldean Oracles*, 91.

100. CO fr. 146 (= Proclus, *In Plat. Resp.* 1.111.3–11), quoted in Johnston, *Hekate Soteira*, 111; cf. Majercik, *Chaldean Oracles*, 105.

101. As we have seen, this object was a golden disk with mystical characters inscribed on it. With a leather cord the theurgist would "swing it around, while reciting magic spells." When it was swung inward, the gods were bound; when outward, they were loosed. Theurgists would then wear these disks or plates as talismans. See Lewy, *Chaldaean Oracles and Theurgy*, 249, 252.

102. Shaw, *Theurgy and the Soul*, 191. The emperor Julian writes to a priest, "not that we may

Through the process described above, the statue would become a mirror in which the god manifested itself on earth to worshipers (Corp. herm. 16.19).[103] "Therefore, my king, adore the statues, because they, too, possess forms from the intelligible cosmos" (Corp. herm. 17). Like the statue, the hierophant himself was transubstantiated into a god, able to command—even berate—the inferior gods because he was no longer human but a divinity superior to them. Porphyry's later turn against theurgy in the person of his student Iamblichus contradicts his own earlier position in *On Statues*. Plato's Socrates would have found the rites distasteful and unnecessary, just as he did the extravagances of Dionysian and Orphic ritualists, but the metaphysical frame for it all was largely his construction.

Alchemy

According to Eliade, "Everywhere we find alchemy, it is always intimately related to a 'mystical' tradition: in China with Taoism, in India with Yoga and Tantrism, in Hellenistic Egypt with gnosis, in Islamic countries with hermetic and esoteric mystical schools, in the Western Middle Ages and Renaissance with Hermetist, Christian and sectarian mysticism, and Cabala."[104] Eliade's own esoteric enthusiasm sometimes led him to downplay the purely natural type of alchemy, but with the qualification "often" (instead of "everywhere and always"), he is right.[105] For Hermeticists at least, the ultimate intent of alchemy was strictly spiritual; material transformations were a means, but the end was the inner transformation of the magus and the supernaturalism of nature.

As strange as physicochemical operations would have seemed to Plato, the goal was no different. Garth Fowden notes, "The alchemists themselves were 'philosophers,' and the aim of their 'philosophy' or 'divine art' was 'the dissolution of the body and the separation of the soul from the body.'"[106] Yet this could happen in this life, before death, through forceful physicospiritual actions. Such practical techniques were based on the methods of the jeweler and glassmaker, while "his theoretical pretensions touched ultimately on the human soul in its relationship

---

regard these things as Gods, but that we may worship the Gods through them (*di' autōn*). . . . When we look at the images of the god, let us not indeed think they are stones or wood, but neither let us think they are the gods themselves" (*Ep.* 19.292a–b). Quoted by Shaw, *Theurgy and the Soul*, 191 n. 11. Translation of Julian from *Works of the Emperor Julian* (ed. Wright, LCL).

103. Copenhaver, *Hermetica*, 208: "Scott II, 460–1 cites passages from Plutarch and Plotinus to show that 'cult-statues' are mirrors in which *noêta* [intelligibles] are reflected."

104. Eliade, *Forge and the Crucible*, 183.

105. See the helpful critique in Principe and Newman, "Historiography of Alchemy."

106. Fowden, *Egyptian Hermes*, 90.

to God." This idea is more Stoic than Platonist, since the form animates within rather than being imposed on matter from without.[107] Physical alchemy was an allegory of the soul.

Karen-Claire Voss describes three stages to this process. Stage one is *nigredo*, the preparation for the great work by first confronting the chaotic and unknowable material—the "dark night of the soul." Stage two is *albedo*, the division of the chaotic substance into polar opposites. "Now that the soul had been 'led out' from the body, there remained the problem of conflict between them. The substances could not be merely superficially reunited; instead, it was necessary to produce a genuine compound"—a third thing.[108] At various stages in the alchemical process, Voss adds, Hermes Trismegistus (Latin: Mercurius) "would intervene in the work by effecting the resolution of opposites."[109] This is stage three, *rubedo*, a movement from division to unification. The successful result from following these steps was the Philosophers' Stone—a completely distinct "third thing." Like a child born to a man and a woman, it was neither the one or the other, nor even simply a mixture of the two. Rather, it was "the Child of the Work," with its union of psychological, philosophical, and practical effects.

The stages of distillation, fermentation, and transmutation were physical methods determined by the Orphic myth of descent and reascent, a "natural supernaturalism."[110] The goal of such transmutation was to return oneself along with nature itself to the "androgynous" unity of the *prima materia* prior to separation into different (and therefore opposite) elements. "It seems clear," says Voss, that "the alchemical model appears to have been based on the 'myth of the eternal return,'" represented by the Hermetic symbol of the snake with its tail in its mouth.[111] She adds, "Ultimately, the alchemist discovers that the Child is his or her true Self."[112] It is "a form of gnosis," a return home to the beginning where one's deepest self has always been in spite of the forgetfulness and drowsiness of forgetful embodiment in the world of becoming.[113] We have already identified the subject-object fluidity in the relation of the human mind to the supreme god, but now it is extended to objects in the world.[114]

---

107. Levere, *Transforming Matter*, 5. Cf. Uždavinys, *Orpheus and the Roots of Platonism*, 58.
108. Voss, "Spiritual Alchemy," 158–59.
109. Voss, "Spiritual Alchemy," 154.
110. I borrow this phrase from Abrams, *Natural Supernaturalism*. It was originally coined by Samuel Taylor Coleridge.
111. Voss, "Spiritual Alchemy," 161–65.
112. Voss, "Spiritual Alchemy," 160–61.
113. Voss, "Spiritual Alchemy," 149.
114. Voss, "Spiritual Alchemy," 152.

Without the story that I have summarized thus far, alchemy would never have emerged in the Western world, as it had centuries earlier in China and elsewhere. However, these Platonic components could take the development only so far. For Platonists the vertical highway consisted of one lane running upward from beautiful things to Beauty itself; for Hermeticists the traffic moved in both directions. To be sure, the goal is ascent and assimilation to the One, but according to the Hermeticists, humans can only rise up to the gods if the gods come down to us. Further, the human being represented the "magnum miraculum" who, as the nexus between animal body and divine soul, was able to facilitate the otherwise harrowing reunion of souls with the One.

Triumph of Theurgic Neoplatonism

Since the soul sinks entirely into the angry waves of matter, Iamblichus insisted, we need divine encounters that touch us at our sensual, physical, and psychological level and lift the soul from danger. The infinite chasm between the One beyond being and knowing must be filled with divine mediators who can appear and speak to us, transform us into their divine likeness, reveal the future, and change mundane circumstances. Beginners, intermediates, and advanced adepts offer different sacrifices according to their movement from material to celestial to supracelestial gnosis. Physical symbols become spiritual technology—transmitters and even conductors that unite the Two Worlds. Damascius (458–538 CE), the last scholiarch of the Athenian school, explains:

> There are those who prefer philosophy, like Porphyry and Plotinus and many other philosophers, and those who prefer theurgy, like Iamblichus, Syrianus, Proclus and the rest of the hieratics. But Plato, realizing that strong arguments can be advanced from both sides, united them in a single truth by calling the philosopher a Bacchus [Dionysus]. For, if the man who has freed himself from generation were to stand in the middle, he would draw both ways to himself. And it is clear that Plato calls the philosopher a Bacchus in his desire to exalt him. (*In Plat. Phaed.* 1.172)[115]

Plotinus did not reject magic and theurgy in general (*Enn.* 4.4.40–44). However, he disdained the vulgar magic of salesmen and gnostics (2.9.1–18). Plotinus said

---

115. Translation quoted from Athanassiadi, *Damascius*, 57. Cited in Shaw, foreword to *Fragments of Numenius of Apamea*, i.

that the gods should come to him (Porphyry, *Vit. Plot.* 10.33–38). This is not because he was irreligious but because he was more divine than the cosmic gods, since his ruling daimon turned out to be a higher god.[116] He was a shaman par excellence. Here he would have been in accord with the Hermetic writers who followed the first treatise of the Corpus Hermeticum. Fowden reminds us, "The Hermetist's was a divinization neither public and official as that of the emperor, nor accorded in consequence of death as was increasingly the custom at this time regardless of social status. It was, rather, deeply private, and the reward of conscious effort—no mere rite of passage," the type of experience that Plotinus experienced several times.[117] Such experiences are in keeping with the idea of "the 'divine man' of late Platonism."[118] Once again, "spiritual, not religious" might be his self-identification at least as correlated with private rather than public religion.

For Plotinus, the soul's "glad release" from its mortal coil was definitely the goal, but he scorned the histrionic escapism of gnostics he encountered in his school and, with a few exceptions, treated the fascination with Greco-Egyptian theurgy in his native Alexandria with polite indifference. In this he was following Plato's Socrates. Plotinus was not a disbeliever in magic.[119] However, one only needed magic and ritual if one was bound to the body, while philosophy freed the soul on its upward journey.[120]

Attracted to theurgy early on, Plotinus's successor Porphyry drew back when he thought that his student Iamblichus had taken it too far. Plotinus acknowledged the novelty of his view of the soul as remaining above in its highest part. Iamblichus countered that all theurgy depends on the belief that the Soul descends entirely into the visible world and the individual soul into a body. The theurgist in his priestly capacity becomes the kind of god who can command the celestial deities. Thus, the theurgist is not blasphemously attacking, commanding, and binding superior gods, as Porphyry charged, but is operating in that higher world as a higher god over lesser deities. All souls are by definition immortal and

---

116. Fowden, *Egyptian Hermes*, 112.
117. E.g., *Enn.* 4.8.1 and Porphyry, *Vit. Plot.* 23.23–40.
118. Fowden, *Egyptian Hermes*, 111.
119. Plotinus, *Enn.* 3.4.3. See Helleman, "Plotinus and Magic," 129–31. Helleman notes, "Both Gnostic and Hermetic texts reveal a worldview characterized by considerable interest in astrology, recognizing limitations on the soul imposed by the planets and celestial entities who are regarded as malevolent" and humans partly of nature and partly divine (129–30). In the Corp. herm. 1, the call is for the soul to ascend from body/fate and to realize its unity with mind, as noted by Copenhaver, *Hermetica*, 288. In more mythical form, this is nevertheless quite close to Plotinus.
120. Plotinus, *Enn.* 5.8.8; cf. *Enn.* 3.2.16; 3.3.6; 4.4.33; 4.4.40; 4.4.43; 5.3.6.; 5.3.17. See also Porphyry, *Vit. Plot.* 10 and 16.2.

therefore deities in their own right. But some are malevolent. The soul is protected by a pneumatic vehicle or astral body (*ochēma*) that it leaves behind after succedding in its harrowing ascent. Harassing the living, some souls in fact are trapped in the sublunar world—"one which has left behind the shell-like earthly body, but which still wanders about in the realms of generation mounted upon a murky and damp pneumatic vehicle" (Iamblichus, *De myst.* 4.13).[121]

Plotinus and Porphyry agreed that "the many," still trapped in the sea of matter, need a theurgic boost, but the philosopher keeps his highest part (the "flower of intellect") above the raging waves. To the contrary, Iamblichus insisted that everyone's soul is completely descended and therefore requires theurgic rescue operations. "Nor do the theurgists 'pester the divine intellect about small matter,'" as Porphyry alleged, "but about matters pertaining to the purification, liberation and salvation of the soul."[122]

Shaw overestimates the return to original Platonism in Iamblichus. We find nothing like Iamblichus's theurgy in Plato's dialogues. On the contrary, Plato was convinced that Dionysian and Orphic cults did not go far enough in demythologizing. We have seen that the Orphic tradition represented by Plato borrowed heavily from the Eleusinian and Dionysian mysteries but, with Dionysus now reconciled to Apollo, transmuted myths and rituals into the gold of philosophical concepts. Proclus presented the best case yet for interpreting Plato as a theurgist, but theurgic Neoplatonists were actually much closer to the *orpheotelestai* criticized by Plato and the author of the Derveni Papyrus.

Furthermore, the idealist ontology of the *Republic* does not allow for genuine theurgy. At no point can the One and its reflection intersect. A statue of Aphrodite may stand for the goddess and remind us to contemplate her beauty, but she does not descend to the statue to occupy it. Soul gives birth to souls but she would never become a soul. Just as the visible realm takes on the character of a prison in book 7, an artist in book 10 is more than a nuisance; the artist is a "creator of appearances" and "what he creates is untrue," a "semblance of existence" and an "imitation thrice removed from the truth." God creates the carpenter, the carpenter creates the bed, and the painter creates the picture of a bed. However, there can be only one true bed, and that is its form. Thus, the better the artist is, the greater the deception he creates. While the *Symposium* suggests a more positive view of beautiful things being able to raise our minds to Beauty itself (209c–210e), appearances are never the reality. "Nor will the beautiful appear to him in the guise

---

121. Besides *De myst.*4.13, Iamblichus discusses this soul-vehicle in 2.4; 2.7; 3.11; cf. Plato, *Phaedr.* 81b–d.

122. Iamblichus, *De myst.* 10.7–8.

of a face or hands or anything else that belongs to the body" (*Symp.* 211a–b). True religion or piety is inward, not outward; it is mystical and does not tie our soul down to even more sensible things.

Plotinus does faithfully represent the allegorization of the Orphic myth, and Iamblichus turned to public religion—in this case, Egyptian (and Syrian) "magic"—against what he regarded as Greek novelties and eclecticism. The founder of theurgic Neoplatonism would have agreed with the minority report in the Hermetic corpus: "For the Greeks have empty speeches, O king, that are energetic only in what they demonstrate [prove], and this is the philosophy of the Greeks, an inane foolosophy of speeches. We, by contrast, use not speeches but sounds that are full of action" (Corp. herm. 16.1–2).[123] Never mind who was right, Iamblichus's brief was adopted wholesale by almost all Neoplatonists until the schools were closed.

Insisting against Plotinus and Porphyry that the soul has sunk completely into matter, Iamblichus taught that the divine self must use certain physical materials, formulas, and words in overtly religious rites to attract the gods. The Chaldean Oracles, supposedly produced in a trance by Julian the Theurgist, were thoroughly bound up with this very conviction. Everyone needs theurgy and not just theology; ritual actions involve material media and not just contemplation informed by logical argument; the descending work of the gods is necessary beyond just the soul's effort of ascent.[124] No one needs theurgy more than the theurgist, who becomes a god through the rites. The goal was as Orphic as ever—the salvation of the soul from the body—but was now achieved through material substances and bodily actions.

Contra Shaw, theurgic Neoplatonism is not the womb of an "incarnational metaphysics" that provides a more sophisticated justification for Christianity. Whatever material media are involved in this process, the goal remains firmly grounded in the Orphic eschatology: saving the soul *from* the body and the visible world. The art of making gods (i.e., enlivened statues) is but a means to that end. Against any charge of materialism, Iamblichus says, "For it ignores the fact that the offering of sacrifices by means of fire is actually such as to *consume and annihilate matter*, . . . elevating it towards the divine and heavenly and immaterial fire, instead of being weighed downwards towards matter and the realm of generation" (*De myst.* 5.11).

---

123. Copenhaver, *Hermetica*, 72–73.

124. In Nietzsche's categorization, Plotinian Neoplatonism is Apollonian while theurgic Neoplatonism is Dionysian. In fact, given the attraction of these later Neoplatonists to the ritualism of the "original" Orphic cult, the comparison is apt.

Not surprisingly, theurgic Neoplatonism was quite popular in its appeal. Stressing ritual over doctrine and promising members the epiphany of rescuing gods in their own world of sense, it placed more demands on the expert in spiritual technology than on the initiates. It could also tolerate and even encourage the incorporation of one's preferred religious background insofar as it could be interpreted according to the Orphic myth. Philosophy could be wedded to the Serapis cult (conveyed to Iamblichus mainly by reading Chaeremon) and the Magical Papyri. The teachings of Pythagoras and Plato were complemented by the Chaldean Oracles and Orphic Hymns. The Orphic Rhapsodies, soon appended to the Neoplatonist canon, contributed to this spiritual intensity. As Majercik observes, "Chaldean notions are also found in the writings of such Platonizing Christians as Arnobius of Sicca (c. 253–327 C.E.), Marius Victorinus (c. 280–363 C.E.), and Synesius of Cyrene (c. 370–413 C.E.)." In fact, the eleventh-century philosopher Michael Psellos preserved many extant fragments in several commentaries on the Oracles.[125]

Yet, as Iamblichus states at the beginning of *On the Mysteries*, Hermes Trismegistus is the fountain of it all (*De myst.* 1.1). Late Neoplatonists found their psychopomp for comprehending all the mysteries of Egypt, Orpheus, Zoroastrian magi, and Indian gymnosophists. Ever since, this "perennial philosophy" has cast a spell across the cultural memory of the West.

Yet it seems that every revival of natural supernaturalism is accompanied (even justified) by the lament for the gods, a doleful nostalgia for the perennial tradition that nourished our enchanted ancestors. Following in the train of earlier prophecies, the lament for Egypt in the Heremetic Asclepius warns of a day when Egypt, "the temple of the whole world," will be desecrated and, "All their holy worship will be disappointed and perish without effect, for divinity will return from earth to heaven and Egypt will be abandoned" (Corp. herm. Ascl. 23–24).[126] After prophesying cosmic, social, and political catastrophes in the near future, Asclepius laments, "how mournful when the gods withdraw from mankind! ... Such will be the old age of the world" (Corp. herm. Ascl. 25–26). It would be like the era before Thoth-Hermes organized civilization under true religion. There is a similar description in Corp. herm. 18 that suggests a provenance during the transition from imperial Rome to Byzantine Egypt.

The lament for the gods—the cry of disenchantment—becomes a familiar refrain, as we will see, down through the modern age, and it is always the justi-

---

125. Majercik, introduction to the *Chaldean Oracles*, 3.
126. The "lament for Egypt" in the Asclepius belongs to a long line of Egyptian apocalypses from the Prophecy of Neferti (1991–1962 BCE), to the Potter's Oracle (third century BCE) and the Oracle of the Lamb (27 BCE–14 CE).

Chapter 6

fication for a new mythology. While eschewing gnostic pessimism and the doctrinal and ethical rigors of Jewish and Christian orthodoxy, Hermeticism privileged theurgy over theology, offering spirituality without religion, experience without dogma, rituals without an institutional authority, a cult without temples.[127] We turn now to the most extreme exit-strategy that evolved in the milieu of Alexandrian Orphism.

---

127. Fowden, *Egyptian Hermes*, 160: "There was no institutional structure to provide formal limits and sanctions—all depended on the personal authority of the teacher. Likewise there was no fixed body of doctrine, and both the manner and content of instruction will have varied widely, to an even greater extent than is reflected in the surviving texts." There is no reason not to imagine that beginners (astrology, alchemy, etc.) sat with adepts for instruction together.

7

Savior *of* or *from* the World?
Christianity and Gnosis

> Rabbi, how shall I attain to the One Who Is, since all these powers and hosts are armed against me?
>
> —First Revelation of James, NHC V 25.10[1]

> When we look back to our example of "evil interpretation," we can see that Irenaeus' characterization, however hostile, nevertheless is accurate. Those who wrote and treasured innovative works like the Gospel of Truth, the Round Dance of the Cross, the Secret Book of John, and the Gospel of Philip were implicitly criticizing, intentionally or not, the faith of most Christians.
>
> —Elaine Pagels[2]

> Perhaps the hate of this school for the corporeal is due to their reading of Plato.
>
> —Plotinus, *Enn.* 2.9.17[3]

Neither the Hebrew prophets nor the New Testament authors sanctify the present order in a locative environment. But it is not the world as such that is evil, since God created and governs it, became incarnate in it, and will return

---

1. Translation by Funk in Meyer, *Nag Hammadi Scriptures*. James is asking Jesus this question in this apocryphal conversation.
2. Pagels, *Beyond Belief*, 138.
3. Translation of the *Enneads* in this chapter from Plotinus, *Enneads* (trans. MacKenna).

to release it from the curse brought upon it by human transgression. This plotline is hardly utopian either, at least according to Smith's definition. The body and the visible world are saved and not escaped. God acts in history instead of calling people out of it. Instead of two worlds, Second Temple Judaism spoke of two ages: "this age" of oppression and death and "the age to come" under the reign of the messiah.[4] These categories are invoked frequently in the New Testament.[5]

Orphism is wholly vertical in its lower to higher orientation: the particulars of historical time to the eternity of universal ideas, corporeal to incorporeal, visible to invisible, division to unity. The Bible moves from promise to fulfillment, charged along the way by God's intervention.

Nevertheless, Judaism and Christianity are given the same allegorizing gloss that Plutarch applied to Egyptian religion. Previously, we saw Philo of Alexandria show how to interpret "the Mosaic philosophy" in an Orphic frame. Some Jewish and Christian teachers later pressed this further. If the utopian sees the visible world and the body as a prison of the divine soul, gnostics represented the furthest extent to which Orphic theosophy could be taken.

Today, the term "Gnosticism" faces the same criticism as the term "Orphism," and for similar reasons. There was no united gnostic religion or church until Manichaeism in the third century. Early Christian opponents referred to specific groups, such as the Valentinians, which were usually formed around a charismatic leader. Ancient Christians even underscored the fissiparous character of the movement. Nevertheless, they recognized affinities shared by these groups that were sufficient to go by the broad label "heresy." Gnostic groups shared fundamental doctrines which, as Plotinus's critique of "the gnostics" shows, suggest that Gnosticism was a Platonic heresy rather than a Christian one, adopting Platonism's allegorical interpretation of myth, radicalizing its contempt for the body, and seeking salvation through a mystical ascent to gnosis: the ostensibly intuitive recognition that God and the individual self are one. Gnostics used the documents now referred to as the Old and New Testaments only as raw material to be allegorized or bowdlerized for teaching a new version of the Orphic way.

Gnostics shared the widespread fear of sinister foes in the heavens as well as on earth. Indeed, they were the most extreme both in their evaluation of the threat and in their escape plan. Throughout the nineteenth and early twentieth centuries learned treatises linked the movement to Iranian/Mesopotamian syn-

---

4. See D. Russell, *Jewish Apocalyptic*, esp. 269; cf. Rowland, *Open Heaven*, esp. 355.

5. For example, they are used by Jesus in the Gospels (Matt 12:32; 13:49; 19:28; 24:3; Mark 4:19; 8:38; 10:30; Luke 18:30; 20:35) and frequently employed in the Pauline Epistles (1 Cor 2:6; 10:11; Eph 1:21; Gal 1:4; 1 Tim 6:19) and Heb 6:5.

cretism (Wilhelm Bousset), Zoroastrianism (R. A. Reitzenstein), and Palestinian/Samaritan gnosis (G. Scholem, K. Rudolph, C. G. Häberl).[6] Attempts have been made even to connect it with Mahayana Buddhism.[7] M. E. Amélineau judged that it was a "soufflé de l'ancienne Égypte."[8] A trend in more recent scholarship has seen these groups in closer connection with Judaism and Christianity.[9] However, these groups referred to as *gnostic* originated in second- and third-century Alexandria, which is where we should expect to see such a harlequin costume patched together from pieces of fabric close to hand. With the collapse of the Old Kingdom there had been a growing spiritual restlessness and anxiety, with the Prophecies of Neferit foretelling a time of turmoil and war. It is the same lament that we find later in Alexandria, with the Potter's Oracle and the Hermetic Asclepius. It is the familiar cry of disenchantment provoking a reenchantment from another quarter.

Gnosis is a uniquely Alexandrian "soufflé" indeed, which means that distinctively Jewish and Christian ingredients are mostly garnishes. Whatever the

---

6. On Zoroastrian influence, see Reitzenstein, *Das iranische Erlösungsmysterium*; Reitzenstein, "Iranischer Erlösungsglaube." For a superb and nuanced critique, see Barr, "Question of Religious Influence." This view is represented by Gershom Scholem, Gilles Quispel, and Robert Grant, among others. Scholem, however, does not believe that all Gnosticism originated in Judaism, but only an important branch that survived in kabbalah. See below for fuller details on this point. A brilliant argument is made by G. Quispel in "Hermes Trismegistus." In the book of Ezekiel, the "Son of Man" is identified with the glory of God. Two centuries before Christ, the Jewish dramatist Ezekiel Tragicus called this glory *phōs* (Light) and identified it with the heavenly/ideal human (*'ādām qadmôn*). This is none other than the "Son of Man" in gnostic literature as well, Quispel argues.

7. See Conze, "Buddhism and Gnosis"; Conze, "Buddhist Prajna and Greek Sophia." Pagels sees Buddhist influence as a "possibility" in *Gnostic Gospels*, xx, but this connection lacks scholarly support.

8. Amélineau, *Essai sur le gnosticisme égyptien*, 10. With better success, Douglas M. Parrott makes firm connections in "Gnosticism and Egyptian Religion."

9. Betz, "Orthodoxy and Heresy," 306. For more recent examples see Turner, *Pattern of Christian Truth*, 57–59. See also the example of "The Preaching of Peter" adduced by Pearson, *Gnosticism and Christianity*, 16–18. Other examples include Meyer, "Gospel of Thomas," 137–38. Meyer states confidently, "The textual evidence for an early date for the Gospel of Thomas thus may rival that of any of the New Testament gospels" (138). Among supporters of his thesis are Koester, *Ancient Christian Gospels*; Meyer, *Gospel of Thomas*; Pagels, *Beyond Belief*; Ehrman, *Lost Scriptures*. For a good summary and rebuttal of the Bauer thesis, see Köstenberger and Kruger, *Heresy of Orthodoxy*. To a large extent, this trend follows Walter Bauer's hypothesis that heresy preceded orthodoxy or claims that these categories did not exist until later centuries. Either way, Bauer's idea is that there were many early Christianities and gnostics represented one party among others until polemical "heresiologists" claimed to speak for the whole movement. Much of what I have to say in the second half of this chapter challenges this account.

Chapter 7

original recipe, the culinary alchemists of the "Platonic underworld" could transmute any foreign dish into merely another course of an Orphic feast.[10] In any case, over the successive occupations by Babylonian, Persian, and Greek empires, Egypt knew how to absorb a variety of cults. In addition, the multicultural society generated by international trade and the attraction of the brightest minds to its academic world made Alexandria rather than Athens the intellectual capital. All of this means that by the time Valentinus arrived on the scene most of the influences mentioned above had been blended. Reading the Corpus Hermeticum, the Chaldean Oracles, and the Orphic Hymns and Rhapsodies prepares us to approach the gnostic literature in a way that reading the Bible does not. Alexandria was where the civilizations involved in the shift to utopian philosophies met.

Sethian and Valentinian Gnosis

J. P. Kenney's verdict on the Valentinian Tripartite Tractate could apply to other gnostic writings: "A cursory reading of its admittedly rather rococo ontology might suggest to an austere student of philosophical theology that there has been a riot in Plato's cave."[11] Here we will focus on two main currents of gnostic thought and then compare for family resemblances.

Sethian Gnosis

Sethian Gnosticism originated in a Jewish milieu. Philo of Alexandria (25 BCE–50 CE) provided a template for assimilating the historical narrative of the Bible to the Orphic metaphysics of ascent. Promises were allegorized and oriented toward individual ascent. In contrast with the "this-worldly" vision of the prophets, 1 Enoch is oriented to "otherworldly journeys and a good deal of cosmological speculation," with Babylonian lore mixed in.[12] After the destruction of the Jewish temple there was a profusion of mystical texts from Hellenistic Judaism (e.g., 4 Ezra, 2 Baruch, Apocalypse of Abraham).[13] Christians had no trouble with

---

10. "Platonic underworld" is John Dillon's famous epithet from *Middle Platonists*, 384–96.
11. Kenney, "Platonism of the *Tripartite Tractate*," 204.
12. Collins, *Apocalyptic Imagination*, 30.
13. See Collins, *Apocalyptic Imagination*; cf. Grant, *Gnosticism and Early Christianity*, 31–34. It does not seem to me that the Essenes were influenced by Hellenistic asceticism but rather by a strong antipathy toward the Jerusalem cult based on the apocalypticism of the Hebrew

this cataclysmic event, since they believed it was predicted by Jesus, who had replaced the temple, but without land and temple individual devotions replaced ritual sacrifices.[14]

In the Jewish phase, Turner says, one phase of Sethianism "conceptualizes the means of salvation as a horizontal, temporally successive sequence of revelatory descents into the world by a heavenly savior," while a second, more Platonizing set teaches "a vertically oriented ascent by which a visionary practitioner enters a succession of mental states in which one is cognitively assimilated to ever higher levels of being (and those above being itself)."[15] Texts such as Zostrianos, Allogenes the Stranger, and Marsanes belong to the second Platonizing phase, distinguished by the prominence of the figure of Zoroaster, and were composed in the late third and early fourth centuries in Alexandria.[16]

Allogenes the Stranger (NHC IX 3) exchanges biblical allusions for central Orphic ascent revelations in Plato's dialogues.[17] The sequence of ascending stages in Allogenes is represented in terms of "a graded series of mental insights cul-

---

prophets. However, we should bear in mind Philo's predestruction tribute to the mystical Jewish Therapeutae near Alexandria as a source for his allegorical exegesis.

14. Levenson, *Sinai and Zion*, 180; cf. Levenson, "Temple and the World."

15. Turner, "Sethian School of Gnostic Thought," 787. The first phase is represented by the Secret Book of John, Revelation of Adam, Three Forms of First Thought, the Gospel of Judas, and perhaps Nature of the Rulers. The second phase is represented by Zostrianos, Allogenes the Stranger, Three Steles of Seth, and Marsanes.

16. Turner, "Zostrianos," in Meyer, *Nag Hammadi Scriptures*, 550–51. These three treatises are mentioned by Plotinus and Porphyry in their critiques. It is interesting how Porphyry distinguishes the groups in *Vit. Plot.* 16: "There were in [Plotinus'] time many Christians and others, and sectarians [*hairetikoi*] who had abandoned the old Philosophy (i.e., Platonism), men of the schools of Adelphius and Aculinus, who possessed a great many treatises of Alexander the Libyan and Philocomus and Demostratus and Lydus, and produced apocalypses by Zoroaster and Zostrianos and Nicotheos and Allogenes and Messus and other people of the kind, deceived themselves and deceiving many, alleging that Plato had not penetrated into the depths of intelligible reality." Translation of Plotinus, *Enneads*, from Armstrong, LCL.

17. For example, Turner refers to "that of Diotima concerning the ascent to the vision of absolute Beauty in the *Symposium* 201d–212a, the parable of the cave in *Republic* VII 514–517a, and the revelation of Er in the *Republic* X 614b–621b." See Turner, introduction to "Allogenes the Stranger" in *Nag Hammadi Scriptures*, 682. Turner adds, "All four clearly share a metaphysics and ontological doctrine characteristic of Plotinus and later Neoplatonists as well as of certain Middle Platonic sources, such as the fragments of Numenius, the *Chaldaean Oracles*, and especially an anonymous *Parmenides Commentary* (which may be pre-Plotinian, even though Pierre Hadot originally ascribed it to Plotinus's disciple Porphyry)." See also Hadot, "Être, vie, pensée chez Plotin." Instead of the Sophia myth (prominent, we will see, in other texts), Turner notes, we find the typical psychology found in the *Phaedo*, the physics of the *Timaeus*, and the negative

minating in a mystical union with the supreme Unknown One, characterized as non-knowing knowledge, thus offering one of the earliest known examples of the doctrine of 'learned ignorance.'"[18] Nicola Denzey Lewis adds, "In fact, *Allogenes* is not really an ascent text at all but a sort of inward journey through various stages of ecstatic contemplation and interiority."[19] The same could be said of Plotinus's use of Heraclitus's dictum: "the way up is the way in."[20]

In its return, the soul progresses from Autogenes (sequential discursive thought) to Protophanes (simultaneous union of knowing subject and known object) and finally to Kalyptos (a direct and intuitive gnosis of absolute being). This noetic ascent bypasses completely the harrowing voyage of the soul past ominous guardians. One only attains contemplation of the Triple Power (Father, Mother, Child) "by transcending intellect altogether by a sudden flash of insight or revelation, which *Allogenes the Stranger* characterizes as a nonknowing knowledge." This is not new but is rooted in "a contemplative Platonism that takes its start in Plato's *Symposium* and leads directly to Plotinus."[21] The ascent in the Platonic Zostrianos (NHC VIII 1) is individualistic, with the "angel of light" giving him a tour of the heavenly ideas.

The work Marsanes (NHC X) is named after the prophet-mystic who, in this text, seeks to establish by way of a direct revelation his authority as the leader of a particular group of theurgic Sethians.[22] There is considerable overlap in this text with Hermeticism, including its emphasis on astral powers (zodiac), angelology,

---

theology of the *Parmenides*. Allogenes seems much less susceptible to Plotinus's criticisms (*Enn.* 2.9; cf. 3.8; 5.5; 5.8) and it may in fact be a response (683).

18. Turner, introduction to "Allogenes the Stranger" in *Nag Hammadi Scriptures*, 683. However, this "learned ignorance" is the final stage of ascent (viz., union) in the Orphic tradition generally (e.g., Pythagoras, Empedocles, Plato).

19. Denzey Lewis, *Introduction to "Gnosticism,"* 253. Denzey Lewis observes, "There is no return journey given."

20. An essay by Hans-Georg Gadamer sheds considerable insight on the use of Heraclitus by Plotinus, especially the interiorization of the statement that "the way up is the way down." See Gadamer, "Heraclitus Studies."

21. Turner, "Zostrianos," 544. See also Eliade, *Shamanism*, 487–94, on the symbol of the ladder: "We have seen countless examples of shamanic ascent to the sky by means of a ladder.... In their funerary texts the Egyptians preserved the expression *asken pet* (*asken* = step) to show that the ladder furnished them by Râ to mount into the sky is a real ladder. 'I set up a ladder to heaven among the gods,' says the Book of the Dead" (487). Eliade also writes on 487–88, "An ascent to heaven by ceremonially climbing a ladder probably formed part of the Orphic initiation," referencing A. B. Cook, *Zeus*, 2.1:124, and Guthrie, *Orpheus and Greek Religion*, 208.

22. Turner, "Marsanes," 629.

numerology and the letters of the Greek alphabet with their combinations, as well as images and emerald stones.[23] Given this association, it is not surprising that Marsanes is the only gnostic text to suggest that the sensible world is worth saving (5.17–6.1) and, unlike the other two Platonizing Sethian treatises, it assumes a less individualistic, more communal, context.[24] Zostrianos and Allogenes the Stranger seem to be seeking rapprochement with Plotinus and his circle, emphasizing individual ascent through contemplation, while Marsanes seems to take the side of Iamblichus with a more communal and ritualistic theurgy.

Like many gnostics, Sethians gave innovative interpretations of biblical passages while nevertheless attacking the whole tenor of biblical teaching. According to Gen 4:25, Seth was the third son of Adam and Eve, "another offspring" given to replace slain Abel. The straightforward interpretation is that God gave a replacement heir. The gnostics interpreted Seth as another kind of being—spiritual, not physical. Seth was the true seed of the *heavenly* Adam and Eve (Sophia).[25] Adam tells Seth that he is "the only child of Adam to have inherited the divine spark of knowledge and thus to have the possibility of returning to his heavenly home above."[26] The soul of this spiritual seed will at last escape "the prison of the body."[27] God's elect, the seed of Seth, are saved by recognizing their unity with the One.

At the most Platonizing end of Sethianism, represented in Zostrianos, we can hardly distinguish their noetic "baptism" from the Hermetic new birth, ascending through the aeons with each realm having its own baptism until, with the fourth, Zostrianos becomes "a perfect angel" (Zost. 1.1–2.24; 4.20–129; 7.22–

---

23. Turner, "Marsanes," 632–33. Turner adds, "This theurgic material, which is reminiscent of the second-century teaching of Marcus the Magician (Irenaeus, *Against Heresies* 1.21) and more distantly of Iamblichus's disciple Theodore of Asine in the early fourth century, focuses on the nature of the soul, both individual and cosmic, the nature of the astral powers that affect the soul, and the means by which the Sethian adept might manipulate these powers to his or her advantage by utilizing the appropriate nomenclature for these realities."

24. Turner, "Marsanes," 633.

25. In the Secret Book of John, Cain and Abel are the offspring of Ialdabaoth by the rape of Eve; in the Nature of the Rulers, Cain is the unfortunate child of the evil creator, but Abel is, along with Seth, the offspring of Adam. In both, however, Seth is distinguished as the true likeness of heavenly Adam.

26. Scopello, "Revelation of Adam," 343.

27. Ap. John 25.16–30.11. All translations of the Secret Book of John, unless otherwise noted, from Meyer, *Nag Hammadi Scriptures*. The NHC III recension of the Secret Book of John is not only longer than the other versions (NHC I, II and BG 2) but includes more detail on Christ ministering to spirits in the prison of this lower world belonging to Sakla.

8.7).²⁸ But then he seeks the ultimate and single reality underlying the self-generated aeons. "For then this type is saved who can pass through them all; he becomes them all. Whenever he wishes, he again parts from all these matters and withdraws into himself; for he becomes divine, having withdrawn into god" (Zost. 7.22–8.7; 42.6–19).²⁹

In Christian baptism one is cleansed from the defilement of sin and death and not of embodiment. Denzey Lewis concludes that "unlike Christian baptism, this rite apparently took place only in the celestial realm."³⁰ For gnostics, baptism is essentially a synonym for gnosis and a recognition of one's inner divinity (Ap. John 31.3–25). Like theurgic Neoplatonists, gnostics saw this as a way to "manipulate the cosmic powers."³¹

Valentinian Gnosis

Valentinian Gnosticism displays little connection to Jewish traditions and therefore less animosity. Valentinian myths diverge from Sethian mostly in the names of the key players rather than their identities or roles in the cosmological process. Unlike the Sethians, this sect did not go through stages from Judaism to Christianity to a purely philosophical vision. Rather, Valentinus was at first a respected Christian presbyter in Rome who, in addition to his public ministry, began to hold private seminars. Einar Thomassen explains, "Characteristic of the Valentinian vision is that the Christian message of salvation is explained by means of the opposition between spirit and matter, an opposition that in turn is derived from the even more basic polarity of oneness and plurality."³² And yet the unknowable forefather, also called Depth (*bythos*), is above all opposition, guaranteeing the triumph of monism.

Like the Sethian elect, the "spiritual" members of humanity in Valentianism are saved because of their inner divinity. Part two of the Valentinian Tripartite Tractate (NHC I 5) begins with the frequent trope of "those on the right" and "those on the left," which alludes to Matthew 25. In the Valentinian version, the final judgment is actually an eternal truth about the nature of souls before their

---

28. Translation of Zostrianos, unless otherwise noted, by Turner in Meyer, *Nag Hammadi Scriptures*.

29. Even if water was involved, it has been transcended by a purely mystical ascent. See Turner, "Zostrianos," 537.

30. Densey Lewis, *Introduction to "Gnosticism,"* 127.

31. Brakke, *Gnostics*, 82.

32. Thomassen, "Valentinian School of Gnostic Thought," 791.

descent into a body (Tri. Trac. 75.17–76.23; 104.4–18).[33] Though less polemical than most gnostic writings, the Tripartite Tractate retains the characteristic antipathy toward the material world.

For the Valentinians as much as for the Sethians, the essence of the fall is the "ignorance of oneself and of that which is." Therefore, sin is ontological rather than the consequence of moral transgression. Although the spirits of the perfect are destined for salvation, they must endure the purgative and dangerous ascent that we have encountered before. The soul may attain out-of-body experiences, but it also still experiences further reincarnations.[34] Reflecting the Alexandrian environment, gnostic archons (rulers) are daimons that harass souls on their flight.[35] Evil therefore is not only essential to the terrestrial realm, as Plato held, but fills the celestial realm.[36] Sethians differed from this cosmology only by correlating the menacing archons (planets and stars) with Hebrew prophets.

FAMILY RESEMBLANCES

It was indeed the era of "philosophy from oracles," as Porphyry's title suggests. Like Hermes Trismegistus, the gnostic Jesus is the common thread. Yet each gnostic group adopted its own psychopomp—Peter, Paul, John, Judas, Mary Magdalene, James, Zostrianos/Zoroaster, or Thomas—as the unique recipient of secrets. The

---

33. Translation of the Tripartite Tractate, unless otherwise noted, from Thomassen in Meyer, *Nag Hammadi Scriptures*.

34. E.g., Apoc. Paul 20.25–21.22; cf. 19.5–7. See Scopello, "Revelation of Paul," 314–16. As she writes on 316: "The depiction of the gatekeeper who guards this heavenly sphere brings to mind passages in the *First Revelation to James* (33,2–27) and Origen's *Against Celsus* (7.31.40) as well as Mandaean literature (*Left Ginza* 3.70)." The flight of the alone to the Alone is fraught with peril and requires passwords. "The three questions of the old man" in the Revelation of Paul "recall the three questions about Gnostic destiny in *Excerpts from Theodotus* 78, transmitted by Clement of Alexandria: 'Where have I come from? Where am I? Where shall I go?'"

35. See Greenbaum, *Daimon in Hellenistic Astrology*, 165. Cf. Burkitt, *Church and Gnosis*, 43. Burkitt adds a noteworthy aside: "It will be noticed that the Pairs are very much like the Hegelian Thesis and Antithesis that between them bring forth a Synthesis. In other words, the Valentinian heavenly hierarchy, know as the Pleroma, is not in essence Mythology but Philosophy." He also points out on pages 42–43 (along with a host of modern interpreters, especially Carl Jüng) that the original *bythos*, the hidden deep that produced the first thought out of itself, corresponds in many ways to the subliminal self as conceived by some modern psychologists."

36. Valentinian references are found in Exeg. Soul 132.2–133.10; Tri. Trac. 93.1; 122.15–17, 21; 128.33; 138.11 and especially Gos. Phil. 65.1–26; 67.1–70.4; 70.9–71.15; 72.17–23; 74.12–24; 76.1–5; 81.34–82.26; 84.14–86.18.

Testimony of Truth (NHC IX 3) may have upbraided Valentinians, Basilidians, and Simonians, but its basic emphases are the same, such as the malicious folly of the biblical creator and the serpent in the garden as the enlightening symbol of Christ.[37] The following beliefs are common among most gnostic groups:

1. *The true God is unknowable and beyond the hierarchy of being and yet identical to one's deepest self.* The paradox of hypertranscendence and hyperimmanence lies at the heart of most mysticism and particularly Orphic-inspired spirituality.[38] The phrase "God is no name and all names" we have met repeatedly in the Hermetic treatises. As Patricia Cox Miller puts it, "That there is a flow at the heart of things, rather than a creator set over against a thing created, seems to be the guiding insight of *On the Origin of the World*."[39] Across the gnostic texts, emanation is the metaphysical stream that pulls theology, Christology, soteriology, ecclesiology, and eschatology into its current. Its epistemological corollary is gnosis: the immediate, intuitive, inward vision of the truth that one has always been identical with God in his or her deepest self. Gnosis is not only a means of attaining salvation but *is* salvation.

"Over against the orthodox Jewish and Christian doctrine of the absolute distinction between God and creatures," notes Elaine Pagels, "Gnostics held that self-knowledge is a knowledge of God; the self and the divine are identical."[40] This could be said of the Orphic tradition generally, as in Celsus's statement: "Plato . . . points to the truth about the highest good when he says that it cannot be expressed in words, but rather comes from familiarity—like a flash from the blue, imprinting itself on the soul."[41] All learning is remembering, so gnosis (the

---

37. Testim. Truth 55.1–18; 56.1–57.8; 58.2–4. See Pearson, "Testimony of Truth," 613. On 614 he writes: "The author then excoriates his opponents for not understanding Christ 'spiritually' (49,10–50,3)." Heavily allegorical throughout, the Testmony of Truth is "based on Alexandrian Jewish (Philonic) and Christian precedents," with a Valentinian view of Christ, humanity, and the resurrection. Composed in Alexandria, the Testimony of Truth is mentioned by Clement of Alexandria (*Strom.* 3.86), so must date to the late second or early third century. Pearson surmises that the author may be Julius Cassianus (615).

38. The Teaching of Silvanus (NHC VII 4) stands midway between the gnostics and the more traditional Platonism of Clement and Origen: God is both hidden and revealed (Teach. Silv. 100.13–117.5). "For no one who wants to can know God as he is, not even Christ or the Spirit, or the chorus of angels, or the archangels." Yet in the next breath: "If you do not know yourself, you will not be able to know any of these." Translation of the Teaching of Silvanus from Pearson in Meyer, *Nag Hammadi Scriptures*, 520–21.

39. Miller, "Plenty Sleeps There," 231.

40. Pagels, introduction to *Gnostic Bible*, xx.

41. Celsus, *On the True Doctrine*, 91–92, from Plato, *Ep.* 341c.

highest kind of knowledge) is not acquired by diligent study or observation but in a sudden and unmediated blast like a flash of lightning. This is how the shaman knows things.

This trope of gnosis as a "flash" beyond discursive thought or observation runs through the various branches of the Orphic tree. Across the Sethian and Valentinian systems, supreme Mind is inaccessible to both the bodily senses and discursive reasoning but not to mystical ecstasy (Gos. Mary 10.1–10). In the Sethian Allogenes the Stranger and the Valentinian Tripartite Tractate alike, the Savior descends to reveal the truth "like a flash of lightning" (Tri. Trac. 89.4–5; 90.13). Those who eat of the "fruit of the Father's *gnosis*" discover the Father within themselves (Gos. Truth 18.25). This "flash" of gnosis characterizes the Hermetic treatises included in the gnostic library.[42] One either "gets it" or does not; the revelatory event cannot be articulated or defended.

Middle Platonists and Christians generally agreed that the essence of the One is incomprehensible, but gnostic writers tend to confuse ineffability with irrationality and treat the latter as proof of gnosis.[43] From the *Symposium* and the *Phaedrus* all the way to Plotinus and the entire Neoplatonic tradition, ecstasy (divine madness) was the final stage that occurred *after* dialogical recollection and contemplation. But the urgency of escape led gnostics to skip reasoning altogether: "Be filled with the spirit but lack in reason, for reason is of the soul," states Jesus in the Secret Book of James (3.38.46–47).[44] No justifications are offered, for these are oracles and not symposia.[45] Gnostics offer an extreme version of the Orphic-Platonic epistemology that characterizes Western rationality: an immediate mystical intuition that transcends not only sense observation but also reason and yet serves as the justification for all arguments.

2. *The Bible is by turns allegorized and rejected.* All the gnostic schools appeal to the Hebrew scriptures and the New Testament. The first Christians, who were Jewish, emphasized the *continuity* between these sets of writings through a promise-fulfillment hermeneutic.[46] Irenaeus later exhibited this approach in his opposition to Marcion and the Valentinians, ensuring that Christianity remained

---

42. See for example Disc. 8–9 58.5, 15, which was was probably attractive to Hermeticists and gnostics alike.

43. See Zost. 61.8–67.37: A divine figure tells Seth, "Do not [attempt to] comprehend it: for this is impossible. Rather if, through a luminous thought, you should happen to understand it, be uncomprehending of it" (60.8–10). Quoted in Brakke, *Gnostics*, 81.

44. Translation of the Secret Book of James by Meyer in Meyer, *Nag Hammadi Scriptures*, 25.

45. Burkitt, *Church and Gnosis*, 48.

46. Burkitt, *Church and Gnosis*, 138.

linked inextricably to the history of Israel. It is the God of Israel who has come to bring redemption to humanity, "to the Jew first and also to the Greek" (Rom 2:10; 1 Cor 1:24; Gal 3:28).

In contrast, gnostic engagement with the Old and New Testaments is characterized by allegorical reinvention and outright rejection. Pearson puts it plainly: "It is axiomatic that once Gnosticism is present Judaism has been abandoned."[47] Orphic emanation-and-return was the truth by which gnostics judged the scriptures, and whereever the Bible could not support this in a "riddling" way, it was rejected.

Herakleon, a disciple of Valentinus, wrote one of the earliest biblical commentaries on the Gospel of John. He approaches the narrative the way Plutarch interpreted the Isis-Osiris myth and Philo exegeted scripture.[48] Jesus going "down to Capernaum" (John 2:12) refers to "the material things to which he descended." Going up to Jerusalem (2:13–15) does not mean literally ascending the physical hill, but "signifies the ascent of the lord from material things to the psychical place, which is an image of Jerusalem" (*Comm. John* 11, 13).[49]

3. *The lower world was created by an inferior and evil ruler*. With the Chaldean Oracles, the Valentinians emphasized the importance of *hōros* (boundary). Sarah Iles Johnston observes that in the gnostic iteration, Sophia "intruded disastrously upon the previously transcendent Paternal Abyss." It is no wonder that intermediaries were called for in such an emergency.[50] Like the fall of the archetypal human, this could potentially be a happy mistake, an opportunity to discover one's divine origin. In common with the broader Orphic-Platonic tradition, the gnostics identified evil—the forgetfulness and fog—with being embodied. This presumed that there had to be a glitch down the line, a weak link in the chain, such as uncooperative matter or perhaps even the unstable World Soul that requires the demiurge's constant attention.[51] This unstable mother was identified as the gnostic Sophia who, in the Gospel of Truth, gives rise to evil by a foolish mistake: "forgetfulness" that "has no root," that is, comes from nowhere, matter as non-

---

47. Pearson, *Gnosticism, Judaism, and Egyptian Christianity*, 51. It is tempting to draw comparisons with German Higher Criticism from 1850 to 1950.

48. For Herakleon's *Commentary on the Gospel of John*, see Barnstone and Meyer, *Gnostic Bible*, 307–25. Translations of Herakleon from this source unless otherwise stated.

49. See also the Gos. Truth 31.35–32.37.

50. Johnston, *Hekate Soteira*, 71–72.

51. As I have noted from Plato, *Pol.* 269d, and other late dialogues, especially the tenth book of the *Laws*.

being.⁵² As we have seen, the fear of Sophia (the World Soul or Dyad) losing her gaze upon the demiurgic Intellect grew intense in Middle Platonism (especially Neopythagoreanism), with considerable grounding in Plato's latest work.

4. *Higher and lower Christs.* Gnostics curved the historical events of Jesus's incarnation, crucifixion, resurrection, bodily ascent, and return at the end of the age into a circle of Orphic descent-and-return. Christ is God incarnate, Col 2:9 explains, "For in him the whole fullness [*plērōma*] of deity dwells bodily." Instead, Valentinians regarded the *plērōma* as a hypostasis containing all the divine beings—much like the Neoplatonic Intellect constituted by all the forms. It is from this *plērōma* that souls have fallen and to which they seek to return. Herakleon interprets the title "Son of Man" without any of its apocalyptic resonances from Ezekiel and Daniel. Instead, he takes it to refer to Jesus's humanity that the disciples mistook for the real Christ. In almost every case, the rejection of a canonical passage is bound up with the contrast between the historical Jesus (matter) and the Christ of gnosis (spirit).⁵³

The author of the Gospel of Judas prefers a Jesus who saves from within by enlightening our own inner divinity. The outer Christ is of no value; it is the Christ within we must follow. In his farewell in the Gospel of Mary, Jesus says, "For the Son of Man exists within you. Follow it" (Gos. Mary 8.11–9.5).⁵⁴ In another text the apostle Paul is made to pray, "I have come from you. You are my mind" (Pr. Paul A.5). He prays for release from his body: "and redeem my eternal enlightened soul and my spirit"—that which was not "made in the image of the animate [soulish] God" (i.e., the demiurge; Pr. Paul A.24, 30).⁵⁵ Jesus is not the creator God in human flesh but the fruit of saving gnosis that the evil creator forbade to Adam and Eve (Gos. Truth 18.11–19.17).⁵⁶ Consequently, far from being the savior *of* the world, the gnostic Jesus by inner enlightenment saves initiates *from* it.

5. *Higher and lower sacraments and churches.* The ontological chasm between spirit and matter extends to rites. In addition to the myriad entities that make up the divine *plērōma* (Fullness), each of these entities has a higher and lower

---

52. This idea is present through the Gospel of Truth and Paraph. Shem 1.16–2.19.

53. According to the Gospel of Philip, "The master said to the disciples, 'Take something from every house and bring it to the Father's house, but do not steal while in the Father's house and take something away" (55.37–56.3). Translation of Gospel of Philip taken from Meyer, *Nag Hammadi Scriptures*. It is the exact opposite instruction that Jesus gives in Luke 9:3–6.

54. Translation from King in Meyer, *Nag Hammadi Scriptures*.

55. From Meyer, *The Nag Hammadi Scriptures*, 17–18. Translations of the Prayer of the Apostle Paul are from this source unless otherwise noted.

56. See the thorough investigation of this work by Gathercole, *Gospel of Judas*.

doppelganger, called a syzygy. The Sethian Five Seals and the Valentinian Bridal Chamber contained initiations that promised to "transform the soul into a 'light being' so that it could not be seen by the celestial demons," as Denzey Lewis explains, giving the soul "celestial passwords" learned in the initiation. Such "ascent formulae" are part of gnosis here and especially in Pistis Sophia and the Books of Jehu, which almost certainly reflect Christian transformation of Egyptian books of the dead.[57] Similar to those found in Bacchic-Orphic tombs, these passwords are the core of some gnostic texts.[58] A Valentinian pastor or bishop would give these passwords to the dying as a form of last rites.[59] Surviving the postmortem journey, not earthly persecution, was the focus of Jesus's instruction to James.[60] Whatever such rites meant, they were external object lessons for an inner truth that is true eternally. At most, bodily rites triggered the soul's memory of its divine origin.[61]

6. *The fundamental soteriology across the texts is return as opposed to resurrection.* The resurrection of the body was unlike anything in the Greco-Roman world, and it was the antithesis of "salvation" in the thinking of Platonists and gnostics alike.[62] Gnostics believed that one's rotting flesh right now serves merely to remind one of where evil comes from and how one must find God within oneself.[63]

---

57. Denzey Lewis, *Introduction to "Gnosticism,"* 185.

58. See the (First) Revelation of James, especially in light of Irenaeus's description of the "Marcosians," that is, the Valentinians who followed Marcus the Magician (*Haer.* 1.21.3–5; 1.13.3–6). All quotations from Irenaeus, including from *Adversus haereses*, are from *ANF* 1. Irenaeus distinguishes three levels of rites according to the Valentinian followers of Marcus the Magician: the holy place (baptism), the holy of the holies (a rite called Redemption), and the Bridal Chamber as the holy of the holies. Although the bulk of references to this "redemption" is found in the Gospel of Philip and the Tripartite Tractate, it is also found in Gos. Truth 16.39; Treat. Res. 46:26. Irenaeus discusses it in *Haer.* 1.21.5.

59. Denzey Lewis, *Introduction to "Gnosticism,"* 185.

60. Denzey Lewis, *Introduction to "Gnosticism,"* 186.

61. Absurd speculations have been drawn from Jesus kissing Mary on the mouth (Gos. Phil. 64.9; cf. 58.30–59.5). From this reference popular fiction writers like Dan Brown and others have hatched the imaginative announcement that they were married or at least sexually engaged. However, this was a common gnostic trope for the spiritual marriage of souls, as in the mention of Jesus kissing James, his own brother, "on the mouth" in 1 Apoc. James 31.4. Translations of this work, unless otherwise noted, from Funk in Meyer, *Nag Hammadi Scriptures*. This represents a failure of imagination and of awareness of Plato. As in the *Phaedrus*, physical acts of love are allegorical tropes of the spiritual-intellectual pursuit.

62. Denzey Lewis, *Introduction to "Gnosticism,"* 177. Here Denzey Lewis is referencing Treat. Res. 48.19.

63. Particularly relevant here are the First and Second Revelations of James (NHC V 3 and V 4), the Secret Book of James (NHC I 2), and especially the Treatise on the Resurrection (NHC I 4).

The true doctrine of the resurrection, Denzey Lewis notes, "is a form of *gnosis* or spiritual awakening to the unreality of the world, which this author sees as an illusion."[64]

Across many gnostic texts, the salvation of the spirituals is the savior's own salvation, since they are all light sparks of his collective identity. Only by regathering these rays to himself (reversion) does he become complete again as the "sun" of the divine All, the Fullness (*plērōma*).[65] To be "dead" is to be "spiritually asleep."[66] Hence, to be "alive"—that is, "saved"—is to be awakened to realize one's inner divine identity. The familiar metaphysics of Parmenidean emanation-and-return is easily recognized beneath the patina of harlequin mythology. The resurrection of Jesus to immortal life and, with him, of believers at the end of the age, was spiritualized as the noetic ascent of those who recognize the inner self's divinity.[67] Jean-Pierre Mahé observes, "Poimandres teaches that salvation consists in 'recognizing oneself as immortal, in knowing that love is the cause of death, and in becoming acquainted with all that exists' (Corpus Hermeticum I, 18)," which, of course, refers to the eternal forms.[68] Similarly, the resurrection has already happened according to Dialogue of the Savior.[69] In contrast with biblical eschatology, this "resurrection" is the gnosis (new birth, Christ within) that liberates the soul from the body.[70] From such family resemblances it seems that we are justified in

---

64. Denzey Lewis, *Introduction to "Gnosticism,"* 179.

65. Hans Jonas puts it well: "On the scale of the total divine drama, this process is part of the restoration of the deity's own wholeness, which in pre-cosmic times has become impaired by the loss of portions of the divine substance. It is through these alone that the deity became involved in the destiny of the world, and it is to retrieve them that its messenger intervenes in cosmic history." See *Gnostic Religion*, 45.

66. Denzey Lewis, *Introduction to "Gnosticism,"* 188.

67. Filoramo, *History of Gnosticism*, 101–27.

68. Mahé, "Discourse on the Eighth and Ninth," 410–11.

69. Madeleine Scopello, introduction to "Dialogue of the Savior," in Meyer, *The Nag Hammadi Scriptures*, 297. An incipient version of this may be indicated by Paul's warning against those who "say the resurrection has already happened" (2 Tim 2:18).

70. Scopello, "Dialogue of the Savior," 49. As she writes on 298, this work shares many similarities with the Secret Book of James, the Secret Book of John, the Gospel of Thomas, the Book of Thomas, and (beyond the Nag Hammadi library) Pistis Sophia. The symposium in the Dialogue of the Savior consists of the typical question-and-answer format. This work is less anticorporeal: The creator made all things through the Logos (129.20–130.22). Scopello writes on 299: "It is maintained that in creation the Father gathered together the water (cf. *Genesis* 1:9–10), and the word came forth and was told to fertilize the earth (a Stoic interpretation of *Genesis*, which may be compared with *Poimandres* 5–14). Nevertheless, the world shows features of deficiency (139,13–20)." See also Gos. Truth 26.27.

Chapter 7

speaking of "Gnosticism." All of these texts bear the characteristics summarized well by van den Broek:

> In the following I shall use the term Gnosticism to indicate the ideas or coherent systems that are characterized by an absolutely negative view of the visible world and its creator and the assumption of a divine spark in man, his inner self, which had become enclosed within the material body as a result of a tragic event in the precosmic world, from which it only can escape to its divine origin by means of the saving gnosis.[71]

"A Riot in Plato's Cave"[72]

One could read Plato's *Statesman*, *Laws* (especially book 10), his seventh *Letter*, and the unwritten doctrines summarized by Aristotle (*Phys.* 209b13–15) and conclude that Plato had turned anxious about the goodness of the world.[73] It may well be, as Dodds argues, that the substance of the Orphic mysteries came to the West by way of the Siberian shamans in the late seventh and early sixth centuries BCE, making their way to Thrace, Sicily, and Italy.[74] As Kurt Rudolph suggests, "one might also refer to the Indian dualism between Being and Appearance or Becoming."[75] Or it may have been born in Egypt, as Uždavinys argues.[76] Regardless, after Plato Western philosophy, spirituality, and religion bled Orphic. To look for direct influences of the Orient at this stage is like explaining the American Revolution as the work of Cromwell.

Gnostic teaching was more conspiracy theory or science fiction than what we know today as philosophy, but it will become apparent in this section that its myths were produced by wild flights of Middle Platonist imagination. Simone Pétrement fails to make her case that Gnosticism is a radicalization of certain New Testament doctrines.[77] There is no Christian doctrine that gnostics overem-

---

71. Van den Broek, "Gnosticism and Hermeticism in Antiquity," 4.
72. I have taken "Riot in Plato's Cave" from John Kenney's essay "Platonism of the *Tripartite Tractate*," 204.
73. Rohde, *Psyche*, 2:260; Armstrong, "Dualism," 37.
74. This is part of Dodds's extended argument in *Greeks and the Irrational*, especially 139–40, where Dodds quotes Rohde's comment.
75. Rudolph, *Gnosis*, 60.
76. Uždavinys, *Orpheus and the Roots of Platonism*.
77. This is the main argument in Pétrement, *Separate God*.

phasize; on the contrary, they repeatedly set their purported visions against the biblical canon.

More plausible is David Brakke's suggestion that gnostics wanted to make Christianity more compelling to a Greco-Roman world at a time when similar hypotheses were being explored and debated by Middle and Neoplatonists.[78] Yet this too obscures the fact that gnostics were apologists for an *alternative* to the teaching of the mainstream church. Hans Jonas does not go too far in concluding, "Gnosticism has been the most radical embodiment of dualism ever to have appeared on the stage of history.... It is a split between self and world, man's alienation from nature, the metaphysical devaluation of nature, the cosmic solitude of the spirit and the nihilism of mundane norms."[79] By contrast, Christianity arose out of the expectations of the Hebrew prophets, affirmed the intrinsic goodness of this world and its creator, and emphasized redemption of matter rather than from matter.[80]

I concur with A. D. Nock's description of Gnosticism as "Platonism run wild."[81] John Dillon includes it among the esoteric streams of the "Platonic underworld."[82] Pétrement calls it "un platonisme romantique."[83] Gnosticism is included in a recent philosophical encyclopedia under "Middle Platonism."[84] In favor of this argument, we have the support of no less than Plotinus.

Before taking up Plotinus's critique of gnostics, it is worthwhile to observe their common horizon. Both shared the Orphic myth of procession and return, *exitus* and *reditus*, the eternal, cyclical movement in which the end is like the beginning.[85] Parmenidean idealism is a common factor. Gnostic cosmology is often considered "the most radical embodiment of dualism ever to have appeared on the stage of history," as in Jonas's description above. However, in contrast with

78. Brakke, *Gnostics*, 52–89.
79. Jonas, *Gnostic Religion*, xxvi.
80. Guthrie, *Numenius*, 34.
81. Nock, *Essays on Religion*, 2:949. Nock says that "few sayings echoed in men's minds more than, 'To discover the Maker and Father of this universe is a task, and after discovering him it is impossible to tell of him to all men' (*Tim*. 28C)." No group believed this more than the gnostics.
82. Dillon, *Middle Platonists*, 216.
83. Nock, *Essays on Religion*, 2:949; Nock, *Le dualism chez Platon*, 129.
84. See Moore, "Middle Platonism."
85. Pépin, "Theories of Procession." Valentinus calls the demiurge "the portrait (εἰκόνα) of the true God and his prophet, while he has given the name of painter (ζωγάφων) to Sophia, whose portrait is a making (πλάσμα), for the glory of the invisible, since from a conjunction there proceed (προέρχεται) only πληρώματα, while from a unique principle there proceed only portraits" (318). See *Enn*. 6.7.36; cf. Plato, *Resp*. 508a–c. Cf. Miller, "Plenty Sleeps There," 231–33.

Neopythagoreans like Numenius, Plutarch, and Atticus, gnostics did not think there were two equally ultimate principles of good and evil. Instead, gnostic texts reflect a dualism nested within an ultimate monism. The evil creator is the offspring of Sophia's mistake. His ignorance and pride lead him to boast that he is the only god.

Like Middle Platonists generally, and certainly Plotinus, gnostics assume a radically transcendent One also called Monad, Perfect Aion, *bythos* (Depth), and the ineffable Father: "He is the Invisible Spirit of whom it is not right to think of him as a god or something similar . . . since everything exists in him."[86] He is above all opposition, including good and evil. Below him is the "fullness of deity" (*plērōma*) consisting of thirty gods and divine powers with Jesus at the top (analogous to the Intellect) and Sophia (World Soul) at the bottom. Names or narratives drawn from Jewish and Christian sources are mere embellishments; the substance is a mishmash of Hellenistic and Egyptian theogonies.

Similarly to Plotinus, gnostics conceive of reality as a single Idea that unfolds into an ontological drama of emanation and return. Especially before his encounter with gnostics, Plotinus exhibits a quite radical dualism. By identifying matter with absolute evil, and the latter with nonexistence, Plotinus took a step beyond Plato closer to the gnostics with their emphasis on the "mindlessness" of matter. He also toyed with the Middle Platonist trope of the World Soul (called Sophia by Philo) as potentially irrational in her association with matter. Once again, he acknowledges the privation theory (i.e., "no self-existent evil"), but only to reject it, concluding that matter cannot exist because it is absolute evil (*Enn.* 1.8.7). Either one must deny that matter exists or deny that it is evil, and Plotinus opts for the former.[87] Armstrong claims Plotinus vacillated between affirming the world order and identifying matter with evil.[88] Focusing on *Enn.* 2.4, Armstrong says that Plotinus draws a distinction between primal (ideal) and actual matter "more sharply than is done anywhere else in the tradition . . . and the relationship of the two matters never seems to be made perfectly clear."[89] Armstrong also points up that the woes of evil are blamed on matter in "where Plotinus identifies the evil body with the feminine."[90] This is inherent in the Pythagorean-Platonic identification

---

86. For Plotinus, too, it is not merely that the finite cannot comprehend the infinite but that the One has no attributes to speak of (*Enn.* 5.5.14).
87. Plotinus, *Enn.* 1.6.5–1.7.7.
88. Armstrong, "Dualism," 40.
89. Armstrong, "Dualism," 38.
90. Armstrong, "Dualism," 43–44.

of instability with the definite Dyad/World Soul.[91] Plotinus does not even think that the soul and the body interact.[92]

However, the marked antithesis of corporeal and incorporeal is founded not on two ultimate principles but on privation: matter's lack of reality. At the end of the day, Plotinus and the gnostics were neither pessimists nor conflict dualists. They simply did not believe that material became shared in real being. They were absolute idealists, like Parmenides and Orphics generally as well as the oldest orthodox school of Hinduism, Advaita Vedanta. The real drama is the fall of divine sparks from the "fullness" (*plērōma*) into illusion. They agreed with Plotinus that, as pure thought, the One is not anything or anyone.[93] It is neither the whole nor a part of reality but beyond all wholes and parts; in fact, beyond all distinctions.[94] Idealist panentheism approximates pantheism, both affirming the *hen kai pan*, "One and All" of Orphism. But this simple unity—the real-in-itself—excludes everything belonging to the realm of corporeality, difference, temporality, and change. Emanation (*aporrhoē*) is the metaphysical engine of procession and reversion from the One to the Intellect and to the World Soul.[95]

Jan Assmann calls this common horizon in third-century Alexandria "cosmotheism." He explains succinctly, "Egypt was connected to Europe in two ways: to Jerusalem via Moses and to Athens via Orpheus. Orpheus brought the idea of *Hen kai pan* to Greece, where it influenced the philosophies of Pythagoras, Herakleitus, Parmenides, the Stoics, and others." This cosmotheism "is the common denominator of Egyptian religion."[96] Moreover, we discover the same basic ideas in Hindu and Buddhist traditions. The "Religion of the One/Brahman," with emanation-and-return as its cosmology and the dualism of corporeal and incorporeal dissolved in a higher monism of pure idea is the broader horizon in which a doctrine like cosmotheism makes sense.[97] This is the metaphysics that Abrams called "natural supernaturalism."

Moreover, with greater stress on the One's transcendence, Plotinus and gnostics alike emphasized that union could be achieved only by a mystical experience beyond rational knowing.[98] Plotinus gave greater place to rational contemplation but,

---

91. Armstrong, "Dualism," 44.
92. Plotinus, *Enn.* 1.1.3.
93. Plotinus, *Enn.* 5.3.10; cf. Perl, "Every Life Is a Thought."
94. Plotinus, *Enn.* 6.9.3; 5.5.12.
95. Plotinus, *Enn.* 5.1.6; 3.8.8.
96. Assmann, *Moses*, 3, 8, 47, 54, 115, 120, 135, 142, 154, 153, 210–18.
97. Pépin, "Theories of Procession," 304, 313–14.
98. Plotinus, *Enn.* 1.4.10; 4.8; 5.3.3; 5.3.14. See Armstrong, *Architecture*, 42–44. Specialists are

like the gnostics, considered this stage preparatory for a higher gnosis through a mystical "flash" of immediate vision. Orphic theosophy assumes that ascent above is the same as descent into oneself.[99] Rising higher into this Intellect within, the soul still yearns to be united to God: "we speak and write impelling toward it and *wakening from reasoning to the vision of it.*"[100] Curtis L. Hancock concludes:

> Faced with these several parallels, one should not be surprised to find the Gnostics charting a mystical ascent much like that presented in the Enneads. Like Plotinus the Gnostics characterize mystical union as the consequence of a preparatory stage consisting of knowledge and purgation. Knowledge in the correct sense occurs on the level of the aeons, which roughly approximates the Plotinian level of Soul and Nous. Experience of the highest level requires a purgation of all association from being, form and duality, properties of the aeons. The mystic must transcend being so as to know "the non-being Existence."[101]

This is true especially of the Platonizing phase of Sethian treatises, which were making the rounds in Plotinus's circle.[102] Plotinus believed that the highest part

---

divided over how seriously Plotinus intends us to take this. Does he mean merely that the One is an "infinite being" and is therefore good, true, and beautiful in a way that we cannot imagine? This seems to be the view of Rist, *Plotinus*, 25. Intellect (Aristotle's self-thinking thought) is for Plotinus the second rather than first hypostasis. Since Intellect thinks itself, thinker and thought are identical. We only know something by its form, but the One transcends form. In fact, the Intellect can be known by its energies, but the One transcends "one-in-many" and thus energies. See Hancock, "Negative Theology in Gnosticism and Neoplatonism," 169, 173. Hancock says on 176 that although "the Gnostics more broadly apply negative theology than the Neoplatonists, the two schools mainly agree in the ways they justify and develop negative theology, at least as applied to the very highest level of reality."

99. Alexander J. Mazur provides a helpful overview of this connection in chapter 4 of *Platonizing Sethian*, 139–230.
100. Plotinus, *Enn.* 6.9.3.3.1–4.14.
101. Hancock, "Negative Theology," 179.
102. Plotinus, *Enn.* 4.8.1; 6.9.9–11, with Plato, *Symp.* 210e–211a, *Ep.* 340c–d; MacKenna, *Enneads*, 11, see also 171 n. 1. Originally, *Enn.* 2.9, entitled "Against the Gnostics," was part of an extended treatise by Plotinus, but Porphyry "hacked it" into four parts, placed in various enneads. If we sew it all back, the main part is *Enn.* 2.9 with 3.8 (chronological number 30), 5.8 (31) and 4.5 (32). See Anton, "Theourgia-Demiourgia," 15. Although "ritual and drama" did not appeal to Plotinus generally, he did even undergo his own initiation of sorts in the Alexandrian shrine (possibly the temple of Serapis itself) with an Egyptian priest prophesying that his spirit-guide (daimon) was actually a god. The attraction to Gnosticism on the part of some of his own students underscores that we are in a fluid context in which traffic moved easily across the borders that we have erected.

of the soul (Intellect) intuits Intellect and therefore knowledge of the forms is possible. Gnostics called this second principle first thought (Protennoia/Mother Barbelo/*nous*). It was as essential for the gnostics as for Plotinus that the highest part of the soul—Intellect—never descended into the body.

However, especially after his confrontation with gnostic students, Plotinus moderated some of his earlier formulations. A century before Plotinus, Celsus was aware that while Christians generally taught "that their God is the same as the God of the Jews," others disputed this and said "that the Son came from their God." This latter group identified themselves as *gnōstikoi* and claimed to be "spirituals" (*pneumatikoi*) rather than mere *psychikoi* like the common herd of Christians.[103] Combining the reports of Celsus, Porphyry, and Plotinus, we may note that the gnostics known to them were (1) heretical Christians (2) who "abandoned" Platonism in order to follow an entirely different religious philosophy, (3) passed off "their own ideas under the name of Zoroaster," and (4) that some of Plotinus's students "still cling to it."[104]

Plotinus has no difficulty suggesting the gnostics' most likely source of inspiration: "Perhaps the hate of this school for the corporeal is due to their reading of Plato *who inveighs against body as a grave hindrance to Soul* and pronounces the corporeal to be characteristically the inferior" (*Enn.* 2.9.17). Plotinus acknowledges this as Plato's view. He never refers to Judaism or Christianity as incubators of the heresy. What he criticizes is how the gnostics "introduce a medley of generation and destruction, how they cavil at the Universe, how they make the Soul blameable for the association with the body, how they revile the Administrator of this All, how they ascribe to the Creator, identified with the Soul, the character and experiences appropriate to partial beings" (2.9.6). Significantly, we find no comparable list in Irenaeus of biblical doctrines that gnostics had exploited, only contradictions. Irenaeus's main concern, as we will see, is their "blasphemous" teaching that evil runs all the way up into the celestial realm.

First, Plotinus defends the World Soul (i.e., the gnostic Sophia). Precisely because it remains steadfast in clinging to the Intellect, the rational part of the soul cannot be bound but instead "imparts life to the body" even while it "admits nothing bodily to itself." The immunity of rational soul is therefore protected, but at the price of denying any real union with the body. One's inner flame "may be quenched," he adds, "but the thing, fire, will exist still; and if fire itself were annihilated that would make no difference to the Soul in the Supreme, but only to the plan of the material world" (*Enn.* 2.9.7). Plotinus allows that the gnostics are

---

103. Nock, *Essays on Religion*, 2:944.
104. Evangeliou, "Plotinus's Anti-Gnostic Polemic," 119.

probably right that this world is unsalvageable, that it is soaked in evil simply by virtue of being material. But he opposes their conclusion that because *we* find ourselves bound by shackles of bodily evil, the Soul is bound as well. The woes of the individual soul in union with a body cannot be extended to the World Soul itself. Hence, Plotinus's strategy against the gnostics is not to affirm the material world but to establish a firewall between it and the upper realm.

Plotinus told us above that goodness accrues to something material only in virtue of its form (*Enn.* 1.8; 2.4). "This positive-negative conception of matter is of the utmost importance for all future religious thinking," says Corrigan. "In later pagan thought, however, this confidence in soul is lost, and the human soul, no longer a *de facto* member of the intelligible, descends into the physical universe."[105] Corrigan is referring to the theurgic Neoplatonism that came to dominate the school from Iamblichus onward. It is no wonder that mind (*nous*) or spirit (*pneuma*) must be posited above the soul, as we find it not only in gnostic thought but also Hermetic theology and the Alexandrian-Christian interpretation of Origen.[106]

Second, Plotinus attacks the gnostics for blaspheming the creator of the world. This would mean, for a follower of the *Timaeus*, no less than the intellectual demiurge. Gnostics did not actually make this correlation but rather, like Plotinus, identified the *Timaeus* demiurge with the Intellect (Logos, Christ, or Savior, depending on the sect). Regardless, Platonists did not believe that the demiurge created matter but tried as best he could to overcome its resistance to form. If Plotinus still thinks that matter is "absolute evil," it is not to be blamed on the artist but on the recalcitrance of its canvas. Of course, the soul longs to return to its homeland. However, where Plotinus sees rungs connecting each level to its superiors in contemplative desire, his opponents see only an unbridgeable chasm. He argues that the gnostics fail to realize the symmetry and coordination of everything within the All.

Third, Plotinus accuses the gnostics of "vulgar magic." This criticism perhaps drew Porphyry back from theurgy. Obsession with magical rites is a weak soul's shortcut, the manipulation of rather than assimilation to God. We do not draw the gods down to us but rise up to them. It was at this point where Egyptian religion (and the Magical Papyri) made the deepest impression on the gnostics and, given the similarity with Porphyry's critique of Iamblichus, may have been the catalyst for Porphyry drawing back from theurgy.

At the same time, we should hesitate to see the gnostics as pioneers of theurgic Neoplatonism. Gnostics exploited spiritual hypochondria; however, with some notable exceptions, they offered a spiritual elixir rather than a physical one. In

---

105. Corrigan, "Body and Soul," 381.
106. Plotinus, *Enn.* 2.9.3–4; 9.3.17; and 2.9.8.

this regard they were actually more like Plotinus than they were the later Neoplatonists. The philosophical Hermetica also represent "new birth in the mixing bowl" as a largely noetic process culminating in gnosis rather than as being associated with physical rites. Moreover, the extent of Plotinus's interest in and approval of magic or theurgy is actually a matter of dispute among specialists. Silence may have been the highest form of worship, but bodily rituals—at least chants and hymns—were also involved at the lower stages of ascent.[107]

Plotinus does not resolve Platonism's inherent contradictions and he refuses to opt for the fatal consistency of the gnostics. "Hence," says Wallis, "Plotinus maintains, in a passage reminiscent of Far Eastern mysticism, the sensible world's excellence stems from the fact that its creator had no intention of producing it, but 'in *not acting* achieved mighty results' (III. 2. I. 34–45)."[108] This is similar to the gnostic Tripartite Tractate, which may have been a rejoinder to Plotinus that softened the myth by suggesting that the "mistake" of the Logos (Sophia) turned out to be a *felix culpa*.

Numenius, Plutarch, and others had been more consistent logically, but to whatever extent Plotinus was at first willing to go down this road, the gnostics caused him to pull back. Perkins summarizes, "Whatever happens in this world, the philosopher can withdraw into the untroubled contemplation of the intelligible realm. The Gnostics, on the other hand, must finally dissolve this world, its order and beauty, in order to transcend it (*Enn.* II.9, 18)."[109]

In Plotinus's view at least, Gnosticism was a corruption of the Orphic core of Platonism. He says gnostics are "people inventing a new jargon to recommend their own school: they contrive this meticulous language as if they had no connection with the ancient Hellenic school, *though the Hellenes knew all this and knew it clearly*, and spoke without delusive pomposity of ascents from the cave and advancing gradually closer and closer to a truer vision." He continues,

> Generally speaking, some of these people's doctrines have been taken from Plato, but others, all the new ideas they have brought in to establish a philosophy of their own, are things they have found outside the truth. For the judgements too, and the rivers in Hades and the reincarnations come from Plato. And the making of a plurality in the intelligible world, Being, and Intel-

---

107. Porphyry, *Vit. Plot.* 10.21–25; cf. Plotinus, *Enn.* 2.3.9; 2.9.18.

108. Wallis, *Neoplatonism*, 86, emphasis added. B. A. G. Fuller pointed out in 1912 that Plotinus adopts Aristotle's idea of perfection as being determined by its class, but it falls into contradiction. All perfection is absolute, yet all but the One is deficient in some degree; hence, not even the One can be perfect if it emanates something less perfect. See Fuller, *Problem of Evil in Plotinus*, 95–96.

109. Perkins, "Beauty, Number, and Loss of Order," 292.

lect, and the Maker different from Intellect, and Soul, is taken from the words in the *Timaeus*.... [But] in general they falsify Plato's account of the manner of the making, and a great deal else, and degrade the great man's teachings as if they had understood the intelligible nature, but he and the other blessed philosophers had not. (*Enn.* 2.9.6)

The gnostics should honor their sources "without in any way disparaging those godlike men, but receiving their teaching with a good grace *since it is the teaching of more ancient authorities* and they themselves have received what is good in what they say from them, *the immortality of the soul, the intelligible universe, the first god, the separation from the body, the escape from becoming to being*. For these doctrines are there in Plato, and when they state them clearly in this way they do well" (2.9.6). J. Zandee observes, "Plotinus opposed the Gnostics very strongly, but is not that the violence which occurs with two spiritual currents that are not far from each other?"[110] Nevertheless, Plotinus's criticisms reveal significant points of difference, especially in blaming the demiurgic Intellect as if it were responsible for evil and in attributing to the World Soul the same bondage to the body that our own souls experience.

GNOSIS AND CHRISTIAN IDENTITY

Even before Plotinus, Celsus recognized Gnosticism as a second-century bricolage of Orphic metaphysics.[111] With embellishments from Egyptian religion and the Greek Magical Papyri, Orphic metaphysics was the most acute product of the Alexandrian imagination that produced Hermeticism and Neoplatonism. A. D. Nock judges, "When the forty works of Gnostics in stone jars were discovered in Egypt, we learned how accurate were Irenaeus, Hippolytus and Epiphanius."[112]

---

110. Zandee, *Terminology of Plotinus*, 4.
111. Celsus recognizes the system, despite its eccentricities. See the reconstructed version of Celsus in Celsus, *On the True Doctrine* (trans. Hoffmann), 98–99: "And so we hear of circles on top of circles and emanations flowing out of emanations," he says, "earthly churches and churches of the circumcision; we witness the Jews flowing from a power represented as a virgin—Prunicus (Sophia)—and another living soul who was killed so that heaven could have life." Their "utterly concocted ideas" are poor imitations of Greek myths, including the war between Kronos and Ophioneus, strife between Zeus and Hera, Heraclitus's Strife and Necessity, "the Titans and the Giants," and "the mysteries related by the Egyptians concerning Typhon, Horus and Osiris."
112. Nock, *Essays on Religion*, 2:956.

This is acknowledged even by scholars partial to Bauer and the gnostics. Elaine Pagels acknowledges that Irenaeus's characterization of gnostic teaching as "'evil interpretation,' . . . however hostile, nevertheless is accurate." Gnostics "were implicitly criticizing, intentionally or not, the faith of most Christians."[113]

In the third century, Porphyry exhibits considerable firsthand knowledge of Christian beliefs and practices, contrasting the sublime contemplation of philosophers with the crass literalism of the Christians. Setting out first to undermine the credibility of the prophecies appealed to by Christians, Porphyry targets the same doctrines identified by Celsus and other earlier critics.[114] It is not difficult to see why Celsus found his gnostic contemporaries in Alexandria more "reasonable." He distinguishes "the church of the multitude" (or "the great church") from "others," mentioning gnostic divergences in some detail. He says that there are "a few moderate, reasonable, and intelligent people who are inclined to interpret its beliefs allegorically, yet it thrives in its purer form among the ignorant."[115] These "others" do not believe that Jesus was really crucified and "speak of two divine sons, locked in combat with one another."[116] Thus, when Irenaeus wrote *Against Heresies* he was not inventing but defending an orthodoxy that was recognizable to Christians, Platonists, and gnostics alike.

CONCLUSION

Platonists like Celsus shared the gnostic judgment that orthodox Christians were intellectual dilettantes preaching "nothing but Christ and him crucified." Obsessed with "earth-bound matters," their souls had lost their wings and could not soar to philosophical heights. In the second century Tertullian and Clement of Alexandria represent widely divergent responses to this charge. Tertullian does not see how philosophy, as currently articulated, is not inherently gnostic.[117] Although his privileged paternity admitted him to a rhetorical education in Carthage, the first Christian to write in Latin concluded, "Indeed heresies are themselves instigated by philosophy. From this source came the Aeons, and I known not what infinite

---

113. Pagels, *Beyond Belief*, 138; cf. Dunderberg, *Beyond Gnosticism*, 7–10.
114. Hoffmann, epilogue to *Porphyry's "Against the Christians,"* 147. Hoffmann notes, "Like Plutarch, he argues that there is one supremely good God who employs a vast array of daimones (some good, some evil) who act as influences in the material world."
115. Celsus, *On the True Doctrine* (trans. Hoffmann), 57.
116. Celsus, *On the True Doctrine* (trans. Hoffmann), 105.
117. Especially illuminating is Roukema, *Gnosis and Faith in Early Christianity*.

Chapter 7

forms, and the trinity of man in the system of Valentinus, who was of Plato's school" (*Praescr.* 3.249).[118]

In sharp contrast, Clement of Alexandria sees the charge as a challenge. The antidote to "false Gnostics," he says, is the "Christian Gnostic." Clement's *Stromateis* (Miscellanies) is a catalogue of wisdom not only in philosophy but also in the arts and sciences drawn from various cultures. His hearty intellectual appetite has rendered this work a major source for historians. Clement is convinced that Moses stands at the head of the noble line of perennial sages and that Plato drew his best ideas from the prophet.[119] In his view, the Greeks pilfered the wisdom of the so-called barbarians, especially the Egyptian and Indian sages. But at the headwaters stood the towering figure of Moses. Clement followed earlier Jewish philosophers in concluding that Musaeus, Orpheus's lieutenant (or perhaps son), was the Greek name for Moses.[120] While Clement was opposed to pagan practices, he was open to pagan learning, even systematically comparing Orphic sayings to those of the Greek philosophers.[121]

It would be a mistake to view Clement as a compromiser. On the contrary, he argues, to deny that there is genuine truth in pagan wisdom is to limit God's providence. Christ himself is the Logos who gives reason to all. "The true light, which gives light to everyone, was coming into the world" (John 1:9). Just as Moses and the Hebrew prophets acted as the pedagogue preparing Israel for Christ, truths taught by the sages of all peoples led the gentiles, like the magi, to Bethlehem. If Christ's seeds of truth have been scattered throughout the world, he reasons, Christians are the proper farmers to harvest them (*Protr.* 1.14, 17).

On the one hand, one can see why Platonism was seen as a suitable handmaiden. What other Greek school taught that there was one sovereign and immutable source of all things? Or that a second hypostasis, the Intellect or Logos,

---

118. Translation from *ANF* 3.

119. Clement's approach was the programmatic statement for all subsequent apologetics seeking a more conciliatory than confrontational approach to philosophy.

120. Similarly, see Artapanus of Alexandria (Jewish historian, third or second century BCE), as noted by Barclay, *Jews in the Mediterranean Diaspora*, 127–31. See also Collins, *Between Athens and Jerusalem*, 37–45. Alexander Polyhistor and Numenius also held this view. So did Clement (*Strom.* 1.23).

121. Thinking they received all of their dogmas from Socrates, they fail to acknowledge their debts. Clement, "exposing their plagiarizing style," compares at length sayings by Orpheus repeated by Solon, Euripides, Sophocles, Thucydides, Heraclitus, the Pythagoreans, and Plato. Euripides repeats Orpheus: "Nothing dies ... dissolved into another thing" (transcribing Chrysippus). "I pass over in silence Heraclitus of Ephesus, who took a very great deal from Orpheus. From Pythagoras, Plato derived the immortality of the soul; and he from the Egyptians" (*Strom.* 6.2–3).

was the craftsman of the world and a third hypostasis, the World Soul, linked individual souls to the "father of all"? Atomists thought there was a god for every atom, Epicureans held that no gods were involved in the world, and Stoics maintained that god *was* the world. For atomists, the gods were efficient but not final causes, while for Aristotle the unmoved mover was the final but not the efficient cause of all. Platonists believed in God's transcendence of the world and his providence over it as both efficient and final cause, the existence of a soul that survives death and the goal of union with the Good.

On the other hand, Tertullian's assessment seems to be supported by the evidence of many centuries. In terms of their most central doctrines, Orphism and Christianity are wholly antithetical. As Andrew Louth points out, Platonism conceives of the soul's search for God "as a return, an ascent to God; for the soul properly belongs with God, and in its ascent it is but realizing its own true nature."

> Christianity, on the other hand, speaks of the Incarnation of God, of his descent into the world that he might give to man the possibility of a communion with God that is not open to him by nature. And yet man is made in the image of God, and so these movements of ascent and descent cross one another and remain—as a fact of experience—in unresolved tension.... Can there, indeed, be such a thing as Christian mystical theology?[122]

It is to Origen next that this question falls, and his answer provoked many of his day and since to repeat Tertullian's query, "What has Jerusalem to do with Athens or the Academy to do with the church?"

---

122. Louth, *Origins of the Christian Mystical Tradition*, viii.

8

Orphic Exegesis
The Eternal Gospel

> For the intellect of the Father declared that all things be divided in threes
> and He nodded his assent to this,
> and all things were so divided.
>
> —Chaldean Oracles fr. 22

> Just as man consists of body, soul and spirit, so in the same way does the Scripture.
>
> —Origen, *Princ.* 4.24[1]

> For the end is always like the beginning.
>
> —Origen, *Princ.* 1.6.2

---

1. All of my quotations from *On First Principles* are taken from the 1973 Butterworth edition and translation. Much of Origen's work was mediated (and translated) by Rufinus, who tried to make Origen (and himself) more amenable to the catholic faith in general and to the Latins in particular. Butterworth therefore includes many citations of *On First Principles* from Jerome. Although Jerome was a critic, his quotations suggest points at which Rufinus modified Origen's bold speculations at their most controversial points. Butterworth helpfully weighs these different translations and frequently places them in parallel lines. Some scholars such as Henri de Lubac and Hans Urs von Balthasar are sympathetic to Origen and his legacy, downplaying the contrast with an "Irenaean" stream. However, the latter rests much of his case on the relative accuracy of Rufinus's Latin translation, as in Balthasar's introduction to *Origen: Spirit & Fire*, 21.

Orphic Exegesis: The Eternal Gospel

Origen of Alexandria was as committed a Christian as one could expect. His mother had to hide his clothes so he would not follow his father, who catechized him, to execution. Origen knew the scriptures deeply and even learned Hebrew, which was rare among patristic writers. Yet, whatever else he was, Origen was a Platonist.[2] His hermeneutical and doctrinal vision is summarized in his statement in his treatise on prayer, "If we understand the ascent of the Son to the Father with holy insight and in a way suitable to God, we shall realize it is the ascent of mind rather than the body" (*Or.* 23.2).[3] Origen agreed with Plato and Philo that the highest stage of reality and therefore meaning was intellectual, not physical or historical. At the literal level of "the many," religions are irreconcilable, but universal spirituality—Orphism—transcends them.[4]

The content and contours of this belief originated in Orphic mysteries as the hermeneutical corollary of Orphic body-soul dualism, which Origen learned from Ammonius Saccas, the Indian émigré of a Christian background who founded the Platonist school in Alexandria. The fifth-century Neoplatonist Hierocles said that Origen and Plotinus were "Ammonius's brightest and most remarkable and illustrious disciples" (*apud* Photius, *Bib.* 214.172a–b; 251.461b).[5] Porphyry relates that Origen dropped in on a seminar in Alexandria to find Plotinus teaching Ammonius's doctrines. Flummoxed, Plotinus said that "it dampens one's enthusiasm for speaking when one sees that one's audience knows already what one is going to say" (*Vit. Plot.* 14.23–25).[6] By his own testimony, Porphyry studied as a youth with

---

2. Digeser, *Threat to Public Piety*, 70. I will not enter this debate further, but refer the reader to Elizabeth DePalma Digeser's persuasive defense of the growing consensus that there is one Ammonius (the reconciler of Plato and Aristotle) and one Origen (the reconciler of Christ and Plato) who was his student. See also the quite thorough analysis of Ramelli, "Origen and the Platonic Tradition," esp. 9–12. Whatever belongs to the rule of faith must be believed by all Christians, he said, but otherwise metaphysical speculations beyond scripture should be left to Christian freedom, he thought (Origen, *Princ.* preface).

3. Translation from Greer, *Origen*.

4. This is the usual dichotomy of the "Philosophical Religion" described so well by Fraenkel, *Philosophical Religions*. The lower religion depends on authority and, taken at face value, is not true; the higher religion, via allegorical interpretation, is the one universal truth attained by autonomous reason.

5. Ramelli, "Origen and the Platonic Tradition," 21. H. Dörrie, Richard Goulet, and, most recently, Mark Edwards, argue that Porphyry mentions a different Origen; see Edwards, *Neoplatonic Saints*, 7; Edwards, "One Origen or Two?" However, the traditional view is defended persuasively in Kettler, "War Origenes Schüler des Ammonius Sakkas?"; Boyarin, "By Way of Apology," 203; Digeser, *Threat to Public Piety*, 27–28. A superb survey is found in Ramelli, "Origen and the Platonic Tradition," 7–9. Later pagan Neoplatonists such as Hierocles and Proclus refer positively to Origen and identify him with distinctive views we find in the Christian Origen's extant works.

6. Plotinus and Origin disagreed over Numenius's interpretation of Plato's "Three Kings"; see Digeser, *Threat to Public Piety*, 75–76.

Chapter 8

Origen in Caesarea or Tyre "around 248–250."[7] He even refers to Origen's library, revealing familiarity with the course Origen taught.[8]

Expounding a "higher gospel," Origen forged the blueprint for an Orphic Christianity that remained powerful and alluring through a millennium of medieval Christendom and on into modernity. Through Origen's Christian Platonism, Orphism found a new form for a new era, making a home both within and outside the established church, and flourishing particularly in the quintessential Byzantine-medieval institution: the monastery.

ORPHIC EXEGESIS: THE GOSPEL OF ASCENT

It was Origen who preserved Celsus's attack and offered a lengthy response. About a century later, Porphyry offered his system in his *Philosophy from Oracles* as a religious creed that could secure imperial harmony against Christianity. It was commissioned by the emperor and displays unabashedly the author's political goals at a time when Christians were studying at pagan academies and rising to distinguished positions at court. Agitated at the same time by Iamblichus's theurgic program, Porphyry felt that the task of holding together the school of Ammonius fell to him as Plotinus's successor. Outlining the perennial wisdom of the revelations given not only to Greeks and Romans but to "Egyptians, Chaldeans and even Jews," he argues that they all teach "One Supreme Being." Even Christianity could be incorporated if just a few beliefs were omitted (viz., Jesus's divinity, salvation exclusively through him, and refusal to participate in the public cult).[9] So, ironically (like Celsus), a polytheist was charging Christians with abandoning monotheism in favor of Christ-worship.[10] He used this tack to unite Romans and "barbarians" in a universal religion that opposed Christianity.

In Porphyry's view, Origen had defended Christian claims only by revising them considerably, slipping out of the noose of alleged biblical contradictions by using a spiritual rather than literal interpretation. Porphyry recognized that the genres of biblical writings—especially historical narrative and apocalyptic—

---

7. Digeser, *Threat to Public Piety*, 26. Digeser notes that this is attested by Athanasius Syrus in his translation of Porphyry's *Isagogē* and Socrates Scholasticus's fifth-century church history (*Hist. eccl.* 3.23.37–39) (76).

8. It would have been from Origen and later from Plotinus that Porphyry would have learned about the secret teachings of Ammonius; see Digeser, *Threat to Public Piety*, 27.

9. Wilken, *Christians as the Romans Saw Them*, 136. This idea is comparable to the view expressed by the liberal theologian Adolf von Harnack, "The Gospel, as Jesus proclaimed it, has to do with the Father only and not with the Son" in *What Is Christianity?*, 144.

10. Wilken, *Christians as the Romans Saw Them*, 151.

were not intended to be subsumed under allegory. Not only did Origen evade the obvious problems in scripture, Porphyry thought, but he employed it to explain away the fact that Christians turned their back on the law of Moses. Judaism was tolerated because its monotheism and aversion to pagan images and rituals were grounded in a very old and venerable law of their nation. Porphyry argued that Christians no longer enjoy this cover of exemption because they do not accept the Mosaic law.

The bulk of Porphyry's *Against the Christians* is devoted to criticism of the Bible and Christian doctrines. Porphyry was quite familiar with Christian doctrines and texts, having even attended Origen's courses (Eusebius, *Hist. eccl.* 6.19.2–5).[11] Jesus's disciples diverged from his basic message, he argues.[12] According to Porphyry, "The new religion focuses on Jesus, whereas the religion of Jesus centered on the supreme God of all," Wilken summarizes, adding, "Porphyry's criticism has a curiously modern ring to it."[13] Christians were arrogant, thinking that their God was the only one and they could be saved in only one way by him.[14] Rather, every nation has a cult suited to its own culture but with a universal core of common belief.[15]

Even before touching the doctrines, Porphyry clashes with Christians at a fundamental level, namely, the role of myth. For him, as for his predecessors, "myths were parables of philosophical truth," as Hoffmann summarizes. "In Christianity," by contrast, "the myth was the truth."[16] So, for example, to the famous Prologue of the Fourth Gospel, a philosopher might have asked, "What is this about?" or "What is the metaphysical truth communicated by the myth of the Word became flesh?" For Christians, however, there was nothing behind the curtain. "The Word became flesh" was the highest truth; it was something that happened in history.

The teaching that Porphyry finds especially offensive is the doctrine of the resurrection of the body: "Just to think of this silly teaching makes me light-headed," he says. Like Celsus, he asks why God would "as you say, 'raise up the rotten and stinking corpses of men,' some of them, no doubt, belonging to worthy men, but others

---

11. See P. F. Beatrice, "Porphyry at Origen's School at Caesarea." Beatrice also quotes the seventh-century Athanasius the Syrian in his preface to Porphyry's *Isogogē*: "Porphyry was a philosopher from the city of Tyre, and he was a disciple of Origen" (271).

12. Wilken, *Christians as the Romans Saw Them*, 153.

13. Wilken, *Christians as the Romans Saw Them*, 154.

14. Porphyry, as quoted in Augustine, *Ep.* 102.8.

15. Wilken, *Christians as the Romans Saw Them*, 163. Wilken adds, "As Symmachus, writing in the later fourth century, puts it in his little treatise defending the altar of Victory in the senate house against Christian efforts to have it removed, 'We cannot attain to so great a mystery by one way' (*Relat.* 10)."

16. Hoffmann, epilogue to *Porphyry's "Against the Christians,"* 161.

having no grace or merit prior to death" (*Christ.* 4.24).[17] The only thing that matters is the soul's ascent through virtue and contemplation, he says (*Marc.* 49).[18] Yet Christians cannot get beyond the physical realm; instead of encouraging the flight of the alone to the Alone, they would rather keep souls bound to their body forever.[19]

Porphyry says that it was from reading the Stoic thinker, magician, and Egyptian priest Chaeremon that Origen "learned the allegorical method of interpreting the mysteries of the Greeks and he applied it to the Jewish scriptures."[20] Given his dislike for both Origen and Egyptian theurgy, it is not surprising that he wanted to pawn Origen off on the Egyptians—keeping him as far away from Ammonius's circle as possible. However, Porphyry knew that Origen was a senior member of the circle to which Plotinus belonged and that there was nothing in Origen's hermeneutic that required an extra-Hellenic explanation. The ascent of mind from the body underwrote the spiritualizing hermeneutic that led to philosophical religion—or "the eternal gospel."[21]

Origen argues against Celsus that anyone who knew how to exegete Plato by finding his inner meaning "under the appearance of myth" would be able to understand why allegorical interpretation of scripture was necessary (*Cels.* 4.39).[22] Although he is considered the source of the "fourfold sense" of scriptural interpretation, Origen does not actually lay out these senses in treating any passage in ascending order. Instead, he believes there is only one true sense: the spiritual (allegorical) meaning. Heine points out, "The literal level, therefore, is discussed only to be dismissed, not to provide edification at its own level."[23] When he says of a given passage, "Taken literally, this cannot be true," he is not saying that the text is wrong; it is a hermeneutical error, not a textual one. It is the spiritual sense that is inspired by the Holy Spirit. The sort of contradictions alleged by Porphyry and acknowledged by Origen vanish when one reads the scriptures the way the Spirit intended.[24]

---

17. Translation from Hoffmann, *Porphyry's "Against the Christians."*

18. Quoted from Hoffmann, epilogue to *Porphyry's "Against the Christians,"* 161.

19. It is ironic that despite the gullibility attributed to Christians, Plato's *Timaeus* asserts that we must rely on the "children of the gods" (poets) who have told us about their ancestors without any proof or evidence (*Tim.* 40a–41e).

20. See fr. 39 of Porphyry, *Christ.* (= Eusebius, *Hist. eccl.* 6.19.8) in van der Horst, *Chaeremon*, 5.

21. This does not render the bodily (literal) interpretation invalid however. See Dawson, "Allegorical Reading," 26–43.

22. "Anagogical" (ascending) is more appropriate than "allegorical" for Origen's hermeneutic, but I will continue to use the familiar term.

23. Heine, introduction to Origen, *Gospel according to John, Books 1–10* (trans. Heine), 12–13.

24. Origen, *Gospel according to John, Books 1–10* (trans. Heine), 257–59, emphasis added; cf. 12–13, 43, 154, 279. All translations of Origen's commentary on John, unless otherwise noted, are from this work.

For Origen, the two levels of meaning, literal and spiritual, represent two gospels: a temporal gospel of "Christ after the flesh" understood by the many and perceptible by the senses, "which all can read," and an "eternal gospel" hidden in the narrative (*Comm. Jo.* 1.43–45). "The spiritual truth is often preserved in the material falsehood, so to speak." Like an exegetical alchemist, one must "translate the gospel perceptible to the senses into the spiritual gospel," says Origen. Scripture leads us from the lower to the higher, from the outer to the inner.[25] Just as the Word became flesh but then left the flesh behind, the literal gospel "is little or nothing, even though the common people believe they receive the things which are revealed from the literal sense." In fact, the historical sense is misleading.

> And wherever it is necessary to preach the literal gospel declaring among the carnal that we "know nothing except Jesus Christ and him crucified," we must do this. But whenever we find those who are established in the Spirit and are bearing fruit in him and desiring the heavenly wisdom, we ought to share with them the Word who was restored from being made flesh to what he was in the beginning with God. (*Comm. Jo.* 1.43–45)

Origen's treatise on the Passover (*Peri Pascha*) provides a clear statement of Origen's spiritual exegesis. He acknowledges that he is going up against the view of "most of the brethren, indeed perhaps all" (*Pasch.* 1.5–8).[26] For Origen the original Passover does not refer to a historical event of Christ in the past, but to his whole, living, and present existence now. As Daly summarizes, "The passover is taking place now; the Hebrew passover does not prefigure the past events of Christ's bodily life, but Christ Himself now saving souls."[27] The Passover is "not a figure or type of the historical passion of Christ but a figure of Christ's passing over to the Father of our own still ongoing passing over with Christ to the Father."[28]

In the treatise itself, Origen says that Egypt "signifies ignorance" (*Pasch.* 43.10). He offers an imaginative interpretation of the celebration in the "first month of the year" and "beginning of months" as referring to the new birth (1.5–10).[29] The

---

25. On Origen's hermeneutic in his John commentary, see Danièlou, *Gospel Message and Hellenistic Culture*, 273–88.

26. Translation of this work, unless otherwise noted, from Origen, *Treatise on the Passover* (trans. Daly). Daly's translation is of Papyrus 88746 in the Museum of Egyptian Antiquities in Cairo; see the critical edition by Scherer, *Entretien d'Origène*.

27. Origen, *Treatise on the Passover* (trans. Daly), 101 n. 35.

28. Origen, *Treatise on the Passover* (trans. Daly), 6–7.

29. Another example of his spiritual interpretation of numbers appears at *Pasch.* 17.10: "that

Chapter 8

fulfillment of this "passing over" is not Christ's suffering, he says, but his passing over from a sensible to intelligible existence, returning to the Father. It is not a historical event pointing to a greater fulfillment in history but an allegory of Christ's ascent that is always occurring. The eating of the Passover lamb is fulfilled not in Christ's death and, sacramentally, in the Eucharist but in spiritual exegesis of scripture (13.15).[30] Origen's interpretation is the same as his Alexandrian predecessor Clement, who was following Philo. "For Philo, the Jewish passover recalled the Exodus and allegorically prefigured the passage of the soul from out of the world of sense into the world of reason," notes Daly. Clement made Passover refer to Christ but also the "passage" from the sensible to the intellectual. "But this is not primarily the historical Christ or the historical event of Christ's life; it is the now living mystical Christ, it is the Christ-event as it is now taking place in the lives of the Christian faithful."[31] "In this search," Daly observes, "his particular Hellenistic-Platonic-Christian view of human and divine reality, without his being aware of how much this view of reality differs from that of the biblical authors, becomes codeterminative of the spiritual meaning he finds in the biblical texts."[32]

THE WORLD BEFORE THIS ONE: ORIGEN'S "ETERNAL GOSPEL"

Paul M. Gould provides a succinct definition of a Christian Platonist as someone who believes in God *and* the *necessary* existence of abstract objects.[33] This puts one in a pickle. Christians believe that God alone is eternal and necessary (e.g., 1 Tim 6:16). Extrapolating God's aseity, immutability, and simplicity from God's name in Exod 3:14 (i.e., "I am"), Philo tried to solve this by locating the forms in the mind of God, so that they were only necessary by virtue of being an eternal act of God's being. However, this does not solve the problem, at least for a monotheist, if God's ideas are not just determinations of what he will create but are themselves real entities identified with God's being. This entails that the ideas and the actualized bearers of them must exist necessarily. Plato and his heirs stress

---

the true Lamb is Christ because of the fact that, being second after the Father, he is taken—I am speaking of the number ten—during the second monad."

30. Origen, *Treatise on the Passover* (trans. Daly), 35; see also 37–45. Karl Rahner offers insight in "Spiritual Senses."

31. Origen, *Treatise on the Passover* (trans. Daly), 10.

32. Origen, *Treatise on the Passover* (trans. Daly), 25.

33. See Gould, *Beyond the Control of God?* This succinct definition was suggested to me by my student Joseph DeAngelo in a theology proper paper, "A Not So Simple Subject: Classical Theism and the Christian Platonism of Alvin Plantinga" (December 2019).

that the Good does not generate the world by choice but instead as a necessary overflow of itself.

Ex nihilo creation entails a total break from the Platonic concept of necessary and eternal forms. On this basis, Irenaeus (*Haer.* 4.19.1) rejects the forms, adding the same argument used by Aristotle that this would produce an infinite series of the form "Human," for example.[34] Alexandrians Clement and Origen, however, are ambivalent concerning creation *ex nihilo* and its implications.[35] Like Platonists generally, Origen views the first principle as supreme, but in quantitative rather than qualitative terms. There is a hierarchical theogony with levels of divinity below the Father, beginning with the Logos and extending all the way down to the form of humanity.[36] The preincarnate Christ is the principle (*archē*) through whom all other creatures exist eternally.[37]

Like the gnostics, Origen believed something happened in the *plērōma*, the realm of the gods, that led to the imprisonment of the soul in this visible world. There is nothing like this in Plato or Plotinus, but there are seeds of it in the Orphic myths of Dionysius and the Titans, in Plutarch's allegorical interpretation of the Isis-Osiris myth, and elsewhere. Note, for example, Origen's interpretation of Gen 1:7 when God seals off the "waters above from the waters below," a text that received a dualistic interpretation by the gnostics.[38] Origen does not see "the waters below" (i.e., matter) as the source of evil per se, but regards embodiment as a punishment for offenses committed prior to this world.[39] If all souls had been as faithful as Jesus's, this world would never have existed. This world, then,

---

34. Sismanian, "Le Nombre et son Ombre," 351.

35. See Origen, *Princ.* 1.6.2; 1.7.1–1.8.4. On the descent of the soul, see 1.3.1. Butterworth observes, "This doctrine of the descent of the soul is found in Plato, *Phaedrus* 246 B–D, a passage clearly referred to by Origen in *Con. Cels.* IV. 40. Jerome says (*Con. Joh. Hieros.* 19), in connexion with this doctrine: 'What you admire so much we long ago despised when we found it in Plato.'" This is also a view put forward by the gnostics, according to Irenaeus (*Haer.* 1.25.4). "Jerome says also in *Con. Joh. Hieros.* 19 that 'Origen used Jacob's ladder to teach that rational creatures descend gradually to the lowest step, namely, to flesh and blood.'" See Origen, *On First Principles* (trans. Butterworth), 41 n. 1.

36. Chadwick, "Beginnings of Christian Thought," 182–92; cf. Scott, *Journey Back to God*, 52. See also the discussion of Origen's Christology below.

37. Panayiotis P. Tzamlikos explains, "He imagines an existence before materiality and temporality; that is, he imagines a 'when' before the cosmos: . . . a reality where there is nothing apart from God himself." See Tzamlikos, *Cosmology and Ontology of Time*, 39. See also Scott, *Journey Back to God*, 55–59.

38. Origen, Homily 1 in Origen, *Homilies on Genesis and Exodus* (trans. Heine), 40. See Pleše, *Poetics of the Gnostic Universe*, 127–28.

39. Origen, *Gospel according to John, Books 1–10* (trans. Heine), 53.

Chapter 8

becomes less a beautiful theater than an enlightened prison complete with continuing education classes. It was created because souls needed a place to fall as a springboard for their return.[40]

With this take on the Orphic myth, Origen defends a view of incarnation that defaults to the Platonic scale of being (*Comm. Jo.* 2.13–17; cf. Plato, *Resp.* 509b; cf. 505a–506e). Yes, the Intellect (Word) and World Soul (Spirit) are hypostases of the One (Father), but the Son is less divine than the Father and the Spirit less divine than the Son. In his commentary on John 1:1, he says that the Word is the next best thing to *the* God. The Father alone is "very God" (2.19). Thus, Origen helps to coin the language of Nicaea and Chalcedon.[41] Nevertheless, many of the conclusions he draws with these categories were rejected at these councils.[42]

For Origen, it is not only that the Son differs qualitatively from the Father, but also that Jesus—his eternal soul—is qualitatively different from the eternal Son. This precosmic union of the human soul of Jesus with the Logos, and the union of the Logos with this human Jesus in the incarnation, tends toward an absorption of his humanity into deity, on the analogy of the lump of iron in the fire. The Word descended to the fallen souls to show them how to return to the Father, "passing from earthly to soulish and finally to spiritual existence" (*Princ.* 4.4.5; 4.9.2; cf. *Or.* 23.3). The call to fellow souls now is to the "ascension of the mind, since only the mind is capable of participation in the Logos."[43] Hence, by leading us even here and now back to contemplation of the Father, "God the Word is the minister of deity to all the other Gods."[44] This precreation myth controls Origen's Christology and soteriology. The eternal Son maintains his divinity by contemplating the Father, and the soul of Jesus was so fixed in this contemplation that it became fused with the Son.[45] Therefore, the chief purpose of the incarnation was to reveal the invisible deity to sensual creatures, Origen says. Having done this, the Logos divests himself of his natural body.[46]

---

40. His parallel to the sending of John the Baptist is Adam being "sent out of the paradise of God," understood allegorically as the first Adam (spiritual) being sent into the second Adam (physical), which is an intriguing choice of Philo over Paul (1 Cor 15:46–49).

41. See Origen, *Princ.* 2.6.2. He also stipulates "that in Christ there is only one nature, his deity, because he is the only-begotten Son of the Father, and another human nature, which in very recent times he took upon him to fulfill the divine purpose" (*Princ.* 1.2.1).

42. The Nicene language of the Son as "very God of very God" and "Light from Light" is directed against Origen's ontological subordinationism.

43. Farrow, *Ascension Theology*, 20.

44. Origen, *Gospel according to John, Books 1–10* (trans. Heine), 99.

45. Origen, *Gospel according to John, Books 1–10* (trans. Heine), 172; cf. 176, 217–18.

46. Trigg notes that nowhere did he affirm resurrection of the body, "and by associating the resurrection of the flesh with the many and the more simple he gave the clear impression to any-

When Celsus mocked the resurrection, Origen said that the pagan philosopher was basing his judgment on the crass literal-historical interpretation of the simple rather than on a spiritual view of the advanced. Origen compares Jesus's resurrection to the reviving of Plato's Er (*Cels.* 2.16).[47] The "spiritual body" of 1 Cor 15:44 indicates that "in the resurrection of the just there will be nothing physical [*animale*] in those who have merited beatitude.... The spirit [*nous*], in its falling, became soul; and the soul, when formed again in virtues, will become spirit again.... It follows from this that God and these beings [rational souls of angels and humans] are *in some way of the divine substance*."[48] At the cross, "the dispensation of the flesh was ended."[49] The ascension is "the ascent of mind rather than the body" (*Or.* 23.2). Those of "perfect faith," then will understand the true, spiritual meaning of Jesus's resurrection.[50] Thus, as in Platonism, the ontological divide is not between creator and created but divine Soul and body (*Princ.* 3.6.8).

Mark Edwards disputes the conclusion of Trigg and others that for Origen there is an end to corporeality.[51] More plausibly, Scott argues that Origen had a more nuanced understanding of "body" and that, "Later hostile interpreters, such as Methodius, Jerome, and Epiphanius, accused Origen of 'spiritualizing' the resurrection body to the point of extinction." Instead, Scott argues that Origen adopts the view that "the soul retains a body to facilitate its postmortem quest for divinization."[52] This fits with the popular view of Origen's day that the

---

one at all familiar with his thought that he rejected it." See Trigg, *Origen*, 214; *Comm. Matt.* 17.29, referencing Isa 40:5. In *Contra Celsum*, Origen basically argues that advanced Christians are better Platonists than are pagan Platonists like Celsus. When Celsus wonders why anyone would want a resurrected body, Origen counters that Celsus has failed to see that this doctrine, "while preached in the churches, is understood more clearly by the intelligent" (*Cels.* 5.18).

47. See also Origen, *Princ.* 4.2.1–4.3.7. This point is argued more fully in *On the Resurrection*, where Origen rejects as a crude myth the idea that our fleshly body will be raised. Although we only have fragments of this work, principally from his contemporary critics, where these critics (especially Methodius and Jerome) agree in their citations, it is reasonable to suggest that they accurately represent his view. Hans Urs von Balthasar notes, "The Alexandrian idea of incarnation always reminds one of the action of a ball which, thrown from great height, in an instant strikes against the ground only to spring up from the earth with tremendous force and return to its starting point." See Balthasar, introduction to *Origen*, 17. This analogy underscores the difference with Irenaeus, who gives more weight to Christ's historical existence and work. For a critical but nuanced interpretation of the view of Origen that I am defending here, see Chadwick, "Origen, Celsus and the Resurrection."

48. See Balthasar, *Origen*, 50–51, emphasis added.

49. Balthasar, *Origen*, 135.

50. Origen, *Gospel according to John, Books 1–10* (trans. Heine), 322, emphasis added.

51. Edwards, "Origen's Two Resurrections," 502.

52. Scott, *Journey Back to God*, 122.

astral "body" in which the soul descends comes to acquire increasingly material vestments, which it then divests itself of these at each level of reascent (based on *Tim.* 41d–e and *Phaedr.* 246a–247b). "For the Neoplatonists, as for the Orphic," says Dodds, "the *kitôn* is always something required in the soul's descent and thereafter sloughed off."[53] This seems to be how Origen thinks of the "spiritual body" of 1 Corinthians 15 (*Princ.* pref. 5).[54]

Regardless of whether Origen adopted the astral body as a temporary vehicle of transportation, the return to the "beginning" is complete disembodiment. Origen can therefore say he believes in the resurrection of the body but understand it the way the Valentinians had—namely, as the replacement of Jesus's natural body with the spiritual church, the eventual restoration of all imprisoned souls to the *plērōma* (*Or.* 23.2).[55] Like Jesus's repatriation, "The soul that will 'climb to the heights of heaven' shall no longer be a man, but according to his word, will be 'like an angel of God'" or perhaps divine; but in either case, "he shall *certainly no longer be a man*."[56] Origen encourages the adept to move from the temporal gospel for the simple to the eternal gospel for the spiritual, fixing our eyes not on Christ crucified and raised in the flesh but on Christ as the postincarnate Word filling the universe (*Princ.* 2.6.7; 2.11.6).[57]

IRENAEAN VERSUS ORIGENIST TRAJECTORIES

Origen did not set out to create a synthesis of Plato and Christ. Rather, he believed that there was already considerable harmony deriving from Plato's knowledge of the Hebrew scriptures and the general enlightening operations of Christ the eternal Logos. Where there was conflict, philosophy knew what to do with scripture.[58] Fraenkel writes, "In ancient Alexandria Plato's model is used in the first centuries of the Common Era to interpret Judaism and Christianity as philosoph-

---

53. Dodds, *Elements of Theology*, 307–8 and 308 n. 1.
54. See also Origen, *Princ.* 3.6.7; cf. Scott, *Journey Back to God*, 125.
55. Greer, *Origen*, 126–27.
56. In the soul's fall before the creation of this world, "because he abandoned life and chose death, man became a human being; and not just a human being, but also earth. . . . In the resurrection, however, the flesh will cleave to the soul and will become a soul which . . . will become 'one spirit with him' (1 Cor 6:17), and become a 'spiritual body' (1 Cor 15:44)." Cf. Origen, *Or.* 23.2.
57. Balthasar, *Origen*, 31.
58. Ramelli, "Origen and the Platonic Tradition," 4. Origen likens Jesus's resurrection to the reviving of Plato's Er (*Cels.* 2.16) and compares the Christian paradise to Plato's ascent of the soul and contemplation of hyperouranios (3.80), which Origen Christianizes (7.44). Origen also assimilates Plato's notion of the deities' purification of the earth through water to the Christian

ical religions, most notably by Philo and Philo's Christian students, Clement and Origen."[59] In this view, the measure of the religion's value is its comportment with philosophy, which leads the soul from the childhood of stories and authorities to individual autonomy.[60]

As we have been seeing, philosophical religion assumes that historical religions, including their scriptures, do not themselves present the truth until they are interpreted allegorically to say in many cases the opposite of their obvious sense. In its simple creed, Christianity is as particular as Judaism or any other religion. It has its own narrative (*mythos*), rites, and way of life, all bound to the body and history. Yet when interpreted philosophically, it is the consummate religion: the ultimate myth underlying the same universal doctrines affirmed by reason (i.e., Orphic presuppositions).

Whenever scripture conflicts with this reason, which is the divine Intellect, the former must be allegorized. Clement and Origen are progenitors of the conviction that Christianity, far from being an odd sect whose gospel is "foolishness to Greeks," conquers and assimilates to itself the sages of all nations who taught the soul's ascent.[61] Philosophy supplies the actual ontological content.[62]

Irenaeus represents a fundamentally different interpretative strategy. Reacting against gnostic allegorizing, his hermeneutic is governed by (1) an ordinary-sense interpretation, (2) Christocentric integration of all scripture in terms of historical promise and fulfillment, and (3) a "presbyterial reading" that eschews idiosyncratic conclusions and instead interprets scripture within the church among its pastors and elders. After carefully summarizing gnostic exploitation of John's Prologue as a myth of the aeons, Ireanaeus concludes that "it simply does not fit with the text."[63]

For Irenaeus, no higher hermeneutic of philosophical religion judges the ordinary sense of scripture. Jesus indeed taught parables, Irenaeus acknowledges, but he explained them and did not give us license to interpret historical narratives parabolically (*Haer.* 4.36).[64] Parables should be interpreted in the light of clearer statements in scripture, he says, so that "the parables will receive a similar inter-

---

concept of purification by Christ (4.20; 4.62). Origen overtly appreciated Plato's criticism of "pagan" mythology as unworthy of the divinities (*Phileb.* 12b; *Cels.* 4.48).

59. Fraenkel, *Philosophical Religions*, xii, 132; see also Walzer, *Galen on Jews and Christians*, 16.
60. Fraenkel, *Philosophical Religions*, 87–88.
61. Fraenkel, *Philosophical Religions*, 89–91.
62. Fraenkel, *Philosophical Religions*, 131.
63. Behr, *Irenaeus of Lyons*, 108.
64. He has an illuminating reading of the parable of the tax collector and the Pharisee at *Haer.* 4.36.

Chapter 8

pretation from all, and the body of truth remain complete, structured harmoniously, an unshaken" (2.27.1).

According to Irenaeus, the ecclesial reading of scripture with Christ as the unifying center began with the apostles themselves, who interpreted the Old Testament as being fulfilled in Christ. While gnostics might gain credit for their myths by taking biblical expressions out of context and allegorizing them, Irenaeus announces that in his fifth book he will draw up "the rest of the words of the Lord, which he taught concerning the Father not by parable but by expressions taken in their obvious meaning, and the exposition of the epistles of the blessed apostle" (*Haer.* 4.41.4).[65] We must be satisfied therefore with revelation and ignore speculative questions, such as what God was doing before he created the world (2.28.3).[66]

For Irenaeus, the gospel is God's descent in the flesh to save the whole person, body and soul (*Haer.* 3.18.1). In contrast with Origen's "ascent of mind," Irenaeus says that Christ did bodily "ascend to the height above, offering and commending to His Father that human nature which had been found, making in His own person the first-fruits of the resurrection of man" (3.19.3). Henri Crouzel observes, "One principle dominates Origen's cosmology: the end is like the beginning."[67] Irenaeus emphasizes the surpassing greatness of bodily resurrection and glorification (2.28.3). While for Origen "the restoration of all things" (Acts 3:21) includes only spirits, Irenaeus says against the gnostics, "neither is the substance nor the essence of the creation annihilated (for faithful and true is He who established it)" (*Haer.* 5.36.1). Origen considered the *apokatastasis* to be the uniting of all spirits in the Logos who is no longer human. In contrast, Irenaeus, drawing on Romans 5 and other biblical passages, describes recapitulation in historical and covenantal terms as being united to Adam as head in a "first covenant," which was a "covenant of law," distinguished from being united to Christ as head in "the gospel covenant" (*Haer.* 1.10.3).[68] He focuses on the economy as it was revealed historically in scripture.

For Irenaeus, everything turned on the activity of the three divine hypostases in this economy, lifting us up from death and bondage to sin rather than on the believer's ascent. The whole human being participates in deification by grace: we become more fully human than ever before and not less (*Haer.* 1.10.3; 1.10.5; 2.28.3; 4.13.1; 4.15.1; 4.16.3).

---

65. Quoted in Behr, *Irenaeus of Lyons*, 97.
66. For a fuller exposition of these points see Behr, *Irenaeus of Lyons*, 118.
67. Crouzel, *Origen*, 205.
68. Cf. *Haer.* 4.13.1; 4.15.1; 4.16.3; and 5.16.3.

Irenaeus's general approach to interpreting scripture led to increasing clarity and consensus regarding two dogmas that decisively separated Christian orthodoxy from the Platonism of Origen and others in the fourth century: creation *ex nihilo* and the consubstantiality of the hypostases or persons of the Trinity. In spite of the continuing attraction of some scholars to the Hellenization thesis of Ritschl and Harnack, both dogmas fought their way to triumph *against* the tide of Platonic-Stoic philosophy. Louth explains how the Trinitarian debates were not only about the immanent relations within the Godhead but also about the relationship of the world to the triune God:

> The problem posed by the Arian controversy was how to rethink the understanding of God's relationship to the world, now that no such intermediate zone could be admitted, and the conclusions of such rethinking were dramatic: Arius consigned the Word to the created order; the Orthodox consigned him to the realm of the (now strictly) divine. Nicaea can then be seen, as Friedo Ricken has put it, as a "crisis for early Christian Platonism." The Orthodox freed themselves from an aspect of Platonism, the implications of which they now fully understood, and attained a new level of clarity in their understanding of the revelation of the Christian God.[69]

Creation and emanation represented irreconcilable maps. If all things were brought into being in the Son by the utterance of the Father, they could not be divine. There is no greater or lesser. Together with the Father, the Son and the Spirit are either God or creatures.

The breadth of agreement regarding *ex nihilo* creation eliminated any ontological *tertium quid* for Origen's subordinationism in the Godhead and pantheism or panentheism in cosmology. As the complicated controversy unfolded, compromise positions proved unsatisfactory to Arians or Homoousions.[70] Instead of a dimmer switch, being was binary. Intermediate divine beings and realms fell out of the picture.[71] For the Arians, Jesus was the first and highest creature while the Nicene Council concluded in 325 that Jesus was "God from God, Light from Light, true God from true God, begotten, not made; of the same essence [*homoousios*] as the Father."[72] If the Nicene consensus had conceded to Helleniz-

---

69. Louth, *Origins of the Christian Mystical Tradition*, 97. *Ex nihilo* creation was adopted from Judaism rather than invented by Christians. See for example Bockmuehl, "Creation ex Nihilo."

70. Such complexities are admirably narrated in Anatolios, *Retrieving Nicaea*, and Ayres, *Nicaea and Its Legacy*.

71. Louth, *Origins of the Christian Mystical Tradition*, 73.

72. Anatolios, *Retrieving Nicaea*, 9.

ing (i.e., Platonism), they would have followed Origen and the semi-Arians (Homoiousians).

Especially through the Trinitarian debates, Athanasius of Alexandria (ca. 296/8–373 CE) underwent a transformation due to a fuller grasp of creation from his early and fairly Origenist treatise *Contra gentes* to his later *De incarnatione*.[73] "This change," Louth observes, "is permanent: nowhere again in Athanasius' writings do we find the idea of divinizing contemplation."

> Indeed, in his *Life of St. Antony*, there is, surprisingly, scarcely any mention of *theoria*, contemplation, at all. One might say that there is in Athanasius a reaction against Origen that is at the same time anti-mystical. And the root of this reaction lies in the perception that the soul is not in any way connatural with God, and certainly not co-eternal with him. The clear assertion of the doctrine of *creatio ex nihilo* which, from Athanasius onwards becomes an accepted premise in patristic theology, has disclosed an ontological gulf between God and the creature and, a fortiori, between God and the soul. And this has led Athanasius to suspect any mysticism whereby the soul becomes divine through contemplation. So he has, at one level at any rate, made a complete break with the Platonist tradition.... Divinization is a result of the Incarnation: it is an act of grace, in the fullest sense of the word.[74]

The whole person is deified—that is, united to God—in a thoroughly creaturely capacity "as he is restored to conformity with the image of God, that is, the Word, by the condescension of the Word himself to our fallen state in the Incarnation."[75] This version of deification is Irenaean rather than Origenist.[76]

By the fifth century, Trinitarian and christological debates were bound up with controversies over asceticism, monasticism, Manichaeism, astrological determinism, and Pelagianism. In many ways, Clark notes, "'Origen' served as a code word for various theological concerns problematic to Christians at the turn of the fifth century."[77] The Second Council of Constantinople (553) condemned Origenism and,

---

73. Louth, *Origins of the Christian Mystical Tradition*, 75–76.
74. Louth, *Origins of the Christian Mystical Tradition*, 76.
75. Louth, *Origins of the Christian Mystical Tradition*, 76–77.
76. Levering, *Jesus and the Demise of Death*, 135 n. 28.
77. Clark, *Origenist Controversy*, 6. Clark puts it this way: "Only Rufinus understood the religious issue confronting Origen that had prompted the writing of *On First Principles*: the need to construct a polemic against Gnostic and astrological determinism that would 'save' human free will and God's justice" (7). On the mediating role of Evagrius of Pontus to subsequent generations, see Ramelli, *Evagrius's "Kephalaia Gnostika."*

according to its extant version, Origen himself.[78] According to the eleventh anathema: "If anyone shall say that the future judgment signifies the destruction of the body and that the end of the story will be an immaterial *physis*, and that thereafter there will no longer be any body matter, but only *nous*, let him be anathema."[79]

CONCLUSION: "THE PLATONISM OF THE FATHERS"

Plotinus repeated Plato's rationale for philosophy: "Since it is here that evils are, and they must necessarily haunt this region, and the soul wants to escape from evils, we must escape from here. What, then, is this escape?" It is "to become as like God as possible" (*Enn.* 1.2.1; Plato, *Theaet.* 176a–b). After Theodosius closed the pagan schools, this *paideia* was carried on mostly in Christian monasticism, true "republics" led by a philosopher-ruler. Eusebius claims that Plato was indebted to Moses, the first such lawgiver, and the Hebrew prophets he describes as early monks—"models of perfection" similar to Pythagoras and Plato.[80] Their goal was "to teach the narratives of the inspired Scripture to those of childish souls in a very simple way just like stories [*mythoi*], but to teach those of a trained disposition the deeper and systematic doctrines of the texts by means of the so-called scond level of interpretation and explanation of the intelligible contents that are hidden from the multitude" (*Praep. ev.* 12.4.2). "These parallels, Eusebius claims, reveal how much Plato is indebted to the Law of Moses," says Fraenkel. "What he shows, in fact, is the opposite: how much the Alexandrian interpretation of the Law of Moses depends on Plato."[81]

As a dedicated follower of Origen, Eusebius believed that only allegorical interpretation could transmute the lead of a literal reading into the gold of philosophical religion. If the Hebrew prophets are correlated with monks, the Christian emperor Constantine is the new Moses. In his *Praise of Constantine* (336 CE) Eusebius claims to have found "'the perfect philosopher-king' [*philosophos basileus*] who, in the footsteps of Moses and Christ, continues the *Logos*'s project of ordering

---

78. Only in the modern era has this condemnation been contested on historical grounds. Some argue that the anathema of the earlier, local synod against Origen was inserted into the Second Council's conclusions; see for example Greer, *Origen*, 3. For the documents and traditional argument, see Price, *Acts of the Council of Chalcedon*.

79. See *NPNF* 14:316–17.

80. Eusebius, *Dem. ev.* 1.2; *Praep. ev.* 7.6.4; 12.29.1. See D. O'Meara, *Platonopolis*, 164–65.

81. Fraenkel, *Philosophical Religions*, 92.

humankind toward what is best." The colony of Magnesia of Plato's *Laws*, says Fraenkel, became Christendom, "a Christian world-state in which all citizens strive to become like God by living a life ordered by reason towards the perfection of reason: 'Yes, this is surely the greatest miracle—that so great a king has cried out at the top of his voice to the whole world and, like some interpreter of the All-Ruling God, has called all under his care to knowledge [*gnôsis*] of the True Being [*ho ôn*].'"[82] For the many, Constantine drove out pagan worship and replaced it with good stories, setting the stage for the few spiritual adepts to attain higher wisdom. "Philosophical doctrines," notes Fraenkel, "can thus be located in, but not learned from, a religious tradition."[83] The many still need the unyielding authority of particular stories, rites, and laws, but Orphic theology transcends them.

It is within this frame, to which Origen contributed significantly, that some Christian theologians wrote, prayed, and taught. The spectrum is represented well by two African bishops: the reluctant Synesius, who confessed his abiding attachment to Neoplatonism and Hermetic beliefs, and Augustine, who grew gradually critical of Neoplatonism and especially of Hermeticism. Certain philosophical convictions, "which have entered the soul through knowledge to the point of demonstration," said Synesius, could not be reconciled with "those 'convictions' which are cherished by the common [Christian] people."[84] He says he cannot accept that the soul was created with the body, as in Genesis 1, and "as for the resurrection such as common belief admits it, I see here an ineffable mystery and I am far from sharing the views of the vulgar crowd thereon."[85] Nevertheless, he was thrust into the episcopal office by Theophilus of Alexandria.

At the other end is Augustine, who converted from Manichaeism with the help of "the Platonist books" (translations of Plotinus and Porphyry) before embracing the Christian faith in which his mother had instructed him. Still in the shadow of Julian's failed attempt to restore paganism and the recent sacking of the empire by Visigoths, Augustine launched out against Hermes Trismegistus and "the raft which is called magic, or sorcery—a name of detestation—or by the more honourable title of 'theurgy.' . . . In fact, both types are engaged in the fraudulent rites of demons, wrongly called angels" (*Civ.* 10.9).[86]

---

82. Fraenkel, *Philosophical Religions*, 143.
83. Fraenkel, *Philosophical Religions*, 14–15.
84. Synesius, *Ep.* 105, quoted in Marrou, "Synesius of Cyrene," 143. Synesius had been a pupil of Hypatia, the Neoplatonic philosopher who was killed by a mob of Christians. See Watts, *City and School*, 197–98.
85. Synesius, *Ep.* 105, quoted in Marrou, "Synesius of Cyrene," 146.
86. Translation of *City of God*, unless otherwise noted, by Knowles and Bettenson. Augustine's lengthy diatribe against Hermes Trismegistus appears in *Civ.* 8.23–26.

Augustine's relation to Plato and Plotinus reflects a combination of attraction and restraint. Platonism had first awakened him from his Manichaean slumbers and drawn him to the One who is the Good and source of all being. "The reason why I have decided to concentrate on the Platonists," he explains, "is that their writings are more generally known" (8.10). Besides, the Platonist recognized that God is immaterial, immutable, simple, impassible, and so forth. Perhaps during his travels Plato learned it from Jeremiah, he suggests.[87] Yet there is a clear tension between Orphic dualism and the scriptures.[88] Augustine feels this tension increasingly. As early as the *Confessions* (12.12.12) he recognized that the doctrine of *ex nihilo* creation established an unbridgeable chasm. The Platonists helped him to believe in one God, the source of all things. "But that the Word was made flesh and dwelt among us, I did not read there." Nor, he adds, did he find in those volumes that God gave all who believe in Christ "the right to become the children of God." "In them no one listens to the voice which says, 'Come unto me all you that labor'" (7.21). "The Platonists, to be sure, do not show quite the folly of the Manicheans," he says in the *City of God*. "All the same, they hold that souls are so influenced by 'earthly limbs and dying members'" that the body is a kind of prison. But we do not seek liberation from the body, says Augustine (*Civ.* 14.5; cf. 13.17).

Augustine's pastoral routine drew him deeply into the scriptures that formed the liturgy and were the basis of his preaching.[89] As he wrote scriptural commentaries, doctrinal summaries, and polemical treatises against Manichaean, Pelagian, and Donatist heresies, Augustine grew more skeptical of Platonism as a handmaiden. Giving his last words on the subject in his *Retractions*, the aged bishop revokes his earlier suggestion that Plato derived some of his beliefs from Moses's writings and contact with Jeremiah. He emphasizes the "literal" sense, he says, "not the allegorical meanings of the text, but the proper assessment of what actually happened" (*Retract.* 22.24).[90] "It is, I suppose, humiliating for learned people to leave the school of Plato to enter that of Christ," he adds (*Civ.* 10.29). "Likewise, the praise with which I so greatly extolled Plato and the Platonists (or the Academic philosophers) was most inappropriate for these impious persons and has rightly displeased me; it is especially in the face of their great errors that Christian teaching must be defended" (*Retract.* 22.24). Yet the imprint of Plato did

---

87. Augustine, *Ver. rel.* 7, noted in *City of God* (ed. Knowles; trans. Bettenson), 304 n. 10.
88. Carlos Steel explains this tension well in "De-Paganizing Philosophy," 32.
89. Sanlon, *Augustine's Theology of Preaching*, 41.
90. Translation of the *Retractions* entitled *Revisions* (trans. Ramsey). We also see this in *On the Literal Interpretation of Genesis* (c. 401–415 CE) after his anti-Manichaean treatises.

not disappear. John Burnaby observes, "Augustine is both the greatest disciple and the profoundest critic of Plotinus."[91]

In this way, Augustine's mature thought reflects a form of chastened, self-critical Christian Platonism that established the creative tension in medieval theology. Yet at the same time, despite anathemas, Origen lived on. Through his many disciples, especially in the monastic movements, he passed on a powerful and essentially Orphic approach to Christianity and the Bible that surged through Western history all the way to the Enlightenment. His "higher gospel" appears in Kant's distinction between "universal religion" and "ecclesiastical faiths," the "Jesus of History" and the "Christ of Faith," and perhaps even our now common dichotomy between "spiritual" and "religious."

---

91. Burnaby, *Amor Dei*, vi. From 1888 to 1920 scholars such as Harnack, Boissier, and Alfaric viewed Augustine as not quite converted from Neoplatonism until quite late in life. Then in 1920 Charles Boyer offered a decisive rebuttal. By mid-century, it was generally thought that Augustine underwent a sincere conversion but remained very Neoplatonic. The trend in Augustine scholarship today is to treat him in his own context. For a good overview of these trends, see J. O'Meara, "Neoplatonism of Saint Augustine," 35.

9

A Christian Reconstruction of Late Neoplatonism
St. Paul's Philosopher-Convert

> I am filled with hilarity & spring, my heart dances, my sight is quickened, I behold shining relations between all beings, and am impelled to write and almost to sing. I think one would grow handsome who read Proclus much and well.
>
> —Ralph Waldo Emerson[1]

> In a fashion beyond words, the simplicity of Jesus became something complex, the timeless took on the duration of the temporal, and, with neither change nor confusion of what constitutes him, he came into our human nature, he who totally transcends the natural order of the world. This is the kind of theurgic lights into which we have been initiated by the hidden tradition of our inspired teachers, a tradition at one with scripture.
>
> —Pseudo-Dionysius (*DN* 1.4)[2]

> Dionysius came, as it were, to a world that already knew him.
>
> —Andrew Louth[3]

It is often supposed that contextualization is the fruit of a peculiarly modern sensitivity to distinct cultural, religious, and social histories. However, from

---

1. Emerson, *Journals and Miscellaneous Notes*, Journal R (1843), 379.
2. Dionysius the Aeropagite, *Pseudo-Dionysius: The Complete Works* (trans. Luibheid), 52. Lit., "theurgic lights"; so I have translated here.
3. Louth, "Reception of Dionysius," 52.

early times Christian thinkers wrestled with the relationship between the two horizons: the biblical world shaped by God's covenant with Israel and the Greek philosophical inheritance that had formed their earlier education. Even Clement and Origen viewed gnostic sects in Alexandria and beyond as a different religion. Yet these early Christian writers carved a riverbed for a significant stream of self-designated "Christian gnosis" that claimed to take captive the highest wisdom of the gentiles to the obedience of Christ. It is ironic that the enemies of pagan idolatry also preserved much of the textual history of that section of the cultural library that has come down to us.

Perhaps more intriguing is that the last—and perhaps the greatest—systematic theologian of the opposing forces became the first significant impact on Byzantine and medieval theology. Proclus of Athens (c. 412–485 CE) influenced Christian theology in some direct ways but especially through his likely pupil who, under the pseudonym of Dionysius the Areopagite, wrote a collection of small books that captured the imagination of Christendom. Leaving out some important details, I focus on the most conspicuous aspects of their contributions at the intersection of pagan and Christian visions of the divine self.

Proclus and the "Shining Relations between All Beings"

Ralph Waldo Emerson exulted that, upon reading Proclus, he felt as if he were dancing.[4] If Hermes Trismegistus is the fountainhead of theurgic Neoplatonism (as Iamblichus assures at the very beginning of the book), Proclus is its systematic theologian. Born eighty-seven years after Iamblichus's death, and a half-century after Emperor Julian's short-lived revival of theurgic paganism, Proclus's cherished world seemed to be in retreat. He came to adulthood in Constantinople at a time when Theodosius I was fending off Gothic invasions while vigorously promoting Nicene orthodoxy and Augustine's *City of God*, with its denunciation of theurgy, appeared in the Western empire. Yet there were still flickering lights. Plutarch of Athens restored Plato's Academy around a theurgic Neoplatonist curriculum based on Iamblichus, and Syrianus, a student of the famous Hypatia, left Alexandria to join him.[5] The school's program is encapsulated in the title of

---

4. Emerson, *Journals and Miscellaneous Notes*, 379.

5. Both the Alexandrian and Athenian branches of Neoplatonism carried the theurgic torch, the latter more aggressive in its paganism. See D. O'Meara's *Platonopolis* for intriguing glimpses of the Iamblichean schools in Syria and Asia Minor (16–18), the Athenian and Alexandrian schools (19–30), and the Iamblichean curriculum, "Minor Mysteries" and religious cult (62–127). Yet, while relations were generally more congenial in Alexandria, they turned deadly

the latter's lost work, *On the Harmony of Orpheus, Pythagoras, and Plato with the Chaldaean Oracles*.[6]

Proclus likewise began his studies in Alexandria, where he also joined various mystery cults but opted finally for the Athenian school to study with Plutarch and Syrianus, the latter soon succeeding the former as scholiarch. He called Syrianus his "fellow Bacchant with Plato" and a "true hierophant of the divine doctrines."[7] According to the biography of Proclus's student Marinus, Proclus "used to experience a dionysiac ecstasy for the first principles" and often beheld them (*Vit. Proc.* 28–29). As Christians removed his beloved Athena from her Parthenon, the divine lady appeared, asking the philosopher to take her into his home. Hekate also appeared to Proclus frequently and, imitating Julian the Theurgist, he often caused rain and averted earthquakes, predicted the future, and received inspired oracles.[8]

For the next fifty years Proclus presided over the Athenian Academy and appointed his student Ammonius as the head of the Alexandrian school, consolidating his leadership of late antique Neoplatonism. Proclus stated that we must "operate logically and intellectually and at the same time with divine inspiration." Because there is theurgy (i.e., the gods reveal themselves) there can be a legitimate science called theology (Proclus, *In Plat. Parm.* 6.1071–1072).[9] The Alexandrian school had no trouble pointing out contradictions, difficulties, and errors in Plato and displayed an interest in reconciling Aristotle to his teacher. However, Proclus was a confirmed heir to the Athenian Academy's respect for Plato's writings as scripture along with the Chaldean Oracles and Orphic Hymns. The highest truth came from the Orphic mysteries, thence Pythagoras, and finally Plato (*In Plat.*

---

when students lynched a classmate who became a Christian and a Christian mob murdered the school's principal, Hypatia, in 415. See Wallis, *Neoplatonism*, 139; cf. Reale, *History of Ancient Philosophy*, 442. Syrianus began his philosophical studies in Alexandria under Hypatia, but after her murder he joined Plutarch in Athens.

6. Bradshaw, *Aristotle East and West*, 142–43. For the most part, Syrianus has been forgotten, but Proclus himself acknowledges him as the source of his system; he chose to be buried in the same tomb so that they might fly to heaven together. As Marrow and Dillon put it, "One reason that Proclus may be unwilling to claim too much credit for the Parmenides Commentary might of course be that in fact very little of it is truly his." See Marrow and Dillon, introduction to Proclus, *Commentary on Plato's Parmenides* (ed. and trans. Marrow and Dillon), xxxvii.

7. Proclus, *In Plat. Parm.* 1.1.

8. See Marinus, *Vit. Proc.* 12, 22, 30. Translation in Edwards, *Neoplatonic Saints*, 58–115. See also Saffrey, "From Iamblichus to Proclus and Damascius," 254–55.

9. Translation, unless otherwise noted, of Proclus, *Commentary on Plato's Parmenides* by Marrow and Dillon, here at 424–25.

Tim. 1.5.25.24–1.5.26.4).[10] Since all truth was Plato's truth, whatever truth that has been said in other schools had already been said better by the philosopher (*In Plat. Tim.* 1.6.30.23; cf. *Theo. Plat.* 1.6.2). He praises "the ways in which [Plato] teaches us the mystical ways of conceiving of things divine."[11]

As Dodds observes, Proclus acclaimed Plato not only "the supreme master" but "definitely an inspired writer" along with Julian the Theurgist, author of the Chaldean Oracles, "whom it is unlawful to disbelieve."[12] For Dodds, though, all of this demonstrates theurgy's role in the decline of Hellenistic thought into gnostic and magical nonsense. "The creator of theurgy was a magician, not a Neoplatonist," said Dodds.[13] "The *De mysteriis* is a manifesto of irrationalism" and "theurgy is the refuge of a despairing intelligentsia."[14] In contrast, Hegel praised the Athenian scholiarch as having restored Plato's philosophy to its pristine luster by understanding its original wells of inspiration.[15]

As Christians enrolled in them, the Neoplatonic schools of Athens and especially Alexandria were roiled in debates about the eternity of the world. For Proclus, the world is an eternally necessary image of the Good. Imaging is not accidental but essential to the being of the cosmos. Hence, if the world is not eternal, the forms—indeed, the One itself—cannot be so. "But if there is no copy when there is no pattern, then there will be no pattern when there will be no copy.... [T]he one is not, if the other is not" (*De aeter. mundi* 2.41).[16] We meet the same aporia we have encountered repeatedly with the analogies of sun and river: transcendent One is not participated or affected in any way by its rays or

---

10. All references to the *Timaeus* commentary are from Tarrant, *Commentary on the Timaeus*.

11. Proclus, *In Plat. Tim.* 1.4; cf. 1.5–6; *Theo. Plat.* 1.1.6; 1.6.16.

12. Dodds, introduction to Proclus, *Elements of Theology*, xii.

13. Dodds, *Greeks and the Irrational*, 283–314, here at 289.

14. Dodds, *Greeks and the Irrational*, 287–88. The heat of his critical, even hostile, approach to the subject should not distract one from his illuminating research.

15. Hegel, *Plato and the Platonists*, 433–34. See also Proclus, *Commentary on Plato's Parmenides* (ed. and trans. Marrow and Dillon), 480. Following Numenius and Iamblichus, the Athenian school adopted a more Neopythagorean triad—the transcendent One with a secondary One (or Monad) and Dyad (the source of multiplicity)—but on this point reverted to the earlier position of Plotinus that the One of the Parmenides is the Good of the *Republic*. See Blumenthal and Lloyd, *Monad and Dyad*, esp. 1–10. A superb collection covering Proclus's life, thought, and influence is d'Hoine and Martijn, *All from One*.

16. Translations of Proclus, *On the Eternity of the World* (*De aeternitate mundi*) from Lang and Macro. The copy must be as ungenerated and indestructible as the paradigm, according to Plato (*Tim.* 29b, 38b–c). "Every producing cause is productive of secondary existences because of its completeness and superfluity of potency" (*Elem. theo.* 27, 30, 32). Thus, the paradigm produces the copy necessarily. Translation from Proclus, *Elements of Theology* (ed. and trans. Dodds).

flow; indeed, effects are always in the cause but never vice versa. Nevertheless, Proclus's main argument is that the One *must* cause exactly what it does in order to be what it "is." "For the maker and the thing generated are simultaneous with one another" (*De aeter. mundi* 16.127; citing Plato, *Phileb.* 26e–27b). So if I walk away from the mirror, would I disappear along with my reflection? If it is the very nature of time to be a "moving image of eternity" (*Tim.* 37d), eternity needs time as much as time needs eternity.

The effect imitates its cause *necessarily*, just as the cause produces the effect by virtue simply of its being. Combining Platonic and Aristotelian concepts, Proclus argues that form is in matter eternally; again, delete the matter and one loses its form. "Matter is something, that is, of the form upon it. In fact, particular matter is matter at that very moment when its form also is. . . . And the matter is ungenerated and incorruptible, so that it should not be the case that matter, when it is absolutely, requires other matter. Therefore, the forms are in matter from eternity and so the cosmos is eternal" (*De aeter. mundi* 11.95).

Proclus never engaged Christians directly, but it is hard to resist the impression that he is trying to provide a pagan alternative to Christianity at the same time colleagues were trying to provide a Christian alternative to paganism. Theurgic Neoplatonism is more religious, not only in terms of appealing to inspired authorities and rites, but in trying to recover a more personal relation to the gods. This is what the average person was missing in the elitism and abstractions of Plotinus's spirituality. In a state of existential anxiety, gnostic sects attracted many who sought an explanation of where they came from, who they are, and where they're going. More importantly, they offered an escape plan. Instead, Christians offered a historical narrative that made sense to many. With little interest in "the many" to begin with, Porphyry was even losing his hold on the court elites who had been students. The future of Neoplatonism lay with Iamblichus, Syrianus, and Proclus.

A deeply committed polytheist, Proclus was hardly interested in harmonizing his staunchly religious Orphic-Platonic school with the newfangled "gospel" sweeping the Mediterranean world. Nevertheless, he himself distinguished the universally applicable system of theo-logic in the *Elements of Theology* from his own commitments expressed in the commentaries on Plato and the texts inspired by his divine spirit: the Orphic theogonies and hymns and the Chaldean Oracles. Substituting the biblical canon, Christians nevertheless found much timber in Proclus's yard to use for their systems.

Proclus's cosmos shares the same milieu as the Chaldean Oracles, philosophical Hermetica, and gnostic texts. It consists of several "fathers," beginning with the "Intelligible Father," the unity from which the gods thought each other as mirrors of their own unity, simplicity, and rest. The Neoplatonic One is like the hypertranscendent Bythos of Alexandrian gnostics. Yet, in contrast with gnostics, Proclus taught that from this simplicity the One emanated matter as the receptacle of the initial qualities (combination of limit/unlimited), yet still without shape, discordant and disordered, but visible (based on *Tim.* 30a). Next, the "Creator-Father" (demiurge/Zeus) organized cosmos according to the vision of the paradigm, focusing on the generation of wholes and universals. He endows eternal matter with corporeal universals. Finally, the "Creator Alone" governs the transition from wholes to parts, universals to particulars, including cycles of birth and death in the corporeal world of becoming.

All of these levels, by the way, correspond to each of the first five hypostases of *Parmenides*: negation by excess (One); affirmation as paradigm (Indivisibles); affirmation and negation (Soul); affirmation as image (Divisibles); negation by defect (Matter). In other words, as the appearances emanate, they become divided; yet it is precisely by such variety of familiar images that revelation reaches us. Just as they do reach us, though, we must recognize through contemplative activity that they are not the reality itself. "But what these causes are we must learn from the family of theologians. Thus we have three causes of participation in forms: the unitary Goodness, the demiurgic power of the Forms, and the aptitude of the beings that receive illuminations from above.... [W]e can see how it possible to liken it to reflections in a mirror" (*In Plat. Parm.* 4.844–845).[17]

Rest and Procession: The One and the Many

Proclus offered an ingenious solution to the aporia of the relation between the One and the many. Giving greater precision to distinctive teachings of later Neoplatonism, Proclus envisions a theurgic cosmology. The "fall" from unity to diversity is less a matter of loss and lack than one of expansion and fullness. Rather than a tragedy, it is a triumphant procession of the Good even to matter itself before drawing all spiritual substances back into its unity. Everything turns on the threefold reality of the One at rest in itself, processing outward into manifestation and relation, and returning the diverse appearances to unity. His *Platonic Theology* is divided into just these three parts (though the third was never finished), and the same pattern governs the Christian imagination all the way to Thomas Aquinas, who structured his *Summa theologiae* according to rest, procession, reversion.

Proclus produces a fascinating myth of his own that he believes (with compelling argument) unites the otherwise contradictory threads of the Platonic di-

---

17. Translations of Proclus, *Commentary on Plato's Parmenides* from Morrow and Dillon, 215; cf. J. Trouillard, *L'Un et l'âme selon Proclos*, 122.

alogues (*In Plat. Parm.* 1.628–629). While Plato was "processing" from Parmenides to Pythagoras, Proclus was always "remaining" in the former (1.712–713). This is not far actually from his student Marinus's description of Socrates, with whom I think Proclus is meant to be identified:

> Parmenides abides in the transcendent One, Zeno projects the many as the One, and Socrates turns back even these many to the Parmenidean One, since the first member in every triad is an analogue of the rest, the second of procession and the third of reversion, and the reversion rounds out a kind of circular path connecting the end with the beginning. (Marinus, *Vit. Proc.* 30)[18]

This compact statement (similar to an allegory in Proclus's Parmenides commentary) underscores the synthetic power of the Orphic myth. Yet it is clear to whom all opinions yield. Like Socrates, Proclus "turns back even these many to the Parmenidean One."[19]

First, with Plotinus, Proclus holds that the One is imparticipable. Taking Plato's statement in the *Resp.* 509b literally, he insists that the One itself is beyond being.[20] Yet the One emanates the cosmos eternally.[21] Participation begins with the second hypostasis, Intellect. However, Proclus argues that all things participate in the imparticipable One. How does he avoid contradiction?

Second, there are three "ones," Proclus tells us: *the* One, the *henadic* ones, and the *individual* ones that constitute the henadic group or "manifold."[22] The henad is a Platonic form, but every henad *is* the One (immutable, incorporeal, simple, etc.) except that it is not self-caused. Astonishingly, he tells us that "each of the gods is nothing else than the One in its participated aspect."[23] But that it is not all:

---

18. Translation in Edwards, *Neoplatonic Saints*, 58–115.

19. Proclus, *In Plat. Tim.* 3.297. Also see OF fr. 54 in Kern, *Orphicorum fragmenta*. The source is Hieronymus of Rhodes or possibly Hellanicus (according to Damascius).

20. As noted in chapter 2, Francis M. Cornford demonstrates the impossibility of this interpretation in *Plato's Cosmology*, 4–5. Not allowing that "the divine Plato" might have changed, much less contradicted, his views, Proclus harmonizes by privileging the *Republic* as the key. Taking *Tim.* 17b literally, as if the dialogue was happening the next day, Proclus insists frankly that the *Timaeus* is simply a recapitulation of the *Republic* (*In Plat. Tim.* 1.4.12). See Proclus, *Commentary on Plato's Parmenides* (ed. and trans. Marrow and Dillon), 394. This work is, in my view, Proclus's crowning achievement and the summative statement of his entire system. See Beierwaltes, *Platonismus und Idealismus*; Beierwaltes, *Proklos*.

21. See the excellent introduction by Helen S. Lang in her and A. D. Marco's translation of Proclus's *On the Eternity of the World*.

22. Proclus, *In Plat. Tim.* 1.205.4–1.206.16; 1.707.9–11; cf. 1.1044.a7–28.

23. Proclus, *Elem. theo.* 124, 111. He adds in proposition 151 a pregnant definition: "All that is

the henads are actually the gods of Homer demoted by Plato to menial tasks in the *Timaeus*, raised anew as the links in the chain from the One to the many.[24] Though it would have surprised Plato, Proclus himself provides an ingenious solution to his One and the Many problem. It is not merely that the One emanates the Many, such that stars are less divine than forms, or that animals are less than humans. Rather, everything participates directly in its own henadic "one" while the wholly unknowable One itself neither participates nor is participated.[25]

At this point, it might seem that there is no possibility of the Many sharing in the divine life of the One. However, it is essential in Proclus's thinking that every henad (divine unity) is exactly the same as the One except for being self-caused. In terms of sovereignty, every henadic god is—in its uppermost part directed at the One—nothing but the One existing in a particular manner. At the level of *paternal* causality, there is no inferior or superior. "Everything paternal [i.e., causative] in the gods is of primal operation and stands in the position of the Good at the head of all the divine orders" (*Elem. theo.* 151).[26] The "primal god" is not "the summit of the intelligible world" (contra Origen and Porphyry) or "a participated henad." The One/Good "is not even a father, but is superior also to all paternal divinity" (*In Plat. Parm.* 6.1070). "Each of the gods is the universe and each in his own way" (*In Plat. Tim.* 1.308) and "each contains all things" (1.308.3–4 and 1.312.21–22).[27] In other words, the One is not even a *supreme* being but is beyond being. Yet every

---

paternal in the Gods is of primal operation [*prōtourgon*] and stands in the position of the Good at the head of all the divine orders [*diakosmēseis*]." Damascius says that there are "seven" in the demiurge and each is "*dis epekeina* (beyond 'twice' or 'twoness,' simple) and containing all that the first does, only particularized in the declension into classes" (*De princ.* 3.30.13–11). Quoted by Butler, "Flower of Fire," 143–44.

24. Proclus, *Elements of Theology* (ed. and trans. Dodds), 215. "For the Procline conception of the Forms as at once paradigmatic and creative, cf. in Parm. 841.26ff., . . . Plot. II.150.15 . . . de myst. 232.12 . . . Syrian. in Metaph. 187.6 . . . ps.-Dion. Div. Nom. 8.6, God creates *kata periousian dunameōs*." See especially Proclus, *Elem. theo.* 113, 119, 127, 133. Also, in proposition 67: "Every plurality has a twofold henad, one that is immanent in it [*syntetagmenē*] and one that transcends it [*exerēmēnē*]."

25. See Proclus, *Commentary on Plato's Parmenides* (ed. and trans. Marrow and Dillon), 242: "This is why Socrates in the *Philebus* (15ab) sometimes calls the Forms heads and sometimes monads: for with respect to the One they are monads because each of them is a plurality and a single being and a life-principle and an intellectual Form, but with respect to the things produced from them and the series which they establish, they are henads." This dipolar theology suggests similarities with process thought (e.g., Whitehead, Hartshorne, and Cobb).

26. Translation from Proclus, *Elements of Theology* (ed. and trans. Dodds), 133.

27. Translation from Proclus, *Commentary on Plato's Timaeus, Book 1* (ed. and trans. Tarrant et al.), vol. 2.

henadic "one" is the One in its imparticipable aspect, and its "many" members participate in it according to its lower aspect.

Third, through its highest part (i.e., the "flower of intellect") every soul shares in the lower part of the soul above it (for example, vegetative souls in the sensual and the sensual in the rational). It is like extension cords, with the leading end of the lower string plugging into the higher at its lowest end. The higher cord does not need the lower one, but the lower one needs the higher in order to be part of the string. The string falls down but can be looped into a circle. That is what Proclus does.[28] The vertical line of descent-ascent becomes a more dynamic movement from rest to procession to reversion: the snake eating its tail.

But henads are living gods, actually descending into plurality through their many participants and then reaching down to draw them back up into their simple unity. A better comparison is the feudal image of the emperor unfolding his realm into increasingly diverse and complex unities of king, knight, mayor, and father; then returning them to his headship through the levels in reverse. The relation is strictly hierarchical: a form does not participate in the individual but vice versa (*In Plat. Parm.* 4.858).[29] The lower entity (Socrates) is united to the higher (human) by its highest part, which, following Hermetic writings and the Chaldean Oracles, he calls the "flower of intellect."[30] The higher up many members are enfolded into the unity above them, the greater their real being is. Through its absolute pole, every henad participates in the relative pole of its superior all the way up the hierarchy, so, for example, by participating in my henad, I am sharing directly in the Good.[31] Every henad is the unity of *a* good, "but not the sum of good: the unitary cause of the latter is pre-established in the First Principle . . .

---

28. The vertical line is emphasized in propositions 1–6 in Proclus, *Elements of Theology* (ed. and trans. Dodds), 3–7; the circular aspect in propositions 7–12 (pp. 9–15); cf. 33 (p. 37).

29. As Proclus puts it, "The fire in us comes from the universal fire, the water in us likewise from the universal water, and so with each of the other two elements. . . . As Socrates says in the *Philebus* (29e), we share in the universal elements, not they in us" (Proclus, *Commentary on Plato's Parmenides* [ed. and trans. Marrow and Dillon], 225).

30. Proclus, *Commentary on Plato's Parmenides* (ed. and trans. Marrow and Dillon), 169; cf. Butler, "Flower of Fire," 142; Majercik, "Chaldean Triads in Neoplatonic Exegesis," 266–67; Majercik, "Chaldean Oracles," 103–4.

31. "Every god is a beneficent henad or a unifying excellence, and has this substantive character qua god (prop. 119); but the primal God is the Good unqualified and Unity unqualified, whilst each of those posterior to him is a particular excellence and a particular henad." While the henadic gods are good (in varying degrees), they are not the Good (prop. 133). Translations of *Elem. theo.* are from Proclus, *Elements of Theology* (ed. and trans. Dodds).

(prop. 8). For not all the gods together may be matched with the One, so far does it overpass the divine multitude" (*Elem. theo.* 133).

Though self-contained unities, henads participate in each other as well. As the emperor remains at rest while producing his likeness in diminishing ranks, the One remains in its transcendent simplicity beyond being while nevertheless processing as "everything in everything," as the Hermetic treatises teach. Moreover, while Plotinus used the face-and-faces image metaphorically, Proclus shares the theurgic belief that these one-many principles are actually the gods of traditional myths:

> Orpheus tells us that all things came to be in Zeus, after the swallowing of Phanes, because, although the cause of all things in the cosmos appeared primarily and in a unified form in him (Phanes), they appear secondarily and in a distinct form in the Demiurge. The sun, the moon, the heaven itself, the elements, and Eros the unifier—all came into being as a unity "mixed together in the belly of Zeus." (*In Plat. Parm.* 3.800)[32]

Zeus (or Phanes/Dionysus) is more than a cipher for the One. The return of the anthropomorphic deities not only transforms spirituality into a religion but injects a dynamism into the cosmological process. Proclus quotes a striking poem from the Chaldean Oracles underscoring this dynamism: "The Intellect of the Father whirred" with the "ideas of every form" that then "leapt out in flight from this single source" by the Father's will. Each had its own "fire of intelligence" and distributed it "among other intelligent beings." Looking to the "eternal intelligible model," "they burst forth ... and scattered through the bodies of the cosmos, swarming like bees about the mighty hollows of the world" (*In Plat. Parm.* 3.800–801).[33] The procession into diversity, materiality, and change is not an evil. On the contrary, such "bursting forth," "scattering," and "swarming" are a necessary part of the procession of the Good into the whole cosmos.

A river becomes more diverse and fragments into streams, but in Proclus's world the streams circle back, flowing toward the unity and purity of the original source. "All that proceeds from any principle and reverts upon it has a cyclical activity ... originating from the unmoved and to the unmoved again returning" (*Elem. theo.* 33). To exist at all is to be dependent on the Good that, in fact, each

---

32. Quoting OF 167b (Kern, *Orphicorum fragmenta*).
33. Quoting *Chaldean Oracles* (Des Places fr. 37).

henad is. It is therefore not a contradiction after all to say that everything participates in the imparticipable One.[34]

Fourth, even matter is swept into this flow of the Good (though of course not in the reversion). Plotinus emphasizes the "nothingness" of matter—so adamantly, in fact, that he turns it into quite something after all: utter darkness, the epitome of ugliness, the source of evil. Matter "begs and bothers, and wants to come inside" and "robs" the soul of its goodness (*Enn.* 1.8). At least in this treatise he approaches the conflict-dualism of Numenius and gnostics, making evil another ultimate cause. In contrast, Proclus does not equate nonbeing with evil but merely with a lack of *any* attributes or qualities of its own, inherently.[35] Crucially, Proclus states that matter is not only no-thing but the *principle* of nothing just as the One is the ultimate source of being. Both the One and matter are beyond being: the former by excess and the latter by lack. "The last is, like the first, perfectly simple, since it proceeds from the First alone; but the First is simple as being above all composition, the other as being beneath it" (*Elem. theo.* 59). This "lack" is not a vice but a virtue. After all, according to Proclus, Plato designates matter as "the place of the forms."[36] In an unusual borrowing from Aristotle, Proclus holds that matter always has form. However, following Plato, he sees this "womb of becoming" as entirely receptive, submitting to the demiurge and his insemination of reason-principles (*Tim.* 48a). Neither the One nor matter is "something" that exists. Precisely because they transcend being, they can be the co-operating cause of all

---

34. Proclus, *Elem. theo.* 3: "All that becomes one does so by participation of unity. For if they already are one, they cannot become one; nothing can become what it already is." The Neoplatonist triad of remaining, processing, and reverting is for Proclus equivalent to the imparticipable, participated, and participating—in other words, the One, henads, and individuals. Just as the procession of all things occurs from the universal and simple to the particular and complex, everything reverts to the Good by diverse individuals being enfolded back up the ascending staircase of unity, level by level. See Proclus, *Commentary on Plato's Parmenides* (ed. and trans. Marrow and Dillon), 139, 142, 178. Proclus adds parenthetically, "(This is the way Plato proceeds in the Sophist, and so also the Socrates of the Philebus)" (142). John Milbank comments in "Christianity and Platonism," 164: "For the same reason, according to the theurgists, the individual good of the philosopher-ruler is inseparable from the good of all the people." Not just aristocratic height, but democratic scope, "for the salvation of all."

35. "From this it is apparent that the principle most remote from the beginning of all things is sterile and a cause of nothing" (*Elem. theo.* 25).

36. *Theo. Plat.* 4.33.22; cf. Plato, *Tim.* 49a, 50d, and 52d. Although Neoplatonists generally identified the "receptacle" with matter, Plato does not; rather, we have seen, the receptacle is space. Especially after the gnostics identified evil with the World Soul, Plotinus could never have entertained the theurgic philosophers' identification of the receptacle or "womb of becoming" with matter. Yet this was a significant step toward matter's rehabilitation.

that exists. As "Father-Creator" the One produces all intelligible reality, including primal matter, but the ideas do not become visible in the realm of generation except through the womb of matter.

Although lacking any goodness of its own, matter is the product of the Good and the condition for the possibility of all goodness in the visible world (*De mal.* 36.16–18).[37] The perfect needs the less perfect; light, shadow; reality, image; fulfillment, emptiness; desire, lack. The *Symposium* reverberates throughout Proclus's theology, stressing the *eros* that yearns to be reunited in the simplicity of its proximate cause and thus directly to the One. Even the lowest things imitate the higher as much as they are able (*In Plat. Parm.* 4.845.3–12).

Fifth, Proclus's solution to the One-and-Many problem allows him to transcend Plotinus's absolute apophaticism. Of course, the One eludes our intellectual grasp. Nevertheless, we may discern causes all the way to the One itself through the effects. This is the beginning of a doctrine of analogy. "Everything divine is by itself ineffable and unknowable to all secondary things because of its superessential unity, but it may be known and apprehended from those that participate it" (*Elem. theo.* 123).

Sixth, theurgic ontology yielded revisions in the status of theological predication. For Proclus at least, this depended in part on contemporary ideas gaining ground, especially Christian ones. Plotinus's absolute apophaticism is grounded in a Parmenidean identity between being and knowing: whatever *is* must be defined and limited (i.e., some*thing*). But the One is beyond being and therefore all definitions and limitations; therefore, no attributes can be predicated of it.

Proclus does not disagree, but by identifying principles with quasi-personal gods, he introduces elements alien to Greek philosophy but familiar to Christians. Greek Gods did not love and care for the salvation of their subjects, and it would be crudely anthropomorphic to imagine the Beautiful as yearning for a human suitor. Proclus also spoke of grace as a gift of the gods to lift up souls to themselves and faith as the means of uniting to them. The contrast of faith and reason's consent, as an intuitive leap versus rational analysis, is the very sort of fideism that Clement censures among some Christians in his *Stromateis*. Christian apologists insisted that faith in Christ be supported by reasonable arguments and evidence. Proclus's account of faith is within the traditional Platonist (Orphic) ambit of an intuitive, mystical, and immediate "flash" that occurs not only in Plato's final release to the One but in Hermetic and gnostic suspension of reason at the mo-

---

37. Translations of Proclus, *On the Existence of Evils*, by Opsomer and Steel.. The One produces limit (form) and unlimited (matter) (*De mal.* 34.12–18; 35.6–20; interpreting *Phil.* 16c).

ment of genuine gnosis. Proclus is the first theologian to articulate this view of faith as a mystical suspension of reason that modernity takes for granted. Echoing the Chaldean Oracles, Proclus insists that faith (*pistis*) leaves reason behind in order to "attain 'the unified silence superior to all.'"[38] Faith does not imply that he disowned theurgy.[39] On the contrary, faith becomes incorporated into it.[40]

Proclus affirms the need for divine grace more than Plotinus and Origen but agrees with all Platonists that the "end" is a release from the body and therefore from the fatigue of generation and becoming, illusion, confusion, ignorance, and desire. The real "I" has the good fortune to participate in the movie, as it were, based on the autobiography of the Good.[41] But when the film is over, I return to

---

38. Proclus elucidates this view in *In Plat. Parm.* 1.109.24–110.2. See Wallis, "Spiritual Importance of Not Knowing," 476. Proclus's biographer and successor, Marinus, describes him as having achieved "a direct intuitive vision of the Forms," and "Marinus's successor, Isidorus . . . is described by his pupil Damascius, the last head of the Athenian school, as having approached the gods within, 'in the hidden depths of unknowing,' which reads like a description of mystical union." Like most ancient Christian writers, Origen eschewed the "ecstasy" associated with union that fascinates Neoplatonists, Hermetists, and gnostics alike. Christian apologists were dedicated to justifying faith with reasonable arguments and evidence. Immediate ecstasy was a controversial subject in the third-century church, especially after the Montanists. See Congar, *I Believe in the Holy Spirit*, 67. "As a Montanist," Congar also observes, "Tertullian made a sharp contrast between the Church of the Spirit and the Church of the bishops, but this was based on a sectarian ecclesiology: the true Church ought, he believed, to be known by the sign of ecstasy. Others should have said that it should be known by the sign of glossolalia."

39. David Bradshaw says, "The important point is that the means of rejoining the One—and thereby sharing in the divine *energeia*—is in Proclus no longer conceived as a magical or theurgical rite, save in a very broad sense, but as reaching out to God in love and silent trust. The resemblance on this point between Proclus and Christianity can hardly fail to be noticed. Is it any wonder that Christians would soon, through Dionysius, find a way of making the Procline ascent their own?" See *Aristotle East and West*, 151–52. Bradshaw may overstate Proclus's downplaying of theurgy (and proximity to Christianity). We have ample evidence from what has been said above that theurgy remained for him the best hope, and it is defended and elaborated in his *On the Hieratic Art*. We also have the summary of the sixth-century Neoplatonist and astrologer Olympiodorus: "Some put philosophy first, as Porphyry, Plotinus &c.; others the priestly art (*hieratikēn*), as Iamblichus, Syrianus, Proclus and all the priestly school." And at this stage at least, Christians considered theurgy illicit, a pagan rival to simple faith in Christ.

40. Shaw, *Theurgy and the Soul*, 204, quoting from Proclus, *In Plat. Crat.* 32.5.

41. The movie analogy is not as far-fetched as it sounds, since we are told in the *Timaeus* that time is a moving image of eternity (37d). The idea is also expressed in gnostic texts such as "Three Forms of the First Thought" (NHC XIII 9.5–8). There are similar appearances in other Sethian texts (e.g., the Secret Book of John and Thunder). For a fascinating study of the connection to Marsanes (from the group of "friends" Plotinus addressed in *Enn.* 2.9), see Birger A.

Chapter 9

what I have always been really: an idea in the Good. Essence rather than existence fills the horizon of interest.[42]

Uniting Above and Below: The One in Us

Following Iamblichus and Syrianus (contra Plotinus), Proclus takes it for granted that "Every particular soul which descends into process descends entirely and there is no part remaining above as it descends" (*Elem. theo.* 211). This is the justification for theurgy, since the whole soul of every person needs to be released from matter through rites that lead from material to contemplative to silent union. The ultimate reality envisioned by Plotinus and Porphyry is assumed by theurgic Neoplatonists: disembodied union of the divine self with the incorporeal One. However, because Soul (both cosmic and individual) descends completely into matter, ascent must begin with material rites.

For Plotinus, just as evil is simply a negation of goodness, complexity is a falling away from simplicity. For Christians, this is not a problem, since the simple God created complex creatures who were totally different from himself. Since being generates from God's free decision (*ex nihilo*) and not as a necessary emanation (*ex deo*), the relation of free agents to a good parent establishes a moral sphere of image and likeness. Ontological difference is not a falling away from some primordial simplicity but a characteristic of the Godhead (three persons, one essence) that finds an analogy in the unity-within-plurality of creation and humanity itself.

It is possible to read Plato (as Plotinus did) as teaching that complexity is simply the negation of simplicity due to materiality. Proclus tried valiantly to counter this. Matter transcends this duality as truly as does the One itself. Embodied soul is the most complex, but instead of representing a deficiency this means that it is the produce of *all* divine causes (*Elem. theo.* 211). Yet how could he prescind from the inspired Plato in maintaining that the end of all things is to revert to an original unity shorn of all particularity? Then it reverts to simplicity, shedding its body and aspects of the soul attached to it. Like the One's emanation, "the soul does not calculate or choose, nor is it in consequence of any calculation or judgement that it animates the body, but simply through being what it is it endows with life that which is adapted to participate it. Its being, therefore, is being alive. If, then, its being is self-derived, and this being is the being alive which is its essential

---

Pearson, "Gnosticism as Platonism." Ebeling notes comparisons with Hermeticism in *Secret History*, 9.

42. See Proclus, *In Plat. Parm.* 1.168, quoting OF 167b from Kern, *Orphicorum fragmenta*.

character, its life too must be self-furnished and self-derived. That is, soul must be self-animated" (*Elem. theo.* 189). Above particular souls, "divine souls" participate in intellectual existence "but fall short of connexion with divine henads, since the intelligence they participate was not divine" (*Elem. theo.* 202).

All souls return to the One, but it is less clear in Plato (relying on Orphic sources) than in Hinduism that the karmic cycle can actually be broken. Proclus is hardly more comforting: "It remains, then, that each soul has a periodic alternation of ascents out of process and descents into process, and this movement is unceasing by reason of the infinitude of time. Therefore each particular soul can descend and ascend an infinite number of times, and this shall never cease to befall every such soul" (*Elem. theo.* 206).

Proclus tells us that the means of return begins with the gracious descent of our leader-gods to bring us back into their unity. From our side, it is the "flower of intellect" that unites with its henad.[43] The soul is "in the middle" (Plato, *Tim.* 34b), mediator between the One and the Many, procession and return, being and becoming (Proclus, *In Plat. Tim.* 2.105). Soul is "Life-principle" (henad) and "living thing" (particular participant, *Elem. theo.* 188). Every soul "is at once a principle of life and a living thing," unparticipated and participated (*Elem. theo.* 188). "Yet it is above every name. This feature of the One is reproduced, but in a different way, by the last of things, which also cannot be represented by a name of its own. . . . But it is named 'Receptacle,' 'Wet Nurse,' 'Matter,' and the 'Substrate,' after the things that come before it, just as the first is named after the things that come after it" (*In Plat. Parm.* 7.513.7–14). What we call "the One" is actually "the understanding of unity which is in ourselves. . . . It is therefore this interior understanding of unity, which is a projection and, as it were, an expression of the One in ourselves, that we call 'the One.' *So the One itself is not nameable, but the One in ourselves*" (7.54.11–14, emphasis added).

As part of this yearning of the gods for their manifold, inspired revelation is sent. Like Christians, Proclus believed that we can talk about the divine not because of rational deduction but because the gods have revealed their nature to us in accommodated ways. He distinguished between knowing the One in its essence and according to its effects:

> It is better, following the decision of Plato, to call it the fount of all divinity, but only in the sense that we term it the beginning and the cause of all things and the end of all things and object of striving for them; for, for its sake all things

---

43. Proclus, *Commentary on Plato's Parmenides* (ed. and trans. Marrow and Dillon), 425. CO fr. 1; cf. fr. 189. Proclus associates this "flower of intellect" with Hekate, notes Butler, "Flower of Fire," 141, 143.

are, and it is the cause of all things, as he says himself in the *Letters* (*Ep.* 312e); by using these terms we do not say what it is in itself, but what relation to it those things have which are after it and of which it is the cause. In a word, then, all divinity is a henad, but the One itself is nothing else than Divinity Itself, through which all gods derive their quality of being gods, even as all intellects derive their qualities as intellects from the primary Intellect, and souls derive their quality of being souls from the primal Soul; for that which primarily is something is the cause for all other things of their being secondarily what it is primarily. (*In Plat. Parm.* 4.1109)

This distinction "not in his essence but according to his works" (effects) was not original with Proclus but was a common rule in Christian theology especially among the fourth-century Cappadocian fathers. This is another example of the interbreeding of pagan Neoplatonism and Christianity in both directions.

Even earlier, St. Paul's statement that all things are from, through, and to God implied effectual, instrumental, and final causality (Rom 11:36). Deliberate or not, such a formula would have found favor uniquely with Platonists, in contrast with Aristotelians (who denied the efficient cause: "from him") and Stoics (who denied the final cause: "to him"). Just as the One is the cause not only of being but of the nonexistent matter that cooperates with the demiurge, perfection flowing from "the efficacious power of the primordial divine Forms" is attained depending on "the appetency of the beings that are shaped in accordance with them. For the creative action of the Forms is not alone sufficient to bring about participation." We must avoid the Aristotelian Scylla of depriving "the divine factor" of its sovereignty as efficient cause, "the efficacious power of the primordial divine Forms," and the Stoic Charybdis of depriving sensible agents its desire "as a collaborator with the agent that can create" (*In Plat. Parm.* 4.842–843).

Yet in the New Testament, the Son is both the transcendent One in essence and the mediator of the cosmological process. Particularly in Johannine and Pauline writings, Jesus is the one by whom all things were created and in whom they exist. By the time Proclus took Athena into his home after Athens's Christian majority had removed her statue, he would have known well such claims concerning Jesus as the following: "He is the image of the invisible God, the firstborn of all creation. For by him all things were created, in heaven and on earth, visible and invisible, whether thrones or dominions or rulers or authorities—all things were created through him and for him. And he is before all things, and in him all things hold together" (Col 1:15–17; cf. John 1:1–18). Drawing on many passages, the formula "from him, through him and to him" was correlated with the Father as originating cause, the Son as the mediator, and the Holy Spirit as the one who restores lost unity with the Father, in the Son. There was no such rapproachment with Platonist theology, but the fundamental agreement on God as the effectual, mediatorial, and final cause was as much Christian as it was Platonic.

Reversion: The End Is Like the Beginning

While Plato allegorized myths, Proclus allegorized Plato, confident that the inspired master correlated a cosmic element with each partner in a dialogue.[44] This is consistent with the exegesis Proclus found in the Orphic literature.[45] The eternal, cyclical process of rest, procession, and reversion (or descent and ascent) is of course rooted in Orphism and formulated beautifully by Plotinus (esp. *Enn.* 5.2.1 and 6.5.7).[46] Nevertheless, Proclus diverges significantly from Plotinus at important points, sometimes in agreement with Origen's cosmology.[47] On distinctives of theurgic philosophy, he demurs from Origen as well. It is not a coincidence that Parmenides, the senior member of the group in Plato's dialogue, is identified by Proclus as "remaining in the One."[48] If Proclus may have been too humble to insert himself into the role of Parmenides, the idea was not lost on his student-biographer, Marinus.[49]

---

44. In fact, following Syrianus, Proclus takes allegorizing to a new level, treating the people, places, and things in the dialogues as symbols of cosmic elements. Matter, form, nature, and the Soul, the Intellect, and the One become personified as partners in the dialogue. According to Marrow and Dillon, in the anonymous *Prolegomena to Platonic Philosophy*—"a product of the 6th-century Alexandrian School, but much dependent on Proclus," we are told, "'As we have seen, then, that the dialogue is a cosmos and the cosmos a dialogue, [so] we may expect to find all the components of the universe in the dialogue.... In the dialogue we have, corresponding to Matter, the characters, the time, and the place in which Plato represents his dialogue as happening.'" Sometimes Plato (as author, not character) presents "divine matters through images, using mathematical terms, those used either in arithmetic or in geometry." In other cases, he uses "dialectical terms," especially in a Pythagorean vein. Thus, says Proclus, "Zeno is an analogue to the Intellect which is participated in by the divine Soul, filled with all the intellectual Forms which he has received into his essence from the immaterial and unparticipated Intellect [Parmenides]; this is why he too strives to 'snatch himself away' (Chald. Or. fr. 3.1) from plurality towards the One Being, imitating the Intellect above him, to which he refers his own perfecting." See Proclus, *Commentary on Plato's Parmenides* (ed. and trans. Marrow and Dillon), 38–39.

45. See Fernández, "Proclus and the Role of Orphism." Cf. de Garcy, "Mystery Religions and Philosophy in Proclus."

46. Proclus, *Elements of Theology* (ed. and trans. Dodds), xviii.

47. A lodestar for this fascinating dependence is Ramelli, "Proclus and Apoktastasis," esp. 102–4. Origen's metaphysics is engaged appreciatively in Proclus, *Plat. Theo.* 2.4 and on many other subjects through his *Timaeus* commentary.

48. Proclus, *Commentary on Plato's Parmenides* (ed. and trans. Marrow and Dillon), 27.

49. Marinus, "Life of Proclus," in Edwards, *Neoplatonic Saints*. For a less sympathetic interpretation see H. J. Blumenberg, "Marius's *Life*."

Chapter 9

The goal of this reversion is assimilation to god (*homoiōsis theō*), based on the *Theaet.* 176a–b. The *Parmenides* is not merely "about all things," says Proclus, but "in so far as all things are deified; for each thing, even the lowest grade of being you could mention, becomes god by participating in unity according to its rank" (*In Plat. Parm.* 1.641). Socrates becomes a god by unity with the henadic Human, souls with the Soul, "twenty-four" with Number, and so forth. However, contrary to Iamblichus, he insists that this can only be assimilation and not absorption, *theōsis* and not *henōsis*. Appealing to Origen, he rejects Plotinus's view that the soul is consubstantial with the Intellect and even the One (*In Plat. Tim.* 34.231.5–11). This reversion leads to Proclus's own version of *apokatastasis* (universal restoration).[50]

Finally, everything returns to its most immediate unity, which is enfolded into its higher unity and so forth, until all that is *real* is *one*. This is not a new state of affairs, however. Reality has always been one, like an accordion that unfolds and returns to rest.[51] Procession necessarily involves a decline from better to worse while reversion is movement from worse to better (*Elem. theo.* 36–37). However, only indivisible substance can revert to its cause. Reversion "is not in the nature of any body" since it is divisible from the soul and lies outside the structure of emanation. "Thus if there is anything which is capable of reverting upon itself, it is incorporeal and without parts" (*Elem. theo.* 15–16).[52] The "All" excludes bodies, which are appearances rather than reality. Whatever is in Zeus's belly is not the visible world but the ideas, but they are one in that "mixture," thus justifying the conclusion that it is another example of a dualism nested within an ultimate monism of pure idea.[53]

The resurrection of the body is the antithesis of Orphic eschatology. Since the end is like the beginning, a reversion to unity is a gradual loss of distinct identity. This qualifies somewhat his denial above that the union entails absorption. In contrast with essence, is existence a dream that is forgotten in the awakening to

---

50. See Ramelli, "Proclus and Apoktastasis." Plato talked about a "great year" that comes along every 36,000 years. The term *apokatastasis* itself comes from the Stoic doctrine of periodical reboots in which the whole cosmos is destroyed and immediately restored right at the moment before the conflagration. Both are based on the myth of eternal recurrence, with infinite time and therefore infinite reversions, and are deterministic. However, Origen's *apokatastasis* is quite different. There is one cycle, in the return of all souls time will come to an end, and how long this takes for any given soul depends on free will and merit.

51. Proclus, *Commentary on Plato's Parmenides* (ed and trans. Marrow and Dillon), 175.

52. This is the same position as Origen's and that of his followers, Gregory of Nyssa and Evagrius. See Ramelli, "Proclus and Apoktastasis," 106.

53. Eric D. Perl describes this development well, though controversially at points, in *Theophany*, 9; cf. 10–11.

true being? In other words, does Proclus finally embrace Parmenides's acosmic idealism? I will let Hegel supply the answer that he found appealing: "the result ensues that only unity is true existence, all other determinations are merely vanishing magnitudes, merely moments, and thus their Being is only an immediate thought."[54] What seemed like reality is an appearance, like the prisoners in Plato's cave who confused the shadows for the truth. Awakening from the dream, we realize what has been true all along.

Proclus's Legacy

Many of Proclus's rules are applicable in Christian theology, particularly to show that causation does not entail movement, change, or loss; the cause is in the effect but not vice versa. Unmistakable echoes are heard in Byzantine and scholastic formulations of divine impassibility: God has no intrinsic relation to creation yet is free to relate creation to himself. Yet a century and more before Proclus, Christians drew on Platonic language and categories to make the same point. God is known not according to his essence but according to his works.

However, there are incommensurable accounts of the metaphysical basis for analogy. There is an unbridgeable gulf between saying, on the one hand, that we know God's attributes insofar as "like produces like" and causes are in the effects and, on the other, insofar as the creation proclaims the invisible attributes of its creator.

We meet again in Proclus the root metaphor of the sun and its rays. Unlike his handling of the One-and-the-Many problem, the scholiarch does not offer a solution to the Platonic aporia of necessary emanation and divine transcendence. On the one hand, overflowing in hypergoodness it shines "without deliberation or choice" but simply "in virtue of its essence." On the other hand, it does so because, "not [being] jealous," it "does not begrudge" sharing its goodness with all things according to their capacity.[55] Even if these personal qualities are intended metaphorically, these two claims cancel out each other. If the One emanates reality necessarily, we cannot praise it for being generous instead of jealous—as if it had any choice in the matter. The Good "is the unmoving cause of all things, as determining their order by his very being."[56] Since it is not by "deliberation or choice," we could substitute that last clause with "necessarily." Moreover, "ev-

---

54. Hegel, *Plato and the Platonists*, 437.
55. Proclus, *Commentary on Plato's Parmenides* (ed. and trans. Marrow and Dillon), 160.
56. Proclus, *Commentary on Plato's Parmenides* (ed. and trans. Marrow and Dillon), 160–61.

erything which is complete (i.e., has realized the full potentialities of its nature) tends to reproduce itself."[57]

Thus everything—the whole cosmos and each of its parts—is a manifestation of the One: "everything in everything." The One is "all names and no name." Every existent is of the same substance as its most proximate cause but in diluted measure: Like produces like (Proclus, *Elem. theo.* 28). This cannot include the One itself, since it transcends being—hence, it has no name, and yet for this very reason it is the cause of all things—and therefore has every name. The cosmos is a god, but not the transcendent god. Appealing to Pythagoras (contra Plutarch, Atticus, and Philo), Proclus sees visible things as images or icons of the divine cosmos, and he employs the mirror analogy throughout the third book of his *Timaeus* commentary.[58] As in Platonism more generally, the outlook is panentheistic.[59]

According to the *Timaeus*, the universe is like the Good eternally and necessarily by virtue of being his offspring. A biomorphic model dominates archaic mythologies, even when philosophers came to give them an allegorical spin. We have seen that in the stories of Homer and Hesiod there is a procession of deities from unity to increasing multiplicity, while in Orphic myths there is a reversion to unity with Zeus (ultimately, Dionysus) having "all gods in his belly." Yet even Socrates still took his ancestors' word for it that he was descended from Zeus through Daedalus to Hephaestus. Spartan and Persian kings trace their lineage to Zeus through Heracles and Achaemenes, respectively (*Alc. maj.* 120e–121a).[60] So when Proclus stipulates, "Every producing cause brings into existence things like to itself before the unlike," he conceives emanation and therefore analogy in biomorphic terms. "But it is necessary that the effect should participate the cause, inasmuch as it derives its being from the latter" (*Elem. theo.* 28). The Many share in the One through an unbroken succession of necessary causes. The biomorphic root-metaphor provided the basis for remarkably similar philosophical doctrines in the Axial Age.

---

57. *Elem. theo.* 25. See also Plotinus, *Enn.* 4.8.6. Compare with Plato, *Resp.* 596a. This theory is implied in Parmenides. As he argues in "The Way of Truth," our experience of reality as many visible things in constant change is an illusion. Being is thought, pure idea (B 2.7–8, 7.1–2), and whatever exists truly—the real—is immutable and eternal, "now all at once, unitarily-uniquely, constantly" (B 8.1–6). He states, "what is there is there without becoming and also without passing away, entire and one in kind [*oulon mounogenes*], without trembling and without outcome" (B 8.1–4). See Woodbury, "Parmenides on Names," 147–49.

58. See books 3 and 4 of Proclus, *In Plat. Tim.* as well as 1.3.31–1.4.5 (based on *Tim.* 34a–b; 62e; 92c). On the mirror analogy, see Proclus, *In Plat. Tim.* 3, on *Tim.* 31b–37c and Proclus, *In Plat. Parm.* 175.

59. See Cooper, *Panentheism*.

60. Translation of *Alcibiades* by Hutchinson in Plato, *Complete Works* (ed. Cooper).

In contrast, the Bible represents a technomorphic (i.e., "making") model. The genesis of all living things is not a necessary emanation from a principle but a contingent creation by a personal God. Instead of being eternal, creation comes into existence in and with time. Time is not a moving image of eternity but a unique index of tensed experience that is intrinsic to creatures. The universe is not a space-time copy of an eternal, necessary, and immutable realm of ideas, a flickering image on the screen of matter. The whole creation displays visibly the existence and invisible attributes of God, but in the way a composition exhibits the nature of its artist, rather than as a mirror reflects the person standing in front of it. Despite its vigorous defense of divine transcendence, Platonism cannot affirm consistently the aseity (independence) of God or a genuine freedom of human agents grounded in their being qualitatively different from God. If the Good is essentially the procession of the All from the real to the apparent, necessity is sovereign over gods and mortals alike. At the end of the day, the Good is nothing other than the world that it must produce exactly as it is and creation is nothing other than the Good's self-manifestation.

According to the biblical traditions, Yahweh is transcendent yet personal agent who created the world from nothing and out of loving freedom rather than any external or internal requirement of his nature. Even if we posit the seminal reasons of things as ideas in God's mind eternally, they remain free self-determinations of what God will create. They are eternal and necessary only in a relative sense (as God's decisions), not absolutely. Whatever God decrees to exist is in conformity with his simple, intellectual, immutable nature but is not required by it. This is because the world is not God, either in reality or appearance. Nothing but God is divine, including angelic rulers, forms, minds, or souls.

The relation of the creation to its creator is not natural (offspring to parent, river to source, rays to sun) but covenantal (servant to king); hence, the dominant images of summoning, decreeing, calling, and sending forth a word. "By the word of the LORD the heavens were made, and by the breath of his mouth all their host" (Ps 33:6). This includes the highest creatures, even celestial servants: "You are the Lord, you alone; you have made heaven, the heaven of heavens, with all their host ... and the host of heaven worships you" (Neh 9:6). Proclus believed that henadic gods mediated the unfolding and enfolding of the cosmos, but Paul says that God created everything through Christ, "visible and invisible, whether thrones or dominions or principalities or authorities" (Col 1:16). The theurgic rites that Proclus practiced zealously involved the worship of these superior intelligences. However, in the Apocalypse John fell down at the feet of the angel who brought him God's words, "but he said to me, 'You must not do that! I am a fellow servant with you and your brothers the prophets, and with those who keep the words of this book.

Worship God'" (Rev 22:9). Even shared terms bear a different connotation; *logos*, for example, is a spoken word rather than silent thought or reason-principle.

It is just these presuppositions that bind biblical traditions to the oral medium and to the irreducible genre of historical narrative. A feature of "axiality" across cultures, we have seen, is the transposition of ritual-founding myths into philosophical ideas. Yet Israel stands out as a glaring exception. The Hebrew prophets bring God's word in the present on the basis of what was spoken in the past and its fulfillment in the future. New Testament writers do not read Israel's narrative as allegories of higher truths but as historical promise leading to historical fulfillment. Contrary to the criticism of philosophers and gnostics, the lack of explicit or formal philosophical system in the Bible is not a deficiency but is integral to its own view of reality. Orphic "reason" is just an alternative theology. The doctrine of creation *ex nihilo* broke the eternal cycle into a historical line with a beginning, middle, and end. And it not only exhibits a technomorphic model in a generic sense but a relationship based on covenant. Taken from the lexicon of international politics rather than religion and philosophy, the covenantal bond between suzerain and vassals forms its own horizon for relating the One and the Many in the historical economy. Not creation in general but human beings are singled out as God's "image and likeness," similar to the way in which a viceroy is the image of the emperor.

Just as this doctrine generates its own ontology, its epistemological corollary is the root-metaphor of *hearing* over *seeing*. Just as all creatures exist as effects of God's speech, they know God by hearing, understanding, receiving God's interpretation of reality. It is consistent with the relation of vassal and suzerain. Rising from myth to doctrine is for ancient philosophers the ascent from believing the testimony one hears based on authority to an intuitive and autonomous vision of the truth itself. Crucially, for Plato and his heirs the antithesis of authority and autonomy is not equivalent to faith and reason, since the vision of the forms is a mystical experience transcending reason. From a biblical perspective, looking for the divine within oneself is the original sin. Recapitulating Adam's trial, Jesus rejected the visions of self-apotheosis conjured by Lucifer, replying not with his own words of wisdom but with "every word that comes from the mouth of God" (Matt 4:4).

And just as the creation of matter, including the visible world and bodies, was pronounced good in Genesis, the whole person—body and soul—is swept into the eschatological consummation of the triune God. Thus, it is crucial to note that in spite of the theurgic practices that "call down" the gods into a temporary illumination of a statue, through which they give oracles, Proclus remains within the Orphic opposition of spirit and matter. Theurgy turns on divine possession, not only of statues but of persons. Proclus emphasizes that those who are directly possessed ("seized by God": *theolēptoi*) are out of their minds and must be led around by a person who is not. Others work themselves up into such a trance through a state of perfect calm, followed by glossolalia and magical formulae. Sometimes material daimons accompany the god's epiphany, terrifying the mediocre medium. In either case, *theagōgia* (*tas entheastikas theagōgias*) draws the divine spirits down to the operator.[61]

In the biblical traditions, however, God ordinarily works through the normal laws he established in the created order. Even in miracles, nature is taken into God's service—not because it possesses natural symbols that correspond to the gods but because God condescends to make creatures analogies of his attributes and works. Moses's staff is not imbued with magical powers but represents God's scepter, which God directs the prophet to use as directed in specific situations. Sometimes Jesus heals simply by his word. At other times, he binds his word to a material sign, as when he mixes his spittle with dirt and places the mud on the eyes of the blind man. In this he shows that he is not a medium, calling down a divinity by employing natural symbols that correspond intrinsically to the nature of the gods, but the Lord of creation who delights in using matter in miraculous as well as providential operations. Just as he made humans from the dust of the ground, he restores them through his creatures.

God reveals plans that could not have been discerned through merely natural discernment, but revelation is not set over against the latter. Inspiration pertains to the writings rather than to the prophets themselves. The prophets are not prepared for their vocation but are ordinary people. They are not shamans or sages but shepherds, farmers, vine dressers, and the like who are taken into God's council to be given a word to bring to God's people. Moreover, in the event of revelation there is no suspension of their natural faculties; the particular cultural-linguistic background and limitations of the writer are fully on display. A physician, Luke addresses his Gospel and the Acts of the Apostles to a certain patron, Theophilus, for whom he seeks to present "an orderly account" drawn from interviewing eyewitnesses.

These few examples hardly comprehend the depth and breadth of disagreement. Nor, however, do they justify vain attempts to break completely from the philosophical milieu of early Christianity. Against Aristotelians, Platonists affirmed the Good as the sole efficient cause of all being, movement and life; against Stoics, as the final cause (chief end); they maintained both against Epicureans. Christians consider as authoritative not only the explicit teachings of scripture in chapter-and-verse but the conclusions that may be deduced from them. Consequently, there are some metaphysical and cosmological doctrines that cannot be

---

61. Proclus, *On the Signs of Divine Possession*, in des Places, *Oracles Chaldaiques*, 219–20.

Chapter 9

accommodated while others, though shared with pagan philosophy, are required by exegetical deduction. Obviously, sorting all of this out belongs to the complicated history of subsequent centuries.

Dionysius the Areopagite: Creative Transposition

Five centuries after Paul's speech to the philosophers in Athens, one of the converts mentioned—Dionysius the Areopagite—appeared with a set of books to his name.[62] In actuality, he was most likely a Syrian monk who had studied under Proclus.[63] Nevertheless, believing that the author was the philosopher converted by Paul's speech in the Areopagus (Acts 17:34), the Palestinian bishop John of Scythopolis introduced him as a nearly apostolic champion of orthodoxy. John viewed Monophysite Christology as part of the broader genus of gnostic Man-

---

62. The account of Paul's speech and passing mention of Dionysius is provided in Acts 17. The primary source for the Pseudo-Dionysian corpus is PG 3–4; cf. Dionysius the Areopagite, *Corpus Dionysiacum I* (ed. Suchla); Dionysius the Areopagite, *Corpus Dionysiacum II* (ed. Heil and Ritter). For historical background on the original text, I have relied on many sources but especially Roques, "Denys l'Areopagite," 3:244–86; Rorem and Lamoreaux, introduction to *John of Scythopolis*. A broad consensus considers the author to have been a student of Proclus, although Ronald F. Hathaway summarizes several other theories well in *Letters of Pseudo-Dionysius*, 31. The latest Dionysius revival is owed to the twentieth-century "ressoursement" (*nouvelle théologie*) movement (e.g., Maurice Blondel, Jean Daniélou, Henri de Lubac, Hans Urs von Balthasar). With special interest in Hermeticism and theurgic Neoplatonism, Jean Trouillard, A.-J. Festugière, Pierre Hadot, and Jean-Luc Marion were also part of this trend among French Catholics. At the same time in Paris a renaissance of Greek patristics emerged through the labors of Russian Orthodox émigrés (e.g., Sergei Bulgakov, Georges Florovsky, Alexander Schmemann, Vladimir Lossky, and John Meyendorff). Once more in Paris, Pseudo-Dionysius received considerable attention among poststructuralist philosophers, sparked especially by Jacques Derrida's exchanges with Jean-Luc Marion. Mary-Jane Rubenstein and Tamison Jones provide helpful summaries in Coakley and Stang, *Rethinking Dionysius the Areopagite*, 195–224. Dionysius figures prominently in diverse retrievals of Neoplatonism, including Radical Orthodoxy and interactions (especially of John Milbank with Slavoj Žižek and Giorgio Ambagen).

63. It is generally agreed that the author of the Dionysian corpus was a Syrian pupil of Proclus in Athens who came to embrace Christianity. Given the pseudonym, the author could not refer to Proclus directly, but there are many statements verbatim from the philosopher especially on evil in chapter 4 of the *Divine Names* (one-sixth of the entire treatise). H. Koch pointed up similarities in "Proklus als Quelle." Since then, comparisons have been multiplied, as evident over the career of Henri-Dominique Saffrey. See in English translation his essay "New Objective Links," 74. See also the fascinating essay by Susan Klitenic Wear, "Pseudo-Dionysius and Proclus." Robbert Maarten van den Berg's *Proclus' Commentary on the Cratylus* is a seminal study for understanding the background to Dionysius's *Divine Names*. Chapters 4–8 are on Proclus, and he devotes chapter 6 to divine names.

ichaeism.⁶⁴ Plato was the fountainhead of it all: "For he says that it is unworthy for the material to live forever with the soul, in that the soul alone exists immortally," and then he lists the gnostics, adding, "Even now there are some who take their stand on the myths—not teachings!—of Origen... these men who are abominable to God and to right-thinking people."⁶⁵ "This is not a fight of words," he adds, "for our salvation is focused on these points."⁶⁶

Who better, therefore, than Paul's converted philosopher to refute the heresies of his own day?⁶⁷ The bishop's *Prologue* praises the philosopher:

> Whoever has been trained with a true knowledge of the invincible traditions of the Church can marvel at the orthodoxy and erudition of Dionysius and [*DN* 17D] can contemplate how the bastard teachings of the Greek philosophers have been restored to the truth.... [S]ome dare to abuse the divine Dionysius with charges of heresy, being themselves absolutely ignorant of matters of heresy. For what could they say of his theology of the only-worshipped Trinity? Or what about Jesus Christ, one of this all-blessed Trinity, the only-begotten Word of God who willed to become fully human?... Or, concerning our general resurrection which will happen with both our body and our soul? And concerning the future judgement of the just and the unjust?⁶⁸

A Syriac version of the *Corpus Dionysiacum*, produced around the same time, came from the so-called Origenist underground that had been influenced by the

---

64. Monophysitism taught that the incarnate Son has one nature, a divine humanity. Apollinarianism held that while Jesus possessed a human body and soul, his mind was substituted for the divine Logos.

65. John of Scythopolis, *SchEH* 173.8. Translation from Rorem and Lamoreaux, *John of Scythopolis*. All references to John of Scythopolis and quotations from his *scholia* are from this volume.

66. John of Scythopolis, *Prol.* 20b. Maximus the Confessor was also a vocal critic of Origenism. On the relation of his *scholia* to John's, see Rorem and Lamoreaux, *John of Scythopolis*, 36–37 n. 57; cf. Suchla, "Die sogenannten Maximus-Scholien"; Suchla, "Die Überlieferung von Prolog und Scholien"; Dionysius the Areopagite, *Corpus Dionysiacum I* (ed. Suchla), 38–54.

67. Rorem and Lamoreaux, *John of Scythopolis*, 146. Space does not allow the many comments John makes about Dionysius "transferring the errors of the Greeks to the truth."

68. His criticisms target the points at which Platonism contradicts the doctrines of *ex nihilo* creation and especially the incarnation and bodily resurrection. John often quotes Plotinus in order to refute his argument with one from Dionysius. "In John's Scholia," Rorem and Lamoreaux inform us, "of the approximately thirty open references to 'the Greeks,' the 'ancients,' or 'the philosophers,' half are clearly negative or critical, while the other half function positively as helpful background for the clarification of difficult Dionysian terminology." See Rorem and Lamoreaux, *John of Scythopolis*, 99–137.

Chapter 9

pioneer of monasticism, Evagrius. The eastern half of Syria was under Sasanian rule, and monks were as familiar as their Egyptian counterparts with Hermes Trismegistus and gnostic literature.[69] Many were Monophysites (teaching that Jesus had only one nature: humanity assimilated to his deity). East Syrian monks considered themselves a direct continuation of the apostolic line via Thomassine gnostics.[70] It was a gnostic stew of Manichaeism, Origenism (especially via Evagrius), and similar sects.

Golitzin notes that among the "holy men" opposing the "clergyman" were the Messalians (lit. "those who pray"). Claiming to receive revelations from angels and visions of the Trinity, they felt they could achieve a "natural union" through the highest faculty of the soul—mind—even apart from preaching and sacraments.[71]

---

69. Drawing on Philo's descriptions in *On the Contemplative Life* (1.2; 3.21–22), Dionysius considers the Therapeutae in Alexandria to be the originators of monasticism. Eusebius concluded that they were Christian monks associated with St. Mark, but this is anachronistic as Philo describes them clearly as Jewish. They are "philosophers," he says repeatedly, and "they live in their soul alone." Based on Philo's account of their ascetic practices and allegorical reading of the Pentateuch, Ekaterina Matusova concludes persuasively that it was an early Jewish gnostic sect employing "Egyptian and Orphic methods" of interpreting scripture much as is found in the Derveni Papyrus in "Allegorical Interpretation of the Pentateuch." East Syria had been a seedbed of gnosticism, which Ephrem the Syrian (306–373) targeted with his popular *Hymns against Heresy*. It was also the home of Numenius and Iamblichus, and Syrians played a large role in theurgic Neoplatonism with its interest in oriental (especially Egyptian) religious rites. Although the Athenian academy was more staunchly pagan than the Alexandrian, there is some evidence of Christians among them and the last scholiarch, Damascius, was Syrian. His triads and apophatic method are very close to the CD and his curriculum consisted largely of Proclus's works. See Hathaway, *Hierarchy and the Definition of Order*, 18–19.

70. Golitzin, "Dionysius Areopagita." In fact, the first mention of "monks" (*monachoi*) is found in the Gospel of Thomas 75: "Jesus said, 'Many are standing at the door, but it is the solitary [*monachos*] who will enter the bridal chamber.'" According to A. L. Frothingham, the East Syrian–Egyptian axis of spirituality was "sentimental" and its mystics were "seers" while West Syrian–Alexandrian mysticism was more "analogical," rising from sensible symbols to pure concepts; see Frothingham, *Stephen bar Sudaili*, 81. A fascinating study that substantiates and qualifies this contrast is Bitton-Ashketony, *Ladder of Prayer*. Among the earliest Syriac Christian communities we know, notes Golitzin, spiritual life required celibacy "seen as restoring the ascetic to something like the status of primeval man, Adam before the Fall"; see Golitzin, *Mystagogy*, 331. Golitzin adds that the asceticism, and the ontological dualism undergirding it, was if anything more extreme than the philosophical schools, abstaining not only from meat but from anything cooked and also from bathing.

71. See Rist, "Mysticism and Transcendence in Later Neoplatonism." Jean Vanneste makes the same argument in *Le mystère de Dieu*, 182–217. However, Vanneste mistakenly attributes this view to Pseudo-Dionysius as well. Dionysius argues repeatedly (e.g., *CH* 4.3) that God's essence can never be seen by mortals but only through the earthly veils he has ordained.

The Messalians held that the ordained ministry had become polluted and was now being replaced by their charismatic order.[72]

This context helps to explain why Dionysius basically accuses his audience of having an overrealized eschatology. We will never know the divine essence, he says, the true sort of "divine enlightenment into which we have been initiated by the hidden tradition of our inspired teachers" is "at one with scripture." It is true that "in time to come, when we have come at last to the blessed inheritance of being like Christ," we will experience the direct vision of his glory as the disciples did in the transfiguration. "But for now, what happens is this. We use whatever appropriate symbols we can for the things of God." The only way and right we have to speak at all about the ineffable God is through the accommodated revelation he has provided. With these analogies we are raised upward toward the truth of the mind's vision, a truth which is simple and one.[73]

Some recent scholars argue that the Syriac version of the *Corpus Dionysiacum* was original and revised significantly by John and his circle until the Greek version became sharply opposed to the Syriac.[74] I do not find this view persuasive. Rather, Dionysius seems to have belonged to an older tradition of Syrian ascetics, who were an extension of the local church, laypeople engaging in diaconal and mis-

---

72. Messalians were flourishing among the small community of Cappadocian Christians in the third and fourth centuries. See Mateo-Seco and Maspero, *Brill Dictionary of Gregory of Nyssa*, 127–28. Anathematized at the Council of Ephesus in 431, they nevertheless gained considerable support among monks in Syria and Asia Minor, including the Studion Monastery, which later became a pro-icon stronghold. Golitzin explores the fascinating dependence of significant later Orthodox ascetics on both Dionysius and the more charismatic emphasis of Evagrius and Macarius in the article "Hierarchy or Anarchy?" As Golitzin notes, Symeon denies that confession and absolution can be performed only by those ordained. While this might have been possible in the better days of Dionysius, it was not any longer. "When time had passed and the bishops became useless," followed by the priests who "became polluted," he says that "it was transferred ... to God's elected people, I mean to the monks" (138). Experience of the Spirit and visions is ordination from above, not below. Nicetas calls the charismatic "the true bishop" (145).

73. All quotes from *DN* 1.4, 53. The *Corpus Dionysiacum* consists of the *Divine Names* (*DN*), the *Mystical Theology* (*MT*), the *Ecclesiastical Hierarchy* (*EH*), and the *Letters* (*Ep.*). Unless otherwise noted, quotations from Dionysius in this chapter are from Dionysius the Areopagite, *Pseudo-Dionysius: The Complete Works* (trans. Luibheid). References are made to the text, followed by page number in this edition.

74. István Perczel offers the most sustained and compelling argument for the "authentic" Dionysius being the "heretical" Syriac version of the Origenist underground; see "Earliest Syriac Reception of Dionysius," 32–36. I am assuming the thesis that the "orthodox" Dionysius came before the one who was "invented" by the underground Origenist Sergius of Resh'ayna. Associated with Sergius is Stephen bar Sudhaili's *Holy Hieropheus*, a gnostic text that spread among the monks but appalled the bishops.

sionary work.[75] This is how Dionysius views the proper role of monks, as the first rank of laypeople operating under the clergy (bishop, presbyters, and deacons; e.g., *EH* 6 and *Ep.* 8).[76]

In any event, it is the Greek version that has come down to us. For John of Scythopolis and other orthodox readers of Dionysius, it did not matter who, when, or where he was in history: "Dionysius came, as it were, to a world that already knew him."[77] He represented the tradition.[78] He was a champion of Nicene Trinitarianism and Chalcedonian Christology on a mission to recall rogue monks back to the "great church" where the true theurgic lights give life, goodness, and being to the whole people of God.

Dionysius the Areopagite exploits the Neoplatonic (particularly Proclean) system while transposing its doctrines into a Christian key. He is not quite "a Christian thinker disguised as a neo-Platonist [seeking] to conquer ground held by neo-Platonism."[79] Much less is he a pagan wolf in sheep's clothing.[80] In contrast

---

75. Called "sons/daughters of the covenant" (Syriac: *bar/bat qyāmâ*), they were not like the example of Antony (251–356), known as "the father of Christian monasticism," promoted by Athanasius's *Life of Antony*. See Theodoret of Cyrrhus, *History of the Monks of Syria* and *Book of Steps*.

76. Golitzin, *Et Introibo ad Altare Dei*, 354–55. His sources are the fourth-century *Demonstrations* of Aphrahat of Persia and the *Hymns* of Ephrem. Golitzin points out also that Dionysius's rite of consecrating a monk in *EH* 6 is his own invention. This background is treated extensively here and in Golitzin, *Mystagogy*.

77. Louth, "Reception of Dionysius," 52.

78. Golitzin puts it well: "Dionysius belongs to the tradition of Christian Platonism and the monastic tradition that runs through all the major figures of the Christian East.... It was for this reason, far more than for any aura which may have attached to his sub-apostolic pseudonym, that he was accepted so quickly and so wholeheartedly in the East, and especially so by the monks... they recognized him for what he was, a spokesman of the Great Tradition." See *Mystagogy*, 52.

79. John of Scythopolis would surely have agreed with this characterization by Lossky, *Vision of God*, 24–25. While I am inclined to this position, I see it as less a matter of disguised sabotage than of an intertextual imagination dominated by Christianity. Even with this agreement, reception histories diverge widely. In the Christian East, Dionysius is read as the fountainhead of the tradition leading to Gregory Palamas, and Byzantine humanists appealed to him for their anti-Palamite cause. For Latins, he anticipated Augustine and either radical mysticism (e.g., Eriugena, Eckhart, Nicholas of Cusa) *or* the scholastic systems of the Franciscans (e.g., Bonaventure) or Dominicans (Albert and Aquinas).

80. Luther judged regarding Dionysius, "Denys is most pernicious; he platonizes more than he christianizes" (*LW* 32:259). Calvin shared Luther's critical stance, but Peter Martyr Vermigli and Martin Bucer were quite sympathetic. See Parker, "Saint Dionysius." The same spectrum may be found in Orthodox and Roman Catholic scholarship. See especially Meyendorff, *Christ in Eastern Christian Thought*, 99–100; cf. Meyendorff, *Byzantine Theology*, 27–29. Similarly, Alexander Schmemann judges that Dionysius fostered "the reduction of the Church to a mysterious

A Christian Reconstruction of Late Neoplatonism: St. Paul's Philosopher-Convert

with these reception histories, some scholars argue that it is no dishonor for a Christian to be a Neoplatonist and that Dionysius was such a philosopher.[81] However, the author tells us that these writings are not intended as a comprehensive system of theology or philosophy. He routinely reminds us of a text in which he treats the subject more fully (usually, his *Theological Representations* and *Outlines of Theology*). Whether these are lost or fictive placeholders, such clues indicate his narrow scope in these extant treatises.[82] He does not offer a philosophical system

---

piety, the dying of its eschatological essence and mission and, finally, the de-Christianizing of this world and its secularization." "But it seems that there is an impulse precisely to return to this very legacy." See *Journals of Father Alexander Schmemann*, 316–17. See also the more recent debate between K. P. Wesche, "Christological Doctrine," and the response by A. Golitzen, "On the Other Hand" in *St. Vladimir's Theological Quarterly* 33 and 34.

81. Challenging this assumption that Neoplatonism is a charge from which to be exonerated or found guilty, a recent trend of scholarship appreciates Dionysius precisely for his Neoplatonism. Besides scholars associated with Radical Orthodoxy, notable examples include Eric D. Perl's *Theophany: The Neoplatonic Philosophy of Dionysius the Areopagite* and the work of John D. Jones, Gregory Shaw, and others cited below. However, this approach divides between those who see the author as a standard-bearer for either Parmenidean/Plotinian idealism or theurgic Neoplatonism. Reaching back to Alexandria with Clement and especially Origen, this approach finds a champion in John Scottus Eriugena, leading to Eckhart, Cusa, Tauler and Pico, Bruno, Böhme, the Cambridge Platonists, and the German and British idealists. This is the location of C. E. Rolt's 1920 English translation and commentary on the *Divine Names* and *Mystical Theology*, which reads the Eriugenist Dionysius through the lens of British idealism, F. H. Bradley, A. E. Taylor, E. S. Brightman, and A. N. Whitehead. Surprisingly, the first English translation of the *Corpus Dionysiacum* was John Parker's 1897 *Dionysius the Areopagite*. Rolt's translation was the first to make a significant impression, going through several editions (SPCK, 1951; Macmillan, 1957, 1963, 1975, 1977; Dover, 2004; Nicholas-Hayes, 2004; Kessinger, 2010). I am citing the Nicholas-Hays 2004 edition. Also representing this interpretation of the *Corpus Dionysiacum* is John Findlay's Gifford Lectures, published as *Discipline of the Cave* (1966) and *Transcendence of the Cave* (1967). Taking a critical stance toward monotheism, he proposed a monistic metaphysics that incorporates much of Hindu and Buddhist elements; cf. Findlay, *Ascent to the Absolute*.

According to the second of these perspectives, Dionysius is seen as a champion of *theurgic* Neoplatonism over against Plotinus's ontology, which they characterize as "gnostic." See Milbank, *Theology and Social Theory*; Milbank, Pickstock, and Ward, *Radical Orthodoxy*; Shaw, *Theurgy and the Soul*; Shaw, "Neoplatonic Theurgy and Dionysius the Areopagite."

82. He explains in the *Mystical Theology*, "In my *Theological Representations*, I have praised the notions which are most appropriate to affirmative theology," such as the Trinity, the incarnation, and "the theology of the Spirit." Next, "In *The Divine Names* I have shown the sense in which God is described as good, existent, life, wisdom, power, and whatever other things pertain to *conceptual* names for God" (i.e., the "attributes of God" in a modern systematic theology) (*MT* 3). Dionysius is often criticized for having a weak pneumatology, but at points such as this one he indicates that he takes it up in another work. It does not matter whether these were actual works now lost or fictive placeholders; the important point is that he recognized the places where his treatises had lacunae and many of these happen to be the very points where he is criticized. Dionysius diverges from Origen also by denying that reason can know God's essence.

with a Christian gloss or seek to incorporate pagan theurgy. Rather, Dionysius exhibits an intertextual imagination that allows him to move effortlessly—perhaps even unconsciously—between his first language and the new grammar that he has come to embrace. Neoplatonic triads are everywhere in the corpus yet everywhere transposed.

First, he transposes the Neoplatonic triad to the Christian Trinity. If Dionysius were to assimilate the Trinity to the Neoplatonic triad, the most obvious result would have been Origen's ontological subordinationism. Or, as some suggest, he would have placed God beyond all affirmative predications of either unity or plurality.[83] However, nothing is clearer in the *Divine Names* than the identical repetition of the Father, the Son, and the Spirit in the divine essence, yet each also bearing incommunicable personal properties. Even in extolling the unity of the Godhead, his purpose is—against the Origenists—to affirm the equality of each person as the one God. Along with the Father, the Son and the Spirit are frequently called "supraessential" (beyond being) and those who rank the persons essentially have "blasphemed" (*DN* 2.1). Dionysius invokes Plotinus's analogy of the circle and its radii, but applies it not to the relation of the cosmos to the One but of the three Trinitarian persons to the one essence in the Godhead (2.5). The doxology that introduces the *Mystical Theology* is not "Unity!" or even "Father!" but "Trinity! Higher than any being, any divinity, any goodness!" (*MT* 1). The three persons are as real for Dionysius as the one essence that they share equally and undividedly (3.1).[84]

Second, there are no divine intermediaries between the Trinity and creation. The triune God, he says, is the sole immediate cause "which produced the sun and which produced everything else" (*DN* 5.8). This "three-person [*trisupostaton*] manifestation of the fecundity beyond being" whom theologians call also "Cause of beings since in its goodness it *employed its creative power to summon all things*

---

83. See throughout Perl, *Theophany.*

84. Confident that they could know God as he is in himself, Arians like Eunomius had merely reified their finite concept of "one" as the "ultimate Godhead" (to use Rolt's term). This was just another futile attempt to grasp the *real* God as if he were a being among beings. Like Gregory of Nyssa, Dionysius insists that a faithful embrace of Trinitarian orthodoxy is inseparable from respect for the mystery that transcends all being and knowing (Brugarolas, *Gregory of Nyssa: Contra Eunomium I*). Based on "the sacred Word of God," he says, "I have discussed all this elsewhere [*Theological Representations*] and I have shown how in scripture all the names appropriate to God are praised regarding the whole, entire, full, and complete divinity rather than any part of it, and that they all refer indivisibly, absolutely, unreservedly, and totally to God in his entirety." Anyone who says that the Son and the Spirit share only a part or lesser measure of divinity "may be said to have blasphemed" (*MT* 3.1).

into being" (1.4).[85] "Nor do we have to do with some other life-producing divinity" (11.36). The henads and other divine principles of Neoplatonism are dehypostatized. Instead, they are simply God's own intentions concerning what he will create. Even the highest angels are the first creatures, "co-workers with God" like the apostles (1 Cor 3:9), he says, not Proclean henads. Instead of being the first gods serving as unities for their respective manifold, they are the first hearers and heralds of God's multifaceted word (*CH* 4.4).

"One truth must be affirmed *above all else*" is that God "*established* the existence of everything and *brought it into being*" (4.1, emphasis added). Unintentionally disclosing his use of the pseudonym, Dionysius even chides Clement of Alexandria by name, who "for some reason declares that the paradigms are the most primal among beings . . . but we should be led through the analogical knowledge of these to the cause of all, as far as this is possible for us" (*DN* 5.9).

It is true that Dionysius does not use the phrase creation out of nothing (*ex ouk ontōn*), although the term "emanation" (*aporrhoē*) appears frequently (*CH* 4.1).[86] Gerson expresses laconically, "The One does not create things *ex nihilo*."[87] Assuming that Dionysius is a Neoplatonic philosopher, Perl concurs that Theophanism (i.e., Platonic emanation) renders meaningless the opposition of "'Neoplatonic necessary procession' and 'Christian free creation. . . . For Dionysius, as for Plotinus, God is nothing but the making of all things, so that the possibility of not making does not arise."[88] *Everything* available to our senses is a manifestation of the One, but it does not really exist.[89] While this description fits Plotinus (and Eriugena), it overlooks Dionysius's key moves. We must attend to how he is using the grammar familiar to his audience and not simply assume that it is univocal with Neoplatonism.

Dionysius does not refer at all to creation as a theophany: a shower of apparent images flowing necessarily from the One.[90] Rather, all three references to theoph-

---

85. For the use of "three-person manifestation," I opt for Jones's rendering in *Pseudo-Dionysius*, 111. Compare also the Luibheid translation of the last phrase, "For all have been brought forward into being through its being-producing goodness." Generally, Jones's translation is less readable but more accurate.

86. Brons, *Gott und die Seinden*, 193–94.

87. Gerson, review of *Dieu sans la puissance*, by Aubry, 28. See Gerson's argument in "Goodness, Unity, and Creation," 35–36.

88. Perl, *Theophany*, 51–52.

89. Perl, *Theophany*, 34: "Wherever we look, we are not seeing God," since he can never be the object of thought, Perl explains. And yet, "wherever we look, we are seeing God, as he appears, for every being, every object of thought, is nothing but a presentation or appearance of God." Cf. Perl, "Neither One nor Many."

90. Contra Perl and other scholars who take a Parmenidean/Plotinian idealist reading. We shall see below that Eriugena introduced this interpretation.

anies in the *Corpus* refer to particular historical events reported "in the scriptural tradition" that Christians had long identified as theophanies (*CH* 4.2–3).[91] When God enlightens, it is a "paternally transmitted enlightenment coming from sacred scripture" (*CH* 1.2). Just as God freely creates whatever he thinks wise, God selects analogies from the creation he has made and, as Dionysius repeats on nearly every page, these are analogies God has revealed in scriptural representations. God is not revealed passively by the cosmos but reveals himself as he pleases through designated images. "This is why we must not dare to resort to words or conceptions concerning that hidden divinity, which transcends being, apart from what the sacred scriptures have divinely revealed" (*DN* 1.1).

Third, Dionysius transposes cosmological terms to a soteriological field. For example, it is God's self-revelation in scripture and providences that "go forth," angels process from heaven to earth to relay messages, and in the church's hierarchy and liturgy God's deifying powers go forth into multiplicity, returning those who have fallen away into division to the unity of divine life in Christ. These are not the necessary overflow of God's being but instead his chosen means of restoring his people.[92]

Most comprehensively, it is "the Providence of Jesus" that emanates from the unity of God's deliberate plan into the diversity of prophecies and rites, returning those fallen to the simplicity of union with God in Christ (*DN* 11.5). The providence of Jesus is the history that gathers around him and moves toward his incarnation. Onto the triadic *cosmological* movement from rest to procession to reversion Dionysius maps a threefold *historical* movement from the old covenant (i.e., the "hierarchy of the law") to the new (i.e., "our hierarchy"), anticipating the "celestial hierarchy" in the age to come.[93] This is the "Providence of Jesus 'who works all things in all,' making that Peace which is ineffable and was foreordained from eternity, reconciling us to himself and in himself to the Father." He refers to the ascension in the flesh as well: "Some [angels] learn that the 'King of Glory,' the

---

91. He refers in *DN* 1.6 to the angel of the Lord theophany in Judges 13, where Manoah asks to know his name. "And the angel of the Lord said to him, 'Why do you ask my name, seeing it is wonderful?'" (13:18). He then links its fulfillment to Christ, who is given "the name above every name" (Phil 2:9). In *CH* 7.1, the seraphim and cherubim receive "the primal theophanies and perfections."

92. See *MT* 5. This comes at the conclusion of a treatise that has emphasized the analogical path. Origen and Dionysius both affirm the anagogical (i.e., "up-lifting") procedure. However, for the latter this is not a stage above an ordinary reading but a way of reading scripture generally. Moreover allegorizing (especially with Origen) sets the true meaning over against the literal, in contrast with an analogical extrapolation from effect to cause.

93. See *EH* 3.3.5; 5.1.1–2; 3.4.12.

one raised up into the heavens *in human form*, is the Lord of the heavenly powers [Ps 24:10]" (*CH* 73, emphasis added).

Greek thought, especially Platonism, waxed eloquent on the ecstasy of the soul for the One, but did not think that the One loved the soul, much less the world. It simply overflowed, unconsciously and necessarily. Yet for Dionysius, God, moved by benevolence toward humanity, undertook to save rebels from their voluntary course.[94] This Good "took upon itself in a most authentic way all the characteristics of our nature, except sin" (*EH* 3.3.11).

> The most evident idea in theology, namely, the sacred incarnation of Jesus for our sakes, is something which cannot be enclosed in words or grasped by any mind, not even by the leaders among the front ranks of the angels. That he undertook to be a man is, for us, entirely mysterious. We have no way of understanding how, in a fashion at variance with nature, he was formed from a virgin's blood. (*DN* 2.9)

For Dionysius, the incarnation of the Son is not a loss of divine transcendence but the apex of the procession. While *remaining* at rest in his divinity, Jesus *processed* into history by assuming a human nature and *returned* in our nature to unite us to himself. "In all this he remains what he is—supernatural, transcendent—and he has come to join us in what we are without himself undergoing change or confusion" (*DN* 2.10).[95] According to Neoplatonism, divine beings never receive anything below them but give to their inferiors, so the Word beyond-being could not have become the *recipient* of being. Dionysius does not believe that the fullness of deity was reflected in Jesus, but rather that in him the fullness of deity *dwelt* (Col 1:19).[96] The providence of Jesus is an arc from the transcendent Trinity (rest) to creation (procession) and deification (reversion).[97] So, what proceeds

---

94. Golitzin, *Mystagogy*, 91. True, Proclus speaks of *erōs*, Golitzen notes, but it is "not at all clear" that it is "a downflowing love coming from God, and certainly not" an ecstatic love. As Balthasar expresses it, "the system of mediation found in Neo-Platonism is undermined in a Christian sense by Denys with his assertion of the immediate relationship of all creatures . . . to a personal God of love." See *Glory of the Lord*, 2:192. Perl challenges this appraisal, arguing that the distinction between God's direct and indirect agency makes no sense in a Neoplatonic framework: God works directly and immediately through hierarchies as light passes through various mirrors; see "Hierarchy and Participation," 18–19.

95. Cf. *EH* 3.3.13; *Ep.* 4.

96. See *DN* 1.4; cf. *DN* 2.9–11; 2.11.

97. Contra Perl, who states up front that in an effort to display Dionysius's Neoplatonic

from God is not his essence or appearances but *providential operations* leading to the incarnation.⁹⁸

For a Neoplatonist, could the incarnation be any more a voluntary act of the Father, in the Son and by the Spirit, than creation? And if everything is naturally God's self-manifestation, is the incarnation unique? How does the emanation of one ray, however luminescent, differ qualitatively from another? Scholars who assume Dionysius is a Neoplatonist philosopher are understandably puzzled when Dionysius identifies emanation with the providence of Jesus. After quoting Dionysius's third letter, Perl says, "The incarnation, then, is the coming forth of God into manifestations. *But this, as we have seen, is what all reality is.*"⁹⁹ Similarly, John D. Jones takes issue with Dionysius: "Yet is it only in the God-man Christ that the divinity takes on being? For the procession and reversion of all beings is the procession and reversion of the divinity out of itself and about itself. . . . But, then, does not the divinity itself take on being in ecstasis? Are not beings an 'incarnation' of the divinity?"¹⁰⁰ Setting aside the Areopagite's Trinitarian theology, Christology, and liturgy, Perl asserts that Dionysius *must* assimilate Christology to cosmology and the incarnation to creation-as-theophany.¹⁰¹ Shaw, Riches, and Milbank argue similarly, but where Perl sees Dionysius as Plotinian, these scholars see him in the line of the ostensibly "incarnational" theology of Iamblichus and theurgic Neoplatonism.¹⁰² This is especially incongruous when Shaw himself observes that theurgic Neoplatonism disdained the body and saw theurgy as the way of release from it. The hierophant performing the operation becomes a *theios*

---

philosophy he will exclude from consideration the author's "trinitarian theology, Christology and liturgy." *Theophany*, 1–5.

98. Golitzin illuminates this point in *Mystagogy*, 172–73.

99. "This formula *assimilate*s the incarnation to Dionysius' Neoplatonic metaphysics, in which God is manifest in and as each and every being." From Perl, *Theophany*, 108, emphasis added.

100. *Pseudo-Dionysius* (trans. J. D. Jones), 60, commenting on *DN* 2.6.

101. "This formula *assimilate*s the incarnation to Dionysius' Neoplatonic metaphysics, in which God is manifest in and as each and every being." See Perl, *Theophany*, 108, emphasis added. This is what Perl wants Dionysius to say, but it is far from what he actually says. This is not surprising, given that Perl says at the outset (1–2) he will exclude Dionysius's discourse on Trinitarian theology, Christology, and liturgy "because it does not contribute to the specifically philosophical understanding of Dionysius" (115 n. 2). Such a question-begging method makes it impossible even to ask whether Christian convictions—everywhere apparent in the *Corpus*—influence his conclusions.

102. See Shaw, preface to *Theurgy and the Soul*, xxiii.

anēr (divine man).¹⁰³ Throughout his corpus, though, Dionysius sees deification as *God's* act of grace, through the word and the sacraments, that incorporates the *whole church* from the leaders to the neophyte.

Where scholars such as Perl interpret Dionysius as a card-carrying Neoplatonist philosopher in the line of Plotinus, Shaw and Milbank see him as the standard-bearer for theurgic Neoplatonism over against Plotinus. Yet both interpretations assimilate the incarnation to a broader metaphysical process. What happens everywhere, always, eternally takes precedence over what happened once but with an everlasting effective history. According to Shaw and Milbank, "*the Incarnation is far greater in scope than the singular event of the life of Jesus.* . . . It is here that Iamblichus's emphasis on the penetration of the One throughout all material existence, provides precisely the metaphysical principle needed to support a more profound and expansive understanding of the Incarnation."¹⁰⁴ Shaw adds, "and I believe we may find clues in that most theurgic and Neoplatonic of Christians, Dionysius the Areopagite." "Yet," he crucially acknowledges, "there is an almost imperceptible shift in Dionysius away from the cosmocentric roots of the Platonic myth."¹⁰⁵ Indeed, this is the case—and the shift is quite perceptible.¹⁰⁶ For Dionysius, Jesus is the only instance of a hypostatic union of God and human nature (*Ep.* 4).

It is one thing to suggest that there are bridges to non-Christian thought and another to conclude that the doctrine of the incarnation requires the broader metaphysical berth of Neoplatonism.¹⁰⁷ By its own common and enthusiastic consent, Platonism is excarnational. For Plotinus and Iamblichus alike, the goal was ascent from the body. Temporary inhabitation of a statue by ritual "enlivening" may be called an epiphany, but it could hardly be considered an incarnation, and the goal of pagan theurgy was to help the soul escape the body rather than to save

---

103. Even Shaw notes (*Theurgy and the Soul*, 57, emphasis added) that according to Iamblichus the gods "shine their light generously on theurgists, calling their souls up to themselves and giving them unification (*henôsis*), accustoming them—while they are yet in bodies—to be *detached* from their bodies and turned to their eternal and noetic principle" (see *De myst.* 1.12). As Shaw writes later on the same page: "To be *in* the body in a divine manner was to be *out of the body* (i.e., free of its material constraints), and Iamblichus maintained that this paradox was integral to every theurgic experience. . . . The theurgist was simultaneously man and god. . . . He became *theios anêr*, universal and divine yet particular and mortal (*DM* 235, 13–14)."

104. Shaw, preface to *Theurgy and the Soul*, xxv, emphasis added.

105. Shaw, preface to *Theurgy and the Soul*, xxvi.

106. Shaw, preface to *Theurgy and the Soul*, xxv.

107. Contra Milbank and Riches, foreword to *Theurgy and the Soul*, v–xviii, and Shaw's argument throughout this impressive work.

both together.[108] Shaw's doctoral supervisor, Birger Pearson, is closer to the truth when he links not Plotinus but Iamblichus to Gnosticism.[109]

Emanation, including creation *ex deo*, is the metaphysical foundation for Platonist panentheistic "natural supernaturalism."[110] Matter, says Plotinus, is "intrin-

---

108. This is evident even in Shaw's passages (e.g., *De myst.* 5.12). Iamblichus answers Porphyry with anything but an "incarnational" riposte: "our sacrificial fire, imitating the activity of the divine fire, destroys everything material in the sacrifices... and frees them from the bonds of matter... and leads our material nature up to the immaterial." Quoted in Shaw, *Theurgy and the Soul*, 43–44. Iamblichus invites, "Recognize, if you will, the lowest of divine beings: the soul purified from the body" (*De myst.* 1.10). The "all things" that are saved, Proclus teaches, are incorporeal ideas. "For the Divine is accessible not to mortals who think corporeally, but 'to all those who, naked, hasten upward toward the heights,' as the oracle says." See CO fr. 116 (= Proclus, *In Plat. Crat.* 88.4–6). In contrast, all of the New Testament testimony to Jesus *requires* looking down to matter to behold here, in the visible world, what God has accomplished (1 John 1:1–4). Shaw states, "Iamblichus's Hermetic position opposed Platonic dualists such as Numenius, who viewed matter as autonomous and evil, and Plutarch, who postulated an evil soul that preceded the World Soul." Against such "Platonic" transcendence, Iamblichus stressed an "'immanentist' Pythagorean metaphysics" (32–33). This seems to be another example of special pleading, setting Iamblichus apart as more affirming of embodiment. Numenius and Plutarch were themselves Neopythagoreans and Iamblichus in many respects develops Numenius's ideas (especially the splitting of the Intellect and the Soul into separate entities, higher and lower).

Moreover, Shaw emphasizes throughout the implications of the undescended soul: gnostic versus incarnation. See also his essay, "Demon est Deus Inversus." "Therefore," says Shaw here, "in spite of Iamblichus's pejorative descriptions of matter in the *De Mysteriis*, it was not viewed negatively, nor was embodiment per se." Though it requires another essay, I believe this is simply a contradiction. I would focus on several questions, such as whether it makes a difference if the highest *part* of the soul remains above or the soul is divided into three (cosmic, rational, irrational) and only the last descends? I would also want to nuance Shaw's now widely adopted contrasts of theurgy with magic not only on the basis of the Magical Papyri and Chaldean Oracles but Iamblichus's *On the Mysteries*. As for purely heavenly ends, "the art of making gods," as the Hermetic Asclepius puts it, leads not to faith (theology) but to a spiritual technology that exploits their services for pragmatic goals (e.g., Julian the Theurgist's rain-making that brought victory to the army, doxological biographies of Iamblichus and Proclus by their students attesting to feats that could only be considered magical).

109. Pearson, "Theurgic Tendencies." Hans Lewy suggested a gnostic influence pervading Iamblichus and later Neoplatonism generally in *Chaldaean Oracles and Theurgy*, 382. Nicola Spanu observes that his description matches what we find in the Greek Magical Papyri. See *Enn.* 6.4 [28].40–44 for his own view of magic. See Spanu, "Magic of Plotinus' Gnostic Disciples."

110. Against Orthodox critics of Dionysius like Wesche, Perl insists that theophany and its hierarchies are "not only consistent with but essential to holy tradition," adding that these doctrines, which happen to distinguish the East most from the West, include the following: "creation as theophany, grace as continuous with nature; knowledge as union of knower and known; Incarnation and sacrament as fulfillment, not exception or addition; liturgy as the realization of the cosmos; mysticism as ontological union rather than psychological condition; sin

sically evil" (*Enn.* 1.8.3). It has "no possible trace of goodness" and is "utterly ugly," which is why we must flee from this world to the next.[111] Shaw, Milbank, and others insist that theurgic Neoplatonism eschews Plotinus's "gnostic" anthropology, yet even Shaw acknowledges that Iamblichus too identified matter with "pollution," "defilement," and "an obstacle to communion with the gods." The union of the soul with the body is "demeaning."[112]

If this is so, then incarnation is unequivocally bad, a decline for a soul and an unimaginable—even blasphemous—fate to attribute to the One itself. Dionysius, however, transposes evil from the ontological sphere to the ethical. There was no cosmological fall of soul into embodiment; rather nature, including both the soul and the body of human beings, was created good but turned away willfully from its Good and embraced death. In fact, he departs explicitly from his teacher Proclus at precisely the point, ironically, where he lifts verbatim much else in his treatment: the problem of evil (*DN* 4). "There is no truth," he says, "in the common assertion that evil is inherent in matter *qua* matter, since matter too has a share in the cosmos, in beauty and form" (*DN* 4.28). The fall into sin is not ontological but ethical.[113] Nor is it the result of ignorance. "Scripture speaks of men who sin knowingly," he says (*DN* 4.35). Just as there is no divine part of humans, there is no inherently evil aspect of their nature.

Fourth, the Corpus Dionysiacum transposes divine henads into ecclesiastical hierarchs. The graded cosmos has been replaced by the triune creator and his

---

as corruption and loss of being, not legalistic transgression; atonement as physical-ontological assumption , not justification or juridical satisfaction; hierarchy as service and love, not oppression and envy." See Perl, "Symbol, Sacrament, and Hierarchy," 355–56. From this familiar list of simplistic antitheses it is easy to see how Perl's polemically charged reading of Dionysius is an exaggeration of genuine elements in the Orthodox tradition (and not without significant development in the West).

111. Plotinus, *Enn.* 1.8.3; 2.16.16–21; 2.16.23–24. Fleeing (a reprise of Plato's point in the *Theaetetus*) is found in *Enn.* 1.2.

112. Shaw, *Theurgy and the Soul*, 44. See also Milbank and Riches, foreword to *Theurgy and the Soul*.

113. *EH* 3.3.11: "From the very beginning human nature has stupidly glided away from those good things bestowed on it by God. . . . There followed the destructive rejection of what was really good, a trampling over the sacred Law laid down in paradise for man. Having evaded the yoke which gave him life, man rebelled against the blessings of God and was left to his own devices, to the temptations and the evil assaults of the devil. And in exchange for eternity he pitiably opted for mortality. Wandering far from the right path, ensnared by destructive and evil crowds, the human race turned away from the true Good and witlessly served neither gods nor friends but its enemies who, out of their innate lack of pity, took the cruelest advantage of its weakness and dragged it down to the deplorable peril of destruction and thus dissolution of being."

good creation, but hierarchy has shifted from cosmology to ecclesiology. It is now through the hierarchy (a term coined by Dionysius) that the rays of the "supra-essential Jesus" reach down to all members and incorporate them into himself as the head of all heads (*EH* 3.7). This is the whole purpose of hierarchy: for the highest to bend down to the lowest through intermediate ministers and bring all into the unity of Christ's visible church.

A good example of this transposition is the way Dionysius relocates the notion of "like produces like" (based on emanation from higher to lower levels) to ecclesiology: Christ "fashions the existence of all things" and "wishes everything to be always akin *to him* and to have *fellowship with him* according to its fitness." This is said in the context not of philosophical speculation but of upbraiding the impetuous monk Demophilus, who arrogantly and publicly criticized a presbyter for dealing mercifully with a penitent (*Ep.* 8).[114] "Jesus, who is the source of all hierarchy, all sanctification, all the workings of God. . . . He assimilates them, as much as they are able, to his own light . . . [and] pulls together many differences" (*EH* 1.2). The reversion from division to unity is clearly relocated to an ecclesiological frame, with the rogue monks especially in view.

The cosmos of Dionysius is the church, the place where the true vision falsely claimed by enthusiasts, whether in the Eleusinian and Orphic mysteries or by rogue monks, is beheld: "So, therefore, let us behold the divine symbols which have to do with the divine birth and let no one who is uninitiated approach this spectacle. For no one with weak eyes can safely look upon the rays of the sun and there is a risk for us when we handle what is above us" (*EH* 2.2.1; cf. *DN* 4.13). This is why the mystery of Christ was not fully revealed to the prophets.

A fifth transposition is from theurgy to liturgy. To be enfolded by the divinizing rays one must participate in Christ's visible body.[115] It is in the church's lit-

---

114. The eighth epistle confirms Dionysius's concern to put the monks in their proper place *within* the church and *after* the clergy rather than before and above the regular ministry of preaching, sacraments, and discipline. Golitzin makes a superb case for the author as one who wants to draw monks from "Messalian" heresy (denying the ecclesiastical offices and sacramental ministry) to the "Great Church." See *Mystagogy*, 1–2. Letter 10 is a major clue to everything, says Golitzin, especially against critics who think the *Corpus Dionysiacum* lacks any eschatology. "It is surely curious that a writer 'devoid of eschatology' should address his concluding remarks to the author [John] of the one and only full-blooded apocalypse to find its way into the NT canon, and do so, moreover, against the background of a Syrian Church which did not accept this book as canonical until very late indeed." At the beginning he says "John is especially dear to him—'more so than for the many,' he says—and then again, toward the end, that he is 'at present engaged in remembering and renewing the truth of your theology' [*Ep.* X 117A and 1120A (208:4–5 and 209:12)]."

115. "Someone might claim that God has appeared himself and without intermediaries to

urgy where God is at work. Christ—through his ministers—catechizes, baptizes, disciplines, and leads the church in prayers, alms, anointing, and cares for the dying. Whenever Dionysius mentions theurgy, it is always the work of God in self-revelation, redemption, and the raising of humanity from division to union with the Father in the Son and by the Spirit.[116] The recalcitrant monks represent division but not for the sake of any universal theophany; this division is a deliberate act for which they are morally culpable. They have imagined themselves as being greater than the whole hierarchy (i.e., body of Christ), experiencing by themselves what no creature can ever know and not waiting, with the rest of the church, to enjoy what is possible for creatures in the eschaton.

The twentieth century was rife with comparisons of Christian sacraments to Greco-Roman mystery cults. Jean Trouillard, a Proclus specialist and student of Maurice Blondel, defended such a connection boldly.[117] However, this project has come under considerable criticism. Among many others, A. D. Nock has shown that there is virtually no evidence of this connection in the New Testament; rather, baptism and the Lord's Supper were rooted in Jewish history and practices (viz., circumcision and Passover).[118] Majercik writes:

> Christian sacramentalism, after all, is based on a theistic view which assumes an essential difference between Creator and creation. Thus, any sacramental act performed here below must ultimately depend for its effect on an irruption of the Divine into an otherwise natural order. In contrast, theurgy is based on an emanationist view which posits a "sympathetic" link between all aspects of the cosmos; the emphasis here is on sameness, not difference. Thus theurgy,

---

some of the saints," Dionysius says. "But in fact it should be realized that scripture has clearly shown that 'no one has ever seen' or every will see the being of God in all his hiddenness." Instead, God revealed himself in creaturely images through the ministry of angels to the prophets and apostles. "In *time to come*," when "as scripture says, 'we shall always be with the Lord,'" we will "enjoy his visible theophanies in perfect contemplation" as the disciples experienced in the transfiguration. In that day, "We shall be 'equal to angels and sons of God, being sons of the resurrection.' This is what the truth of scripture affirms. But *for now*, what happens is this. We use whatever appropriate symbols we can for the things of God." These "analogies" then halt as "we approach the ray which transcends being" (*DN* 1.4). I have changed Luibheid's rendering of *theophaneias* as "the sight of God" to "theophanies." John D. Jones translates it in the singular form in *Pseudo-Dionysius*, 112. The plural underscores that "theophany" is not a general phenomenon but a particular event. Moreover, Dionysius makes it clear that even these special theophanies are not "for now" but for "when we see the Lord."

116. Shaw, "Neoplatonic Theurgy and Dionysius the Areopagite," 573, 576.
117. Trouillard, "La théurgie païenne," 15:58–83.
118. Nock, *Essays on Religion*, 2:791–820.

unlike Christian sacramentalism, depends not on any inbreaking of the Divine but, rather, on a recognition of the Divine presence in even the basest matter. (In this regard, see, e.g., Proclus, *El. Th.*, props. 144 and 145.) It is on this point, then, that theurgy and Christian sacramentalism part company.[119]

Like Gregory of Nyssa, Dionysius calls the divine names in scripture "statues" of this theurgy.[120] As in scripture itself, in baptism and the Eucharist we see God at work reaching down to the lowest level and raising all to fellowship with him. "The reception of the most divine Eucharist is a symbol of participation in Jesus" (*CH* 1.3). The cosmos does not naturally reveal God's grace in the providence of Jesus, but God himself selects the analogies he will use to knit people to himself. Dionysius explains that the old covenant was laden with images (e.g., the temple cult) while "our covenant" is simpler, less enigmatic (*EH* 5.2).[121]

Beyond these divinely authorized portraits, we cannot speculate, much less represent them in art. Dionysius stipulated, "We must not have pictures," even of "revealing symbols of Scripture," since they are already the earthly images he has selected (*CH* 2.1).[122] In brief, all images are restricted to "the initiation of our founders"—the prophets and apostles whose inspired tradition was "passed onto us by the divinely transmitted scriptures." "Furthermore, we say that these writings are to be honored, whatever our inspired initiators set down for us in the holy tablets of written scripture" (*EH* 1.4). This is consistent with the policy of the ancient church, including the Council of Elvira (300–309): "Pictures are not to be

---

119. Majercik, introduction to *Chaldean Oracles*, 24–25.

120. Saffrey relates a scholia at the beginning of chapter 9 of the *Divine Names* where John of Scythopolis explains: "'Well,' he says, 'we must examine also all that is manifested to us from these statues that are the divine names, *toutôn tôn theônumikôn agalmatôn*.' I am obliged to translate literally this, at first sight, very strange expression: 'those statues that are the divine names.'" Saffrey notes, "The comparison of the divine names with the statues of the gods is habitual in the Athenian Neoplatonists," including Proclus, *Theo. Plat.* 1.29. "As theurges animate the statues of the gods and there demonstrate their presence, so language in composing the names of the gods expresses their nature and makes them present intellectually." See "New Objective Links," 67.

121. His liturgy by which cosmic return of those fallen from God's goodness consists of the Word (reading, singing, and preaching of scripture) and the sacraments (baptism and the Eucharist). To complete the triad, he adds anointing with oil. Though practiced in the Syrian church, Dionysius is the first to include it as a sacrament.

122. Justin Martyr testifies that artistic representations of God (including Christ) are forbidden. Irenaeus complained that the gnostics painted images of Christ in violation of scripture in *Haer.* 1.25.6; 2.13.3, 4, 8. Even the Hermes-friendly Lactantius went so far as to conclude, "there is no true religion wherever there is a statue or image" (*Inst.* 2.18). Translation from Lactantius, *Divine Institutes* (trans. McDonald). "It is sinful to set up an image of God in a Christian temple," says Augustine, *De fide et symbolo* 7.14; cf. *De diversis quaestionibus* 78.

placed in churches, so they do not become objects of worship or adoration."[123] Later departures from this consensus—especially the introduction of statues into Western veneration—may exhibit similarities with pagan theurgy, but making such comparisons concerning Dionysius's day is anachronistic.

Sixth and finally, Dionysius transposes emanation to eschatology. By participating in Christ's providential activity—his descent and reversion to the Father—human beings share in deifying grace. God's activity, he says, is focused on "recalling and resurrecting of those who have fallen away from it." *Recalling* (i.e., reversion) he equates with *resurrection* (*DH* 1.3). "The whole person" (*holous hēmas*) is saved, "body and soul," the body sharing in "the honors" of salvation.

> That is why divine justice links the body with the soul when final judgment is rendered to the soul, for the body also partook of the same journey along the road of holiness or impiety. Hence the blessed ordinances grant divine communion to both the one and the other.... Thus the entire person is made holy, the work of his salvation is all-embracing, and the full rites make known the totality of the resurrection that is to come. (*EH* 7.3.9)

Moreover, Dionysius rejects the Origenist *apokatastasis*. According to Orphic eschatology—gnostic, Hermetic, Neoplatonic, kabbalistic—biblical narratives of historical events are allegorized as precosmic stages of fall and return that occur within God.[124] This was exactly the doctrine taught by Syrian gnostic Stephen ben Sadhaili, whose *Book of Holy Hierotheos* pretended to be Dionysius's muse: "All nature will be confused with the Father," he said. "Nothing will perish or be destroyed, but all will return, be sanctified, united, and confused. Thus God will be all in all. Even hell will pass away and the damned return."[125]

However, Dionysius is explicit in his rejection of this view. Only those who are united to Christ share in his resurrection.[126] He says that "in the times to come it

---

123. Not merely a synod, this was the first of a series of broader councils leading up to the First Ecumenical Council (Nicaea). See Grigg, "Aniconic Worship," 428–33.

124. Frothingham, *Stephen bar Sudaili*, 60–61. He adds, "The mystical pantheism of the monks of Egypt and Syria from the IV to the VI century . . . are facts too well-known to require proof. In both there flourished every degree of pantheism and pan-nihilism, from the gross and material form of the Euchites to the spiritualized forms of the kabbalists, Neo-Platonic and Origenist sects." Stephen's "thought was dominated by gnostic-kabbalistic elements." Hermetic interests (astrology and alchemy) were integral to oriental gnosis, and the *Book of Holy Hierotheus* connects the process of emanation and return to astronomical-astrological theories of the day. Intriguingly, along with an alleged autobiography, two texts on astronomical and meteorological topics have been assigned to the Syriac Dionysian material.

125. Quote from the *Book of Holy Hierotheos* from Frothingham, *Stephen bar Sudaili*, 110–11.

126. See especially *EH* 7.3.1–11.

is not God who will rightly separate himself from the wicked but, rather, it is the wicked who will separate themselves completely from God" (*Ep.* 10). Elsewhere he adds that "with undeviating power [God] gives Himself for the Deification of those that turn to him" and "bestows a Divine Similitude upon those that turn to him" (*DN* 9.5–6).[127] As John of Scythopolis interprets him, Dionysius is so explicit on this point "because of those who claim that along with the saints even these [demons] are saved in the 'restoration' mythologized by them" (*SchEH* 173.1).

---

127. Translation here from Dionysius, *Dionysius the Areopagite* (trans. Rolt), 164–65. Rolt's translation (active rather than passive voice) is more accurate here than Luibheid's: "With unswerving power he gives himself outward for the sake of the divinization of those who are returned to him."

10

Cosmotheism as Philosophical Religion
Eriugena's Dionysius

> No one goes to heaven except by philosophy.
>
> —John Scottus Eriugena[1]

The subtitle of Seyyed Hossein Nasr's survey *Islamic Philosophy from Its Origin to the Present: Philosophy in the Land of Prophecy* captures well the tension between Hebraic and Greek discourses.[2] Prophecy looks forward to new events while "axial" philosophy has a cyclical view of time drawn into the stream of procession and return. For Jews and Christians, the end cannot be like the beginning because the world is not a natural overflow of the One but a history in which a personal and communicative God acts. Emmanuel Levinas expresses the contrast well: "To the myth of Ulysses returning to Ithaca wish to oppose the story of Abraham who leaves his fatherland forever for a yet unknown land and forbids his servants to even bring back his son to the point of departure."[3]

However, as Jan Assmann observes, from Egypt—via Jerusalem and Athens—came the prophetic monotheism of Moses and the cosmotheism of Orpheus. "The opposite of monotheism is not polytheism, nor even idol-worship, but cosmotheism, the religion of an immanent god and a veiled truth that shows and conceals itself in a thousand images that illuminate and complement, rather than logically exclude, one another."[4] Cosmotheism "seems to be the common denominator

---

1. Quote taken from Johannes Scottus Eriugena, *Iohannis Scotti Annotationes in Marcianum* (ed. Lutz), 64. The Latin reads: Memo intrat in coelum nisi per philosophiam.
2. Fraenkel, *Philosophical Religions*, 87–88.
3. Levinas, "Trace of the Other," 348.
4. Assmann, *Price of Monotheism*, 43.

of Egyptian religion, Alexandrinian (Neoplatonic, Stoic, Hermetic) philosophy, and Spinozism, including the medieval traditions such as alchemy and the kabbalah that might have served as intermediaries."[5] The West opted for monotheism officially; "above all, however, we can see that the rejected alternative, the cosmotheism driven out by monotheism, has constantly shadowed the religious and intellectual history of the West, and in certain phases even struck at its heart."[6]

Gilles Quispel reminds us, "Orphic mysteries were celebrated until the end of Hellenism in Alexandria: their myth of the world egg [upper half of shell became heaven, lower half earth] was still told there in the first centuries of the Christian Era."[7] By this time writers referred to Orphism, almost always with respect, as simply the ancient wisdom tradition of the Greeks.[8] However, given its utopian emphases, it was destined to be a phenomenon that refused all definition, limitation, or boundary. "All the theology of the Greeks comes from Orphic mystagogy," according to the pagan Proclus.[9] Alexandrian gnosis was the common property of all parties, so that Proclus could draw upon even Origen at certain points.[10] Even when the mysteries fell silent and the schools were closed, Orpheus's euphonious voice could be heard in the deserts and secluded monastic houses where the heritage of pagan antiquity was not only preserved and curated but from which the most sensitive bricoleurs continued the philosophical tradition.

In Western antiquity, "philosophy" was not a university major, far less a secular discipline. On the one hand, the denotation was broad: "love of wisdom." Philosophers were simply truth-seekers. The personification of wisdom (*sophia*) and truth (*alētheia*) as gods underscores the religious roots. On the other hand, ironi-

---

5. Assmann, *Moses*, 141–42.
6. Assmann, *Price of Monotheism*, 43.
7. Quispel, "Reincarnation and Magic," 172–73.
8. Though every renaissance involves reconstruction, Neoplatonists had some direct lines of historical continuity. The scholiarchs (at least of Athens) were initiated into the mysteries despite the decline of Eleusis as a religious center, and they were steeped not only in the Chaldean Oracles but in Orphic theogonies and hymns that we do not possess.
9. Proclus, *Theo. Plat.* 1.6 (= testamenta 250 in Kern, *Orphicorum fragmenta*).
10. Hermeticists and later Neoplatonists would speak about the central role of the human, part divine and part animal, imitating the demiurge by looking up to the Real and down to assist fellow appearances, with gnostics being less sanguine. Nevertheless, the Orphic *mythos*, understood as the *logos*, was antithetical to any notion of the natural equality of body and soul, much less to the salvation of the body and the visible world through the incarnation of a god. The supposed incarnation of the supreme principles, even the One itself, was tantamount to saying that the source of all being became evil. The spectrum is broad, of course, and I have not identified Origen's *apokotastasis* with reincarnation, although it also belongs to this broader Alexandrian milieu.

cally, the connotation was narrower. Analogous to its emergence throughout the Persian Empire, philosophy arose in Greece through the impetus of new religious concepts and ways of conceiving reality that were more mystical, speculative, abstract, and transcendent. It was part of the shift from a locative to a utopian outlook, characterized by new myths and doctrines identified with Orpheus.

Orphism was not a school or sect but a tradition sharing common intuitions that focused on the soul's immortality (and thus, divinity), bodily incarceration, various reincarnations, and eventual return to the unity of the All. This powerful trend reconfigured the entire horizon of late archaic Greece, fostered the classical age, and became the dominant philosophical tradition of the West. It is this specific tradition, I have argued, that constitutes what Carlos Fraenkel describes as "philosophical religion."

Any concrete religion forged by historical accidents could be transmuted by Orphic alchemy into the gold of abstract thought. Through allegorical interpretation, myth became metaphysics, divine beings became principles, rituals became symbols of ideas. Religion came to belong to the realm of ever-changing shadows that yielded nothing more than opinion, but philosophy grasped *That Which Is* by a single vision of gnosis. Consequently, Orphism never became a world religion. Instead, Western civilization came to assume that it was Reason itself.

We may picture this as a pyramid with lines radiating downward from a single point in expanding diversity. At its base, the lower world is the realm of shadows: the historical, visible, temporal level of shifting appearances. Limited, defined, and bounded by a body and the physical and moral laws of the visible world, the soul longs to reascend together with the rest of separated ideas to the absolute unity of its source. Analogous to the Soul's division into separate bodies, truth is divided into separate religions and schools. As ardent souls tend to the mending of their spiritual wings, they are able to transcend the divisions of body-bound creeds and behold with a single vision the Real itself. No longer requiring authorities and mediating institutions of the divided realm below, the Orphic soul traverses the shaman's path from authority to autonomy.

As the pagan schools eventually closed, it was mainly in certain monastic houses where the entrancing song of Orpheus could be heard. Like Pythagoras and Plato, the abbot was the philosopher-king, guiding initiates from authority to autonomy. Rising from the lower world and its temporal gospel to the eternal gospel, the ascent of the soul followed the Orphic course from Pythagoras to Proclus. Beginning with purgation, novitiates withdrew from the world, and through rigorous asceticism emptied their thoughts of matters associated with the body. Through contemplation, they came to understand that the literal meaning of scripture, tied to the body and history, could be transcended by spiritual exegesis and exercises. Finally, the perfect achieved union with the Real through an unobscured and unmediated vision of the mind. The thinker and the object of thought became one in the beatific vision. Throughout the Byzantine-medieval centuries, it was monks who not only preserved and curated the Orphic tradition but were Christendom's most profound theologians, scientists, and formulators of philosophical religion.

Influential Byzantine and medieval manifestations of this Orphic-orthodox tension appear in Pseudo-Dionysius, who represents a *creative transposition* of Neoplatonic themes to distinctive Christian doctrines, and John Scottus Eriugena, who articulated a medieval *philosophical religion*. There are of course many representatives in between we could engage, but the goal of this chapter is to explore these distinctive appropriations of Neoplatonic philosophy.

Eriugena: Cosmology as Theophany

At precisely the points where Augustine, Dionysius, and Maximus transferred Neoplatonic cosmology to Trinitarian theology, the incarnation, and the liturgical reversion of believers to God, Eriugena transfers them back to what Bernhard Blankenhorn describes as a "quasi-pantheistic theology."[11] Like Origen, he can say that his system is "consistent with the Faith and with the Catholic creed" only as it is interpreted according to his philosophy, which he identifies with reason itself.

John Scottus Eriugena's treatise on the Eucharist was charged with teaching Origenist symbolism, and his *Treatise on Divine Predestination* was judged as both Origenist and Pelagian by two councils in 859 and 865.[12] He rejected not only divine predestination but also foreknowledge.[13] His *Periphyseon* (*On the Division*

---

11. Blankenhorn, *Mystery of Union with God*, 39–40, referring to the *Parisian Scholia* on the *Mystical Theology* (5.108); John Scottus Eriugena, *Periph.* 2.136.24–38.13; 142.35–44.16.

12. Helpful in placing Eriugena in his ninth-century context is Deirdre Carabine's *John Eriugena Scotus*, 13–28. In 827 Charlemagne's son Louis the Pious received from the Byzantine emperor Michael the Stammerer the gift of a Greek manuscript of the *Corpus Dionysiacum*, which eventually his son Charles the Bald put in the hands of Hilduin, abbot of Saint-Denis for translation. Hilduin's erroneous identification of the Pseudo-Areopagite with Denis, the third-century martyr and patron saint of France, turned out to be more successful than his translation (c. 838), so the honor was given to Eriugena.

13. As he writes in *Div. praed.* 9.6–7, God cannot even foreknow evil because it does not exist. These terms are "metaphorically applied to God." See Eriugena, *Treatise on Divine Predestination* (trans. Brennan).

of Nature) reveals the unique metaphysics that Eriugena presupposed when he came to translate the Dionysian corpus.

The essential difference between Dionysius and Eriugena is the qualitative distinction between God and creation. Dionysius affirms the orthodox Christian belief that God is simple, immutable, impassible, eternal, and self-existent. In contrast, Eriugena assumes the univocity of being that was formulated first by Parmenides. Being comprehends both God and the world, such that in making the world God makes himself, unfolding from simplicity into complexity. Emanation is a process occurring within the divine life that is simultaneously God's act of making the world.

First, Eriugena returns Trinitarian theology to emanation. It is Eriugena who first uses "theophany" to summarize Dionysian theology.[14] Whereas Dionysius identified theophanies with God's revelation in scripture, Eriugena returns the concept to its original habitat. Of several definitions, the clearest is "the manifestation of the unmanifest in both intelligible and sensible appearance" (*Periph.* 3.633a).[15] "Nature" (*physis*) is for Eriugena the "general name for all things that are and all things that are not," including "both God and the creature" (1.441a; 2.524d). It is not Eriugena the protonominalist but a radical Christian Neoplatonist who returns to Parmenides's univocity of being: "It follows that we ought not to understand God and the creature as two beings distinct from one another but as one and the same and the Creator of all things created in all things and the maker of all things made in all things."[16] We have seen the same formula in Hermetic treatises.[17] Nature simply *is* the eternal procession of this purely ideal One into multiplicity and back again to unity.

Far from rejecting the plurality of the divine persons, Eriugena sees it as paradigmatic for a theophanic cosmology. At rest, "God" is nonexistent.[18] But supraessential divinity becomes personal and self-conscious as Father in the procession

14. Eriugena introduces this theme near the beginning of *Periphyseon*.
15. Translation of *Periphyseon*, unless otherwise noted, from Sheldon-Williams. It is also the Neoplatonic triad of rest, procession, and reversion, summarized by proposition 35 of Proclus's *Elements of Theology*: "Every effect remains in its cause, proceeds from it, and converts to it." In its absolute nature, nonbeing; in its manifestation, all being; in its reversion, absorbed back into absolute unicity. Other definitions of theophanies given in *Periphyseon* are "certain divine apparitions comprehensible to the intellectual nature" (1.446c–d), "the forms of visible and invisible things through whose order and beauty God's existence is made known" (1.919c), or even "willings" (*voluntates*) of divine mind (2.529b), which seems somewhat contradictory of the other definitions. On this point see Moran, "Spiritualis Incressatio," 136.
16. Moran, "Spiritualis Incressatio," 145, quoting *Periph.* 3.678c.
17. Moran, "Spiritualis Incressatio," 138–39. Cf. *Periph.* 679b.
18. Blankenhorn, *Mystery of Union with God*, 39–40.

of the cosmos, which is identical to the immanent procession of the Son.[19] "God, who is unknowable even to himself . . . beings to know itself in something" (*Periph.* 3.689b). The no-thing becomes some-thing.[20] The *nihil* from which God creates is not literally nothing but God's own nonbeing.[21] This is what he means by saying that "God is effected or made in His effects."[22]

The divine nature creates itself (*ac per hac se ipsum creat*), he says, and thus "allows itself to appear in its theophanies, willing to emerge from the most hidden recesses of its nature in which it is unknown even to itself . . . but descending into the principles of things, and, as it were, creating itself, it begins to know itself in something." The emanation of the Son is the paradigm of this broader procession, as the Spirit is for the reversion. And the reversion of creation is identical to the immanent procession of the Spirit. The immanent Trinity comes into being with the economy; cosmology and Christology merge. In this dialectic (reminiscent of the philosophical Hermetica), identity (sameness) is discovered paradoxically in the opposite (difference) (*Periph.* 3.689a–b). The opposite of the Father is the Son, and the opposite of Spirit is matter, so the Absolute (identified with the Father) pluralizes and materializes itself, as the Father comes from unconscious nonbeing into goodness through the Son.[23] In creating itself, the Trinity generates the cosmos.[24]

Second, Eriugena returns God's predeterminations to primordial divine principles.[25] Dionysius had used Plotinus's analogy of radii drawn from the center to

---

19. Moran, "Spiritualis Incressatio," 138–39.
20. Carabine, *John Eriugena Scotus*, 45–66.
21. Sheldon-Williams, introduction to Eriugena, *Periphyseon*, 9.
22. Sheldon-Williams, introduction to Eriugena, *Periphyseon*, 10. "Therefore," says Sheldon-Williams, "*nihilum* can only denote the Superessence of Him Who is nothing of the things that are, *qui Melius nesciendo scitur* (686A 4–687A 3). . . . Therefore the *nihilum* out of which all things were made is, exclusively, the Divine Superessence (687A 3–B9) . . . therefore God is effected or made in His effects (687B 9–688A 1)." Very important commentary on this point is given by Moran, "Spiritualis Incressatio," 136.
23. Unlike Augustine, Eriugena cannot defend the consubstantiality of the Son with the Father because he has adopted wholesale the emanationist ontology. For Plotinus, the soul in its highest aspect (*intellectus*) bears an immediate relationship to the second hypostasis, the Intellect (*nous*), where participation begins. For Augustine, however, this immediate relationship is with God himself. One attains self-consciousness by turning inward, going deeper into oneself, and it is not surprising that we find here his much-debated psychological analogy of the Trinity. It is not "like produces like" for Augustine, but "same produces same—eternally," which is *not* a creature.
24. Moran, "Johannes Scottus Eriugena."
25. Fokin, "Intelligible Triad," 65–66. Fokin points out that from Porphyry on, this Being-Life-Mind triad is interpreted as "three gods," and Sethian gnostics, especially those in the circle of Plotinus, adapted the triad to their "Triple-Powered One" (50–52). Fokin refers to Augustine,

the circumference of the circle only in relation to the Trinity, but Eriugena returns the analogy to its original cosmological habitat.[26] The world is an exhaustive and necessary emanation not of God's will—the "providence of Jesus"—but of his being (*Periph.* 3.637a). He wants to affirm that the primordial causes are completely simple in the unity of the Word (Neoplatonic Intellect) but are nevertheless plural in their apparent emanation.[27]

Eriugena's moves reflect a uniquely Western (Orphic) corollary of the Hindu dualism that surrenders finally to a monistic idealism in which nothing exists but pure thoughts.[28] Eriugena offers a "radical version of immaterialism and intellectualism," notes Moran.[29] Humans are co-demiurges as divine and human intellect in the undistinguishable simplicity of nature makes itself eternally. Like God, our divine intellect must be drawn from the excessive fecundity of its unconscious nonbeing to Being itself, and return to its absolute simplicity in Mind, overcoming the transgression of thinking reality is corporeal.[30] To be sure, there are impor-

---

Civ. 10.23, 29; Porphyry, *De regressu animae*, fr. 8. They are Proclus's "intellective gods" (henads). However, as Fokin shows, for Dionysius Being, Life, and Intelligence are divine names—attributes of the simple essence—rather than divine beings. God's processions (*proodoi*) or manifestations (*ekphanesis*) are not creatures in general but the divine names in scripture. With regard to the act of creation, however, Dionysius refers to God's providence through the words or reasons (*logoi*) (50–52). Marius Victorinus and Maximus correlate the triad with the persons of the Trinity. However, Maximus again interprets it in more cosmic terms: the Father (essence), the Son (difference), and the Spirit (movement). There are many shared sources (especially since Maximus lived for a time in Rome and Carthage), but for the more Dionysian Maximus the canvas is the whole world more than simply the soul. Augustine is partial to the Plotinian-Porphyrian psychological emphasis of Victorinus, but he does not correlate the triad with the persons of the Trinity. This is true of Dionysius as well. In short, according to Fokin, Being, Life, and Intelligence for both Augustine and Dionysius are neither "gods" nor even persons of the Godhead but attributes of the one God (59–64).

26. This intellectual triad finds its source in unsystematized comments in the *Sophist* and *Timaeus* (and book 5 of Aristotle's *Metaphysics*). Though never quite as developed as the more important triad of the One, Intellect, and Soul, this subordinate triad was correlated with the triad of rest, procession, and reversion. See Plotinus, *Enn.* 1.6.7; 3.9.5; 5.1.6; 5.2.1; 5.4.2; 5.6.5; 6.7.16 and Proclus, *Elem. theo.* 35.

27. W. Norris Clarke is right: "It is not clear how he can have it both ways, though if he is to remain both a good Christian and a good Neoplatonist he must try. Here we have the latent tension between the conflicting demands of the two traditions coming sharply to a head, since Eriugena pushes each one all the way to the limit." Clarke, *Creative Renewal of Saint Thomas Aquinas*, 76.

28. Moran summarizes, "Here we find a monism where the material principle has been reabsorbed into the One and the One is understood according to the model of a mind coming to know itself." See "Spiritualis Incressatio," 128.

29. Moran, "Spiritualis Incressatio," 123.

30. Moran, "Spiritualis Incressatio," 146.

tant differences between Platonic idealism and the modern version.[31] However, if one defines idealism as "a monism of mind," Eriugena certainly qualifies.[32]

Third, Eriugena returns Dionysius's soteriological transpositions to an emanative paradigm. Human beings in particular are the microcosm of the cosmic Son: the other in whose emanation God creates himself (*a se ipso creatur*).[33] The preincarnate mind of humans is identical to the divine Mind, as will be the postincarnate condition.[34] For Eriugena, "their being *in* God is not other than their being *God*, since God is simple and contains no divisions or distinctions." Corporeal things are *not* corporeal.[35] More like Parmenides than Plato, Eriugena denies not only that matter is eternal but that it exists at all. Similar to Origen and Gregory of Nyssa, Eriugena leans toward a conception of matter as a "thickening of spirit."[36] Nature, comprehending God and creation, is pure thought. If creation *ex nihilo* is true, the world can hardly be a theophany. "For if all things that are, are eternal in the creative Wisdom, how are they made out of nothing?" (*Periph.* 3.636a).[37]

Fourth, Eriugena returns the incarnation to emanation. There is no historical incarnation of the Son, no Dionysian exultation in the paradox of the simple and incorporeal assuming complexity and materiality.[38] In a striking passage, Eriugena describes what a Christian might expect to be the incarnation:

> God, by manifesting Himself, in a marvelous and ineffable manner, creates Himself in the creature, the invisible making Himself visible and the incomprehensible and the hidden revealed and the unknown known and being without form and species formed and specific and the superessential essential and the

---

31. Burnyeat, "Idealism in Greek Philosophy."
32. Williams, "Philosophy," 204–5. An important treatment of Platonism, idealism, and Eriugena is Beierwaltes, "Die Wiederentdeckung des Eriugena"; cf. Beierwaltes, *Denken des Einen*.
33. Eriugena, *Periph.* 1.454a; cf. *Periph.* 4.755b; 4.761a; 4.817d; 4.846a. See Carabine, *John Eriugena Scotus*, 67–78.
34. Moran explains: "Moreover, by extension, the prelapsarian human mind knows the essence of all things, the essences that are in the mind of God and contained explicitly in the mind of Christ, the perfect man.... Moreover this nature is mind" which "has a 'memory of eternal things' (*PP* 4.755c). It is only by the freedom of the will that man is an animal (*PP* 4.755d), and, in the return, there is an absorption of body into soul and soul into mind." Moran mentions Werner Beierwaltes's apt description "the mind's road to God is also the journey of God within God, *itinerarium dei in deum*, as it were." See "Spiritualis Incressatio," 146.
35. Moran, "Spiritualis Incressatio," 142.
36. Cf. Moran, "Spiritualis Incressatio," 144–45.
37. The whole project is a dialogue between "Nutritor" and "Alumnus," both representing Eriugina's views. Here the speaker is Alumnus.
38. See Eriugena's commentary on Dionysius's *Celestial Hierarchy* (140b).

supernatural natural and the simple composite and the accident-free subject to accident and accident and the infinite finite and the uncircumscribed circumscribed and the supratemporal temporal and the Creator of all things created in all things and the Maker of all things made in all things. (*Periph.* 3.678c)

This is almost a verbatim quotation of Dionysius's statement of the paradoxical character of the incarnation (*DN* 2.10). However, unlike Dionysius, Eriugena qualifies, "And I am *not* speaking of the Incarnation of the Word and His taking of manhood on Himself, but of the ineffable descent of the Supreme Goodness, which is Unity in Trinity, into the things that are so as to make them be" (*Periph.* 3.678d, emphasis mine). Rather than transferring cosmology to the metaphysics of the incarnation, Eriugena moves deliberately in the opposite direction. There cannot be any reality to the incarnation because there cannot be any reality to creation as something other than God. To become incarnate is to be an appearance, not the reality.[39]

Fifth, Eriugena returns eschatology to the eternal cycle where the end is like the beginning.[40] Eriugena takes to its extreme the cyclical telos of Orphism: the end is like the beginning. "If God created the world out of absolutely nothing at all," Eriugena reasons, "then it ends in absolutely nothing at all."[41] But for Eriugena, in the end, everything reverts to the "*principles* of visible things" (*Periph.* 4.843b, emphasis added). Reversion includes all, but deification, achieved by some, leads to complete identity with God.[42] It is not that bodies are left behind but rather that they are recognized as the simulacra that they have always been.[43]

In considering the creation days of Genesis, Eriugena treats each day as an allegory of theophany. On the second day, according to Augustine's literal commentary, "the waters below the firmament are the seas and rivers, and those above are the vapours suspended in the air as clouds." However, like Origen, Eriugena

---

39. E.g., *Periph.* 2.530d; 4.755b; 5.893c; 5.925a–b.
40. Van Nieuwenhove, *Introduction to Medieval Theology*, 69.
41. Sheldon-Williams, introduction to Eriugena, *Periphyseon* (trans. Sheldon-Williams), 11. "The descent from *nihil* to *esse* does not involve a divine causality *ad extra* . . . for the descent from the Primordial Cause to the effects, like the descent from the Word to the Causes, occurs within God himself."
42. Eriugena notes that "deification" is rarely discussed in Latin theology (*Periph.* 5.1015c).
43. Rorem, "Early Latin Dionysius," 72–73. "To Eriugena, the very first sentence in the Dionysian corpus, that is, in chapter one of *The Celestial Hierarchy*, was the key. He first provides the original text, in translation (as here in capitals): 'BUT ALSO EVERY PROCESSION OF THE MANIFESTATION OF THE LIGHTS, MOVED BY THE FATHER, COMING FORTH INTO US EXCELLENTLY AND GENEROUSLY, LIKE A UNIFYING POWER, AGAIN FILLS US AND TURNS US TO THE UNITY AND DEIFYING SIMPLICITY OF THE GATHERING FATHER.'"

interprets it allegorically as dividing between three realms: "the wholly corporeal, the wholly spiritual, and that which is intermediate between body and spirit."[44] Eriugena says that the final state is being "changed into God Himself," when everything "will be resolved into the things from which they are taken," which means purified of everything bodily and diverse.[45]

Since the end is like the beginning, reversion is not a personal conversion to God as it was for Augustine, Dionysius, and Maximus but a cosmological return from multiplicity, individuality, and corporeality to pure idea. The body is resolved into the four elements from which it was taken—never to rise again, just as sense is resolved again into intellect, and all (including the Trinity) resolved back into the unity of the supraessence (*Periph.* 3.626d–628a). "The Return and the resurrection are one and the same thing," says Eriugena (3.279d; cf. 3.646d–649d). In fact, the procession and reversion are one and the same thing, eternally and in reality, although in appearance they seem to be a process (3.529a; cf. 2.649d).

The fifth book of the *Periphyseon* reprises Origen's *apokatastasis*, with the fallen angels and even the devil restored (5.923c–941b). Sin is ignorance and the "fire" of which scripture speaks is not a real place to which some are sent. Rather, it is an existential state of mind. "In it beyond doubt there will dwell the blessed no less than the damned," but the blessed see it as intellectual light and the damned see it as tormenting. "One and the same water sustains the swimmer and suffocates the drowning man."[46]

Like most advocates of philosophical religion, Eriugena wants to save the appearances—religion—by translating into allegorical truth what is absurd or offensive to reason.[47] Like Origen, he can say that his system is "consistent with the Faith and with the Catholic creed" only as interpreted according to his philosophy, which he identifies with reason itself. Thus, he can say, "No one goes to heaven except by philosophy."[48] One can hardly consider the defenses of *ex nihilo*

---

44. Sheldon-Williams, introduction to Eriugena, *Periphyseon* (trans. Sheldon-Williams), 13, quoting from 3.694d–696b.

45. *Periph.* 3.666a. Cf. 5.876a; 5.895a; 5.907a; 5.912c–d; 5.979d. On the return, see Carabine, *John Eriugena Scotus*, 93–108.

46. John Scottus Eriugena, *Div. praed.* 17.8. Referring to the liberal arts handbook of Martianus Capella, Prudentius added, "Your Capella has led you into a labyrinth, because you have tied yourself more to the meditation of his work than to the truth of the Gospel." See PL 115:1294a. Nevertheless, Eriugena displayed his skills as a biblical grammarian and allegorical exegete in a commentary on John and *Glossae divinae historiae*.

47. Sheldon-Williams, introduction to Eriugena, *Periphyseon* (trans. Sheldon-Williams), 19, quoting from *Periph.* 3.723a–724b; cf. 3.690b–c.

48. Quote from Eriugena, *Iohannis Scotti Annotationes in Marcianum* (ed. Lutz), 64, 23–24.

creation by John Philoponus, Gregory of Nazianzus, Augustine, and Maximus less philosophical or less reasonable, but Eriugena equated reason with an alternative religion. He acknowledges, "For almost all the commentators on Holy Scripture agree in this, that the Creator of the universal creature made whatever he willed to be made not out of something but out of nothing at all." He confesses that he would take this on scriptural authority, but "I feel myself to be surrounded on all sides by the dark clouds of my thoughts" (*Periph.* 3.635b). These traditional teachers described as biblical commentators earlier "are now dismissed as the unintillegent [*qui minus intelligent*]. . . . The correct interpretation of *nihil* is not *omnino nihil* but the purity of the Divine Goodness which descends from non-being into being."[49] Thus, a philosophical religion trumps a religion based on revelation not as a license to freethinking skeptics but because Orphic theology has been equated with reason and reason with God.[50]

Eriugena influenced the more daring varieties of mystics at the fountainhead of modernity. The condemnation of the *Periphyseon* as pantheistic in 1210 and 1225 alongside the denunciation of Pope Gregory XIII in 1585 measures its far greater impact on the later medieval and early modern world than in Eriugena's own day. The *Periphyseon* became a centerpiece of the twelfth-century Plato renaissance centered at the seminary of Chartres and Nicholas of Cusa's proto-Renaissance project. But for the most part, the only access of medievals to Eriugena was the popular *Clavis physicae* (*The Key to Nature*), by a twelfth-century monk who patched together various quotes clumsily.[51] Not only were there bricoleurs of ancient bricoleurs, but there were also bricoleurs of these commentators. Mostly ignorant of Greek, scholastic theologians depended on such summaries.

The spread of Eriugena's daring theses among speculative mystics led to a combustible elixir. "When Dionysius is mixed with Augustine to construct a Latin erotic mysticism, especially strong at the end of the Middle Ages and at the beginning of modernity," says Hankey, "the difference between self and God seems to disappear."[52] Laeszek Kołakowski summarizes:

> It has since been essential to all Northern mysticism of the pantheistic kind, and we can trace it in different variations almost from one generation to an-

---

49. Sheldon-Williams, introduction to Eriugena, *Periphyseon* (trans. Sheldon-Williams), 9.
50. Marler, "Authority in the Periphyseon," esp. 96.
51. This monk was Honorius Augustodensis (Honorius of Atun). Until 1682, when a complete copy was discovered in Oxford, the *Periphyseon* was disseminated mostly in this form, which may explain partially the Scot's obscurity.
52. Hankey, "Denys and the Later Platonic Trails," 501. This cannot be attributed to Augustine directly, however. Eriugena reworked Augustinian materials as yet another Orphic bricoleur.

other, from the Carolingian renaissance to Hegel. Speaking in the most general terms, it is in the idea of the potential Absolute (a semi-Absolute, if this expression can be permitted) which attains the full actuality by evolving out of itself a non-absolute reality characterized by transience, contingency, and evil; such non-absolute realities are a necessary phase of the Absolute's growth towards self-realization, and this function justifies the course of world history.[53]

The human soul also attains infinite divinity through this process, liberated from its alienation from creation and from the dualism of subject and object.[54]

Schopenhauer was not wide of the mark when he suggested that Eriugena was a major influence on Hegel's *Phenomenology of Spirit*, both directly and also indirectly through Cusa, Ficino, and Pico della Mirandola, Böhme, Bruno, Malebranche, and Spinoza.[55] It may well represent the dominant influence today not only among theosophists and New Agers but in philosophical theology (especially at the intersection with the natural sciences) and popular theosophy.[56]

---

53. Kołakowski, *Main Currents of Marxism*, 21.
54. Kołakowski, *Main Currents of Marxism*, 21–22.
55. Schopenhauer observed, "Altogether one might be surprised that pantheism did not gain complete victory over theism already in the seventeenth century; since the most original, beautiful and thorough European expositions of it (for compared to the *Upanishads* of the *Vedas* all of that is nothing) all became known during that period, namely through *Bruno, Malebranche, Spinoza*, and *Scotus Erigena*. The latter was rediscovered in Oxford, after having been forgotten and lost for many centuries, and first appeared in print in 1681, four years after Spinoza's death. This seems to prove that the insight of individuals cannot prevail as long as the spirit of the age is not ripe to receive it. In our time, on the other hand [1851], pantheism, even if only in Schelling's eclectic and confused revival, has become the dominant mode of thought of scholars and even educated people. For Kant had gone before with his overthrow of theistic dogmatism and had cleared the way for it, whereby the spirit of the age got prepared, just as a ploughed field for the seed." Schopenhauer, *Panerga and Paralipomena*, 1:9.
56. Brierley, "Potential of Panentheism for Dialogue"; cf. Thomas, "Problems in Panentheism." Panentheism appears also in Polkinghorne, "Christianity and Science," and Griffin, "Process Thought and Natural Theology." In much of the theological engagement with science over recent decades, panentheism has taken the lead. "In certain theological circles," notes R. T. Mullins, "panentheism is all the rage," but his attempts to define it in distinction to theism and pantheism fail. See Mullins, "Difficulty with Demarcating Panentheism." In the same vein, also Cocke, "Panentheism and Classical Theism." See also Diller and Kasher, *Models of God and Alternative Ultimate Realities*, especially Philip Clayton's "Introduction to Panentheism" (371–80) and the essays on Pseudo-Dionysius (783–92) and Nicholas of Cusa (381–98) by Nancy J. Shaffer, on Eckhart (801–10) by Dietaer Mieth, and on Hegel (421–30) by Glenn Alexander Magee.

Far from Home: Dionysius in the High Middle Ages

Though adopted by the most radical mystics, Eriugena's interpretation of Dionysius was not universally accepted. Commentaries on the *Corpus Dionysiacum* became a mark of distinction for a mature theologian, Bonaventure, Albert, and Aquinas being key examples. Aquinas quotes the Pseudo-Areopagite more times than any nonbiblical author except Augustine. However, he highlights Dionysius's analogical ontology and epistemology over against Eriugena. It is beyond our scope to pursue his rich interpretations—and diversions—but it will suffice to say that no Latin theologian captured the specific purpose of these brief treatises. They all saw it as something like a broader cosmological system.

What we have instead, at least among those whose formulations achieved broad assent, is an intertextual imagination at work—a relative fusion of horizons.[57] At least in my reading, Dionysius represents vividly the power of the Christian imagination to hold its own against philosophical determination. Yet the medieval imagination was less transfixed by his Tolkienesque way of mapping the "providence of Jesus" onto a Neoplatonic framework. In contrast with Dionysius's reconstructed deployment of pagan *allusions* in the service of Christocentric *narrative*, the medieval imagination assumed he was talking about Christendom.

In the Dionysian corpus there is a hierarchy of the law and of the gospel as well as the celestial hierarchy we will share in fully after the resurrection. It was not merely the Areopagite's fondness for "threes" that led him to omit a *terrestrial* hierarchy. We will never know if he had any interest in the constitutions of nations because he does not mention temporal polities. His ecclesiastical hierarchy has little to do with either the caesaropapism of the East or the papalism of the later Latin church. And he certainly has no conception of hierarchy as encompassing secular society, as in feudalism. If he has assimilated cosmology to Christology, ecclesiology, and liturgy, we should not be surprised that deification so flooded his mind that the arrangement of secular society was beyond his scope, perhaps even his interest.[58]

---

57. This phrase was coined in Gadamer, *Truth and Method*. On the one hand, we all have a finite horizon of our own time and place that limits our vision. We see things from a certain vantage point. Yet understanding can be achieved across horizons. Thus, "working out the hermeneutical situation means acquiring the right horizon of inquiry for the questions evoked by the encounter with tradition" (269). I only qualify this fusion as "relative" because I think that a genuinely universal understanding always remains particular, limited, and relative to one's own horizon.

58. In his day, of course, the emperor was the philosopher-ruler of the Christian state. Diony-

However, the medieval church added the fourth hierarchy in which the specific person, Jesus of Nazareth, must be absent not so that the Spirit can descend to unite sinners to himself as he himself promised, but so that the church can replace his natural body. Douglas Farrow goes so far as to conclude that "western ecclesiology ... *requires* a completely absent Christ if it is to provide instead that miraculous eucharistic one who will underwrite the programme of the church, a programme always in danger of becoming fully immanentist, and hence, absolutist, in nature."[59] Especially with Duns Scotus, he notes, the church was fused with Mary and "the west began to look towards the idea of the Logos incarnate in all things, and to explore more confidently a ubiquitarian Christology."

> His lead was followed by Nicholas of Cusa, who situated the ascended Christ in a place that cannot really be defined in terms of place, at once "the centre and the inclusive periphery of all spiritual beings," and thus also of the cosmos as such. The resurgence of Neoplatonism and even of Hermeticism, that *prisca theologia* which the later Middle Ages shared with the Renaissance, must also be taken into account here. It testifies to the tenacity of a pre-Christian sacramentalist worldview, of panentheism. That was a worldview naturally resistant to the hard edge of biblical eschatology, but quite comfortable with a hidden Christ who is always ascending and a Mary who is always bringing him down again; with an endless liturgical rhythm in which the Parousia (not unlike the philosophers' stone) is always within reach yet forever receding.[60]

The particularity of Jesus, enthroned in our flesh, with the church awaiting his return ("in the same way" the disciples saw him leave, Acts 1:11) became subservient to a worldwide conquest in which an absent Jesus opened up space for an active church as his supposed embodiment on earth. In the medieval church, the Dionysian hierarchy of Jesus became a fully immanent hierarchy at the price of a docetic Christology. The church replaced Jesus as his ongoing incarnation. This fateful conclusion can be summed up thus: the Christ needs the church as a *pneuma* needs a *sōma*. Farrow cuts to the joint: "Where the church is seen as the express image of an ascending Christ who is all but absorbed into the divine Reason, ecclesiology is bound to move along an absolutist course."[61] At

---

sius may have taken this context for granted, but he does not even mention it. This is surprising, given the elaborate religious aura and rites associated with the East's "caesaropapism."

59. Farrow, *Ascension and Ecclesia*, 163. Farrow, I do not think, is imputing this view at all to Pseudo-Dionysius himself but to his medieval interpreters.

60. Farrow, *Ascension and Ecclesia*, 159.

61. Farrow, *Ascension and Ecclesia*, 159.

the turn of the thirteenth century, Pope Boniface VIII brought this course to its consummation.[62]

A patient reading of the *Corpus Dionysiacum* yields the impression that this construction is not only independent of but wholly inimical to Dionysius's teaching. Yet, for the most part, the corpus known to Latins was a hodgepodge that Blankenhorn calls the *Parisian Scholia*, which was taken from Eriugena's translation but with significant revision by Anastasius with the scholia of John of Scythopolis and Maximus. It was the handbook used by Hugh of St. Victor, Albert, and Aquinas.[63] Neither the high scholastic nor the radical mystical receptions of Dionysius had very much to do with his principal agenda. There was, we may say, no genuine fusion of horizons.

In the "age of faith" between the fall of Rome and the Renaissance, these two cosmic stories battled for the allegiance of those inhabiting Christendom, as shown by the influential examples of Dionysius and Eriguena, with many subtler engagements omitted from our scope. The final chapter traces a third trajectory, represented by Gemistos Plethon, whose attempt to revive pre-Christian Platonism "outside the gates" led him to Florence where he helped spark the Renaissance.

---

62. Hankey, "Denys and the Later Platonic Trails," 501.
63. Blankenhorn, *Mystery of Union with God*, 31–33. Cf. Forrai, "Notes of Anastasius," 77–78.

11

Prophetic Gnosis
Dreaming of Utopia

> In a nutshell: Plethon discerned the connection between secularism and paganism that lies at the centre of the project of modernity.
>
> —Niketas Sinossoglou[1]

As I argued at the beginning of this volume, the so-called Axial Age is not an event that happened once and for all around the sixth century BCE. Instead, it is an ongoing process that is frequently identified with modernity. It is a transition from a locative to a utopian outlook, fueled by the discovery of the self as a divine spark imprisoned in an alien cage from which it seeks liberation. The religious quest is construed as being less about dogmas and rituals than about eternal truths revolving around this goal of escaping natural limitations and discovering one's unity with the divine All.

The ongoing effects of the Axial revolution are exhibited in internal debates over self-definition across the new religions, generating different schools. Emerging under the auspices of the powerful magi of the Neo-Persian (Sasanid) Empire (224–651 CE), Zoroastrian orthodoxy demanded strict adherence to dualism. The Hindu Classical Age (320–550 CE) under the Gupta Empire brought greater doctrinal refinement attended by the emergence of divergent schools (*darsanas*). Refinement continued well into the Middle Ages, as six schools of orthodoxy (*astika*) were defined against heterodoxy (*nastika*).[2] And just two centuries after its origin,

---

1. Sinossoglou, *Radical Platonism in Byzantium*, 426.
2. The former came to be defined by three principles: (1) authority of the Vedas, (2) the concept that the *atman* is *brahman*, and (3) belief in the afterlife and *devas* (divine beings). See Doniger, *On Hinduism*, 46. Sankhya, Yoga, Nyaya, Vaisheshika, Mimamsa, and Vedenta are

Islam was led by Al-Kindi into its golden age of *fasafa* (philosophy), which lasted until Averroes (Ibn Rushd) in the twelfth century. Islamic philosophy dug deep trenches that carried all four streams of Alexandrian gnosis into the Middle Ages. Due to space limitations, I cannot pursue these sources here, which is a tragedy, since late Neoplatonic and Hermetic traditions were mediated largely by Arabic translations of Greek sources (including influential pseudepigraphal works that inspired much of medieval alchemy). Jewish gnosis produced kabbalism, which flourished in Christian and Islamic circles. Sporadic movements arose in southern Italy and France that appear to have had a fairly direct connection to southern European missionaries of ancient gnostic sects.[3] Especially as these communities attracted members of the nobility and priests, including higher clerics, these Cathars ("Pure Ones," also Albigensians) provoked the first medieval Inquisition.[4]

Closer to home, Almaric of Bena, a distinguished late twelfth-century professor at the University of Paris, was compelled to recant several pantheistic theses. Appealing to Eriugena's views, Almaric taught that God is all (*omnia sunt deus*) and that all things are one because whatever is, is God (*omnia unum, quia quidquid est, est Deus*). This entailed perfectionism, since the soul is God and God cannot sin. Other teachings included that heaven and hell are within us, gnosis of our divinity as the true resurrection, and that all souls will be saved. Soon after Almaric's death in 1209, ten followers were burned at the city's gates, and Almaric's body was exhumed and burned. Believing that he was ushering in the age of the Spirit, Almaric represents the confluence of Joachite prophecy and pantheistic gnosis that we explore in this concluding chapter.[5]

History and Gnosis: Utopian Dreams in the Age of the Spirit

Central to my narrative is the way in which modernity—in particular, the utopian notion of the divine self—was gestating in the womb of Christendom. Officially rejected, Orphic theology nevertheless flourished as a philosophical and spiritual enterprise. Carlos Steel observes, "Eriugena's model was too unorthodox in

---

considered *astika*, whereas Jain and Buddhist religions are considered *nastika*. See Plott et al., *Axial Age*, 63: "The Buddhist schools reject any Ātman concept. As we have already observed, this is the basic and ineradicable distinction between Hinduism and Buddhism." All of these definitions continue to be debated.

3. R. I. Moore, "Medieval Europe," 137. See Pegg, *Most Holy War*; Costen, *Cathars and the Albigensian Crusade*.
4. See Graham-Leigh, *Southern French Nobility*.
5. Russell, *Influence of Amalric of Bene*.

its conclusions to have any future in the middle ages." It was to Augustine and the Aristotelian comeback that medieval scholasticism gave the palm.[6] This is true generally, but only if we concentrate on the architects of scholastic theology. The *Clavis physicae*, an abridged form of Eriugena's *Periphyseon*, became very influential in the twelfth-century renaissance in which the Chartres school especially took Platonic realism to the extreme. Aquinas criticized this trend sharply.[7] For the most part, Eriugena is ignored by the great thirteenth-century theologians. Nevertheless, Eriugena was assured enduring influence in the more radical currents of Neoplatonic mysticism that shaped modernity. Eriugena's *Periphyseon* influenced Meister Eckhart and the Rhineland mystics along with Nicholas of Cusa and a host of Renaissance thinkers, and it was also pivotal for Hegel's system centuries later.

However, what happens when philosophy and prophecy converge? This is precisely what happened in the twelfth century when the Cistercian monk Joachim of Fiore developed a remarkably influential system of eschatology.

Marking Time

For what can we hope? Eschatology—*ta eschata*, "last things"—pertains to the meaning of history disclosed by its culmination. We have seen at length that Orphic time is cyclical, pictured by the snake eating its tail. The end is like the beginning, time being a moving picture of eternity. Yet I have said little about the biblical view of time, which is fundamental for understanding Joachim's project.

Arguably, the Bible may be described as an eschatological vision based on the pattern of divine promise and fulfillment. Along with creaturely existence more generally, time is not a shadowy appearance or image but has its own reality dependent on but distinct from God's eternity. After humanity fell, however, history itself held no potential for bringing about the consummation; it would have to descend from heaven as a gift. At various points history seems to come to a standstill as Israel too violates the covenant; but it is kept moving forward by God's pledge of a "new covenant" beyond the exile. It is the mighty acts of God in judgment and salvation that charge the horizontal axis with hope and meaning. Instead of two worlds, the New Testament speaks of two ages: "this age" under judgment and "the age to come" when God's Messiah delivers his people.[8] Jesus and Paul invoke these categories frequently.[9] M. H. Abrams puts it this way:

---

6. Steel, "De-Paganizing Philosophy," 36.

7. See Macierowski, "Thomistic Critique."

8. See D. S. Russell, *Method and Message of Jewish Apocalyptic*, especially 269; cf. Rowland, *Open Heaven*, especially 355.

9. Jesus appeals to the distinction in the Gospels (Matt 12:32; 13:49; 19:28; 24:3; Mark 4:19;

While the main line of change in the prominent classical patterns of history, whether primitivist or cyclical, is continuous and gradual, the line of change in Christian history (and this difference is pregnant with consequences) is right-angled: the key events are abrupt, cataclysmic, and make a drastic, even an absolute, difference. Suddenly, out of nothing, the world is created by divine fiat. There is a precipitous fall from a deathless felicity into a mortal life of corruption and anguish in a stricken world. The birth of the Redeemer, at a precise instant in time, is the crisis, the absolute turning point in the plot which divides the reign of law and promise from the reign of grace and fulfillment and assures the happy outcome. The visible denouement of the plot, however, awaits Christ's second Advent, which will bring an immediate restoration of lost happiness on earth.[10]

Gerhard von Rad goes so far as to suggest that through its history of promise oriented toward future fulfillment a historical consciousness arose uniquely in Israel.[11] Atheist philosopher Mark C. Taylor puts it well: "Beginning . . . Middle . . . End. From the 'tick' of Genesis to the 'tock' of Apocalypse, the history of the West runs its course. . . . History, as well as self, is a theological notion."[12]

Many Jews of Jesus's day were expecting this messianic reign to involve the judgment of gentile oppressors and the restoration of Israel's theocracy. The New Testament counters the expectation of the messianic age in terms of a geopolitical kingdom. Instead, it announces the reign of Christ as a present reality, but in two phases, following his own journey from humiliation to glory. Between Christ's two advents there will be a long period of travail. Besides experiencing natural disasters and wars, the church will endure persecution. Nevertheless, despite its weak appearance in the eyes of the world, the church will not only endure but flourish. "And this gospel of the kingdom will be proclaimed throughout the whole world as a testimony to all nations, and then the end will come" (Matt 24:3–14).

Consequently, the New Testament comforts believers with the hope of Christ's return "at the end of the age" (Dan 12:13; Matt 13:39, 41, 49; 24:3; 28:20). In one place, however, there is mention of "a thousand years." "They came to life and reigned with Christ for a thousand years" (Rev 20:4; cf. vv. 5–7). Most ancient Christian writers interpreted the "thousand years" (*chilia etē*) in Revelation 20 symbolically, consistent with the figurative use of numbers throughout the Apocalypse.[13] Com-

---

8:38; 10:30; Luke 18:30; 20:35), and it is found frequently in the Pauline Epistles (1 Cor 2:6; 10:11; Eph 1:21; Gal 1:4; 1 Tim 6:19) as well as in Hebrews 6:5.

10. Abrams, *Natural Supernaturalism*, 36–37.
11. Von Rad, *Old Testament Theology*, vols. 1 and 2.
12. Mark C. Taylor, *Erring*, 53.
13. The definitive study on this point is Charles E. Hill, *Regnum Caelorum*. Although mil-

paring Revelation 20 with such passages as Jesus's Olivet discourse (Matt 24), these early Christians concluded that the thousand years symbolizes the completion of Christ's conquest of the nations by his word and Spirit.

However, as early as the second century, a sect formed around a certain Montanus, who claimed that the Holy Spirit had descended not at Pentecost but in his own person: "I am the Father, the Word, and the Paraclete."[14] Assisted by two young women, Prisca and Maximilla, he taught that the first two dispensations had failed but the third had appeared with the Spirit's incarnation in himself. The New Jerusalem would be established in his native Phrygia, and all would experience God through direct revelations, visions, glossolalia, and healings. After the failure of its prophecies, the movement lost credibility among adherents. Yet its combination of millennial fervor, spiritual enthusiasm, and restorationist ecclesiology would be revived at various points throughout church history. The Sibylline Oracles, composed by Alexandrian Gnostics between the second and fourth centuries, included prophecies of a world emperor who will lead a final crusade against the enemies of God's people and a glorious reign of the saints before the end of the world.[15]

Eusebius (260–339) was a devotee of Origen, even the savior of his library. But he lived in a different time. Rather than being a victim of persecution, he was an acolyte of the first Christian emperor. Like Moses by anticipation, Constantine by imitation was the philosopher-king who made the kingdom of Christ visible throughout the world. He gave laws, uprooted paganism, and became the universal bishop, presiding at synods. Eusebius writes, "Our divinely favored emperor, receiving, as it were, a transcript of the divine sovereignty, directs, in imitation of God himself, the administration of this world's affairs." With divine mandate, therefore, he "subdues and chastens the open adversaries of the truth in accordance with the usages of war" (*Orat.* 1.6–2.5). This expectation of a geopolitical kingdom is similar to that of Jesus's contemporaries, but for Eusebius the messianic age is associated with a nascent Christendom.

---

lenarianism (or millennialism) is more familiar today, for most of church history this position was called *chiliasm* (following the Greek over the Latin). In modern times, three schools of interpretations have been identified and defended: premillennialism, postmillennialism, and amillennialism. *Premillennialists* hold that Christ will return before the millennium. *Postmillennialists* generally teach that Christ will return after a golden age of extraordinary blessing throughout the world through wide-scale conversion to the gospel. *Amillennialists* maintain that the "thousand years" referred to in Revelation 20 is symbolic and represents the present era of Christ's reign in grace, to be consummated at his return in glory.

14. Didymus, *De Trinitate* 3.41.
15. Barnes, *Prophecy and Gnosis*, 20.

An important fourth-century theologian in North Africa, Tychonius, rejected Eusebius's triumphalistic vision even though Theodosius I had now declared Nicene Christianity the imperial faith.[16] Tychonius provided the broader hermeneutical markers for an amillennial interpretation of the book of Revelation that had been widely assumed among early Christian writers.[17] He believed that the New Jerusalem was not the empire but the church that even now "is coming down from heaven like a bride prepared for her bridegroom" (Rev 21:2). Drawn from every nation but identified with no worldly empire, this kingdom grows even amid opposition. Christ will return at the end of history to open the seals of history, judge the living and the dead, and usher his elect into his everlasting Sabbath.

Augustine adopted Tychonius's seven rules for interpreting the Apocalypse.[18] In fact, he quoted his fellow African extensively in *On Christian Doctrine*, and Tychonius's non-extant *City of God* likely influenced Augustine's own masterpiece. Only at Christ's second advent will the City of God encompass the kingdoms of this age, and the timing is unknown to us.[19] Bernard McGinn observes, "The authority of these Fathers of the Church effectively squashed any crudely literal interpretation of the millennium of Apocalypse 20 for much of the next 1,000 years."[20]

However, millennialism was given fresh impetus with the rise of Islam. Adopting the pseudonym of a popular fourth-century bishop, a late seventh-century Syrian Christian laid out an elaborate prophetic timetable. The *Apocalypse of Pseudo-Methodius* expects the rise of antichrist and the great tribulation followed by the cleansing of the church, the conversion of the Jews, and the defeat of Islam. What is new in this millennialist scheme is the idea of a messianic Roman emperor who will defeat Christ's enemies (represented as Gog and Magog).[21] Islam, ironically, developed remarkably similar millennial eschatologies.[22]

---

16. Tyconius was also a mild Donatist, which contributed to his anti-imperialist eschatology.

17. Tyconius, *The Book of Rules*.

18. West and Zimdars-Swartz, *Joachim of Fiore*, 11.

19. See Markus, *Saeculum*, and his *Christianity and the Secular*.

20. McGinn, "Wrestling with the Millennium," 151.

21. Griffith, *Church in the Shadow of the Mosque*, 34. See also Alexander, *Byzantine Apocalyptic Traditions*.

22. Abbas Amanat documents this in fascinating detail down to the present regime in Iran in *Apocalyptic Islam and Iranian Shi'ism*. Especially significant, despite Sunni and Shia disagreements, is the general expectation of a great tribulation for the righteous under the reign of an antichrist figure. Jesus ('Isa) is expected to return in preparation for the revealing of the messiah (*mahdi*), followed by the final defeat of the wicked, the resurrection of the dead, the final judgment, and the destiny of heaven or hell. Overall, Islamic eschatology is premillennial. See Poston, "Second Coming of 'Isa."

Chapter 11

There was considerable apocalyptic fervor in the Middle Ages. Following the Venerable Bede and Gregory of Tours, a number of scholars produced chronologies aimed at predicting when Christ would return. Millennialism received a boost from the approach of the year 1000.[23] Afterward, doomsday prophecies were common as daily events were often read through a prism of apocalyptic pessimism.

Joachim of Fiore: Gnosis Historicized

The stage is set for Joachim of Fiore, one of the most fascinating visionaries whose influence will be seen throughout the rest of this project.[24] Born in Calabria (southern Italy) in 1135, Joachim said that he experienced a vision during a trip to

---

23. One prominent movement, backed by the church, was called the Peace of God. Beginning in Aquitaine in the ninth century, the Peace of God movement was the first to adopt a postmillennial perspective: Jesus returning after a period of Christian reign over the world. Especially as the year 1000 approached, this extremely popular movement, backed by the church, envisioned the return of the nations to Zion, the Holy Sepulchre. The Peace of God movement was a catalyst in the Crusades, yet by the late twelfth century it lost its prestige amid charges of "Manichean" influences. See the essays in Head and Landes, *Peace of God*, especially Landes, "Between Aristocracy and Heresy."

24. On Joachim of Fiore's "three ages," see especially Reeves, *Joachim of Fiore*; McGinn, *Calabrian Abbot*; West and Zimdars-Swartz, *Joachim of Fiore*. Radical Anabaptists like Thomas Müntzer saw their movement as a fulfillment of the Joachite prophecy. Lessing appropriated for the Enlightenment the Joachite prophecy of a "third age" when the inner light of reason would transcend any need for external authority or its mediation to us in creaturely forms. See Lessing, "Education of the Human Race," 96–97. This significance of Joachim for Hegel's thought is treated in fascinating detail by Cyril O'Regan, *Heterodox Hegel*, 270–85. In that work, O'Regan also provides tremendous insight into Hegel's dependence on ancient Gnosticism and its trajectory to the modern era. Yong, *Spirit Poured Out on All Flesh*, 248–49, points out the adaptation of Joachim's thesis by Wesley's successor, John Fletcher, with the dispensation of the Father corresponding to God's work among nonbelievers, the dispensation of the Son corresponding to God's work among Jews, gentile monotheists, and the disciples of Jesus ("carnal" and "imperfect" during Jesus's ministry), and the dispensation of the Spirit making perfection possible through the baptism of the Spirit. Yong even points out the similarities with Joachim's speculations (249) and draws on Fletcher's view that "Deists, Socinians, Unitarians, and even Arians," as well as adherents of other religions, are also children of God in whom the Spirit is at work (248–50). Explicit appeals to Joachim's trinitarian apocalyptic (however revised) are remarkably plentiful in contemporary theologies, especially those which display a creative reappropriation of Hegelian thinking. In fact, Jürgen Moltmann displays this interest throughout his remarkable series of studies in dogmatics, and the dust jacket of *History and the Triune God* reproduces Joachim's chart of the three ages. In volume 2 of my project, Joachim's philosophy of history will be elaborated and its formative influences within modernity will be traced.

the Holy Land, on Mount Tabor, after which he committed himself to preaching. After a period as an independent itinerant, he entered the Benedictine monastery in Corazzo; when he became abbot there, he required strict observance of the Cistercian rules.[25] Pope Lucius III relieved him of his burdensome administrative duties so that he could begin writing a three-part project. He offered the monk any monastery of his choosing. Joachim began the first volume in Casamari in 1183.[26] He began to grow restless with the failures of the Cistercian reform. Vocal opponents in the order, of the stature of Geoffrey of Auxerre (a close friend of Bernard of Clairvaux), expressed alarm at his millennialism as a "Jewish dream."[27] Nevertheless, in 1196 Pope Celestine III allowed Joachim to establish his own order of St. Giovanni in Fiore. For this enterprise he received considerable gifts from Emperor Henry VI and his wife.[28]

The relationship between monks and clergy had always been a delicate dance. To some extent, tensions between the church and monastic communities anticipate the anti-institutionalism and indeed anti-ecclesiastical path along which modernity traveled. However, Joachim gave this an eschatological justification. Joachim's interpretation of the salutation in the book of Revelation in terms of three stages correlated with the particular persons of the Trinity: "grace from he who is [the Son], and who was [the Father], and who is to come [the Spirit]" (Rev 1:4). He drew from Revelation 11:3 and 12:6 the number of 1260 days, which he took to be the year in which the Age of the Spirit would dawn.[29] The final age

---

25. West and Zimdars-Swartz, *Joachim of Fiore*, 3–4. The authors add, "The two primary sources of knowledge about Joachim of Fiore's life are the biographies left to us by Joachim's secretary, Luke of Cosenza, *Virtutum Beati Joachimi synopsis*, and the anonymous *Vita beati Joachimi abbatis*," along with some autobiographical remarks in his writings (1).

26. The *Harmony of the New and Old Testaments* (*Liber Concordie novi ac veteris Testamenti*) laid out his philosophy of history, with correspondences between biblical prophecy and contemporary events (*The Book of Concordance*, trans. Randolph Daniel in McGinn, *Apocalyptic Spirituality*, 120). The second volume, a commentary on the book of Revelation (*Expositio in Apocalypsim*), provided an exegetical basis for his interpretation of prophetic history; the third is *Psaltery of Ten Strings* (*Psalterium decem chordarum*). Cf. West and Zimdars-Swartz, *Joachim of Fiore*, 7.

27. West and Zimdars-Swartz, *Joachim of Fiore*, 4. Lutheran and Reformed confessions would also use this language. In context, this was not anti-Semitic but was based on the belief that, contrary to first-century Jewish expectation, Jesus inaugurated a spiritual kingdom rather than a geopolitical theocracy.

28. West and Zimdars-Swartz, *Joachim of Fiore*, 5.

29. Knox, *Enthusiasm*, 23.

will "last to the end of the world."[30] The "Age of the Father" (from Adam to Christ) was the order of the married, the time of the Law and the Letter (literal sense) of Scripture. The Age of the Son (from Christ to St. Benedict) is the order of the clergy, the time of the institutional church with its external ministry of preaching and sacraments. However, just as the new covenant made the old obsolete, the "eternal gospel" of the Age of the Spirit will replace the "temporal gospel" of the new covenant. It will be the order of the monk.[31]

Though convinced that the thousand years of Revelation 20 refers to a literal reign of the saints on earth prior to Christ's return, Joachim was not committed to a literal thousand years. It would certainly not be a "carnal" era of sensual pleasure, McGinn notes, "but for Joachim involved the contemplative monastic utopia of the *tertius* status, the third era of the Holy Spirit." McGinn adds, "The 'refreshment of the saints' after Antichrist seems to have had some role in Joachim's revival of millenarianism, but what is significant about the Calabrian abbot's view is that he was the first to link a spiritualizing and non-chronological millennial perspective back to the text of Apocalypse 20. In this, as in much else, Joachim stands out as the foremost Christian millenarian since John of the Apocalypse. The influence exerted by the Calabrian abbot was far-reaching, even if often realized in tortuous and indirect ways."[32]

Though often attended by bold claims of visions and prophecies, millennialism typically was not associated with gnostic ideas. The expectation of a this-worldly kingdom was quite different from the ascent of mind. Origen in fact taught that there is a "temporal gospel" for the many (viz., "Christ and him crucified") and an "eternal gospel" deciphered by the spiritual.[33] Yet it was one of Joachim's achievements to integrate prophecy and gnosis. Effectively, he laid the ladder of the monk's ascent on its side. It was a new age in the middle of history, but one characterized by the sort of enlightenment that was reserved previously for the most ardent monk. Bernard McGinn reckons that "the period 1200–1350 was argu-

---

30. McGinn, *Apocalyptic Spirituality*, 102. Joachim thought in pictures and charts, which is why his *Book of Figures* (collected by his followers) was so successful in communicating his ideas. See Reeves and Hirsch-Reich, *Figure of Joachim of Fiore*, 20–74.

31. The *Harmony of the New and Old Testaments* (*Liber de concordia Novi ac Veteris Testamenti*) laid out Joachim's philosophy of history with correspondences between biblical prophecy and contemporary events. A second volume, a commentary on the book of Revelation (*Expositio in Apocalypsim*), provided an exegetical basis for his interpretation of prophetic history. His third volume is entitled *Psaltery of Ten Strings* (*Psalterium decem chordarum*). Cf. West and Zimdars-Swartz, *Joachim of Fiore*, 7.

32. McGinn, "Wrestling with the Millennium," 150, 152.

33. Cf. Farrow, *Ascension Theology*, 20–21.

ably the richest era for the production of mystical literature in the whole history of Christianity."[34] Yet the ascent from purgation to illumination and finally union would no longer be a rare experience of spirituals but a universal phenomenon. Everyone would be a monk.

In this lies Joachim's great significance for modernity. Joining a religious order was of course voluntary. The laity and secular clergy revered their ascetic brothers and sisters as much as they felt relieved not to follow their solemn vows. It is quite a different matter to announce a dawning era in which the whole world will become a giant monastery. Though it was in history, the Age of the Spirit was not of history. Or rather, it was history spiritualized along the following correlates:

Father	Son	Spirit
Married	Clergy	Monks
Purgation	Illumination	Union
Law	Gospel	Ecstasy
Literal	Moral	Allegorical
Fleshly	Soulish	Spiritual
Infancy (Authority)	Adolescence (More Freedom)	Adulthood (Autonomy)

This glorious era began with the rule of St. Benedict (the order of the monks) but would be realized fully in 1260. It is the time of perfection (union) in love: universal, intuitive, rational-spiritual unity. Since everyone will know God immediately, the external ministry of preaching and sacraments will come to an end; the visible church, a mere shadow, will be extinguished by the light of invisible union of souls. In fact, infidels and Christians will be merged, knowing God through immediate revelation.[35]

Joachim also wrote a commentary on the Gospel of John, articulating his philosophy of history, as well as various tracts, "including *Adversus Iudaeos* in which Joachim wished to prepare the Jews for their inevitable conversion expected at the beginning of the third age." The *Liber Figurarum* may have been written by Joachim or a student but summarized his basic ideas and was the primary medium for conveying Joachite thought throughout Europe.[36] As we will see in volume

---

34. McGinn, *Flowering of Mysticism*, x.

35. Joachim clearly defines these three ages in his *Book of Concordance*, book 2, part 1, chapters 9–10 (in McGinn, *Apocalyptic Spirituality*, 102). For studies of Joachim see especially Reeves, *Joachim of Fiore*; McGinn, *Calabrian Abbot*; Williams, "Recent Scholarship on Joachim"; Cohen, *Pursuit of the Millennium*; Knox, *Enthusiasm*; West and Zimdars-Swartz, *Joachim of Fiore*.

36. West and Zimdars-Swartz, *Joachim of Fiore*, 8.

2, crusaders and colonizers, princes and peasants, preachers and philosophers appealed directly to these prophecies as empowering visions of a new world.

The original "Orphic" shift, marking the transition from archaic to classical Greece, represented a utopian spirituality that was otherworldly. The escape of the divine self from its incarceration in the visible world and the body, history, and the public world of "the many" is unlikely to set its sights on transforming social life here and now. The *Republic* and *Laws* seem to entertain the possibility (or prove the impossibility) of such a city below. Stoic political philosophy enjoyed considerable influence especially in the Roman era. Yet for the most part, utopia lies above, within the self, or in a past epoch.

To become a harbinger of modernity, a utopian outlook had to become both immanent and imminent, incarnating itself in history. The Orphic ontology remains, but in a Joachite perspective escaping from the flesh to the spirit refers to dynamic ages more than static realms. Modernity required a transition from a locative to a utopian outlook. There are many other factors besides Joachite eschatology to account for this shift, and Jewish and Islamic apocalypticism flourished over these same centuries. Indeed, according to Said Amir Arjomand, "The apocalyptic perspective that underlies both political messianism and astrological millennialism was integrated into pristine Islam by Muhammad."[37] However, in the West at least it is unlikely that this transition could have appeared, at least in its historical form, apart from the influence of Joachim of Fiore and the many disciples who invoked (and forged) his name. The movement of the Spirit would be discerned not only in isolated times and places but in the movement of history, in the transition from dependence on ecclesiastical and political authority to enlightened adulthood. No longer looking back to a golden age or to the return of Christ at a future point that cannot be determined, Joachim has proposed a new way of looking at the present as bristling with portents of a dawning era of universal enlightenment, beginning in 1260. As it turned out, this would be fifty-eight years after Joachim's death.

Joachim disdained Islam, naming his contemporary Saladin the antichrist. Yet a number of later thinkers were drawn to his vision of an enlightened Age of the Spirit in which all people know God apart from external authorities and priestly mediation. Writing around the time of Constantinople's collapse, Nicholas of Cusa argued that the three monotheistic religions were agreed at the highest level and differed only in rituals, although the cardinal was the first to require Jews to wear the star of David to indicate their foreign identity. In spite of its villainous

---

37. Arjomand, "Messianism, Millennialism and Revolution," 125.

role in Joachim's scheme, Islamic writers—Shias especially—were influenced by his outlook.[38]

Among the lasting influences of the mass expulsion of Jews from the Iberian Peninsula in 1492 was the spread of Sephardic mysticism throughout Europe. This horrific episode provoked widespread despair among Jews and hope that the messiah's arrival was imminent. This was Abraham Abulafia's emphasis, as he combined kabbalism with the prophecies of Joachim of Fiore.[39] Like Meister Eckhart, notes Scholem, Abulafia exhibits the typical combination of rationalist and mystic. He found kindred souls in non-Jews. "I saw that they belong to the 'pious of the gentiles,' and that the words of fools of whatever religion need not be heeded, for the Torah has been handed over to the masters of true knowledge."[40] In 1280, he made his way to Rome to see Pope Nicholas III to announce himself as the Messiah. The pope ordered him to be burned once he entered the gate, but he died of a stroke in the middle of the night. After twenty-eight days in prison, Abulafia was released.[41] His own messianic claims failed to materialize, but many Sephardic Jews remained messianic in orientation. In fact, this is commonly identified as Safed mysticism because many of those expelled made their way to that Galilean city, which in fact became the center of Jewish kabbalah.

Among such individuals was Isaac Luria (1534–1572), arguably the most important figure in Jewish mysticism. Whatever unity kabbalah possesses as a system is due largely to Luria's formulations. He brought together the various types of kabbalah that had often viewed each other with suspicion: theosophical, ecstatic, and magico-theurgical. In the next century, Sabbatai Zevi (1626–1676), advocating a messianic millennialism, gathered a large following. Arrested by the Ottoman emperor for claiming to take over the world and rebuild the temple in Jerusalem, he converted to Islam to escape execution. In all of these circles—"Twelver" Shia and Sufi Islam, Jewish kabbalah, and esoteric Christian mysticism—the eschatology of Joachim of Fiore was a direct influence.[42]

The alliance of Joachite eschatology and kabbalistic speculation was not arbitrary. According to Reeves, "When Joachim sought to penetrate to the still center

---

38. Amanat, *Apocalyptic Islam*; Griffith, *Church in the Shadow of the Mosque*, 34; cf. Alexander, *Byzantine Apocalyptic Traditions*.

39. Hames, "From Calabria Cometh the Law." See also Scholem's in-depth study, "Abraham Abulafia."

40. Scholem, "Abraham Abulafia," 129.

41. Scholem, "Abraham Abulafia," 128.

42. See the fascinating work of Amanat, *Apocalyptic Islam*.

of all being in the Godhead, he fastened on the geometrical figure of the circle ... he found his solution this time, not in a vision, but in a *figura* of Petrus Alphonsi, a converted Spanish Jew."[43] Alphonsi tried to create a Christian type of kabbalah.[44] According to Joachim's scheme, the world will be evangelized. "In addition, as the institutional church is transformed into the spiritual church, so the kingdoms of this world will yield to the kingdom of God. The entire globe will be 'spiritualized' and heaven will descend upon earth."[45]

Besides grafting an Orphic vision of the cosmological return to a historical consciousness, Joachim completes his massive contribution to modernity by giving a starring role to human beings as agents in bringing about the age of freedom. The self is not only divine and a magus but becomes a history-transforming agent. In biblical eschatology the faithful beseech God, "Oh that you would rend the heavens and come down" (Isa 64:1), or cry, "How long, O Lord?" (Rev 6:10). The spotlight is on God as the savior and judge, intervening in this passing evil age: "For the Lord himself will descend from heaven with a cry of command, with the voice of an archangel, and with the sound of the trumpet of God. And the dead in Christ will rise first" (1 Thess 4:16).

However, Joachim envisions an unprecedented and global crisis in which the godly themselves must intervene to turn the darkness into dawn. A cast of villains wreaks havoc on the world. Three popes and the emperor encouraged Joachim in this project, having appreciated his correspondences to biblical prophecy and contemporary events. However, it was only shortly before he died that his writings began to circulate and readers discovered that the antichrist will be a pope, a ruler of the Holy Roman Empire will be the wicked world ruler, and Rome is "Babylon."[46] Yet the people of God ensure the triumph of the angelic pope and godly world emperor.

So, one might wonder: Should we be working to overthrow the current emperor and the pope? Abolish all authority and law, close all the churches, and suspend preaching and sacraments? Have we passed already from the order of priests? The revolutionary potential of Joachite prophecy seems so familiar to us that we can forget how discomfiting it could be to those in ecclesiastical and

43. Reeves, *Joachim of Fiore and the Prophetic Future*, 19.
44. Moltmann, *History and the Triune God*, 104.
45. Knight, "John Fletcher's Influence," 29: in the dispensation of the Spirit, "one who is introduced to this dispensation by the baptism of the Holy Spirit comes to know Christ in a way far superior to that of the flesh or the senses. Here one knows deliverance from the power of sin and is filled with the Holy Spirit." Cf. Burgess, *Holy Spirit*, 129–31.
46. Whalen, *Dominion of God*, 29.

secular power. However, those most dissatisfied with the current state of affairs—especially the lower classes—would draw upon Joachim directly.

In some ways the projects of Eriugena and Joachim are comparable. They share an imagination inspired by the triad of rest, procession, and reversion with the Trinity as the template. Both believe that the end point of humanity is being folded back into the immediate relation to God. Modern thinkers like Hegel saw enough similarity to appeal to both in their construction of speculative philosophy. Yet while Eriugena's trinitarian scheme remains in the ambit of an emanationist cosmology, Joachim's is a process in history. This is what makes the Calabrian monk a harbinger of modernity.

JOACHIM'S LEGACY: THE SPIRITUAL FRANCISCANS

The Fourth Lateran Council (1215) condemned Joachim's view of the Trinity as tritheistic.[47] Thomas Aquinas criticized Joachim's teaching on the same grounds.[48] Yet what is surprising is that his novel—and potentially revolutionary—eschatology was not addressed in these judgments. This would soon change. Taking his prophecies in a more radical direction, his followers separated from the Conventual Franciscans to form a Spiritual Franciscan order. It is not surprising that Joachim's order faded, given its inherent bias against institutions. However, as usual, anti-institutional enthusiasm eventually adopts an institutional form.

The Spiritual Franciscans pressed the Joachimist vision even further, arguing that the Age of the Spirit would overthrow the reign of the pope. At last, sacraments and church would be unnecessary, for the Spirit would teach everyone. This was hardly unexpected, though, given the fact that 1260 was not far in the distance. A spiritual history was central to the group, and they went beyond Joachim in naming contemporary figures as part of the end-time cast of characters. Pope Boniface VIII and his successor Benedict XI were cast as "the mystical Antichrist" along with the Holy Roman Emperor Frederick II.

Joachim's writings grew in popularity and "were widely disseminated in the second half of the thirteenth and in the fourteenth centuries."[49] His enduring fame is evident in the proliferation of pseudo-Joachimite texts. Only about sixteen

---

47. McGinn, *Apocalyptic Spirituality*, 98.
48. *Summa theol.* I, q. 39, a. 5.
49. Reeves, *Joachim of Fiore*, preface: "Thirty-eight houses were founded in Calabria and sixty altogether. Yet, though the cult of its founder was devoutly maintained down to the seventeenth century, it steadily declined in strength after the mid-fourteenth century until in 1570 it was reunited with its parent order."

of the fifty works attributed to him are likely authentic.[50] "Spirituals" continued to flourish independently of any institution, and Joachite speculations permeated the Franciscan Order itself. Indeed, as Savonarola's career attests, Dominicans could be drawn to the Joachite prophecies.

Bonaventure (1221–1274), who had been the general of the Franciscan Friars Minor, drew upon Joachim's prophecies to support his order's historical credibility. Dante acknowledged his debt to Joachim and, in the *Paradisio*, placed him next to Bonaventure and Francis in the circle of the Sun.[51] Reeves states the ambiguity well: "When handbooks of saints and heretics began to appear in print in the fifteenth and sixteenth centuries, he found a place in both" and the debate "has gone on ever since."[52] McGinn points to Dante's verses in canto 33, lines 115–20:

> That light supreme, with its fathomless / Clear substance, showed, to me three spheres, which bare / Three hues distinct, and occupied one space; / The first mirrored the next, as though it were / Rainbow from rainbow, and the third seemed flame / Breathed equally from each of the first pair.[53]

In 1254, a famous Franciscan, Gerardus de Borgo San Donino, announced the completion of the old and new covenants, asserting "that all authority had been passed on to the Eternal Evangel and the Holy Spirit."[54] The Lateran Council condemned Gerardus's trinitarian tract, and Pope Alexander IV added his condemnation. The Council of Arles condemned any notion of the three ages along with Joachim's writings in 1260.[55] To be sure, Gerardus went further than Joachim, but he was basing his conclusions on Joachim's text.[56] Among the condemnations of Arles are these:

> They dare to claim with their blasphemous and impious mouths that the spiritual gospel of the Son is only literal, compared with the gospel of the Spirit.... They also add to their teaching a certain triad of life, which varies from what they said about time. First they have proposed a time in which men lived according to the flesh. Second they interpose a period between flesh and

---

50. West and Zimdars-Swartz, *Joachim of Fiore*, 7.
51. West and Zimdars-Swartz, *Joachim of Fiore*, 9.
52. Reeves, *Joachim of Fiore*, 28.
53. McGinn, *Apocalyptic Spirituality*, 106. McGinn provides an excellent overview of the Spiritual Franciscans as a preface to his selections from their writings on pp. 149–82.
54. Schmidt-Biggemann, *Philosophia Perennis*, 390.
55. Schmidt-Biggemann, *Philosophia Perennis*, 390. See also Reeves, *Joachim of Fiore*, 27.
56. West and Zimdars-Swartz, *Joachim of Fiore*, 6.

spirit, reaching to the present time. From this there is to follow another one, in which they will live according to the spirit, and this will last until the end of the world.[57]

Franciscans generally, with their devotion to poverty, were tinged with or at least suspected of having Joachite sympathies. Ever since Gerard's trial by the University of Paris, papal condemnation, and incarceration in 1255, medicants in general were considered rogue. The combination of elements "led the Franciscans to build a sacramental and preaching organization separate from and in rivalry with the established Church."[58] Fra Angelo Clareno, a leader of the Spiritual Franciscans in Spain, created his own unauthorized order of Fraticelli (brothers), but after his death in 1337 his followers became more radical. Fra Angelo's teachings, like Joachim's, contained elements that clashed with his insistence that they were not schismatics, and his followers were less conflicted. Reeves points out that Fra Angelo's disciples "looked for the manifestation of Antichrist in a pseudo-pope and the final overthrow of the 'carnal church.'"[59] Reeves continues:

> Clearly many found these ideas attractive. In Florence, Fraticelli almost gained official approval during the anti-papal War of the Eight Saints. The signoria was ready to use any stick to beat the *"Chiesa carnale"*—the term used in its propaganda—and the shopkeeper/artisan class was receptive of Fraticellian ideas. But especially their campaign against the rich chimed with the aspirations of the sweated workers.... Prophecies circulating at this time exalted the cause of the common people and looked for a humble leader who would bring peace and renewal. When the revolution failed and the government made its peace with the papacy, official cooperation with the Inquisition in suppressing heresy was resumed, but heresy and prophecy remained associated with social unrest.[60]

Throughout the thirteenth century, such sects taught that Rome was "the Babylonish Whore," but "there would be a new outpouring of the Holy Spirit" leading to the triumph of the gospel throughout the world.[61] "The Apostolic Brethren," followers first of Gerard Segarelli and then Fra Dolcino, "carried repudiation of ecclesiastical authority to extremes," Reeves notes.

57. Schmidt-Biggemann, *Philosophia Perennis*, 390.
58. West and Zimdars-Swartz, *Joachim of Fiore*, 105.
59. Reeves, *Joachim of Fiore*, 40.
60. Reeves, *Joachim of Fiore*, 40.
61. Reeves, *Joachim of Fiore*, 44.

Authority was now transferred to the Apostoli. The outward transfer of authority, which they expected soon after 1300, would be accomplished by the violence of revolution. Pope Boniface VIII, the cardinals, prelates, clergy, and all religious would be exterminated by the sword of God, wielded by a new emperor. Dolcino believed that this emperor would be Frederick, King of Sicily, in whose favour he cited many scriptural passages.[62]

This would be the great tribulation preceding the golden Age of the Spirit.

After the holocaust a new and holy pope would be chosen by God and under his obedience would be placed the Apostolic order, with all the remnant who had been saved from the sword by divine grace and chose to become *Apostoli*. Then there would be a new outpouring of the Spirit. A second manifesto, issued after the death of Boniface VIII, revises the time schedule a little, but still expects the general destruction of clergy and religious in 1305.[63]

Throughout the twelfth and thirteenth centuries there were forms of mysticism that seemed to draw more indirectly on Joachite influences. In Germany (Erfurt for example) there were complaints of Joachimist heresy.[64] A cult gathered around a certain Guglielma upon her death in 1282. "The Holy Spirit had become incarnate in her, transferring authority from the pope to her followers." Though it soon disappeared, its followers were drawn from the upper classes. In others, there is "a strange mixture of Catharism and Joachimism."[65] This perhaps qualifies my attempt above to distinguish Joachite gnosis from gnostic heresy as such, although Joachim himself would have repudiated such conclusions. Indeed, the Cathari ("Pure Ones") and Albigensians represented fresh eruptions of Gnosticism, sharply contrasting everything visible, external, and material to that which is invisible, internal, and immaterial. The church was an entirely invisible and spiritual entity, without any formal ministry of preaching, sacraments, or discipline. The only sacrament was the *consolomento*, a laying on of the hands to bestow the Spirit with the evidence of speaking in unknown languages.

The Inquisition was inaugurated to extirpate these sects, and it led to massive slaughter of whole villages. Yet the movements had been quite popular not only among peasants but among priests and even higher clergy. The Holy Office could

---

62. Reeves, *Joachim of Fiore*, 48.
63. Reeves, *Joachim of Fiore*, 49.
64. Reeves, *Joachim of Fiore*, 52–53.
65. Reeves, *Joachim of Fiore*, 50.

not extirpate all gnostic sects, and it is understandable how Joachite anticipations of the abolition of church and state would be attractive to some.

Also in the thirteenth century, a lay Christian movement arose calling itself Brethren of the Free Spirit.[66] There is some question as to the extent of Meister Eckhart's involvement, but there is a close affinity between his writings and the movement's central ideas. They advocated antinomian, perfectionistic, and individualistic teachings that were a combination of gnostic and Montanist elements. There is some evidence that they possessed some of the gnostic gospels, and writers such as Sister Catherine interpreted the story of Jesus in a manner closer to these writings rather than the canonical gospels. In a dialogue with her confessor—possibly Eckhart—Sister Catherine records, "Father rejoice with me, I have become God.... When I looked into myself I saw God within me and everything he has ever created in heaven and earth.... I am established in the pure Godhead, in which there never was form or image." A little later she continues:

> I am where I was before I was created: that place is purely God and God. There are neither angels nor saints, nor choir, nor this nor that. Many people speak of eight heavens and of nine choirs. They are not where I am. You should know that everything stated in such a way and presented to people in images is but an incitement to seek God. Realise that in God is nothing but God. You must also understand that no soul may come unto God before it has become God as it was before it was created. No one may come into the naked Godhead except the one who is naked as he was when he flowed out of God. The masters say that no one may enter here as long as he has any attachment to lower things, even if it is only as much as the tip of a needle can carry.[67]

In addition to their charismatic emphases, the Brethren adopted Joachim of Fiore's millenarianism and interpreted contemporary events as the fulfillment of biblical prophecy. The world is coming to an end, and the institutional church seemed to be merely part of the perishing world. For the Brethren of the Free Spirit, there were no sacraments, no clerical or secular authorities, no gender distinction, and a communion of property. Declared heretical by Pope Clement V and the Council of Vienna (1311–1312), the Brethren were targeted for persecution by the emperor.

All of these various sects flourished during the Western Schism (1309–1417), with rival popes, Christian armies locked in brutal conflict (such as the Hun-

---

66. Lerner, *Heresy of the Free Spirit*.
67. "Sister Catherine Treatise," trans. Elvira Borgstaedt, in McGinn, *Meister Eckhart*, 347–88.

dred Years' War) that were interrupted occasionally by crusades, the Black Death, widespread crop failures across Europe, and the rise of the Inquisition. It was an ideal time for prophets who could persuade people that such perplexing events were foretold explicitly in Scripture and that they were mere birthpangs of the new age.

At least for the Franciscans of both orders, everything came to a head in 1322. Under Pope Gregory VII, the Gregorian reform (1050–1080) had in fact added expectations (such as poverty) to the traditional description of Acts 4.[68] However, Pope John XXII commissioned a sweeping investigation of the writings of a famous Spiritual Franciscan, Peter Olivi. But it widened to encompass the Franciscan Order, particularly the ideal of poverty. The pope condemned the idea as without foundation in Christ's teaching, the apostles' doctrine or example, and the history of the church. The "Spirituals" were assuming that everything went wrong between the death of the apostles and St. Francis.[69]

The Spiritual Franciscans in Italy themselves divided into various sects, united only by the name of "Brothers" (Fraticelli), and in the fourteenth century they declared themselves sworn enemies of the Roman Church and the papacy.[70] "In Inquisitorial proceedings a major accusation against Joachites was the claim to greater perfection than Christ and the Apostles, yet the Joachite was almost driven into this extreme position for it was in the nature of the 'myth' that the future must transcend the past."[71] Reeves adds,

> These show clearly whither the logic of the Joachimist hope could lead. If the whole hierarchy of the Church opposed the perfection of the future *status* entrusted to the few, then it could not be the true Church but the expected Antichrist. Thus they developed the mentality of the exclusive sect, for "always the many have persecuted the poor faithful of Christ." The fatal agent of the Church's seduction had been John XXII. If anyone persistently denied the poverty of Christ, he was a manifest heretic whom to obey was contrary to God and the Rule.[72]

The election of John XXII was rescinded by the Council of Basel, so it was not as if Franciscans stood alone. According to the Spiritual Franciscans, John XXII

---

68. West and Zimdars-Swartz, *Joachim of Fiore*, 106.
69. West and Zimdars-Swartz, *Joachim of Fiore*, 105–6.
70. Reeves, *Joachim of Fiore*, 40.
71. Reeves, *Joachim of Fiore*, 57.
72. Reeves, *Joachim of Fiore*, 40.

and his successors were the true schismatics, and some of the Fraticelli even "asserted that John XXII was the mystic Antichrist and that the Roman Church was the synagogue of the devil; to all it was clear that the Pope had no power to touch the Rule and Testament of St. Francis." As Reeves observes,

> The Fraticelli saw themselves as the saving remnant gathered into the frail bark of the true church, the Noah's Ark of the last age. In the sixth age of the Church Christ had sent St Francis, another Noah, to build a new ark, the Ark of the Evangelical Rule, in which the seed of the elect would be saved from the deluge of the unfaithful.... After the Deluge would come the *renovatio*, when the Gospel would be preached by twelve poor evangelical men—the last in a long sequence of twelves starting from the patriarchs.[73]

The later controversy surrounding the English Franciscan, William of Ockham, must be seen in this context. Fleeing to the protection of the Holy Roman Emperor Ludwig of Bavaria, William of Ockham declared Pope John a heretic for condemning St. Francis, his order, and the vow of poverty. He took the further step of arguing that Emperor Ludwig should take the supremacy over the church from the pope. While Pope John questioned the apostolic and ecclesiastical justification for their order, the Friars Minor answered that they were "new apostles" (*novi apostoli*) like those that had been raised up throughout church history but outside the walls of the established church to follow the example of Christ.

Throughout the thirteenth and fourteenth centuries, the Augustinian interpretation of the Apocalypse by Nicholas of Lyra (d. 1329) was ranged against the Joachite reading. Besides Franciscans like Peter John Olivi and John of Rupescissa, the commentary by Dominican Annius of Viterbo "is an exegetical example of the flood of millennial prophecy that swept over Italy between c. 1475 and 1525, both among the clergy and with wandering male and female seers. Many of the clerical representatives of this Renaissance millenarianism were active at the Fifth Lateran Council (1512–17). The most interesting was Egidio of Viterbo ([c. 1465]–1532)—humanist, apocalypticist, cabbalist, as well as general of the Augustinians, papal preacher, and eventually cardinal."[74]

Nicholas of Cusa, who initially had defended conciliarism against papalism, was an important mediator of both gnostic and Joachite streams. In fact, if we find in Joachim himself a convergence of mystical Neoplatonist, enthusiast, and

---

73. Reeves, *Joachim of Fiore*, 40.
74. McGinn, "Wrestling with the Millennium," 156.

utopian rivers, the cardinal represents not only these but also Hermetic and Nominalist currents. In a passing remark in the *City of God*, Augustine compared epochs of human history to Christ's personal development from infancy to adulthood.[75] In this optimistic amillennialism, the bishop of Hippo had in mind the progress of the gospel, but it could serve as a suggestive template for broader history. It did so for Joachim and also for Nicholas of Cusa.[76]

Intellect lies buried in the infant and begins to display itself later on, Cusa says. The age of the cutting of foreskin and sacrifice corresponds to the era of the martyrs and living under "the Christian law." "The time approaches in which Christ, as one having power, will elevate [us] more clearly unto spiritual understanding, as if He were about to cross over from this world unto the Father through mortification of the flesh by way of most bitter sensory suffering, because the senses are at odds with the spirit."[77] For his first seventeen years, Jesus "was not seen to do anything," just as there was inactivity in the church "for eight hundred fifty years." "But on the basis of this [inference] He will now very soon begin to appear as One who has power; and His appearance will last one hundred fifty years. Then there will follow the final persecution of crucifixion; then [will come] resurrection and the ascension of the mystical body unto the Church Triumphant."[78] Cusa is convinced that this comports with Daniel and Ezekiel:

> The time of John's preaching will come forthwith, in order that we may do penance. (Here consider that there are, perhaps, still forty years for Christ to be manifest to all nations successively; and He will experience suffering.) After He has thus appeared for one hundred fifty years and a few more, the final tribulation will come—[a tribulation] than which there was never a greater one, viz., that of the crucifixion. But there will follow immediately the resurrection and, after some years, the ascension. And [this] will be the end of the world. These are the likely [sequences]; but they are not certain to us.[79]

The abbot's influence in Renaissance Florence extended to Spanish and Portuguese explorations, Columbus filling his journals and his *Book of Prophecies* with appeals to his role in fulfilling Joachim's prophecies. In fact, his goal in mining

---

75. Augustine, *Civ. Dei* 16.2.
76. See Nicholas of Cusa, "Domine, in Lumine Vultus Tui," in *Nicholas of Cusa's Early Sermons*, 379–80. Cusa compares the epochs to Christ's infancy (gentile wisdom), circumcision (the old law), and ministry (the new law).
77. Nicholas of Cusa, "Domine, in Lumine Vultus Tui," 380–81.
78. Nicholas of Cusa, "Domine, in Lumine Vultus Tui," 381.
79. Nicholas of Cusa, "Domine, in Lumine Vultus Tui," 381–82.

gold was not to enrich Portuguese coffers but to rebuild the temple in Jerusalem.[80] Franciscan missions to the Americas were inspired by the abbot's vision. The Order had been granted nearly full oversight of New Spain, which, along with a papal encyclical, justified Diego de Landa's ruthless campaign of terror against the Mayan civilization in the Yucatán. "The evangelical prophecies over Jerusalem have been fulfilled," he declared, convinced that the natives were at least spiritual if not physical descendants of the Jews. Like any heretics, such precious souls must be saved from idolatry through the most severe measures. Though recalled to account for his atrocities against natives deemed too childish to fall under the Inquisition's policies, Philip II sent him back as the second bishop of Yucatán.[81] Yet, also based on the Joachite prophecies, many other Franciscan missionaries opposed Spanish authorities and sought to create an environment in which the "chosen people" could be "elevated" from paganism to mature autonomy.[82]

Meanwhile, as we will see in volume 2, Joachite millennialism was integral to Renaissance utopianism from Thomas More's *Utopia* and Tomaso Campanella's *City of the Sun* to Anabaptist revolts, the Thirty Years' War, and the radical pietist and puritan spirits of the seventeenth century. Positive references to the Calabrian abbot are found among the writings of New England colonialists such as Cotton Mather, Jonathan Edwards, and George Whitefield as well as pietist sects from Germany and Switzerland who established utopian communities in Pennsylvania. He reemerges in the gnostic apocalypticism of Jakob Böhme, through whom Lessing, Schelling, Hegel, and other thinkers found their way to Joachim as a major source of inspiration. Joachim's enduring influence is evident across the political spectrum, from Friedrich Engels[83] to the German Nationalist historian Oswald Spengler, who judged, "His teaching moved the best of the Franciscans and the Dominicans, Dante, Thomas Aquinas, in their inmost souls and awakened a world-outlook which slowly but surely took entire possession of the historical sense of our Culture."[84] Roger Garaudy, a communist philosopher and, ironically, also a Holocaust denier, observed that the "first great revolutionary movements in Europe" were "more or less imbued with the ideas of Joachim of Fiore."[85]

The Joachite philosophy of history not only was novel with respect to the present and future, but offered a new interpretation of the past: a telling of the story

80. Cf. Prosperi, "New Heaven and New Earth."
81. David, "'Evangelical Prophecies over Jerusalem."
82. This story is told in fascinating detail in Phelan, *Millennial Kingdom of the Franciscans*.
83. See Ben Jones, *Apocalypse without God*, 119–42.
84. Spengler, *Decline of the West*, 139, although Aquinas considered his trinitarian doctrine tritheistic.
85. Garaudy, "Faith and Revolution," 66.

that gives primary place to the revolutionaries seeking the Age of the Spirit instead of the gradual extension and dominion of the institutional church. Eric Voegelin concludes that medieval "gnosis" spawned countless end-times scenarios, but nothing as extreme or as enduring as "the fallacious construction of history that characterizes modernity since Joachim." It fuels the drive not only for utopian meaning in history but for certainty. There may be trials and tribulations greater than anything seen before, but they are but the prelude to the golden age. Joachim leads souls out of a medieval pessimism that views history as decline into an optimism that empowers and justifies the "civilizational expansiveness of Western society" of the early modern era. "It is a coming-of-age in search of its meaning" that will no longer put up with the worsening world until Christ's return. It is also an impulse that makes it difficult to live patiently in our given world.[86]

In brief, the church through the schools kept a wary eye on pantheism while incorporating the non-Eriugenist Dionysian legacy. For many others, though, gnosis was preferred above Scripture and sacraments, and Jewish and Arab philosophers were introducing Latins to Hermes Trismegistus, kabbalah, and radical Neoplatonism. Whatever the age was, it was not dark, dead, or silent but one of the most productive eras of Christian engagement with its Orphic legacy. And through Savonarola, the Age of the Spirit coincided with the Golden Age of Florence.

Philosophical Religion as the Culmination of Historical Reason

Apart from Joachite intervention, Orphic ascent may have remained an ideal pursued by hardy spiritual athletes. Joachim called upon the testimony of Origen concerning an "eternal gospel" that supersedes the temporal gospel even as the latter superseded the law. But similarities are superficial. Despite the monastic ideal governing both, Origen's third age was fulfilled beyond time and space. Joachite enlightenment is in the tradition of Origen's inner light, but ascent from dependence on the authority of scripture's ordinary sense to the autonomy of immediate vision is fulfilled *within* history. Far broader in its exhilarating appeal, this utopian vision was something to which everyone could relate because it involved everyone. This version of utopianism was more tangible, concrete, and relevant. In short, the goal of philosophical religion became imaginable and even realizable in the historical consciousness. History itself became the macrocosmic soul or spirit unfolding in diverse appearances until its final consummation in this world.

86. Voegelin, *New Science*, 191.

Prophetic Gnosis: Dreaming of Utopia

Marxist philosopher Ernst Bloch noted that "Eastern reason . . . pulled away from the letter of the text, transforming it into a mere shell." This was evident in Islamic philosophy:

> The mystical movements also supported, in a strange way, the distance of such thinkers from the believers in scripture. In the Orient, much like later in Europe with the Albigensians and Meister Eckhart, this found expression in a number of people's movements against nobility and the church. These movements, particularly within the Iranian elite, formed a lasting defense against Arabic Islam; here it took on Neoplatonist traits. Aristotle himself was often viewed by Avicenna in a Neoplatonic and even Gnostic light. This type of Syrian-Iranian influence is unmistakable in Baghdad's cultural circle, a group inherently alien to the Qur'an as well as to Islamic ritual practice. In Baghdad, and still more in Basra, there was a continuation of the old Iranian [Zoroastrian] myth of light, which was itself one of the origins of mystical gnosis, of light's journey and homecoming.[87]

At the beginning of the tenth century, this metaphysics of light undergirded the metaphysics of Avicenna (Ibn Sina) more than any Islamic orthodoxy.

> It interacted with the Sufis, the Persian mystical sect that, without regard to the Qur'an and not mediated through the mosque, taught the pouring back of the soul into the cosmic ur-light. He also had contact with the Brethren of Purity of Basra, a learned sect founded in 950, who, in an encyclopedia still available today, wrote in Neoplatonist terms of the light-origin of the world so as to thereby gain reciprocal knowledge of the return of the world and soul, a sort of travel guide to the ur-light.[88]

Bloch observes, "This is all mysticism and, as such, not yet worldliness; as mentioned, this mysticism—a peculiar yet undeniable ally—stood side by side with naturalism in the struggle with the church and scriptural orthodoxy." Not only for Sufis but for mystical philosophers generally "positive faith dissolves in the inner view of the All-One," feeling himself above all religions, which are at best "pedagogical steps to a 'pneumatic' truth; they are ultimately dimmers of the Light, lands of deception."[89]

---

87. Bloch, *Avicenna and the Aristotelian Left*, 8.
88. Bloch, *Avicenna and the Aristotelian Left*, 8.
89. Bloch, *Avicenna and the Aristotelian Left*, 8–9.

It is all quite similar to the heterodox mystical traditions of Christendom, says Bloch, with Joachim of Fiore's "Age of the Spirit" and Eckhart's "deification of humanity, the deification of reason" paving the way for the Enlightenment. With the revolutionary Anabaptists and the return of an "only half-hidden neo-Stoicism," Bloch concludes, "Avicenna's unitas intellectus [unity of Intellect] was at work alongside other traditions."[90]

In the train of Eriugena's version of Dionysian mysticism, the Dominican monk Meister Eckhart (1260–1327) preached, "The eye with which I see God is the eye with which God sees me. God's eye and my eye are the same. If God did not exist, I would not exist; if I did not exist, God would not exist either."[91] Sharing in divinity, the imperishable divine spark (*scintalla animae*) is superior even to the highest flame of reason (*apex mentis superior enim scintilla rationalis*).[92] Like Eriugena, Eckhart's monism loses the paradoxical Christology of Chalcedon defended by Dionysius himself. Not even distinctions in the Godhead remain.[93] Everything "outer," even concerning Jesus and his human ministry, is dispensable; it is the birth of God in the soul that is real.[94] The eternal generation of the Son from the Father is identical with Eckhart's: "He generates me his Son without any distinction."[95]

From Schopenhauer to the present, many modern scholars have compared his views with Zen Buddhism. T. D. Suzuki observes, "From these passages we see that the biblical creation is thoroughly contradicted; it has not even a symbolic meaning for Eckhart, and, further God is not at all like the God conceived by most Christians."[96] In contrast with the Thomistic formulation of analogy (tacking closely to that of Pseudo-Dionysius), he concludes, "All creatures are pure nothing."[97] Oliver Davies notes that at the end of the day the only difference between God and creatures for Eckhart is that the properties exist according to perfect unity in the former and in multiplicity in the latter."[98]

---

90. Bloch, *Avicenna and the Aristotelian Left*, 19.
91. Quoted from Eckhart's sermon "True Heading" found in *Meister Eckhart's Sermons* (trans. Field), 29.
92. Des Places, *Études platoniciennes*, 383–85.
93. Meister Eckhart, *Sermons and Treatises*, 85.
94. Also from "True Hearing"; see *Meister Eckhart's Sermons* (trans. Field), 29.
95. Quoted in McGinn, "Meister Eckhart on God," 129–30. As McGinn notes, in his *Defense* (*Rechtfertigungsschrift*), Eckhart insisted "that he had never taught that a part of the soul was uncreated, a position that may seem contradictory to assertions in his surviving works." In any case, he stood by his idea of the birth of the Word in the soul and other teachings that, to many, savored pantheism (130).
96. Suzuki, *Mysticism*, 9.
97. *In agro dominico* art. 26 (D 976), taken from Eckhart, *Predigten* 4: "Omne datum optimum" in Eckhart, *Die deutschen Werke*, 1:69.8–70.1. Quoted in McGinn, "Meister Eckhart on God," 131, 133.
98. Davies, "Revelation and the Politics of Culture," 119.

The condemnations of Eckhart's pantheistic theses were critical in showing exactly the boundary that could not be crossed, although numerous mystics and sects ignored them up to and including the Anabaptists.[99] Eckhart and the Rhineland mystics pursued Eriugena's Neoplatonic idealism, and Nicholas of Cusa brought it to the doorstep of the Renaissance. Eriugena and Joachim may have lost the patronage of the church, but they prepared the ground for powerful currents that shaped the course of modernity.

Nicholas of Cusa also poured himself into the study of Eckhart's writings, possessing an especially well-read copy of Eriugena's *Periphyseon*. Dionysius is ever present throughout Nicholas of Cusa's sermons as well as treatises. Over against the Plotinian way of *theōria*, Nicholas followed the theurgic path, with a Proclean ladder that was alive with heavenly beings reaching down to lift their inferiors up to a higher participation in the Good in a cycle of *noblèsse oblige*. Instead of merely flowing down, therefore, the grace of being was circulating.[100] Yet Moran puts it well: "Of course, it is almost impossible to separate the Dionysian influence from what is purely Eriugenian, but we can say that Cusanus was his greatest disciple and that it was through Cusanus (and his admirers Bruno and Descartes) that Eriugena's thought came to affect the formation of the modern mind."[101] "He had the greatest knowledge of the Platonic tradition of anyone prior to Ficino," notes Moran, even tracing Dionysius's dialectic back to the *Parmenides*.[102]

Moreover, he drew liberally on Hermes Trismegistus, whom he saw as the fountainhead of wisdom that led to Zoroaster, Orpheus, and Plato. It is not odd to hear Nicholas say in a sermon, "For Trismegistus, who somehow has investigated almost all truth, has often described the power and majesty of the Word."[103] He drew freely on the kabbalah as well, even in his sermons.[104] As with the broader "Orphic" tradition, Nicholas believed that only the *prudentiores philosophi* such as Proclus, Dionysius, and Eckhart could discern the truth hidden under the "con-

---

99. Thomas Müntzer wrote, "When St. Paul told Timothy to 'Preach the Word,' he did not mean that word that merely beats the air, but the secret, inborn Word." See Müntzer, "Sermon to the Princes." Eckhart was also a personal favorite of Hegel's. Ernst Benz observes that the continuity between German medieval mysticism and German idealistic philosophy has been thoroughly recognized at least since Wilhelm Dilthey; see Benz, *Mystical Sources of German Romantic Philosophy*, 2. For this connection especially between Hegel and Eckhart (as well as ancient Gnosticism), see also O'Regan, *Heterodox Hegel*.

100. See Sermon 21 in *Cusa's Early Sermons* (trans. Hopkins), 348.

101. Moran, *Philosophy of John Scottus Eriugena*, 281.

102. Moran, "Nicholas of Cusa and Modern Philosophy," 174. See Nicholas of Cusa, *On Learned Ignorance*, 146.

103. See Sermon 1 in *Cusa's Early Sermons* (trans. Hopkins), 7.

104. Sermon 20 in *Cusa's Early Sermons* (trans. Hopkins), 320–21.

traditions and even 'absurdities' in a literal reading of the biblical narratives."[105] Indeed, for Nicholas, "spiritual body" in the resurrection means a "subtle" body.[106] It is true that Jesus ate and drank with the disciples after his resurrection, "although the food that was eaten and swallowed was not turned into the nature of His body but was vaporized, even as water is vaporized."[107] Similar to Origen, Nicholas's Christology is interpreted within the *exitus-reditus* pattern, as the Jesus of history returns to his status that allows him to be absolute maximality.[108]

The cosmological process of enfolding and unfolding is theogonic. Nicholas of Cusa's recurring language of "separation and conjunction" is drawn from theurgic Neoplatonism (especially Hermeticism), which emphasizes the emergence of a third thing from two opposite principles. "In the history of Hermetic tradition," Ebeling relates, "the *Tabula Smaragdina* was the most important text for alchemists and Paracelsists." It was especially in this text that Nicholas discovered this alchemical language.[109] Theurgy—the great work of the magus—was seen as the separation and union of things in the world. As the antipode of the good, even evil has its place in the cosmic alchemy.

The world, including humans, exists as God's own process of self-manifestation. Creatures therefore have no actual existence except as this divine unfolding. At rest with himself in unity, God manifests himself not only in but as the world in plurality. Inwardly, God has no names; outwardly, he has all names. In a 1440 sermon preached in Augsburg, Nicholas of Cusa argues that because God is the absolute *One*, he enfolds all multiplicity in his simple being, "beyond all opposition and contradictoriness."[110] He does not mean simply that God is in all things as their cause; rather, he is their essence.[111]

To the extent that the Orphic trajectory has been ignored, we will be inclined to emphasize modernity's discontinuity with all that went before it. When the absolute transcendence and unknowability of God is emphasized, greater stress is placed on the mystical leap that is above not only the historical particularities of a given religion but above reason itself. In fact, the fourth step of ascent for Nicholas is "by means only of reason," the fifth "is beyond reason," but the sixth is not only beyond reason "but at times is contrary to reason."[112]

---

105. Gandillac, "Neoplatonism and Christian Thought," 150.
106. Sermon 12 in *Cusa's Early Sermons* (trans. Hopkins), 268.
107. Sermon 12 in *Cusa's Early Sermons* (trans. Hopkins), 269.
108. Nicholas of Cusa, *On Learned Ignorance*, 141.
109. Ebeling, *Secret History*, 57.
110. Sermon 22 in *Cusa's Early Sermons* (trans. Hopkins), 359–60, emphasis added.
111. Sermon 22 in *Cusa's Early Sermons* (trans. Hopkins), 361.
112. Sermon 5 in *Cusa's Early Sermons* (trans. Hopkins), 91–92, emphasis added. Thus, Neoplatonism and Nominalism sit comfortably together.

Finally, Nicholas of Cusa is often credited with a modern historicism in which consciousness evolves through successive stages. This stands in contrast with the ancient and medieval prejudice for what is oldest. Yet this also may be seen more as a radicalization rather than rejection of medieval influence. In the end, Gandillac explains, Nicholas incorporates in *De docta ignorantia* 2.8–11 a more Stoic conception of *spiritus*, "an immense dynamic whole that has often been compared to the world of Leibniz to the extent to which everything in it depends on everything and corresponds to everything (*quodlibet in quolibet*).... And without evoking any astral influence, he then outlines—in the line of the myth of Protagoras taken up and adapted by Gregory of Nyssa in the Creation of Man—a history of humanity at first deprived, then raised up, through culture and technology, to the true religion."[113]

Yet it is difficult not to associate this view of history as a succession of unfolding stages toward perfection with Joachim of Fiore, on whom he draws directly.[114] The ascent now occurs in historical epochs toward the beatific vision in which all share in the monk's experience. This historical evolution is actually part of Nicholas's cosmology: the idea of creatures as enfolding in God and unfolding in creation. This fusion of Christian Neoplatonism, Hermeticism, and Joachite eschatology will become a powerful force in modernity, even in secularized forms.[115] Nicholas of Cusa has been nicknamed aptly as "Gatekeeper of the New Age."[116]

Beyond the Gates

Concluding our exploration, we now trace the philosophical religion exemplified by Eriugena to the threshold of the Florentine Renaissance.[117] Our study thus far has been centered on the West, but profound shifts from locative (Orthodox) religion to utopian (spiritual-Platonic) faith were occurring in the Byzantine world over a long period. The same war of the philosophers—Aristotle and Plato—was

---

113. Gandillac, "Neoplatonism and Christian Thought," 154.

114. Nicholas of Cusa, "Coniectura de novissimis diebus," 932–35. See Zivadinovic, "Joachim of Fiore's Historical-Continuous Method." Nicholas in his sermon "Domine, In Lumine Vultus Tui" correlates the ages of history with the ages of Israel's history and the stages of Christ's life, leading him to posit an imminent tribulation (crucifixion) and vindication (resurrection/ascension). See *Cusa's Early Sermons* (trans. Hopkins), 379–82.

115. Balthasar, "Patristik, Scholastik, und wir," 88, translation in Oakes, *Pattern of Redemption*, 120.

116. Haubst, *Nikolaus von Kues*.

117. See Celenza, "Revival of Platonic Philosophy," 75–80.

playing out in the East as in the West, with Gemistos Plethon (1355–1452) leading the call to an ostensibly pristine Platonism.

While drawing generously upon classical philosophy, scholastic theologians were careful to remain within the gates of Christian belief and were assisted in this by the magisterium. If Eriugena and Eckhart were judged to have crossed the border into pantheistic territory, others with similar convictions, such as the cardinal Nicholas of Cusa, escaped unscathed. However, Gemistos Plethon was explicitly and unapologetically pagan.[118] Rather than simply translate the beliefs of the many into philosophical religion, Plethon (adopting Plato's name in Greek) sought to revive not only a pre-Christian but a pre-Neoplatonic Platonism. Nevertheless, Zoroaster and the magi along with the Chaldean Oracles and Proclus played an important part in his theories.[119]

Yet the end is never a return to the beginning, of course. Plethon's Plato renaissance was the fruit of centuries beginning with the so-called "first Byzantine humanism" that emerged in the ninth century and was signaled by an imperial decree for copying Hellenistic sources, including works of Proclus and his successors of the New Athenian Academy.[120] However, Plethon's vision was as opposed to both Christianity and theurgic excess as Plato's was to the state religion of Athens and to rituals generally. Although he never saw his project realized fully in his island-state of Mistra, he built the sails for his eponym's voyage into the Renaissance. This episode completes the story of the Orphic myth and its ancient Christian reception leading up to the Renaissance.

Seeking wisdom "outside the gates" was not off-limits, as we have seen, but it required discernment and submission to scriptural authority.[121] Orpheus, Zoroaster, Hermes Trismegistus, "our divine Plato," Iamblichus, and Proclus were

---

118. I have avoided using the term "pagan" anachronistically to describe those who were simply citizens of the Roman Empire, much less the Greeks before them. In Tertullian's day, Christians thought of themselves as a "third race," neither Jewish nor gentile but drawing citizens from both. Calling themselves *milites Christi* (soldiers of Christ), Christians early on referred to their polytheistic neighbors as Hellenes or gentiles. Only in Constantine's wake did the term "pagan" emerge as consciousness of being a third race faded into the state privileges granted to the church. Now non-Christians were described as "peasantry" (*paganus*), although in truth the majority of the population, including wealthy and powerful elites, remained committed to the old religion. See Brown, "Pagan," 625–26. In the Byzantine Empire, however, "pagan" is an appropriate emic term.

119. Hanegraaff, *Esotericism and the Academy*, 38.

120. Sinossoglou, *Radical Platonism in Byzantium*, 62: "Proclus' commentary on the *Republic* and the *Timaeus*, Damascius' commentary on the *Parmenides*, Olympiodorus' commentaries on the *Gorgias, Alcibiades I, Phaedo* and *Philebus,* and the works of Albinus and Maximus of Tyre."

121. See Gregory of Nazianzus, *Oration* 21. Text in PG 35:1088.15–18.

rediscovered in the West well into the Middle Ages and mostly through Arabic scholars, but they had never faded from the cultural imagination of the Christian East.[122] Michael Psellos, appointed "Consult of Philosophers" by Constantine IX and the head of the new university of Constantinople, believed that the ascent of the soul "is not a gift of divine grace, but a philosophical quest" initiated by one's own discursive reasoning. Just as others claimed higher truth in allegorizing biblical narratives (e.g., Moses's ascent of Mount Sinai), Psellos sought it in Hellenic myths as well, but the meaning he found was not Christian.[123]

With Plethon three centuries later, we are back in the milieu of Middle Platonism, especially Hermeticism and the Chaldean Oracles. Reaching back before theurgic Neoplatonism, however, Plethon sought to recover what he thought was the original Platonism.[124] Plethon also followed the emperor Julian over Proclus (and Neoplatonism generally) in attributing Being to the One.[125] No longer supraessential, the One *is* Being itself (*Ad bess.* 1.460.34–461.1).[126] There is no question of panentheism; Plethon's Platonism is pantheism full stop.[127] For Proclus, the levels proceed from the One to Being, then the Intellect, Soul, and finally Body.[128] "If we are to point at the most probable target of Plethon's criticism of Proclus," argues Hladký, "it seems that it is the extremely complicated succession of divine generations described in Orphic poems."[129] Instead, Plethon returns to the more austere triad of Plotinus: "(1) the One, (2) Intellect and (3) the Soul."[130]

Besides Plato (including the second *Letter*), Plethon's debts are mainly to Julian's *Oration to the King Sun*, the Chaldean Oracles, and Plutarch's *Isis and Osiris*.[131] The major difference between Plethon and Proclus—in fact, with the

---

122. Sinossoglou, *Radical Platonism in Byzantium*, 64–71. "Byzantine humanism maintained the core of a die-hard Hellenic naturalistic paradigm that persistently challenged Christian exclusivity, revelation and soteriology and whose exponents in the ninth century are to be found among the high-profile advocates of secular education with excellent connections at court" (71).

123. Plested, "Philosophy," 2:44–47. Edward Siecienski relates that the emperor Isaac I Comnenos moved against the patriarch, Michael Caerularios, exiling and deposing him on the charges of treason, heresy, and witchcraft. Ironically, it was Psellos who drew up the charges and gave his eulogy. Siecienski, "Michael Caerularios," 1:94. See also Sinossoglou, *Radical Platonism in Byzantium*, 79.

124. Hladký, *Philosophy of Gemistos Plethon*, 168–69.
125. Sinossoglou, *Radical Platonism in Byzantium*, 243–50.
126. Hladký, *Philosophy of Gemistos Plethon*, 171.
127. Hladký, *Philosophy of Gemistos Plethon*, 81, from *De diff.* 10.336.20–25.
128. Hladký, *Philosophy of Gemistos Plethon*, 172.
129. Hladký, *Philosophy of Gemistos Plethon*, 173.
130. Hladký, *Philosophy of Gemistos Plethon*, 173–74.
131. Hladký, *Philosophy of Gemistos Plethon*, 175, 182.

entire Platonic tradition—lies in the first point that Hladký mentioned: the One or Zeus was not beyond Being, constituting a radically monistic idealism. Plethon outlines what he takes to be Plato's ontology, which fits my own interpretation of Plato's *Timaeus*:

> 1. Being *is* the supreme *genus*. Nothing exists outside Being—not even god... 2. It is logically necessary to assume causes mediating between Being *qua* Being and the world of becoming and corruption. God is not beyond logical and ontological necessity... 3. A pagan theogony and cosmogony is substituted for Christian *ktisiology* [doctrine of creation]. This cancels the distinction between creation according to god's free will... and the eternal generation... of Christ/Logos in the Trinity... 4. Multi-causalism carries a deterministic dimension, according to which freedom consists in discovering and aligning oneself to necessity/fate rather than in escaping the compulsion of logical and ontological necessity through Christ/Logos.[132]

I have interpreted Plato as divided on the question of the Good, with the *Republic* (509c) stipulating it as "beyond being" and the *Timaeus* representing it as within being as the demiurgic craftsman. It is understandable that Zeno and the Stoics took Plato in the latter, more pantheistic, direction. Plethon follows this latter course, but in an idealistic (Parmenidean) direction. The result is "Plethon's re-sacralisation of *cosmos* and Being."[133]

Following Aristotle, Aquinas observed that Parmenides founded the notion of being as univocal. "In a manner presumably very unnerving for any carrier of 'pagan' and monist tendencies such as Plethon and Spinoza, the Proclan commentary on the *Parmenides* ends with a frustrating concession to *silence*."[134] This ultimate "silence" can only be grounded in a view of God as beyond being. This is Plethon's greatest disagreement with Proclus. The world is not just full of resemblances to the hyperessential God, as Proclus and Dionysius would have it, but is simply God. God *is* reality and reality *is* God. Beyond the ideal world there is no God. Dispensing with *ex nihilo* creation, Plethon emphasizes the necessary emanation of the cosmos from "Zeus." Moreover, Christ is no longer the Logos in whom all things hold together; univocal kinship with the Father is now possessed by all levels of

---

132. In Sinossoglou, *Radical Platonism in Byzantium*, 223.
133. Sinossoglou, *Radical Platonism in Byzantium*, 224.
134. Sinossoglou, *Radical Platonism in Byzantium*, 240–41, citing Wippel, *Metaphysical Thought of Thomas Aquinas*, 70–71.

intelligible being. "Divested of its uniqueness, Christology is rendered obsolete."[135] For Plethon, though, this is not a potential danger but an intentional outcome.

Plethon's naturalism points toward what we call modernity. While the gods were real and busy in the universe of Iamblichus and Proclus, for Plethon they are back to serving as symbols for intellectual or natural principles. Thus, there is little need for theurgy, a point from which Ficino will demur. Plethon begins with the Chaldean Oracles, although Proclus's commentary, available to Psellos in the eleventh century by this point, had disappeared. There is also no Hekate and the theurgic context of the Oracles is ignored.[136] Zeus, Hera, and the rest of the divinities are equated with natural entities and processes. For Plethon, "the divine" is not personal and does not intervene, especially not due to prayers or manipulation by mortals. At this point, Plethon's God is like the One of Plato and Plotinus, shining forth its rays of being in an eternal gesture without any variation. The cosmos turns silently on its axis in a circular motion. Justice does not vary and there is no such thing as grace. To whatever extent one lives virtuously and rationally in this immutable order, wings are repaired for the return flight. We are far from third-century Alexandria, with philosophers seeking pupils by proffering various methods of salvation. Absent from Plethon's mind are the cries, "The foes! The foes!" More like Plotinus, his flight is intellectual and his salvation is philosophy.

Plethon sucks out the juice of Orphic metaphysics while leaving the theurgic skin behind. For Psellos and more so Plethon, the Chaldean Oracles were naturalized.[137] "They are not messages from the world beyond or god any longer," Sinnosglous notes. Plethon's source for the Oracles is Psellos, who was influenced by Proclus's commentary. However, "The Plethonean editorial work on the *Oracles* is a conscious move towards the secularization of their contents."[138] In this context, "secularisation" means downplaying the religious-theurgic aspects. There is a distinctly "modern" sensibility at work. With transcendence reduced to immanence, he even seeks to avoid the mystical elements that were integral to Plato's philosophy and the spiritual life of Plotinus and Porphyry.[139]

In resacralizing the world, Plethon has no need of the Christian God.[140] "In a nutshell: Plethon discerned the connection between secularism and paganism

---

135. Sinossoglou, *Radical Platonism in Byzantium*, 250–53.
136. Hladký, *Philosophy of Gemistos Plethon*, 35, 37–38.
137. Sinossoglou, *Radical Platonism in Byzantium*, 214.
138. Sinossoglou, *Radical Platonism in Byzantium*, 215.
139. Sinossoglou, *Radical Platonism in Byzantium*, 216.
140. Sinossoglou, *Radical Platonism in Byzantium*, 18. What we find especially in Plethon, says

that lies at the centre of the project of modernity."[141] Both in the *Memoranda* presented to the emperor and the despot of Morea and, more fully, in the *Nomoi*, Plethon lays out "the constitution for a utopian pagan city-state."[142] Acknowledging Plato, Zoroaster, and the Stoics as his main sources, he nevertheless diverges at key points. Socrates said that true defenders of justice should stay out of politics and live a private life (Plato, *Apol.* 31d–32a). If one wanted to join the true philosophers, Plotinus stipulated, "put away authority and office" (*Enn.* 1.4.14).[143] Plotinus was at first thrilled with the plan to establish a "city of philosophers," called Platonopolis in southern Italy, but when that fell through, perhaps he was even more confident that Plato's Socrates was right.

But Plethon was among the first to fuse the spiritual-philosophical utopianism with an early modern revolutionary spirit.[144] In his view, religion is epiphenomenal to politics. Instead, philosophy—"common notions" (actually his version of Platonism)—would be the basis for a concrete experiment that could be universalized.[145] For him, a secular Platonism required a political state, which of course would have to be achieved by revolution. There are some striking similarities with Joachim of Fiore's more religious vision. In both, the golden age now lies in the near future rather than in the past, and it will be a complete renovation, even revolution, all at once. Sinossoglou points out, "The most significant conceptual shift in the *Memoranda* consists in recovering this Platonic sense of the word σωτηρία [salvation] as preservation of political entities and abandoning Christian *Heilsgeschichte* [salvation history] which has salvation as redemption at its centre." Political salvation depends on its constitution.[146]

Modeled on Plato's *Laws*, Plethon's political treatise the *Nomoi* was explicit in theology as well as politics. Its theology is a mélange of Zoroastrian mysticism and astrology wrapped around an Orphic core. In his exile on the island of Mistra, Plethon's teaching attracted many students, including Bessarion, and Mistra became a center for Hellenistic revival. It was not a cosmopolitan outlook, however. Justinian's universal Christian empire was a fraud, Plethon thought, and he asked the emperor

---

Sinossoglou, are the following commitments: (1) "epistemic optimism"; (2) "a pagan ontology" replacing the one ineffable God with "a humanly cognizable" Good *qua* Being; (3) "a multi-causalist or 'polytheist' metaphysical model that eliminates contingency and substitutes the determinist notion of *heimarmene* or fate for Christian free will"; and (4) "political utopianism."

141. Sinossoglou, *Radical Platonism in Byzantium*, 426.
142. Sinossoglou, *Radical Platonism in Byzantium*, 5.
143. Translation from Plotinus, *Enneads* (trans. MacKenna).
144. Hladký, *Philosophy of Gemistos Plethon*, 19.
145. Hladký, *Philosophy of Gemistos Plethon*, 27.
146. Sinossoglou, *Radical Platonism in Byzantium*, 345.

to turn the peninsula into a cultural island with a centralized monarchy. In this absolute rule of the philosopher-king, land and property would be owned publicly. Christians, homosexuals, and other deviants would be burned at the stake.[147]

Sinnosoglou notes, "Two competing and mutually exclusive notions of utopianism evolved."[148] Gennadius Scholar, future patriarch of Constantinople, was a formidable opponent of Plethon. In the new age conceived by Scholarios's millennialist eschatology, there would be more religious freedom than envisioned in Plethon's state. Yet just as the philosopher is the center of Plethon's scheme, the monk dominates Scholarios eschatology precisely as in Joachim of Fiore. Scholarios predicted the end of time in 1492 or 1513.[149] "What is striking in this type of eschatology is the absence of the Church in the Last Days," says Petre Guran. There are prophets and emperors, but the institutional church seems to have little place.[150] "It is striking to discover in this particular conception of the monk put forth by the Hesychasts a resemblence with the eschatological aspects of Western spirituality in the works of Joachim da Fiore, Peter Olivi, and Master Ekchart."[151] In Gregory of Palamas, the historical resurrection is a sorrow. Palamas does not believe in the end of the age in the future. Rather, he embraces a realized eschatology in which the Tabor experience constitutes the "consummation of time" here and now.[152] Palamite eschatology was fully realized and ahistorical.[153]

The wide influence of Joachim of Fiore cannot be denied. In a letter to Pope Nicholas V, George of Trezibond, very obsessed with the end times, wrote, "There is no one, I believe, Most Blessed Father, who has studied the book and the prophecy of the Abbot Ioachim more than I."[154] But Plethon is nonplussed by any of this prophecy wrangling. Joachim's idea of an imminent transcendence of religious authority appealed to Plethon, but he does not attach any significance to eschatology. Instead, he grounds his utopian futurism in an optimistic view of human reason, of epistemology, and therefore of the potential here and now to create a just society.

To whatever extent Pico's *Oration* can be considered "the charter of modernity," as it often is, no new note is struck. In spite of the tendency of some to lay the blame for modern voluntarism and individualism on nominalism (especially Scotus and Ockham), its influence is all but absent, except perhaps as an element

---

147. Burns, *Cambridge History of Medieval Political Thought*, 649–52.
148. Sinossoglou, *Radical Platonism in Byzantium*, 323.
149. Guran, "Eschatology and Political Theology," 73.
150. Guran, "Eschatology and Political Theology," 76.
151. Guran, "Eschatology and Political Theology," 82.
152. Guran, "Eschatology and Political Theology," 78–79.
153. Guran, "Eschatology and Political Theology," 82.
154. Quoted by Lobovikova, "George of Trebizond's Views on Islam," 348.

in the overall Neoplatonist perspective of Nicholas of Cusa. The optimistic, even Promethean, individualism is Hermetic. And the shift from the intellect to the will as the divine core of the self, though Franciscan, is also evident in Eckhart and the Rhineland mystics.

Building on his anthropological optimism, Plethon's utopianism was fueled by an *optimistic epistemology*.[155] Plato said, "To discover the Maker and Father of this Universe would be a task indeed" (*Tim.* 28c), but not impossible at least for the few. The eyes get dizzy at such heights, to be sure, but for the adept philosopher, the "eyes of the soul" capture the vision (*Soph.* 254a–b). Origen accepted this theological optimism, telling Celsus, "Plato does not say that god is indescribable and nameless, but that *although he can be described it is only possible to declare him to a few*" (*Cels.* 7.42.20–43.4). This passage scandalized Palamas, while Barlaam followed Plato and Origen. It represented to the Palamites the humanistic rationalism of the Arians (especially Eunomius). The heart of the Platonist error, Palamas said, was its goal of making "the mind 'go out,' not only from fleshly thoughts, but out of the body itself."[156] The wise are able after all to unite both worlds in themselves and to know Being, whether divine or creaturely, as it is in itself. But it is not just contemplation but transformation that is made possible by this optimism. According to the *Nomoi*, "Along with other important teachers we assert that man's happiness [*eudaimonia*] depends upon the accomplishment of actions that accord with his kinship [*syngeneia*] with the gods."[157] Plethon's epistemic optimism fits with his political utopianism. As with the knowledge of God, it is difficult but not impossible.[158]

Plethon did not expect any climax to history, but did anticipate an eternal cycle of emanation and reversion. Much like Marx's rejection of Hegel's teleological view of history, Plethon believed that utopia had to be created and not awaited. Philosophy would bring unity where Christianity only brought division and obscurantism. For George Scholarios and Plethon alike, the crisis of Byzantium portended a radically new era, but for the former it was the return of Christ for a final battle with the antichrist, while for Plethon it was the emergence of the Hellenistic human from the ashes of a Christian empire. Scholarios held out hope for religious ecumenism under the new order, while Plethon envisioned a

---

155. Sinossoglou, *Radical Platonism in Byzantium*, 182.
156. Sinossoglou, *Radical Platonism in Byzantium*, 195–96.
157. Plethon, *Nomoi* 248 (3.43.82–88), quoted in Sinossoglou, *Radical Platonism in Byzantium*, 175; emphasis added.
158. Sinossoglou, *Radical Platonism in Byzantium*, 181.

strictly secular political community whose constitution would be modeled on Plato's *Republic* and *Laws*.

In book 1 of the *Nomoi* Plethon attacks the view that God is qualitatively different. Here he breaks not only from the religious exclusivism of Christian claims to revelation but from "those versions of Platonism that prioritize the ineffability of the divine." Common notions (a Stoic idea) not only ground belief in God's existence but become the authoritative foundation for all doctrine. Everyone is after the same thing: "a communal intellection of Zeus," of whom we are (in the intellect) a part.[159] We have encountered the same Stoicized Platonism in the Hermetic treatises. In his *Reply to Certain Questions* (1440/1443), says Sinossoglou, "For the first time Plethon advanced the idea featured in the *Nomoi* that the mixture of mortality and immortality in man serves universal harmony and accounts for man's participation in the All." This is why the soul may expect many transmigrations (reincarnations). It is "the divine element in us" (*Tim.* 90c) that inspires Platonists of all times, and Plethon's idea of the soul as *methorion* (borderline) between the two worlds is the same as the *copula mundi* (bond of the world) that we find in Pico, Ficino, and Pomponazzi.[160]

After the Council of Florence, George of Trebizond recalled:

> I myself heard him at Florence ... asserting that in a few more years the whole world would accept one and the same religion with one mind, one intelligence, one teaching. And when I asked him "Christ's or Muhammad's?," he said, "Neither; but it will not differ much from paganism." ... I heard, too, from a number of Greeks who escaped here from the Peloponnese that he openly said before he died ... that not many years after his death Muhammad and Christ would collapse and the true truth would shine through every region of the globe.[161]

This distinctively "modern" element in Plethon is similar to Nicholas of Cusa's reconciliation of faiths based on philosophical religion. Despite his disinterest in theurgy, *technē* is at least as important as *theōria* in the ascent of humanity. Spiritual technology can never be far off wherever the self is constructed as a magus, the fulcrum between the two worlds, incorporeal reality, and corporeal illusion. But the "natural supernaturalism" is under human control. It is up to us whether

---

159. Sinossoglou, *Radical Platonism in Byzantium*, 169–70.
160. Sinossoglou, *Radical Platonism in Byzantium*, 183–84, 195.
161. George of Trezibond, *Comparatio Platonis et Aristotolis*, fol. Vb3, quoted in Hanegraaff, *Esotericism and the Academy*, 38.

we advance civilization by returning to its pagan origins. Plethon's *Nomoi*, says Sinossoglou, "affirms the ability of man to compensate for the deficiencies and limitations of his mortal body by means of *technai*, technological progress and the manipulation of the power of animals according to human will." Influenced deeply by Plethon, "Pico did his very best to integrate these ideas into his Judeo-Christian outlook by putting a biblical plot at the service of pagan Platonic epistemological optimism."[162] Yet it is Platonic, requiring no revelation or grace.

The search for utopia coincides with the search for the *Philosophia perennis*. According to Plato's Socrates, Solon learned something of his own culture's hoary past from an old Egyptian priest. Even before Pythagoras, there had been talk of journeys to the East—Egypt, Persia, India—to discover older and wiser medicine for the soul. The Bible also relates Egyptian and Persian connections with Joseph in Egypt, Moses's schooling in Egyptian wisdom, Solomon's court, and Daniel's time in Babylon. Ficino made much of these connections, coining the term *prisca theologia* (ancient theology) for the tradition that he thought led from Zoroaster to Orpheus and from thence to Pythagoras, Socrates, and "our divine Plato," on to the Chaldean Oracles, the Corpus Hermeticum, and Proclus.

Plethon had no use for this idea, given the way in which he seems to skip over much of Platonism to Plato himself. Moreover, his perennial philosophy had to omit Moses and Christ. Based on lectures in Florence attended by Ficino, Pico, and others during the ecclesiastical council in 1439, Plethon's *On the Differences of Aristotle from Plato* sought to convert his hosts to Plato, who was at this point little known to Latins.[163]

Following Plato's *Republic*, Plethon's *Nomoi* contrasts poet-sophists and philosopher-lawgivers.[164] The latter are always true geniuses and founders, while the former are the theologian-priests who keep the masses in bondage to authority and the images and rituals of this world. The lawgivers form his perennial philosophy and turn out to be the same figures that we find in gnostic, Hermetic, and late Platonist texts. Not surprisingly, Parmenides heads Plethon's list of the wisest sages, followed by Timaeus of Locri, Plutarch, Plotinus, Porphyry, and Iamblichus. "It is also interesting to note that all the persons in the list who are, in some way, followers of Pythagoras," Hladký observes. "This provides a connection between Zoroastrian Magi and Plato. As is well known and as Plethon certainly could not ignore, the Neoplatonists Porphyry and Iamblichus both admired the ancient sage,

---

162. Sinossoglou, *Radical Platonism in Byzantium*, 165.
163. Hladký, *Philosophy of Gemistos Plethon*, 39, 42–43.
164. Hladký, *Philosophy of Gemistos Plethon*, 53–54.

and each of them wrote an account of the life of Pythagoras." Plato himself supplies his approval of Zoroaster in the *First Alcibiades*.[165]

Plethon also includes the Egyptians among the most ancient; though corrupted by ridiculous rites, they did at last incorporate Zoroaster. Given the similarities with Orphic doctrines, especially reincarnation, he asserts that the Indians had Dionysus (Bacchus) as their lawgiver and, finally, via Pythagoras, Plato became the steward of Zoroaster's doctrines.[166] Hladký concludes:

> By this conception of the *philosophia perennis* Plethon influenced other thinkers in the Renaissance and later, one of the earliest of them being most probably Francesco Filefo in 1464, a humanist who knew Gemistos personally.... However, the most famous case is that of Marsilo Ficino who originally held Hermes Trismegistus to be the first sage in the line of the wise men in his ancient theology (*prisca theologia*), but under Plethon's influence opted for Zoroaster.[167]

The Orphic mysteries become incorporated in the perennial tradition but, as in Pythagoras and Plato, tamed into a more contemplative sort of ecstasy.

There is something analogous—at least on the surface—between Plethon's project and that of Plato's Socrates. Both wanted to revise or jettison the old myths in favor of new ones and interpret all of them as allegories of principles rather than anthropomorphic persons. Nature—that is, the cosmos, everything in being as well as becoming—is itself supernatural, though in differing grades. Both were accused of atheism, but for neither of them is this charge quite accurate. Plato's Orphism is still alive with its talk of the soul's being overwhelmed by the ecstasy of divine vision. As Hladký explains, "Plethon rejects the presentation of the gods known from ancient Greek mythology and wants to conceive a new theology that is more in accordance with his rational philosophy." This is what makes his project of Hellenizing distinctly modern, in contrast with the frank supernaturalism of Julian's pagan revival.[168]

The alluring stranger beyond those gates has always been Orpheus. Wherever the historical eschatology of the Bible is transformed into a vertical ascent, Orpheus sings. Where we find *ex nihilo* creation elided in favor of emanation, a natural supernaturalism—pantheism or panentheism—prevails. When Chris-

---

165. Hladký, *Philosophy of Gemistos Plethon*, 56.
166. Hladký, *Philosophy of Gemistos Plethon*, 45.
167. Hladký, *Philosophy of Gemistos Plethon*, 203–4.
168. Hladký, *Philosophy of Gemistos Plethon*, 47.

tian theologians appeal to a perennial philosophy or *prisca theologia* that grants to Greek philosophy a pedagogical role in the history of redemption analogous to Moses and the prophets, Orphic philosophy is predictably the determining authority and allegorizing the method of interpretation. Above all, wherever we discern a quasi-docetic eschatology that leaves the body and the visible world behind, we are in an Orphic rather than biblical atmosphere. This includes an emphasis on "God" as a cipher for the "Whole" and a subordinate Christology that privileges the *logos asarkos* in eternity over and above the *logos ensarkos* in time.[169] And that, I suggest, is the nucleus of what it means, at least in a formerly Christian civilization, to be spiritual rather than religious.

---

169. Farrow, *Ascension and Ecclesia*, 163.

Works Cited

Abrams, M. H. *Natural Supernaturalism: Tradition and Revolution in Romantic Literature*. New York: Norton, 1973.
Adams, Peter Mark. *Mystai: Dancing Out the Mysteries of Dionysos*. London: Scarlet, 2019.
Aeschylus. *Agamemnon, Libation-Bearers, Eumenides, Fragments*. Edited and translated by Herbert Weir Smyth. LCL. Cambridge: Harvard University Press, 1926.
———. *Attributed Fragments*. Edited and translated by Alan H. Sommerstein. LCL. Cambridge: Harvard University Press, 2008.
———. *Suppliant Maidens, Persians, Prometheus, Seven against Thebes*. Edited and translated by Herbert Weir Smyth. LCL. Cambridge: Harvard University Press, 1922.
Agostini, Domenico, and Samuel Thrope, eds. and trans. *The Bundahišn: The Zoroastrian Book of Creation*. Oxford: Oxford University Press, 2020.
Akeroyd, J. R. "Cannabis." Page 78 in *Psilotaceae to Platanaceae*. Vol. 1 of *Flora Europaea*. Edited by T. G. Tutin et al. Cambridge: Cambridge University Press, 1993.
Albert, K. *Grieschische Religion und platonische Philosophie*. Hamburg: Mainer, 1980.
Alexander, P. J. *Byzantine Apocalyptic Traditions*. Berkeley: University of California Press, 1985.
Allen, James P. *Middle Egyptian Literature: Eight Literary Works of the Middle Kingdom*. Cambridge: Cambridge University Press, 2015.
Allum, Nick, and Paul Stoneman. "Astrology in Europe." Pages 301–22 in *The Culture of Science: How the Public Relates to Science across the Globe*. Edited by Martin W. Bauer, Rajesh Shukla, and Nick Allum. London: Routledge, 2012.
Al-Rawi, Ahmed K. "The Arabic Ghoul and Its Western Transformation." *Folklore* 120.3 (2009): 291–306.
Amanat, Abbas. *Apocalyptic Islam and Iranian Shi'ism*. London: I. B. Tauris, 2009.
Amélineau, M. E. *Essai sur le gnosticisme égyptien*. Anales de musée Guimet 14. Paris: Ministère de l'instruction publique, 1888.

Ames, Roger T. "*Yin* and *Yang*." Pages 846–47 in *Encyclopedia of Chinese Philosophy*. Edited by Antonio S. Cua. London: Routledge, 2002.

Annas, Julia. *An Introduction to Plato's Republic*. Oxford: Clarendon, 1981.

———. *Platonic Ethics, Old and New*. Ithaca: Cornell University Press, 1999.

Anotolios, Khaled. *Retrieving Nicaea: The Development and Meaning of Trinitarian Doctrine*. Grand Rapids: Baker Academic, 2011.

Anthony, David W. *The Horse, the Wheel, and Language: How Bronze Age Riders from the Eurasian Steppes Shaped the Modern World*. Princeton: Princeton University Press, 2007.

Anton, John P. "Theourgia-Demiourgia: A Controversial Issue in Hellenistic Thought." Pages 9–31 in *Neoplatonism and Gnosticism*. Edited by Richard T. Wallis. Albany: SUNY Press, 1992.

Aristotle. *The Complete Works of Aristotle*. Edited by Jonathan Barnes. 2 vols. Princeton: Princeton University Press, 1984.

Arjomand, Said Amir. "Messianism, Millennialism and Revolution in Early Islamic History." Pages 106–25 in *Imagining the End: Visions of Apocalypse from the Ancient Middle East to Modern America*. Edited by Abbas Amanat and Magnus T. Bernhardsson. London: I. B. Tauris, 2002.

Armstrong, A. H. "The Ancient and Continuing Pieties of the Greek World." Pages 66–101 in *Classical Mediterranean Spirituality: Egyptian, Greek, Roman*. Edited by A. H. Armstrong. New York: Crossroad, 1986.

———. *The Architecture of the Intelligible Universe in the Philosophy of Plotinus*. Cambridge: Cambridge University Press, 1940.

———. "Dualism: Platonic, Gnostic, and Christian." Pages 33–54 in *Neoplatonism and Gnosticism*. Edited by Richard T. Wallis. Albany: SUNY Press, 1992.

Armstrong, Karen. *The Great Transformation: The Beginning of Our Religious Traditions*. New York: Knopf, 2006.

Arnason, Johann P. "Rehistoricizing the Axial Age." Pages 337–65 in *The Axial Age and Its Consequences*. Edited by Robert N. Bellah and Hans Joas. Cambridge: Harvard University Press, 2012.

Arnim, Hans von, ed., *Stoicorum Veterum Fragmenta*. 3 vols. Leipzig: Teubner, 1903–1905.

Assmann, Jan. "Cultural Memory and the Myth of the Axial Age." Pages 366–407 in *The Axial Age and Its Consequences*. Edited by Robert N. Bellah and Hans Joas. Cambridge: Harvard University Press, 2012.

———. *Death and Salvation in Ancient Egypt*. Translated by David Lorton. Ithaca, NY: Cornell University Press, 2005.

———. Foreword to *The Secret History of Hermes Trismegistus: Hermeticism from Ancient to Modern Times*, by Florian Ebeling. Translated by David Lorton. Ithaca, NY: Cornell University Press, 2007.

———. *The Invention of Religion: Faith and Covenant in the Book of Exodus*. Translated by Robert Savage. Princeton: Princeton University Press, 2018.

———. *Moses the Egyptian: The Memory of Egypt in Western Monotheism*. Cambridge: Harvard University Press, 1997.

———. *Of God and Gods: Egypt, Israel and the Rise of Monotheism*. Madison: University of Wisconsin Press, 2008.

———. *The Price of Monotheism*. Translated by Robert Savage. Stanford, CA: Stanford University Press, 2010.

Astore, Rocco A. "Unveiling Ultimate Reality in Plato's *Allegory of the Cave* and the *Bhagavad Gita*." *Inquiries Journal* 11.9 (2019): 1.

Athanassakis, Apostolos N., and Benjamin M. Wolkow. *The Orphic Hymns: Translation, Introduction, and Notes*. Baltimore: Johns Hopkins University Press, 2013.

Atherton, Patrick. "The City in Ancient Religious Experience." Pages 314–36 in *Classical Mediterranean Spirituality: Egyptian, Greek, Roman*. Edited by A. H. Armstrong. New York: Crossroad, 1986.

Augustine. *City of God*. Edited by David Knowles. Translated by Henry Bettenson. New York: Penguin, 1976.

———. *Revisions*. Translated by Boniface Ramsey. Works of Saint Augustine. Hyde Park, NY: New City, 2010.

Ayres, Lewis. *Nicaea and Its Legacy: An Approach to Fourth-Century Trinitarian Theology*. Oxford: Oxford University Press, 2006.

Bagshaw, Hilary B. P. *Religion in the Thought of Mikhail Bakhtin*. London: Routledge, 2016.

Baltes, M. "Numenios von Apamea und der platonische *Timaios*." *VC* 29 (1975): 241–70.

Balthasar, Hans Urs von. *The Glory of the Lord*. Translated by Andrew Louth et al. 7 vols. San Francisco: Ignatius, 1982–1989.

———. Introduction to *Origen: Spirit & Fire; A Thematic Anthology of His Writings*. Edited by Hans Urs von Balthasar. Translated by Robert J. Daly, SJ. Washington, DC: Catholic University of America Press, 1984.

———. "Patristik, Scholastik, und wir." *Theologie der Zeit* 3 (1939): 65–104.

Barclay, John M. G. *Jews in the Mediterranean Diaspora*. Berkeley: University of California Press, 1996.

Bar-Kochva, Bezalel. *The Image of Jews in Greek Literature: The Hellenistic Period*. Berkeley: University of California Press, 2010.

Barnes, Jonathan. *The Presocratic Philosophers*. New York: Routledge, 1983.

Barnes, Robin Bruce. *Prophecy and Gnosis: Apocalypticism in the Wake of the Lutheran Reformation*. Stanford, CA: Stanford University Press, 1988.

Barnstone, Willis, and Marvin Meyer, eds. *The Gnostic Bible*. Rev. ed. Boston: Shambhala, 2009.

Barr, James. "The Question of Religious Influence: The Case of Zoroastrianism, Judaism, and Christianity." *JAAR* 53.2 (1985): 201–36.

Basham, A. L. *The Origin and Development of Classical Hinduism*. Edited by Kenneth G. Zysk. Oxford: Oxford University Press, 1989.

Basu, B. D. *Sacred Books of the Hindus*. Delhi: Gyan Books, 1925.

Baumgarten, Murray. "Carlyle's 'Spiritual Optics.'" *Victorian Studies* 11.4 (1968): 503–22

Beatrice, P. F. "Porphyry at Origen's School at Caesarea." Pages 267–84 in *Origeniana Duodecima*. Edited by B. Bitton-Ashkelony et al. Leuven: Peeters, 2019.

Beckman, G. "Primordial Obstetrics: 'The Song of Emergence' (CTH 344)." Pages 25–34 in *Hethitische Literatur. Überlieferungsprozesse, Textstrukturen, Ausdrucksformen und Nachwirken* 31. Edited by Manfred Hutter and Sylvia Hutter-Barunser. Münster: Ugarit-Verlag, 2001.

Beckwith, Christopher. *Greek Buddha: Pyrrho's Encounter with Early Buddhism in Central Asia*. Princeton: Princeton University Press, 2015.

Behr, John. *Irenaeus of Lyons: Identifying Christianity*. Oxford: Oxford University Press, 2013.

Beierwaltes, Werner. *Denken des Einen: Studien zur neoplatonischen Philosophie und ihrer Wirküngsgeschichte*. Frankfurt am Main: Klostermann, 1985.

———. "Die Wiederentdeckung des Eriugena im Deuthschen Idealismus." Pages 188–201 in *Platonismus und Idealismus*. Frankfurt am Main: Klostermann, 1972.

———. *Platonismus und Idealismus*. 2nd ed. Frankfurt am Main: Klostermann, 2004.

———. *Proklos: Grundzüge seiner Metaphysik*. Jena: Klostermann, 1975.

Bell, H. Idris. *Cults and Creeds in Graeco-Roman Egypt*. 2nd ed. Liverpool: Liverpool University Press, 1954.

Bellah, Robert N. *Beyond Belief: Essays on Religion in a Post-Traditional World*. New York: Harper & Row, 1970.

———. "The Heritage of the Axial Age: Resource or Burden?" Pages 447–68 in *The Axial Age and Its Consequences*. Edited by Robert N. Bellah and Hans Joas. Cambridge: Belknap Press of Harvard University Press, 2012.

———. "What Is Axial about the Axial Age?" *European Journal of Sociology* 46 (2005): 69–89.

Benso, Silvia. "The Breathing of the Air: Presocratic Echoes in Levinas." Pages 9–23 in *Levinas and the Ancients*. Edited by Brian Schroeder and Silvia Benso. Bloomington: Indiana University Press, 2008.

Benz, Ernst. *The Mystical Sources of German Romantic Philosophy*. Translated by Blair R. Reynolds and Eunice M. Paul. Allison Park, PA: Pickwick, 1983.

Berg, Robbert Maarten van den. *Proclus' Commentary on the Cratylus in Context: Ancient Theories of Language and Naming*. Leiden: Brill, 2007.

Berlin, Isaiah. "The Birth of Greek Individualism: A Turning-Point in the History of

Political Thought." Pages 287–321 in *Liberty: Collected Essays of Isaiah Berlin*. Edited by Henry Hardy. Oxford: Oxford University Press, 2002.

Bernabé, Alberto. "Autour du mythe orphique sur Dionysos et les Titans: Quelque notes critiques." Pages 25–39 in *Des Géants à Dionysos: Mélanges offerts à F. Vian*. Edited by Domenico Accorinti and Pierre Chuvin. Alessandria, Italy: Edizioni dell'Orso, 2003.

———. "The Derveni Theogony: Many Questions and Some Answers." *HSCP* 103 (2007): 99–133

———. "The Gods in Ancient Orphism." Pages 422–41 in *The Gods in Ancient Greece: Identities and Transformations*. Edited by Jan N. Bremmer and Andrew Erskine. Edinburgh: Edinburgh University Press, 2010.

———. "Imago Inforum Orphica." Pages 95–130 in *Mystic Cults in Magna Graecia*. Edited by Giovanni Casadio and Patricia Johnston. Austin: University of Texas Press, 2009.

———. "La teogonía órfica citada en las *Pseudocle-mentina*." *Adamantius* 14 (2008): 79–99.

———. "La toile de Pénélope: a-t-il existé un mythe orphique dur Dionysos et les Titans?" *Revue de l'histoire des religions* 219.4 (2002): 401–33.

———. *Poetae Epici Graeci* 1. Leipzig: K. G. Sauer, 1987.

Bernabé, Alberto, Miguel Herrero de Jáuregui, Ana Isabel Jiménez San Cristóbal, and Raquel Martín Hernández, eds. *Redefining Dionysos*. Berlin: de Gruyter, 2013.

Bernabé, Alberto, and Ana Isabel Jiménez San Cristóbal. *Instrucciones para el más allá: Las laminillas órficas de oro*. Madrid: Clásicas, 2001.

———. *Instructions for the Netherworld: The Orphic Gold Tablets*. Leiden: Brill, 2007.

———. "Two Aspects of the Orphic Papyrological Tradition." Pages 17–44 in *Presocratics and Papyrological Tradition: A Philosophical Reappraisal of the Sources*. Edited by Christian Vassallo. Berlin: de Gruyter, 2019.

Bernabé Pajares, Alberto, and Ricardo Olmos Romera. *Poetarum epicorum Graecorum: Testimonia et fragmenta. Bibliotheca scriptorum Graecorum et Romanorum Teubneriana*. 2 vols. in 4 parts. Leipzig: Teubner, 1987–2007.

Betegh, Gábor. *The Derveni Papyrus: Cosmology, Theology and Interpretation*. Cambridge: Cambridge University Press, 2004.

Betz, Hans Dieter, ed. *The Greek Magical Papyri in Translation Including the Demotic Spells*. Chicago: University of Chicago Press, 1986.

———. "Orthodoxy and Heresy in Primitive Christianity: Some Critical Remarks on Georg Strecker's Republication of Walter Bauer's *Rechtgläubigkeit und Ketzerei im ältesten Christentum*." *Int* 19.3 (1965): 299–311.

Bhattacharji, Sukumari. *The Indian Theogony: A Comparative Study of Indian Mythology from the Vedas to the Puranas*. Cambridge: Cambridge University Press, 1970.

Bitton-Ashketony, Brouria. *The Ladder of Prayer and the Ship of Stirrings: The Praying Self in Late Antique East Syrian Christianity.* Leuven: Peeters, 2019.

Black, Jeremy, and Andrew Green. *Gods, Demons and Symbols of Ancient Mesopotamia.* Austin: University of Texas Press, 1992.

Black, Jeremy et al. "Inana's Descent to the Nether World: Translation." *Electronic Text Corpus of Sumerian Literature.* n.d. https://etcsl.orinst.ox.ac.uk/section1/tr141.htm.

Blankenhorn, Bernhard. *The Mystery of Union with God: Dionysian Mysticism in Albert the Great and Thomas Aquinas.* Washington, DC: Catholic University of America Press, 2016.

Bloch, Ernst. *Avicenna and the Aristotelian Left.* Translated by Loren Goldman and Peter Thompson. New York: Columbia University Press, 2019.

Bloom, Allen, trans. *The Republic of Plato.* New York: Basic Books, 1968.

Blumenberg, H. J. "Marius's *Life*: A Neoplatonic Biography." *Byzantion* 54/2 (1984): 649–94.

Blumenthal, H. J., and A. C. Lloyd. *Monad and Dyad as Cosmic Principles in Syrianus: Soul and the Structure of Being in Late Neoplatonism.* Liverpool: Liverpool University Press, 1982.

Bockmuehl, Markus. "Creation ex Nihilo in Palestinian Judaism and Early Christianity." *SJT* 65.3 (2013): 253–70.

Bodine, Joshua. "The Shabaka Stone: An Introduction." *Studia Antiqua* 7.1 (2009): 1–21.

Boll, Franz. *Studien über Claudius Ptolemaus: Ein Beitrag zur Geschichte der griechischen Philosophie und Astrologie.* Leipzig: Teubner, 1894.

Bolton, James David. *Aristeas of Proconnesus.* Oxford: Clarendon, 1962.

Bos, Abraham P. "The 'Vehicle of Soul' and the Debate over the Origins of this Concept." *Phil* 151.1 (2013): 31–50.

Boyarin, Daniel. "By Way of Apology: Dawson, Edwards, Origen." *SPhilo* 16 (2004): 188–217.

Boyce, Mary. *A History of Zoroastrianism under the Achaemenids.* Leiden: Brill, 2015.

———. "On the Zoroastrian Temple Cult of Fire." *JAOS* 95.3 (1975): 454–66.

Boyd, James W. "Symbols of Evil in Buddhism." *Journal of Asian Studies* 31 (1971): 63–75.

Bradshaw, David. *Aristotle East and West: Metaphysics and the Division of Christendom.* Cambridge: Cambridge University Press, 2008.

Brakke, David. *The Gnostics: Myth, Ritual, and Diversity in Early Christianity.* Cambridge: Harvard University Press, 2010.

Breasted, J. H. *The Dawn of Conscience.* New York: Scribner's Sons, 1933.

Bremmer, Jan N. *Initiation in the Mysteries of the Ancient World.* Berlin: de Gruyter, 2014.

———. "Scapegoat Rituals in Ancient Greece." *HSCP* 87 (1983): 299–320.

Brereton, Joel P., and Stephanie W. Jamison. *The Rigveda: A Guide.* Oxford: Oxford University Press, 2020.

Brierley, Michael W. "The Potential of Panentheism for Dialogue between Science and Religion." Pages 635–51 in *The Oxford Handbook of Religion and Science*. Edited by Philip Clayton and Zachary Simpson. Oxford: Oxford University Press, 2006.

Brisson, Luc. "La figure de Chronos dans la Théogonie Orphique et ses antécédents Iraniens." Pages 37–55 in *Mythes et représentations du temps*. Edited by Dorian Tiffeneau. Paris: CNRS, 1985.

———. *Plato the Myth Maker*. Translated and edited by Gerard Naddaf. Chicago: University of Chicago Press, 1998.

———. "Proclus et l'orphisme." Pages 43–103 in *Proclus lecteur et interprète des anciens*. Edited by Jean Pepin and H. D. Saffrey. Paris: Editions du Centre Nationale de la reserche scientifique, 1987.

———. Review of *Orphic Tradition and the Birth of the Gods*, by Dwayne A. Meisner. *Bryn Mawr Classical Review* (May 2019). https://bmcr.brynmawr.edu/2019/2019.05.55/.

Brock, Sebastian P. "Dionysius the Areopagite, Pseudo-." In *Gorgias Encyclopedic Dictionary of the Syriac Heritage: Electronic Edition*. Edited by S. P. Brock, Aaron M. Butts, George A. Kiraz, and Lucas Van Rompay. https://gedsh.bethmardutho.org/entry/Dionysius-the-Areopagite-Pseudo-.

Broek, Roelof van den. "Gnosticism and Hermeticism in Antiquity: Two Roads to Salvation." Pages 1–20 in *Gnosis and Hermeticism from Antiquity to Modern Times*. Edited by Roelof van den Broek and Wouter J. Hanegraaff. Albany: SUNY Press, 1998.

Broek, Roelof van den, and Wouter J. Hanegraaff, eds. *Gnosis and Hermeticism from Antiquity to Modern Times*. Albany: SUNY Press, 1998.

Brons, Julius. *Gott und die Seinden: Untersuchungen zum Verhältnis von neuplatonischer Metaphysik und christlicher Tradition bei Dionysius Areopagita*. Göttingen: Vandenhoeck & Ruprecht, 1976.

Brooks, David. "The Too-Muchness of Bono." *Atlantic*, December 2022. https://www.theatlantic.com/magazine/archive/2022/12/u2-bono-memoir-surrender/671894/.

Brown, Garrett Wallace. "Cosmopolitanism." In *The Concise Oxford Dictionary of Politics*. Edited by Iain McLean and Alistair McMillan. 3rd ed. Oxford: Oxford University Press, 2009.

Brown, N. O. "The Apocalypse of Islam." *Social Text* 8 (1983): 155–71.

Brown, Peter. "Pagan." In *Late Antiquity: A Guide to the Postclassical World*. Edited by Glen Warren Bowerstock, Peter Brown, and Oleg Grabar. Cambridge: Belknap Press of Harvard University Press, 1999.

Bruce, Steve. *Secularization: In Defence of an Unfashionable Theory*. Oxford: Oxford University Press, 2011.

Brugarolas, Miguel, ed. *Gregory of Nyssa:* Contra Eunomium I. *An English Translation with Supporting Studies.* Leiden: Brill, 2018.

Buck, Adriaan de, and Alan Gardiner. *The Egyptian Coffin Texts.* 7 vols. Chicago: University of Chicago Oriental Institution, 1935–1961.

Buckareff, Andrei A., and Yugi Nagasawa, eds. *Alternative Concepts of God: Essays on the Metaphysics of the Divine.* Oxford: Oxford University Press, 2016.

Budge, E. A. Wallis. *The Dwellers on the Nile.* 1926. Repr., New York: Dover, 1977.

Burge, Ryan P. *The Nones: Where They Came From, Who They Are, and Where They Are Going.* Minneapolis: Fortress, 2021.

Burgess, Stanley M. *The Holy Spirit: Medieval Roman Catholic and Reformation Traditions.* Peabody, MA: Hendrickson, 1997.

Burkert, Walter. *Ancient Mystery Cults.* Cambridge: Harvard University Press, 1987.

———. *Babylon, Memphis, Persepolis: Eastern Contexts of Greek Cultures.* Cambridge: Harvard University Press, 2007.

———. *Greek Religion.* Translated by John Raffin. Cambridge: Harvard University Press, 1985.

———. *Homo Necans: The Anthropology of Ancient Greek Sacrificial Ritual and Myth.* Translated by Peter Bing. Berkeley: University of California Press, 1983.

———. "Killing in Sacrifice: A Reply [to Bruno Dumbrowski]." *Numen* 25 (1978): 77–79.

———. *Lore and Science in Ancient Pythagoreanism.* Translated by Edwin L. Minar. Cambridge: Harvard University Press, 1972.

———. *The Orientalizing Revolution: Near Eastern Influence on Greek in the Early Archaic Age.* Translated by Margaret E. Pinder. Cambridge: Harvard University Press, 1998.

Burkitt, F. C. *Church and Gnosis: A Study of Christian Thought and Speculation in the Second Century.* Cambridge: Cambridge University Press, 1932.

Burnaby, John. *Amor Dei: A Study in the Religion of St. Augustine.* London: Hodder & Stoughton, 1938.

Burnet, John. *Early Greek Philosophy.* London: Black, 1892.

Burns, James Henderson. *The Cambridge History of Medieval Political Thought c. 350–c. 1450.* Cambridge: Cambridge University Press, 1988.

Burnyeat, Myles. "Idealism in Greek Philosophy." *Philosophical Review* 91 (1982): 3–40.

Burton, Tara Isabella. "The Rise of Progressive Occultism." *American Interest* 15.1 (June 7, 2019). https://www.the-american-interest.com/2019/06/07/the-rise-of-progressive-occultism/.

———. *Strange Rites: New Religions for a Godless World.* New York: Public Affairs, 2020.

Busker, Bianca. "Why Witchcraft Is on the Rise." *Atlantic*, March 2020. https://www.theatlantic.com/magazine/archive/2020/03/witchcraft-juliet-diaz/605518/.

Bussanich, John. "The Roots of Platonism and Vedānta: Comments on Thomas McEvilley." *International Journal of Hindu Studies* 9.1–3 (2005): 1–20.

Butler, E. M. *Ritual Magic*. Cambridge: Cambridge University Press, 1949.

Butler, Edward P. "Flower of Fire: Hekate in the *Chaldean Oracles*." Pages 140–57 in *Bearing Torches: A Devotional Anthology for Hekate*. Edited by Sannion et al. Eugene, OR: Biblioteca Alexandrina, 2009.

Campbell, Joseph. *Hero with a Thousand Faces*. Princeton: Princeton University Press, 1949.

Carabine, Deirdre. *John Eriugena Scotus*. Oxford: Oxford University Press, 2000.

Carod-Artal, F. J. "Psychoactive Plants in Ancient Greece." *Neuroscience and History* 1.1 (2013): 28–38.

Casadesús Bordoy, Francesc. "Dionysian Enthusiasm in Plato." Pages 386–400 in *Redefining Dionysos*. Edited by Alberto Bernabé, Miguel Herrero de Jáuregui, Ana Isabel Jiménez San Cristóbal, and Raquel Martín Hernández. Berlin: de Gruyter, 2013.

Casanova, José. "Religion, the Axial Age, and Secular Modernity in Bellah's 'Theory of Religious Evolution.'" Pages 191–221 in *The Axial Age and Its Consequences*. Edited by Robert N. Bellah and Hans Joas. Cambridge: Harvard University Press, 2012.

Cashford, Jules. trans. *The Homeric Hymns*. New York: Penguin, 2003.

Cavelli-Sforza, Luigi Luca. *The History and Geography of Human Genes*. Princeton: Princeton University Press, 1994.

Celenza, Christopher S. "Pythagoras in the Renaissance: The Case of Marsilio Ficino." *Renaissance Quarterly* 52 (1999).

———. "The Revival of Platonic Philosophy." Pages 72–96 in *The Cambridge Companion to Renaissance Philosophy*. Edited by James Hankins. Cambridge: Cambridge University Press, 2007.

Celsus. *On the True Doctrine*. Translated by R. Joseph Hoffmann. New York: Oxford University Press, 1987.

Chadwick, Henry. "Origen, Celsus and the Resurrection of the Body." *HTR* 41 (1948): 83–102.

———. "Philo and the Beginnings of Christian Thought." Pages 182–92 in *The Cambridge History of Later Greek and Early Medieaval Philosophy*. Edtied by A. H. Armstrong. Cambridge: Cambridge University Press, 1967.

Chaeremon. *Chaeremon: Egyptian Priest and Stoic Philosopher; The Fragments Collected and Translated with Explanatory Notes; Reprint with a Preface, Addenda et Corrigenda*. Edited by P. W. van der Horst. Leiden: Brill, 1984.

Chrysanthou, Anthi. *Defining Orphism: The Beliefs, the 'Telestae' and the Writings*. Berlin: de Gruyter, 2020.

Chulev, Basil. *Bronze Volute Wine Kraters from Macedon*. Skopje, Macedonia: Macedon-Hegmon Editions, 2014.

Clark, Elizabeth A. *The Origenist Controversy: The Cultural Construction of an Early Christian Debate*. Princeton: Princeton University Press, 1992.

Clark, Peter. *Zoroastrianism: An Introduction to an Ancient Faith*. Sussex, UK: Sussex Academic Press, 2001.

Clarke, Michael. *Flesh and Spirit in the Songs of Homer: A Study of Words and Myths*. Oxford: Clarendon, 1999.

Clarke, W. Norris. *The Creative Renewal of Saint Thomas Aquinas: Essays in Thomistic Philosophy, New and Old*. New York: Fordham University Press, 2009.

Clay, Jenny Strauss. *The Politics of Olympus: Form and Meaning in the Major Homeric Hymns*. London: Duckworth, 2006.

Clayton, Philip. "Introduction to Panentheism." Pages 371–80 in *Models of God and Alternative Ultimate Realities*. Edited by Jeanine Diller and Asa Kasher. Dordrecht: Springer, 2013.

Clayton, Philip, and Arthur Peacocke, eds. *In Whom We Live and Move and Have Our Being: Panentheistic Reflections on God's Presence in a Scientific World*. Grand Rapids: Eerdmans, 2004.

Cleary, Thomas, trans. *The Secret of the Golden Flower*. New York: HarperOne, 1991.

Clegg, Jerry S. "Plato's Vision of Chaos." *ClQ* 26.1 (1976): 52–61.

Clement. *Stromateis, Books 1–3*. Translated by John Ferguson. The Fathers of the Church: A New Translation 85. Washington, DC: Catholic University of America Press, 1991.

Clymer, R. Swinburne. *Philosophy of Fire*. Quakertown, PA: The Philosophical Publishing Co., 1920; repr., New Orleans: Cornerstone, 2016.

Coakley, Sarah, and Charles M. Stang, eds. *Rethinking Dionysius the Areopagite*. Oxford: Wiley-Blackwell, 2009.

Cocke, B. P. "Panentheism and Classical Theism." *Sophia* 52 (2013): 52–75.

Cohen, Norman. *The Pursuit of the Millennium: Revolutionary Messianism in Medieval and Reformation Europe and Its Bearings on Modern Totalitarian Movements*. New York: Pimlico, 1993.

Collins, John J. *The Apocalyptic Imagination: An Introduction to Jewish Apocalyptic Literature*. 2nd ed. Grand Rapids: Eerdmans, 1998.

———. *Between Athens and Jerusalem: Jewish Identity in the Hellenistic Diaspora*. Grand Rapids: Eerdmans, 1999.

Compton, Todd M. *Victim of the Muses: Poet as Scapegoat, Warrior and Hero in Greco-Roman and Indo-European Myth and History*. Washington, DC: Center for Hellenic Studies, 2006.

Congar, Yves. *I Believe in the Holy Spirit*. New York: Seabury, 1983.

Conwell, E. B., and A. E. Gough. *The Sarva-Darsana-Samgraha: Review of the Different Systems of Hindu Philosophy*. London: Taylor & Francis, 2001.
Conze, Edward. "Buddhism and Gnosis." Pages 651–67 in *The Origins of Gnosticism: Colloquium of Messina, 13–18 April 1966*. Edited by Ugo Bianchi. Leiden: Brill, 1967.
———. "Buddhist Prajna and Greek Sophia." *Religion* 5.2 (1975): 160–67.
Coogan, Michael D., and Mark S. Smith, trans. and eds. *Stories from Ancient Canaan*. 2nd ed. Louisville: Westminster John Knox, 2012.
Cook, A. B. *Zeus: A Study in Ancient Religion*. 3 vols. Cambridge: Cambridge University Press, 1914–1940.
Cooper, John W. *Panentheism: The Other God of the Philosophers from Plato to the Present*. Grand Rapids: Baker Academic, 2006.
Copenhaver, Brian P. *Hermetica: The Greek Corpus Hermeticum and the Latin Asclepius in a New English Translation with Notes and Introduction*. Cambridge: Cambridge University Press, 1992.
Copenhaver, Brian P., and C. Schmitt. *Renaissance Philosophy*. Oxford: Oxford University Press, 1992.
Copleston, Frederick. *A History of Philosophy*. Garden City, NJ: Doubleday, 1993.
———. *Religion and the One: Philosophies East and West*. London: Continuum, 1982.
Corbin, Henry. *Alone with the Alone: Creative Imagination in the Sufism of Ibn 'Arabi*. Princeton: Princeton University Press, 1998.
———. *Cyclical Time and Ismaili Gnosis*. London: Routledge, 2013.
Cordovero, Moses. *Introduction to Kabbalah: An Annotated Version of His "Or Ne'erav."* Translated by Ira Robinson. New York: Yeshiva University Press, 1994.
Cornford, F. M. *Greek Religious Thought from Homer to the Age of Alexander*. London: Dent & Sons, 1923.
———. "Pattern of Ionian Cosmology." Pages 21–31 in *Theories of the Universe from Babylonian Myth to Modern Science*. Edited by Milton K. Munitz. New York: Free Press, 1957.
———. *Plato and Parmenides*. London: Routledge, 1939.
———. *Plato's Cosmology: The "Timaeus" of Plato*. Indianapolis: Hackett, 1997.
———. *Plato's Theory of Knowledge*. Chelmsford, UK: Courier, 2013.
Corrigan, Kevin. "Body and Soul in Ancient Religious Experience." Pages 360–83 in *Classical Mediterranean Spirituality: Egyptian, Greek, Roman*. Edited by A. H. Armstrong. New York: Crossroad, 1986.
Costen, Michael D. *The Cathars and the Albigensian Crusade*. Manchester: Manchester University Press, 1997.
Coxon, A. H. *The Fragments of Parmenides: A Critical Text with Introduction, Translation, the Ancient Testimonia and a Commentary*. Translated by Richard McKirahan. Rev. ed. Las Vegas: Parmenides, 2009.

Creighton, J. *Coins and Power in Late Iron Age Britain*. Cambridge: Cambridge University Press, 2000.

———. "Visions of Power: Imagery and Symbols in Late Iron Age Britain." *Brittania* 26 (1995): 285–301.

Crouzel, Henri. *Origen: The Life and Thought of the First Great Theologian*. Translated by A. S. Worrall. San Francisco: Harper & Row, 1989.

Csikszentmihalyi, Mihaly. *Flow: Studies of Enjoyment*. Chicago: University of Chicago Press, 1974.

Curd, Patricia. *The Legacy of Parmenides: Eleaetic Monism and Later Presocratic Thought*. Princeton: Princeton University Press, 1998.

Curd, Patricia, and Daniel W. Graham, eds. *The Oxford Handbook of Presocratic Philosophy*. Oxford: Oxford University Press, 2008.

Czigany, L. G. "The Use of Hallucinogens and the Shamanistic Tradition of the Finno-Ugrian People." *The Slavonic and East European Review* 58.2 (1980): 212–17.

Dalferth, Ingolf U. "The Idea of Transcendence." Pages 146–88 in *The Axial Age and Its Consequences*. Edited by Robert N. Bellah and Hans Joas. Cambridge: Harvard University Press, 2012.

Dalley, Stephanie, trans. *Myths from Mesopotamia: Creation, the Flood, Gilgamesh, and Others; A New Translation*. Oxford: Oxford University Press, 2008.

Damascius. *The Philosophical History*. Edited and translated by Polymnia Athanassiadi. Athens: Apamea Cultural Association, 1999.

Daniélou, Alain. *Gods of Love and Ecstasy: The Traditions of Shiva and Dionysus*. Rochester, VT: Inner Traditions, 1992.

Danièlou, Jean. *Gospel Message and Hellenistic Culture*. Translated by J. A. Baker. Philadelphia: Westminster, 1973.

David, Mark Evan. "'The Evangelical Prophecies over Jerusalem Have Been Fulfilled': Joachim of Fiore, the Jews, Fray Diego de Landa and the Mayans." *Journal of Medieval Iberian Studies* 5.1 (2013): 86–103.

Davies, Oliver. "Revelation and the Politics of Culture: A Critical Assessment of the Theology of John Milbank." Pages 112–25 in *Radical Orthodoxy: A Catholic Enquiry*. Edited by Laurence Paul Hemming. Aldershot, UK: Ashgate, 2009.

Davis-Kimball, Jeannine, Vladimir A. Bashilov, and Leonid T. Yablonsky. *Nomads of the Eurasian Steppes in the Early Iron Age*. Berkeley, CA: Zinat, 1995.

Dawson, David. "Allegorical Reading and the Embodiment of the Soul in Origen." Pages 26–43 in *Christian Origins: Theology, Rhetoric and Community*. Edited by Lewis Ayres and Gareth Jones. London: Routledge, 1998.

Day, John. *Yahweh and the Gods and Goddesses of Canaan*. Sheffield: Sheffield Academic Press, 2000.

Debiasi, Andrea. "The *Alcmeonis* between the Theban and the Trojan Cycles." Pages 261–80 in *The Greek Epic Cycle and Its Ancient Reception: A Companion*. Edited by Marco Fantuzzi and Christos Tsagelis. Cambridge: Cambridge University Press, 2015.

Demetrius. *On Style*. Translated by W. Rhys Roberts. Cambridge: Cambridge University Press, 1902.

Denzey Lewis, Nicola. *Introduction to "Gnosticism": Ancient Voices, Christian Worlds*. Oxford: Oxford University Press, 2013.

Derrida, Jacques. *L'écriture et la Différence*. Paris: Editions de Seuil, 1979.

———. *Writing and Difference*. Translated by Alan Bass. Chicago: University of Chicago Press, 1978.

Desmond, William D. *Cynics*. Berkeley: University of California Press, 2008.

Des Places, Édouard. *Études platoniciennes, 1929–1979*. Leiden: Brill, 2015.

Detienne, Marcel. "Forgetting Delphi between Apollo and Dionysus." *CP* 96.2 (2001): 147–58.

Deusson, Paul, and Alfred Shenington Geden. *The Philosophy of the Upanishads*. Edinburgh: T&T Clark, 1906.

Deutsch, Nathaniel. "Dangerous Ascents: Rabbi Akiba's Water Warning and Late Antique Cosmological Traditions." *Journal of Jewish Thought and Philosophy* 8 (1988): 1–12.

Dhalla, Maneckji Nusservanji. *Zoroastrian Theology: From the Earliest Times to the Present Day*. New York: Columbia Press, 1941; repr., London: Forgotten Books, 2018.

d'Hoine, Pieter, and Marije Martijn, eds. *All from One: A Guide to Proclus*. Oxford: Oxford University Press, 2017.

Diels, H., and W. Kranz. *Die Fragmente der Vorsokratiker*. 6th ed. Berlin: Weidmann, 1951–1952.

Digeser, Elizabeth DePalma. *A Threat to Public Piety: Christians, Platonists, and the Great Persecution*. Ithaca, NY: Cornell University Press, 2012.

Diller, Jeanine, and Asa Kasher, eds. *Models of God and Alternative Ultimate Realities*. Dordrecht: Springer, 2013.

Dillon, John. *The Heirs of Plato: A Study of the Old Academy, 347–274 BC*. Oxford: Oxford University Press, 2003.

———. *The Middle Platonists: 80 B.C. to A.D. 220*. Ithaca, NY: Cornell University Press, 1996.

———. *Morality and Culture in Ancient Greece*. Bloomington: Indiana University Press, 2004.

———. "Plutarch and Second-Century Platonism." Pages 214–29 in *Classical Mediterranean Spirituality: Egyptian, Greek, Roman*. Edited by A. H. Armstrong. New York: Crossroad, 1986.

Diodorus Siculus. *On Egypt. Book 1 of Diodorus Siculus' Historical Library*. Translated by Edwin Murphy. Jefferson, NC: McFarland, 1985.

Diogenes Laertius. *Lives of Eminent Philosophers*. Translated by R. D. Hicks. 2 vols. LCL. Cambridge: Harvard University Press, 1925.

Dionysius the Areopagite. *Corpus Dionysiacum I: Pseudo-Dionysius Areopagita*. Edited by B. R. Suchla. Berlin: de Gruyter, 1990.

———. *Corpus Dionysiacum II: Pseudo-Dionysius Areopagita*. Edited by G. Heil and A. M. Ritter. Berlin: de Gruyter, 1991.

———. *Dionysius the Areopagite: On the Divine Names and the Mystical Theology*. Translated by C. E. Rolt. New York. Macmillan, 1920.

———. *Dionysius the Areopagite, Works*. Translated by John Parker. London: Parker, 1897.

———. *Pseudo-Dionysius: The Complete Works*. Translated by Colm Luibheid. Mahwah, NJ: Paulist, 1987.

———. *Pseudo-Dionysius: The Divine Names, The Mystical Theology, Translated from the Greek with an Introductory Study*. Translated by John D. Jones. Milwaukee: Marquette University Press, 2011.

Dobbin, Robert, trans. *The Cynic Philosophers from Diogenes to Julian*. New York: Penguin Classics, 2013.

Dobredojde Macedonia Welcome Centre. "The Maenad of Tetovo." *Dobredojde Macedonia Welcome Centre Magazine*. September 2014. http://www.dmwc.org.mk/wp-content/uploads/2017/01/The_Maenad_of_Tetovo.pdf.

Dodd, C. H. *The Bible and the Greeks*. London: Hodder & Stoughton, 1935.

Dodds, E. R. *The Greeks and the Irrational*. Berkeley: University of California Press, 1951.

———. *Pagan and Christian in an Age of Anxiety*. New York: Norton, 1965.

Domaradzki, Mikolaj. "Of Nymphs and Sea: Numenius on Souls and Matter in Homer's *Odyssey*." *Greece & Rome* 67.2 (2020): 139–50.

Doniger, Wendy. *On Hinduism*. Oxford: Oxford University Press, 2014.

———. *Splitting the Difference: Genders and Myth in Ancient Greece and India*. Chicago: Chicago University Press, 1999.

Dörrie, Heinrich. *Platonica Minora*. Munich: Fink, 1976.

Drews, Robert. *The End of the Bronze Age: Changes in Warfare and the Catastrophe ca. 1200 B.C.* Princeton: Princeton University Press, 1993.

Drugaş, Şerban G. P. "The Name of Zalmoxis and Its Significance in the Dacian Language and Religion." *Hiperboreea* 3.2 (2016): 5–66

Dunand, Francois, and Christiane Zivie-Coche. *Gods and Men in Egypt: 3000 BCE to 395 CE*. Ithaca, NY: Cornell University Press, 2004.

Dunderberg, Ismo. *Beyond Gnosticism: Myth, Lifestyle, and Society in the School of Valentinus*. New York: Columbia University Press, 2008.

Duplouy, Alain. *Construire la Cité: Essai de sociologie historique sur les communautés de l'archaïsme grec*. Paris: Les Belles Lettres, 2019.

———. "Epimenides the Cretan: A History of Athens (6th–5th c. BC)." *CHS Research Bulletin* 7 (2019). http://nrs.harvard.edu/urn-3:hlnc.essay:DuplouyA.Epimenides_the_Cretan.2019.

Ebeling, Florian. *The Secret History of Hermes Trismegistus: Hermeticism from Ancient to Modern Times*. Translated by David Lorton. Ithaca, NY: Cornell University Press, 2007.

Edelstein, L., and I. G. Kidd. *Posidonius*. Vol. 1: *The Fragments*. Cambridge: Cambridge University Press, 2005.

Edmonds, Radcliffe G., III. "Dionysos in Egypt? Epaphian Dionysos in the Orphic Hymns." Pages 415–32 in *Redefining Dionysos*. Edited by Alberto Bernabé, Miguel Herrero de Jáuregui, Ana Isabel Jiménez San Cristóbal, and Raquel Martín Hernández. Berlin: de Gruyter, 2013.

———. *Redefining Ancient Orphism: A Study in Greek Religion*. Cambridge: Cambridge University Press, 2013.

———. "Tearing Apart the Zagreus Myth: A Few Disparaging Remarks on Orphism and Original Sin." *ClAnt* 18.1 (1999): 35–73.

Edwards, Mark, ed. *Neoplatonic Saints: The Lives of Plotinus and Proclus by Their Students*. Liverpool: Liverpool University Press, 2000.

———. "One Origen or Two? The Status Quaestionis." *Symbolae Osloenses* 89 (2015): 81–103.

———. "Origen's Two Resurrections." *JTS* 46.2 (1995): 502–18.

Ehrman, Bart D. *Lost Scriptures: Books That Did Not Make It into the New Testament*. Oxford: Oxford University Press, 2003.

Eliade, Mircea. *The Forge and the Crucible: The Origins and Structures of Alchemy*. 2nd ed. Chicago: University of Chicago Press, 1978.

———. *Myth and Reality*. New York: Harper & Row, 1963.

———. *Myth of Eternal Return: Cosmos and History*. Translated by W. R. Trask. Princeton: Princeton University Press, 1971.

———. *Sacred and Profane: The Nature of Religion*. New York: Harper Torchbooks, 1959.

———. *Shamanism: Archaic Techniques of Ecstasy*. Princeton: Princeton University Press, 1964.

———. *Zalmoxis: The Vanishing God*. Chicago: University of Chicago Press, 1972.

Eliade, Mircea, and Willard R. Trask. "Zalmoxis." *HR* 11.3 (1972): 257–302.

Emerson, Ralph Waldo. *Journals and Miscellaneous Notes, 1841–1843*. Edited by William H. Gilman. Cambridge: Harvard University Press, 1960.

Erlandson, Sven. *Spiritual but Not Religious: A Call to Religious Revolution in America*. Bloomington: iUniverse, 2000.

Euripides. *The Bacchae, Iphigenia in Aulis, The Cyclops, Rhesus*. Edited by David Greene and Richmond Lattimore. 3rd ed. Chicago: University of Chicago Press, 2013.

Works Cited

Evangeliou, Christos. "Plotinus's Anti-Gnostic Polemic and Porphyry's *Against the Christians*." Pages 111–28 in *Neoplatonism and Gnosticism*. Edited by Richard T. Wallis. Albany: SUNY Press, 1992.

Farrow, Douglas. *Ascension and Ecclesia*. Grand Rapids: Eerdmans, 2009.

———. *Ascension Theology*. London: Bloomsbury, 2011.

Feldman, Michal, et al. "Ancient DNA Sheds Light on the Genetic Origins of Early Iron Age Philistines." *Science Advances* 5.7 (2019): 1–10.

Fernández, Antoni Bordoy. "Proclus and the Role of Orphism." Pages 123–48 in *Greek Philosophy and the Mystery Cults*. Edited by María José Martín-Velasco and María José García Blanco. Newcastle upon Tyne: Cambridge Scholars Press, 2016.

Feuchtwang, Stephan. "Chinese Religions." Pages 143–72 in *Religions in the Modern World*. Edited by Linda Woodhead, Christopher Partridge, and Hiroko Kawanami. 3rd ed. London: Routledge, 2016.

———. *Religions in the Modern World: Traditions and Transformations*. 3rd ed. London: Routledge, 2016.

Ficino, Marsilio. *Philebus Commentary*. Edited by M. J. B. Allen. Berkeley: University of California Press, 1975.

Filoramo, Giovanni. *A History of Gnosticism*. Translated by Anthony Alcock. Oxford: Blackwell, 1990.

Findlay, John N. *Ascent to the Absolute*. London: Allen & Unwin, 1970.

———. *The Discipline of the Cave*. London: Allen & Unwin, 1966.

———. *The Transcendence of the Cave*. London: Allen & Unwin, 1967.

Fitch, W. T. "The Biology and Evolution of Music: A Comparative Perspective." *Cognition* 100 (2006): 173–215.

Flood, Gavin D. *An Introduction to Hinduism*. Cambridge: Cambridge University Press, 2018.

Foerster, Werner. *Gnosis: A Selection of Gnostic Texts*. Translated by R. M. Wilson. 2 vols. Oxford: Clarendon, 1972–1974.

Fokin, Alexey R. "The Doctrine of the 'Intelligible Triad' in Neoplatonism and Patristics." StPatr 58 (2013): 45–72.

Fol, Alexander, and Ivan Marazov. *Thrace and the Thracians*. New York: St. Martin's, 1977.

Foley, Helen P., ed. *The Homeric Hymn to Demeter: Translation, Commentary, and Interpretive Essays*. Princeton: Princeton University Press, 1994.

Fontenrose, Joseph Eddy. *Didyma: Apollo's Oracle, Cult, and Companions*. Berkeley: University of California Press, 1988.

———. *Python: A Study of the Delphic Myth and Its Origins*. Berkeley: University of California Press, 1959.

Forrai, Réka. "The Notes of Anastasius on Eriugena's Translation of the *Corpus Dionysiacum*." *Journal of Medieval Latin* 18 (2008): 74–100.

Fowden, Garth. *The Egyptian Hermes: A Historical Approach to the Late Pagan Mind*. Princeton: Princeton University Press, 1986.

———. "The Pagan Holy Man in Late Antique Society." *JHS* 102 (1982): 33–59.

Fowler, Robert L. *Early Greek Mythography*. Vol. 2. Oxford: Oxford University Press, 2013.

Fox, Robin Lane. *Alexander the Great*. New York: Penguin, 1986.

———. *Traveling Heroes: Greeks and Their Myths in the Epic Age of Homer*. New York: Vintage, 2008.

Fraenkel, Carlos. *Philosophical Religions from Plato to Spinoza: Reason, Religion, and Autonomy*. Cambridge: Cambridge University Press, 2012.

Frankfort, Henri. *Ancient Egyptian Religion: An Interpretation,* London: Dover, 2011.

Freeman, Kathleen. *Ancilla to the Pre-Socratic Philosophers*. Cambridge: Harvard University Press, 1983.

Frothingham, A. L. *Stephen bar Sudaili, The Syrian Mystic and The Book of Hierotheos*. Leiden: Brill, 1886; repr., Eugene, OR: Wipf & Stock, 2010.

Froude, James Anthony. *Thomas Carlyle: A History of the First Forty Years of His Life, 1795–1835*. New York: Harper and Brothers, 1882.

Fuller, B. A. G. *The Problem of Evil in Plotinus*. Cambridge: Cambridge University Press, 1912.

Gadamer, Hans-Georg. *The Beginning of Philosophy*. Translated by Rod Coltman. London: Continuum, 2000.

———. "Heraclitus Studies." Pages 202–42 in *The Presocratics after Heidegger*. Edited by David C. Jacobs. Albany: SUNY Press, 1999.

———. *Truth and Method*. Translated by J. Wiensheimer and D. G. Marshall. 2nd ed. London: Bloomsbury, 2013.

Gandillac, Maurice de. "Neoplatonism and Christian Thought in the Fifteenth Century." Pages 143–68 in *Neoplatonism and Christian Thought*. Edited by Dominic J. O'Meara. Albany: State University of New York Press, 1982.

Gantz, Timothy. *Early Greek Myth*. Baltimore: Johns Hopkins University Press, 1996.

Garaudy, Roger. "Faith and Revolution." *Ecumenical Review* 25 (1973): 66.

Garcy, Jésus de. "Mystery Religions and Philosophy in Proclus." Pages 149–70 in *Greek Philosophy and the Mystery Cults*. Edited by María José Martín-Velasco and María José García Blanco. Newcastle upon Tyne: Cambridge Scholars Press, 2016.

The Gathas: The Sublime Book of Zarathustra. Translated by Parvis Koupai. Nivelles, Belgium: European Centre for Zoroastrian Studies, 2007.

Gathercole, Simon. *The Gospel of Judas: Rewriting Early Christianity*. Oxford: Oxford University Press, 2007.

Gennep, Arnold van. *The Rites of Passage.* Chicago: University of Chicago Press, 1961.

Gerson, Lloyd. "Goodness, Unity, and Creation in the Platonic Tradition." Pages 29–42 in *The Ultimate Why Question: Why Is There Anything at All Rather Than Nothing Whatsoever?* Edited by John F. Wippel. Washington, DC: Catholic University of America Press, 2012.

———. Review of *Dieu sans la puissance*, by Gwenaëlle Aubry. *Bryn Mawr Classical Review* (January 2008). https://bmcr.brynmawr.edu/2008/2008.01.28/.

Gier, Nicholas. *Spiritual Titanism: Indian, Chinese, and Western Perspectives.* Albany: SUNY Press, 2000.

Gilson, Étienne. *God and Philosophy.* New Haven: Yale University Press, 1941.

Ginzburg, Carlo. *Threads and Traces: True False Fictive.* Translated by Anne C. Tedeschi and John Tedeschi. Berkeley: University of California Press, 2012.

Girardot, J. Norman. *Myth and Meaning in Early Taoism: The Theme of Chaos (Hun-Tun).* Berkeley: University of California Press, 1983.

Glück, Louise. *Averno.* New York: Farrar, Straus & Giroux, 2006.

Godwin, William. *Lives of the Necromancers.* London: Frederick J. Mason, 1834.

Goldhill, Simon. "The Great Dionysia and Civic Ideology." Pages 97–129 in *Nothing to Do with Dionysos? Athenian Drama in Its Social Context.* Edited by John J. Winkler and Froma I. Zeitlin. Princeton: Princeton University Press, 1990.

Golitzin, Alexander. "Dionysius Areopagita: A Christian Mysticism?" *ProEccl* 12.2 (2003): 161–212.

———. *Et Introibo ad Altare Dei: The Mystagogy of Dionysius Areopagita, with Special Reference to Its Predecessors in the Eastern Christian Tradition.* Thessalonica: Patriarchal Institute of Patristic Studies, 1994.

———. "Hierarchy or Anarchy? Dionysius Areopagita, Symeon the New Theologian, Nicetas Stethatos and Their Common Roots in Ascetic Tradition." *SVTQ* 38.2 (1994): 131–79.

———. *Mystagogy: A Monastic Reading of Dionysius Areopagita.* Edited by Bogdan G. Bucur. Collegeville, MN: Liturgical Press, 2013.

———. "On the Other Hand: A Response to Fr Paul Wesche's Recent Article on Dionysius in *St Vladimir's Theological Quarterly*, Vol. 33, No. 1." *SVTQ* 34 (1990): 305–23.

Gombrich, Richard. *What the Buddha Thought.* Sheffield: Equinox, 2012.

Gonda, Jan. "The Śatarudriya." Pages 75–92 in *Sanskrit and Indian Studies: Essays in Honour of Daniel H. H. Ingalls.* Edited by M. Nagatomi, B. K. Matilal, J. M. Masson, and E. C. Dimock Jr. Dordrecht: Reidel, 1980.

González-Reimann, Luis. "Cosmic Cycles, Cosmology, and Cosmography" Pages 1:411–28 in *Brill's Encyclopedia of Hinduism.* Edited by Knut A. Jacobsen et al. Leiden: Brill, 2009.

Gough, A. E. *The Philosophy of the Upanishads and Ancient Indian Metaphysics*. London: Routledge, 1975.

Gould, Paul M. *Beyond the Control of God? Six Views on the Problem of God and Abstract Objects*. London: Bloomsbury, 2014.

Graf, Fritz. "The Bridge and the Ladder." Pages 19–33 in *Heavenly Realms and Earthly Realities in Late Antique Religions*. Edited by Ra'anan S. Boustan and Anette Yoshiko Reed. Cambridge: Cambridge University Press, 2004.

———. "Dionysian and Orphic Eschatology: New Texts and Old Questions." Pages 239–58 in *Masks of Dionysus*. Edited by Thomas Carpenter and Christopher Faraone. Ithaca, NY: Cornell University Press, 1993.

———. *Magic in the Ancient World*. Cambridge: Cambridge University Press, 1997.

Graf, Fritz, and Sarah Iles Johnston. *Ritual Texts for the Afterlife: Orpheus and the Bacchic Gold Tablets*. London: Routledge, 2007.

Graham, Daniel. *Explaining the Cosmos: The Ionian Tradition of Scientific Philosophy*. Princeton: Princeton University Press, 2006.

Graham-Leigh, Elaine. *The Southern French Nobility and the Albigensian Crusade*. Suffolk: Boydell & Brewer, 2005.

Granger, Herbert. "The Theologian Pherekydes of Syros and the Early Days of Natural Philosophy." *HSCP* 103 (2007): 135–63.

Grant, Michael. *The Ancient Mediterranean*. New York: Scribner's Sons, 1969.

Grant, Robert M. *Gnosticism and Early Christianity*. New York: Columbia University Press, 1959.

Graves, Robert. *Greek Gods and Heroes*. New York: Rosetta, 2014.

———. *The Greek Myths*. Harmondsworth: Penguin, 1964.

Graziosi, Barbara. *Inventing Homer: The Early Reception of Epic*. Cambridge: Cambridge University Press, 2007.

Greenbaum, Dorlan Gieseler. *The Daimon in Hellenistic Astrology: Origins and Influence*. Leiden: Brill, 2015.

Greer, Rowan A., ed. *Origen: An Exhortation to Martyrdom, Prayer, and Selected Works*. Mahwah, NJ: Paulist, 1979.

Grene, David, and Richmond Lattimore, eds. *The Complete Greek Tragedies*. 2nd ed. 9 vols. Chicago: University of Chicago Press, 1960.

Griffin, David Ray. *Panentheism and Scientific Naturalism: Rethinking Evil, Morality, Religious Experience, Religious Pluralism, and the Academic Study of Religion*. Claremont, CA: Process Century, 2014.

———. "Process Thought and Natural Theology." Pages 453–71 in *The Oxford Handbook of Religion and Science*. Edited by Philip Clayton and Zachary Simpson. Oxford: Oxford University Press, 2006.

Griffith, Sidney Harrison. *The Church in the Shadow of the Mosque: Christians and Muslims in the World of Islam.* Princeton: Princeton University Press, 2008.

Griffiths, Alan H. "Abaris." In *The Oxford Classical Dictionary.* Edited by Simon Hornblower and Anthony Spawforth. 3rd ed. Oxford: Oxford University Press, 2003.

Griffiths, J. Gwyn. "Allegory in Greece and Egypt." *Journal of Egyptian Archaeology* 53 (December 1967): 79–102.

———. "The Great Egyptian Cults of Oecumenical Spiritual Significance." Pages 39–65 in *Classical Mediterranean Spirituality: Egyptian, Greek, Roman.* Edited by A. H. Armstrong. New York: Crossroad, 1986.

Grigg, Robert. "Aniconic Worship in the Apostolic Tradition: A Note on Canon 36 of the Council of Elvira." *Church History* 45 (1976): 428–33.

Griswold, H. D., and Hervey De Witt. *The Religion of the Rigveda.* Delhi: Banarsidass, 1971.

Guran, Petre. "Eschatology and Political Theology in the Last Centuries of Byzantium." *Revue des études Sud-est européeanes* 45 (2007): 73–87.

Guthrie, Kenneth Sylvan. *Numenius of Apamea: The Father of Neo-Platonism. Works, Biography, Message, Sources, and Influence.* London: George Bell & Sons, 1917.

———, trans. *The Pythagorean Sourcebook and Library.* Grand Rapids: Phanes, 1988.

Guthrie, W. K. C. *A History of Greek Philosophy.* 6 vols. Cambridge: Cambridge University Press, 1962–1981.

———. *Orpheus and Greek Religion: A Study of the Orphic Movement.* Princeton: Princeton University Press, 1993.

Haage, Bernhard Dietrich. *Alchemie in Mittelalter: Ideen und Bilder von Zosimos bis Paracelsus.* Darmstadt: Artemis & Winkler, 2000.

Hadot, Pierre I. "Être, vie, pensée chez Plotin et avant Plotin." Pages 107–57 in *Les sources de Plotin.* Edited by E. R. Dodds et al. Geneva: Fondation Hardt, 1960.

———. "The Spiritual Guide." Pages 436–59 in *Classical Mediterranean Spirituality: Egyptian, Greek, Roman.* Edited by A. H. Armstrong. New York: Crossroad, 1986.

Halfwassen, Jens. "Monism and Dualism in Plato's Doctrine of Principles." Pages 143–59 in *The Other Plato: The Tübingen Interpretation of Plato's Inner-Academic Teachings.* Edited by Dmitri Nikulin. Albany: SUNY Press, 2012.

———. "Speusipp und die metaphysische Deutung von Platons 'Parmenides.'" Pages 330–73 in *HEN KAI PLETHOS / Einheit und Vielheit: Festschrift für Karl Bormann zum 65. Geburtstag.* Edited by Ludwig Hagemann and Reinhold Glei. Echter: Oros, 1993.

Haller, John S., Jr. *The History of New Thought: From Mind Cure to Positive Thinking and the Prosperity Gospel.* West Chester, PA: Swedenborg Foundation, 2012.

Hamerton-Kelly, Robert G. "Some Techniques of Composition in Philo's Allegorical Commentary with Special Reference to *De Agricultura*—a Study in the Hellenistic Midrash." Pages 45–56 in *Jews, Greeks and Christians: Religious Cultures* in *Late Antiquity; Essays in Honor of William David Davies.* Edited by Robert G. Hamerton-Kelly and Robin Jerome Scroggs. Leiden: Brill, 1976.

Hames, Harvey J. "From Calabria Cometh the Law, and the Word of the Lord from Sicily: The Holy Land in the Thought of Joachim of Fiore and Abraham Abulafia." *Mediterranean Historical Review* 20.2 (2005): 187–99.

Hancock, Curtis L. "Negative Theology in Gnosticism and Neoplatonism." Pages 167–86 in *Neoplatonism and Gnosticism.* Edited by Richard T. Wallis. Albany: SUNY Press, 1992.

Hanegraaff, Wouter J. *Esotericism and the Academy: Rejected Knowledge in Western Culture.* Cambridge: Cambridge University Press, 2012.

Hankey, Wayne J. "Denys and the Later Platonic Trails." Pages 496–510 in *The Oxford Handbook of Catholic Theology.* Edited by Lewis Ayres and Medi Ana Volpe. Oxford: Oxford University Press, 2019.

Hankins, J. *Plato in the Italian Renaissance.* 2 vols. Leiden: Brill, 1990.

Hard, Robin. *The Routledge Handbook of Greek Mythology.* London: Routledge, 2004.

Harland, Philip. "Orphic Bone Tablets (V BCE)." *Associations in the Greco-Roman World: An Expanding Collection of Inscriptions, Papyri, and Other Sources in Translation.* October 1, 2020. http://www.philipharland.com/greco-roman-associations/?p=15649.

Harnack, Adolf von. *What Is Christianity?* Translated by T. B. Sanders. Philadelphia: Fortress, 1986.

Harner, M. J., ed. *Hallucinogens and Shamanism.* Oxford: Oxford University Press, 1973.

Harris, Max. *Sacred Folly: A New History of the Feast of Fools.* Ithaca, NY: Cornell University Press, 2014.

Harrison, Jane Ellen. *Prolegomena to the Study of Greek Religion.* Princeton: Princeton University Press, 1922.

Hart, George. *Routledge Dictionary of Egyptian Gods and Goddesses.* London: Routledge, 2019.

Harvey, Paul. "Theatre." Pages 422–24 in *The Oxford Companion to Classical Literature.* Edited by Paul Harvey. Rev. ed. Oxford: Oxford University Press, 1946.

Hathaway, Ronald F. *Hierarchy and the Definition of Order in the Letters of Pseudo-Dionysius: A Study in the Form and Meaning of the Pseudo-Dionysian Writings.* The Hague: Nijhoff, 1969.

Haubst, Rudolf. *Nikolaus von Kues: "Pförtner der neuen Zeit."* Trier, Germany: Paulinus, 1988.

Head, Thomas, and Richard Landes, eds. *The Peace of God: Social Violence and Religious Response in France around the Year 1000.* Ithaca, NY: Cornell University Press, 1992.

Heelas, Paul, and Linda Woodhead. *The Spiritual Revolution: Why Religion Is Giving Way to Spirituality.* Malden, MA: Blackwell, 2005.

Hegel, G. W. F. *Plato and the Platonists*. Vol. 2 of *Lectures on the History of Philosophy*. Translated by E. S. Haldane and Francis H. Simson. London: Routledge & Kegan Paul, 1894.

Heidel, Alexander. *The Gilgamesh Epic and Its Old Testament Parallels*. Chicago: University of Chicago Press, 1963.

Heider, G. C. "Molech." Pages 581–85 in *Dictionary of Deities and Demons in the Bible*. Edited by Karel van der Toorn, Bob Becking, and Pieter van de Horst. 2nd ed. Grand Rapids: Eerdmans, 1999.

Helleman, Wendy Elgersma. "Plotinus and Magic." *International Journal of the Platonic Tradition* 4.2 (2010): 114–46.

Heraclitus. *Fragments: A Text and Translation with a Commentary*. Translated by T. M. Robinson. Toronto: University of Toronto Press, 1987.

Herodotus. *The Histories*. Translated by Aubrey de Sélincourt. London: Penguin, 2003.

Hesiod. *Theogony*. Translated by M. L. West. Oxford: Clarendon, 1966.

———. *Theogony and Works and Days*. Translated by M. L. West. Oxford: Oxford University Press, 1988.

Hill, Charles E. *Regnum Caelorum: Patterns of Millennial Thought in Early Christianity*. 2nd ed. Grand Rapids: Eerdmans, 2001.

Himmelfarb, Martha. "Revelation and Rapture: The Transformation of the Visionary in the Ascent Apocalypses." https://www.marquette.edu/maqom/himmelfarbrev.pdf. Accessed May 10, 2023.

Hladký, Vojtěch. *The Philosophy of Gemistos Plethon: Platonism in Late Byzantium, between Hellenism and Orthodoxy*. Farnham, UK: Routledge, 2014.

Hoffmann, R. Joseph. *Porphyry's "Against the Christians": The Literary Remains*. New York: Prometheus, 1994.

Homer. *The Iliad*. Translated by Robert Fagles. New York: Penguin, 1998.

———. *The Odyssey*. Translated by Robert Fitzgerald. New York: Farrar, Straus & Giroux, 1998.

"Homeric Hymns." In *The Concise Oxford Companion to Classical Literature*. Edited by M. C. Howatson and Ian Chilvers. Oxford: Oxford University Press, 1996.

Hoppál, Mihály. "Eco-Animism of Siberian Shamanhood." Pages 17–26 in *Shamans and Traditions*. Budapest: Akadémiai Kiadó, 2007.

———. *Sámánok Eurázsiában*. Budapest: Akadémiai Kiadó, 2004.

Hornung, Erik. *Conceptions of God in Ancient Egypt: The One and the Many*. Ithaca, NY: Cornell University Press, 1996.

Horst, P. W. van der. *Chaeremon: Egyptian Priest and Stoic Philosopher*. Leiden: Brill, 1987.

Hunter, R. *The Hesiodic Catalogue of Women: Constructions and Reconstructions*. Cambridge: Cambridge University Press, 2005.

Hurst, P. T. *Flesh of the Gods: The Ritual Uses of Hallucinogens*. London: Allen & Unwin, 1972.
Hutton, Ronald. *Shamans: Siberian Spirituality and the Western Imagination*. London: Bloomsbury, 2007.
———. *The Triumph of the Moon: A History of Modern Pagan Witchcraft*. Oxford: Oxford University Press, 2001.
Huxley, Aldous. *The Perennial Philosophy*. New York: Harper & Bros., 1945.
Iamblichus. *Iamblichi Chalcidensis in Platonis dialogos commentariorum fragmenta*. Edited by John Dillon. Leiden: Brill, 1973.
———. *On the Mysteries*. Translated by Emma C. Clarke, John M. Dillon, and Jackson P. Hershbell. Atlanta: Society of Biblical Literature, 2003.
———. *On the Mysteries of the Egyptians, Chaldeans, and Assyrians*. Translated by Thomas Taylor. Chiswick, UK: Whittingham, 1821.
Indich, William. *Consciousness in Advaita Vedanta*. London: Banarsidass, 2000.
Inglehart, Ronald, and Christian Welzel. *Modernization, Cultural Change and Democracy: The Human Development Sequence*. Cambridge: Cambridge University Press, 2005.
Inwood, Brad, and Lloyd P. Gerson, trans. *The Stoics Reader: Select Writings and Testimonia*. Indianapolis: Hackett, 2008.
Irani, D. J., and Rabindranath Tagore. *The Divine Songs of Zarathushtra*. New York: Macmillan, 1924.
Jaeger, Werner. "The Greek Concept of Immortality." In *Immortality and Resurrection: Death in the Western World; Two Conflicting Currents of Thought*. Edited by Krister Stendahl. New York: Macmillan, 1965.
———. *Theology of the Early Greek Philosophers*. Oxford: Clarendon, 1947.
Jamison, Stephanie W., and Joel P. Brereton. *The Rigveda: Earliest Religious Poetry of India*. Oxford: Oxford University Press, 2015.
Janko, Richard. "The Derveni Papyrus." *ZPE* 141 (2002): 93–128.
———. "The Derveni Papyrus: An Interim Text." *ZPE* 141 (2002): 1–62.
———. "The Derveni Papyrus (Diagoras of Melos, *Apopyrgizontes Logoi*?): A New Translation." *CP* 96 (2001): 1–32.
———. *Homer, Hesiod and the Hymns: Diachronic Development in Epic Diction*. Cambridge: Cambridge University Press, 1982.
———. "The Physicist as Hierophant: Aristophanes, Socrates, and the Authorship of the Derveni Papyrus." *ZPE* 118 (1997): 61–94.
———. "Reconstructing (Again) the Opening of the Derveni Papyrus." *ZPE* 166 (2008): 37–51.
Jansen, W., ed. *Der Kommentar des Clarembaldus von Arras zu Boethius* De Trinitate. Breslau, 1926.

Jaruszynski, Piotr. *Science in Culture.* Amsterdam: Rodopi, 2007.
Jaspers, Karl. *The Origin and Goal of History.* Translated by Michael Bullock. London: Routledge & Kegan Paul, 1953.
Jáuregui, Miguel Herrero de. "The Construction of Inner Religious Space in Wandering Religion of Classical Greece." *Numen* 62 (2015): 667–97.
Joas, Hans. "The Axial Age Debate as Religious Discourse." Pages 9–29 in *The Axial Age and Its Consequences.* Edited by Robert N. Bellah and Hans Joas. Cambridge: Harvard University Press, 2012.
Johannes Scottus Eriugena. *Iohannis Scotti Annotationes in Marcianum.* Edited by Cora E. Lutz. Cambridge: Medieval Academy of America, 1939.
———. *Periphyseon (The Division of Nature).* Translated by I. P. Sheldon-Williams. Revised by John J. O'Meara. Washington, DC: Dumbarton Oaks, 1987.
———. *Treatise on Divine Predestination.* Translated by Mary Brennan. Notre Dame: University of Notre Dame Press, 2002.
Johnson, Patricia Cannon. "The Neoplatonists and the Mystery Schools of the Mediterranean." Pages 143–61 *The Library of Alexandria: Centre of Learning in the Ancient World.* Edited by Roy MacLeod. London: I. B. Tauris, 2005.
Johnson, Will J. *Harmless Souls: Karmic Bondage and Religious Change in Early Jainism with Special Reference to Umâsvâti and Kundakunda.* Delhi: Banarsidass, 1995.
Johnston, Sarah Iles. "Crossroads." *ZPE* 88 (1991): 217–24.
———. *Hekate Soteira: A Study of Hekate's Roles in the Chaldean Oracles and Related Literature.* Atlanta: Scholars Press, 1990.
Jonas, Hans. *The Gnostic Religion: The Message of the Alien God and the Beginnings of Christianity.* 3rd ed. Boston: Beacon, 2001.
Jones, Ben. *Apocalypse without God: Apocalyptic Thought, Ideal Politics, and the Limits of Utopian Hope.* Cambridge: Cambridge University Press, 2022.
Jones, Frederick Stanley. "The Orphic Cosmo-Theogony in the Pseudo-Clementines." Pages 71–82 in *Les polémiques religieuses du Ier au IVè siècle de notre ère.* Edited by Guillaume Bady and Dianne Curry. Paris: Beauchesne, 2011.
Jones, Tamsin. "Dionysius in Hans Urs von Balthasar and Jean-Luc Marion." Pages 213–24 in *Rethinking Dionysius the Areopagite.* Edited by Sarah Coakley and Charles M. Stang. Oxford: Wiley-Blackwell, 2009.
Jourdan, Fabienne. *Orphée et les chrétiens: La réception du mythe d'Orphée dans la littérature chrétienne grecque des cinq premiers siècles.* 2 vols. Paris: Les Belles Lettres, 2010–2011.
Julian. *The Works of the Emperor Julian.* Edited by W. C. Wright. 3 vols. LCL. Cambridge: Harvard University Press, 1913–1923.
Kalligas, Paul. *The Enneads of Plotinus: A Commentary.* 2 vols. Princeton: Princeton University Press, 2014–2023.

Kampakoglou, Alexandros. "Melampus in Callimachus and Hesiod." *CJ* 113.1 (2017): 1–24.

Katz, Jerry, ed. *One: Essential Writings on Nonduality.* Boulder: Sentient, 2007.

Kellens, Jean, and Éric Pirart. *Les textes vieil-avestiques.* 3 vols. Wiesbaden: Reichert, 1998–1991.

Kenney, John Peter. "Monotheistic and Polytheistic Elements." Pages 269–92 in *Classical Mediterranean Spirituality: Egyptian, Greek, Roman.* Edited by A. H. Armstrong. New York: Crossroad, 1986.

———. "The Platonism of the *Tripartite Tractate* (NH I, 5)." Pages 187–206 in *Neoplatonism and Gnosticism.* Edited by Richard T. Wallis. Albany: SUNY Press, 1992.

Kenny, Anthony. *Ancient Philosophy.* Vol. 1 of *A New History of Western Philosophy.* Oxford: Oxford University Press, 2004.

Kent, Roland G. *Old Persian: Grammar, Texts, Lexicon.* 2nd ed. New Haven: American Oriental Society, 1953.

Kerényi, Carl. *Dionysus: Archetypal Image of the Indestructible Life.* Translated by Ralph Manheim. Princeton: Princeton University Press, 1976.

———. *Eleusis: Archetypal Image of Mother and Daughter.* Princeton: Bollingen, 1967.

Kern, Otto. *Orphicorum fragmenta.* Berlin: Weidmanns, 1922.

Kettler, F. H. "War Origenes Schüler des Ammonius Sakkas?" Pages 327–34 in *Epektasis: Mélanges patristiques offert au Cardinal Jean Daniélou.* Edited by J. Fontaine and C. Kannengiesser. Paris: Beauchesne, 1972.

Kingsley, K. Scarlett, and Richard Parry. "Empedocles." *The Stanford Encyclopedia of Philosophy.* April 7, 2020. https://plato.stanford.edu/entries/empedocles/.

Kingsley, Peter. "An Introduction to the Hermetica: Approaching Ancient Esoteric Tradition." Pages 17–40 in *From Poimandres to Jacob Böhme: Gnosis, Hermeticism and the Christian Tradition.* Edited by Roelof van den Broek and Cis van Heertum. Leiden: Brill, 2000.

Kirk, G. S. *Myth: Its Meaning and Function in Ancient and Other Cultures.* Berkeley: University of California Press, 1970.

Kirk, G. S., J. E. Raven, and M. Schofield. *The Presocratic Philosophers: A Critical History with a Selection of Texts.* 2nd ed. Cambridge: Cambridge University Press, 2003.

Knight, John A. "John Fletcher's Influence on the Development of Wesleyan Theology in America." *Wesleyan Theological Journal* 13 (1978): 13–33.

Knox, Ronald. *Enthusiasm.* Notre Dame: University of Notre Dame Press, 1994.

Koch, H. "Proklus als Quelle des Pseudo-Dionysius Areopagita in der Lehre vom Bösen." *Phil* 54 (1895): 438–54.

Koch-Westenholz, Ulla. *Babylonian Liver Omens: The Chapters Manzazu, Padanu, and Pan Takalti of the Babylonian Extispicy Series Mainly from Assurbanipal's Library.* Chicago: University of Chicago Press, 2000.

Koester, Helmut. *Ancient Christian Gospels*. Harrisburg, PA: Trinity Press International, 1990.

Kołakowski, Leszek. *Chrétiens sans Église: La conscience religieuse et le lien confessionnel au XVIIe siècle*. Translated by Anna Posner. Paris: Gallimard, 1969.

———. *Main Currents of Marxism*. Translated by P. S. Falla. Rev. ed. New York: Norton, 2005.

Kolenkaya-Bostanci, Neyir. "The Evolution of Shamanism Rituals in Early Prehistoric Periods of Europe and Anatolia." *Colloquium Anatolicum* 13 (2014): 185–204.

Köstenberger, Andreas, and Michael Kruger, *The Heresy of Orthodoxy: How Contemporary Culture's Fascination with Diversity Has Reshaped Our Understanding of Early Christianity*. Wheaton, IL: Crossway, 2010.

Kotwick, Mirjam. *Der Papyrus von Derveni: Grieschish-deutsch. Sammlung Tusculum*. Berlin: de Gruyter, 2017.

Krämer Hans Joachim. *Plato and the Foundations of Metaphysics: A Work on the Theory of the Principles and Unwritten Doctrines of Plato with a Collection of the Fundamental Doctrines*. Translated by John R. Catan. Albany: SUNY Press, 1990.

———. "Plato's Unwritten Doctrine." Pages 65–82 in *The Other Plato: The Tübingen Interpretation of Plato's Inner-Academic Teachings*. Edited by Dmitri Nikulin. Albany: SUNY Press, 2012.

Kreyenbroek, Philip G. "Cosmogony and Cosmology in Zoroastrianism and Mithraism." Pages 303–29 in vol. 6, facsimile 3 of *Encyclopedia Iranica*. Edited by E. Yarshater. Leiden: Brill, 1993.

Krisnananda, Swami. *Daily Invocations*. Rishikesh: Divine Life Society, 2015.

Kroll, Paul K. *A Student's Dictionary of Classical and Medieval Chinese*. Rev. ed. Leiden: Brill, 2017.

Kroner, Richard. *Speculation and Revelation in Modern Philosophy*. Philadelphia: Westminster, 1961.

Kuehn, Manfred. "Acosmism." In *The Cambridge Dictionary of Philosophy*. Edited by Robert Audi. 3rd ed. Cambridge: Cambridge University Press, 2015.

Kuhn, Thomas. *The Structure of Scientific Revolutions*. Chicago: University of Chicago Press, 1962.

Lactantius. *The Divine Institutes, Books I–VII*. Translated by Mary F. McDonald. Washington, DC: Catholic University of America Press, 1964.

Laks, André. *The Concept of Presocratic Philosophy: Its Origin, Development, and Significance*. Translated by Glen W. Most. Princeton: Princeton University Press, 2006.

Laks, A., and G. W. Most, eds. *Studies on the Derveni Papyrus*. Oxford: Oxford University Press, 1997.

———, eds. *Western Greek Thinkers, Part 2*. Vol. 5 of *Early Greek Philosophy*. LCL. Cambridge, MA: Harvard University Press, 2016.

Lambert, W. G. "An Address of Marduk to the Demons." *AfO* 17 (1954–1956): 310–21.

Landes, Richard. "Between Aristocracy and Heresy: Popular Participation in the Limousin Peace of God, 994–1033." Pages 184–218 in *The Peace of God: Social Violence and Religious Response in France around the Year 1000*. Edited by Thomas Head and Richard Landes. Ithaca, NY: Cornell University Press, 1992.

Lane, Eugene, ed. *Cybele, Attis, and Related Cults: Essays in Memory of M. J. Vermaseren*. Leiden: Brill, 1996.

Lang, Philippa. *Science: Antiquity and Its Legacy*. London: Bloomsbury, 2015.

Lännström, Anna. "A Religious Revolution? How Socrates Undermined the Practice of Sacrifice." *Ancient Philosophy* 31.2 (2010): 261–74.

Larson, G. J. *Classical Sāṁkhya: An Interpretation of Its History and Meaning*. London: Banarsidass, 1998.

Larson, James G., and Ram Shankar Bhattacharya, eds. *Sāṁkhya: A Dualist Tradition in Indian Philosophy*. Princeton: Princeton University Press, 1987.

Latura, George. "Plato's Visible God: The Cosmic Soul Reflected in the Heavens." *Religions* 3 (2012): 880–86.

Lebedev, Andrei V. "The Theogony of Epimenides of Crete and the Origin of the Orphic-Pythagorean Doctrine of Reincarnation." [In Russian] Pages 550–84 in *Indo-European Linguistics and Classical Philology XIX: Proceedings of the 19th Conference in Memory of Professor Joseph M. Tronsky*. Edited by Nikolai N. Kazansky. St. Petersburg: Nauka, 2015.

Ledger, Gerald R. *Re-Counting Plato: A Computer Analysis of Plato's Style*. Oxford: Clarendon, 1989.

Leeming, David A. *Creation Myths of the World: An Encyclopedia*. 2nd ed. 2 vols. Santa Barbara, CA: ABC-CLIO, 2010.

———. *The Oxford Companion to World Mythology*. Oxford: Oxford University Press, 2005.

Lefkowitz, Mary, and James Romm, eds. *The Greek Plays: Sixteen Plays by Aeschylus, Sophocles, and Euripides*. New York: Random House, 2017.

Lerner, Robert. *The Heresy of the Free Spirit in the Later Middle Ages*. Berkeley: University of California Press, 1972.

Lesko, Leonard H. "Ancient Egyptian Cosmogonies and Cosmology." Pages 88–122 in *Religion in Ancient Egypt: Gods, Myths, and Personal Practice*. Edited by Byron E. Shafer. Ithaca, NY: Cornell University Press, 1991.

Lessing, Gotthold Ephraim. "The Education of the Human Race." Pages 82–98 in *Lessing's Theological Writings: Selections in Translation*. Translated by Henry Chadwick. 2nd ed. Stanford, CA: Stanford University Press, 1967.

Levenson, John D. *Sinai and Zion: An Entry into the Hebrew Bible*. New York: Harper One, 1987.

Works Cited

———. "The Temple and the World." *Journal of Religion* 64 (1984): 275–98.

Levere, Trevor H. *Transforming Matter: A History of Chemistry from Alchemy to the Buckyball.* Baltimore: Johns Hopkins University Press, 2001.

Levering, Matthew. *Jesus and the Demise of Death.* Waco, TX: Baylor University Press, 2012.

Levin, David Michael, ed. *Modernity and the Hegemony of Vision.* Berkeley: University of California Press, 1993.

Levinas, Emmanuel. "The Trace of the Other." Pages 345–59 in *Deconstruction in Context.* Edited by M. C. Taylor. Chicago: University of Chicago Press, 1986.

Lévi-Strauss, Claude. *The Savage Mind.* Chicago: University of Chicago Press, 1966.

Lewy, Hans. *Chaldaean Oracles and Theurgy: Mysticism, Magic and Platonism in the Later Roman Empire.* Paris: Institut d'Études Augustiniennes, 2001.

Lincoln, Bruce. "Competing Discourses: Rethinking the Prehistory of *Mythos* and *Logos*." *Arethusa* 30.3 (1997): 341–67

———. *Theorizing Myth: Narrative, Ideology and Scholarship.* Chicago: University of Chicago Press, 1999.

Lindberg, David C. *The Beginnings of Western Science.* Chicago: University of Chicago Press, 2007.

Linforth, I. N. *The Arts of Orpheus.* Berkeley: University of California Press, 1941.

———. "Two Notes on the Legend of Orpheus." *TAPA* 62 (1931): 5–17.

Lisi, Francisco L. "Individual Soul, World Soul and the Form of the Good in Plato's *Republic* and *Timaeus*." *Etudes Platonisciennes* 4 (2007): 105–18.

Lloyd, G. E. R. "The Hot and Cold, the Dry and the Wet in Greek Philosophy." *JHS* 84 (1964): 92–106.

Lobovikova, Ksenia. "George of Trebizond's Views on Islam and Their Eschatological Background." Pages 346–65 in *Patrologia Pacifica: Selected Papers Presented to the Asia Pacific Early Christian Studies Society; Fifth Annual Conference (Sendai, Japan, September 10–12, 2009) and other Patristic Studies.* Edited by Vladimir Baranov and Kazuhiko Demura. Piscataway, NJ: Gorgias, 2010.

Locke, Liz. "Orpheus and Orphism: Cosmology and Sacrifice at the Boundary." *Folklore Forum* 28.2 (1997): 11

Lombardo, Stanley. *Parmenides and Empedocles: The Fragments in Verse Translation.* Eugene, OR: Wipf & Stock, 1982.

Long, A. A., and D. N. Sedley. *The Hellenistic Philosophers.* 2 vols. Cambridge: Cambridge University Press, 1987.

López-Ruiz, Carolina. *When the Gods Were Born: Greek Cosmologies and the Near East.* Cambridge: Harvard University Press, 2010.

Lossky, Vladimir. *The Vision of God.* Translated by Asheleigh Moorhouse. London: Faith Press, 1964.

Louth, Andrew. *The Origins of the Christian Mystical Tradition: From Plato to Denys.* Oxford: Oxford University Press, 2007.

———. "The Reception of Dionysius Up to Maximus the Confessor." Pages 43–52 in *Rethinking Dionysius the Areopagite.* Edited by Sarah Coakley and Charles M. Stang. Oxford: Wiley-Blackwell, 2009.

Lowe, John J. *Participles in Rigvedic Sanskrit: The Syntax and Semantics of Adjectival Verb Form.* Oxford: Oxford University Press, 2015.

Luck, Georg. *Arcana Mundi: Magic and the Occult in the Greek and Roman Worlds; A Collection of Ancient Texts.* Baltimore: Johns Hopkins University Press, 2006.

Lyotard, Jean-François. *The Postmodern Condition: A Report on Knowledge.* Minneapolis: University of Minnesota Press, 1984.

Macierowski, Edward Michael. "The Thomistic Critique of Avicennian Emanationism from the Viewpoint of the Divine Simplicity with Special Reference to the *Summa contra gentiles.*" PhD diss., University of Toronto, 1979.

MacIntyre, Alasdair. "Myth." Pages 434–37 in vol. 5 of *Encyclopedia of Philosophy.* Edited by Paul Edwards. New York: Macmillan, 1967.

Mackenzie, Donald A. *Myths of Babylonia and Assyria.* New York: Scribner's Sons, 1915.

MacLeod, Roy, ed. *The Library of Alexandria: Centre of Learning in the Ancient World.* London: I. B. Tauris, 2010.

Macurdy, Grace Harriet. "Klodones, Mimallones and Dionysus Pseudanor." *Classical Review* 27.6 (1913): 191–92.

———. *Troy and Paeonia: With Glimpses of Ancient Balkan History and Religion.* New York: Columbia University Press, 1925.

Mahé, Jean-Pierre. "The Discourse on the Eighth and Ninth." Pages 408–12 in *The Nag Hammadi Scriptures: The Revised and Updated Translation of Sacred Gnostic Texts.* Edited by Marvin Meyer. New York: HarperOne, 2007.

Mair, Victor H. "Chuang Tzu." In vol. 2 of *Indiana Companion to Traditional Chinese Literature.* Edited by William Nienheuser. Bloomington: Indiana University Press, 1998.

———. *Tao Te Ching: The Classic Book of Integrity and the Way, by Lao Tzu; An Entirely New Translation Based on the Recently Discovered Ma-wang-tui Manuscripts.* New York: Bantam, 1990.

———. *Wandering on the Way: Early Taoist Tales and Parables of Chuang Tzu.* New York: Bantam, 1994.

Majercik, Ruth. "The Chaldean Oracles and the School of Plotinus." *The Ancient World* 29 (1988): 91–105.

———. *The Chaldaean Oracles—Text, Translation and Commentary.* Leiden: Brill, 1989.

———. "Chaldean Triads in Neoplatonic Exegesis: Some Reconsiderations." *ClQ* 51.1 (2001): 265–96.

Malandra, William W. "Zoroastrianism: Historical Review Up to the Arab Conquest." *Encyclopaedia Iranica*. July 20, 2005. https://www.iranicaonline.org/articles/zoroastrianism-i-historical-review.

Malkovsky, Bradley J. "Samkara on Divine Grace." Pages 1–17 in *New Perspectives on Advaita Vedānta: Essays in Commemoration of Professor Richard De Smet, S.J.* Edited by Bradley J. Malkovsky. Leiden: Brill, 2000.

Mallory, J. P. *In Search of the Indo-Europeans: Language, Archaeology and Myth*. London: Thames and Hudson, 1989.

Mallory, J. P., and Victor H. Mair. *The Tarin Mummies: Ancient China and the Mystery of the Earliest Peoples from the West*. London: Thames and Hudson, 2000.

Mansfield, Jaap. *Heresiography in Context: Hippolytus'* Elenchos *as a Source for Greek Philosophy*. Leiden: Brill, 1992.

Marciano, M. Laura Gemelli. "Images and Experience: At the Roots of Parmenides' Aletheia." *Ancient Philosophy* 28 (2008): 21–48.

Markus, Robert. *Christianity and the Secular*. South Bend: University of Notre Dame Press, 2006.

———. *Saeculum: History and Society in the Theology of St. Augustine*. Cambridge: Cambridge University Press, 1989.

Marinus of Samaria. *The Life of Proclus or Concerning Happiness*. Translated by Kenneth S. Guthrie. Grand Rapids: Phanes, 1986.

Marler, J. C. "Dialectical Use of Authority in the Periphyseon." Pages 95–113 in *Eriugena: East and West. Papers of the Eighth International Colloquium of the Society for the Promotion of Eriugenian Studies, Chicago and Notre Dame, 18–20 October 1991, Notre Dame Conferences in Medieval Studies*. Edited by Bernard McGinn and Willemein Otten. Notre Dame, IN: University of Notre Dame Press, 1994.

Marrou, Henri Irénée. "Synesius of Cyrene and Alexandrian Neoplatonism." Pages 126–50 in *The Conflict between Paganism and Christianity in the Fourth Century*. Edited by Arnaldo Momigliano. Oxford: Clarendon, 1963.

Martin, Wayne M. "Stoic Self-Consciousness." Pages 342–68 in *The Transcendental Turn*. Edited by Sebastian Gardner and Matthew Grist. Oxford: Oxford University Press, 2015.

Mateo-Seco, Lucas Francisco, and Giulio Maspero, eds. *The Brill Dictionary of Gregory of Nyssa*. Leiden: Brill, 2010.

Matthews, Roger, and Cornelia Roemer, eds. *Ancient Perspectives on Egypt*. London: Routledge, 2003.

Matusova, Ekaterina. "Allegorical Interpretation of the Pentateuch in Alexandria: Inscribing Aristobulus and Plato in a Wider Literary Context." SPhiloA 22 (2010): 1–51.

Matveychev, O. A. "Hermotimus of Clazomenae as Anaxagoras's Predecessor." *Vestnik Permskogo universiteta. Filosofia. Psihologia. Sociologia* 3 (2020): 355–64.

Mazur, Alexander J. *The Platonizing Sethian Background of Plotinus' Mysticism*. Leiden: Brill, 2020.

McConnel, D. R. *A Different Gospel*. Peabody, MA: Hendrickson, 1994.

McEvilley, Thomas. *The Shape of Ancient Thought: Comparative Studies in Greek and Indian Philosophies*. New York: Allworth, 2002.

McFarlane, Thomas J. "Process and Emptiness: A Comparison of Whitehead's Process Philosophy and Mahayana Buddhist Philosophy." *Center for Integral Science*. http://www.integralscience.org/whiteheadbuddhism.html.

McGinn, Bernard, ed. *Apocalyptic Spirituality: Treatises and Letters of Lactantius, Adso of Montier-En-Der, Joachim of Fiore, the Spiritual Franciscans, Savonarola*. New York: Paulist, 1979.

———. *The Calabrian Abbot: Joachim of Fiore in the History of Western Thought*. New York: Harper & Row, 1985.

———. *The Flowering of Mysticism: Men and Women in the New Mysticism (1200–1350)*. New York: Crossroad, 1998.

———, ed. *Meister Eckhart: Preacher and Teacher*. New York: Paulist, 1986.

———. "Meister Eckhart on God as Absolute Unity." Pages 128–39 in *Neoplatonism and Christian Thought*. Edited by Dominic J. O'Meara. Albany: SUNY Press, 1982.

———. "Wrestling with the Millennium: Early Modern Catholic Exegesis of Apocalypse 20." In *Imagining the End: Visions of Apocalypse from the Ancient Middle East to Modern America*. Edited by Abbas Amanat and Magnus T. Bernhardsson. London: I. B. Tauris, 2002.

McInerney, Jeremy. "Parnassus, Delphi, and the Thyiades." *GRBS* 38.3 (1997): 263–83.

McKirahan, Richard D. *Philosophy before Socrates: An Introduction with Texts and Commentary*. 2nd ed. Indianapolis: Hackett, 2010.

McNicholl, Stephen Peter. "Reason, Religion and Plato: Orphism and the Mathematical Mediation between Being and Becoming." PhD diss., University of Canterbury, 2003.

Mead, G. R. S. *Orpheus*. 1896; repr. London: Watkins, 1965.

———. *Thrice-Greatest Hermes: Studies in Hellenistic Theosophy and Gnosis*. London: Theosophical Pub. Society, 1906.

Megino, Carlos. "Presence in Stoicism of an Orphic Doctrine on the Soul Quoted by Aristotle (*De Anima* 410b 27 = *OF* 421)." Pages 139–46 in *Tracing Orpheus: Studies of Orphic Fragments*. Edited by Miguel Herrero de Jáuregui et al. Berlin: de Gruyter, 2012.

Mehr, Frahang. *The Zoroastrian Tradition: An Introduction to the Ancient Wisdom of Zarathushtra*. Costa Mesa, CA: Mazda Publishers, 2003.

Meier, Christian. *A Culture of Freedom: Ancient Greece and the Origins of Europe*. Oxford: Oxford University Press, 2011.

Meisner, Dwayne. *Orphic Tradition and the Birth of the Gods*. Oxford: Oxford University Press, 2018.

Meister Eckhart. *Die deutschen Werke*. Edited by Josef Quint and Georg Steer. 5 vols. Stuttgart: Kohlhammer, 1936–2016.

———. *Meister Eckhart's Sermons*. Translated by Claud Field. London: Allenson, 1904.

———. *Sermons and Treatises*. Translated by Maurice O'Connell Walshe. Rockport, MA: Element Books, 1987.

Merkelbach, R., and M. L. West. *Fragmenta Hesiodea*. Oxford: Oxford University Press, 1967.

Merlan, Philip. "Religion and Philosophy from Plato's *Phaedo* to the *Chaldean Oracles*." *Journal of the History of Philosophy* 1 (1963): 163–76.

Meyendorff, John. *Byzantine Theology: Historical Trends and Doctrinal Themes*. New York: Fordham University Press, 1979.

———. *Christ in Eastern Christian Thought*. Crestwood, NY: St. Vladimir's Seminary Press, 1975.

Meyer, Marvin. *The Gospel of Thomas: The Hidden Sayings of Jesus*. New York: HarperCollins, 2004.

———. "The Gospel of Thomas with the Greek Gospel of Thomas." Pages 133–38 in *The Nag Hammadi Scriptures: The Revised and Updated Translation of Sacred Gnostic Texts*. Edited by Marvin Meyer. New York: HarperOne, 2007.

———, ed. *The Nag Hammadi Scriptures: The Revised and Updated Translation of Sacred Gnostic Texts*. New York: HarperOne, 2007.

Michaels, Axel. *Hinduism: Past and Present*. Princeton: Princeton University Press, 2004.

Milbank, John. "Christianity and Platonism in East and West." Pages 149–203 in *A Saint for East and West: Maximus the Confessor's Contribution to Eastern and Western Christian Theology*. Edited by Daniel Haynes. Eugene, OR: Wipf & Stock, 2019.

———. *Theology and Social Theory: Beyond Secular Reason*. 2nd ed. Oxford: Wiley-Blackwell, 2006.

Milbank, John, Catherine Pickstock, and Graham Ward. *Radical Orthodoxy: A New Theology*. London: Routledge, 1998.

Milbank, John, and John Riches. Foreword to *Theurgy and the Soul: The Neoplatonism of Iamblichus*, by Gergory Shaw. 2nd ed. Brooklyn, NY: Angelico, 2014.

Miller, Patricia Cox. "'Plenty Sleeps There': The Myth of Eros and Psyche in Plotinus and Gnosticism." Pages 18–40 in *Neoplatonism and Gnosticism*. Edited by Richard T. Wallis. Albany: SUNY Press, 1992.

Moltmann, Jürgen. *History and the Triune God*. New York: Crossroad, 1992.

Moore, Edward. "Middle Platonism." *Internet Encyclopedia of Philosophy*. n.d. https://www.iep.utm.edu/midplato/.

Moore, R. I. "Medieval Europe." Pages 129–47 in *Imagining the End: Visions of Apocalypse from the Ancient Middle East to Modern America*. Edited by Abbas Amanat and Magnus T. Berharndsson. London: I. B. Tauris, 2002.

Moran, Dermot. "Johannes Scottus Eriugena." Pages 33–45 in *Medieval Philosophy of Religion*. Edited by Graham Oppy and N. N. Trakakis. London: Routledge, 2013.

———. "Nicholas of Cusa and Modern Philosophy." Pages 173–92 in *The Cambridge Companion to Renaissance Philosophy*. Edited by James Hankins. Cambridge: Cambridge University Press, 2007.

———. *Philosophy of John Scottus Eriugena: A Study of Idealism in the Middle Ages*. New York: Cambridge University Press, 1989.

———. "Spiritualis Incressatio: Eriugena's Intellectualist Immaterialism; Is It an Idealism?" Pages 123–50 in *Eriugena, Berkeley and the Idealist Tradition*. Edited by Stephen Gersh and Dermot Moran. Notre Dame: University of Notre Dame Press, 2006.

Moreschini, Claudio. *Dall' Asclepius al Crater Hermetis: Studi sull'Ermetismo latino trado-antico e rinascimentale*. Pisa: Giardini, 1985.

Mourelatos, Alexander. *The Route of Parmenides*. New Haven: Yale University Press, 1970.

Müller, Karl Otfried. *History of the Literature of Ancient Greece*. 2 vols. London: Baldwin & Cradock, 1840.

Müller, Max, trans. *The Upanishads: Parts I and II*. New York: Dover, 1962.

Mullins, R. T. "The Difficulty with Demarcating Panentheism." *Sophia* 55 (2016): 325–46.

Müntzer, Thomas. "Sermon to the Princes." Pages 11–31 in *The Radical Reformation*. Edited and translated by Michael G. Baylor. Cambridge: Cambridge University Press, 1991.

Murdock, Jacob M. "Lethe and the Twin Bodhisattvas of Forgiveness and Forgetfulness." MA thesis, Pacifica Graduate Institute, 2017.

Muscolino, Guiseppe. "Porphyry and Black Magic." *International Journal of the Platonic Tradition* 9 (2015): 1460–58.

Nakamura, Hajime. *Indian Buddhism: A Survey with Bibliographical Notes*. Delhi: Banarsidass, 1999.

Nasr, S. H. *Islamic Philosophy from Its Origins to the Present: Philosophy in the Land of Prophecy*. Albany: SUNY Press, 2006.

National Science Foundation. "Chapter 7: Science and Technology: Public Attitudes and Understanding." *Science and Engineering Indicators 2014*. February 2014. https://www.nsf.gov/statistics/seind14/content/chapter-7/chapter-7.pdf.

Neusner, Jacob, and William Scott Green, eds. *Dictionary of Judaism in the Biblical Period: 450 BCE to 600 CE*. 2 vols. New York: Macmillan, 1996.

Nicholas of Cusa. "Coniectura de novissimis diebus." Pages 932–35 in *Opera Omnia*. Basel: Petrina, 1565.

———. *Nicholas of Cusa's Early Sermons: 1430–1441*. Translated by Jasper Hopkins. Loveland, CO: Banning, 2003.

———. *On Learned Ignorance: A Translation and an Appraisal of "De Docta Ignorantia."* Translated by Jasper Hopkins. Minneapolis: Banning, 1985.

Nietzsche, Friedrich. *The Birth of Tragedy and the Case of Wagner*. Translated by Walyer Kaufmann. New York: Vintage Books, 1967.

Nikulin, Dmitri, ed. *The Other Plato: The Tübingen Interpretation of Plato's Inner-Academic Teachings*. Albany: SUNY Press, 2012.

———. "Plato: Testimonia et Fragmenta." Pages 1–38 in *The Other Plato: The Tübingen Interpretation of Plato's Inner-Academic Teachings*. Edited by Dmitri Nikulin. Albany: SUNY Press, 2012.

Nilsson, Martin P. "Early Orphism and Kindred Religious Movements." *HTR* 28.3 (1935): 181–230.

———. *Early Orphism and Kindred Religious Movements*. Cambridge: Harvard University Press, 1935.

———. *Greek Popular Religion*. New York: Columbia University Press, 1947.

Nissinen, Martii. *Ancient Prophecy: Near Eastern, Biblical, and Greek Perspectives*. Oxford: Oxford University Press, 2017.

Nock, A. D. *Essays on Religion and the Ancient World*. Edited by Zeph Stewart. 2 vols. Oxford: Clarendon, 1972.

———. *Le dualism chez Platon, les Gnostiques et les Manichéens*. Paris, 1947.

Nock, A. D., and A.-J. Festugière, eds. and trans. *Corpus Hermeticum*. 4 vols. Paris: Belles Lettres, 1946–1954.

Numenius. *Fragments of Numenius of Apamea*. Translated by Robert Petty. Wiltshire: Prometheus Trust, 2012.

Oakes, Edward T. *Pattern of Redemption: The Theology of Hans Urs von Balthsasar*. New York: Continuum, 2005.

Ober, Josiah, and Barry Strauss. "Drama, Political Rhetoric, and the Discourse of Athenian Democracy." Pages 237–70 in *Nothing to Do with Dionysos? Athenian Drama in Its Social Context*. Edited by John J. Winkler and Froma I. Zeitlin. Princeton: Princeton University Press, 1990.

Oldenberg, Hermann. *The Religion of the Veda*. Translated by Shridhar B. Shrotri. Delhi: Molitel Banassidass, 1988.

Olivelle, Patrick. *The Asraman System: The History and Hermeneutics of a Religious Institution*. Oxford: Oxford University Press, 1993.

———. "Caste and Purity: A Study in the Language of the Dharma Literature." *Contributions to Indian Sociology* 32.2 (1998): 199–203.

———. "The Renouncer Tradition." Pages 271–87 in *The Blackwell Companion to Hinduism*. Edited by Gavin Flood. Oxford: Blackwell, 2003.

———. *Upaniṣads*. Oxford: Oxford University Press, 1996.

O'Meara, Dominic J. *Platonopolis: Platonic Political Philosophy in Late Antiquity*. Oxford: Clarendon, 2005.

O'Meara, John J. "The Neoplatonism of Saint Augustine." Pages 34–41 in *Neoplatonism and Christian Thought*. Edited by Dominic J. O'Meara. Albany: SUNY Press, 1982.

Ong, Walter, SJ. *The Presence of the Word: Some Prolegomena for Cultural and Religious History*. New Haven: Yale University Press, 1967.

Oppenheim, A. Leo. "The Seafaring Merchants of Ur." Pages 155–63 in *Ancient Cities of the Indus*. Edited by Gregory Possehl. New Delhi: Vikas, 1979.

O'Regan, Cyril. *The Heterodox Hegel*. Albany: SUNY Press, 1994.

Origen. *Commentary on the Gospel according to John, Books 1–10*. Translated by Ronald E. Heine. Washington, DC: Catholic University of America Press, 1989.

———. *Homilies on Genesis and Exodus*. Translated by Ronald E. Heine. Washington, DC: Catholic University of America Press, 1981.

———. *On First Principles*. Translation by G. W. Butterworth. Gloucester, UK: Smith, 1973.

———. "On Prayer." Pages 81–170 in *Origen: An Exhortation to Martyrdom, Prayer, and Selected Works*. Translated by Rowan A. Greer. Mahwah, NJ: Paulist, 1979.

———. *On the True Doctrine: A Discourse against the Christians*. Translated by R. Joseph Hoffman. Oxford: Oxford University Press, 1987.

———. *Treatise on the Passover and Dialogue of Origen with Heraclides and His Fellow Bishops on the Father, the Son, and the Soul*. Translated by Robert J. Daly. Ancient Christian Writers. New York: Paulist, 1992.

Page, Denys L. *Poetae Melici Graeci*. Oxford: Oxford University Press, 1962.

Pagels, Elaine. *Beyond Belief: The Secret Gospel of Thomas*. New York: Random House, 2003.

———. *The Gnostic Gospels*. New York: Random House, 1989.

———. Introduction to *The Gnostic Bible*. Edited by Willis Barnstone and Marvin Meyer. Rev. ed. Boston: Shambhala, 2009.

Paglia, Camille. *Sexual Personae: Art and Decadence from Nefertiti to Emily Dickinson*. New York: Vintage Books, 1990.

Palmer, John. "Parmenides." *Stanford Encyclopedia of Philosophy* at https://plato.stanford.edu/entries/parmenides/. October 19, 2020. Accessed December 20, 2022.

———. *Plato's Reception of Parmenides*. Oxford: Clarendon, 1999.

Paramananda, Swami. *Plato and Vedic Idealism*. Boston: Vedanta Centre, 1924.

Parke, H. W. *A History of the Delphic Oracle*. Oxford: Oxford University Press, 1939.

Parker, Eric M. "'Saint Dionysius': Martin Bucer's Transformation of the Pseudo-Areopagite." Pages 121–45 in *From Rome to Zurich, between Ignatius and Vermigli: Essays in Honor of Patrick Donnelly*. Edited by Kathleen M. Comerford, Gary W. Jenkins, and W. J. Torrence Kirby. Leiden: Brill, 2017.

Parker, Robert. "Early Orphism." Pages 483–510 in *The Greek World*. Edited by Anton Powell. London: Routledge, 1995.

———. *Miasma: Pollution and Purification in Early Greek Religion*. Oxford: Clarendon, 1996.

Parrott, Douglas M. "Gnosticism and Egyptian Religion." *NovT* 29.1 (1987): 73–93.

Pearson, Birger A. *Gnosticism and Christianity in Roman and Coptic Egypt*. London: T&T Clark, 2004.

———. "Gnosticism as Platonism: With Special Reference to Marsanes (NHC 10, 1)." *HTR* 77 (1984): 55–72.

———. *Gnosticism, Judaism, and Egyptian Christianity*. Minneapolis: Fortress, 1990.

———. "The Testimony of Truth." Pages 612–16 in *The Nag Hammadi Scriptures: The Revised and Updated Translation of Sacred Gnostic Texts*. Edited by Marvin Meyer. New York: HarperOne, 2007.

———. "Theurgic Tendencies in Gnosticism and Iamblichus' Conception of Theurgy." Pages 253–76 in *Neoplatonism and Gnosticism*. Edited by Richard T. Wallis. Albany: SUNY Press, 1992.

Pegg, Mark Gregory. *A Most Holy War: The Albigensian Crusade and the Battle for Christendom*. Oxford: Oxford University Press, 2008.

Pépin, Jean. "Theories of Procession in Plotinus and the Gnostics." Pages 299–323 in *Neoplatonism and Gnosticism*. Edited by Richard T. Wallis. Albany: SUNY Press, 1992.

Perczel, István. "The Earliest Syriac Reception of Dionysius." Pages 27–41 in *Re-thinking Dionysius the Areopagite*. Edited by Sarah Coakley and Charles M. Stang. Oxford: Wiley-Blackwell, 2009.

Perkins, Pheme. "Beauty, Number, and Loss of Order in the Gnostic Cosmos." Pages 277–96 in *Neoplatonism and Gnosticism*. Edited by Richard T. Wallis. Albany: SUNY Press, 1992.

Perl, Eric D. "'Every Life Is a Thought': The Analogy of Personhood in Neoplatonism." *Philosophy and Theology* 18 (2006): 143–67.

———. "Hierarchy and Participation in Cionysois the Areopagite and Greek Neoplatonism." *American Catholic Philosophical Quarterly* 68 (Winter 1994): 15–30.

———. "Neither One nor Many: God and the Gods in Plotinus, Proclus, and Aquinas." *Dionysius* 28 (2010): 167–91.

———. "Symbol, Sacrament, and Hierarchy in Saint Dionysios the Areopagite." *GOTR* 39.3–4 (1994): 311–55.

———. *Theophany: The Neoplatonic Philosophy of Dionysius the Areopagite.* Albany: SUNY Press, 2008.

Peters, L. G., and D. Price-Williams. "Towards and Experiential Analysis of Shamanism." *American Ethnologist* 7 (1980): 397–418.

Pétrement, Simone. *The Separate God: The Christian Origins of Gnosticism.* New York: Harper & Row, 1993.

Petridou, Georgia. "'Blessed Is He, Who Has Seen': The Power of Ritual Viewing and Ritual Framing in Eleusis." *Helios* 40.1–2 (2013): 309–41.

Pew Research Center. "About Three-in-Ten U.S. Adults Are Now Religiously Unaffiliated." December 14, 2021. https://www.pewresearch.org/religion/2021/12/14/about-three-in-ten-u-s-adults-are-now-religiously-unaffiliated/.

———. "Being Christian in Western Europe." May 29, 2018. https://www.pewresearch.org/religion/wp-content/uploads/sites/7/2018/05/Being-Christian-in-Western-Europe-FOR-WEB1.pdf.

———. "Few Americans Blame God or Say Faith Has Been Shaken Amid Pandemic, Other Tragedies." November 23, 2021. https://www.pewresearch.org/religion/wp-content/uploads/sites/7/2021/11/PF_23.11.21_problem_of_evil.pdf.

———. "In U.S., Decline of Christianity Continues at Rapid Pace." October 17, 2019. https://www.pewforum.org/2019/10/17/in-u-s-decline-of-christianity-continues-at-rapid-pace/.

———. "'New Age' Beliefs Common among Both Religious and Nonreligious Americans." October 1, 2018. https://www.pewresearch.org/fact-tank/2018/10/01/new-age-beliefs-common-among-both-religious-and-nonreligious-americans/.

Pfeiffer, Rudolf. *History of Classical Scholarship from the Beginning to the End of the Hellenistic Age.* Oxford: Clarendon, 1968.

Phelan, John Leddy. *The Millennial Kingdom of the Franciscans in the New World.* Berkeley: University of California Press, 1970.

Phillips, E. D. "The Legend of Aristeas: Fact and Fancy in Early Greek Notions of East Russia, Siberia, and Inner Asia." *Artibus Asiae* 18.2 (1955): 161–77.

Phillips, Stephen. *Yoga, Karma and Rebirth: A Brief History and Philosophy.* New York: Columbia University Press, 2009.

Philo of Alexandria. *On the Confusion of Tongues, On the Migration of Abraham, Who Is the Heir of Divine Things?, On Mating with the Preliminary Studies.* Translated by F. H. Colson and G. H. Whitaker. LCL. Cambridge: Harvard University Press, 1932

———. *Philo's Works.* Edited by F. H. Colson and G. H. Whitaker. LCL. Cambridge: Harvard University Press, 1932; repr. 1985.

———. *The Works of Philo*. Translated by Charles Duke Yonge. London: Bohn, 1854–1890; repr., Peabody, MA: Hendrickson, 1995.
Pickard-Cambridge, Arthur. *The Drama Festivals of Athens*. 2nd ed. Oxford: Clarendon, 1968.
Pindar. *The Complete Odes*. Translated by Anthony Verity. Oxford: Oxford University Press, 2007.
Places, É. des, ed. *Oracles Chaldaiques*. Paris: Les Belles Lettres, 1971.
Plato. *Complete Works*. Edited by John M. Cooper. Indianapolis: Hackett, 1997.
———. *Euthyphro, Apology Crito, Phaedo*. Translated by Benjamin Jowett. Amherst, NY: Prometheus, 1988.
———. *Phaedrus*. Translated with introduction and commentary by R. Hackforth. Cambridge: Cambridge University Press, 1952.
———. *Plato I, Euthyphro, Apology, Crito, Phaedo, Phaedrus*. Translated by Harold North Fowler. LCL. Cambridge: Harvard University Press, 1914.
———. *Plato IX, Timaeus. Critas. Cleitophon. Menexenus. Epistles*. Translated by R. G. Bury. LCL. Cambridge: Harvard University Press, 1929.
———. *Timaeus and Critias*. Translated with introduction and appendix on Atlantis by Desmond Lee. London: Penguin, 1977.
Pleše, Zlatko. *Poetics of the Gnostic Universe in Narrative and Cosmology in the Apocalypse of John*. Nag Hammadi and Manichaean Studies 52. Leiden: Brill, 2006.
Plested, Marcus. "Philosophy." Pages 447–49 in vol. 2 of *The Encyclopedia of Eastern Orthodox Christianity*. Edited by John Anthony McGuckin. 2 vols. Oxford: Wiley-Blackwell, 2001.
Plotinus. *The Enneads*. Translated by A. H. Armstrong. LCL. Cambridge: Harvard University Press, 1984.
———. *The Enneads*. Translated by Stephen MacKenna. Burdett, NY: Larson, 1992.
Plott, John C., with James Michael Dolin and Russell E. Hatton. *The Axial Age*. Vol. 1 of *Global History of Philosophy*. Edited by Robert C. Richmond. Delhi: Banarsidass, 1963.
Plutarch. *Moralia, Volume V: Isis and Osiris. The E at Delphi. The Oracles at Delphi No Longer Given in Verse. The Obsolescence of Oracles*. Translated by Frank Cole Babbitt. LCL. Cambridge: Harvard University Press, 1936.
Poehlmann, Egert. "Agon Music and Theatre." Pages 317–46 in *Theatre World: Critical Perspectives on Greek Tragedy and Comedy*. Edited by Andreas Fountoulakis, Andreas Markantonatos, and Georgios Vasilaros. Berlin: de Gruyter, 2017.
Polkinghorne, John. "Christianity and Science." Pages 57–70 in *The Oxford Handbook of Religion and Science*. Edited by Philip Clayton and Zachary Simpson. Oxford: Oxford University Press, 2006.
Porphyry. *Porphyry to Gaurus on How Embryos Are Ensouled and What Is in Our Power*. Edited by James Wilberding. London: Bloomsbury Academic, 2011.

Poston, Larry. "The Second Coming of 'Isa: An Exploration of Islamic Premillennialism." *Muslim World* 100 (2010): 100–116.

Power, Timothy Conrad. *The Culture of Kitharôidia*. Washington, DC: Center for Hellenic Studies, 2010.

Preus, Anthony. *Historical Dictionary of Greek Philosophy*. New York: Rowman & Littlefield, 2015.

Price, Richard, ed. *The Acts of the Council of Chalcedon*. 3 vols. Liverpool: University of Liverpool Press, 2009.

Principe, Lawrence M., and William R. Newman. "Some Problems with the Historiography of Alchemy." Pages 388–432 in *Secrets of Nature: Astrology and Alchemy in Early Modern Europe*. Edited by William R. Newman and Anthony Grafton. Cambridge: MIT Press, 2006.

Pritchard, James B., ed. *Ancient Near Eastern Texts Relating to the Old Testament*. 3rd ed. Princeton: Princeton University Press, 2001.

Proclus. *Commentary on Plato's Parmenides*. Edited and translated by Glenn R. Marrow and John M. Dillon. Princeton: Princeton University Press, 1987.

———. *Commentary on Plato's Timaeus*. Edited and translated by Harold Tarrant et al. 6 vols. Cambridge: Cambridge University Press, 2006–2017.

———. *The Elements of Theology*. Edited and translated by E. H. Dodds. Oxford: Clarendon, 1963.

———. *On the Eternity of the World (De Aeternitate Mundi)*. Translated by Helen S. Lang and A. D. Macro. Berkeley: University of California Press, 2001.

———. *On the Existence of Evils (de Mal.)*. Translated and edited by Jan Opsomer and Carlos Steel. Ithaca, NY: Cornell University Press, 2003.

Prosperi, Andriano. "New Heaven and New Earth: Prophecy and Propaganda at the Time of the Discovery and Conquest of the Americas." Pages 279–302 in *Prophetic Rome in the High Renaissance Period*. Edited by Marjorie Reeves. Oxford: Oxford University Press, 1992.

Provan, Iain. *Conventional Myths: The Axial Age, Dark Green Religion, and the World That Never Was*. Waco, TX: Baylor University Press, 2013.

Quispel, Gilles. "Hermes Trismegistus and the Origins of Gnosticism." *VC* 46 (1992): 1–19.

———. "Reincarnation and Magic in the Asclepius." Pages 167–231 in *From Poimandres to Jacob Böhme: Gnosis, Hermeticism and the Christian Tradition*. Edited by Roelof van den Broek and Cis van Heertum. Leiden: Brill, 2000.

Rad, Gerhard von. *Old Testament Theology*. Vol. 1: *The Theology of Israel's Historical Traditions*. New York: Harper, 1962.

———. *Old Testament Theology*. Vol. 2: *The Theology of Israel's Prophetic Traditions*. New York: Harper, 1967.

Rahner, Karl. "The Spiritual Senses according to Origen." Pages 81–103 in volume 16 of *Theological Investigations*. New York: Seabury, 1979.

Ram, Indranie. "Plato and Vedanta." *Phronoimon* 6.1 (2005): 59–69.

Ramelli, Ilaria L. E. *Evagrius's Kephalaia Gnostika: A New Translation of the Unreformed Text from the Syriac*. Atlanta: SBL Press, 2015.

———. "Origen and the Platonic Tradition." *Religions* 8 (2017): 1–21.

———. "Proclus and Apoktastasis." Pages 95–122 in *Pseudo-Dionysius and His Legacy*. Edited by Danielle Layne and David D. Butorac. Millennium Studien 65. Berlin: de Gruyter, 2017.

Reale, Giovanni. *Origins to Socrates*. Vol. 1 of *A History of Ancient Philosophy*. Translated by John R. Catan. Albany: SUNY Press, 1987.

Redfield, J. "The Politics of Immortality." Pages 3:103–117 in *Orphisme et Orphée: En l'honneur de Jean Rudhardt*. Edited by P. Borgeaud. Geneva: Librairie Droz, 1991.

Redford, Donald B. *Egypt, Canaan, and Israel in Ancient Times*. Princeton: Princeton University Press, 1992.

———. "Ptah." Pages 75–76 in vol. 3 of *Oxford Encyclopedia of Ancient Egypt*. Edited by Donald Redford. Oxford: Oxford University Press, 2001.

Reed, Anette Yoshiko. "Heavenly Ascent, Angelic Descent and the Transmission of Knolwedge in 1 Enoch 6–16." Pages 47–66 in *Heavenly Realms and Earthly Realities in Late Antique Religions*. Edited by Ra'anan S. Boustan and Anette Yoshiko Reed. Cambridge: Cambridge University Press, 2004.

Reese, Gustave. *Music in the Middle Ages with an Introduction on the Music of Ancient Times*. New York: Norton, 1940.

Reeves, Marjorie. *Joachim of Fiore and the Prophetic Future: A Medieval Study in Historical Thinking*. London: SPCK, 1976.

Reeves, Marjorie, and B. Hirsch-Reich. *The Figure of Joachim of Fiore*. Oxford: Oxford University Press, 1972.

Reid, Jane Davidson. *The Oxford Guide to Classical Mythology in the Arts, 1300–1990s*. Oxford: Oxford University Press, 1994.

Reiman, Donald H., and Sharon B. Powers, eds. *Shelley's Poetry and Prose*. New York: Norton, 1977.

Reitzenstein, Richard. *Das iranische Erlösungsmysterium: Religionsgeschichtliche Untersuchungen*. Bonn: Marcus & Weber, 1921.

———. "Iranischer Erlösungsglaube." *ZNW* 20 (1921): 1–23.

Repstad, Pål. "Has the Pendulum Swung Too Far? The Construction of Religious Individualism in Today's Sociology of Religion." *Temenos* 37/38 (2001): 181–90.

Rickert, Thomas. "Parmenidean Ontological Enaction, and the Prehistory of Rhetoric." *Philosophy and Rhetoric* 47 (2014): 427–93.

Ricoeur, Paul. *The Symbolism of Evil*. Translated by Emerson Buchanan. New York: Harper & Row, 1967.

Ridley, Ronald Thomas. *Akhenaten: A Historian's View*. Cairo: American University in Cairo Press, 2019.

Riedweg, Christoph. *Pythagoras: His Life, Teachings and Influence*. Ithaca, NY: Cornell University Press, 2005.

Riffard, Pierre A. *Dictionnaire de l'ésoterisme*. Paris: Payot, 1983.

Rist, John M. "Mysticism and Transcendence in Later Neoplatonism." *Hermes* 92 (1964): 213–25.

———. "Plotinus and the 'Daimonion' of Socrates." *Phoenix* 17.1 (1963): 13–24.

———. *Plotinus and the Road to Reality*. Cambridge: Cambridge University Press, 1967.

Robson, Eleanor. "Empirical Scholarship in the Neo-Assyrian Court." Pages 603–30 in *The Empirical Dimension of Ancient Near Eastern Studies*. Edited by Gebhard J. Selz and Klaus Wagensonner. Münster: LIT Verlag, 2011.

Roetz, H. *Confucian Ethics of the Axial Age*. Albany: SUNY Press, 1993.

Rohde, Erwin. *Psyche: The Cult of Souls and the Belief in Immortality*. Translated by W. B. Hillis. 8th ed. London: Routledge, 2001.

Roller, Lynn Emrich. *In Search of God the Mother: The Cult of Anatolian Cybele*. Berkeley: University of California Press, 1999.

———. "The Phrygian Character of Kybele: The Formation of an Iconography and Cult Ethos in the Iron Age." Pages 189–98 in *Anatolian Iron Ages 3: The Proceedings of the Third Anatolian Iron Ages Colloquium*. Edited by A. Çilingiroğlu and D. H. French. London: British Institute, 1994.

Roques, René. "Denys l'Areopagite." Pages 244–86 in vol. 3 of *Dictionnaire de spiritualité: ascetique et mystique, doctrine et histoire*. Paris: Beauchesne, 1957.

Rorem, Paul. "The Early Latin Dionysius: Eriugena and Hugh of St. Victor." Pages 601–14 in *Re-thinking Dionysius the Areopagite*. Edited by Sarah Coakley and Charles M. Stang. Oxford: Wiley-Blackwell, 2009.

Rorem, Paul, and John C. Lamoreaux. *John of Scythopolis and the Dionysian Corpus: Annotating the Areopagite*. Oxford: Clarendon, 1998.

Roth, Ann M. "Father Earth, Mother Sky: Beliefs about Conception and Fertility." Pages 187–201 in *Reading the Body: Representations and Remains in the Archaeological Record*. Edited by Alison E. Rautman. Philadelphia: University of Pennsylvania Press, 2000.

Rouget, Gilbert. *Music and Trance: A Theory of the Relations between Music and Possession*. Translated by Brunhilde Biebuyck. Chicago: University of Chicago Press, 1985.

Roukema, Reimer. *Gnosis and Faith in Early Christianity: An Introduction to Gnosticism*. Harrisburg, PA: Trinity Press International, 1999.

Rowland, Christopher. *The Open Heaven: A Study of Apocalyptic in Judaism and Early Christianity*. New York: Crossroad, 1982.
Rubarth, Scott. "Stoic Mind." *Internet Encyclopedia of Philosophy*. n.d. https://iep.utm.edu/stoicmind/.
Rubenstein, Mary-Jane. "Dionysius, Derrida, and the Critique of 'Ontotheology.'" Pages 195–212 in *Re-thinking Dionysius the Areopagite*. Edited by Sarah Coakley and Charles M. Stang. Oxford: Wiley-Blackwell, 2009.
Ruck, Carla P., et al. "Ethnogens." Pages 137–40 in *The Road to Eleusis: Unveiling the Secrets of the Mysteries*. Edited by R. Gordon Wasson, Albert Hofmann, and Carla P. Ruck. Berkeley, CA: North Atlantic, 2008.
Rudolph, Kurt. *Gnosis: The Nature and History of Gnosticism*. Translated and edited by Robert McLachlan Wilson. San Francisco: Harper & Row, 1977.
Runia, David. *Philo and the Church Fathers: A Collection of Essays*. Leiden: Brill, 1995.
Russell, Bertrand. *A History of Western Philosophy*. London: Allen & Unwin, 1947.
Russell, D. S. *The Method and Message of Jewish Apocalyptic, 200 BC–AD 100*. London: SCM, 1964.
Russell, J. B. *The Influence of Amalric of Bene in Thirteenth Century Pantheism*. Berkeley: University of California Press, 1957.
Ruzsa, Frenc. "Sankhya." *Internet Encyclopedia of Philosophy*. n.d. https://iep.utm.edu/sankhya/.
Saffrey, Henri-Dominique. "From Iamblichus to Proclus and Damascius." Pages 250–65 in *Classical Mediterranean Spirituality, Egyptian, Greek, Roman*. Edited by A. H. Armstrong. New York: Crossroad, 1986.
———. "Les Néoplatoniciens et les oracles, chaldaïques." *Revue des Études Augustiniennes* 27 (1981): 209–25.
———. "New Objective Links between the Pseudo-Dionysius and Proclus." Pages 54–63 in *Neoplatonism and Christian Thought*. Edited by Dominic J. O'Meara. Albany: SUNY Press, 1982.
———. "The Piety and Prayers of Ordinary Men and Women in Late Antiquity." Pages 195–213 in *Classical Mediterranean Spirituality, Egyptian, Greek, Roman*. Edited by A. H. Armstrong. New York: Crossroad, 1986.
Salles, Ricardo. "The Stoic World Soul and the Theory of Seminal Principles." Pages 44–66 in *World Soul: A History*. Edited by James Wilberding. Oxford: Oxford University Press, 2021.
Samuel, Geoffrey. *Mind, Body, Culture: Anthropology and the Biological Interface*. Cambridge: Cambridge University Press, 1980.
———. *The Origins of Yoga and Tantra: Indic Religions to the Thirteenth Century*. Cambridge: Cambridge University Press, 2008.

Sanderson, Stephen K. *Religious Evolution and the Axial Age*. London: Bloomsbury, 2018.

Sanlon, Peter. *Augustine's Theology of Preaching*. Minneapolis: Fortress, 2014.

Sargent, Lyman Tower. "The Necessity of Utopian Thinking: A Cross-National Perspective." Pages 1–14 in *Thinking Utopia: Steps into Other Worlds*. Edited by Jörn Rüsen, Michael Fehr, and Thomas Rieger. New York: Berghahn, 2005.

Sarton, George. *A History of Science*. Vol. 1: *Ancient Science through the Golden Age of Greece*. New York: Norton, 1952.

Schaeffer, Jonathan. "Monism: The Priority of the Whole." *Philosophical Review* 119 (2010): 31–76.

Scherer, J. *Entretien d'Origène avec Héraclide et les évêques ses collegues sur le Père, le Fils et l'âme*. Cairo: Institut français d'Archéologie orientale, 1949.

Schibli, Hermann S. *Pherecydes of Syros*. Oxford: Clarendon, 1990.

Schmemann, Alexander. *Journals of Father Alexander Schmemann, 1973–1983*. Crestwood, NY: St. Vladimir's Seminary Press, 2000.

Schmidt, Michael. *The First Poets: Lives of the Ancient Greek Poets*. London: Weidenfeld & Nicolson, 2004.

Schmidt-Biggemann, William. *Philosophia Perennis: Historical Outlines of Western Spirituality in Ancient, Medieval and Early Modern Thought*. Dordrecht: Springer, 2004.

Schmithausen, Lambert. *The Problem of the Sentience of Plants in Early Buddhism*. Tokyo: International Institute for Buddhist Studies, 1991.

Schofield, Malcolm. "Plato and Practical Politics." Pages 291–302 in *Greek and Roman Thought*. Edited by M. Schofield and C. Rowe. Cambridge: Cambridge University Press, 2000.

Scholem, Gershom. "Abraham Abulafia and the Doctrine of Prophetic Kabbalism." Pages 124–55 in *Major Trends in Jewish Mysticism*. New York: Schocken Books, 1995.

Schopen, Gregory. *Bones, Stones, and Buddhist Monks: Collected Papers on the Archaeology, Epigraphy and Texts of Monastic Buddhism in India*. Honolulu: University of Hawaii Press, 1997.

Schopenhauer, Arthur. *Panerga and Paralipomena*. Vol. 1 of *The Cambridge Edition of the Works of Schopenhauer*. Edited by Sabine Rohert and Christopher Janaway. Cambridge: Cambridge University Press, 2014.

Schwartz, Benjamin I. "The Age of Transcendence." *Daedalus* 104.2 (1975): 1–7.

Scopello, Madeleine. "The Revelation of Adam." Pages 343–46 in *The Nag Hammadi Scriptures: The Revised and Updated Translation of Sacred Gnostic Texts*. Edited by Marvin Meyer. New York: HarperOne, 2007.

———. "The Revelation of Paul." Pages 313–16 in *The Nag Hammadi Scriptures: The Re-*

vised and Updated Translation of Sacred Gnostic Texts. Edited by Marvin Meyer. New York: HarperOne, 2007.

Scott, Mark S. M. *Journey Back to God: Origen on the Problem of Evil.* Oxford: Oxford University Press, 2012.

Scott, Michael. *Delphi: A History of the Center of the Ancient World.* Princeton: Princeton University Press, 2015.

Scott, Walter, ed. and trans. *Hermetica: The Ancient Greek and Latin Writings Which Contain Religious or Philosophical Teachings Attributed to Hermes Trismegistus.* 4 vols. 1924. Repr., Boston: Shambhala, 1985.

Seaford, Richard. *Dionysos.* London: Routledge, 2006.

———. *Money and the Early Greek Mind: Homer, Philosophy, Tragedy.* Cambridge: Cambridge University Press, 2004.

Sedley, David. "'Becoming like God' in the *Timaeus* and Aristotle." Pages 327–39 in *Interpreting the Timaeus-Critias: Proceedings of the IV Symposium Platonicum.* Edited by Tomás Calvo and Luc Brisson. Sankt Augustin, Germany: Academia Verlag, 1997.

Seeskin, Kenneth. "Platonism, Mysticism and Madness." *The Monist* 59 (October 1976).

Shaked, Shaul. Foreword to *The Bundahišn: The Zoroastrian Book of Creation.* Edited and translated by Dominic Agostini and Samuel Thrope. Oxford: Oxford University Press, 2020.

Sharma, B. N. K. *History of the Dvaita School of Vedanta and Its Literature.* 3rd ed. Delhi: Motilal Banarsidass, 2008.

Sharma, Chandradhar. *A Critical Survey of Indian Philosophy.* London: Motilal Banarsidass, 2000.

Sharples, R. W. "On Fire in Heraclitus and in Zeno of Citium." *ClQ* 34.1 (1984): 231–35.

Shaw, Carl A. *Satyric Play: The Evolution of Greek Comedy and Satyr Drama.* Oxford: Oxford University Press, 2014.

Shaw, Gregory. "Demon est Deus Inversus." *Gnosis: The Journal of Gnostic Studies* 1 (2016): 177–95.

———. "Living Light: An Exploration of Divine Embodiment." Pages 59–87 in *Seeing with Different Eyes: Essays in Astrology and Divination.* Edited by Patrick Curry and Angela Voss. Newcastle, UK: Cambridge Scholars Press, 2007.

———. "Neoplatonic Theurgy and Dionysius the Areopagite." *Journal of Early Christian Studies* (Winter 1999).

———. *Theurgy and the Soul: The Neoplatonism of Iamblichus.* University Park: Pennsylvania State University Press, 1995.

Sholem, Gershom. *Major Trends in Jewish Mysticism.* New York: Schocken Books, 1961.

Sider, David. "Notes on Two Epigrams of Philodemus." *AJP* 103.2 (1982): 208–13.

Siecienski, Edward. "Michael Caerularios (d. 1059)." Page 94 in vol. 1 of *The Encyclo-*

pedia of Eastern Orthodox Christianity. Edited by John Anthony McGuckin. 2 vols. Oxford: Wiley-Blackwell, 2001.

Sinha, Nandlal. *The Samkhya Philosophy.* New Delhi: Hard Press, 2012.

Sinossoglou, Niketas. *Radical Platonism in Byzantium: Illumination and Utopia in Gemistos Plethon.* Cambridge: Cambridge University Press, 2011.

Sismanian, Ara Alexandru. "Le Nombre et son Ombre (Résumé)." Pages 351–80 in *Neoplatonism and Gnosticism.* Edited by Richard T. Wallis. Albany: SUNY Press, 1992.

Skjærvø, P. O. "The State of Old-Avestan Scholarship." *JAOS* 117.1 (1997): 103–14.

Small, Jocelyn Penny. *Cacus and Marsyas in Etrusco-Roman Legend.* Princeton: Princeton University Press, 1982.

Smith, Andrew, ed. *Porphyrii philosophi fragmenta.* Stuttgart: Teubner, 1993.

———. "Religion, Magic, and Theurgy in Porphyry." Pages 1–10 in *Plotinus, Porphyry and Iamblichus: Philosophy and Religion in Neoplatonism.* Farnham, UK: Ashgate Variorum, 2011.

Smith, Homer W. *Man and His Gods.* New York: Grosset & Dunlap, 1952.

Smith, Jonathan Z. *Drudgery Divine: On the Comparison of Early Christianities and the Religions of Late Antiquity.* Chicago: University of Chicago Press, 1990.

———. *Map Is Not Territory: Studies in the History of Religions.* 2nd ed. Chicago: University of Chicago Press, 1993.

Smith, Shellie A. "Identifying an Archetype: The Hipponion Tablet and Regional Variations in the Orphic Gold Lamellae." *Proceedings from the Document Academy* 1.1 (2014): Art. 8.

Smith, William. "Thales." Page 1016 in *Dictionary of Greek and Roman Biography and Mythology.* Boston: Little, Brown, 1870.

Snell, Bruno. *The Discovery of the Mind in Greek Philosophy and Literature.* Translated by T. G. Rosenmeyer. New York: Harper, 1960.

Sourvinou-Inwood, Christiane. *Reading Greek Death: To the End of the Classical Period.* Oxford: Oxford University Press, 1996.

Souza, Rafael Sampaio Octaviano de, et al. "Jurema-Preta (Mimosa tenuiflora [Willd.] Poir.): A Review of Its Traditional Use, Phytochemistry and Pharmacology." *Brazilian Archives of Biology and Technology* 51.5 (2008): 937–47.

Spanu, Nicola. "The Magic of Plotinus' Gnostic Disciples in the Context of Plato's School of Philosophy." *JLARC* 7 (2013): 1–14.

Spengler, Oswald. *The Decline of the West.* Translated by C. F. Atkinson. Rev. ed. 2 vols. New York: Knopf, 1926.

Staal, J. F. *Advaita and Neoplatonism: A Critical Study in Comparative Philosophy* (Madras: University of Madras, 1961.

Stafford, Betty. "Dvaita, Advaita, and Viśiṣṭādvaita: Contrasting Views of Mokṣa." *Asian*

Philosophy: An International Journal of the Philosophical Traditions of the East 20 (2010): 215–24.

Stavrakopoulou, Francesca. "The Jerusalem Tophet Ideological Dispute and Religious Transformation." *Studi Epigrafici e Linguistici* 30 (2013): 137–58.

Steel, Carlos. "De-Paganizing Philosophy." Pages 19–38 in *Paganism in the Middle Ages: Threat and Fascination*. Edited by Carlos Steel, John Marenbon, and Werner Verbeke. Leuven: Leuven University Press, 2012.

Stépanoff, Charles. "Shamanistic Ritual and Ancient Circumpolar Migrations: The Spread of the Dark Tent Tradition through North Asia and North America." *Anthropological Currents: Report* 62.2 (2021): 239–46.

Stoker, Valerie. "Madhva (1238–1317)." *Internet Encyclopedia of Philosophy*. Accessed June 25, 2022.

Stoyanov, Yuri. *The Other God: Dualist Religions from Antiquity to the Cathar Heresy*. New Haven: Yale University Press, 2000.

Strickmann, Michel. *Chinese Magical Medicine*. Stanford, CA: Stanford University Press, 2002.

Suchla, Beate Regina. "Die sogenannten Maximus-Scholien des Corpus Dionysiacum Areopagiticum." *NAWG* 3 (1980): 31–55.

———. "Die Überlieferung von Prolog und Scholien des Johannes von Skythopolis zum griechischen Corpus Dionysiacum Areopagiticum." StPatr 18.2 (1989): 78–83.

Sujato, Bhante, and Ajahn Brahmali. *The Authenticity of the Early Buddhist Texts*. Kandy, Sri Lanka: Buddhist Publication Society, 2016.

Sullivan, Bruce M. *The A to Z of Hinduism*. Lanham, MD: Rowman & Littlefield, 2001.

Suzuki, T. D. *Mysticism: Christian and Buddhist*. London: Routledge, 2002.

Takács, Sarolta A. "Politics and Religion in the Bacchanalian Affair of 186 B.C.E." *HSCP* 100 (2000): 301–10.

Tarn, William Woodthorpe. *The Greeks in Bactria and India*. Cambridge: Cambridge University Press, 1951.

Tarrant, Harold. *Proclus' Commentary on Plato's Timaeus, Book 1: Proclus on the Causes of the Cosmos and Creation*. Vol. 2. Cambridge: Cambridge University Press, 2007.

Tate, J. "The Beginnings of Greek Allegory." *Classical Review* 41 (1927): 214–15.

Taylor, Charles. *A Secular Age*. Cambridge: Belknap Press of Harvard University Press, 2007.

Taylor, Mark C. *Erring: A Postmodern A/theology*. Chicago: University of Chicago Press, 1987.

Taylor, Thomas. *The Eleusinian and Bacchic Mysteries*. New York: Bouton, 1875.

Teeter, Emily. *Religion and Ritual in Ancient Egypt*. Cambridge: Cambridge University Press, 2011.

Te Velde, Herman. "Seth." In *The Oxford Encyclopedia of Ancient Egypt*. Edited by Donald Redford. Oxford: Oxford University Press, 2001.

Theodoret of Cyrrhus. *The Book of Steps: The Syriac Liber Graduum*. Translated by Robert A. Kitchen and Martien F. G. Parmentier. Kalamazoo, MI: Cistercian, 2004.

———. *A History of the Monks of Syria*. Translated by R. M. Price. Kalamazoo, MI: Cistercian, 1985.

Theophrastus. *The Characters of Theophrastus*. Edited and translated by J. M. Edmonds. London: Heinemann, 1929.

Thomas, Owen C. "Problems in Panentheism." Pages 652–64 in *The Oxford Handbook of Religion and Science*. Edited by Philip Clayton and Zachary Simpson. Oxford: Oxford University Press, 2006.

Thomassen, Einar. "The Valentinian School of Gnostic Thought." Pages 790–94 in *The Nag Hammadi Scriptures: The Revised and Updated Translation of Sacred Gnostic Texts*. Edited by Marvin Meyer. New York: HarperOne, 2007.

Thompson, R. C. *Semitic Magic: Its Origins and Development*. London: Luzac, 1908.

Tierney, Michael. "A New Ritual of the Orphic Mysteries." *ClQ* 2 (1922): 77–87.

Tillich, Paul. *A History of Christian Thought*. New York: Simon & Schuster, 1972.

Timalsina, Sthaneshwar. "Purusavâda: A Pre-Sankara Monistic Philosophy as Critiqued by Mallavâdin." *Journal of Indian Philosophy* 45.5 (2017): 939–59.

Toorn, Karel van der, et al. *Dictionary of Deities and Demons in the Bible*. Grand Rapids: Eerdmans, 1999.

Trigg, Joseph W. *Origen*. The Early Church Fathers. New York: Routledge, 1998.

Trivedi, Saam. "Idealism and Yogacara Buddhism." *Asian Philosophy* 15.3 (2005): 231–46.

Trouillard, Jean. "La théurgie païenne." Pages 58–83 in vol. 15 of *Encyclopedia Universalis*. Chicago: Encyclopedia Brittanica, 1968–1974.

———. *L'Un et l'âme selon Proclos*. Paris: Les Belles Lettres, 1982.

Tsagalis, Christos. "Peisistratus." Pages 193–95 in *The Cambridge Guide to Homer*. Edited by Corinne Ondine Pache. Cambridge: Cambridge University Press, 2020.

Tsantsanoglou, K., G. M. Parássoglou, and T. Kouremenos, eds. *The Derveni Papyrus: Edited with Introduction and Commentary*. Florence, Italy: Olschki, 2006.

Tschannen, Olivier. "The Secularization Paradigm: A Systematization." *JSSR* 30 (1991): 395–415.

Turchi, Nicola. *Le religion dei misteri nel mondo anticho*. Genoa: Fratelli Melita, 1987.

Turner, H. E. W. *The Pattern of Christian Truth: A Study in Relations between Orthodoxy and Heresy in the Early Church*. Eugene, OR: Wipf & Stock, 2004.

Turner, Jason. "Logic and Ontological Pluralism." *Journal of Philosophical Logic* 41 (2012): 419–48.

Turner, John D. "Allogenes the Stranger." Pages 679–74 in *The Nag Hammadi Scriptures: The Revised and Updated Translation of Sacred Gnostic Texts*. Edited by Marvin Meyer. New York: HarperOne, 2007.

———. "Marsanes." Pages 629–34 in *The Nag Hammadi Scriptures: The Revised and*

Works Cited

  Updated Translation of Sacred Gnostic Texts. Edited by Marvin Meyer. New York: HarperOne, 2007.

———. "Ontological Pluralism." *Journal of Philosophy* 107.1 (2010): 5–34.

———. *Sethian Gnosticism in the Platonic Tradition.* Leuven: Peeters, 2001.

———. "The Sethian School of Gnostic Thought." Pages 784–89 in *The Nag Hammadi Scriptures: The Revised and Updated Translation of Sacred Gnostic Texts.* Edited by Marvin Meyer. New York: HarperOne, 2007.

———. "Zostrianos." Pages 537–44 in *The Nag Hammadi Scriptures: The Revised and Updated Translation of Sacred Gnostic Texts.* Edited by Marvin Meyer. New York: HarperOne, 2007.

Turner, Victor. *From Ritual to Theatre: The Human Seriousness of Play.* Village Station, NY: PAJ Publications, 1982.

———. *The Ritual Process: Structure and Anti-Structure.* London: Routledge, 1995.

Tyconius. *The Book of Rules.* Translated by William S. Babcock. Atlanta: Scholars Press, 1989.

Tzamlikos, Panayiotis P. *Origen: Cosmology and Ontology of Time.* Leiden: Brill, 2006.

UNESCO. "The Derveni Papyrus: The Oldest 'Book' of Europe." n.d. https://en.unesco.org/memoryoftheworld/registry/577.

Ustinova, Yulia. *Caves and the Ancient Greek Mind.* New York: Oxford University Press, 2009.

Uždavinys, Aglis. *Orpheus and the Roots of Platonism.* London: Mathison Trust, 2011.

Vamvacas, Constantine J. *The Founders of Western Thought: The Presocratics.* New York: Springer, 2009.

Vanamali, Mataji Devi. *Shiva: Stories and Teachings from the Shiva Mahapurana.* Rochester, VT: Inner Traditions, 2013.

Vanneste, Jean. *Le mystère de Dieu: Essai sur la structure rationnelle de la doctrine mystique du pseudo-Denys l'Aréopagite.* Rome: Pontificia Universitas Gregoriana, 1955.

Van Nieuwenhove, Rik. *An Introduction to Medieval Theology.* Cambridge: Cambridge University Press, 2012.

Ventris, Michael, and John Chadwick. *Documents in Mycenaean Greek.* 2nd ed. Cambridge: Cambridge University Press, 1973.

Vernant, Jean-Pierre. *Les origins de le pensée grecque.* Paris: Presses Universitaires de France, 1962.

———. *The Origins of Greek Thought.* Ithaca, NY: Cornell University Press, 1982.

Versnel, H. S. "Deisidaimonia." *Oxford Classical Dictionary Online.* December 22, 2015. https://oxfordre.com/classics/view/10.1093/acrefore/9780199381135.001.0001/acrefore-9780199381135-e-2073#acrefore-9780199381135-e-2073.

Voegelin, Eric. *In Search of Order*. Vol. 5 of *Order and History*. Edited by Elias Sandoz. Columbia: University of Missouri Press, 2000.

———. *Israel and Revelation*. Vol. 1 of *Order and History*. Edited by Maurice P. Hogan. Columbia: University of Missouri Press, 2001.

———. *The New Science of Politics: An Introduction*. Chicago: University of Chicago Press, 1987.

Vos, R. L. "Atum." Pages 119–24 in *Dictionary of Deities and Demons in the Bible*. Edited by Karel van der Toorn, Bob Becking, and Pieter van de Horst. 2nd ed. Grand Rapids: Eerdmans, 1999.

Voss, Karen-Claire. "Spiritual Alchemy." Pages 147–81 in *Gnosis and Hermeticism from Antiquity to Modern Times*. Edited by Roelof van den Broek and Wouter J. Hanegraaff. Albany: SUNY Press, 1998.

Vroom, H. H. *No Other Gods: Christian Belief in Dialogue with Buddhism, Hinduism and Islam*. Grand Rapids: Eerdmans, 1996.

Vyas, R. T. "The Concept of Prajapati in Vedic Literature." *Bharatiya Vidya* 38 (1978): 95–101.

Wagner, Peter. *Modernity as Experience and Interpretation: A New Sociology*. London: Polity, 2008.

Wallace, Robert. *The World of Leonardo: 1452–1519*. New York: Time, 1972.

Wallis, A. "The Spiritual Importance of Not Knowing." In *Classical Mediterranean Spirituality: Egyptian, Greek, Roman*. Edited by A. H. Armstrong. New York: Crossroad, 1986.

Wallis, R. T. *Neoplatonism*. Indianapolis: Hackett, 1995.

Walsh, P. G. "Making a Drama out of a Crisis: Livy on the Bacchanalia." *GR* 43.12 (1996): 188–203.

Walzer, Richard. *Galen on Jews and Christians*. Oxford: Oxford University Press, 1949.

Wang, Dingding, et al. "Analysing the Carlyle Letters Online." in *Congress 2012*. Edited by Clare Mills, Michael Pidd, and Esther Ward. Sheffield: Digital Humanities Institute, 2012. https://www.dhi.ac.uk/openbook/chapter/dhc-ogihara.

Wasson, R. Gordon. *Mushroom of Immortality*. New York: Harcourt Brace Jovanovich, 1972.

Wasson, R. Gordon, Albert Hofmann, and Carla P. Ruck, eds. *The Road to Eleusis: Unveiling the Secrets of the Mysteries*. Berkeley, CA: North Atlantic Books, 2008.

Watkins, C. *How to Kill a Dragon: Aspects of Indo-European Poetics*. Oxford: Oxford University Press, 1995.

Watson, Burton, ed. and trans. *The Complete Works of Chuang Tzu*. New York: Columbia University Press, 1968.

Watts, Edward J. *City and School in Late Antique Athens and Alexandria*. Berkeley: University of California Press, 2006.

Wear, Sarah Klitenic. "Pseudo-Dionysius and Proclus on *Parmenides* 137d: On Parts and Wholes." Pages 219–32 in *Proclus and His Legacy*. Edited by Danielle Layne and David Buterac. Berlin: de Gruyter, 2017.

Wesche, K. P. "Christological Doctrine and Liturgical Interpretation in Pseudo-Dionysius." *SVTQ* 33 (1989): 53–73.

West, D. R. "Gello and Lamia: Two Hellenic Daemons of Semitic Origin." *UF* 23 (1991): 361–68.

West, Delno C., and Sandra Zimdars-Swartz. *Joachim of Fiore: A Study in Spiritual Perception and History*. Bloomington: Indiana University Press, 1983.

West, M. L. "Conjectures on 46 Greek Poets." *Philologus* 110 (1966).

———. *Early Greek Philosophy and the Orient*. Oxford: Clarendon, 1971.

———. *The East Face of Helicon: West Asiatic Elements in Greek Poetry and Myth*. Oxford: Clarendon, 1999.

———, ed. *Greek Epic Fragments*. Cambridge: Harvard University Press, 2003.

———. *The Hesiodic Catalogue of Women: Its Nature, Structure and Origins*. Oxford: Clarendon, 1985.

———, ed. *Homeric Hymns, Homeric Apocrypha, Lives of Homer*. Cambridge: Harvard University Press, 2003.

———. *Indo-European Poetry and Myth*. Oxford: Oxford University Press, 2007.

———. *The Orphic Poems*. Oxford: Oxford University Press, 1983.

———. "The Orphics of Olbia." *ZPE* 45 (1982): 17–29.

———. *Studies in Aeschylus*. Stuttgart: Teubner, 1990.

———. *Theogony*. Oxford: Clarendon, 1966.

———. "Three Presocratic Cosmologies." *Classical Review* 13 (1963): 154–76.

Westmoreland, Perry L. *Ancient Greek Beliefs*. Chicago: Lee & Vance, 2007.

Whalen, Brett Edward. *Dominion of God: Christendom and Apocalypse in the Middle Ages*. Cambridge: Harvard University Press, 2009.

Widengren, Geo. *Die Religionen Irans*. Stuttgart: Kohlhammer, 1965.

Wiggermann, Frans A. M. *Mesopotamian Protective Spirits: The Ritual Texts*. Groningen: Styx & PP, 1992.

Wilamowitz-Moellendorff, Ulrich von. *Der Glaube der Hellenen*. 2 vols. Berlin: Weidmannsche Buchhandlung, 1931–1932.

Wilberding, James. "The World Soul in the Platonic Tradition." Pages 15–43 in *World Soul: A History*. Edited by James Wilberding. Oxford: Oxford University Press, 2021.

Wilhelm, Richard, trans. *The I Ching or Book of Changes*. 3rd ed. Princeton: Princeton University Press, 1967.

Wilken, Robert L. *The Christians as the Romans Saw Them*. New Haven: Yale University Press, 1984.

Wilkinson, Richard H. *Complete Gods and Goddesses of Ancient Egypt.* London: Thames & Hudson, 2003.

Williams, Ann. "Recent Scholarship on Joachim of Fiore and His Influence." In *Prophecy and Millennialism.* Edited by Ann Williams. London: Longman, 1981.

Williams, Bernard. "Philosophy." Pages 202–55 in *The Legacy of Greece: A New Appraisal.* Edited by M. I. Finley. Oxford: Clarendon, 1981.

Williams, M., and J. Creighton. "Shamanic Practice and Trance Imagery in the Iron Age." Pages 49–60 in *Celtic Coinage: New Discoveries, New Directions.* Edited by P. de Jersey. Oxford: BAR International Series, 2006.

Williams, Paul. *Mahâyâna Buddhism: The Doctrinal Foundations.* 2nd ed. London: Routledge, 2009.

Wippel, John F. *The Metaphysical Thought of Thomas Aquinas.* Washington, DC: Catholic University of America Press, 2000.

Wittgenstein, Ludwig. "Remarks on *The Golden Bough*." *Human World* 3 (1971): 28–41.

Woodbury, Leonard. "Parmenides on Names." *HSCP* 63 (1958): 145–60.

Woudhuisen, F. C. *The Language of the Sea Peoples.* Amsterdam: Najade, 1992.

Wright, M. R. "Presocratic Cosmologies." Pages 413–33 in *The Oxford Handbook of Presocratic Philosophy.* Edited by Patricia Curd and Daniel W. Graham. Oxford; Oxford University Press, 2008.

Wright, Robert. *The Evolution of God.* Boston: Little, Brown, 2009.

Xella, P. "'Tophet': An Overall Interpretation." Pages 259–81 in *The Tophet in the Ancient Mediterranean.* Edited by P. Xella. Verona, Italy: Essedue, 2013.

Xenophanes. *Fragments and Commentary.* Edited and translated by Arthur Fairburns. London: Pauls, Trench & Trubner, 1898.

Yakar, J. "The Nature of Prehistorical Anatolian Religions: An Etnoarchaeological Perspective." *Colloquium Anatolicum* 8 (2009): 291–324.

Yates, Frances. *Giordano Bruno and the Hermetic Tradition.* Chicago: University of Chicago Press, 1991.

Yong, Amos. *The Spirit Poured Out on All Flesh.* Grand Rapids: Baker Academic, 2005.

Zandee, Jan. *The Terminology of Plotinus and Some Gnostic Writings, Mainly the Fourth Treatise of the Jung Codex.* Leiden: Nederlands Instituut voor Nabje Oosten, 1961.

Zeller, Eduard. *Outlines of the History of Greek Philosophy.* Translated by L. R. Palmer. 13th ed. New York: Meridian, 1950.

Zhmud, Leonid. "Pythagorean Communities: From Individuals to a Collective Portrait." *Hyperboreus* 16 (2010): 311–27.

Zielinski, Thaddeus. "Hermes und die Hermetik I." *AR* 8 (1905): 321–72.

———. "Hermes und die Hermetik II." *AR* 9 (1906): 25–60.

Zivadinovic, Dojcin. "The Origins and Antecedents of Joachim of Fiore's Historical-Continuous Method of Prophetic Interpretation." PhD diss., Andrews University, 2017.

Index of Authors

Abrams, M. H., 20, 141, 278, 303, 390–91
Adams, P. M., 86
Agostini, D., 60, 146
Akeroyd, J. R., 88
Albert, K., 175
Alexander, P. J., 393, 399
Allen, J. P., 63–64
Allum, N., 3
Al-Rawi, A. K., 40
Amanat, A., 393, 399
Amélineau, M. E., 287
Anatolios, K., 325
Annas, J., 176, 184
Anthony, D. W., 5, 34, 81, 106
Anton, J. P., 271, 304
Arjomand, S. A., 398
Armstrong, A. H., 79–80, 96, 203, 223, 229, 232, 234, 300, 302–3
Armstrong, K., 12
Arnason, J. P., 8
Arnim, H. von, 219
Assmann, J., 12–13, 15, 21–22, 30–31, 55, 60–61, 63–67, 87, 116, 124–25, 252–53, 257, 303, 373–74
Astore, R. A., 147
Athanassakis, A. N., 76–77, 100, 106, 135, 138, 152
Atherton, P., 243
Ayres, L., 325

Bagshaw, H. B. P., 88
Baltes, M., 228
Balthasar, H. U. von, 312, 321–22, 363, 415
Barclay, J. M. G., 310
Bar-Kochva, B., 118
Barnes, J., 167
Barnes, R. B., 392
Barnstone, W., 429
Barr, J., 287
Basham, A. L., 214
Bashilov, V. A., 23
Basu, B. D., 149
Baumgarten, M., 20
Beatrice, P. F., 315
Beckman, G., 136
Beckwith, C., 128, 212
Behr, J., 323–24
Beierwaltes, W., 337, 380
Bell, H. I., 220
Bellah, R. N., 15–16
Benso, S., 164
Benz, E., 413
Berg, R. M. van den, 354
Berlin, I., 80
Bernabé, A., 75, 86, 94–96, 99, 101, 105–7, 121, 135–37, 151–53, 170
Betegh, G., 104–6, 132, 135–36, 140–41, 143, 165, 171, 178, 193
Betz, H. D., 270, 287

479

Index of Authors

Bhattacharji, S., 148
Bhattacharya, R. S., 148
Bitton-Ashketony, B., 356
Black, J., 40, 49
Blankenhorn, B., 376–77, 387
Bloch, E., 411–12
Bloom, A., 184
Bloom, H., 26
Blumenberg, H. J., 181, 347
Blumenthal, H. J., 334
Bockmuehl, M., 325
Boll, F., 221
Bolton, J. D., 27
Bos, A. P., 260
Boyarin, D., 313
Boyce, M., 165
Boyd, J. W., 249
Bradshaw, D., 238, 270, 333, 343
Brahmali, A., 214
Brakke, D., 292, 295, 301
Breasted, J. H., 63–64
Bremmer, J. N., 82, 91, 100, 105, 118, 152–53
Brereton, J. P., 58, 81, 123, 127–28, 138, 142–43, 145
Brierley, M. W., 384
Brisson, L., 135–36, 140, 182
Broek, R. van den, 256, 263–64, 300
Brons, J., 361
Brooks, D., 19
Brown, G. W., 207
Brown, P., 416
Bruce, S., 3
Brugarolas, M., 360
Buck, A. de, 64
Buckareff, A. A., 254
Budge, E. A. W., 62
Burge, R. P., 2
Burgess, S. M., 400

Burkert, W., 12, 26, 34, 39–42, 45, 47, 49, 58, 74, 79–81, 84, 89–93, 96–99, 108, 110, 135–36, 152–53, 160, 170, 196, 211
Burkitt, F. C., 222, 293, 295
Burnaby, J., 330
Burnet, J., 113–14, 164
Burns, J. H., 421
Burnyeat, M., 380
Burton, T. I., 3
Bury, R. G., 173
Busker, B., 3
Butler, E. P., 338–39, 345
Butterworth, G. W., 312, 319

Campbell, J., 74
Carabine, D., 376, 378, 380
Carod-Artal, F. J., 87
Casanova, J., 25
Cashford, J., 74, 85
Cavelli-Sforza, L. L., 5
Celenza, C. S., 266, 415
Chadwick, H., 74, 319, 321
Chrysanthou, A., 98–99
Chulev, B., 76
Clark, E. A., 326
Clark, P., 139
Clarke, E. C., 272
Clarke, M., 100
Clarke, W. N., 379
Clay, J. S., 80, 82
Clayton, P., 254, 384
Clegg, J. S., 229
Clymer, R. S., 165
Coakley, S., 354
Cocke, B. P., 384
Cohen, N., 397
Collins, J. J., 242, 288, 310
Compton, T. M., 180
Congar, Y., 343

Conwell, E. B., 208
Conze, E., 287
Coogan, M. D., 154
Cook, A. B., 290
Cooper, J. M., 59, 118
Cooper, J. W., 20, 123, 350
Copenhaver, B. P., 27, 226, 255, 257, 259–60, 264, 271, 277, 280, 282
Copleston, F. C., 9, 123, 141, 155
Corbin, H., 26
Cordovero, M., 258
Cornford, F. M., 100, 124, 150, 194, 202, 337
Corrigan, K., 306
Costen, M. D., 389
Coxon, A. H., 111, 168
Creighton, J., 23
Crouzel, H., 324
Csikszentmihalyi, M., 72
Curd, P., 155, 167, 169, 198
Czigany, L. G., 53

Dalferth, I. U., 15
Dalley, S., 47, 142, 209
Daly, R. J., 317–18
Daniélou, A., 128, 354
Danièlou, J., 317
David, M. E., 409
Davies, O., 412
Davis-Kimball, J., 23
Dawson, D., 316
Day, J., 41
Debiasi, A., 73
Denzey, L., 290, 292, 298–99
Derrida, J., 181, 354
Desmond, W. D., 206–7
Des Places, E., 412
Detienne, M., 92
Deusson, P., 145

Deutsch, N., 241
De Witt, H., 6
Dhalla, M. N., 139
d'Hoine, P., 334
Diels, H., 111
Digeser, E. D., 313–14
Diller, J., 384
Dillon, J. M., 196, 204, 206, 214, 216, 224, 226, 228–30, 234–35, 242, 244, 272, 288, 301, 333, 347
Dobbin, R., 206–7
Dodd, C. H., 260
Dodds, E. R., 50, 80, 96, 101, 174–77, 179, 194, 244, 253, 261, 300, 322, 334
Domaradzki, M., 232–33
Doniger, W., 140, 388
Dörrie, H., 256, 313
Drews, R., 7
Drugaş, S. G. P., 117
Dunand, F., 147
Dunderberg, I., 309
Duplouy, A., 109–10, 119

Ebeling, F., 254–56, 344, 414
Edelstein, L., 222
Edmonds, R. G., 95, 98, 107, 115, 130, 152, 165
Edwards, M., 236, 313, 321, 337, 347
Ehrman, B. D., 287
Eliade, M., 23, 52–55, 57, 72, 87, 112, 117, 128, 175, 210, 277, 290
Erlandson, S., 1
Evangeliou, C., 305

Farrow, D., 320, 386, 396, 426
Feldman, M., 7
Ferguson, J., 212
Fernández, A. B., 347
Festugière, A. J., 259–60, 354
Feuchtwang, S., 258

Index of Authors

Filoramo, G., 299
Findlay, J. N., 359
Fitch, W. T., 53
Flood, G. D., 145, 214
Foerster, W., 153
Fokin, A. R., 378–79
Fol, A., 78, 86–87, 117, 185
Foley, H. P., 82–83
Fontenrose, J. E., 46, 222
Forrai, R., 387
Fowden, G., 256–57, 259, 263, 269, 277, 280, 284
Fowler, R. L., 144
Fox, R. L., 72, 219
Fraenkel, C., 28–29, 233, 235, 313, 323, 327–28, 373, 375
Frankfort, H., 140
Freeman, K., 103, 114, 126, 133, 155–57, 160
Frothingham, A. L., 356, 371
Fuller, B. A. G., 307

Gadamer, H., 24, 174, 290, 385
Gandillac, M., 414–15
Gantz, T., 34, 72–73, 77–78, 85, 91, 107, 111, 131
Garaudy, R., 409
Garcy, J., 347
Gardiner, A., 64
Gathercole, S., 297
Geden, A. S., 145
Gennep, A., 73
Gerson, L. P., 217, 219, 361
Gier, N., 139
Gilson, E., 215
Ginzburg, C., 27
Girardot, J. N., 146, 148
Glück, L., 78
Godwin, W., 93
Goldhill, S., 88
Golitzin, A., 356–59, 363, 368

Gombrich, R., 69–70, 139, 141, 161
Gonda, J., 139
González-Reimann, L., 208
Gough, A. E., 148, 208
Gould, P. M., 318
Graf, F., 96–99, 153, 242
Graham, D., 155, 169
Graham-Leigh, E., 389
Granger, H., 109, 132, 162
Grant, M., 8
Grant, R. M., 287–88
Graves, R., 46, 145, 153
Graziosi, B., 104
Green, A., 49
Green, W. S., 236
Greenbaum, D. G., 293
Greer, R. A., 322, 327
Griffin, D. R., 20–21, 384
Griffith, S. H., 393, 399
Griffiths, A. H., 110
Griffiths, J. G., 62–63, 220
Grigg, R., 371
Griswold, H. D., 6
Guran, P., 421
Guthrie, K. S., 213, 222, 231–34, 236–37, 301
Guthrie, W. K. C., 91, 93, 110, 173, 190, 198, 290

Haage, B. D., 212
Häberl, C. G., 287
Hackforth, R., 180, 184–85, 193, 200
Hadot, P. I., 100, 289, 354
Halfwassen, J., 216
Haller, J. S., 3
Hamerton-Kelly, R. G., 73
Hames, H. J., 399
Hancock, C. L., 304
Hanegraaff, W. J., 21, 256, 416, 423
Hankey, W. J., 383, 387

Index of Authors

Hankins, J., 252
Hard, R., 3
Harland, P., 97
Harnack, A. von, 314
Harner, M. J., 53
Harris, M., 88
Harrison, J. E., 94–95
Hart, G., 124, 146
Harvey, P., 84–85
Hathaway, R. F., 354, 356
Haubst, R., 415
Head, T., 394
Heelas, P., 1, 30
Heidel, A., 124
Heider, G. C., 41
Heine, R. E., 316
Helleman, W. E., 280
Hershbell, J. P., 272
Hicks, R. D., 109
Hill, C. E., 391–92
Himmelfarb, M., 270
Hirsch-Reich, B., 396
Hladký, V., 417–20, 424–25
Hoffmann, R. J., 308–9, 315–16
Hofmann, A., 81
Hoppál, M., 23, 53
Hornung, E., 134–35
Horst, P. W. van der, 316
Hunter, R., 77
Hurst, P. T., 53
Hutton, R., 23
Huxley, A., 27

Indich, W., 149
Inwood, B., 217, 219
Irani, D. J., 124

Jaeger, W., 100
Jamison, S. W., 58, 81, 123, 127–28, 138, 142–43, 145
Janko, R., 77, 105, 171–72

Jaruszynski, P., 270
Jaspers, K., 10–15, 27, 30
Jáuregui, M. H. de, 189
Jiménez San Cristóbal, A. I., 96, 99, 101, 106, 152
Joas, H., 12
Johnson, P. C., 202–3, 238, 244
Johnson, W. J., 70, 161
Johnston, S. I., 97–99, 153, 248–50, 268, 274–76, 296
Jonas, H., 299, 301
Jones, B., 409
Jones, F. S., 107
Jones, J. D., 359, 364, 369
Jones, T., 354, 361
Jourdan, F., 107

Kalligas, P., 153
Kampakoglou, A., 116
Kasher, A., 384
Katz, J., 148
Kellens, J., 122
Kenney, J. P., 217, 288, 300
Kenny, A., 173
Kerényi, C., 75, 82, 88, 94, 116
Kern, O., 101, 156, 187, 197
Kettler, F. H., 313
Kidd, I. G., 222
Kingsley, K. S., 109, 114, 119
Kirk, G. S., 105, 132–33, 154, 165, 167, 217
Knight, J. A., 400
Knox, R., 395, 397
Koch, H., 354
Koester, H., 287
Kolakowki, L., 5, 383–84
Kolenkaya-Bostanci, N., 54
Köstenberger, A., 287
Kotwick, M., 105
Koupai, P., 61
Kouremenos, T., 105

Index of Authors

Krämer, H. J., 204
Kranz, W., 111
Kreyenbroek, P. G., 143, 146
Krisnananda, S., 148
Kroll, P. K., 70
Kroner, R., 21
Kruger, M., 287
Kuehn, M., 171

Laks, A., 105, 111, 161
Lambert, W. G., 44
Lamoreaux, J. C., 354–55
Landes, R., 394
Lane, E., 76
Lang, H. S., 334, 337
Lang, P., 210
Lännström, A., 177
Larson, G. J., 149–50
Larson, J. G., 148
Latura, G., 200
Ledger, G. R., 173
Lee, D., 199
Leeming, D. A., 76, 147
Lefkowitz, M., 75, 87–88, 184
Lerner, R., 405
Lesko, L. H., 140
Levenson, J. D., 289
Levere, T. H., 278
Levering, M., 326
Levin, D. M., 181
Levinas, E., 238, 373
Lévi-Strauss, C., 25, 104
Lewy, H., 242, 247–48, 251, 269, 275–76, 366
Lincoln, B., 102–3, 182
Lindberg, D. C., 196
Linforth, I. M., 91, 95
Lloyd, A. C., 334
Lloyd, G. E. R., 163

Locke, L., 138
Lombardo, S., 157, 168, 184
Long, A. A., 217–18
López-Ruiz, C., 72
Lossky, V., 354, 358
Louth, A., 237–38, 240, 311, 325–26, 331, 358
Lowe, J. J., 6
Luck, G., 56
Lutz, C. E., 382
Lyotard, J. F., 12

Macierowski, E. M., 390
MacIntyre, A., 182
MacKenna, S., 304
Mackenzie, D. A., 40
Macleod, R., 212, 220
Macurdy, G. H., 76
Magee, G. A., 384
Mahé, J. P., 299
Mair, V. H., 6, 147–48, 150
Majercik, R., 249–50, 257, 265, 267–69, 273–74, 276, 283, 369–70
Malandra, W. W., 55, 61, 122
Mallory, J. P., 5–6
Mansfield, J., 230
Marazov, I., 78, 86–87, 117, 185
Marciano, M. L. G., 167
Marco, A. D., 337
Marincola, J., 116
Marion, J., 354
Markus, R., 393
Marler, J. C., 383
Marrou, H. I., 328
Marrow, G. R., 333, 347
Martijn, M., 334
Martin, W. M., 102, 217
Maspero, G., 357
Mateo-Seco, L. F., 357

Index of Authors

Matthews, R., 220
Matusova, E., 356
Mazur, A. J., 304
McConnel, D. R., 3
McEvilley, T., 28, 58–59, 113–15, 125, 128–29, 132, 139, 141, 148, 168–69, 207–8, 212
McFarlane, T. J., 150
McGinn, B., 393–97, 401–2, 405, 407, 412
McInerney, J., 75
McKirahan, R. D., 121, 155, 159–60, 164, 166
McNicholl, S. P., 87, 100, 193
Mead, G. R. S., 225
Megino, C., 172, 208
Mehr, F., 61
Meier, C., 7, 9
Meisner, D. A., 72, 95, 104, 107–8, 110, 131, 133–36, 143–45
Merlan, P., 247
Meyendorff, J., 354, 358
Meyer, M., 287, 289, 292–96
Michaels, A., 148, 191, 214
Mieth, D., 384
Milbank, J., 341, 354, 359, 364–65, 367
Miller, P. C., 294, 301
Moltmann, J., 394, 400
Moore, E., 301
Moore, R. I., 389
Moran, D., 377–80, 413
Moreschini, C., 259
Most, G. W., 105
Mourelatos, A., 167
Müller, K. O., 119
Müller, M., 67, 148–49, 164
Mullins, R. T., 384
Murdock, J. M., 153
Muscolino, G., 251

Nagasawa, Y., 254
Nakamura, H., 151
Nasr, S. H., 258
Neusner, J., 236
Newman, W. R., 277
Nikulin, D., 204, 216, 229
Nilsson, M. P., 82, 153
Nissinen, M., 39, 41, 43–44, 46
Nock, A. D., 259, 301, 305, 308, 369
Nye, A., 181

Ober, J., 84
Oldenberg, H., 81
Olivelle, P., 128, 130, 138, 149, 161, 191, 214
O'Meara, D. J., 327, 332
O'Meara, J. J., 330
Ong, W., 81
Oppenheim, A. L., 59
O'Regan, C., 394, 413

Page, D. L., 91
Pagels, E., 285, 287, 294, 309
Paglia, C., 1
Palmer, J., 98, 132
Paramananda, S., 148
Parássoglou, G. M., 105
Parke, H. W., 74
Parker, E. M., 358–59
Parker, R., 43, 46, 83, 136, 153
Parrott, D. M., 287
Parry, R., 109, 114, 119
Peacocke, A., 254
Pearson, B. A., 272, 287, 294, 296, 343–44, 366
Pegg, M. G., 389
Pépin, J., 301, 303
Perczel, I., 357
Perkins, P., 307
Perl, E. D., 348, 359–61, 363–67

Index of Authors

Peters, L. G., 55
Pétrement, S., 300–301
Petridou, G., 82
Petty, R., 222, 228, 233, 236
Pfeiffer, R., 89
Phelan, J. L., 409
Phillips, E. D., 27
Pickard-Cambridge, A., 88
Pickstock, C., 359
Pirart, E., 122
Pleše, Z., 319
Plott, J. C., 389
Polkinghorne, J., 384
Poston, L., 393
Power, T. C., 26, 108
Powers, S. B., 175
Preus, A., 26, 108
Price, R., 327
Price-Williams, D., 55
Principe, L. M., 277
Pritchard, J. B., 146
Prosperi, A., 409
Provan, I., 12

Quispel, G., 252, 287, 374

Rad, G. von, 391
Rahner, K., 318
Ram, I., 148
Ramelli, I. L. E., 313, 322, 326, 347–48
Raven, J. E., 105, 132–33, 154, 165, 167, 217
Reale, G., 91, 223–24, 228, 230, 232, 236–41, 244, 333
Redfield, J., 115
Redford, D. B., 7, 140
Reed, A. Y., 242
Reese, G., 108
Reeves, M., 394, 396–97, 399–404, 406–7

Reid, J. D., 93–94
Reiman, D. H., 175
Reitzenstein, R. A., 119, 287
Repstad, P., 1
Richardson, N., 73, 85, 90
Riches, J., 364–65, 367
Rickert, T., 111–12, 167
Ricoeur, P., 24
Ridley, R. T., 124
Riedweg, C., 206
Riffard, P. A., 266
Rist, J. M., 266, 304, 356
Robinson, T. M., 102
Robson, E., 41
Roemer, C., 220
Roetz, H., 175
Rohde, E., 151, 300
Roller, L. E., 76–77
Rolt, C. E., 359–60
Romera, R. O., 101, 105
Romm, J., 75, 87–88, 184
Rorem, P., 354–55, 381
Roth, A. M., 62
Rouget, G., 56–57, 102, 179, 181
Roukema, R., 309
Rowland, C., 286
Rubarth, S., 141
Rubenstein, M. J., 354
Ruck, C. P., 81, 87
Rudolph, K., 287, 300
Runia, D., 237
Russell, B., 245
Russell, D. S., 286, 390
Russell, J. B., 389
Ruzsa, F., 148

Saffrey, H., 243, 269, 333, 354, 370
Salles, R., 218–19

Samuel, G., 55, 58, 128–29, 138–40, 171, 214
Sanderson, S. K., 124
Sanlon, P., 329
Sargent, L. T., 211
Sarton, G., 63, 154–55, 157–59, 161, 163–64, 172, 174
Schaeffer, J., 16
Schibli, H., 109, 132, 144
Schmemann, A., 354, 358–59
Schmidt, M., 92
Schmidt-Biggemann, W., 262, 402–3
Schmithausen, L., 161
Schmitt, C., 27
Schofield, M., 105, 132–33, 154, 165, 167, 173, 217
Scholem, G., 287, 399
Schopen, G., 214
Schwartz, B. I., 14
Scopello, M., 291, 293, 299
Scott, M., 42, 59, 74, 76, 89
Scott, M. S. M., 319, 321
Scott, W., 259, 262
Seaford, R., 8, 122, 243
Sedley, D. N., 176, 217–18
Seeskin, K., 176
Sélincourt, A. de, 96, 103
Shaffer, N. J., 384
Shaked, S., 122
Sharma, B. N. K., 148
Sharma, C., 148
Sharples, R. W., 165
Shaw, C. A., 85
Shaw, G., 231, 242, 246, 261–63, 268–69, 272–73, 277, 279, 281–82, 343, 359, 364–67, 369
Sheldon-William, I. P., 378, 381–83
Sholem, G., 241, 270

Sider, D., 76
Siecienski, E., 417
Sinha, N., 149
Sinossoglou, N., 388, 416–24
Sismanian, A. A., 319
Skjærvø, P. O., 58
Smith, A., 251
Smith, H. W., 62, 140
Smith, J. Z., 18–19, 209, 211, 260
Smith, M. S., 154
Smith, S. A., 107
Smith, W., 160
Snell, B., 50, 80, 103
Sommerstein, A. H., 85–86, 93
Sourvinou-Inwood, C., 47
Souza, R. S. O. de, 23
Spanu, N., 366
Spengler, O., 409
Staal, J. F., 148
Stafford, B., 148
Stang, C. M., 354
Stavrakopoulou, F., 41
Steel, C., 329, 389–90
Stépanoff, C., 54
Stoker, V., 148
Stoneman, P., 3
Stoyanov, Y., 86, 189, 225–26
Strauss, B., 84
Suchla, B. R., 355
Sujato, B., 214
Sullivan, B. M., 214
Suzuki, T. D., 412

Tagore, R., 124
Takács, S. A., 89
Tarn, W. W., 212
Tarrant, H., 334, 338
Tate, J., 102

Index of Authors

Taylor, C., 4, 12, 17, 25
Taylor, M. C., 391
Taylor, T., 123, 170, 182
Teeter, E., 66
Te Velde, H., 7
Thomas, O. C., 384
Thomassen, E., 292–93
Thompson, R. C., 209
Thrope, S., 60, 146
Tierney, M., 94
Tillich, P., 4
Timalsina, S., 148
Toorn, K. van der, 81
Trask, W. R., 117
Trigg, J. W., 320–21
Trouillard, J., 336, 354, 369
Tsagalis, C., 89
Tsantsangolou, K., 105
Tschannen, O., 28
Turchi, N., 175
Turner, H. E. W., 287
Turner, J., 10, 123
Turner, J. D., 10, 247, 289–92
Turner, V., 71–72, 88
Tzamlikos, P. P., 319

Ustinova, Y., 111–12
Uždavinys, A., 99, 173, 278, 300

Vamvacas, C. J., 164
Vanamali, M. D., 128
Vanneste, J., 356
Van Nieuwenhove, R., 381
Ventris, M., 74
Verity, A., 85, 90, 152
Vernant, J. P., 115, 162
Versnel, H. S., 253
Voegelin, E., 12, 410

Vos, R. L., 140
Voss, K., 278
Vroom, H. H., 148
Vyas, R. T., 140

Wallace, R., 262
Wallis, A., 343
Wallis, R. T., 307, 333
Walsh, P. G., 89
Walzer, R., 323
Ward, G., 359
Wasson, R. G., 81
Watkins, C., 122
Watson, B., 147, 151
Watts, E. J., 328
Wear, S. K., 354
Weber, M., 21, 25, 27
Wesche, K. P., 359, 366
West, D. C., 393–97, 402–3, 406
West, D. R., 40
West, M. L., 23–24, 26, 34, 39, 59, 71, 73, 77, 89, 92–95, 97–98, 100, 106–8, 110, 117–19, 125, 129, 131, 133–34, 136–39, 143–44, 156–57, 197, 217–18
Westmoreland, P. L., 222
Whalen, B. E., 400
Widengren, G., 122
Wiggermann, F. A. M., 209
Wilamowitz-Moellendorff, U. von, 95
Wilberding, J., 200–201
Wilhelm, R., 147
Wilken, R. L., 314–15
Wilkinson, R. H., 67, 140, 146–47, 165
Williams, A., 397
Williams, B., 380
Williams, M., 23
Williams, P., 69, 149
Wippel, J. F., 418

Wolkow, B. M., 76–77, 100, 106, 135, 138, 152
Woodbury, L., 350
Woodhead, L., 1, 30
Woudhuisen, F. C., 7
Wright, R., 55, 171

Xella, P., 41

Yablonsky, L. T., 23
Yakar, J., 53

Yates, F., 252, 259–60
Yong, A., 394

Zandee, J., 308
Zeller, E., 218, 244–45
Zhmud, L., 118
Zielinski, T., 259
Zimdars-Swartz, S., 393–97, 402–3, 406
Zivadinovic, D., 415
Zivie-Coche, C., 147

Index of Subjects

absolute principle. *See* monism
acosmism, 171n231, 235, 348–49
afterlife
    Egyptian conception, 63–66, 116n218, 222–23
    Greek conception, 47–49, 70, 78, 182–83, 188
    Hindu conception, 67
    Mesopotamian conception, 49–50
    Taoist conception, 70
allegory, 94–95, 102–3, 106–7, 126–27, 143n106, 172–73, 177, 184, 195, 204n84, 225–26, 232–33, 235–38, 257, 282, 286, 288–89, 291, 294n37, 295–97, 298n61, 309, 313n4, 314–22, 327, 329, 347, 350, 356, 375, 381–82, 397
androgyny, 40, 62, 75–77, 128, 137–38, 146, 278
annihilationism, 66
apeiron, 123, 155, 162–67
apokatastasis, 208, 324, 348, 371, 382
asceticism, 18n66, 86, 128, 206–7, 226n71, 244, 246, 260, 288n13, 356–57, 374–75, 395–97, 403, 406
astrology
    and diviners, 41, 273
    and fate, 222, 239, 271–72
    and fear, 211, 221, 230
    and science, 2–3, 159n174, 221–22
atheism
    anachronistic, 126, 136, 161, 163, 171
    numerical adherents, 1, 3
atman, 10, 67, 69, 149–51, 388n2, 389n2
Axial Age
    birth of, 10–12, 122
    concept, 15
    cosmology, 16–17, 22, 24, 75, 123–24, 373
    criticism of, 13
    epistemology, 17
    ethics, 17–18
    politics, 18, 100
    psychology, 17
    and spiritualism, 12, 30
    trade, 8

beatific vision, 176, 191, 376, 415
bisexuality, 75, 134, 137–39, 250
body
    as astral, 321–22
    as change, 201
    as evil, 152, 261–62, 305, 364, 382
    as good, 264, 316, 327, 329
    as penalty, 152–53, 162, 173, 186–87, 190, 193–94, 232, 253, 319
    as prison, 15, 23–24, 26, 70, 74, 94, 96, 98, 100, 103, 106, 149–53, 158, 175, 177, 187, 190, 199–200, 240–41, 245,

Index of Subjects

262–64, 270, 274–75, 282, 286, 291, 297, 308, 319, 322, 329, 344, 365, 375
and resurrection, 298–99, 315, 321, 324, 328, 348, 371, 382, 414
salvation, 371
brahman, 10, 67–69, 123, 129, 133, 138–39, 145–51, 161–62, 170, 303
bricolage, 25n94, 99n137, 104, 115, 120, 131, 174, 178, 189, 259, 308, 374, 383
Bronze Age
biomorphic, 135, 137, 150, 350
collapse, 7–8, 22–23, 122
ritual purity, 42
Buddhism
and axiality, 14
cosmology, 149n131, 160–61
and demons, 249
as heretical, 389n2
meditation, 274
origins, 122
and reincarnation, 17, 69–70
and rejection, 15–16
renounce, 17–18
and ritual, 70
and self, 69

chaos to cosmos
doctrine, 17, 51, 55–56, 66–67, 74, 156
modified, 160
origins, 6–7, 34
and salvation, 18–19
Christianity
baptism, 292
cosmology, 285–86, 294–95, 301, 310–11, 385
eschatology, 390–401, 404–6, 408–10, 421, 425
and myth, 323
and Platonism, 310–11, 314, 317–19,

321–23, 325, 327–30, 346–47, 349, 353–56, 358–61, 365, 377, 407–8
redemptive history, 295–96, 315, 318, 323, 330, 335, 352–53, 362, 370–71, 373, 390–92
and salvation, 315, 324, 362
suppression, 5
syncretism, 212
theophany, 361–62, 369n115, 377
as true, 315
church, 368–69, 386–87, 396, 400, 404–5
civilization
advance of, 8
archetypal, 18
cities, 6
migration, 5–8
unity, 8
community
imperial, 8
as restrictive, 4
as society, 9
writing, 9
Confucianism, origins of, 122
cosmic egg, 134, 140–48, 157, 160, 163, 193, 374
cosmic tree, 67, 144
cosmotheism, 21–22, 31, 114, 124–25, 130–31, 142, 160, 168–69, 303, 373–74, 400
cult
and culture, 7, 30
mystery, 24, 26, 75, 79–81, 83, 87n81, 89, 91, 99, 107, 118, 175, 180, 220, 242–44, 269, 333, 369, 374n8
culture, evolution of, 19
curse
disease, 42–43, 88, 249
fall, 285–86, 367n113, 391
family, 48
misfortune, 44–45, 89, 120
Cynics, 128, 206–8

Index of Subjects

daimon. *See* demon
death
  bound, 56–57
  as gateway, 83
  as inevitable, 35–38, 48–50
  as positive, 117, 183–84, 194
deification, 98, 226, 230, 262–63, 321, 326, 363, 365, 368–69, 371, 381, 385
demiurge, 106, 133–42, 146–47, 154–56, 160, 162–66, 195–203, 213–16, 224, 229–31, 250–51, 256–58, 263–64, 267, 270, 296–97, 306, 308, 336, 338–41, 346, 374n10, 379, 418
democracy, 27, 52, 60, 109, 111, 113, 119, 157, 210
demon
  appeasement, 45
  as divine, 223, 225
  ghouls, 40, 250
  as hostile, 66, 222, 230, 248, 270, 280–81, 293
  as intermediary, 223, 230, 242, 263, 265, 268, 272, 328, 353, 361
  spirits, 43–44, 249, 262
dismemberment, 53, 66n116, 74, 78, 82, 90, 93, 97, 100, 108, 130, 139, 225–26
divination, 41–42, 44, 53, 57, 59, 87n80, 114, 271, 275
divinity
  assimilation, 176
  being, 11, 133, 223–24, 337–39, 379–80, 417
  cosmic principles, 22, 113, 126, 133–34, 137, 155n161, 156–57, 159–65, 168–69, 197, 199, 217, 256, 268–69, 339, 344, 347n44, 419
  cosmogonic origins, 6, 132–34, 136, 213
  emanation, 9–11, 15–17, 23–24, 67, 101, 114, 117, 126–27, 130–31, 133, 137, 139–44, 146–47, 149–50, 157–58, 162–63, 170–71, 196–97, 200, 204, 231, 237–38, 294, 302–4, 325, 336–38, 344, 348–50, 361, 364, 366, 368–69, 377–82, 401, 425
  as evil, 203–4
  as the Good, 162, 196–97, 200, 202–4, 211, 223–24, 227–28, 230, 233, 237, 247, 249, 311, 319, 329, 334, 336, 338–44, 349–51, 353, 363, 413, 418
  henad, 337–41, 345–48, 351, 360–61, 367–68, 379n25
  immanence, 15, 17, 25, 126n21, 224, 246, 265, 419
  incarnation, 119, 127, 134, 404
  incomprehensible, 295
  as mediator, 201, 249
  as one, 166
  procession, 130, 167, 215, 301, 303, 336–41, 345–48, 350–51, 361–64, 373, 377–79, 382, 401, 417
  reversion, 27, 299, 303, 336–37, 339–40, 347–50, 362–64, 368, 370, 376–79, 381–82, 401, 422
  self-generation, 75, 337–38, 344–45, 351, 364, 378, 380, 414
  and simplicity, 15, 137, 150, 195, 198, 336, 340
  transcendent, 10, 17, 133, 150, 224, 259, 302, 311, 334–35, 340, 349, 351
  as triad, 62, 146n121, 205, 229, 250, 265, 334n15, 337, 341, 360, 362, 378–79, 417
  unmoved mover, 215–16, 311, 349
  warrior-kings, 6–7
  within, 28
  as world soul, 20, 124, 126–27, 145, 159, 161, 163–64, 172, 196, 198–204, 213–16, 223–24, 228–32, 242, 249–51, 265,

267–69, 273, 275–76, 296–97, 302–3, 305–8, 311, 320, 341n34, 366n108
drugs, 23, 53, 81, 87n81, 114, 116
dualism
  body and soul, 175, 194–95, 201, 226n68, 227, 258, 275, 303, 313, 321, 328, 344, 352, 356n70, 374n10, 422, 426
  combining, 162–63, 165–66, 169, 196–97, 203, 218, 227
  complexity and simplicity, 343–44
  conflict, 223–24, 229, 231–35, 248, 258–60, 262, 279, 301–3, 341
  as doctrine, 166, 189–90, 197–98
  earth and heaven, 15–17, 144, 202–3
  as false, 168–69
  good and evil, 130, 138, 146, 202, 227–29, 260–61, 414
  life and death, 189
  light and darkness, 122n6, 130, 138, 150
  list, 147nn126–27
  male and female, 137–38, 150, 168
  mind and matter, 26, 105, 108, 114, 138, 141–42, 150, 159, 197, 233, 239–40, 274–75, 316, 352, 423, 426
  as monism, 214
dyad, 147, 157, 195–97, 199, 202–3, 214–15, 223–24, 228–32, 234, 251, 267, 297, 303, 334n15

elements. *See* divinity: cosmic principles
empiricism
  argument, 163, 196
  critique of, 15, 17, 165, 182
enchantment, 12, 21, 24–25, 28, 61, 283, 287
Enuma Elish, 6, 34, 39, 135
Epic of Gilgamesh, 35–36, 38–39, 44, 49–51

evil
  as imperfection, 216
  as necessary, 218, 231, 250, 336, 414, 423
  origins, 213–16, 229
  as pervasive, 221, 227–28, 302
  as privation, 202, 204, 223, 344
  ex nihilo, 20, 170, 197, 319, 325–26, 329, 344, 351–52, 361, 380–83, 391, 418, 425

faith
  age of, 387
  consistency of, 313, 376, 382
  as irrational, 256, 321, 342–43, 352, 411
  as reasonable, 240, 342–43

gnosis
  baptism, 291–92
  as certain, 17, 75, 182, 261, 295, 410
  and learned ignorance, 290
  and salvation, 21, 26, 151, 153, 226–27, 278, 289, 294, 297, 299–300, 304, 404
Gnosticism
  as heretical, 305–6, 309
  radical dualism, 301, 305
  Sethian, 288–300, 304–5
  Valentinian, 292–300, 322
God. *See also* divinity
  aseity, 318, 351, 377
  as creator, 20–21, 30, 38, 124, 325–26, 344, 349, 351, 353, 360, 367–69
  energies, 238, 346, 349
  essence, 238, 346, 349, 356n71, 357, 360, 364, 414
  as eternal, 377
  as Father, 133, 230n83, 248–49, 264, 295, 299n70, 301n81, 311, 313, 317, 320, 324, 340, 346, 362, 369, 371, 377–79, 394n24, 397, 405, 408, 412, 418, 422
  as free, 351
  as good, 237

Index of Subjects

as human, 264
as immutable, 310, 318, 329, 351, 377
as impassible, 349, 377
love of, 363
as personal, 21, 29, 237, 240, 351
predestination, 376–77
providence of, 310, 362–64, 370–71, 379
as simple, 318, 329, 344, 351, 377, 380, 414
as sovereign, 237, 239
as transcendent, 16, 21, 124, 237, 240, 314, 351
union, 304, 311, 326, 344, 348, 356, 362, 368–69, 371, 376, 397
as unknowable, 294, 345
as Yahweh, 22, 30, 237, 240, 351

gods
anthropomorphic, 125–27, 166, 340, 342
appeasement, 55
Bronze Age, 6–7
as capricious, 35–36, 38–39, 43, 45–48, 61–62, 103, 126
celestial, 126, 200, 211, 261, 268, 273, 280
as divine, 103
and fate, 50–51, 64–65, 101
as ubiquitous, 79

grace, divine, 342–43, 345, 365, 370–71, 390
guilt, 43–47, 50, 64–65, 153, 177, 179, 232, 234

Hen kai pan, 30, 303
Hermeticism, 125n16, 212, 227, 230, 247, 253–64, 266–67, 269–73, 277–84, 290–91, 307, 328, 332, 335–36, 374n10, 378, 386, 414–15
hieroi logoi. See logos: as story
Hinduism
and afterlife, 67
and axiality, 14
caste, 142, 191
cosmology, 141–42, 148n128, 150n138, 160–61, 167
origins, 122, 127, 145n115, 191n59
reincarnation, 191, 345
and ritual, 70
and utopianism, 138–40

humanity
as cosmic, 141, 191n60, 193, 260–61
as divine, 264
as free, 351
as *imago dei*, 38, 240, 344, 352
as microcosm, 17, 23, 27, 123–24, 141, 150, 158, 163n197, 164, 193, 198–99, 213, 232, 258, 262, 380
origins, 221–22
as responsible, 239
as threefold, 193, 306
as twofold, 276
unity, 13–14

ignorance
learned, 290
as misguided, 190, 260, 293, 302, 343, 366
as ultimate, 180

Iliad, 36–38, 43, 51, 72
immanence. See divinity: immanence
incubate, 53, 72n4, 73–74, 82, 84, 87n81, 111–12, 119, 167
individualism
and autonomy, 75, 175, 179, 205, 212, 323
and epistemology, 17, 21, 68–69, 82–83, 86, 422
as essential, 1
and insecurity, 212
origins, 60, 420–21
and secularism, 4

494

Index of Subjects

and spiritualism, 80
and writing, 9
Indo-Aryans, migration of, 5–6, 58, 122
Indo-Iranian, migration of, 5, 23, 122
Intellect, the. *See* demiurge
interpretation. *See also* allegory
  ecclesial, 323–24
  fourfold, 316–17
  literal, 87, 95, 103, 131, 154, 179, 196, 225–26, 239, 296, 314, 316–17, 321, 323, 327, 329, 362, 375, 381, 396, 413
  spiritual, 314, 317–18, 321, 375, 382, 396, 414
Israel
  eschatology, 67n121
  law, 41n27
  monotheism, 9n36, 21–22, 122–24, 237, 315
  prophets, 122, 352–53, 373
  technomorphic, 135, 351–52
  temple, 288–89

Jainism
  cosmology, 149n131, 160–61
  as heretical, 389n2
  origins, 122
  reincarnation, 70
  and ritual, 70
Jesus Christ
  advent, 391–92
  ascension, 321
  as creator, 368
  as divine, 320, 322, 325, 346, 362–63
  as incarnate, 297, 320, 322, 324, 326, 362–65, 367, 380–81
  as Logos, 310, 319–20, 322, 352, 386, 418
  as mediator, 346, 351
  and miracles, 353
  as preincarnate, 319
  resurrection of, 299, 321, 324, 371
  as Son, 320, 325
  as truth, 30, 310
  as Word, 317–18, 320, 379
  justice, 18, 45–47, 60–61, 64–67, 101, 177, 185–86, 188–90, 348n50, 371–72, 420

kabbalah, 139, 238, 242, 258n26, 287n6, 371, 374, 389, 399–400, 410, 413
karma, 65, 67 146n116, 191

locative cosmos
  belief, 33, 63n105, 123
  bounded, 56, 73, 127, 151, 270
  fate, 50, 64–65
  human passivity, 38–40, 55–56, 72n4
  immorality, 7
  interconnected, 41, 50, 55
  as preservation, 18, 39, 50, 56–57, 78, 80
logos
  divine, 164–65
  doctrine, 237, 240
  fiery, 217–19, 256
  as rationalism, 11, 25
  as story, 98, 100, 103–5, 107, 156n167, 184–86, 188, 190, 225
  as true, 102, 182

magic
  alchemy, 22, 74n15, 246, 253, 266, 271, 277–79, 371n124, 374, 389
  amulets, 40, 219, 249
  animal, 116, 119, 129–30
  bounded, 253
  curses, 129, 192
  death, 64, 66, 208
  definition, 246, 268
  divine, 61–63, 83, 127
  dualism, 53
  as evil, 328
  healing, 46, 82, 112, 114, 118, 128, 167, 219

495

Index of Subjects

oracles, 247–48, 250
as philosophy, 114, 129–30, 225, 245–46, 333
protective, 40, 221–22, 230, 242, 249–50
and science, 253, 265–66
skill, 129
theurgy, 245–48, 260, 265–77, 279–84, 291, 306–7, 316, 328, 332–35, 341–44, 347, 352–53, 359–60, 364–71, 413–14, 419, 423
wheel, 274–76
matter. *See also* dualism: mind and matter
as created, 351
as eternal, 197, 334–35, 337
as evil, 156, 202–3, 211, 224, 228, 234, 261, 303, 305–6, 341, 366n108, 367
as good, 325, 329, 342, 366n108
as lower, 147, 150, 166, 203, 217, 230, 260, 279, 296, 320, 380
medicine, 219n42
metempsychosis, 64n111, 184, 191
mind
as cosmic, 105, 114, 123, 136–38, 140–41, 159, 195, 217–18, 249, 260, 262, 270, 275, 295, 380
as divine, 51, 193, 380
as real, 123
monad, 123, 133, 147, 155, 157, 162, 169, 195–97, 202–4, 215, 223–24, 228n74, 230, 232n89, 237, 250n169, 267, 302, 318n29, 328n25, 334n15
monarchy. *See also* philosopher: as ruler
divine hero, 6, 18, 34–35, 63, 106, 176
as mediator, 55
monism
definition, 16, 123
dualism, 147, 214, 234, 292, 348, 379
existence, 138, 167–68
and monotheism, 22

numerical, 131
priority, 123, 130–36, 138–41, 143, 149, 156, 158, 160–67, 170–71, 195–97, 204–5, 211, 213–15, 223–24, 228–29, 259, 264, 279, 281, 292, 301–3, 306, 308, 334–36, 338, 341, 343, 345–46, 383–84, 388, 411–12, 414, 418–19
strict, 167–68, 223, 229
substance, 123, 146–47, 162, 165, 167, 171, 196–97, 217–19, 227, 232, 234, 258, 337, 348, 350, 375, 377, 380–81
monotheism
decline, 4, 22, 25n91, 31
misunderstanding, 123–24, 166, 314
movement, 16, 374
and science, 163
mummification, 60n94, 64n111, 66
music
classical, 27, 108, 119n231
and magic, 92, 97, 119, 266
and mania, 19, 40, 44, 46, 53, 74, 77
as religious, 92
theory, 213
therapy, 26, 108, 110, 113n204
mysticism
definition, 246, 397
internal, 60
and madness, 178–80, 270
and philosophy, 107, 205, 352, 411
and rationalism, 177–78, 295, 303, 334, 342–43, 352, 399, 414
secret, 80, 106–7
as self-abandonment, 240
mythos
as false, 102, 182
as myth, 11, 25, 205
as narrative, 323
myths
Adamic, 24
and critical thought, 154, 179, 189

as narrative, 6–7, 9, 11, 14, 16, 20–21, 25, 61–65, 67, 72–74, 80, 87n81, 89–91, 93–95, 98–100, 103–4, 106, 114–15, 117, 127, 130–33, 142, 164, 177, 179, 182–83, 185–86, 188–89, 225–27, 241, 315–16, 327, 337, 373, 385
Orphic, 24–25, 67, 103–4, 115–20, 143–45, 225, 230, 236, 278, 347, 350, 374–75

natural supernaturalism
and autonomy, 29–30
belief, 271, 283, 366, 419, 423–26
definition, 20, 22, 141, 163, 217–18, 269, 275, 303
as ideal, 27–28
as scientific naturalism, 20–21, 158, 171–72
nature. *See* matter
Neoplatonism, 29, 94, 96, 101, 104, 152n148, 176n16, 205–6, 212, 215, 221, 223–24, 226, 230, 235–36, 242–44, 246–50, 255–58, 264–70, 273n81, 279–88, 292, 295–97, 304n98, 306–8, 313, 322, 328–30, 331–36, 341n34–36, 342–46, 354–56, 358–79, 385, 389–90, 411–17
New Age
numerical adherents, 2n12
tenets, 2, 115, 384

Odyssey, 36, 38, 47–49, 72
One, the. *See* monism
one and many problem, the, 8–10, 14–16, 23, 26, 30–31, 114, 123, 125, 130, 132–35, 137, 141, 147–48, 157, 162, 165–66, 168–70, 195, 197–99, 205, 214–15, 336, 338, 340–42, 349–50, 352, 377
Orphism
autonomy, 30
cosmology, 130–31, 134
as cult, 23–24, 80, 97–100
definition, 24

Greek, 17
influence, 25–26, 28–29, 95, 192–93
origins, 105
as philosophy, 153–54, 173–75, 375
as private, 101
reality of, 94–102
as salvation, 153–54
Ouroboros, 67, 390

panentheism
belief, 160–61, 350, 386, 425
definition, 20
and monism, 9n36, 123, 136, 138, 141, 158, 163, 170–72, 197, 205, 213, 303
and Western modernity, 4
pantheism
belief, 68–69, 160–61, 217, 259, 413, 417, 425
definition, 20
divinization, 11, 28
and monism, 9n36, 123, 136, 138, 158, 163, 170–72, 197, 213, 303, 389
and Western modernity, 4, 22
philosopher
as certain, 182
as divine, 175, 184, 194
as ecstatic, 102, 174–75, 178, 180–82
as ideal, 192, 194–95
as inspired, 107, 111, 334
as magician, 114, 266, 268–69, 277, 334
as mystic, 242
as physician, 59, 114
as ruler, 18, 327, 375, 392, 421, 424
as shaman, 176, 178
philosophy
becoming, 17, 127, 130–31, 133, 154, 184, 195–99, 202, 216, 250, 263, 278, 300, 308, 336, 341, 343, 345, 350n57, 418, 425
being, 10–11, 14–15, 17, 130–31, 147–48, 150, 184, 195, 197–98, 216, 233, 250,

Index of Subjects

300, 304n98, 308, 320, 337, 345, 349, 418–19
Eastern, 26, 29, 73, 132, 424
and ecstasy, 234, 245, 272, 333, 363, 425
as enlightenment, 178–79, 206–7
epistemology, 17, 26, 28, 68–69, 80–81, 106, 131, 138, 150–51, 167–68, 180–82, 185, 194–95, 239, 352, 375, 422
forms, 11, 15, 176, 179, 191, 195, 198, 200, 202, 215–16, 281, 318–19, 334–35, 337, 341–42, 346, 382
goal, 179
Greek, 15, 26, 111
harmonization, 236
idealism, 20, 123, 141, 217, 259, 281–82, 301–3, 348–49, 359n81, 379–80, 413, 418
materialism, 158, 196–97, 216–19, 259–60, 282
natural, 154–57, 160–66
nonbeing, 202, 341, 378–79
origins of, 11, 107–8, 111, 115, 119, 154–56, 161, 174, 245, 254–55, 300
particulars, 198, 217n33
perennial, 27–28, 94–95, 257, 265, 283, 313–15, 323, 335, 424–26
pessimism, 223
potency and act, 216
as reflective, 104, 180–81, 253, 290, 295, 303–4, 307
salvation, 270, 280, 419
and theology, 215, 333, 374–75, 384, 420
transcendence, 10, 15, 18, 25, 90, 123, 149, 419
universals, 198, 217n33
physician, 46, 58–59, 112–14, 120, 219n42
poet
and ecstasy, 180

as hearer, 181
as inspired, 40, 102, 112, 181, 424
as mediator, 39, 181
as theologian, 91, 126, 166–67, 179, 244n143
prayer
as magic, 129
priest
as magician, 246
as mediator, 265, 275
as purifier, 46
as ritualist, 79, 244n143
prophecy
external, 60, 373
millennial, 399–407
and philosophy, 390–92
prophet
frenzy, 39–40, 54–55, 59, 179
as hearer, 181
as inspired, 183–84
as mediator, 42, 75, 181
as mystic, 246
purification
as atonement, 44–45, 96
as cleansing, 46, 65
and disease, 26, 43, 109, 114
and ritual, 42, 95, 177, 179, 307
soul, 177–78, 188–89, 239, 281
and wisdom, 178
reason
as Orphic, 235, 352, 375
as standard, 17, 421
reflexivity, 15, 208
reincarnation
belief, 2, 17, 24, 30, 90, 97–98, 100, 108–10, 118, 128, 157, 184–85, 199–200, 207–8, 245, 375, 423, 425
divine, 82

Index of Subjects

doctrine, 9–10, 113, 124, 188, 190–92, 293, 345
escape, 149, 153–54
origins, 64n111, 96, 111n189, 116
religion
  canon, 14
  and caves, 16, 27, 72–73, 79, 82, 84, 88, 94, 109, 111–12, 119–20, 131–34, 143–44, 167–68, 177, 195, 232
  continuation of, 4
  definition, 1
  and demythologization, 227, 235, 281, 286, 425
  experiential, 80, 177
  philosophical, 28–31, 244–45, 323, 375–76, 382–83, 410, 415–16
  philosophical development, 9, 11, 123
  pilgrimage, 243
  positive, 21
  public, 26, 30, 42–43, 57–58, 80, 89–91, 102, 115, 176, 235, 265, 274, 280
  and rationalism, 11, 167, 382–83
  tradition, 9–11
  unaffiliated, 2n7, 3
  universal, 127
resurrection. *See also* body: and resurrection
  belief, 30
  as new birth, 74
revelation
  divine, 2, 29, 167–68, 178, 180, 240, 247, 324, 353, 357, 362
  experiential, 30, 102–3, 138
ritual
  initiatory, 81–83, 100–101, 176, 273–74
  precision, 43–44, 51, 80, 269, 275
  stabilizing, 6–7, 18, 40, 51, 55, 74
  as symbolic, 226–27
Romanticism, 12, 20, 24–25, 27, 253, 413

sacraments, 369–70, 386, 404–5
sacrifice
  animal, 40, 43, 45–48, 86n78, 88, 90n88, 116
  god, 51–52, 75, 139, 142, 191n60
  human, 40–41, 46, 116
sage
  as autonomous, 26
  and ecstasy, 180
  as shaman, 120, 138, 157, 353
salvation
  assurance, 220
  as contemplation, 230, 246, 303–4, 307, 326, 336, 343–44, 375
  as escape, 230, 234, 247, 304, 327
  as world rejection, 15, 17–18
secularism
  philosophy and, 374
  and spirituality, 1–4, 13, 17–21, 25–28, 30–31, 415, 419–20
self
  discovery, 388
  as divine, 5, 11, 33, 58, 106, 119–20, 141–42, 148–49, 151, 175, 177, 192, 194–95, 231, 262, 270, 280, 282, 292, 294, 297, 299, 332, 344–45, 352, 383, 389, 398, 400, 405, 422
  revolutionary, 400–401
  universality, 11
shaman
  and animals, 53, 97, 116
  and chaos, 77, 88
  as convert, 83
  as divine, 52, 55–56, 58, 73, 109, 113, 120, 135, 150, 157, 175, 280
  and ecstasy, 52–53, 56, 59, 74, 76, 114, 180, 295
  Greek examples, 26–27, 132
  as healer, 109, 112, 266

499

Index of Subjects

as individualist, 101
as medium, 23, 56–57, 177
as modern-self, 19, 120
origins, 23, 52, 54, 87n80, 108–10, 116–17, 119, 128, 174n6, 300
as renunciate, 17, 128–29
as revolutionary, 58, 207
as ruler, 135
as seer, 181–82
as spiritualist, 54, 57, 74, 86–87, 112, 181–82, 253–54, 263
as temple, 55
as transformer, 25
as utopian, 23, 54–55, 67–68, 72, 78, 208, 211–12, 261, 265, 375
shame, 50–51, 177, 206
sin
  as ethical, 367
  as ignorance, 382
  as ontological, 293
singer
  as mythologist, 100
  as transitional, 90–92
skepticism, and knowledge, 17
soul
  composition, 164, 195, 198–200, 267, 278, 305, 321, 326, 344, 348, 380
  and deification, 262–63, 269, 321
  as divine, 152–53, 158, 198, 200, 208, 218, 245, 264, 267, 292–93, 345, 375, 384, 412, 423
  dual, 232, 234–35
  and enlightenment, 28, 82–83, 106, 148, 177, 180, 320, 375, 396
  and freedom, 9, 18, 23, 65, 149, 151, 199–200, 211, 233, 240, 260, 279–80, 291, 323, 327, 344, 365
  immortality, 24, 96–97, 100, 108–9, 114, 118, 138, 140, 151, 153, 158–59, 173, 179–80, 185–88, 190–91, 194, 196, 235, 240, 245, 280–81, 308, 311, 375
  incarnation, 153, 176, 182, 190–92, 195, 199, 222, 232, 234, 260
  as mediator, 114
  morality, 263
  nature, 21
  as real, 17, 72
  and recollection, 181–82, 187, 192, 194, 298
  salvation, 80, 176, 222, 253, 269, 282, 299, 343, 371, 384, 417
  and slavery, 4, 15, 23–24
  transfiguration, 66
  transmigration, 67, 94, 96, 158
  trilevel, 199–200
  as ubiquitous, 218–19
spirituality
  and atheism, 3
  definition, 1
  and religion, 29, 102, 255–56, 280, 420, 426
  rise of, 31
  speculative thought, 11
Stoicism, 30, 80n45, 104, 141n95, 164, 196n68, 207–8, 211, 216–21, 227, 237, 255n10, 256, 258–62, 273, 278, 299n70, 311, 325, 346, 348n50, 398, 415, 418, 420, 423
suffering
  escape, 149
  inevitable, 232
superstition, rise of, 2–3
tai chi, 123, 133, 147
tao, 123, 162, 258n26
Taoism
  and afterlife, 70
  cosmology, 133, 145–47, 151–52
  and monism, 201

500

origins, 122
and rejection, 15–16, 152
temple
  house of god, 55, 79
  initiatory, 79–80
theater
  and cult, 84–87, 90
  and madness, 74
  as propaganda, 85–86, 95
  and ritual, 71–72, 127
theogonic-cosmological myths, as epics, 6, 58. *See also* myths
theogony, 77, 104–9, 130–37, 140, 156n167, 160–61, 165, 170, 197n70, 228, 249, 319, 418
theology, origins of, 119, 156–57
time, sacred, 55, 75–76, 78–79, 90, 185
tragedians, 84–85, 117
trance, 23, 26, 42, 44, 52–53, 56–57, 59n91, 102, 108, 113n204, 178–79, 181, 269n67, 353
Transcendence, Age of, 15–17
transcendence, definition, 15. *See also* philosophy: transcendence
transmigration. *See* reincarnation
Trinity, 124n14, 320, 324–25, 344, 346–47, 352, 360, 364, 369, 378–79, 381–82, 395–97, 401–2, 412
truth
  deceptive, 180
  exclusive, 13
  and illusion, 16–18, 69, 131, 138, 148n128, 149–51, 166, 168, 170–71, 181, 191n59, 199, 258n26, 281–82, 299, 303, 349, 350n57, 375, 412, 423
  inward, 21, 28–30, 68, 102–3, 106, 175, 177–78, 205, 239, 260–61, 282, 290, 375

objective, 1
as revealed, 168, 180, 185, 240
Scripture, 22, 247
universal, 16, 18, 334

Upanishads, 10, 67–68
Ur, 5
utopian cosmos
  afterlife, 78–79, 83–84, 97, 179–80, 182
  belief, 33, 115, 123, 138, 270, 410–11
  communities, 122
  destiny, 60, 177, 188, 192, 398
  egalitarian, 80, 88
  as escape, 19, 23, 70, 210–11
  as freedom, 125, 151, 374
  madness, 76–77, 87–88, 176
  revolution, 210, 389, 398, 410, 420–22, 424
  three-tier, 52–53, 55–57, 65, 67, 70, 140–41, 382

vegetarianism, 96–97, 191n59, 234

Wicca, rise of, 3
wilderness, 39, 53, 74–75, 77, 89, 130
world soul. *See* divinity: as world soul

yin/yang, 133, 147, 258n26

zodiac, 159n174, 222, 233, 290
Zoroastrianism
  and axiality, 14
  cosmology, 60–61, 139, 146, 227–28, 248–49, 265–66, 388
  eschatology, 61
  monotheism, 122n6
  origins, 122
  scriptures, 124n13